THE PSYCH SOLUTION

STUDENT RESOURCES

- Full Text (print/online)
- Student Progress Tracker
- Chapter Review Cards
- Chapter Videos
- Studyboard Quiz

- Studyboard Flashcards
- Interactive Figures
- Animated Tutorials
- Games: Beat the Clock & Crossword Puzzles

Students sign in at **www.cengagebrain.com**

INSTRUCTOR RESOURCES

- All Student Resources
- A Guide to DSM-5
- First Day of Class Instructions
- LMS Integration
- Instructor's Manual
- Test Bank
- PowerPoint® Slides
- Instructor Prep Cards

Instructors log in at **www.cengage.com/login**

Print

PSYCH4 delivers all of the foundational content for the **Psychology** course through a visually engaging and easy-to-reference print experience. Chapter Review Cards in the back of the textbook provide a compact tool for studying on the go.

PSYCH Online

Explore **PSYCH4** anywhere, anytime, and on most devices – including smartphones! Collect notes and create **StudyBits™** from interactive content throughout the product. Then tag, organize, make flashcards, and take practice quizzes to **learn Psychology YOUR way**.

PSYCH4

Spencer A. Rathus

Vice President, General Manager, 4LTR Press and the Student Experience: Neil Marquardt

Product Director, 4LTR Press: Steven E. Joos

Product Manager: Clinton Kernen

Marketing Manager: Andrew Ginsberg

Content Developer: Sarah Dorger

Product Assistant: Mandira Jacob

Content Project Manager: Darrell E. Frye

Manufacturing Planner: Ron Montgomery

Marketing Communications Manager: Eric Low

Production Service: Integra Software Services Pvt. Ltd.

Sr. Art Director: Bethany Casey

Internal Designer: Joe Devine/Red Hangar Design

Cover Designer: Joe Devine/Red Hangar Design

Cover Image: © Stuart Jenner/Shutterstock.com

Intellectual Property

    Analyst: Deanna Ettinger

    Project Manager: Brittani Morgan

Vice President, General Manager, Social Science & Qualitative Business: Erin Joyner

Product Director: Jon-David Hague

Product Manager: Clay Austin

Internal Ads:

    © iStockphoto.com/dashadima | © Cengage Learning 2011

    © iStockphoto.com/A-Digit | © Cengage Learning 2011

For product information and technology assistance, contact us at
Cengage Learning Customer & Sales Support, 1-800-354-9706

For permission to use material from this text or product, submit all requests online at **www.cengage.com/permissions**
Further permissions questions can be emailed to
permissionrequest@cengage.com

Library of Congress Control Number: 2014958535

Student Edition + PSYCH Online ISBN 13: 978-1-305-09192-4

Student Edition with CD ISBN 13: 978-1-305-11186-8

Cengage Learning
20 Channel Center Street
Boston, MA 02210
USA

Cengage Learning is a leading provider of customized learning solutions with office locations around the globe, including Singapore, the United Kingdom, Australia, Mexico, Brazil, and Japan. Locate your local office at:
www.cengage.com/global

Cengage Learning products are represented in Canada by Nelson Education, Ltd.

To learn more about Cengage Learning Solutions, visit
www.cengage.com

Purchase any of our products at your local college store or at our preferred online store **www.cengagebrain.com**

Printed in the United States of America
Print Number: 01   Print Year: 2014

SPENCER A. RATHUS

PSYCH 4

BRIEF CONTENTS

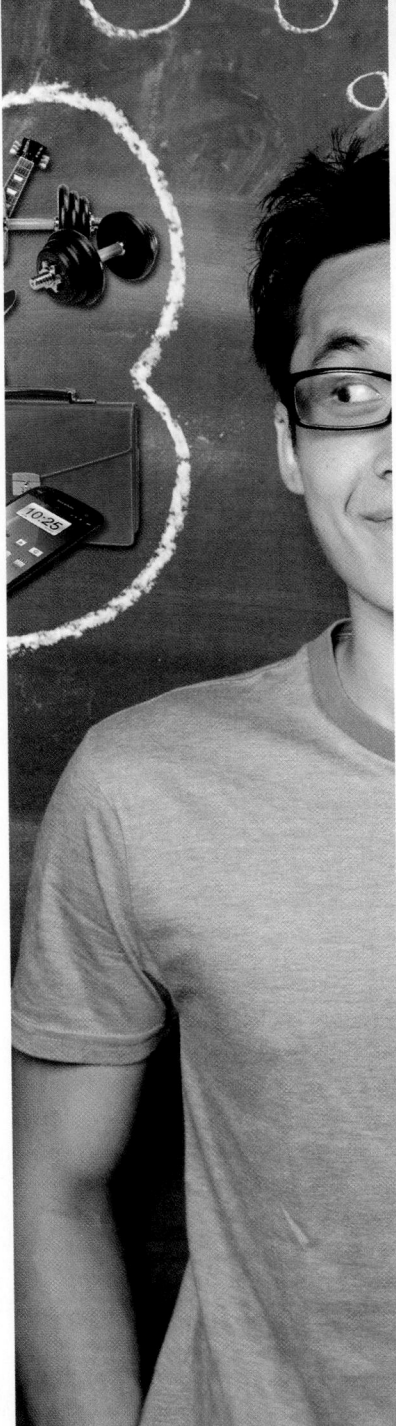

CONTENTS

amana images inc./Alamy

marco betti/Alamy

es/Laurence Mouton/PhotoAlto/Alamy

Steve Raymer/Encyclopedia/Corbis

LEARNING YOUR WAY

Go to **www.cengagebrain.com** to access **PSYCH Online!**

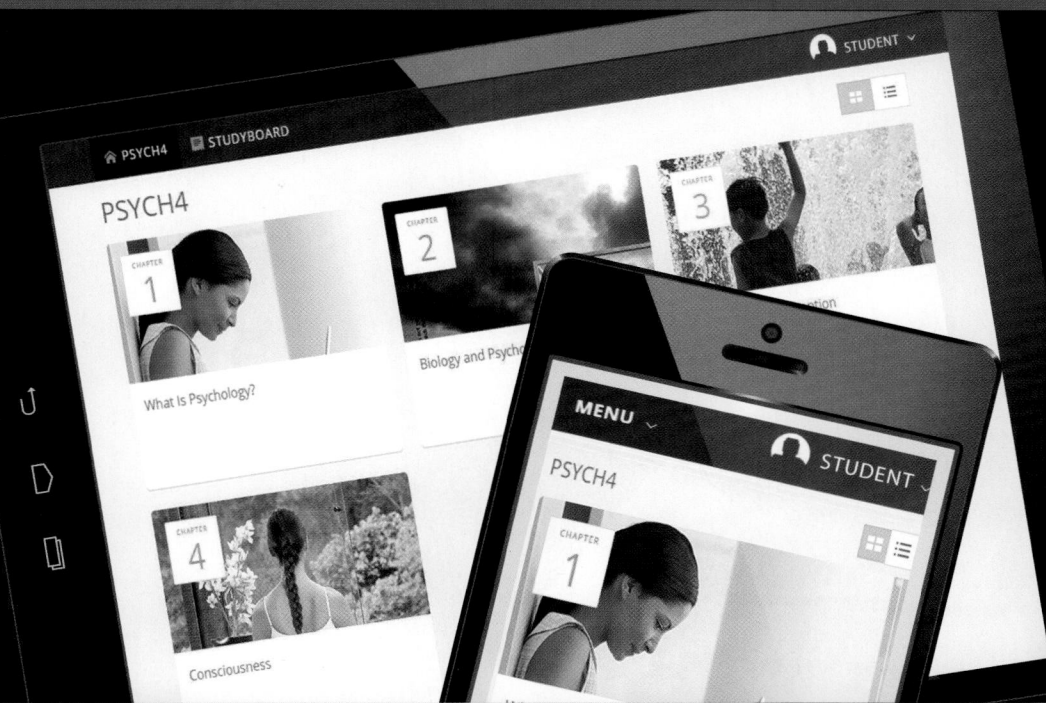

Reading YOUR Way
- Explore Full Text Content
- Interact with Figures & Videos
- Review Chapter Summaries

Studying YOUR Way
- Tag & Organize Notes & Highlights
- Make Your Own Flashcards
- Rate Your Understanding & Take Quizzes
- Track Your Progress

Learning YOUR Way
Read, Study, Take Notes Anytime, Anywhere – Even Smart Phones!

 Follow us at
www.facebook.com/4ltrpress

1 | What Is Psychology?

Masterfile

LEARNING OUTCOMES

After studying this chapter, you will be able to...

1-1 Define psychology.

1-2 Describe the various fields of psychology.

1-3 Describe the origins of psychology and identify people who made significant contributions to the field.

1-4 Identify the theoretical perspectives from which today's psychologists view behavior and mental processes.

1-5 Explain how psychologists study behavior and mental processes, focusing on critical thinking, research methods, and ethical considerations.

After you finish this chapter, go to **PAGE 27** for **STUDY TOOLS**

My favorite place: The checkout counter of the supermarket. After being buffeted about by the crowds in the aisles and trying to convince myself that I really will survive until the people in line ahead of me are checked out, I am rewarded by the display of all the supermarket tabloids. The headlines cry out. Each week, there are 10 new sightings of Elvis and 10 new encounters with extraterrestrials. There are 10 new "absolutely proven effective" ways to take weight off and 10 new ways to conquer stress and depression. There are 10 new ways to tell if your partner has been cheating and, of course, 10 new predictions by astrologers and psychics.

Extraterrestrials regularly kidnap us Earthlings. Although they possess the technology to leap between the stars, aliens must apparently prod and poke us to figure out how we work. While we update our iPhones with the latest apps and music, and download the latest ringtones, tabloid drawings suggest that aliens have been flying the same-model flying saucer for decades. Their sense of style is nothing to text home about.

Although we can find some humor in tales of abduction by aliens, psychologists and other scientists are interested in the questions these tales raise about human nature and the distinction between sensationalism and science. What do we know about people who claim to have been abducted by

aliens? How can we sort truth from fiction and decide whether we will believe the "kidnap victims"?

Psychologists who have studied reported alien kidnappings conclude that the kidnappings never occurred. However, the people making the claims are not necessarily mentally ill, nor are they necessarily lying (Ladd & Borshuk, 2013). By and large, these are people who have "remembered" their "experiences" while undergoing therapy, often under hypnosis. Tales of alien abduction are widely known throughout our culture, so it is not at all surprising that the "memories" of these "kidnap" victims would tend to coincide (Meyersburg et al., 2009; Swami et al., 2009).

"Abductees" generally claim that they are awakened in their sleep by the aliens and unable to move. Psychologists know that many of our voluntary muscles—the ones involved in movement—are "paralyzed" when we sleep, which is why we usually don't thrash about (and assault our bed partners) when we dream (Torontali et al., 2014). *Hallucinations*—seeing and hearing things that are not really there—are quite common as we are waking from a sleep-paralyzed state, and it seems that the reported experiences of "abductees" fit the pattern.

Psychologists also know that people are quite open to suggestion (Bernstein & Loftus, 2009; Vyse, 2014). Memories are not perfect snapshots. When trial

Bloomberg/Getty Images

witnesses are asked leading questions—questions that might encourage them to recall events in a certain way—the opposing attorney will usually object ("Leading the witness, your Honor"). Sometimes, the person interviewing the supposed kidnap victim asks leading questions, looking for experiences with aliens.

All in all, "UFO memories may be constructed from bits and pieces of sleep-related hallucinations, nightmares, and media attention and fixed solidly into place with the suggestion of hypnosis and the validation of support groups" (Clark & Loftus, 1996). "Abductees" may also be trying to escape, temporarily, from their humdrum lives—as might be buyers of supermarket tabloids (Clancy et al., 2002).

Psychologists have thus worked to "explain" how it can be that many people report being abducted by aliens and being subjected to tests by them.

But is there *scientific evidence* that people have been abducted by aliens? In sum, when we subject the stories in the supermarket tabloids to scientific analysis, we usually find that they fall short of any reasonable requirements of evidence.

This book will take you on a journey. It's not a journey into outer space. It's a journey into the inner space of thinking critically about the world around you, about stories and arguments made by other people, about human behavior and mental processes. In our overview of reported alien abductions, we touched on people's memories, the state of consciousness known as sleep, hallucinations, hypnosis, the search for stimulating events, social influences on witnesses, and the effects of social support and the media. All these, and much, much more, lie within the science of psychology. We will see who psychologists are, what they do, what they have learned, and perhaps most important, how they sort out truth from fiction.

1-1 PSYCHOLOGY AS A SCIENCE

Psychology is the scientific study of behavior and mental processes. Topics of interest to psychologists include the nervous system, sensation and perception, learning and memory, intelligence, language, thought, growth and development, personality, stress and health, psychological disorders, ways of treating those disorders, sexual behavior, and the behavior of people in social settings such as groups and organizations.

Sciences have certain goals. Psychology, like other sciences, seeks to describe, explain, predict, and control the events it studies. Psychology thus seeks to describe, explain, predict, and control *behavior and mental processes*. Note that the goal of *controlling* behavior and mental processes doesn't mean that psychologists seek ways to make people do their bidding, like puppets on strings. Rather, psychologists seek to understand the factors that influence behavior and apply this knowledge for the public good—for example, to help individuals cope with problems such as anxiety and depression.

When possible, descriptive terms and concepts—such as anxiety and depression—are interwoven into **theories**. Theories propose reasons for relationships among events, as in perception of a threat can arouse feelings of anxiety. They allow us to derive explanations and predictions. Many psychological theories combine statements about behavior (such as eating or aggression), mental processes (such as attitudes and mental images), and biological processes. For instance, many of our responses to drugs such as alcohol and marijuana can be measured as overt behavior, and they are presumed to reflect our (mental) expectations of the drugs and the biological effects of the drugs themselves.

A satisfactory psychological theory allows us to predict behavior. For instance, a theory of hunger should allow us to predict when people will or will not eat. If our observations cannot be adequately explained by, or predicted from, a given theory, we should consider revising or replacing it.

The remainder of this chapter presents an overview of psychology as a science. You will see that psychologists have diverse interests and fields of specialization. We discuss the history of psychology and the major perspectives from which today's psychologists view behavior. Finally, we consider the research

psychology the science that studies behavior and mental processes

theory a set of hypothesized statements about the relationships among events

👍 Truth or Fiction? 👎

WHAT DO YOU THINK? Folklore, common sense, or nonsense? Select T for "truth" or F for "fiction," and then check the accuracy of your answers as you read through the chapter.

T	F	More than 2,000 years ago, Aristotle wrote a book on psychology with contents similar to the book you are now holding.
T	F	The ancient Greek philosopher Socrates suggested a research method that is still used in psychology.
T	F	Men receive the majority of doctoral degrees in psychology.
T	F	Even though she had worked to complete all the degree requirements, the first female president of the American Psychological Association turned down the doctoral degree that was offered to her.
T	F	You could survey millions of voters and still not accurately predict the outcome of a presidential election.
T	F	In many experiments, neither the participants nor the researchers know who is receiving the real treatment and who is not.

methods psychologists use to study behavior and mental processes.

1-2 WHAT PSYCHOLOGISTS DO

Psychologists share a keen interest in behavior, but they may differ markedly in other ways. Psychologists engage in research, practice, and teaching. Some researchers engage primarily in basic, or pure, research. **Pure research** is undertaken because the researcher is interested in the research topic. Pure research has no *immediate* application to personal or social problems and has therefore been characterized as research for its own sake. However, although pure research is sparked by curiosity and the desire to know and understand, today's pure research frequently enhances tomorrow's way of life. For example, pure research on learning and motivation in pigeons, rats, and monkeys done early in the 20th century has found applications in today's school systems. It has shown, for example, that learning often takes time and repetition and also profits from "booster shots" (repetition after the learning goal has been reached). Pure research into the workings of the nervous system has enhanced knowledge of disorders such as epilepsy, Parkinson's disease, and Alzheimer's disease. Other psychologists engage in **applied research**, which is designed to find solutions to specific personal or social problems.

Many psychologists do not conduct research. Instead, they *practice* psychology by applying psychological knowledge to help individuals change their behavior so that they can meet their own goals more effectively. Still other psychologists primarily teach. They share psychological knowledge in classrooms, seminars, and workshops. Psychologists may also engage in all three: research, practice, and teaching.

1-2a FIELDS OF PSYCHOLOGY

Psychologists are found in a number of specialties. Although some psychologists wear more than one hat, most carry out their functions in the following fields.

Clinical psychologists help people with psychological disorders adjust to the demands of life. Clinical psychologists evaluate problems such as anxiety and depression through interviews and psychological tests. They help clients resolve problems and change self-defeating behavior. For example, they may help clients face "threats," such as public speaking, by exposing them

gradually to situations in which they make presentations to actual or virtual groups (see virtual therapy in Chapter 13). Clinical psychologists are the largest subgroup of psychologists (see Figure 1.1). *Counseling psychologists*, like clinical psychologists, use interviews and tests to define their clients' problems. Their clients typically have adjustment problems but not serious psychological disorders. For example, clients may have trouble making academic or vocational decisions or making friends in college.

School psychologists are employed by school systems to identify and assist students who have problems that interfere with learning. They help schools make decisions about the placement of students in special classes. *Educational psychologists*, like school psychologists, attempt to facilitate learning, but they usually focus on course planning and instructional methods for a school system rather than on individual children. Educational psychologists research issues such as how learning is affected by psychological factors such as motivation and intelligence, sociocultural factors such as poverty and acculturation, and teachers.

Developmental psychologists study the changes—physical, cognitive, social, and emotional—that occur throughout the life span. They attempt to sort out the influences of heredity and the environment on development.

Personality psychologists identify and measure human traits and determine influences on human thought processes, feelings, and behavior. They are particularly concerned with issues such as anxiety, aggression, and gender roles.

Social psychologists are concerned with the nature and causes of individuals' thoughts, feelings, and behavior in social situations. Whereas personality psychologists tend to look within the person to explain behavior, social psychologists tend to focus on social influences.

Environmental psychologists study the ways that people and the environment—the natural environment and the human-made environment—influence one another. For example, we know that extremes of temperature and loud noises interfere with learning in school. Environmental psychologists study ways to encourage people to recycle and to preserve bastions of wilderness.

Psychologists in all specialties may conduct experiments. However, those called *experimental psychologists* specialize

pure research research conducted without concern for immediate applications

applied research research conducted in an effort to find solutions to particular problems

Fuse/Jupiter Images

HUMAN SERVICE PROVIDER SUBFIELDS
- Clinical Child Psychology
- School Psychology
- Counseling Psychology
- Clinical Psychology

WORK SETTING
- Schools/Educational
- Business & Government
- Independent Practice
- Other Human Service
- Hospitals
- College or University

TYPE OF DEGREE
- Psy.D.
- Ph.D.

MEMBERS OF MINORITY GROUPS
- American Indian
- Latin American
- African American
- Asian American

GENDER
- Men
- Women

■ APA Members
■ New Doctorates

0% 10% 20% 30% 40% 50% 60% 70% 80% 90%

More women and members of ethnic minorities are entering the field of psychology today. The percentage of new psychologists with Psy.D. degrees is also growing.

Source: Adapted from the American Psychological Association (2009). *Doctoral Psychology Workforce Fast Facts*. Health Service Provider Subfields. Center for Workforce Studies. http:// research.apa.org/ fastfacts-09.pdf. © Copyright 2009 APA Center for Workforce Studies. Washington, DC; and from American Psychological Association (2014). 2013 APA Directory. Compiled by Center for Workforce Studies, Tables 1, 2, 3, 4. APA Center for Workforce Studies. Washington, DC.

in basic processes such as the nervous system, sensation and perception, learning and memory, thought, motivation, and emotion. For example, experimental psychologists have studied what areas of the brain are involved in processing math problems or listening to music. They use people or animals such as pigeons and rats to study learning.

Industrial psychologists focus on the relationships between people and work. *Organizational psychologists* study the behavior of people in organizations such as businesses. *Human factors psychologists* make technical systems such as automobile dashboards and computer keyboards more user-friendly. *Consumer psychologists* study the behavior of shoppers in an effort to predict and influence their behavior. They advise store managers on how to lay out the aisles of a supermarket in ways that boost impulse buying, how to arrange window displays to attract customers, and how to make newspaper ads and television commercials more persuasive.

Health psychologists study the effects of stress on health problems such as headaches, cardiovascular disease, and cancer. Health psychologists also guide clients toward healthier behavior patterns, such as exercising and quitting smoking.

pumkinpie/Alamy

Why are TV crime shows so popular? Why are people fascinated by psychopaths? Why do so many boys and men enjoy playing videogames such as Theft Grand Auto, God of War, Call of Duty, and Battlefield? Psychologists investigate the origins of aggression and violence. They have found that aggressive people and mass murders are more likely to play violent videogames. Does this mean that violent videogames cause violent behavior? Could it also mean that violent individuals are more likely to seek out the games? (More on this in Chapter 5.)

Forensic psychologists apply psychology to the criminal justice system. They deal with legal matters such as whether a defendant was sane when he or she committed a crime. Forensic psychologists may also treat psychologically ill offenders, consult with attorneys on matters such as picking a jury, and analyze offenders' behavior and mental processes. They may conduct research on matters ranging from evaluation of eyewitness testimony to methods of interrogation.

Sport psychologists help athletes concentrate on their performance and not on the crowd, use cognitive strategies such as positive visualization (imagining themselves making the right moves) to enhance performance, and avoid choking under pressure.

1-3 WHERE PSYCHOLOGY COMES FROM: A HISTORY

Have you heard the expression "Know thyself"? It was proposed by the ancient Greek philosopher Socrates more than 2,000 years ago. Psychology, which is in large part the endeavor to know ourselves, is as old as history and as modern as today. Knowledge of the history of psychology allows us to appreciate its theoretical conflicts, its place among the sciences, the evolution of its methods, and its social and political roles.

Another ancient contributor to psychology was the Greek philosopher Aristotle (384–322 BCE). Aristotle argued that human behavior, like the movements of the stars and the seas, is subject to rules and laws. Then he delved into his subject matter topic by topic: personality, sensation and perception, thought, intelligence, needs and motives, feelings and emotion, and memory.

Other ancient Greek philosophers also contributed to psychology. Around 400 BCE, Democritus suggested that we could think of behavior in terms of a body and a mind. (Contemporary psychologists still talk about the interaction of biological and mental processes.) He pointed out that our behavior is influenced by external stimulation. Democritus was one of the first to raise the

ARISTOTLE

Although he lived 2,400 years ago, the Greek philosopher Aristotle made many contributions to contemporary psychology:

1 He argued that science could rationally treat only information gathered by the senses.

2 He numbered the so-called five senses of vision, hearing, smell, taste, and touch.

3 He explored the nature of cause and effect.

4 He pointed out that people differ from other living things in their capacity for rational thought.

5 He outlined laws of associationism that have lain at the heart of learning theory for more than 2,000 years.

6 He also declared that people are more motivated to seek pleasure and avoid pain—a view that remains as current today as it was in ancient Greece.

The Art Gallery Collection/Visual Arts Library/Alamy

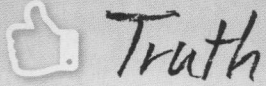 **Truth**

| **T** | F | More than 2,000 years ago, Aristotle wrote a book on psychology with contents similar to the book you are now holding. |

It is true that Aristotle wrote a book on psychology with contents similar to the book you are now holding more than 2,000 years ago. In fact, the outline for this book could have been written by Aristotle. His *peri psyches* begins with a history of psychological thought and historical perspectives on the nature of the mind and behavior.

question of whether there is free will or choice. Putting it another way, where do the influences of others end and our "real selves" begin?

Socrates suggested that we should rely on rational thought and

introspection deliberate looking into one's own cognitive processes to examine one's thoughts and feelings

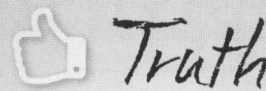 **Truth**

| **T** | F | The ancient Greek philosopher Socrates suggested a research method that is still used in psychology. |

Yes, Socrates did suggest a research method that is still used in psychology—introspection. The method is based on Socrates' advice to "know thyself," which has remained a motto of psychology ever since.

introspection—careful examination of one's own thoughts and emotions—to gain self-knowledge. He also pointed out that people are social creatures who influence one another.

Had we room enough and time, we could trace psychology's roots to thinkers farther back in time than the ancient Greeks, and we could trace its development through the great thinkers of the Renaissance. As it is, we must move on to the development of psychology as a laboratory science during the second half of the 19th century. Some historians set the marker date at 1860. It was then that Gustav Theodor Fechner (1801–1887) published his landmark book *Elements of Psychophysics*, which showed how physical events (such as lights and sounds) are related to psychological sensation and perception. Fechner also showed how we can scientifically measure the effect of these events. Most historians set the debut of modern psychology as a laboratory science in the year 1879, when Wilhelm Wundt established the first psychological laboratory in Leipzig, Germany.

1-3a STRUCTURALISM

The German psychologist Wilhelm Wundt (1832–1920) looked as if he were going to be a problem child. He did poorly in elementary school—his mind would wander—and he had to repeat a grade. Eventually he attended medical school because he wanted to earn a good living. But he did not like working with patients and dedicated himself to philosophy and psychology.

Like Aristotle, Wundt saw the mind as a natural event that could be studied scientifically, like light, heat, and the flow of blood. Wundt used introspection to try to discover the basic elements of experience.

Wundt and his students founded the school of psychology called *structuralism*. **Structuralism** attempted to break conscious experience down into *objective* sensations, such as sight or taste, and *subjective* feelings, such as emotional responses, and mental images such as memories or dreams. Structuralists believed that the mind functions by combining objective and subjective elements of experience.

1-3b FUNCTIONALISM

Toward the end of the 19th century, psychologist William James (1842–1910) became a major figure in the development of psychology in the United States. He focused on the relation between conscious experience and behavior. He argued, for example, that the stream of consciousness is fluid and continuous. Introspection convinced him that experience cannot be broken down into objective sensations and subjective feelings as the structuralists maintained.

William James was a founder of the school of **functionalism**, which focused on behavior as well as the mind or consciousness. Functionalists looked at how our experience helps us function more adaptively in our environments—for example, how habits help us cope with common situations. (When eating with a spoon, we do not create an individual plan to bring each morsel of food to our mouths.) They also turned to the laboratory for direct observations as a way to supplement introspection. Structuralists tended to ask, "What are the pieces that make up thinking and experience?" In contrast, functionalists tended to ask, "How do behavior and mental processes help people adapt to the requirements of their lives?"

James was also influenced by Charles Darwin's (1809–1882) theory of evolution. Earlier

WILHELM WUNDT

Wilhelm Wundt, the founder of structuralism, attempted to break down conscious experience into sensations such as sight and taste, emotions, and mental imagery.

WILLIAM JAMES

William James wrote the first modern psychology textbook in 1890. He wrote, "I wished, by treating Psychology like a natural science, to help her become one."

in the 19th century, the British naturalist Darwin had argued that organisms with adaptive features—that is, the "fittest"—survive and reproduce. Functionalists adapted Darwin's theory and proposed that adaptive behavior patterns are learned and maintained. Maladaptive behavior patterns tend to drop out, and only the fittest behavior patterns survive. These adaptive actions tend to be repeated and become habits. James wrote that "habit is the enormous flywheel of society." Habit keeps the engine of civilization running.

1-3c BEHAVIORISM

Imagine you have placed a hungry rat in a maze. It meanders down a pathway that ends in a T. It can then turn left or right. If you consistently reward the rat with food for turning right at this point, it will learn to turn right when it arrives there, at least when it is hungry. But what does the rat *think* when it is learning to turn right?

Does it seem absurd to try to place yourself in the "mind" of a rat? So it seemed to John Broadus Watson (1878–1958), the founder of American behaviorism. Watson was asked to consider the contents of a rat's "mind" as one of the requirements for his doctoral degree, which he received from the University of Chicago in 1903. Functionalism was the dominant view

structuralism the school of psychology that argues that the mind consists of three basic elements—sensations, feelings, and images—that combine to form experience

functionalism the school of psychology that emphasizes the uses or functions of the mind rather than the elements of experience

of psychology at the University of Chicago, and functionalists were concerned with the stream of consciousness as well as observable behavior. But Watson (1913) believed that if psychology was to be a natural science, like physics or chemistry, it must limit itself to observable, measurable events—that is, to behavior alone—hence the term *behaviorism*.

Behaviorism is the school of psychology that focuses on learning observable behavior. The term *observable* refers to behaviors that are observable by means of specialized instruments, such as heart rate, blood pressure, and brain waves. These behaviors are *public*—they can be measured easily and different observers would agree about their existence and features. Given their focus on behavior, behaviorists define psychology as the scientific study of *behavior*, not of *behavior and mental processes*.

B. F. Skinner (1904–1990) also contributed to behaviorism. He believed that organisms learn to behave in certain ways because they have been **reinforced** for doing so—that is, their behavior has a positive outcome. He demonstrated that laboratory animals can be trained to carry out behaviors through strategic use of reinforcers, such as food. He trained rats to turn in circles, climb ladders, and push toys across the floor Because Skinner demonstrated that remarkable combinations of behaviors could be taught by means of reinforcement, many psychologists adopted the view that, in principle, one could explain complex human behavior in terms of thousands of instances of learning through reinforcement (see Figure 1.2).

1-3d GESTALT PSYCHOLOGY

In the 1920s, another school of psychology—**Gestalt psychology**—was prominent in Germany. In the 1930s, the three founders of the school—Max Wertheimer (1880–1943), Kurt Koffka (1886–1941), and Wolfgang Köhler (1887–1967)—left Europe to escape the Nazi threat. They carried on their work in the United States, giving further impetus to the growing American ascendance in psychology.

Gestalt psychologists focused on perception and how perception influences thinking and problem solving. The German word *Gestalt* translates roughly to "pattern" or "organized whole." In contrast to behaviorists, Gestalt psychologists argued that we cannot hope to understand human nature by focusing only on overt behavior. In contrast to structuralists, they claimed that we cannot explain human perceptions, emotions, or thought processes in terms of basic units. Perceptions are *more* than the sums of their parts: Gestalt psychologists saw our perceptions as wholes that give meaning to parts, as we see in Figure 1.3.

behaviorism the school of psychology that defines psychology as the study of observable behavior and studies relationships between stimuli and responses

reinforcement a stimulus that follows a response and increases the frequency of the response

Gestalt psychology the school of psychology that emphasizes the tendency to organize perceptions into wholes and to integrate separate stimuli into meaningful patterns

FIG.1.2 THE POWER OF REINFORCEMENT

Behaviorists have shown that we can teach animals (and people) complex behaviors by first reinforcing approximations to the goal or target behavior. For example, we might first drop a food pellet into our feathered friend's cage when she drops the star anywhere on the tray, and then demand closer tries before reinforcing her. With people, of course, we can reinforce desired behavior by saying things like "Good" and "That's right," or "You're getting there."

Tom McHugh/Science Source

FIG.1.3   GESTALT PSYCHOLOGY AND THE IMPORTANCE OF CONTEXT

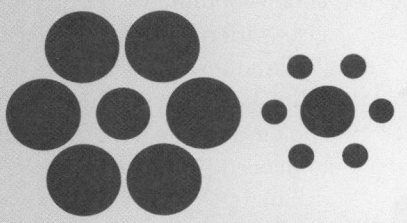

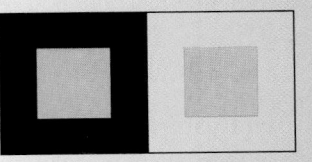

A. Are the dots in the center of the configurations the same size? Why not take a ruler and measure them?

B. Is the second symbol in each line the letter *B* or the number *13*?

C. Which of the gray squares is brighter?

© 2012 Cengage Learning®

Gestalt psychologists have shown that we tend to interpret objects and people according to their context. You interpret somebody's running toward you differently when you are in a dark alley or watching a football game. Interpret the examples shown above.

Gestalt psychologists showed that we tend to perceive separate pieces of information as integrated wholes depending on the contexts in which they occur. In Figure 1.3A, the dots in the centers of the configurations are the same size, yet we may perceive them as being different in size because of their surroundings. The second symbol in each line in part B is identical, but in the top row we may perceive it as a B and in the bottom row as the number 13. The symbol has not changed, but its context has. The inner squares in part C are equally bright, but they do not appear so because of their contrasting backgrounds.

Gestalt psychologists believed that learning could be active and purposeful, not merely responsive and mechanical as in Watson's and Skinner's experiments. They demonstrated that much learning, especially in problem solving, is accomplished by *insight*, not by mechanical repetition.

Consider Köhler's classic research with chimpanzees, as shown in Figure 1.4. At first, the chimp is unsuccessful in reaching bananas suspended from the ceiling. Then he suddenly stacks the boxes and climbs up to reach the bananas. It seems the chimp has experienced a sudden reorganization of the mental elements of the problem—that is, he has had a "flash of insight." Köhler's findings suggest that we often manipulate the elements of problems until we group them in such a way that we can reach a goal. The manipulations may take

FIG.1.4   GESTALT PSYCHOLOGY: SOME INSIGHT INTO INSIGHT

Have you ever had an "Aha experience?" The chimpanzee from Köhler's research is shown here having just such an experience. At first, he cannot reach the bananas hanging from the ceiling. After some time has passed, he has an apparent "flash of insight" and rapidly piles the boxes on top of one another to reach the fruit.

© 2012 Cengage Learning®

quite some time as mental trial and error proceeds. But once the proper grouping has been found, we seem to perceive it all of a sudden.

1-3e PSYCHOANALYSIS

Psychoanalysis is the name of both the theory of personality and the method of psychotherapy developed by Sigmund Freud (1856–1939). As a theory of personality, psychoanalysis proposes that much of our lives is governed by unconscious ideas and impulses that originate in childhood conflicts. As a method of psychotherapy, psychoanalysis aims to help patients gain insight into their conflicts and to find socially acceptable ways of expressing wishes and gratifying needs. We'll discuss psychoanalysis in more depth in Chapter 10.

Mansell/Time Life Pictures/Getty Images

SIGMUND FREUD

Sigmund Freud, the founder of psychoanalysis, is the often the first person that comes to mind when people are asked to name a psychologist.

The history of psychological thought has taken many turns, and contemporary psychologists differ in their approaches. Today, there are several broad, influential perspectives in psychology: biological, cognitive, humanistic–existential, psychodynamic, learning, and sociocultural. Each approaches its topics in its own way.

1-4a THE BIOLOGICAL PERSPECTIVE

Psychologists with a **biological perspective** seek the relationships between the brain, hormones, heredity, and evolution, on the one hand, and behavior and mental processes on the other. Psychologists assume that thoughts, fantasies, and dreams—and the inborn or instinctive behavior patterns of various species—are made possible by the nervous system and especially by the brain.

Biologically oriented psychologists also study the role of heredity in behavior and mental processes such as psychological disorders, criminal behavior, and thinking. Generally speaking, our heredity provides a broad range of behavioral and mental possibilities. Environmental factors interact with inherited factors to determine specific behavior and mental processes.

Biologically oriented psychologists focus on the evolution of behavior and mental processes as well. Charles Darwin argued that in the age-old struggle for existence, only the fittest (most adaptive) organisms manage to reach maturity and reproduce. For example, fish that swim faster or people who are naturally immune to certain diseases are more likely to survive and transmit their genes to future generations. Therefore, species tend to evolve in adaptive directions. Evolutionary psychologists suggest that much human social behavior, such as aggressive behavior and mate selection, has a hereditary basis. People may be influenced by social rules, cultural factors, and personal choice, but evolutionary psychologists believe that inherited tendencies sort of whisper in people's ears and tend to move, them in certain directions.

1-4 HOW TODAY'S PSYCHOLOGISTS VIEW BEHAVIOR AND MENTAL PROCESSES

Today, we no longer find psychologists who describe themselves as structuralists or functionalists. Although the school of Gestalt psychology gave birth to current research approaches in perception and problem solving, few would label themselves Gestalt psychologists. But we do find Gestalt *therapists* who focus on helping clients integrate conflicting parts of their personality (making themselves "whole"). The numbers of orthodox behaviorists and psychoanalysts have been declining (Robins et al., 1999). Many contemporary psychologists in the behaviorist tradition look on themselves as social–cognitive theorists.

psychoanalysis the school of psychology that emphasizes the importance of unconscious motives and conflicts as determinants of human behavior

biological perspective the approach to psychology that seeks to understand the nature of the links between biological processes and structures such as the functioning of the brain, the endocrine system, and heredity, on the one hand, and behavior and mental processes, on the other

1-4b THE COGNITIVE PERSPECTIVE

Psychologists with a **cognitive** perspective venture into the realm of mental processes to understand human nature. They investigate the ways we perceive and mentally represent the world, how we learn, remember the past, plan for the future, solve problems, form judgments, make decisions, and use language. Cognitive psychologists, in short, study those things we refer to as the *mind*.

The cognitive tradition has roots in Socrates' advice to "Know thyself" and in his suggested method of introspection. We also find cognitive psychology's roots in structuralism, functionalism, and Gestalt psychology, each of which, in its own way, addresses issues that are of interest to cognitive psychologists.

CHARLES DARWIN

In the mid-nineteenth century, the British naturalist Charles Darwin presented his theory that the animal and plant species that occupy the world today—including homo sapiens (us)—have evolved from earlier species.

Mary Evans/Science Source

1-4c THE HUMANISTIC-EXISTENTIAL PERSPECTIVE

The humanistic–existential perspective is cognitive in flavor, yet it emphasizes the role of subjective (personal) experience. Let's consider each of the parts of this perspective: *humanism* and *existentialism.*

Humanism stresses the human capacity for self-fulfillment and the central roles of consciousness, self-awareness, and decision making. Humanists believe that self-awareness, experience, and choice permit us, to a large extent, to "invent ourselves" and our ways of relating to the world as we progress through life. Consciousness—our sense of being in the world—is seen as the force that unifies our personalities. *Existentialism* views people as free to choose and as being responsible for choosing ethical conduct. Grounded in the work of Carl Rogers (1951) and Abraham Maslow (1970), the humanistic–existential perspective has many contemporary adherents (Elkins, 2009).

1-4d THE PSYCHODYNAMIC PERSPECTIVE

In the 1940s and 1950s, psychodynamic theory dominated the practice of psychotherapy and was influential in scientific psychology and the arts. Most psychotherapists were psychodynamically oriented. Many renowned artists and writers consulted psychodynamic therapists as a way to liberate the expression of their unconscious ideas. Today, Freud's influence continues to be felt, although it no longer dominates psychotherapy. Contemporary psychologists who follow theories derived from Freud are likely to call themselves *neoanalysts.* Famous neoanalysts such as Karen Horney (1885–1952) and Erik Erikson (1902–1994) focused less on unconscious processes and more on conscious choice and self-direction.

1-4e PERSPECTIVES ON LEARNING

Many contemporary psychologists study the effects of experience on behavior. Learning, to them, is the essential factor in describing, explaining, predicting, and controlling behavior. The term *learning* has different meanings to psychologists of different persuasions, however. Some students of learning find roles for consciousness and insight. Others do not. This distinction is found today among those who adhere to the behavioral and social–cognitive perspectives.

Early proponents of behaviorism, like John B. Watson, viewed people as doing things because of their learning histories, their situations, and rewards, not because of conscious choice. Like Watson, contemporary behaviorists emphasize environmental influences and the learning of habits through repetition and reinforcement. **Social–cognitive theorists**, in contrast, suggest that people can modify and create their environments. They also grant *cognition* a key role. They note that people engage in intentional learning by observing others. Since the 1960s, social–cognitive theorists have gained influence in the areas of personality development, psychological disorders, and psychotherapy.

> **cognitive** having to do with mental processes such as sensation and perception, memory, intelligence, language, thought, and problem solving
>
> **social–cognitive theory** a school of psychology in the behaviorist tradition that includes cognitive factors in the explanation and prediction of behavior; formerly termed *social learning theory*

1-4f THE SOCIOCULTURAL PERSPECTIVE

The profession of psychology focuses mainly on the individual and is committed to the dignity of the individual. However, many psychologists believe we cannot understand people's behavior and mental processes without reference to their diversity (Alarcón et al., 2009).

The **sociocultural perspective** addresses many of the ways that people differ from one another. It studies the influences of ethnicity, gender, culture, and socioeconomic status on behavior and mental processes (Comas-Diaz & Greene, 2013). For example, what is often seen as healthful, self-assertive, outspoken behavior by most U.S. women may be interpreted as brazen behavior in Latin American or Asian American communities.

sociocultural perspective the view that focuses on the roles of ethnicity, gender, culture, and socioeconomic status in behavior and mental processes

gender the culturally defined concepts of *masculinity* and *femininity*

ETHNICITY One kind of diversity involves ethnicity. Members of an *ethnic group* share their cultural heritage, race, language, or history. The experiences of various ethnic groups in the United States highlight the impact of social, political, and economic factors on human behavior and development (Phinney & Baldelomar, 2011).

In the 1940s, Kenneth Bancroft Clark (1914–2005) and Mamie Phipps Clark (1917–1983) conducted research that showed the negative effects of school segregation on African American children. In one such study, African American children were shown white and brown dolls and asked to "Give me the pretty doll," or "Give me the doll that looks bad." Most children's choices showed that they preferred the white dolls over the brown ones. The Clarks concluded that the children had swallowed the larger society's prejudiced views that favored European Americans. The Clark's research was cited by the Supreme Court in 1954 when it overturned the "separate but equal" schools doctrine that had allowed inequalities in school services for various ethnic groups.

Latin American and Asian American psychologists have also made their mark. Jorge Sanchez was among the first to show how intelligence tests are culturally biased—to the disadvantage of Mexican American children. Latina American psychologist Lillian Comas-Diaz (e.g., 2013) has edited a journal on multicultural mental health. Asian American psychologist Richard M. Suinn (e.g., 2001) studies mental health and the development of identity among Asians and Asian Americans.

Figure 1.1 shows that the percentage of psychologists from ethnic minorities is higher among psychologists with new doctorates than among APA members who include psychologists from older generations. Psychologists are becoming more diverse.

GENDER Gender refers to the culturally defined concepts of *masculinity* and *femininity*. Gender is not fully defined by anatomic sex.

David Buffington/Photodisc/Getty Images

Psychologists focus on the individual but believe that we cannot understand individuals without referring to their diversity, such as their gender, their ethnic backgrounds, and their physical condition.

How did "the Doll Experiment" by Kenneth Clark and Mamie Phipps Clark influence a Supreme Court decision?

Eudora Welty/Historical Premium/Corbis

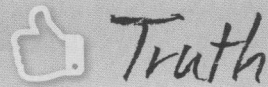
It involves a complex web of cultural expectations and social roles that affect people's self-concepts and hopes and dreams as well as their behavior. Just as members of ethnic minority groups have experienced prejudice, so too have women.

Although American women have attended college only since 1833, when Oberlin College opened

its doors to women, most American college students today are in fact women. Women APA members outnumber APA members (refer back to Figure 1.1 on page 4), and their numbers are growing dramatically, as shown by the percentage of new doctorates received by women (American Psychological Association, 2009, 2012).

Women have made indispensable contributions to psychology. Mary Whiton Calkins (1863–1930) introduced the method of paired associates to study memory (see Chapter 7), discovered the primacy and recency effects, and engaged in research into the role of the frequency of repetition in the vividness of memories. Calkins had studied psychology at Harvard University, which she had to attend as a "guest student," because Harvard was not yet admitting women. When she completed her Ph.D. requirements, Harvard would not award her the degree because of her sex. Instead, Harvard offered to grant her a doctorate from its sister school, Radcliffe. As a form of protest, Calkins declined the offer. Even without the Ph.D., Calkins went on to become president of the American Psychological Association.

In more recent years, Mary Salter Ainsworth (1913–1999) revolutionized our understanding of attachment between parents and children by means of her cross-cultural studies. Elizabeth Loftus (e.g., Laney & Loftus, 2009) has shown that our memories are not snapshots of the past. Instead, they often consist

© Archives of the History of American Psychology, The Center for the History of Psychology—The University of Akron

MARY WHITON CALKINS

At a time when men dominated the discipline of psychology, Mary Whiton Calkins was one of the pioneers who fought the male-centered bias and encouraged psychology to incorporate the values of the "new woman" (D. Rogers, 2009). She pioneered research in memory at Wellesley College, where she founded a psychology laboratory in 1891. She introduced the method of paired associates, discovered the primacy and recency effects, and engaged in +G3 research into the role of the frequency of repetition in the vividness of memories.

of something old (what actually happened), something new (i.e., influenced by more recent events), something borrowed (e.g., further shaped by our biases and prejudices), and something blue (altered by tinges of color or emotion).

The contributions of members of diverse ethnic groups and women have broadened our understanding of the influences of ethnicity and gender on behavior and mental processes. They have also increased our knowledge of differences among Europeans. For example, Southern European singles (from Italy, Greece, and Portugal, for example) are more likely than Northern European singles (from the United Kingdom, France, Germany, and Scandinavia) to live with their parents until they get married (Giuliano, 2007). The researcher suggests that the family ties of Southern Europeans seem to be relatively stronger.

> **critical thinking** a way of evaluating the claims and comments of other people that involves skepticism and examination of evidence

HOW PSYCHOLOGISTS STUDY BEHAVIOR AND MENTAL PROCESSES

Does alcohol cause aggression? Does watching violence on television cause children to be violent? Why do some people hardly ever think of food, whereas others are obsessed with it and snack all day? Why do some unhappy people attempt suicide, whereas others don't? How does having people of different ethnic backgrounds collaborating in their work affect feelings of prejudice?

Many of us have expressed opinions—maybe strong opinions—on questions like these. But as we saw in our discussion of people who claim to be abducted by aliens from outer space, scientists insist on evidence. Psychologists, like other scientists, use careful means to observe and measure behavior and the factors that influence behavior.

The need for evidence is one of the keys to critical thinking. Critical thinking is a life tool for all of us as well as a pathway toward scientific knowledge.

1-5a CRITICAL THINKING

Psychologists are guided by scientific principles, and one hallmark of science is critical thinking. **Critical thinking** has many meanings. On one level, it means taking nothing for granted—not believing things just because they are in print or because they were uttered by authority figures or celebrities. On another level, critical thinking refers to a process of thoughtfully analyzing and probing the questions, statements, and arguments of others.

PRINCIPLES OF CRITICAL THINKING

1. *Be skeptical.* Keep an open mind. Politicians and advertisers try to persuade you. Are some of your attitudes and beliefs superficial or unfounded? Accept nothing as the truth until you have examined the evidence.

2. *Insist on evidence.* It is not sufficient that an opinion is traditional, that it appears in print or on the Internet, or that it is expressed by a doctor or a lawyer. Ask for evidence.

3. *Examine definitions of terms.* Some statements are true when a term is defined in one way, but not when it is defined in another way. Consider the statement, "Head Start programs have raised children's IQs." The correctness of the statement depends on the definition of IQ. (You will see later in the text that *IQ* is not the same thing as *intelligence.*)

4. *Examine the assumptions or premises of arguments.* Consider the statement that one cannot learn about human beings by engaging in research with animals. One premise in the statement seems to be that human beings are not animals. We are, of course.

5. *Be cautious in drawing conclusions from evidence.* For many years, studies had shown that most clients who receive psychotherapy improve. It was therefore generally assumed that psychotherapy worked. Some 40 years ago, however, psychologist Hans Eysenck pointed out that most psychologically troubled people who did *not* receive psychotherapy also improved. The question thus becomes whether people receiving psychotherapy are *more* likely to improve than those who do not. Current research on the effectiveness of psychotherapy therefore compares the benefits of therapy techniques to the benefits of other techniques or no treatment at all. Be especially skeptical of anecdotes. When you hear "I know someone who …," ask yourself whether this person's reported experience is satisfactory as evidence.

6. *Consider alternative interpretations of research evidence.* Does alcohol cause aggression? Later in the chapter we report evidence that there is a *connection*, or *correlation*, between alcohol and aggression. But does the evidence show that drinking *causes* aggression? Might other factors, such as gender, age, or willingness to take risks, account for both drinking and aggressive behavior?

7. *Do not oversimplify.* Most human behavior involves complex interactions of genetic and environmental influences. For example, consider the issue of whether psychotherapy helps people with psychological problems. A broad answer to this question—a simple yes or no—might be oversimplifying. It is more worthwhile to ask: What *type* of psychotherapy, practiced by *whom*, is most helpful for *what kind of problem?*

8. *Do not overgeneralize.* Again, consider the statement that one cannot learn about humans by engaging in research with animals. Is the truth of the matter an all-or-nothing issue? Are there certain kinds of information we can obtain about people from research with animals? What kinds of things are you likely to learn only through research with people?

9. *Apply critical thinking to all areas of life.*

1-5b THE SCIENTIFIC METHOD

The **scientific method** is an organized way of using experience and testing ideas to expand and refine knowledge. Psychologists do not necessarily follow the steps of the scientific method as we might follow a recipe in a cookbook, but research is guided by certain principles.

Psychologists usually begin by *formulating a research question.* Research questions can have many sources. Our daily experiences, psychological theory, and even folklore all help generate questions for research. Daily experience in using day-care centers may motivate us to conduct research on whether day care affects the development of social skills or the bonds of attachment between children and their parents. Social–cognitive principles of observational learning may prompt research on the effects of television violence. Research questions may also arise from common knowledge. Consider familiar adages such as "misery loves company" and "opposites attract." Psychologists may ask: *Does* misery love company? *Do* opposites attract?

A research question may be studied as a question or reworded as a *hypothesis* (see Figure 1.5). A **hypothesis**

scientific method an organized way of using experience and testing ideas to expand and refine knowledge

hypothesis in psychology, a specific statement about behavior or mental processes that is tested through research

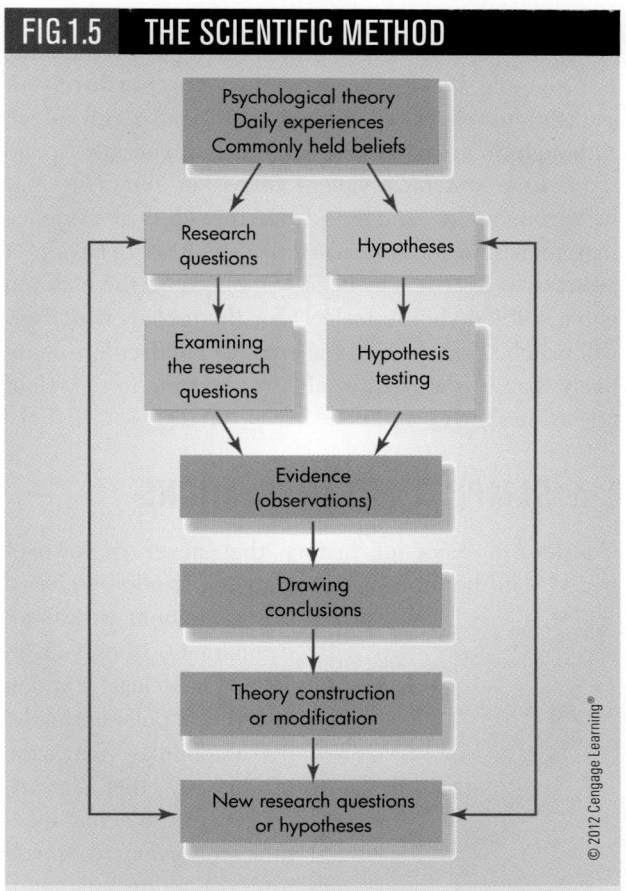

FIG.1.5   THE SCIENTIFIC METHOD

© 2012 Cengage Learning®

The scientific method is a systematic way of organizing and expanding scientific knowledge.

is a statement about behavior or mental processes that is testable through research. A hypothesis about day care might be that preschoolers who are placed in day care will acquire greater social skills in relating to peers than preschoolers who are cared for in the home.

Psychologists next examine the research question or *test the hypothesis* through controlled methods such as the experiment. For example, we could take a group of preschoolers who attend day care and another group who do not and introduce each to a new child in a controlled setting such as a child-research center. We could then observe how children in each group interact with the new acquaintance.

Psychologists draw conclusions about their research questions or the accuracy of their hypotheses on the basis of their observations or findings. When their observations do not bear out their hypotheses, they may modify the theories from which the hypotheses were derived. Research findings often suggest refinements to psychological theories and new avenues of research. In our research on day care, we might find that children in day care show greater social skills than children who are cared for in the home (Belsky et al., 2001).

As psychologists draw conclusions from research evidence, they are guided by principles of critical thinking. For example, they try not to confuse **correlations**—or associations—between findings with cause and effect. Although more aggressive children apparently spend more time watching violent television shows, it may be erroneous to conclude from this kind of evidence that television violence *causes* aggressive behavior. A **selection factor** may be at work because the children being studied choose (select) for themselves what they will watch. Perhaps more aggressive children are more likely than less aggressive children to tune in to violent television shows.

1-5c SAMPLES AND POPULATIONS

Consider a piece of history that never quite happened: The Republican candidate Alf Landon defeated the incumbent president, Franklin D. Roosevelt, in 1936. Or at least Landon did so in a poll conducted by a popular magazine of the day, the *Literary Digest*. In the actual election, however, Roosevelt routed Landon by a landslide. In effect, the *Digest*

correlation an association or relationship among variables, as we might find between height and weight, or between study habits and school grades

selection factor a source of bias that may occur in research findings when participants are allowed to choose for themselves a certain treatment in a scientific study

You may ask 20,000 people like this who they will vote for in the U.S. presidential election, but it will probably not help you determine the winner. Wealthy people tend to vote Republican, and in order to make your prediction, you need to sample people who represent the target population—that is, Americans of various income levels who are likely to vote.

accomplished something like this when they predicted a Landon victory. How was so great a discrepancy possible?

The *Digest*, you see, had surveyed voters by phone. Today, telephone sampling is still widely practiced, but the *Digest* poll was taken during the Great Depression, when people who had telephones were much wealthier than those who did not. People at higher income levels are also more likely to vote Republican, in this case, for Landon. Question: Is telephone sampling valid if it omits people—like many college students!—whose only telephone is a cellphone?

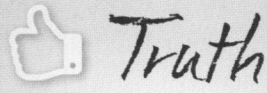 *Truth*

T F You could survey millions of voters and still not accurately predict the outcome of a presidential election.

It is true that you could survey millions of voters and still not predict the outcome of a presidential election. Samples must be *representative*; size alone may not matter.

The *Digest* poll failed because of its method of sampling. A **sample** is a segment of a **population** that must be drawn so that it accurately *represents* that population. Only representative samples allow us to *generalize*—or *extend*—our findings from research samples to target populations, such as U.S. voters, and not subgroups such as southern Californians or European American members of the middle class.

1-5d PROBLEMS IN GENERALIZING FROM PSYCHOLOGICAL RESEARCH

Many factors must be considered when interpreting the accuracy of the results of scientific research. One is the nature of the research sample. Later in the chapter, we consider research in which the participants were drawn from a population of college men who were social drinkers. That is, they tended to drink at social gatherings but not when alone. Who do college men represent other than themselves? To whom can we extend, or generalize, the results? For one thing, they do not extend to college women, who, as we see in Chapter 4, are affected more quickly than men are by alcohol.

Also, compared to the general adult male population, college men are younger and score higher on intelligence tests. Social drinkers may also differ biologically and psychologically from alcoholics, who have difficulty controlling their drinking.

> "ALL GENERALIZATIONS ARE DANGEROUS, EVEN THIS ONE."
>
> ALEXANDRE DUMAS

By and large, we must also question whether findings of research with men can be generalized to women, and whether research with European American men can be extended to members of ethnic minority groups.

RANDOM AND STRATIFIED SAMPLING One way to achieve a representative sample is by means of random sampling. In a **random sample**, each member of a population has an equal chance of being selected to participate. Researchers can also use a **stratified sample**, which is selected so that identified subgroups in the population are represented proportionately in the sample. For instance, 13% of the American population is African American. A stratified sample would thus be 13% African American. As a practical matter, a large randomly selected sample will show reasonably accurate stratification. A random sample of 1,500 people will represent the broad American population reasonably well. However, a sample of 20,000 European Americans or men will not.

Large-scale magazine surveys of sexual behavior ask readers to fill out and return questionnaires. Although many thousands of readers complete the questionnaires and send them in, do the survey respondents represent the American population? Probably not. These and similar studies may be influenced by **volunteer bias**. People who offer or volunteer to participate in research studies differ systematically from people who do not. In the case of research on sexual behavior, volunteers may represent subgroups of the population—or of readers of the magazines in question—who are willing to disclose intimate information and therefore may also be likely to be more liberal in their sexual behavior (Rathus et al., 2011). Volunteers may also be more interested in research than other people, as well as have more spare time. How might such volunteers differ from the population at large? How might such differences slant or bias the research outcomes?

1-5e METHODS OF OBSERVATION

Many people consider themselves experts on behavior and mental processes. How many times, for example, have you or someone else been eager to share a life experience that proves some point about human nature?

We see much during our lifetimes, but our personal observations tend to be fleeting and unsystematic. We sift through experience for the things that interest us. We often ignore the obvious because it does not fit our assumptions about the way things ought to be. Scientists, however, have devised more controlled ways of observing others. Let's consider three of them: the case study, the survey, and naturalistic observation.

sample part of a population

population a complete group of interest to researchers, from which a sample is drawn

random sample a sample drawn so that each member of a population has an equal chance of being selected to participate

stratified sample a sample drawn so that identified subgroups in the population are represented proportionately in the sample

volunteer bias a source of bias or error in research reflecting the prospect that people who offer to participate in research studies differ systematically from people who do not

THE CASE STUDY Case studies collect information about individuals and small groups. Many case studies are clinical; that is, they are descriptions of a person's psychological problems and how a psychologist treated them. Case studies are sometimes used to investigate rare occurrences, as in the case of Chris Sizemore, who was diagnosed with dissociative identity disorder ("multiple personalities"). A psychiatrist identified three distinct personalities in Chris. Her story was made into a movie called *The Three Faces of Eve* (a fictitious name). One personality, "Eve White," was a mousy, well-meaning woman. "Eve Black," a flirtatious and promiscuous personality sometimes emerged and took control of Eve. A third personality, "Jane," was well-adjusted and integrated parts of the personalities of the Eves.

Case studies are subject to inaccuracies. We find gaps and factual errors in people's memories (Bernstein & Loftus, 2009). People may also distort their pasts to please or to antagonize the interviewer. Interviewers may also have certain expectations and may subtly encourage participants to fill in gaps in ways that are consistent with these expectations. Psychoanalysts, for example, have been criticized for guiding people who seek their help into viewing their own lives from the psychodynamic perspective (Hergenhahn & Henley, 2014). No wonder, then, that many people provide "evidence" that is consistent with psychodynamic theory—such as, "My parents' inept handling of my toilet training is the source of my compulsive neatness." However, interviewers of *any* theoretical viewpoint may indirectly prod people into saying what they want to hear.

THE SURVEY Just as computers and pollsters predict election results and report national opinion on the basis of scientifically selected samples, psychologists conduct **surveys** to learn about behavior and mental processes that cannot be observed in the natural setting or studied experimentally. Psychologists conducting surveys may employ questionnaires and interviews or examine public records. One of the advantages of the survey is that by distributing questionnaires and analyzing answers with a computer, psychologists can study many thousands of people at a time (Schwartz, 2007).

One of the best-known surveys, the so-called Kinsey reports, provided surprising information about people's sexual behavior during the middle of the 20th century, a time of widespread sexual repression in the United States. Alfred Kinsey and his colleagues published two surveys of sexual behavior, based on interviews: *Sexual Behavior in the Human Male* (1948) and *Sexual Behavior in the Human Female* (1953). The nation was shocked to hear that masturbation was virtually universal in his sample of men in a day when masturbation was still widely thought to impair health. At the time, it was also widely believed that nearly all single women were virgins. Yet Kinsey found that about one woman in

case study a carefully drawn biography that may be obtained through interviews, questionnaires, and psychological tests

survey a method of scientific investigation in which a large sample of people answer questions about their attitudes or behavior

In the film biography *Kinsey*, Liam Neeson played Alfred Kinsey, the scientist who investigated human sexuality during a time when even talking about sex was considered indecent.

three who remained single at age 25 reported having engaged in sexual intercourse.

Surveys, like case studies, also have sources of inaccuracy (Schwartz, 2007). People may recall their behavior inaccurately or deny or lie about it. Some people try to ingratiate themselves with their interviewers by answering in a socially desirable direction. The Kinsey studies all relied on male interviewers, but it has been speculated that female interviewees might have been more open with female interviewers. Similar problems may occur when interviewers and the people surveyed are from different ethnic or socioeconomic backgrounds. Other people may falsify attitudes and exaggerate problems to draw attention to themselves or to intentionally foul up the results.

Consider some survey errors caused by inaccurate self-reports of behavior. If people brushed their teeth as often as they claimed and used the amount of toothpaste they indicated, three times as much toothpaste would be sold in the United States as is actually sold (Koerber et al., 2006). People also over report the extent to which they follow doctors' orders (Wilson et al., 2009) and underreport how much they smoke (Swan et al., 2007). Why do you think this is so?

NATURALISTIC OBSERVATION You use **naturalistic observation**—that is, you observe people in their natural habitats—every day. Naturalistic observation allows psychologists and other scientists to observe behavior where it happens, or "in the field." Observers use unobtrusive measures to avoid interfering with the behaviors they are observing. For example, Jane Goodall has observed the behavior of chimpanzees in their natural environment to learn about their social behavior, sexual behavior, use of tools, and other facts of chimp life (Peterson, 2006; Pusey et al., 2008). Her observations have shown us that (a) we were incorrect to think that only humans use tools and (b) kissing on the lips, as a greeting, is used by chimps as well as humans.

1-5f CORRELATION

Are people with higher intelligence more likely to do well in school? Are people with a stronger need for achievement likely to climb higher up the corporate ladder? What is the relationship between stress and health?

Such questions are often answered by means of the **correlational method**. Correlation follows observation. By using the correlational method, psychologists investigate whether observed behavior or a measured trait

Jane Goodall's naturalistic observations revealed that chimpanzees—like humans—use tools and greet one another with a kiss.

Kay & Karl Ammann/BRUCE COLEMAN INC./Alamy

is related to, or correlated with, another. Consider the variables of intelligence and academic performance. These variables are assigned numbers such as intelligence test scores and academic averages. Then the numbers are mathematically related and expressed as a **correlation coefficient** (r). A correlation coefficient is a number that varies from $r = +1.00$ to $r = -1.00$.

Studies report *positive correlations* between intelligence test scores

naturalistic observation
a scientific method in which organisms are observed in their natural environments

correlational method
a mathematical method of determining whether one variable increases or decreases as another variable increases or decreases

correlation coefficient
a number between +1.00 and −1.00 that expresses the strength and direction (positive or negative) of the relationship between two variables

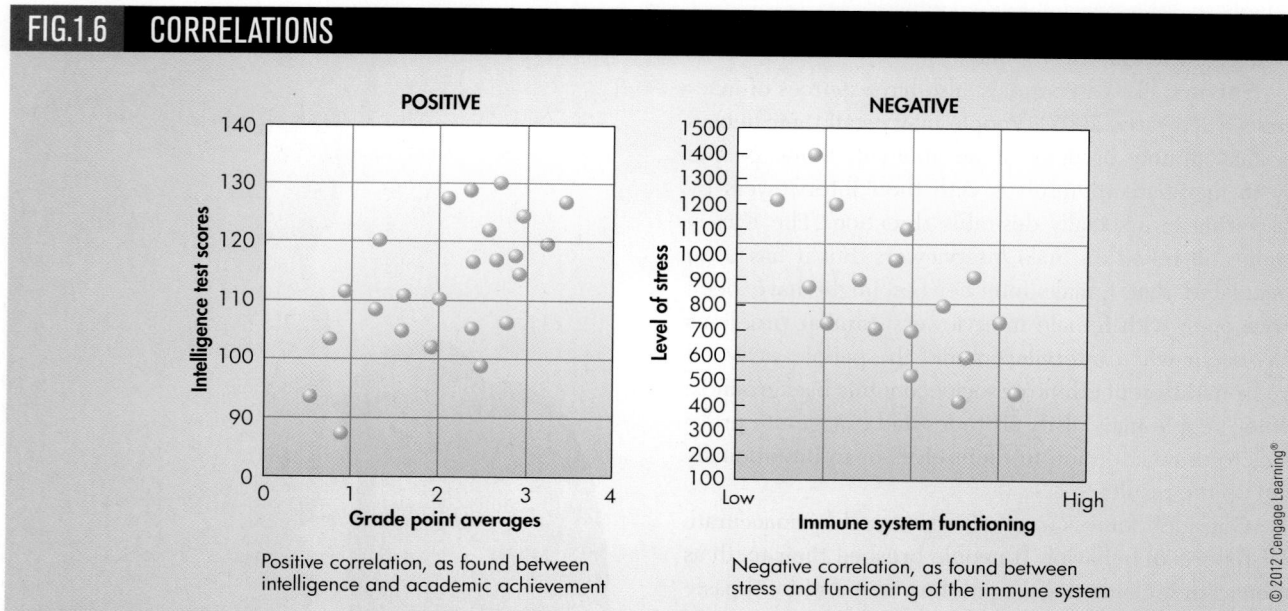

FIG.1.6 CORRELATIONS

POSITIVE

Intelligence test scores / Grade point averages

Positive correlation, as found between intelligence and academic achievement

NEGATIVE

Level of stress / Immune system functioning

Negative correlation, as found between stress and functioning of the immune system

© 2012 Cengage Learning®

When there is a positive correlation between variables, as there is between intelligence and achievement, one increases as the other increases. By and large, the higher people score on intelligence tests, the better their academic performance is likely to be, as in the diagram on the left. (Each dot represents an individual's intelligence test score and grade point average.) But there is a negative correlation between stress and health. As the amount of stress we experience increases, the functioning of our immune system tends to decrease.

and academic achievement, as measured, for example, by grade point averages. That is, the higher people score on intelligence tests, the better their academic performance is likely to be. Intelligence test scores tend to be positively correlated (about $r = +0.30$ to $r = +0.60$) with academic achievement (see Figure 1.6). But factors *other* than performance on intelligence tests also contribute to academic success. These include desire to get ahead, self-discipline, ability to manage stress, and belief in one's ability to succeed (Duckworth & Seligman, 2005; Jennings et al., 2009; Thomas, 2008).

Many correlations are *negative correlations;* that is, as one variable increases, the other variable decreases. For example, there is a negative correlation between stress and health. As the amount of stress affecting us increases, the functioning of our immune system decreases. Under high levels of stress, many people show poorer health.

What kinds of correlations (positive or negative) would you expect to find among behavior patterns such as the following: Churchgoing and crime? Language ability and musical ability? Grades in school and delinquency? Why?

Correlational research may suggest, but does not prove, cause

experiment a scientific method that seeks to confirm cause-and-effect relationships by introducing independent variables and observing their effects on dependent variables

and effect. For example, it may seem logical to assume that high intelligence makes it possible for children to profit from education. However, research has also shown that education contributes to higher scores on intelligence tests (Nisbett, 2009). Preschoolers who are placed in stimulating Head Start programs later attain higher scores on intelligence tests than age-mates who did not have this experience. What of the link between stress and health? Does stress impair health, or is it possible that people in poorer health encounter more stress?

1-5g THE EXPERIMENTAL METHOD

The preferred method for answering questions about cause and effect is the experiment. In an **experiment**, a group of participants obtains a treatment, such as a dose of alcohol, a change in room temperature, or perhaps an injection of a drug. The participants are then observed to determine whether the treatment makes a difference in their behavior. Does alcohol alter the ability to take tests, for example? What are the effects of differences in room temperatures and the level of background noise?

Experiments allow psychologists to control the experiences of participants and draw conclusions about cause and effect. A psychologist may theorize that alcohol leads to aggression because it reduces fear of

What kind of correlation would you expect between teenagers' grades in school and their numbers of delinquent acts? Why?

independent variable. The presence of an independent variable is manipulated by the experimenters so that its effects may be determined. The independent variable of alcohol may be administered at different levels, or doses, from none or very little to enough to cause intoxication or drunkenness.

The measured results, or outcomes, in an experiment are called **dependent variables.** The presence of dependent variables presumably depends on the independent variables. In an experiment to determine whether alcohol influences aggression, aggressive behavior would be a dependent variable. Other dependent variables of interest might include sexual arousal, visual-motor coordination, and performance on cognitive tasks such as math problems.

In an experiment on the relationships between temperature and aggression, temperature would be an independent variable and aggressive behavior would be a dependent variable. We could set temperatures from below freezing to blistering hot and study the effects of these extremes on aggression. We could also use a second independent variable such as social provocation; we could insult some participants but not others and see whether insults affect their level of aggression. This method would allow us to study how two independent variables—temperature and social provocation—affect aggression, by themselves and together.

EXPERIMENTAL AND CONTROL GROUPS Ideal experiments use experimental groups and control groups. Participants in **experimental groups** obtain the treatment. Members of **control groups** do not. Every effort is made to ensure that all other conditions are held constant for both groups. This method enhances the researchers' confidence that the outcomes of the experiment are caused by the treatments and not by chance factors or chance fluctuations in behavior.

For example, in an experiment on the effects of alcohol on aggression, members of the experimental group would ingest alcohol, and members of the control group would not (Eriksson, 2008). The researcher would then measure how much aggression was shown by each group.

consequences or because it energizes the activity levels of drinkers. But the theory needs to be tested. In one approach, the psychologist may devise a treatment in which participants receive various doses of alcohol and the outcomes on their behavior are measured. Let's follow the example of the effects of alcohol on aggression to further our understanding of the experimental method.

INDEPENDENT AND DEPENDENT VARIABLES In an experiment to determine whether alcohol causes aggression, participants are given an amount of alcohol and its effects are measured. In this case, alcohol is an

independent variable a condition in a scientific study that is manipulated so that its effects may be observed

dependent variable a measure of an assumed effect of an independent variable

experimental groups in experiments, groups whose members obtain the treatment

control groups in experiments, groups whose members do not obtain the treatment, while other conditions are held constant

liquidlibrary(RF)/Getty Images/Jupiter Images

BLINDS AND DOUBLE BLINDS One experiment on the effects of alcohol on aggression (Boyatzis, 1974) reported that men at parties where beer and liquor were served acted more aggressively than men at parties where only soft drinks were served. But participants in the experimental group knew they had drunk alcohol, and those in the control group knew they had not. Aggression that appeared to result from alcohol might not have reflected drinking per se. Instead, it might have reflected the participants' expectations about the effects of alcohol. People tend to act in stereotypical ways when they believe they have been drinking alcohol (Eriksson, 2008). For instance, men tend to become less anxious in social situations, more aggressive, and more sexually aroused. To what extent do these behavior patterns reflect the direct effects of alcohol on the body, and to what extent do they affect people's *beliefs* about the effects of alcohol?

In medicine, physicians sometimes give patients **placebos** (a fake treatment, such as sugar pills, that appears to be genuine) when the patient insists on having a medical cure but the physician does not believe that medicine is necessary. When patients report that placebos have helped them, it is because they expected the pills to be of help and not because of the biochemical effects of the pills. Placebos are not limited to sugar pills. Interestingly, the taste of vodka and tonic water is almost impossible to distinguish from tonic water alone. Therefore, tonic water can be used as a placebo in experiments on the effects of alcohol. Moreover, if participants believe they have drunk alcohol but have actually been given tonic water only, we may conclude that changes in their behavior result from their beliefs about the effects of alcohol and not from alcohol itself.

Well-designed experiments control for the effects of expectations by creating conditions under which participants are unaware of, or **blind** to, the treatment. Placebos are one way of keeping participants blind as to whether they have received a particular treatment. Yet researchers may also have expectations. They may be "rooting for" a certain treatment outcome, a phenomenon known as *experimenter bias*. For instance, tobacco company executives may wish to show that cigarette smoking is harmless. In such cases, it is useful if the people measuring the experimental outcomes

are unaware of which participants have received the treatment. Studies in which neither the participants nor the experimenters know who has obtained the treatment are called **double-blind studies**.

Neither the participants nor the researchers know who is receiving the real treatment in many experiments. For example, the Food and Drug Administration requires double-blind studies before it allows the marketing of new drugs. The drug and the placebo look and taste alike. Experimenters assign the drug or placebo to participants at random. Neither the participants nor the observers know who is taking the drug and who is taking the placebo. After the final measurements have been made, a neutral panel (a group of people who have no personal stake in the outcome of the study) judges whether the effects of the drug differed from those of the placebo.

In one double-blind study on the effects of alcohol on aggression, Alan Lang and his colleagues (1975) pretested a highball of vodka and tonic water to determine that it could not be discriminated by taste from tonic water alone. They then recruited college men who described themselves as "social drinkers" to participate in the study. Some of the men drank vodka and tonic water. Others drank tonic water only. Of the men who drank vodka, half were misled into believing they had drunk tonic water only (see Figure 1.7). Of those who drank tonic water only, half were misled into believing their drink contained vodka. Thus, half the participants were blind to their treatment. Experimenters defined aggression as pressing a lever that participants believed would deliver an electric shock to another person. The researchers who measured the men's aggressive responses were also blind concerning which participants had drunk vodka.

The research team found that men who believed that they had drunk vodka responded more aggressively

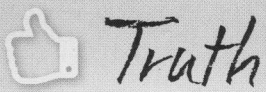

T F   In many experiments, neither the participants nor the researchers know who is receiving the real treatment and who is not.

It is true that neither the participants nor the researchers know who is receiving the real treatment in many experiments. This "double-blind" method controls for the effects of participants' and researchers' expectations.

placebo a bogus treatment that has the appearance of being genuine

blind in experimental terminology, unaware of whether or not one has received a treatment

double-blind study a study in which neither the subjects nor the observers know who has received the treatment

FIG.1.7 THE SIGNIFICANCE OF DOUBLE BLIND STUDIES

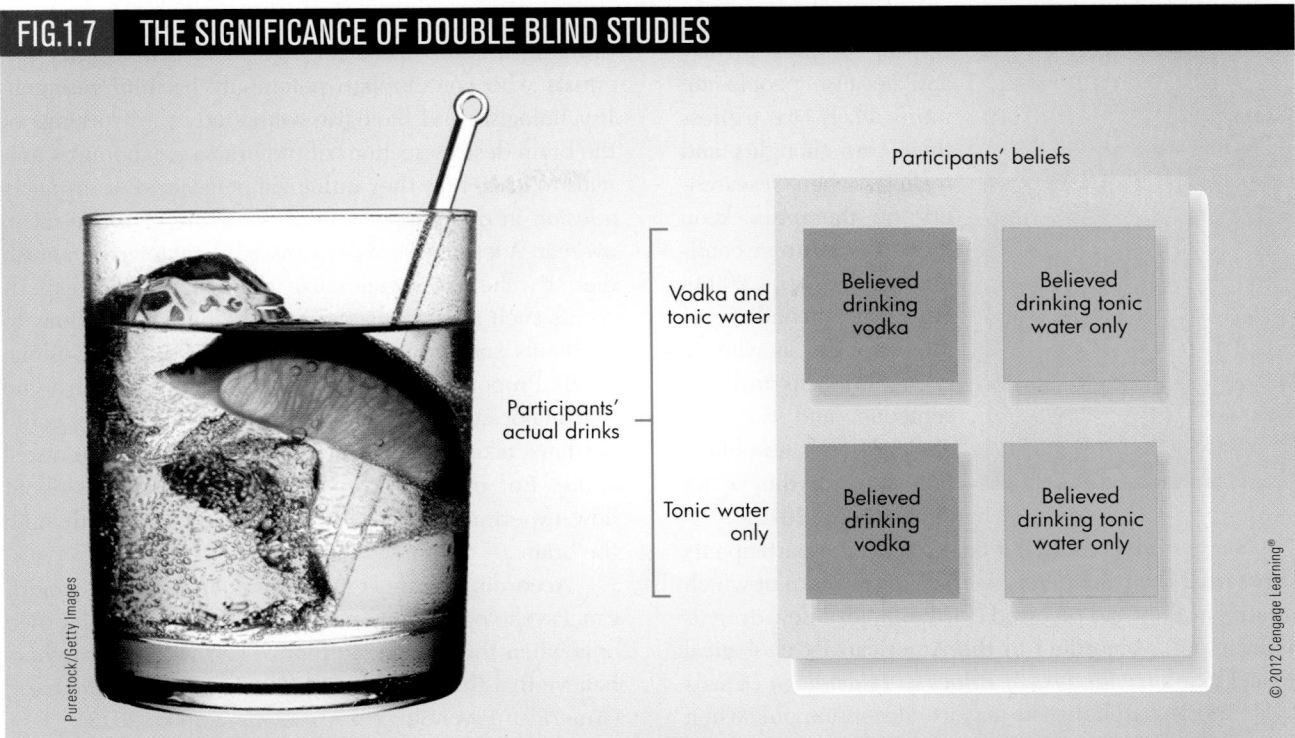

In the Lang Study on alcohol and aggression, the subjects were kept "blind" as to whether or not they had actually drunk alcohol by using tonic to mask the presence or absence of vodka. Blind studies allow psychologists to control for the effects of subjects' expectations.

(selected a higher level of shock) in response to a provocation than men who believed that they had drunk tonic water only. The actual content of the drink was immaterial. That is, the men's *belief* about what they drank affected their behavior more than what they actually consumed. The results of the Lang study differ dramatically from those reported by Boyatzis, perhaps because the Boyatzis study did not control for the effects of expectations or beliefs about alcohol.

1-5h ETHICS OF RESEARCH WITH HUMANS

If the Lang group were running their experiment today rather than in the 1970s, they would probably have been denied permission to do so by a university ethics review committee. Why? Because the researchers gave some participants alcohol to drink—a potentially harmful treatment, especially to participants who might have drinking problems—and deceived the entire group about the purposes and methods of the study. Was their method ethical?

Psychologists adhere to a number of ethical standards that are intended to promote individual dignity, human welfare, and scientific integrity. The standards are also intended to ensure that psychologists do not undertake research methods or treatments that are harmful. In virtually all institutional settings, including colleges, hospitals, and research foundations, ethics review committees help researchers consider the potential harm of their methods and review proposed studies according to ethical guidelines. When such committees find that proposed research might be unacceptably harmful to participants, they may withhold approval until the proposal has been modified. Ethics review committees also weigh the potential benefits of research against the potential harm.

Today, individuals must provide **informed consent** before they participate in research (Knaus et al., 2012). Having a general overview of the research and the opportunity to choose not to participate apparently give them a sense of control and decrease the stress of participating (Fisher, 2009). Is there a way in which participants in the Lang study could have provided informed consent? What do you think?

Psychologists keep the records of research participants and clients

informed consent a participant's agreement to participate in research after receiving information about the purposes of the study and the nature of the treatments

confidential because they respect people's privacy and because people are more likely to express their true thoughts and feelings when researchers or therapists keep their disclosures confidential (Fisher, 2009). Sometimes, conflicts of interest arise, as when a client threatens to harm someone, and the psychologist feels an obligation to warn the victim (Knaus et al., 2012).

Some studies could not be conducted if participants know what the researchers were trying to learn or which treatment they had received (for example, a new drug or a sugar pill). According to the American Psychological Association's *Handbooks of Ethics in Psychology* (Knaus et al., 2012), psychologists may use deception only when they believe the benefits of the research outweigh its potential harm, when they believe the individuals might have been willing to participate if they had understood the benefits of the research, and when participants are **debriefed** afterward—that is, the purposes and methods of the research are explained.

Participants in the Lang study on alcohol and aggression were deceived in two ways. The researchers (a) misinformed them about what they were drinking and (b) told them they were shocking other participants when they were actually only pressing switches on an unconnected control board. (*Aggression* was defined for purposes of the study as pressing these switches.) The study could not have been run without deception, but the ethics of deceiving research participants remains debated.

1-5i ETHICS OF RESEARCH WITH ANIMALS

Psychologists and other scientists frequently use animals to conduct research that cannot be carried out with humans. For example, experiments on the effects of early separation from the mother have been done with monkeys and other animals. Such research has helped psychologists investigate the formation of parent–child bonds of attachment.

debrief to explain the purposes and methods of a completed procedure to a participant

Experiments with infant monkeys highlight some of the ethical issues faced by psychologists and other scientists who contemplate potentially harmful research. Psychologists and biologists who study the workings of the brain destroy sections of the brains of laboratory animals to learn how they influence behavior. For instance, a lesion in one part of a brain structure causes a rat to overeat. A lesion elsewhere causes the rat to go on a crash diet. Psychologists generalize to humans from experiments such as these in the hope of finding solutions to problems such as eating disorders (Mehta & Gosling, 2008). Proponents of the use of animals in research argue that major advances in medicine and psychology could not have taken place without them (Ringach & Jentsch, 2009). For example, we would know much less about how experimental drugs affect cancerous growths and the brain.

According to the ethical guidelines of the American Psychological Association, animals may be harmed only when there is no alternative and when researchers believe that the benefits of the research justify the harm (American Psychological Association, 2002; 2012).

Now that we have an overview of psychology as a science, we will move on to the connections between psychology and biology in Chapter 2. Psychologists assume that our behaviors and our mental processes are related to biological events. In Chapter 2 we consider the evidence for this assumption.

BonkersAboutScience/Alamy

Researchers in many fields—including psychology, biology, and medical sciences—use animals for studies they could or would not run with human participants. In such cases, psychologists have strict standards as to how animals are to be cared for and treated.

STUDY TOOLS 1

IN THE BOOK, YOU CAN:

☐ Check your understanding of what you've read with the quizzes that follow.

☐ Rip out the chapter review card at the back of the book to have a summary of the chapter and the key terms handy.

ONLINE AT CENGAGEBRAIN.COM YOU CAN:

☐ View a learning module on the difference between scientific and armchair psychology.

☐ Prepare for tests with quizzes.

☐ Review the key terms with Flash Cards.

☐ Play games to master concepts.

FILL-INS

Answers can be found in the back of the book.

1. Psychology is defined as the study of _____ and mental processes.

2. _____ psychologists evaluate problems such as anxiety and depression through interviews and psychological tests.

3. _____ founded the school of structuralism.

4. _____ psychologists saw our perceptions as wholes that give meaning to parts.

5. _____ psychologists note that only the fittest organisms reach maturity and reproduce, thereby transmitting their genes to future generations and causing species to evolve in adaptive directions.

6. Kenneth and Mamie Phipps _____ conducted research that influenced a Supreme Court decision on segregated schools.

7. Samples must accurately represent the target _____.

8. In the _____ method, a large sample of people answer questions about their attitudes or behavior.

9. Ideal experiments use experimental groups and _____ groups.

10. Psychologists adhere to _____ standards that help promote the dignity of the individual, maintain scientific integrity, and protect research participants and clinical clients from harm.

MULTIPLE CHOICE

1. **Psychology is defined as the scientific study of**
   a. behavior and mental processes.
   b. diagnosis and treatment of behavioral disorders.
   c. conscious and unconscious mental processes.
   d. the mind.

2. **School psychologists are employed by school districts to**
   a. develop achievement and aptitude tests.
   b. identify and assist students who have problems that interfere with their learning.
   c. assess the development of children in the school system.
   d. develop curriculum for teachers to deliver.

3. **What distinguished Wilhelm Wundt's contribution from other contributions to psychology?**
   a. He wrote the first textbook of psychology.
   b. He defined psychology as the science of behavior.
   c. He established psychology as a laboratory science.
   d. He studied insight in lower animals.

4. **The school of psychology that places unconscious impulses and desires at the center of human behavior is**
   a. psychoanalysis.
   b. humanism-existentialism.
   c. functionalism.
   d. Gestalt psychology.

5. **The first female president of the American Psychological Association was**
   a. Mary Ainsworth.   c. Karen Horney.
   b. Elizabeth Loftus.   d. Mary Whiton Calkins.

6. **A(n) _____ is a specific statement about behavior or mental processes that is tested through research.**
   a. observation   c. theory
   b. scientific method   d. hypothesis

7. **In a _____, each member of a population has an equal chance of being selected to participate.**
   a. random sample   c. stratified sample
   b. selection sample   d. free sample

8. **A disadvantage of survey research is _____. For example, people tend to overrate behaviors like church attendance and proper hygiene.**
   a. inaccurate self-report
   b. too much detail
   c. that people are too honest
   d. too few survey companies

9. **You design a test of intelligence. On the theory that intelligence is related to academic performance, you use _____ to test the relationship between performance on your new test and grades in school.**
   a. an experimental method
   b. a test-retest method
   c. the correlational method
   d. naturalistic observation

10. **Dr. Liu was interested in testing the effects of violent television on six-year-old children. She showed one group a particularly violent episode of *Power Rangers* and another group watched a short nonviolent episode of an old Bill Cosby show. She then observed the groups in the playground and measured their behaviors. What is the dependent variable in this study?**
   a. Bill Cosby and his family
   b. violent or nonviolent television show
   c. the behavior on the playground
   d. the amount of time watching television

2 | Biology and Psychology

Colin Anderson/Photographer's Choice/Getty Images

LEARNING OUTCOMES

After studying this chapter, you will be able to...

2-1 Describe the nervous system, including neurons, neural impulses, and neurotransmitters

2-2 List the structures of the brain and their functions

2-3 Explain the role of the endocrine system and list the endocrine glands

2-4 Describe evolutionary psychology and the connections between heredity, behavior, and mental processes

After you finish this chapter, go to **PAGE 59** for the **STUDY TOOLS**

"Gage is no longer Gage," said those who had known him before the accident.

There are many key characters in the history of psychology, and some of them did not arrive there intentionally. One of these was a promising railroad worker who was helping our young nation stretch from coast to coast. His name was Phineas Gage. Gage was highly admired by his friends and coworkers. But all that changed one day in 1848. While he was tamping down the blasting powder for a dynamite charge, Gage accidentally set the powder off. The inch-thick metal tamping rod shot upward through his cheek and brain and out the top of his head.

If the trajectory of the rod had been slightly different Gage would have died. Although Gage fell back in a heap, he was miraculously alive. His coworkers watched in shock as he stood up a few moments later and spoke. While the local doctor marveled at the hole through Gage's head, Gage asked when he'd be able to return to work. Two months later, Gage's external wounds had healed, but the psychological aspects of the wound were now obvious. His former employer, who had regarded him as "the most efficient and capable foreman in their employ previous to his injury" (Harlow, 1868) refused to rehire him because he had changed so much

The equilibrium or balance, so to speak, between his intellectual faculties and animal propensities, seems to have been destroyed. He is ... irreverent, indulging at times in the grossest profanity (which was not previously his custom). [He showed little consideration for other people, was] impatient of restraint or advice when it conflicts with his desires ... obstinate, yet capricious and vacillating, devising many plans of future operation which are no sooner arranged than they are abandonee in turn for others ... But all had not been lost in Gage's brain. In fact, many of his intellectual skills were just fine, apparently untouched.

Generations of researchers—including psychologists, physicians, biologists, and neuroscientists—have wondered how the damage to Gage's brain might have caused the changes in his personality. Perhaps the trajectory of the rod spared parts of the frontal lobes that are involved in language and movement but damaged areas connected with personality and emotional response (Giudotti, 2012; Van Horn et al., 2013). In this chapter, we will learn about the frontal lobes of the brain and much more. We will travel from the small to the large—from the microscopic brain cells that hold and transmit information, to the visible structures that provide the basis for functions such as memory, speech, sensation, thought, planning, and voluntary movement.

> "**Gage** is no longer **Gage,**" said those who had known him before the accident.

 ## 2-1 THE NERVOUS SYSTEM: ON BEING WIRED

The nervous system is a system of nerves involved in thought processes, heartbeat, visual-motor coordination, and so on. The nervous system consists of the brain, the spinal cord, and other parts that make it possible for us to receive information from the world outside and to act on the world. It is composed of cells, most of which are *neurons.* Here we begin our study of the nervous system.

2-1a NEURONS: INTO THE FABULOUS FOREST

Within our brains lies a fabulous forest of nerve cells, or neurons. **Neurons** are specialized cells of the nervous system that conduct impulses. Neurons can be visualized as having branches, trunks, and roots—something like trees. As we voyage through this forest, we see that many nerve cells lie alongside one another as in a thicket of

neuron a specialized cell of the nervous system that receives and transmits messages

trees. But neurons can also lie end to end, with their "roots" intertwined with the "branches" of the neurons that lie below. Neurons receive "messages" from a number of sources such as light, other neurons, and pressure on the skin, and they can pass these messages along in a complex biological dance. We are born with more than 100 billion neurons. Most of them are found in the brain.

The nervous system also contains **glial cells**. Glial cells remove dead neurons and waste products from the nervous system; nourish and insulate neurons; form a fatty, insulating substance called *myelin;* and play a role in neural transmission of messages (Rozanski et al., 2013). But neurons occupy center stage in the nervous system. The messages transmitted by neurons somehow account for phenomena ranging from the perception of an itch from a mosquito bite to the coordination of a skier's vision and muscles to the composition of a concerto to the solution of an algebraic equation.

Neurons vary according to their functions and their location. Neurons in the brain may be only a fraction of an inch in length; whereas neurons in the legs can be several feet long. Most neurons include a cell body, dendrites, and an axon (see Figure 2.1). The cell body contains the core or *nucleus* of the cell. The nucleus uses oxygen and nutrients to generate the energy needed to carry out the work of the cell. Anywhere from a few to several hundred short fibers, or **dendrites**, extend like roots from the cell body to receive incoming messages from thousands of adjoining neurons.

Each neuron has an **axon** that extends like a trunk from the cell body. Axons are very thin, but those that carry messages from the toes to the spinal cord extend several feet in length—even though they remain microscopic! Like tree trunks, axons can branch in different directions. Axons end in small, bulb-shaped structures called *axon terminals* or *terminal buttons*. Neurons carry messages in one direction only: from the dendrites or cell body through the axon to the axon terminals. The messages are then transmitted from the terminal buttons to other neurons, muscles, or glands.

As a child matures, the axons of neurons become longer and the dendrites and terminals proliferate, creating vast interconnected networks for the transmission of complex messages. The number of glial cells also increases as the nervous system develops, contributing to its dense appearance.

MYELIN The axons of many neurons are wrapped tightly with white, fatty **myelin** that makes them look like strings of sausages under the microscope (Figure 2.1). The fat insulates the axon from electrically charged atoms, or *ions*, found in the fluids that surround the nervous system. The myelin sheath minimizes leakage of the electrical current being carried along the axon, thereby allowing messages to be conducted more efficiently.

Myelination is part of the maturation process that leads to a child's ability to crawl and walk during the first year. Infants are not physiologically "ready" to engage in visual-motor coordination and other activities until the coating process reaches certain levels. In people with the disease multiple sclerosis, myelin is replaced with a hard fibrous tissue that throws off the timing of nerve impulses and disrupts muscular control.

AFFERENT AND EFFERENT NEURONS If someone steps on your toes, the sensation is registered by receptors or sensory neurons near the surface of your

glial cells cells that remove dead neurons and waste products from the nervous system, nourish and insulate neurons, form myelin, and play a role in neural transmission of messages

dendrites root-like structures, attached to the cell body of a neuron, that receive impulses, or incoming messages, from other neurons

axon a long, thin part of a neuron that transmits impulses to other neurons from bulb-shaped structures called *axon terminals or terminal buttons*

myelin a fatty substance that encases and insulates axons, facilitating transmission of neural impulses

Truth or Fiction?

WHAT DO YOU THINK? Folklore, common sense, or nonsense? Select T for "truth" or F for "fiction," and check the accuracy of your answers as you read through the chapter.

T	F	A single cell can stretch all the way from your spine to your toe.
T	F	Messages travel in the brain by means of electricity.
T	F	A brain cell can send out hundreds of messages each second—and manage to catch some rest in between.
T	F	Fear can give you indigestion.
T	F	The human brain is larger than that of any other animal.
T	F	If a surgeon were to stimulate a certain part of your brain electrically, you might swear that someone had stroked your leg.
T	F	Charles Darwin was nearly excluded from the voyage that led to the development of his theory of evolution because the captain of the ship did not like the shape of his nose.

FIG.2.1 THE ANATOMY OF A NEURON

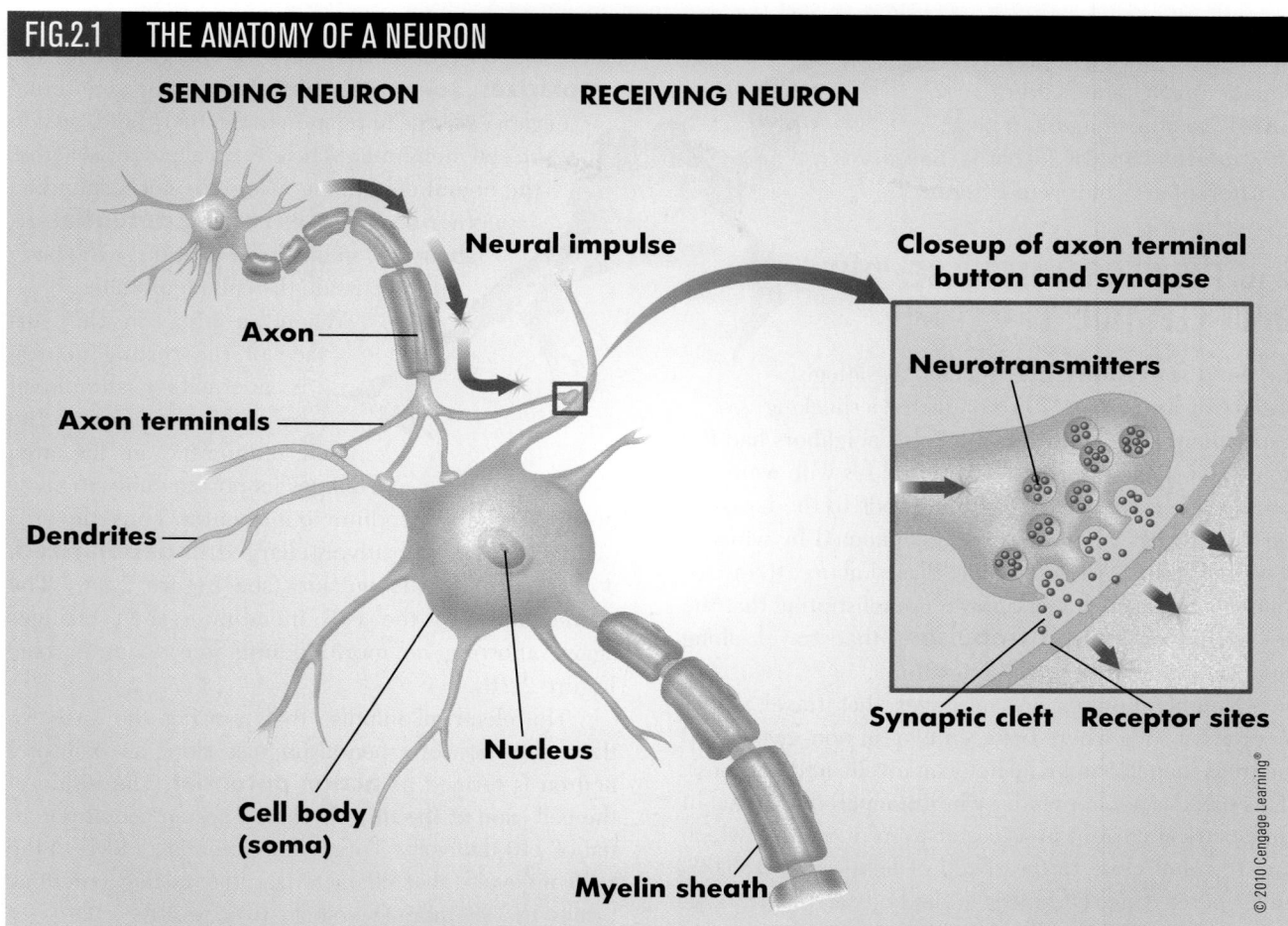

SENDING NEURON **RECEIVING NEURON**

Neural impulse

Closeup of axon terminal button and synapse

Axon

Axon terminals

Neurotransmitters

Dendrites

Nucleus

Synaptic cleft   Receptor sites

Cell body (soma)

Myelin sheath

© 2010 Cengage Learning®

"Messages" enter neurons through dendrites, are transmitted along the trunk-like axon, and then are sent from axon terminal buttons to muscles, glands, and other neurons. Axon terminal buttons contain sacs of chemicals called *neurotransmitters*. Neurotransmitters are released into the *synaptic cleft*, where many of them bind to *receptor sites* on the dendrites of the receiving neuron.

skin. Then it is transmitted to the spinal cord and brain through *sensory neurons,* or **afferent neurons**, which can be as long as two to three feet in length. In the brain, subsequent messages might be conveyed by associative neurons that are only a few thousandths of an inch long. You experience the pain through this process and perhaps entertain some rather nasty thoughts about the perpetrator, who is now apologizing and begging for understanding.

Long before you arrive at any logical conclusions, however, *motor neurons,* or **efferent neurons**, send messages to your foot so that you withdraw it and begin an impressive hopping routine. Efferent neurons transmit messages from the brain or spinal cord to muscles and glands. Other efferent neurons stimulate glands so that your heart is beating more rapidly, you are sweating, and the hair on the back of your arms has become erect! Being a good sport, you say, "Oh, it's nothing." But considering all the neurons involved, it really is something, isn't it?

In case you think that afferent and efferent

👍 *Truth*

| **T** | F | A single cell can stretch all the way from your spine to your toe. |

It is true that a single cell can stretch all the way from your spine to your toe, yet it is "microscopic" because of its thinness.

afferent neurons neurons that transmit messages from sensory receptors to the spinal cord and brain; also called *sensory neurons*

efferent neurons neurons that transmit messages from the brain or spinal cord to muscles and glands; also called *motor neurons*

neurons will be hard to distinguish because they sound pretty much the SAME to you, remember that they *are* the "SAME." That is, Sensory is to Afferent as Motor is to Efferent.

2-1b THE NEURAL IMPULSE: "THE BODY ELECTRIC"[1]

In the 18th century, the Italian physiologist Luigi Galvani (1737–1798) conducted a shocking experiment in a rainstorm. While his neighbors had the sense to remain indoors, Galvani and his wife were out on the porch connecting lightning rods to the heads of dissected frogs whose legs were connected by wires to a well of water. When lightning blazed above, the frogs' muscles contracted. Galvani was demonstrating that the messages—or **neural impulses**—that travel along neurons are electrochemical in nature.

Neural impulses are messages that travel within neurons at somewhere between two (in non-myelinated neurons) and 225 miles an hour (in myelinated neurons). This speed is not impressive when compared with that of an electrical current in a toaster oven or a lamp, which can travel at close to the speed of light—over 186,000 miles per second. Distances in the body are short, however, and a message will travel from a toe to the brain in perhaps 1/50th of a second.

AN ELECTROCHEMICAL VOYAGE The process by which neural impulses travel is electrochemical. Chemical changes take place within neurons that cause an electrical charge to be transmitted along their lengths. Neurons and body fluids contain *ions*—positively or negatively charged atoms. In a resting state—that is, when a neuron is not being stimulated by its neighbors—negatively charged chloride (Cl–) ions are plentiful within the neuron, contributing to an overall negative charge in relation to the outside. The difference in electrical charge readies, or **polarizes**, a neuron for firing by creating an internal negative charge in relation to the body fluid outside the cell membrane. The electrical potential across the neural membrane when it is not responding to other neurons—its **resting potential**—is about –70 millivolts in relation to the body fluid outside the cell membrane.

When an area on the surface of the resting neuron is adequately stimulated by other neurons, the cell membrane in the area changes its permeability to allow positively charged sodium ions to enter. Thus, the area of entry becomes positively charged, or **depolarized**, with respect to the outside (see Figure 2.2A). The permeability of the cell membrane then changes again, allowing no more sodium ions to enter (see Figure 2.2B).

The electrical impulse that provides the basis for the conduction of a neural impulse along an axon of a neuron is termed its **action potential**. The inside of the cell axon at the disturbed area has an action potential of 110 millivolts. This action potential, added to the −70 millivolts that characterizes the resting potential, brings the membrane voltage to a positive charge of about +30 to +40 millivolts (see Figure 2.2). This inner change causes the next section of the cell to become permeable to sodium ions. At the same time, other positively charged (potassium) ions are being pumped out of the area of the cell that was previously affected, which returns the area to its resting potential. In this way, the neural impulse is transmitted continuously along an axon. Because the impulse is created anew as it progresses, its strength does not change.

FIRING: HOW MESSAGES VOYAGE FROM NEURON TO NEURON The conduction of the neural impulse along the length of a neuron is what is meant by *firing*. When a rifle fires, it sends a bullet speeding through its barrel and discharges it at more than 1,000 feet per second. Neurons also fire, but instead of having a barrel, a neuron has an axon. Instead of discharging a bullet, it releases *neurotransmitters*.

Some neurons fire in less than 1/1,000th of a second. When they fire, neurons transmit messages to other neurons, muscles, or glands. However, neurons will not fire unless the incoming messages combine to reach a certain strength, which is defined as the *threshold* at which a

neural impulse the electrochemical discharge of a nerve cell, or neuron

polarize to ready a neuron for firing by creating an internal negative charge in relation to the body fluid outside the cell membrane

resting potential the electrical potential across the neural membrane when it is not responding to other neurons

depolarize to reduce the resting potential of a cell membrane from about 70 millivolts toward zero

action potential the electrical impulse that provides the basis for the conduction of a neural impulse along an axon of a neuron

[1]From Walt Whitman's *Leaves of Grass*.

FIG.2.2 | CHANGES IN ELECTRICAL CHARGES AS A NEURAL IMPULSE IS TRANSMITTED ALONG THE LENGTH OF AN AXON

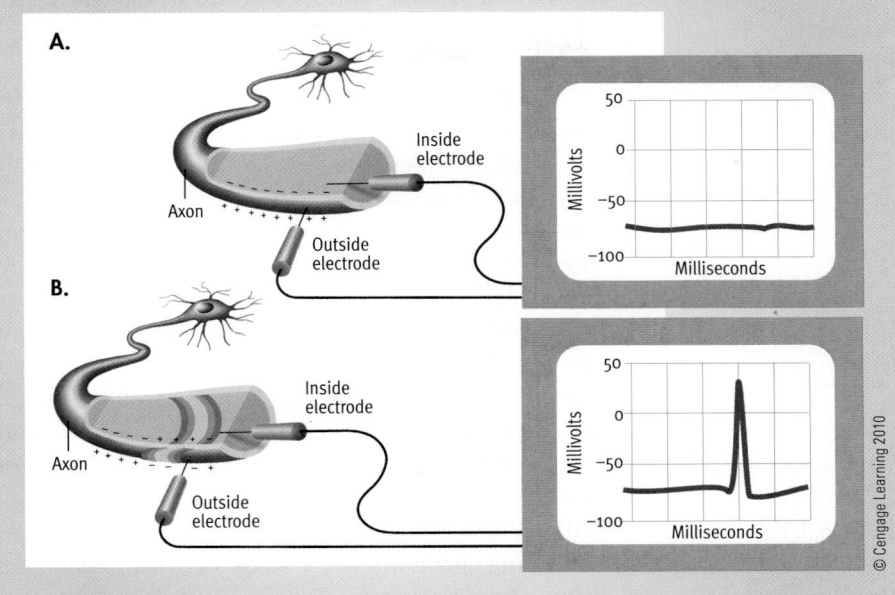

Electrical charges inside and outside axons are measured by microscopic glass tubes placed inside and outside the cell membranes of axons. As shown in part A, when an axon is at rest, it has a negative charge of about 270 millivolts. But when sodium ions enter and the area of entry is depolarized, as shown in part B, the charge in that part of the axon rises to 130 to 140 millivolts. The change causes the next part of the cell membrane to become permeable to sodium ions, continuing the transmission of the neural impulse along the axon.

Source: Weiten *Psychology*, 8e. Copyright © 2010. Cengage Learning.

neuron will fire. A weak message may cause a temporary shift in electrical charge at some point along the cell membrane, but this charge will dissipate if the neuron is not stimulated to its threshold.

Every time a neuron fires, it transmits an impulse of the same strength. This occurrence is known as

T	F	A brain cell can send out hundreds of messages each second—and manage to catch some rest in between.

It is true that neurons in the brain can send out hundreds of messages each second—and manage to catch some rest in between. That "rest" is termed the *refractory period.*

the **all-or-none principle**. That is, either a neuron fires or it doesn't. Neurons fire more often when they have been stimulated by larger numbers of other neurons. Stronger stimuli cause more frequent firing, but again, the strength of each firing remains the same.

For a few thousandths of a second after firing, a neuron is in a **refractory period**; that is, it is insensitive to messages from other neurons and will not fire. This period is a time of recovery during which sodium is prevented from passing through the neuronal membrane. Because such periods of "recovery" might occur hundreds of times per second, it seems a rapid recovery and a short rest indeed.

THE SYNAPSE: ON BEING WELL-CONNECTED A neuron relays its message to another neuron across a junction called a **synapse**. A synapse consists of an axon terminal from the transmitting neuron, a dendrite, or the body of a receiving neuron, and a fluid-filled gap between the two that is called the *synaptic cleft* (see Figure 2.1). Although the neural impulse is electrical, it does not jump across the synaptic cleft like a spark. Instead, when a nerve impulse reaches a synapse, axon terminals release chemicals into the synaptic cleft like myriad ships being cast into the sea. Scientists have identified a few dozen of these chemicals to date. Let's consider a few that are usually of the greatest interest to psychologists.

all-or-none principle the fact that a neuron fires an impulse of the same strength whenever its action potential is triggered

refractory period a phase following firing during which a neuron is less sensitive to messages from other neurons and will not fire

synapse a junction between the axon terminals of one neuron and the dendrites or cell body of another neuron

© Cengage Learning 2010

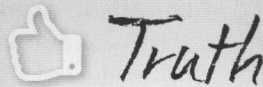
2-1c NEUROTRANSMITTERS: THE CHEMICAL KEYS TO COMMUNICATION

Sacs called *synaptic vesicles* in the axon terminals contain **neurotransmitters**—the chemical keys to communication (see Figure 2.1). When a neural impulse (action potential) reaches the axon terminal, the vesicles release varying amounts of neurotransmitters into the synaptic cleft. From there, they influence the receiving neuron.

Each kind of neurotransmitter has a unique chemical structure, and each can fit into a specifically tailored harbor, or **receptor site**, on the receiving cell (see Figure 2.1). The analogy of a key fitting into a lock is often used to describe this process. Once released, not all molecules of a neurotransmitter find their way into receptor sites of other neurons. "Loose" neurotransmitters are usually either broken down or reabsorbed by the axon terminal (a process called *reuptake*).

Some neurotransmitters act to *excite* other neurons—that is, to cause other neurons to fire. Other neurotransmitters *inhibit* receiving neurons. That is, they prevent the neurons from firing. The sum of the stimulation—excitatory and inhibitory—determines whether a neuron will fire.

Neurotransmitters are involved in physical processes such as muscle contraction and psychological processes such as thoughts and emotions. Excesses or deficiencies of neurotransmitters have been linked to psychological disorders such as depression and schizophrenia. Let's consider the effects of some neurotransmitters that are of interest to psychologists: acetylcholine (ACh), dopamine, norepinephrine, serotonin, GABA, and endorphins.

Acetylcholine (ACh) is a neurotransmitter that controls muscle contractions. It is excitatory at synapses between nerves and muscles that involve voluntary movement but inhibitory at the heart and some other locations. The effects of the poison *curare* highlight the functioning of ACh. Curare is extracted from plants by South American indigenous people and used in hunting. If an arrow tipped with curare pierces the skin and the poison enters the body, it prevents ACh from binding to the receptor sites on neurons. Because ACh helps muscles move, curare causes paralysis. The victim is prevented from contracting the muscles used in breathing and dies from suffocation. Botulism, a disease that stems from food poisoning, prevents the release of ACh and has the same effect as curare.

ACh is normally prevalent in a part of the brain called the **hippocampus**, a structure involved in the formation of memories (Park & Spruston, 2012). When the amount of ACh available to the brain decreases, as in Alzheimer's disease, memory formation is impaired (Oz et al., 2013). In one experiment, researchers decreased the ACh available to the hippocampus of laboratory rats. As a result, the rats were incapable of learning their way through a maze, apparently because they could not remember which way to turn at various choice points (Egawa et al., 2002).

Dopamine is a neurotransmitter that acts in the brain and affects the ability to perceive pleasure, voluntary movement, and learning and memory. Nicotine, alcohol, and many other drugs are pleasurable because they heighten levels of dopamine. Deficiencies of dopamine are linked to Parkinson's disease, in which people progressively lose control over their muscles (Choi et al., 2012). They develop muscle tremors and jerky, uncoordinated movements.

The psychological disorder *schizophrenia* is characterized by confusion and false perceptions, and it has been linked to dopamine. People with schizophrenia may have more receptor sites for dopamine in an area of the brain that is involved in emotional responding. For this reason, they may "overutilize" the dopamine available in the brain (Fusar-Poli & Meyer-Lindenberg, 2013). Overutilization is connected with hallucinations and disturbances of thought and emotion. The phenothiazines, a

neurotransmitters chemical substances involved in the transmission of neural impulses from one neuron to another

receptor site a location on a dendrite of a receiving neuron tailored to receive a neurotransmitter

acetylcholine (ACh) a neurotransmitter that controls muscle contractions

hippocampus a structure of the brain that is involved in memory formation

dopamine a neurotransmitter that affects the ability to perceive pleasure, voluntary movement, and learning and memory; it is involved in Parkinson's disease and appears to play a role in schizophrenia

Stephen Jaffe/AFP/Getty Images

The boxer Muhammad Ali and the actor Michael J. Fox are two of the better-known individuals who are living with Parkinson's disease. Parkinson's disease is linked to deficiencies of the neurotransmitter dopamine. Dopamine is also involved in the experiencing of pleasure.

Serotonin is a neurotransmitter that is involved in emotional arousal and sleep. Deficiencies of serotonin have been linked to eating disorders, alcoholism, depression, aggression, and insomnia (Kamphuis et al., 2012; Risch et al., 2009). The drug LSD decreases the action of serotonin and is also believed to increase the utilization of dopamine, which may be the mechanism by which it produces hallucinations.

Gamma-aminobutyricacid (GABA) is another neurotransmitter of great interest to psychologists. One reason is that GABA is an inhibitory neurotransmitter that may help calm anxiety reactions (Shen et al., 2013). Tranquilizers and alcohol may quell anxiety by binding with GABA receptors and amplifying its effects. One class of anti-anxiety drug may also increase the sensitivity of receptor sites to GABA. Other studies link deficiencies of GABA to depression (Karolewicz et al., 2009).

Endorphins are inhibitory neurotransmitters. The word *endorphin* is the contraction of *endogenous morphine*. *Endogenous* means "developing from within." Endorphins occur naturally in the brain and in the bloodstream and are similar to the narcotic morphine in their

group of drugs used in the treatment of schizophrenia, inhibit the action of dopamine by blocking some dopamine receptors (Neve, 2009). Because of their action, phenothiazines may have Parkinson's-like side effects, which are usually lessened by lowering the dosage or prescribing other drugs.

Norepinephrine is produced largely by neurons in the brain stem and acts both as a neurotransmitter and as a hormone. It is an excitatory neurotransmitter that speeds up the heartbeat and other body processes and is involved in general arousal, learning and memory, and eating. Excesses and deficiencies of norepinephrine have been linked to mood disorders. Deficiencies of both ACh and norepinephrine particularly impair memory formation (Qi & Gold, 2009).

The stimulants cocaine and amphetamine ("speed") boost norepinephrine (as well as dopamine) production, increasing the firing of neurons and leading to persistent arousal. Amphetamines both facilitate the release of these neurotransmitters and prevent their reuptake. Cocaine also blocks reuptake.

functions and effects. They lock into receptor sites for chemicals that transmit pain messages to the brain. Once the endorphin "key" is in the "lock," the pain-causing chemicals are locked out. Endorphins may also increase our sense of competence, enhance the functioning of the immune system, and be connected with the pleasurable "runner's high" reported by many long-distance runners (Weinstein & Weinstein, 2013).

There you have it—a fabulous forest of

norepinephrine a neurotransmitter whose action is similar to that of the hormone epinephrine and that may play a role in depression

serotonin a neurotransmitter involved in emotional arousal and sleep; deficiencies of serotonin have been linked to eating disorders, alcoholism, depression, aggression, and insomnia

gamma-aminobutyric acid (GABA) an inhibitory neurotransmitter that apparently helps calm anxiety

endorphins inhibitory neurotransmitters that occur naturally in the brain and in the bloodstream and are similar to the narcotic morphine in their functions and effects

neurons in which billions upon billions of axon terminals are pouring armadas of neurotransmitters into synaptic clefts at any given time. The combined activity of all these neurotransmitters determines which messages will be transmitted and which ones will not. You experience your sensations, your thoughts, and your control over your body as psychological events, but the psychological events come from billions upon billions of electrochemical events.

We can think of neurons as the microscopic building blocks of the nervous system. Millions upon millions of these neurons gather together to form larger, visible structures that we think of as the parts of the nervous system. We discuss those parts next.

2-1d THE PARTS OF THE NERVOUS SYSTEM

The nervous system consists of the brain, the spinal cord, and the **nerves** linking them to the sensory organs, muscles, and glands. As shown in Figure 2.3, the brain and the spinal cord make up the **central nervous system**. If you compare your nervous system to a computer, your central nervous system would be your central processing unit (CPU).

The sensory (afferent) neurons, which receive and transmit messages to the brain and spinal cord, and the motor (efferent) neurons, which transmit messages from the brain or spinal cord to the muscles and glands, make up the peripheral nervous system. In the comparison of the nervous system to a computer, the **peripheral nervous system** makes up the nervous system's peripheral devices— keyboard, mouse, DVD drive, and so on. You would not be able to feed information to your computer's central processing unit without these *peripheral* devices. Other peripheral devices, such as your monitor and printer, allow you to follow what is happening inside your CPU and see what it has done.

THE PERIPHERAL NERVOUS SYSTEM: THE BODY'S PERIPHERAL DEVICES The peripheral nervous system consists of sensory and motor neurons that transmit messages to and from the central nervous

nerve a bundle of axons from many neurons

central nervous system the brain and spinal cord

peripheral nervous system the part of the nervous system consisting of the somatic nervous system and the autonomic nervous system

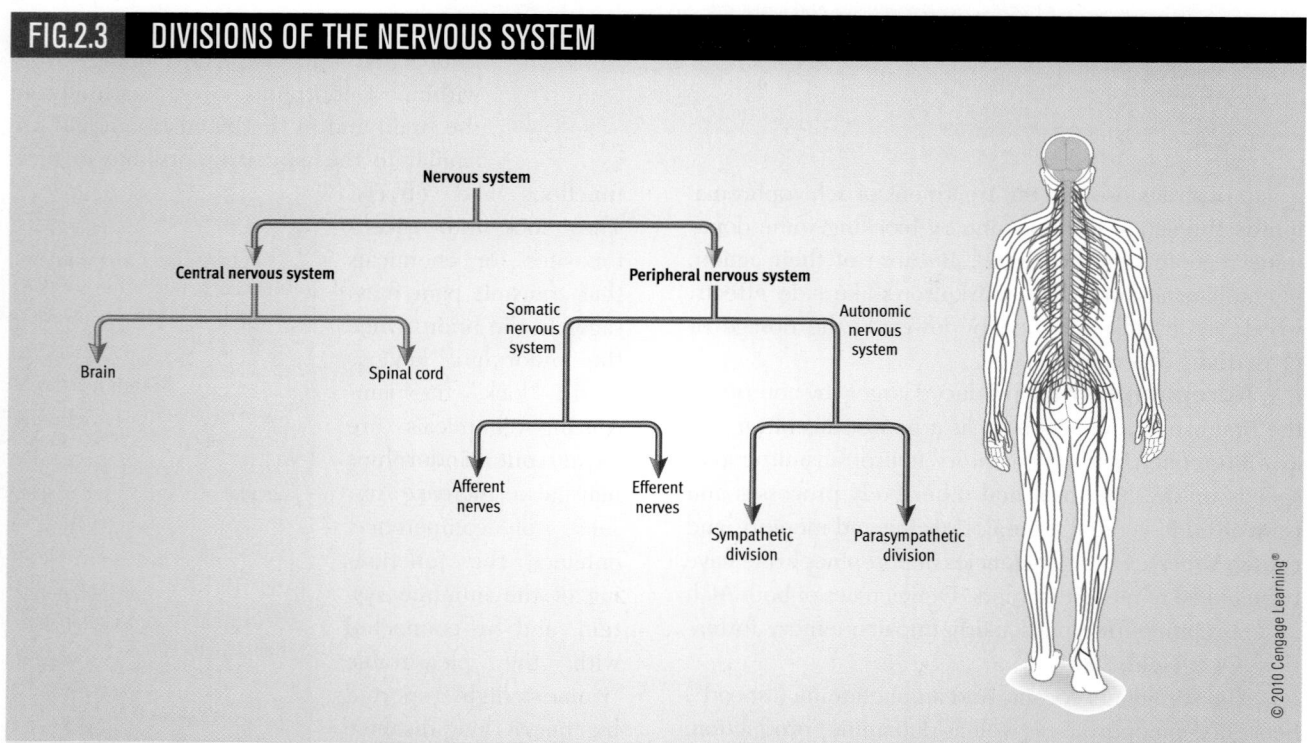

FIG.2.3   DIVISIONS OF THE NERVOUS SYSTEM

© 2010 Cengage Learning®

The nervous system contains two main divisions: the central nervous system and the peripheral nervous system. The central nervous system consists of the brain and spinal cord. The peripheral nervous system contains the somatic and autonomic systems. In turn, the autonomic nervous system has sympathetic and parasympathetic divisions.

system. Without the peripheral nervous system, our brains would be like computers without keyboards, mouses, DVDs, or other ways of inputting information. There would also be no monitors, printers, modems, or other ways of displaying or transmitting information. We would be isolated from the world. We would not be able to perceive it; we would not be able to act on it. The two main divisions of the peripheral nervous system are the *somatic nervous system* and the *autonomic nervous system.*

The **somatic nervous system** contains sensory (afferent) and motor (efferent) neurons. It transmits messages about sights, sounds, smells, temperature, body positions, and so on, to the central nervous system. Messages transmitted from the brain and spinal cord to the somatic nervous system control purposeful body movements such as raising a hand, winking, or running, as well as the tiny, almost imperceptible movements that maintain our balance and posture.

The **autonomic nervous system (ANS)** also has afferent and efferent neurons and regulates the glands and the muscles of internal organs. Thus, the ANS controls activities such as heartbeat, respiration, digestion, and dilation of the pupils. These activities can occur automatically, while we are asleep. But some of them can be overridden by conscious control. You can breathe at a purposeful pace, for example. Methods like biofeedback and yoga also help people gain voluntary control of functions such as heart rate and blood pressure.

The ANS also has two branches, or divisions: *sympathetic* and *parasympathetic*. These branches have largely opposing effects. Many organs and glands are stimulated by both branches of the ANS (see Figure 2.4). When organs and glands are simultaneously stimulated by both divisions, their effects can average out to some degree. In general, the **sympathetic division** is most active during processes that involve spending body energy from stored reserves, such as a fight-or-flight response to a predator or when you find out that your rent is going to be raised. The **parasympathetic division** is most active during processes that replenish reserves of energy, such as eating. When we are afraid, the sympathetic division of the ANS accelerates the heart rate. When we relax, the parasympathetic division decelerates the heart rate. The parasympathetic division stimulates digestive processes, but the sympathetic branch, which can be activated by fear, inhibits digestion. Thus, fear can give you indigestion. The ANS is of particular interest to psychologists because its activities are linked to various emotions such as anxiety and love.

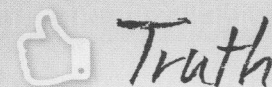
THE CENTRAL NERVOUS SYSTEM: THE BODY'S CENTRAL PROCESSING UNIT The central nervous system consists of the spinal cord and the brain. The **spinal cord** is a true "information superhighway"—a column of nerves as thick as a thumb. It transmits messages from sensory receptors to the brain and from the brain to muscles and glands throughout the body. The spinal cord also carries out some "local government." That is, it responds to some sources of external stimulation through spinal reflexes. A **spinal reflex** is an unlearned response to a stimulus that may require only two neurons—a sensory neuron and a motor neuron (see Figure 2.5). In some reflexes, a third neuron, called an *interneuron*, transmits the neural impulse from the sensory neuron through the spinal cord to the motor neuron.

The spinal cord and brain contain gray matter and white matter. **Gray matter** consists of non-myelinated neurons. Some of these are

somatic nervous system the division of the peripheral nervous system that connects the central nervous system with sensory receptors, skeletal muscles, and the surface of the body

autonomic nervous system (ANS) the division of the peripheral nervous system that regulates glands and activities such as heartbeat, respiration, digestion, and dilation of the pupils

sympathetic division the branch of the ANS that is most active during emotional responses, such as fear and anxiety, that spend the body's reserves of energy

parasympathetic division the branch of the ANS that is most active during processes (such as digestion) that restore the body's reserves of energy

spinal cord a column of nerves within the spine that transmits messages from sensory receptors to the brain and from the brain to muscles and glands throughout the body

spinal reflex a simple, unlearned response to a stimulus that may involve only two neurons

gray matter the grayish neurons and neural segments that are involved in spinal reflexes

FIG.2.4 THE BRANCHES OF THE AUTONOMIC NERVOUS SYSTEM (ANS)

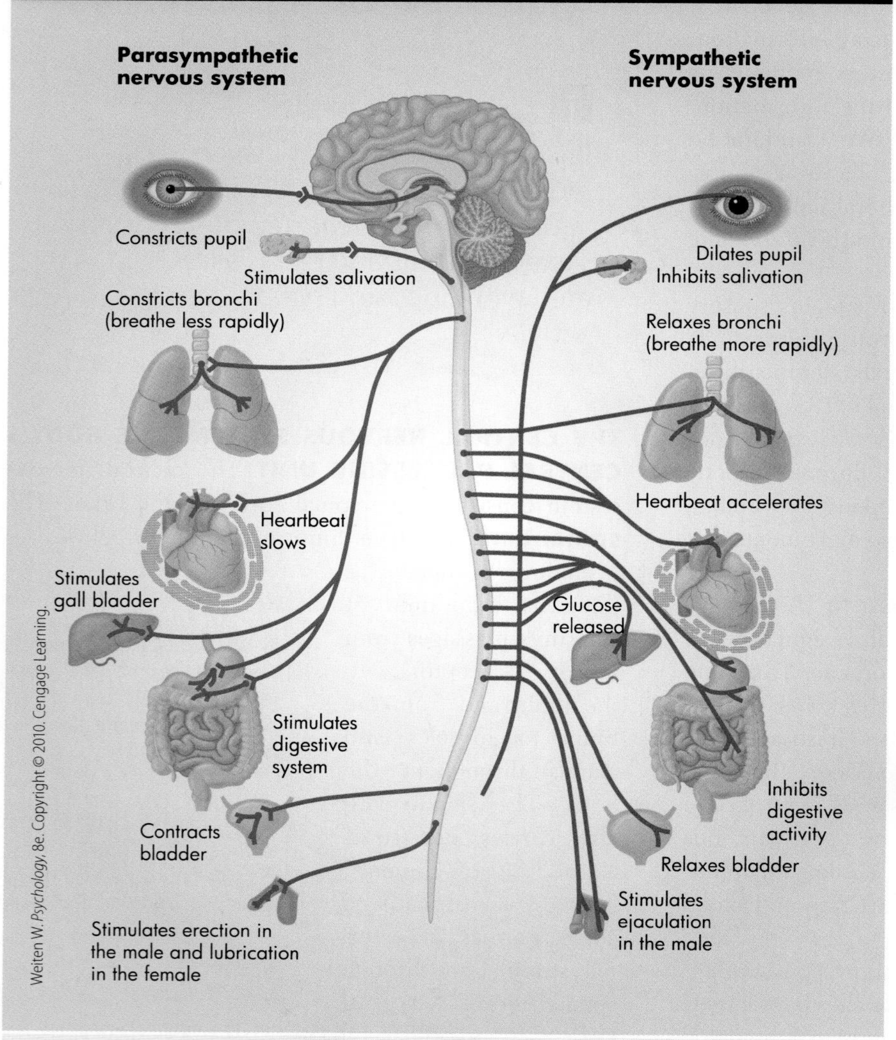

Parasympathetic nervous system

Sympathetic nervous system

Constricts pupil

Stimulates salivation

Constricts bronchi (breathe less rapidly)

Dilates pupil
Inhibits salivation

Relaxes bronchi (breathe more rapidly)

Heartbeat slows

Heartbeat accelerates

Stimulates gall bladder

Glucose released

Stimulates digestive system

Inhibits digestive activity

Contracts bladder

Relaxes bladder

Stimulates erection in the male and lubrication in the female

Stimulates ejaculation in the male

Weiten W. Psychology, 8e. Copyright © 2010. Cengage Learning.

The parasympathetic branch of the ANS generally acts to replenish stores of energy in the body. The sympathetic branch is most active during activities that expend energy. The two branches of the ANS frequently have antagonistic effects on the organs they service.

involved in spinal reflexes. Others send their axons to the brain. **White matter** is composed of bundles of longer, myelinated (and thus whitish) axons that carry messages to and from the brain. A cross-section of the spinal cord shows that the gray matter, which includes cell bodies, is distributed in a butterfly pattern (see Figure 2.5).

The spinal cord is also involved in reflexes. We blink in response to a puff of air in our faces. We swallow when food accumulates in the mouth. A physician may tap below the knee to elicit the knee-jerk reflex, a sign that the nervous system is operating adequately. Sexual response involves many reflexes. Urinating and defecating are reflexes that occur in response to pressure in the bladder and the rectum. It is your central nervous system that makes you so special. Other species see more sharply, smell more keenly, and hear more acutely. Other species run faster, or fly through the air, or swim underwater, without the benefit of artificial devices such as airplanes and submarines. But it is your central nervous system that enables you to use symbols and language, the abilities that allow people not only to adapt to their environment but also to create new environments and give them names (Bandura, 1999).

white matter axon bundles that carry messages to and from the brain

2-2 THE BRAIN: WIDER THAN THE SKY

When I was a child, I was told that the human nervous system is more complex than that of any other animal and that our brains are larger than those of any other animal. Now, this last piece of business is not quite true. A human brain weighs about three pounds, but the brains of elephants and whales may be four times as heavy. Still, our brains account for a greater part of our body weight than do those of elephants or whales. Our brains weigh about 1/60th of our body weight. Elephant brains weigh about 1/1,000th of their total weight, and whale brains are a paltry 1/10,000th of their weight.

Philosophers and scientists have wondered about the functions of the brain throughout history. Scientists today generally agree that the mind is a function of the brain (American Psychological Association, 2008; Landau, 2012). Some engage in research that attempts to pinpoint exactly what happens in certain parts of the brain when we are listening to music

FIG.2.5   THE REFLEX ARC

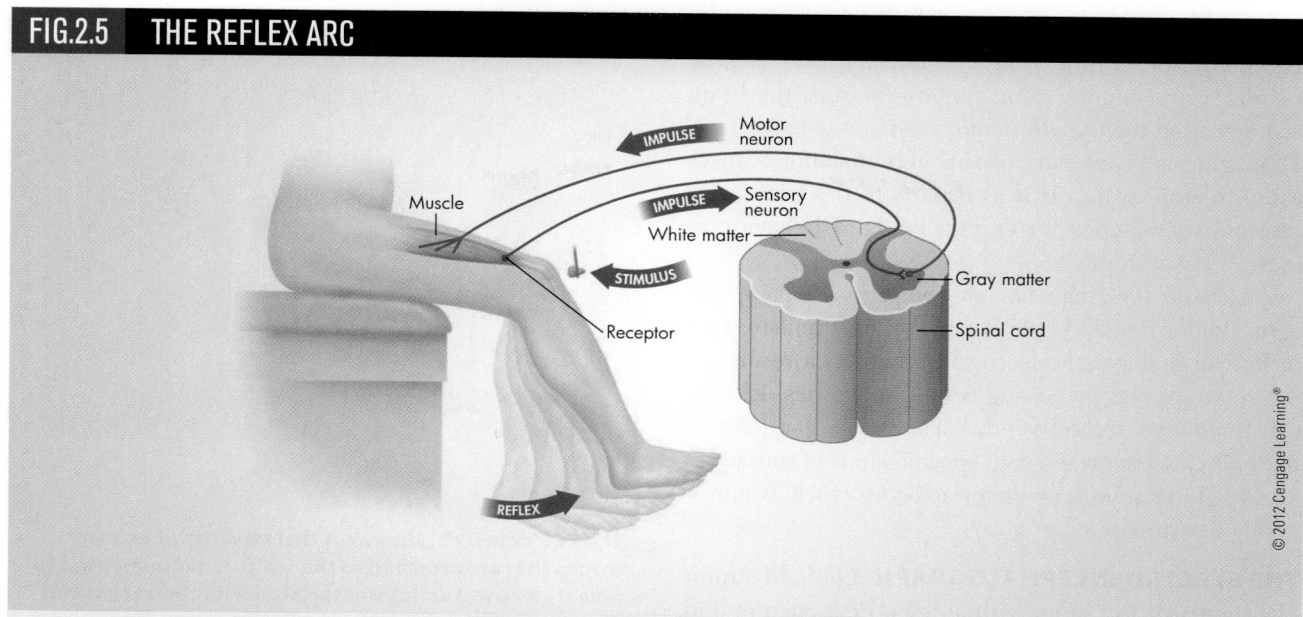

Reflexes are inborn, stereotyped behavior patterns that have apparently evolved because they help individuals adapt to the environment even before they can understand and purposefully manipulate the environment. Here we see a cross-section of the spinal cord, highlighting a sensory neuron and a motor neuron, which are involved in the knee-jerk reflex. In some reflexes, interneurons link sensory and motor neurons.

"THE BRAIN—IS WIDER THAN THE SKY—
FOR—PUT THEM SIDE BY SIDE—
THE ONE THE OTHER WILL CONTAIN
WITH EASE—AND YOU—BESIDE—"

EMILY DICKINSON, AMERICAN POET,
1830–1886

Fiction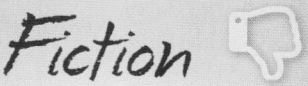

T **F**   The human brain is larger than that of any other animal.

It is not true that the human brain is larger than that of any other animal. However, our brains account for a larger percentage of our body weight than do the brains of larger animals such as elephants or whales.

or trying to remember someone's face. At other times—as in the case of Phineas Gage—knowledge has almost literally fallen into their laps. From injuries to the head—some of them minimal, some horrendous—we have learned that brain damage can impair consciousness, perception, memory, and abilities to make plans and decisions. In some cases, the loss of large portions of the brain may result in little loss of function. But the loss of smaller portions in certain locations can cause language problems, memory loss, or death. It has been known for about two centuries that damage to the left side of the brain is connected with loss of sensation or movement on the right side of the body, and vice versa. Thus, it has been assumed that the brain's control mechanisms cross over from right to left, and vice versa, as they descend into the body.

Accidents provide unplanned—and uncontrolled—opportunities of studying the brain. Still, scientists learn more about the brain through methods like experimentation, electroencephalography, and brain scans.

2-2a EXPERIMENTING WITH THE BRAIN

The results of disease and accidents (as in the case of Phineas Gage) have shown us that brain injuries can be connected with changes in behavior and mental processes. Scientists have also purposefully damaged part of the brain in laboratory animals to observe the results. For example, damaging one part of the brain region called the *hypothalamus* causes rats to overeat. Damaging another part of the hypothalamus causes them to stop eating. It is as if parts of the brain contain on-off switches for certain kinds of behavior, at least in lower animals.

Because the brain has no receptors for pain, surgeon Wilder Penfield (1969) was able to stimulate parts of human brains with electrical probes. As a result, his patients reported perceiving certain memories. Electrical stimulation of the brain has also shown that parts of the brain are connected with specific kinds of sensations (as of light or sound) or motor activities (such as movement of an arm or leg).

THE ELECTROENCEPHALOGRAPH Penfield stimulated parts of the brain with an electrical current and asked people to report what they experienced. Researchers have also used the **electroencephalograph (EEG)** to record the natural electrical activity of the brain. The EEG (see Figure 2.6) detects minute amounts of electrical activity—called *brain waves*—that pass between the electrodes. Certain brain waves are associated with feelings of relaxation, with various stages of sleep, and with neurological problems such as epilepsy.

BRAIN-IMAGING TECHNIQUES When Phineas Gage had his fabled accident, the only ways to look into the brain were to drill holes or crack it open, neither of which would have contributed to the well-being of the subject. But in the latter years of the 20th century, researchers developed imaging techniques that use the computer's ability to generate images of the parts of the brain from sources of radiation.

electroencephalograph (EEG) a method of detecting brain waves by means of measuring the current between electrodes placed on the scalp

computerized axial tomography (CAT or CT scan) a method of brain imaging that passes a narrow X-ray beam through the head and measures the structures that reflect the beams from various angles, enabling a computer to generate a three-dimensional image

positron emission tomography (PET scan) a method of brain imaging that injects a radioactive tracer into the bloodstream and assesses activity of parts of the brain according to the amount of glucose they metabolize

magnetic resonance imaging (MRI) an imaging method that places a person in a magnetic field and uses radio waves to cause the brain to emit signals that reveal shifts in the flow of blood, which, when the brain is being scanned, indicate brain activity

functional MRI (fMRI) a form of MRI that enables researchers to observe the brain "while it works" by taking repeated scans

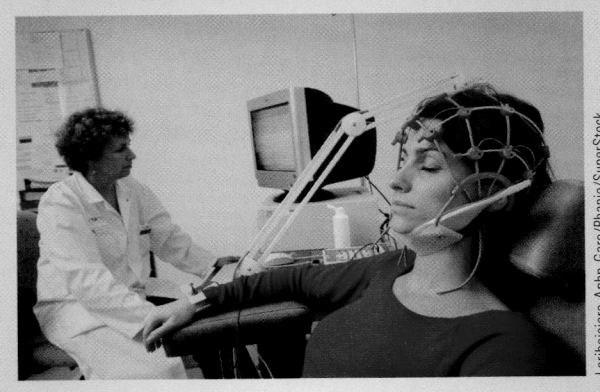

FIG.2.6 THE ELECTROENCEPHALOGRAPH (EEG)

Lariboisiere-Aphp-Garo/Phanie/SuperStock

The EEG detects brain waves that pass between electrodes that are attached to the scalp. It has been used to reveal electrical activity associated with relaxation and the stages of sleep.

Computerized axial tomography (CAT or CT scan), shown in Figure 2.7A, passes X-rays through the head and measures the structures that reflect the beams from various angles, generating a three-dimensional image. The CAT scan reveals deformities in shape and structure that are connected with blood clots, tumors, and other health problems.

A second method, **positron emission tomography (PET scan)**, shown in Figure 2.7B, forms a computer-generated image of the activity of parts of the brain by tracing the amount of glucose used (or metabolized) by these parts. More glucose is metabolized in more active parts of the brain. To trace the metabolism of glucose, a harmless amount of a radioactive compound, called a *tracer*, is mixed with glucose and injected into the bloodstream. When the glucose reaches the brain, the patterns of activity are revealed by measurement of the positrons—positively charged particles—that are given off by the tracer.

A third imaging technique is **magnetic resonance imaging (MRI)**, which is shown in Figure 2.7C. In MRI, the person lies in a powerful magnetic field and is exposed to radio waves that cause parts of the brain to emit signals, which are measured from multiple angles. MRI relies on subtle shifts in blood flow. (More blood flows to more active parts of the brain, supplying them with oxygen.) **Functional MRI (fMRI)** provides a more rapid picture and therefore enables researchers to observe the brain "while it works" by taking repeated scans while subjects engage in activities such as mental processes and voluntary movements. fMRI can be used to show which parts of the brain are active when we are, say, listening to

FIG.2.7   BRAIN IMAGING TECHNIQUES

A. Computerized axial tomography (the CAT scan) passes a narrow X-ray beam through the head and measures structures that reflect the rays from various angles, enabling a computer to generate a three-dimensional image.

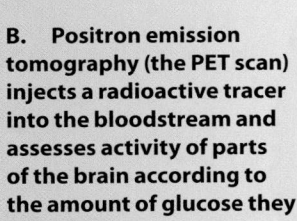

Detectors

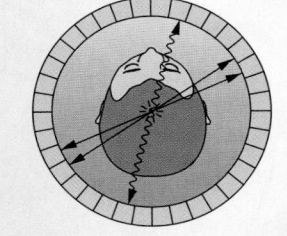

A. CAT scan

Moving X-ray source

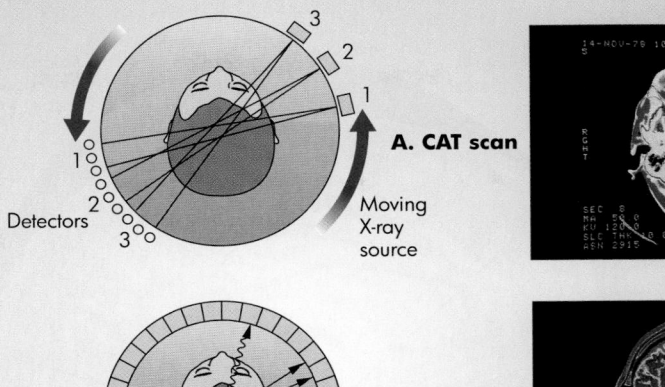

Ohio Nuclear Corporation/Science Source

B. Positron emission tomography (the PET scan) injects a radioactive tracer into the bloodstream and assesses activity of parts of the brain according to the amount of glucose they metabolize.

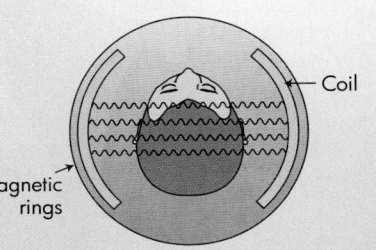

B. PET scan

Jupiter Images

C. Magnetic resonance imaging (MRI) places a person in a magnetic field and uses radio waves to cause the brain to emit signals which reveal shifts in the flow of blood which, in turn, indicate brain activity.

Coil

C. MRI

Magnetic rings

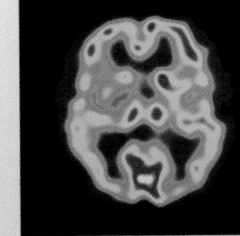

Department of Nuclear Medicine, Charing Cross Hospital/Science Source

© 2012 Cengage Learning®

music, using language, or playing chess (Krueger et al., 2008; Newman et al., 2009; Stocco & Anderson, 2008).

Some researchers consider the prefrontal cortex to be the "executive center" of the brain, where decisions are made to keep information in working memory and to solve problems. The prefrontal cortex is the part of the frontal lobe (see Figure 2.10) that is closest to the front of the brain. Research with the PET scan and MRI supports the view that the prefrontal cortex is where we process much of the information involved in making plans and solving problems (Gilbert et al., 2008; Wang et al., 2008).

2-2b A VOYAGE THROUGH THE BRAIN

Let's begin our tour of the brain with the *hindbrain,* where the spinal cord rises to meet the brain (see Figure 2.8). Here we find three major structures: the *medulla,* the *pons,* and the *cerebellum.* Many pathways pass through the **medulla** to connect the spinal cord to higher levels of the brain. The medulla regulates basic functions such as heart rate, blood

pressure, and respiration. (In fact, Gage survived his accident because his medulla escaped injury.) The medulla also plays roles in sleeping, sneezing, and coughing. The **pons** is a bulge in the hindbrain that lies forward of the medulla. *Pons* is the Latin word for "bridge"; the pons is so named because of the bundles of nerves that pass through it. The pons transmits information about body movement and is involved in functions related to attention, sleep and arousal, and respiration.

Behind the pons lies the **cerebellum** ("little brain" in Latin). The cerebellum has two hemispheres that are involved in maintaining balance and in controlling motor (muscle) behavior. You may send a command from your forebrain to get up and walk to the ref rigerator, but your cerebellum is key to organizing the information

medulla an oblong area of the hind-brain involved in regulation of heartbeat, blood pressure, movement, and respiration

pons a structure of the hindbrain involved in respiration, attention, and sleep and arousal

cerebellum a part of the hindbrain involved in muscle coordination and balance

FIG.2.8 THE PARTS OF THE BRAIN

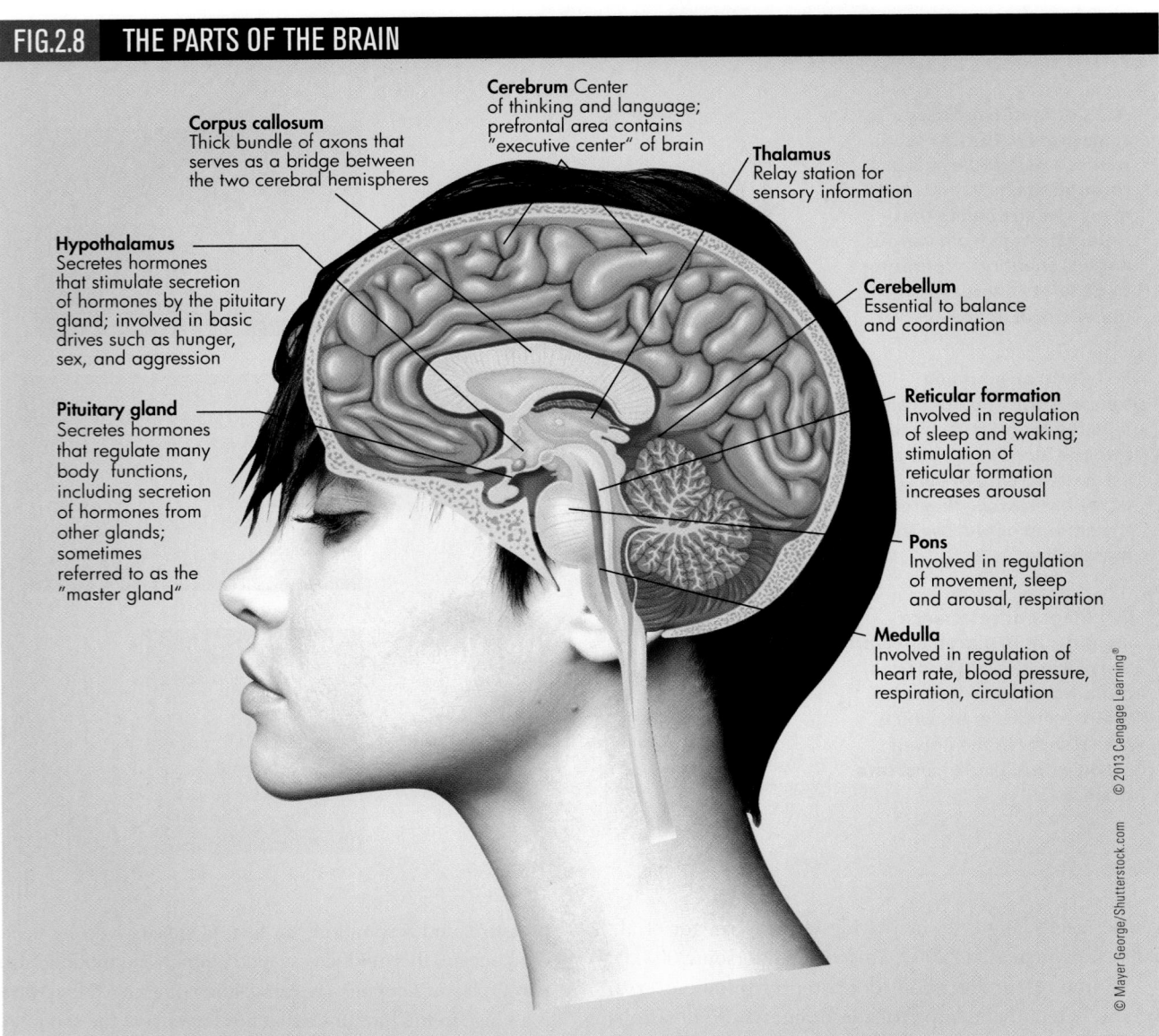

Corpus callosum
Thick bundle of axons that serves as a bridge between the two cerebral hemispheres

Cerebrum Center of thinking and language; prefrontal area contains "executive center" of brain

Thalamus
Relay station for sensory information

Hypothalamus
Secretes hormones that stimulate secretion of hormones by the pituitary gland; involved in basic drives such as hunger, sex, and aggression

Cerebellum
Essential to balance and coordination

Pituitary gland
Secretes hormones that regulate many body functions, including secretion of hormones from other glands; sometimes referred to as the "master gland"

Reticular formation
Involved in regulation of sleep and waking; stimulation of reticular formation increases arousal

Pons
Involved in regulation of movement, sleep and arousal, respiration

Medulla
Involved in regulation of heart rate, blood pressure, respiration, circulation

© 2013 Cengage Learning®

© Mayer George/Shutterstock.com

The view of the brain, split top to bottom, shows some of the most important structures. Note how close the hypothalamus is to the pituitary gland, which allows the hypothalamus to readily influence the pituitary gland. The "valleys" in the cerebrum are called *fissures*.

that enables you to engage in these movements. The cerebellum allows you to place one leg in front of the other and reach your destination without tipping over. Injury to the cerebellum may impair motor coordination and cause stumbling and loss of muscle tone.

As we tour the hindbrain, we also find the lower part of the **reticular formation**. That is where the reticular formation begins, but it ascends through the mid-brain into the lower part of the forebrain. The reticular formation is vital in the functions of attention, sleep, and arousal. Injury to the reticular formation may result in a coma. Stimulation of the reticular formation causes it to send messages to the cerebral cortex (the large wrinkled mass that you think of as your brain), making us more alert to sensory information. In classic neurological research, Giuseppe Moruzzi and Horace Magoun (1949) discovered that electrical stimulation of the reticular formation of a sleeping cat caused it to awaken at once. But when the reticular formation was severed from higher parts of the brain, the cat fell into a coma from which it would not awaken. Drugs known as central nervous system depressants, such as alcohol, are thought to work, in part, by lowering the activity of the reticular formation.

reticular formation a part of the brain involved in attention, sleep, and arousal

Key areas of the forward most part of the brain, or forebrain, are the *thalamus*, the *hypothalamus*, the *limbic system*, and the *cerebrum*. The **thalamus** is located near the center of the brain and could be said to lie between the forebrain and the midbrain. It consists of two joined egg-shaped structures. The thalamus serves as a relay station for sensory stimulation. Nerve fibers from sensory systems enter from below; their information is then transmitted to the cerebral cortex by fibers that exit from above. For example, the thalamus relays sensory input from the eyes to the visual areas of the cerebral cortex. The thalamus also regulates sleep and attention in coordination with other brain structures, including the reticular formation.

The **hypothalamus** lies beneath the thalamus and above the pituitary gland. It weighs only four grams, yet it is vital in the regulation of body temperature, concentration of fluids, storage of nutrients, and motivation and emotion. Experimenters learn many of the functions of the hypothalamus by implanting electrodes in parts of it and observing the effects of electrical stimulation. They have found that the hypothalamus is involved in hunger, thirst, sexual behavior, caring for offspring, and aggression. Among lower animals, stimulation of various areas of the hypothalamus can trigger instinctual behaviors such as fighting, mating, or nest building.

Canadian psychologists James Olds and Peter Milner (1954) made a splendid mistake in the 1950s. They were attempting to implant an electrode in a rat's reticular formation to see how stimulation of the area might affect learning. Olds, however, was primarily a social psychologist and not a biological psychologist. He missed his target and found a part of the animal's hypothalamus instead. Olds and Milner dubbed this area the "pleasure center" because the animal would repeat whatever it was doing when it was stimulated. The term *pleasure center* is not used frequently because it appears to attribute human emotions to rats. Yet the "pleasure centers" must be doing something right, because rats stimulate themselves in these centers by pressing a pedal several thousand times an hour, until they are exhausted (Olds, 1969).

The hypothalamus is important to humans as well as to lower animals. Unfortunately (or fortunately), our "pleasure centers" are not as clearly defined as those of the rat. Then, too, our responses to messages from the hypothalamus are less automatic and relatively more influenced by higher brain functions—that is, cognitive factors such as thought, choice, and value systems.

The **limbic system** forms a fringe along the inner edge of the cerebrum and is fully evolved only in mammals (see Figure 2.9). It is made up of several structures, including the amygdala, hippocampus, and parts of the hypothalamus. It is involved in memory and emotion and in the drives of hunger, sex, and aggression. People with hippocampal damage can retrieve old memories but cannot permanently store new information. As a result, they may reread the same newspaper day in and day out without recalling that they read it before. Or they may have to be perpetually reintroduced to people they have met just hours earlier (Squire, 2004).

thalamus an area near the center of the brain involved in the relay of sensory information to the cortex and in the functions of sleep and attention

hypothalamus a bundle of nuclei below the thalamus involved in body temperature, motivation, and emotion

limbic system a group of structures involved in memory, motivation, and emotion that forms a fringe along the inner edge of the cerebrum

FIG.2.9 THE LIMBIC SYSTEM

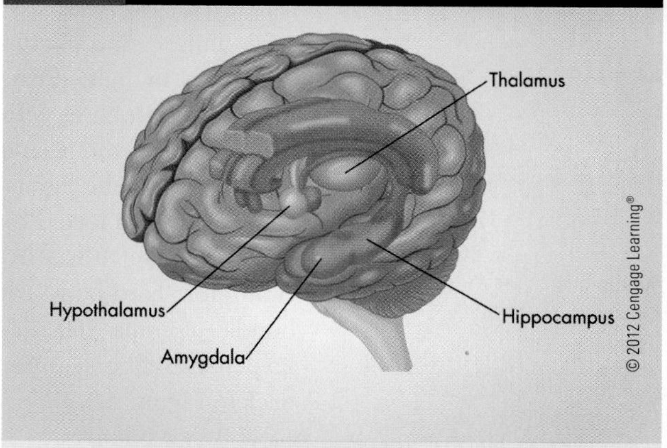

© 2012 Cengage Learning®

The limbic system is made up of structures that include the amygdala, the hippocampus, and parts of the hypothalamus. It is evolved fully only in mammals and forms a fringe along the inner edge of the cerebrum. The limbic system is involved in memory and emotion, and in the drives of hunger, sex, and aggression.

The **amygdala** is near the bottom of the limbic system and looks like two little almonds. Studies using lesioning and electrical stimulation show that the amygdala is connected with aggressive behavior in monkeys, cats, and other animals. Early in the 20th century, Heinrich Klüver and Paul Bucy (1939) lesioned part of the amygdala of a rhesus monkey. Rhesus monkeys are normally a scrappy lot and try to bite or grab at intruders, but destruction of this animal's amygdala made it docile. No longer did it react aggressively to people. It even allowed people to poke and pinch it. Electrical stimulation of the part of the amygdala that Klüver and Bucy had destroyed, however, triggers a "rage response." For example, it causes a cat to hiss and arch its back in preparation to attack. The amygdala is also connected with a fear response (Ahs et al., 2009; Feinstein et al., 2010). If you electrically stimulate another part of the amygdala, the cat cringes in fear when you cage it with a mouse.

The amygdala is also connected with vigilance. It is involved in emotions, learning, and memory, and it behaves something like a spotlight, focusing attention on matters that are novel and important to know more about.

Only in humans does the **cerebrum** make up such a large part of the brain (refer back to Figure 2.8). The cerebrum is responsible for thinking and language. The surface of the cerebrum—the **cerebral cortex**—is wrinkled, or convoluted, with ridges and valleys. The convolutions allow a great deal of surface area to be packed into the brain— and surface area is apparently connected with cognitive ability. Valleys in the cortex are called *fissures*. A key fissure almost divides the cerebrum in half, creating two hemispheres with something of the shape of a walnut. The hemispheres are connected by the **corpus callosum** (Latin for "hard body"), a bundle of some 200 million nerve fibers (refer back to Figure 2.8).

2-2c THE CEREBRAL CORTEX

The cerebral cortex is the part of the brain that you usually think of as your brain. *Cortex* is a Latin word meaning "bark," as in the bark of a tree. Just as the bark is the outer coating of a tree, the cerebral cortex is the outer coating of the cerebrum. Despite its extreme importance and its creation of a world of civilization and culture, it is only about 1/8th of an inch thick.

The cerebral cortex is involved in almost every bodily activity, including most sensations and responses. It is also the part of the brain that frees people from the tyranny of genetic dictates and instinct. It is the seat of thinking and language, and it enables humans to think deeply about the world outside and to make decisions.

The cerebral cortex has two hemispheres, left and right. Each of the hemispheres is divided into four lobes, as shown in Figure 2.10. The *frontal lobe* lies in front of the central fissure and the *parietal lobe* behind it.

The *temporal lobe* lies below the side, or lateral, fissure—across from the frontal and parietal lobes. The *occipital lobe* lies behind the temporal lobe and behind and below the parietal lobe.

When light strikes the eyes, neurons in the occipital lobe fire, and as a result, we "see" (that is, the image is projected in the brain). Direct artificial stimulation of the occipital lobe also produces visual sensations. If neurons in the occipital region of the cortex were stimulated with electricity, you would "see" flashes of light even if it were pitch-black or your eyes were covered. The hearing or auditory area of the cortex lies in the temporal lobe along the lateral fissure. Sounds cause structures in the ear to vibrate. Messages are relayed from those structures to the auditory area of the cortex; when you hear a noise, neurons in this area are firing.

Just behind the central fissure in the parietal lobe lies a sensory area called the **somatosensory cortex**, which receives messages from skin senses all over the body. These sensations include warmth and cold, touch, pain, and movement. Neurons in different parts of the sensory cortex fire, depending on whether you wiggle your finger or raise your leg.

Many years ago it was discovered that patients with injuries to one hemisphere of the brain would show sensory or motor deficits on the opposite side of the body below the head. This led to the recognition that sensory and motor nerves cross in the brain and elsewhere. The left hemisphere controls, acts on, and receives inputs from the right side of the body. The right hemisphere controls, acts on, and receives inputs from the left side of the body. The motor area of the cerebral cortex, or **motor cortex**, lies in the frontal lobe, just across the valley of the central fissure from the somato–sensory cortex. Neurons firing in the motor cortex cause parts of our body to move. More than 100 years ago, German scientists electrically stimulated the motor cortex in dogs and

amygdala a part of the limbic system that apparently facilitates stereotypical aggressive responses

cerebrum the large mass of the fore-brain, which consists of two hemispheres

cerebral cortex the wrinkled surface area (gray matter) of the cerebrum

corpus callosum a thick fiber bundle that connects the hemispheres of the cortex

somatosensory cortex the section of cortex in which sensory stimulation is projected. It lies just behind the central fissure in the parietal lobe

motor cortex the section of cortex that lies in the frontal lobe, just across the central fissure from the sensory cortex; neural impulses in the motor cortex are linked to muscular responses throughout the body

FIG.2.10 THE GEOGRAPHY OF THE CEREBRAL CORTEX

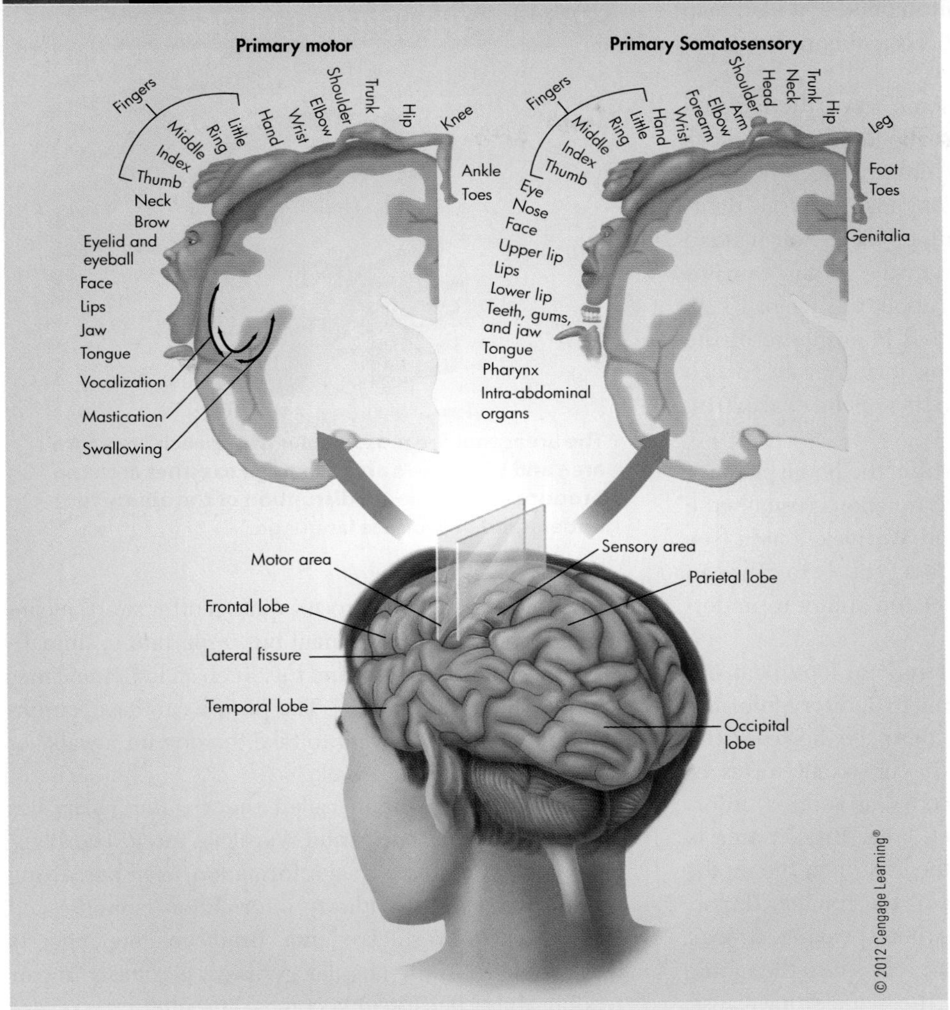

Primary motor

Fingers
Little
Middle
Ring
Index
Thumb
Neck
Brow
Eyelid and eyeball
Face
Lips
Jaw
Tongue
Vocalization
Mastication
Swallowing
Hand
Wrist
Elbow
Shoulder
Trunk
Hip
Knee
Ankle
Toes

Primary Somatosensory

Fingers
Little
Middle
Ring
Index
Thumb
Hand
Wrist
Forearm
Elbow
Arm
Shoulder
Head
Neck
Trunk
Hip
Leg
Foot
Toes
Genitalia
Eye
Nose
Face
Upper lip
Lips
Lower lip
Teeth, gums, and jaw
Tongue
Pharynx
Intra-abdominal organs

Motor area
Frontal lobe
Lateral fissure
Temporal lobe

Sensory area
Parietal lobe
Occipital lobe

© 2012 Cengage Learning®

The cortex has four lobes; frontal, parietal, temporal, and occipital. The visual area of the cortex is in the occipital lobe. The hearing or auditory cortex lies in the temporal lobe. The motor and somatosensory areas—shown below—face each other across the central fissure. Note that the face and the hands are "super-sized" in the motor and somatosensory areas. Why do you think this is so?

in the *prefrontal* region of the brain—that is, in the frontal lobes, near the forehead—are the brain's executive center. It appears to be where we solve problems and make plans and decisions.

Executive functions like problem solving also require memory, like the memory in your computer. Association areas also provide the core of your working memory (Rawley & Constantinidis, 2008). They are connected with various sensory areas in the brain and can tap whatever sensory information is needed or desired. The prefrontal region thus retrieves visual, auditory, and other memories and manipulates them; similarly, a computer retrieves information from files in storage and manipulates it in working memory.

Certain neurons in the visual area of the occipital lobe fire in response to the visual presentation of vertical lines. Others fire in response to presentation of horizontal lines. Although one group of cells may respond to one aspect of the visual field and another group of cells may

observed that muscles contracted in response (Fritsch & Hitzig, 1870/1960). Since then, neuroscientists have mapped the motor cortex in people and lower animals by inserting electrical probes and seeing which muscles contract. For example, José Delgado (1969) caused one patient to make a fist even though he tried to prevent his hand from closing. The patient said, "I guess, doctor, that your electricity is stronger than my will" (Delgado, 1969, p. 114).

THINKING, LANGUAGE, AND THE CORTEX Areas of the cerebral cortex that are not primarily involved in sensation or motor activity are called *association areas.* They make possible the breadth and depth of human learning, thought, memory, and language. The association areas

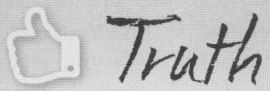
👍 *Truth*

T F If a surgeon were to stimulate a certain part of your brain electrically, you might swear that someone had stroked your leg.

It is true that if an area of your somatosensory cortex is stimulated with an electrical probe, it might seem to you as if someone is touching your arm or leg. The actual source of the stimulation might be unclear to you.

respond to another, association areas put it all together. As a result, we see a box or an automobile or a road map and not a confusing array of verticals and horizontals.

LANGUAGE FUNCTIONS In some ways, the left and right hemispheres of the brain duplicate each other's functions. In other ways, they differ. The left hemisphere contains language functions for nearly all right-handed people and for two out of three left-handed people (Pinker, 2007). However, the brain remains "plastic," or changeable, through about the age of 13. As a result, children who lose the left hemisphere of the brain because of medical problems may transfer speech functions to the right hemisphere (Guediche et al., 2014; Mercado, 2008).

Two key language areas lie within the hemisphere of the cortex that contains language functions (usually the left hemisphere): Broca's area and Wernicke's area (see Figure 2.11). Damage to either area is likely to cause an **aphasia**—that is, a disruption of the ability to understand or produce language.

Wernicke's area lies in the temporal lobe near the auditory cortex. It responds mainly to auditory information (sounds). As you are reading this page, however, the visual information is registered in the visual cortex of your occipital lobe. It is then recoded as auditory information as it travels to Wernicke's area. Broca's area is located in the frontal lobe, near the section of the motor cortex that controls the muscles of the tongue, throat, and other areas of the face used when speaking. Broca's area processes the information and relays it to the motor cortex. The motor cortex sends the signals that cause muscles in your throat and mouth to contract. If you are "subvocalizing"—saying what you are reading "under your breath"—that is because Wernicke's area transmits information to Broca's area via nerve fibers.

People with damage to Wernicke's area may show **Wernicke's aphasia**, which impairs their abilities to comprehend speech and to think of the proper words to express their own thoughts. Ironically, they usually speak freely and with proper syntax. Wernicke's area is essential to understanding the relationships between words and their meanings. When Broca's area is damaged, people usually understand language well enough but speak slowly and laboriously, in simple sentences. This pattern is termed **Broca's aphasia**.

aphasia a disruption in the ability to understand or produce language

Wernicke's aphasia a language disorder characterized by difficulty comprehending the meaning of spoken language

Broca's aphasia a language disorder characterized by slow, laborious speech

FIG.2.11 **BROCA'S AND WERNICKE'S AREAS OF THE CEREBRAL CORTEX**

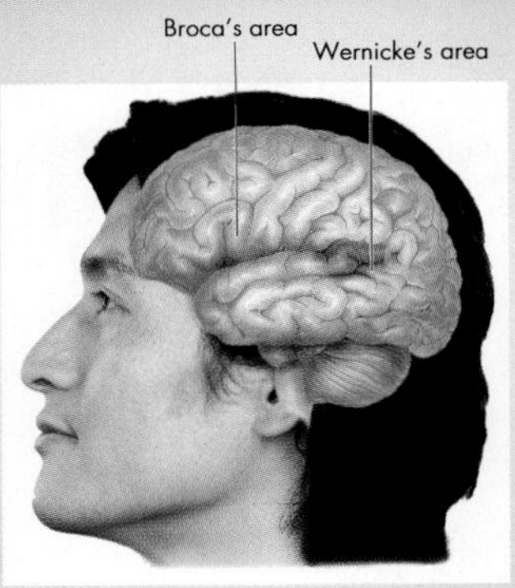

Siri Stafford/Digital Vision (RF)/Jupiter Images

The areas that are most involved in speech are Broca's area and Wernicke's area. Damage to either area can produce an aphasia—a disruption of the ability to understand or produce language.

Some people with Broca's aphasia utter short, meaningful phrases that omit small but important grammatical words such as *is, and,* and *the.* Such an individual may laboriously say "walk dog." The phrase can have various meanings, such as "I want to take the dog for a walk" or "Take the dog out for a walk."

A part of the brain called the *angular gyrus* lies between the visual cortex and Wernicke's area. The angular gyrus "translates" visual information, as in perceiving written words, into auditory information (sounds) and sends it on to Wernicke's area. Brain imaging suggests that problems in the angular gyrus can seriously impair reading ability because it becomes difficult for the reader to segment words into sounds (Ye et al., 2014).

2-2d LEFT BRAIN, RIGHT BRAIN?

You may have heard that some people are "left-brained," whereas others are "right-brained." The notion is that the hemispheres of the brain are involved in very different kinds of intellectual and emotional functions and responses. According to this view, left-brained people would be primarily logical and intellectual. Right-brained people would be intuitive, creative, and emotional. Those of us who are fortunate enough to have our brains "in balance" would presumably have the best of it—the capacity for logic combined with emotional richness.

Like many other popular ideas, the left-brain versus right-brain notion is exaggerated. Research does suggest that in right-handed individuals, the left hemisphere is relatively more involved in intellectual undertakings that require logical analysis and problem solving, language, and mathematical computation

(Corballis, 2009). The other hemisphere (typically the right hemisphere) is usually superior in visual-spatial functions (it's better at putting puzzles together), recognition of faces, discrimination of colors, aesthetic and emotional responses, understanding metaphors, and creative mathematical reasoning. Despite these differences, the hemispheres of the brain do not act independently such that some people are truly left-brained and others are right-brained (American Psychological Association, 2008). The functions of the left and right hemispheres overlap to some degree, and they tend to respond simultaneously as we focus our attention on one thing or another.

Whether we are talking about language functions or being "left-brained" or "right-brained," we are talking about people whose hemispheres of the cerebral cortex communicate back and forth.

2-2e HANDEDNESS

Being left-handed was once seen as a deficiency. Left-handed students were made to learn to write with their right hands. We are usually labeled right-handed or left-handed on the basis of our handwriting preferences, yet some people write with one hand and pass a football with the other.

Being left-handed appears to provide a somewhat-greater-than-average probability of language problems, such as dyslexia and stuttering, and health problems such as migraine headaches and allergies (Lundborg, 2014). But there may also be advantages to being left-handed. Left-handed people are more likely than right-handed people to be numbered among the ranks of gifted artists, musicians, and mathematicians (Lundborg, 2014).

The origins of handedness may have a genetic component. In the English royal family, Queen Elizabeth II and Princes Charles and William are both left-handed, as was Queen Elizabeth's mother. On the other hand, a recent study of more than 27,000 Dutch and Australian twin families found that heritability makes only about a 24% contribution to the likelihood of being right- or left-handed (Medland et al., 2008).

2-2f SPLIT-BRAIN EXPERIMENTS

A number of people with severe cases of **epilepsy** have split-brain operations in which much of the corpus callosum is severed (refer back to Figure 2.8). The purpose of the operation is to confine seizures to one hemisphere of the cerebral cortex rather than allowing a neural tempest to reverberate. Split-brain operations do seem to help people with epilepsy.

People who have undergone split-brain operations can be thought of as winding up with two brains, yet under most circumstances their behavior remains ordinary enough. Still, some aspects of hemispheres that have stopped talking to each other are intriguing.

As reported by pioneering brain surgeon Joseph Bogen (1969, 2000), each hemisphere may have a "mind of its own." One split-brain patient reported that her hemispheres frequently disagreed on what she should be wearing. What she meant was that one hand might undo her blouse as rapidly as the other was buttoning it.

Another pioneer of split-brain research, Michael Gazzaniga (American Psychological Association, 2008), found that people with split brains whose eyes are closed may be able to verbally describe an object such as a key when they hold it in one hand, but not when they hold it in the other hand. If a person with a split brain handles a key with his left hand behind a screen, tactile impressions of the key are projected into the right hemisphere, which has little or no language ability (see Figure 2.12). Thus, he will not be able to describe the key. If he holds it in his right hand, he will have no trouble describing it because sensory impressions are projected into the left hemisphere of the cortex, which contains language functions. To further confound matters, if the word *ring* is projected into the left hemisphere while the person is asked what he is handling, he will say "ring," not "key."

This discrepancy between what is felt and what is said occurs only in people with split brains. Even so, people who have undergone split-brain operations tend to lead largely normal lives. And for the rest of us, the two hemispheres work together most of the time, such as when we are playing the piano or solving math problems.

2-3 THE ENDOCRINE SYSTEM

The body has two types of **glands**: glands with ducts and glands without ducts. A *duct* is a passageway that carries substances to specific locations. Saliva, sweat, tears, and breast milk all reach their destinations through ducts. A number of substances secreted by *ductless* glands have effects on behavior and mental

epilepsy temporary disturbances of brain functions that involve sudden neural discharges

gland an organ that secretes one or more chemical substances such as hormones, saliva, or milk

FIG.2.12   THE SPLIT-BRAIN EXPERIMENT

Left field   Front   Right field

Left eye
Right eye
Optic nerve
Corpus callosum
Left hemisphere
Right hemisphere
Line of incision

Key   Ring
Speech

© 2012 Cengage Learning®

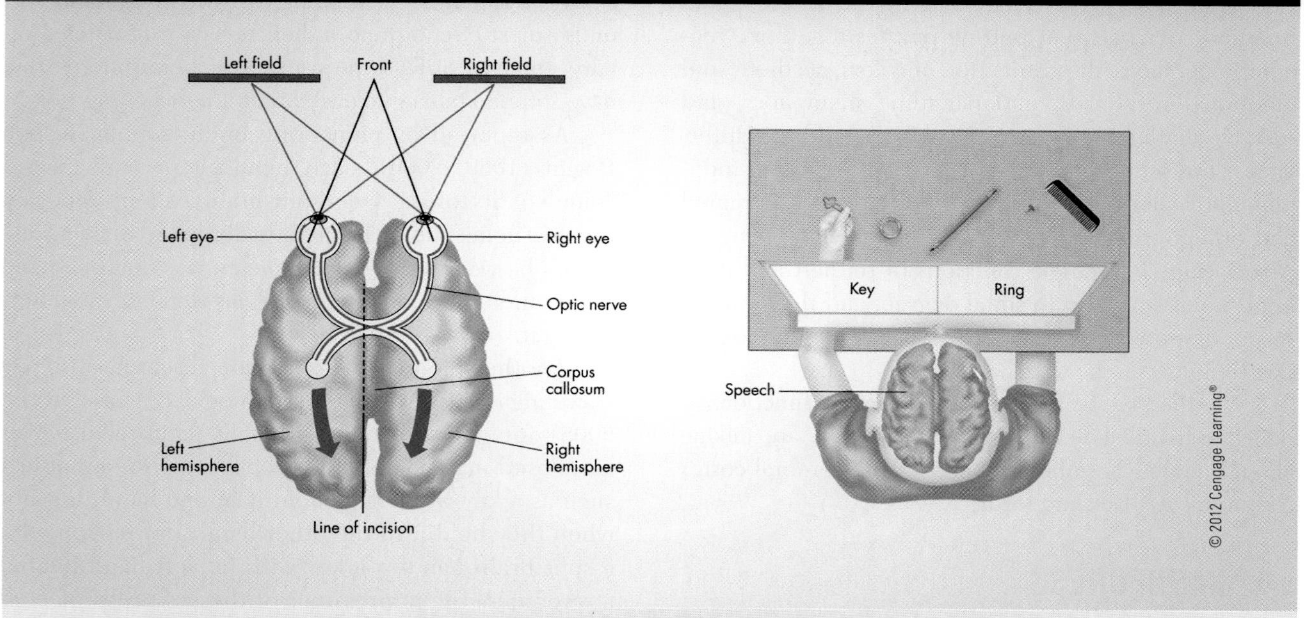

In the detailed drawing of the brain, we see that visual sensations in the *left* visual field are projected in the occipital cortex of the *right* hemisphere, while visual sensations from the *right* visual field are projected in the occipital cortex in the *left* hemisphere. In the diagram of the split-brain experiment, a person with a severed corpus callosum handles a key with his left hand and perceives the written word in his left visual field. The word "key" is projected in the right hemisphere. Speech, however, is usually a function of the left hemisphere. The written word "ring," perceived by the right visual field, is projected in the left hemisphere. So, when asked what he is handling, the split-brain subject reports "ring," not "key."

processes. The ductless glands make up the **endocrine system** (see Figure 2.13), and they release **hormones** into the bloodstream. Hormones are then picked up by specific receptor sites and regulate growth, metabolism, and some forms of behavior. That is, they act only on receptors in certain locations.

Much hormonal action helps the body maintain steady states— fluid levels, blood sugar levels, and so on. Bodily mechanisms measure current levels; when these levels deviate from optimal, they signal glands to release hormones. The maintenance of steady states requires feedback of bodily information to glands. This type of system is referred to as a *negative feedback loop*. When enough of a hormone has been secreted, the gland is signaled to stop.

2-3a THE PITUITARY AND THE HYPOTHALAMUS

The pituitary gland and the hypothalamus work in close cooperation. The **pituitary gland** lies

endocrine system the body's system of ductless glands that secrete hormones and release them directly into the bloodstream

hormone a substance secreted by an endocrine gland that regulates various body functions

pituitary gland the gland that secretes growth hormone, prolactin, antidiuretic hormone, and other hormones

FIG.2.13   THE ENDOCRINE GLANDS

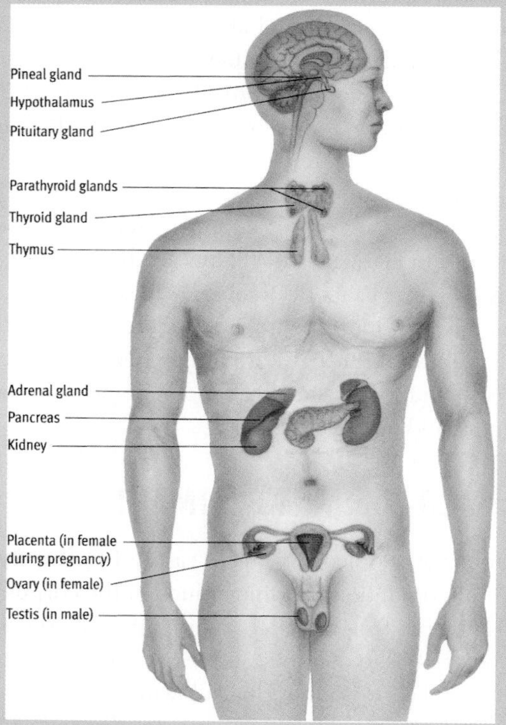

Pineal gland
Hypothalamus
Pituitary gland
Parathyroid glands
Thyroid gland
Thymus
Adrenal gland
Pancreas
Kidney
Placenta (in female during pregnancy)
Ovary (in female)
Testis (in male)

Weiten W. Psychology, 8e. Copyright © 2010. Cengage Learning: Fig. 3.24 on p. 109.

below the hypothalamus. Although the pituitary is only about the size of a pea, it is so central to the body's functioning that it has been dubbed the "master gland."

The anterior (front) and posterior (back) lobes of the pituitary gland secrete hormones that regulate the functioning of many other glands. *Growth hormone* regulates the growth of muscles, bones, and glands. Children whose growth patterns are abnormally slow may catch up to their age-mates when they obtain growth hormone. *Prolactin* regulates maternal behavior in lower mammals such as rats and stimulates production of milk in women. As a water conservation measure, *vasopressin* (also called *antidiuretic hormone*) inhibits production of urine when the body's fluid levels are low. Vasopressin is also connected with stereotypical paternal behavior in some mammals. *Oxytocin* stimulates labor in pregnant women and is connected with maternal behavior (cuddling and caring for young) in some mammals (Champagne et al., 2009). Obstetricians can induce labor by injecting pregnant women with oxytocin. During nursing, stimulation of the nerve endings of the nipples signals the brain to secrete oxytocin, which then causes the breasts to eject milk.

Although the pituitary gland may be the "master gland," the master has a "commander": the hypothalamus. We know today that the hypothalamus regulates much pituitary activity. The hypothalamus secretes a number of releasing hormones, or "factors," that stimulate the pituitary gland to secrete related hormones. For example, growth hormone releasing factor (hGRF) causes the pituitary to produce growth hormone. Blood vessels between the hypothalamus and the pituitary gland provide a direct route for these factors.

2-3b THE PINEAL GLAND

The pineal gland secretes the hormone *melatonin,* which helps regulate the sleep-wake cycle and may affect the onset of puberty. Melatonin may also be connected with aging. In addition, it appears that melatonin is a mild sedative, and some people use it as a sleeping pill (Srinivasan et al., 2014). Melatonin may be used to help people adjust to jet lag (Srinivasan et al., 2014).

2-3c THE THYROID GLAND

The thyroid gland could be considered the body's accelerator. It produces *thyroxin,* which affects the body's *metabolism*—the rate at which the body uses oxygen and produces energy. Some people are overweight because of *hypothyroidism,* a condition that results from too little thyroxin. Thyroxin deficiency in children can lead to *cretinism,* a condition characterized by stunted growth and mental retardation. Adults who secrete too little thyroxin may feel tired and sluggish and may put on weight. People who produce too much thyroxin may develop *hyperthyroidism,* which is characterized by excitability, insomnia, and weight loss.

2-3d THE ADRENAL GLANDS

The adrenal glands, located above the kidneys, have an outer layer, or cortex, and an inner core, or medulla. The adrenal cortex is regulated by the pituitary hormone ACTH (adrenocorticotrophic hormone). The adrenal cortex secretes hormones known as *corticosteroids,* or cortical steroids. These hormones regulate the heartbeat, increase resistance to stress, promote muscle development, and cause the liver to release stored sugar, making more energy available in emergencies, such as when you see another car veering toward your own. Epinephrine and norepinephrine are secreted by the adrenal medulla. *Epinephrine,* also known as adrenaline, is manufactured exclusively by the adrenal glands, but norepinephrine (noradrenaline) is produced elsewhere in the body. (Norepinephrine acts as a neurotransmitter in the brain.) The sympathetic branch of the autonomic nervous system causes the adrenal medulla to release a mixture of epinephrine and norepinephrine that helps arouse the body to cope with threats and stress. Epinephrine is of interest to psychologists because it has emotional as well as physical effects. It intensifies most emotions and is central to the experience of fear and anxiety.

2-3e THE TESTES AND THE OVARIES

The testes and ovaries also produce steroids, among them testosterone and estrogen. (Testosterone is also produced in smaller amounts by the adrenal glands.) About six weeks after conception, the male sex hormone testosterone causes the male's sex organs to develop. In fact, if it were not for the secretion of testosterone at this time, we would all develop the external genital organs of females. During puberty, testosterone stokes the growth of muscle and bone and the development of primary and secondary sex characteristics. *Primary sex characteristics* are directly involved in

> "MY NOSE HAD SPOKEN FALSELY."
>
> CHARLES DARWIN, ENGLISH NATURALIST AND GEOLOGIST, 1809–1882

✱ Steroids, Behavior, and Mental Processes

Professional wrestler Chris Benoit and Nancy Benoit—before his double murder and suicide that took their lives and the life of their 7-year-old son.

Steroids increase muscle mass, heighten resistance to stress, and increase the body's energy supply by signaling the liver to release glucose into the bloodstream. The steroid testosterone is connected with the sex drive in both males and females (females secrete some testosterone in the adrenal glands). Anabolic steroids (synthetic versions of the male sex hormone testosterone) have been used, sometimes in tandem with growth hormone, to enhance athletic prowess. Not only do these steroids enhance athletic prowess, but they are also connected with self-confidence and aggressiveness. Anabolic steroids are generally outlawed in sports; however, many athletes, such as professional wrestler Chris Benoit, have used them. Benoit, sadly, may be best known for murdering his wife and his son before taking his own life. Benoit had had a number of explosive outbursts, and it has been suggested that he might have been experiencing "road rage" due to his use of anabolic steroids to pump up his muscle mass and his competitiveness.

reproduction and include the increased size of the penis and the sperm-producing ability of the testes. *Secondary sex characteristics,* such as the presence of a beard and a deeper voice, differentiate males from females but are not directly involved in reproduction.

The ovaries produce estrogen and progesterone as well as small amounts of testosterone. (Estrogen is also produced in smaller amounts by the adrenal glands.) Estrogen fosters female reproductive capacity and secondary sex characteristics such as accumulation of fatty tissue in the breasts and hips. Progesterone stimulates growth of the female reproductive organs and prepares the uterus to maintain pregnancy. Estrogen and testosterone have psychological effects as well as biological effects, which we will explore further in Chapter 9.

2-4 EVOLUTION AND HEREDITY

Charles Darwin almost missed the boat—literally. Darwin had volunteered to serve on an expeditionary voyage on the *H.M.S. Beagle.* However, he was nearly prevented from undertaking his historic voyage

due to the shape of his nose. The captain of the ship, Robert Fitz-Roy, believed that you could judge a person's character by the outline of his facial features, and Darwin's nose didn't fit the bill. But Fitz-Roy relented, and in the 1830s, Darwin undertook the historic voyage to the Galápagos Islands that led to the development of his theory of evolution.

In 1871 Darwin published *The Descent of Man,* which made the case that humans, like other species, were a product of evolution. He argued that the great apes (chimpanzees, gorillas, and so on) and humans were related and shared a common primate ancestor (see Figure 2.14). Evidence from fossil remains suggests that such a common ancestor might have lived about 13 million years ago (Moyà-Solà et al., 2004). Many people ridiculed Darwin's views because they were displeased with the notion that they might share ancestry with apes. Others argued that Darwin's theory contradicted the Bible's Book of Genesis, which stated that humans had been created in one day in the image of God.

The concept of a *struggle for existence* lies at the core of Darwin's theory of evolution. At the Galápagos Islands, Darwin found himself immersed in the unfolding of a

FIG.2.14 THE HUMAN SKELETON AND THE SKELETONS OF SOME RELATIVES

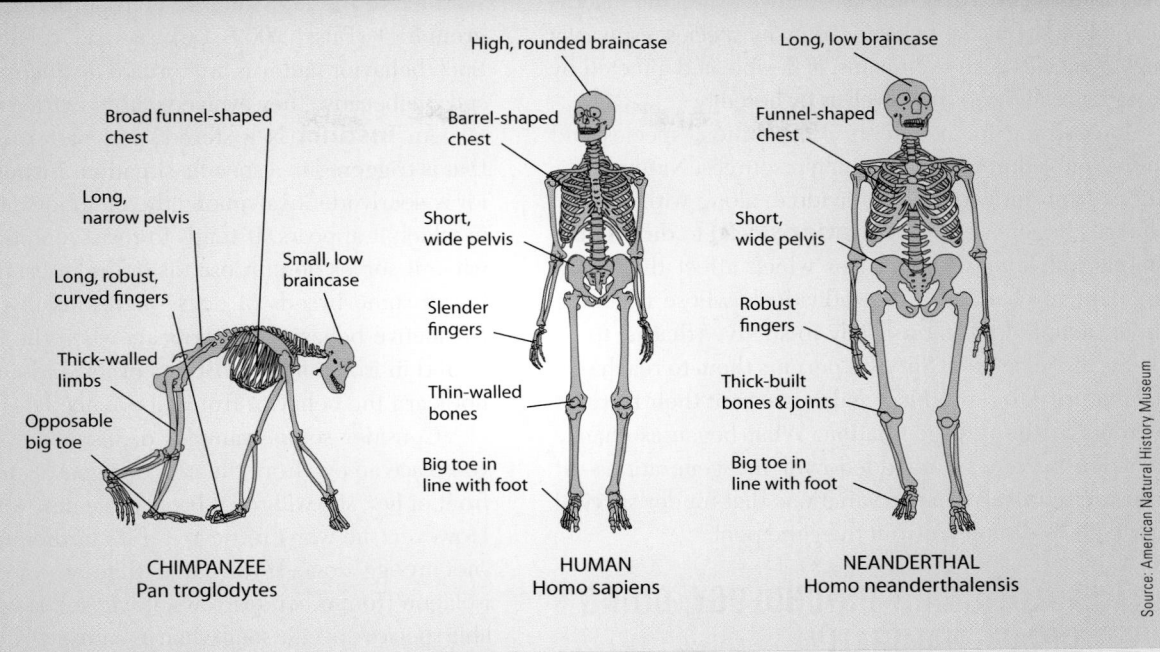

CHIMPANZEE
Pan troglodytes

HUMAN
Homo sapiens

NEANDERTHAL
Homo neanderthalensis

Source: American Natural History Museum

The idea that humans were genetically related to monkeys and other animals was so divergent from other 19th century views of our species that Darwin was initially reluctant to discuss his theory of evolution. *The Descent of Man,* **published in 1871, made the case that humans, like other species, were a product of evolution. Darwin believed that the great apes (chimpanzees, gorillas, and so on) shared a common primate ancestor. We did not descend from Neanderthals, but we coexisted with them for thousands of years. Neanderthals became extinct some 35,000 years ago.**

huge game of "Survivor," with animals and plants competing for food, water, territory, even light. But here the game was for real, and the rewards had nothing to do with fame or fortune. The rewards were reaching sexual maturity and transmitting one's genes into subsequent generations.

As described by evolutionary theory, some creatures have adapted successfully to these challenges, and their numbers have increased. Others have not met the challenges and have fallen back into the distant mists of time. Evidence suggests that 99.99% of all species that ever existed are now extinct (Gould, 2002). Which species prosper and which fade away are determined by **natural selection**; that is, species that are better adapted to their environment are more likely to survive and reproduce.

When we humans first appeared on Earth, our survival required a different sort of struggle than it does today. We fought or fled from predators such as leopards. We foraged across parched lands for food. But because of the evolution of our intellect, we prevailed. Our numbers have increased. We continue to transmit the traits that led to our selection down through the generations by means of genetic material whose chemical codes are only now being cracked.

Just what is handed down through the generations? The answer is biological, or physiological, structures and processes. Our biology serves as the material base for our behaviors, emotions, and cognitions (our thoughts, images, and plans). Biology somehow

natural selection the concept that holds that adaptive genetic variations among members of a species enable individuals with those variations to survive and reproduce

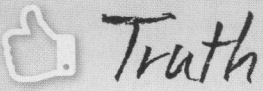

| T | F | Charles Darwin was nearly excluded from the voyage that led to the development of his theory of evolution because the captain of the ship did not like the shape of his nose. |

It is true that Darwin was almost prevented from undertaking his historic voyage because the ship captain did not like the shape of his nose. But the captain relented and, as they say, the rest is history.

gives rise to specific behavioral tendencies in some organisms, such as the chick's instinctive fear of the shadow of the hawk. But the behavior of many species, especially higher species such as humans, is flexible and affected by experience and choice, as well as by heredity.

According to the theory of evolution, species and individuals compete for the same resources. Natural variations from individual to individual, along with sudden changes in genes called **mutations**, lead to differences among individuals, differences which affect the ability to adapt to change. Those individuals whose traits are better adapted are more likely to survive (that is, to be "naturally selected"). Survival permits them to reach sexual maturity, to reproduce, and to transmit their features or traits to the next generation. What began as chance variation becomes embedded over the generations—if it fosters survival. Chance variations that hinder survival are likely to disappear from the gene pool.

2-4a EVOLUTIONARY PSYCHOLOGY: DOING WHAT COMES NATURALLY

These same concepts of *adaptation* and *natural selection* have also been applied to psychological traits and are key concepts in **evolutionary psychology**. Evolutionary psychology studies the ways in which adaptation and natural selection are connected with mental processes and behavior (Plomin et al., 2013). Over the eons, evolution has provided organisms with advantages such as stronger fins and wings, sharper claws, and camouflage. Human evolution has given rise to various physical traits and also to such diverse activities as language, art, committed relationships, and warfare.

One of the concepts of evolutionary psychology is that not only physical traits but also many patterns of behavior, including social behavior, evolve and can be transmitted genetically from generation to generation. Behavior patterns that help an organism to survive and reproduce may be transmitted to the next generation. Such behaviors are believed to include aggression, strategies of mate selection, even altruism (that is, self-sacrifice of the individual to help perpetuate the family grouping) (Buss, 2009; Lukaszewski & Roney, 2009). Such behavior patterns are termed *instinctive* or *species-specific* because they evolved within certain species.

An **instinct** is a stereotyped pattern of behavior that is triggered in a specific situation. Instinctive behavior is nearly identical among the members of the species in which it appears. It tends to resist modification, even when it serves no purpose (as in the interminable barking of some breeds of dogs) or results in punishment. Instinctive behavior also appears when the individual is reared in isolation from others of its kind and thus cannot learn the behavior from experience.

Consider some examples of instinctive behavior. If you place an egg from the nest of a goose a few inches in front of her, she will roll it back to the nest with her beak. However, she won't retrieve it if it's farther away—in the "not my egg" zone. If you rear a white-crowned sparrow in isolation from other sparrows, it will still sing a recognizable species-specific song when it matures. The male stickleback fish instinctively attacks fish (or pieces of painted wood) with the kinds of red bellies that are characteristic of other male sticklebacks. Many psychologists consider language to be "instinctive" among humans. Psychologists are trying to determine what other kinds of human behavior may be instinctive. However, even instinctive behavior can be modified to some degree by learning, and most psychologists agree that the richness and complexity of human behavior are made possible by learning.

2-4b HEREDITY, GENETICS, AND BEHAVIORAL GENETICS

Heredity defines one's *nature*, which is based on biological structures and processes. Heredity refers to the biological transmission of traits that have evolved from generation to generation. Fish are limited in other ways by their natural traits. Chimpanzees and gorillas can understand many spoken words and express some concepts through nonverbal symbol systems such as American Sign Language. Apes cannot speak, however, apparently because of limitations in the speech areas of the brain.

The subfield of biology that studies heredity is called **genetics**. The field of genetics looks at both species-specific behavior patterns (instincts) and individual differences among the members of a species. *Behavioral genetics* focuses on the contribution of genes to behavior.

Behavioral genetics bridges the sciences of psychology and biology. It is concerned with the genetic transmission of traits that give rise to patterns of behavior. Psychologists are thinking in terms of behavioral genetics

mutation a sudden variation in an inheritable characteristic, as distinguished from a variation that results from generations of gradual selection

evolutionary psychology the branch of psychology that studies the ways in which adaptation and natural selection are connected with mental processes and behavior

instinct a stereotyped pattern of behavior that is triggered by a particular stimulus and nearly identical among members of a species, even when they are reared in isolation

heredity the transmission of traits from parent to offspring by means of genes

genetics the area of biology that focuses on heredity

when they ask about the inborn reasons why individuals may differ in their behavior and mental processes. For example, some children learn language more quickly than others. Part of the reason may lie in behavioral genetics—their heredity. But some children also experience a richer exposure to language at early ages.

Heredity appears to be a factor in almost all aspects of human behavior, personality, and mental processes (Plomin & Asbury, 2005; Plomin & Haworth, 2009; Stone et al., 2012). Examples include sociability, shyness, social dominance, aggressiveness, leadership, thrill seeking, effectiveness as a parent or a therapist, happiness, even interest in arts and crafts (Blum et al., 2009; Ebstein et al., 2010; Leonardo & Hen, 2006).

Heredity is apparently involved in psychological disorders ranging from anxiety and depression to schizophrenia, bipolar disorder, alcoholism, and personality disorders (Dworzynski et al., 2009; Lewis et al., 2013; Viding et al., 2013). These disorders are discussed in Chapter 12, but here we can note that a study of 794 pairs of female twins by Kendler and his colleagues (2000) found six aspects of psychological health that were connected with genetic factors: feelings of physical well-being, social relationships, anxiety and depression, substance abuse, use of social support, and self-esteem.

The Kendler group also found, however, that the family environment contributed strongly to social relationships, substance abuse, and social support. Although psychological health is influenced by environmental factors, our understanding of the role of heredity continues to expand. Unlocking these mysteries depends on how well we understand genes and chromosomes.

2-4c GENES AND CHROMOSOMES

Genes are the most basic building blocks of heredity. Genes regulate the development of specific traits. Some traits, such as blood type, are controlled by a single pair of genes. (One gene is derived from each parent.) Other traits are determined by combinations of genes. The inherited component of complex psychological traits, such as intelligence, is believed to be determined by combinations of genes. It is estimated that the cells within your body contain 20,000 to 25,000 genes (International Human Genome Sequencing Consortium, 2004).

Genes are segments of **chromosomes**. That is, chromosomes are made up of strings of genes. Each cell in the body contains 46 chromosomes arranged in 23 pairs. Chromosomes are large complex molecules of **DNA** (short for *deoxyribonucleic acid*), which has several chemical components. The tightly wound structure of DNA was first demonstrated in the 1950s by James Watson and Francis Crick. DNA takes the form of a double helix—a twisting molecular ladder (see Figure 2.15). The "rungs" of the ladder are made up of chemicals whose names are abbreviated as A, T, C, and G. A always links up with T to complete a rung, and C always combines with G. Therefore, you can describe

gene a basic unit of heredity, which is found at a specific point on a chromosome

chromosome a microscopic rod-shaped body in the cell nucleus carrying genes that transmit hereditary traits from generation to generation; humans normally have 46 chromosomes

DNA acronym for deoxyribonucleic acid, the substance that forms the basic material of chromosomes; it takes the form of a double helix and contains the genetic code

FIG. 2.15 CELLS, CHROMOSOMES, AND DNA

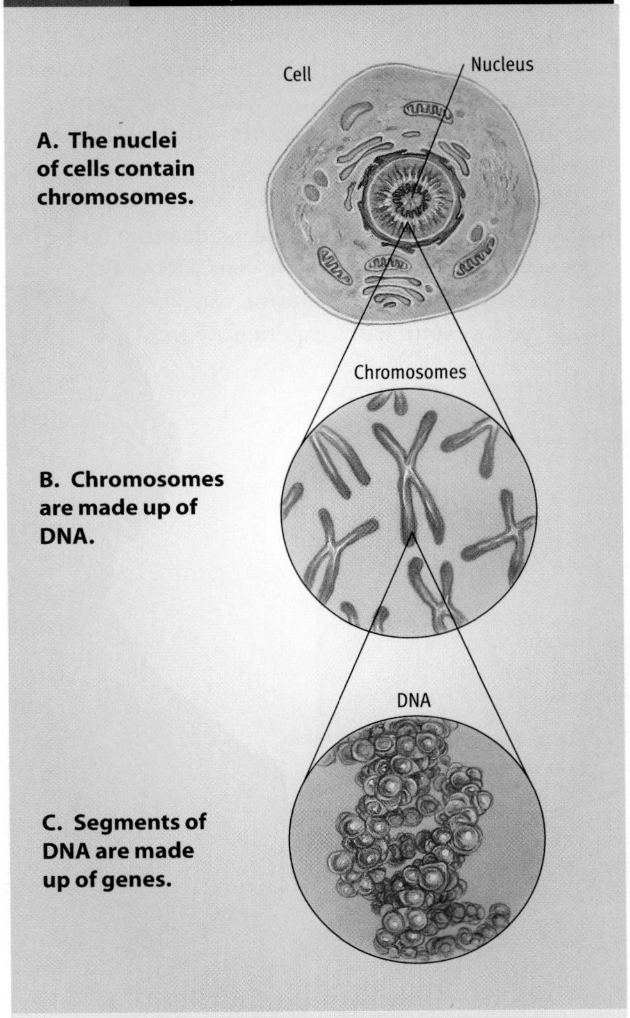

Cell
Nucleus

A. The nuclei of cells contain chromosomes.

Chromosomes

B. Chromosomes are made up of DNA.

DNA

C. Segments of DNA are made up of genes.

The genetic code—that is, the order of A, G, T, and C—determines your species and all those traits that can be inherited, from the color of your eyes to predispositions toward many psychological traits and abilities, including sociability and musical talent.

the *genetic code* in terms of the nucleotides you find along just one of the rungs—CTGAGTCAC and so on. A single gene can contain hundreds of thousands of base pairs. So if you think of a gene as a word, it can be a few hundred thousand letters long and completely unpronounceable.

A group of scientists working together around the globe—referred to as the Human Genome Project—has learned that the sequencing of your DNA consists of about three billion DNA sequences spread throughout your chromosomes (Plomin & Schalkwyk, 2007). These sequences—the order of the chemicals we call A, T, C, and G—caused you to grow arms and not wings, and skin rather than scales. Psychologists debate the extent to which genes influence complex psychological traits such as intelligence, aggressiveness, and happiness, and the appearance of psychological disorders such as schizophrenia. Some traits, such as eye color, are determined by a single pair of genes. Other traits, especially complex psychological traits such as sociability and aggressiveness, are thought to be **polygenic**—that is, influenced by combinations of genes.

Your genetic code provides your **genotype**—that is, your full genetic potential, as determined by the sequencing of the chemicals in your DNA. But the person you see in the mirror was also influenced by your early experiences in the home, injuries, adequacy of nourishment, educational experiences, and numerous other environmental influences. Therefore, you see the outer appearance of your phenotype, including the hairstyles of the day. Your **phenotype** is the manner in which your genetic code manifests itself because of your experiences and environmental circumstances. Your genotype enables you to acquire language. Your phenotype reveals that you are likely to be speaking English if you were reared in the United States or Spanish if you were reared in Mexico (or both, if you are Mexican American).

Your genotype provides what psychologists refer to as your **nature**. Your phenotype represents the interaction of your nature (heredity) and your **nurture** (environmental influences) in the origins of your behavior and mental processes. Psychologists are especially interested in the roles of nature and nurture in intelligence and psychological disorders. Our genotypes provide us with physical traits that set the stage for certain behaviors. But none of us is the result of heredity alone. Environmental factors such as nutrition, learning opportunities, cultural influences, exercise, and (unfortunately) accident and illness also determine our phenotypes and whether genetically possible behaviors will be displayed. Behavior and mental processes represent the interaction of nature and nurture. A potential Shakespeare who is reared in poverty and never taught to read or write will not create a *Hamlet*.

We normally receive 23 chromosomes from our father's sperm cell and 23 chromosomes from our mother's egg cell (ovum). When a sperm cell fertilizes an ovum, the chromosomes form 23 pairs. The 23rd pair consists of **sex chromosomes**, which determine whether we are female or male. We all receive an X sex chromosome (so called because of the X shape) from our mother. If we also receive an X sex chromosome from our father, we develop into a female. If we receive a Y sex chromosome (named after the Y shape) from our father, we develop into a male.

When people do not have the normal number of 46 chromosomes (23 pairs), physical and behavioral abnormalities may result. Most persons with **Down syndrome**, for example,

Behavior and mental processes represent the interaction of nature and nurture. A potential Shakespeare who is reared in poverty and never taught to read or write will not create a Hamlet.

polygenic referring to traits that are influenced by combinations of genes

genotype one's genetic makeup, based on the sequencing of the nucleotides we term A, C, G, and T

phenotype one's actual development and appearance, as based on one's genotype and environmental influences

nature the inborn, innate character of an organism

nurture the sum total of the environmental factors that affect an organism from conception onward

sex chromosomes the 23rd pair of chromosomes, whose genetic material determines the sex of the individual

Down syndrome a condition caused by an extra chromosome on the 21st pair and characterized by mental deficiency, a broad face, and slanting eyes

have an extra, or third, chromosome on the 21st pair. Persons with Down syndrome have a downward-sloping fold of skin at the inner corners of the eyes, a round face, a protruding tongue, and a broad, flat nose. They are cognitively impaired and usually have physical problems that cause death by middle age.

2-4d KINSHIP STUDIES

Kinship studies are ways in which psychologists compare the presence of traits and behavior patterns in people who are biologically related or unrelated to help determine the role of genetic factors in their occurrence. The more *closely* people are related, the more *genes* they have in common. Identical twins share 100% of their genes (see Figure 2.16). Parents and children have 50% of their genes in common, as do siblings (brothers and sisters). Aunts and uncles related by blood have a 25% overlap with nieces and nephews. First cousins share 12.5% of

their genes. If genes are involved in a trait or behavior pattern, people who are more closely related should be more likely to show similar traits or behavior. Psychologists and behavioral geneticists are especially interested in running kinship studies with twins and adopted individuals (Plomin & Haworth, 2009).

TWIN STUDIES The fertilized egg cell (ovum) that carries genetic messages from both parents is called a *zygote*. Now and then, a zygote divides into two cells that separate, so that instead of developing into a single person, it develops into two people with the same genetic makeup. Such people are identical, or **monozygotic (MZ) twins**. If the woman releases two ova in the same month and they are both fertilized, they develop into fraternal,

> **monozygotic (MZ) twins**
> twins that develop from a single fertilized ovum that divides in two early in prenatal development; MZ twins thus share the same genetic code; also called *identical twins*

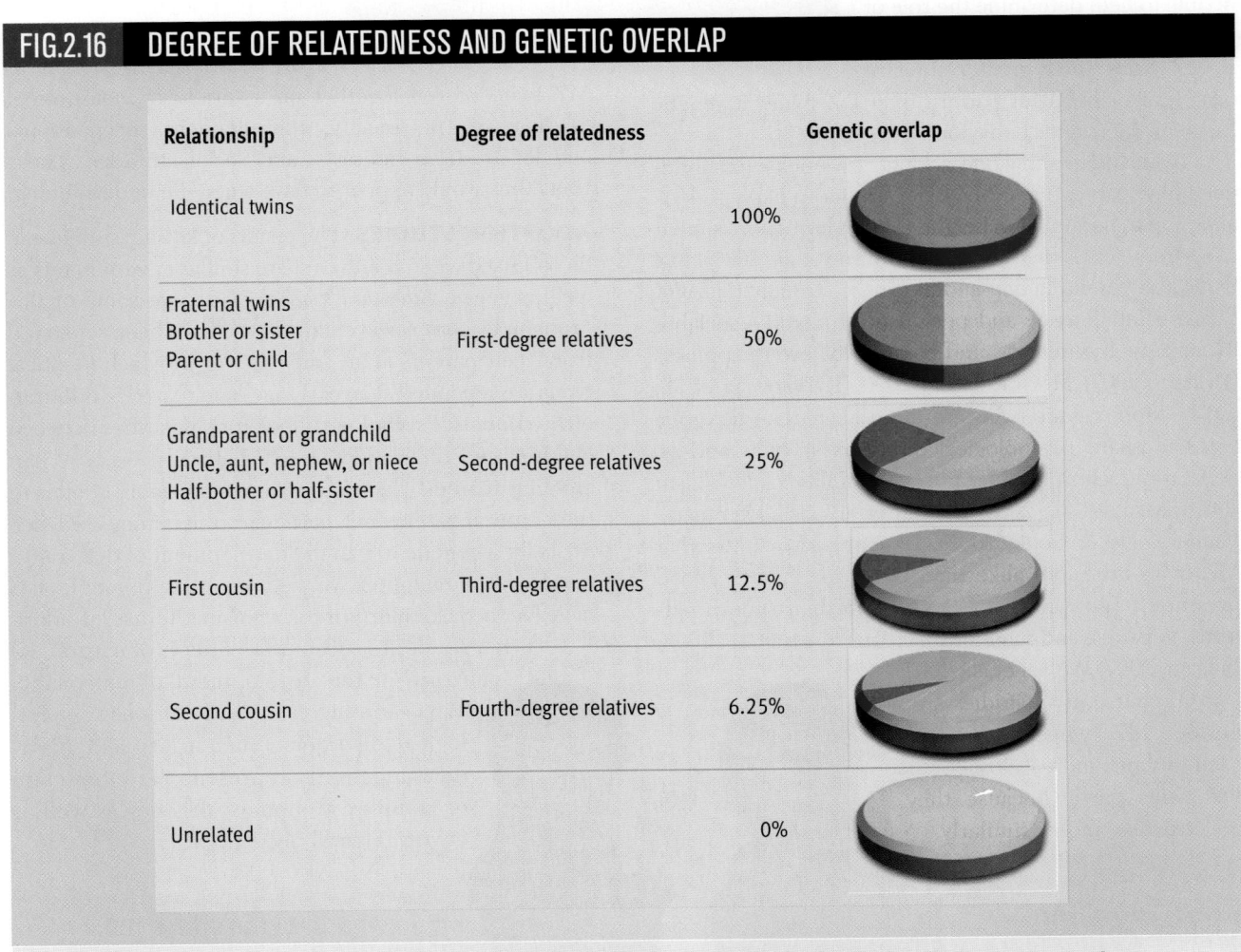

FIG.2.16   DEGREE OF RELATEDNESS AND GENETIC OVERLAP

Relationship	Degree of relatedness	Genetic overlap
Identical twins		100%
Fraternal twins Brother or sister Parent or child	First-degree relatives	50%
Grandparent or grandchild Uncle, aunt, nephew, or niece Half-bother or half-sister	Second-degree relatives	25%
First cousin	Third-degree relatives	12.5%
Second cousin	Fourth-degree relatives	6.25%
Unrelated		0%

Identical twins have the greatest genetic overlap: 100%. Parents and children have only a 50% genetic overlap.

Source: Weiten, *Psychology: Themes & Variations, Briefer Version*, 9E, 2014, p. 87

People with Down syndrome have characteristic facial features and often develop health problems that lead to death in middle age.

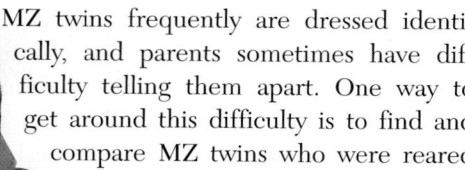

or **dizygotic (DZ) twins**. DZ twins, like other siblings, share 50% of their genes. MZ twins are important in the study of the relative influences of nature (heredity) and nurture (the environment) because differences between MZ twins are the result of nurture. (They do not differ in their heredity—that is, their nature—because their genetic makeup is the same.)

Twin studies compare the presence of traits and behavior patterns in MZ twins, DZ twins, and other people to help determine the role of genetic factors in their occurrence. If MZ twins show greater similarity on a trait or behavior pattern than DZ twins, a genetic basis for the trait or behavior is suggested.

Twin studies show how strongly genetic factors influence physical features. MZ twins are more likely to look alike and to be similar in height, even to have more similar cholesterol levels than DZ twins (Souren et al., 2007). MZ twins also resemble one another more strongly than DZ twins in intelligence and personality traits like sociability, anxiety, friendliness, and conformity, even happiness (Lykken, 2007; McCrae et al., 2000; Trzaskowski et al., 2013). Monozygotic twins are more likely than dizygotic twins to share psychological disorders such as autism, depression, schizophrenia, and vulnerability to alcoholism (Dworzynski et al., 2009; Plomin et al., 2013; Veenstra-Vanderweele & Cook, 2003). Research also shows that MZ twins are more alike than DZ twins in their blood pressure, brain wave patterns, even in their speech patterns, gestures, and mannerisms (Ambrosius et al., 2008; Lykken, 2007; Wessel et al., 2007).

Of course, twin studies are not perfect. MZ twins may resemble each other more closely than DZ twins partly because they are treated more similarly.

MZ twins frequently are dressed identically, and parents sometimes have difficulty telling them apart. One way to get around this difficulty is to find and compare MZ twins who were reared in different homes. Then, any similarities between MZ twins reared apart could not be explained by a shared home environment and would appear to be largely a result of heredity. In the fascinating Minnesota study of twins reared apart (McGue & Christensen, 2013), researchers have been measuring the physiological and psychological characteristics of 56 sets of MZ adult twins who were separated in infancy and reared in different homes.

In sum, MZ twins reared apart are about as similar as MZ twins reared together on a variety of measures of intelligence, personality, temperament, occupational and leisure-time interests, and social attitudes. These traits thus would appear to have a genetic underpinning.

ADOPTION STUDIES The results of kinship studies can be confused when relatives share similar environments as well as genes. *Adoption studies* overcome some of this problem by comparing children who have been separated from their parents at an early age (or in which identical twins are separated at an early age) and reared in different environments. Psychologists look for similarities between children and their adoptive and natural parents. When children reared by adoptive parents are more similar to their natural parents in a particular trait, strong evidence exists for a genetic role in the development of that trait.

In later chapters we will see that psychologists have been particularly interested in the use of adoption studies to sort out the effects of nature and nurture in the development of personality traits, intelligence, and various psychological disorders. Such traits and disorders apparently represent the interaction of complex groupings of genes as well as environmental influences.

dizygotic (DZ) twins twins that develop from two fertilized ova and who are thus as closely related as brothers and sisters in general; also called *fraternal twins*

Monozygotic twins share 100% of their genes, whereas dizygotic share 50% of their genes.

Michael Greenlar/The Image Works

Image Source Photography/Veer

STUDY TOOLS 2

IN THE BOOK, YOU CAN:

- ☐ Check your understanding of what you've read with the quizzes that follow.
- ☐ Rip out the chapter review card at the back of the book to have a summary of the chapter and the key terms handy.

ONLINE AT CENGAGEBRAIN.COM YOU CAN:

- ☐ Learn more about the workings of the brain in a learning module on split-brain patients.
- ☐ Practice retrieving what you've learned using the interactive figures on neurons and the nervous system.
- ☐ Explore the brain's organization, structure, and function in a short video.
- ☐ Prepare for tests with quizzes
- ☐ Review the key terms with Flash Cards.
- ☐ Play games to master concepts.

FILL-INS

Answers can be found in the back of the book, starting on page XXX.

1. Neurons transmit messages to other neurons by means of chemical substances called _____.

2. Neurons have a cell body, or soma; dendrites, which receive "messages"; and a(n) _____, which extends from the cell body and transmits messages.

3. The axons of many neurons have a fatty insulating sheath called _____.

4. It is theorized that people with the psychological disorder called _____ apparently overutilize the neurotransmitter dopamine.

5. The _____ nervous system regulates the glands and involuntary activities such as heartbeat and digestion.

6. The brain structure called the _____ is involved in balance and coordination.

7. The concept of a struggle for _____ lies at the core of the theory of evolution.

8. Stereotypical behavior patterns that have evolved within a species are called _____.

9. People with _____ syndrome have an extra chromosome on the 21st pair.

10. The behavior of _____ twins is of special interest to psychologists because their genetic endowment is the same.

MULTIPLE CHOICE

1. **An axon's length can range from a few millimeters to**
   a. 1 inch.
   b. 12 inches.
   c. several feet.
   d. up to a mile.

2. **A neuron can fire up to a limit of about _____ times per second.**
   a. 40
   b. 400
   c. 4,000
   d. 40,000

3. **If someone steps on your toes, resulting in pain and the movement of your foot, which of the following describes this process?**
   a. Afferent neurons transmit the sensation of pain to the spinal cord and to the brain followed by efferent neurons sending the message to your foot to move.
   b. Efferent neurons transmit the sensation of pain to the spinal cord and to the brain followed by afferent neurons sending the message to your foot to move.
   c. Efferent neurons transmit the sensation of pain to the spinal cord and to the brain followed by efferent neurons sending the message to your foot to move.
   d. Afferent neurons transmit the sensation of pain to the spinal cord and to the brain followed by afferent neurons sending the message to your foot to move.

4. **When Charlotte hears something embarrassing, she blushes. Being a student of psychology, she knows that this condition is controlled by the**
   a. motor cortex.
   b. autonomic nervous system.
   c. somatosensory cortex.
   d. motor nervous system.

5. **Wernicke's aphasia causes**
   a. impairment of one's ability to comprehend speech and to think of the proper words to express his or her own thoughts.
   b. one to speak slowly and laboriously in simple sentences.
   c. serious impairment in reading.
   d. an inability to segment words in sounds while reading.

6. **An editor gets so upset that she is late in working on a manuscript that she throws up her lunch. This probably occurred because of activity of the**
   a. longest neurons in her body.
   b. corpus callosum.
   c. parasympathetic division of her autonomic nervous system.
   d. sympathetic division of her autonomic nervous system.

7. **Ellen loses weight and becomes somewhat agitated. Her doctor is most likely to theorize that she is suffering from a deficiency of**
   a. epinephrine.
   b. dopamine.
   c. cortisol.
   d. thyroxin.

8. **_____ are the most basic building blocks of heredity.**
   a. Genes
   b. Hormones
   c. Neurons
   d. Neurotransmitters

9. **Dizygotic twins**
   a. develop when two ova are fertilized.
   b. share 100% of their genes.
   c. are referred to as identical twins.
   d. demonstrate differences that are the result of nurture.

10. **"Messages" travel within neurons by means of _____ and from neuron to neuron by means of _____.**
    a. electricity, electricity
    b. neurotransmitters, neurotransmitters
    c. neurotransmitters, electricity
    d. electricity, neurotransmitters

ONE APPROACH.
70 UNIQUE SOLUTIONS.

3 | Sensation and Perception

Chung Sung-Jun/Getty I...

LEARNING OUTCOMES

After studying this chapter, you will be able to...

3-1 Define and differentiate between sensation and perception

3-2 Identify the parts of the eye; explain the properties of light and the theories of color vision

3-3 Describe the organization of visual perceptions

3-4 Identify the parts of the ear; explain how the sense of hearing works

3-5 Describe the chemical senses

3-6 Describe the skin senses and discuss theoretical explanations for pain

3-7 Describe the kinesthetic and vestibular senses

3-8 Explain why psychologists are skeptical about extrasensory perception

After you finish

this chapter, go

to **PAGE 89** for

STUDY TOOLS

The tsunami that hit the coast of southern Asia a decade ago killed as many as a quarter of a million people. The people were caught off guard, but not the animals.

Along the western coast of Thailand, elephants giving rides to tourists began to trumpet agitatedly hours before the tsunami, just about when the earthquake that fractured the ocean floor sent the big waves rushing toward the shore. An hour before the waves slammed into the area, the elephants began wailing. Before the waves struck, they trooped off to higher ground. Elephants, tigers, leopards, deer, wild boar, water buffalo, monkeys, and reptiles in Sri Lanka's Yala National Park escaped the tsunami unharmed.

People have observed that animals appear to detect earthquakes, hurricanes, volcanic eruptions, and tsunamis before the earth starts shaking. Some animals are apparently supersensitive to sound, others to temperature, touch, or vibration, which gives them advance warning of coming disaster.

Elephants are particularly sensitive to ground vibrations and probably sensed in their feet and trunks the earthquake that caused the tsunami. Some birds, dogs, tigers, and elephants can sense sound waves whose frequencies are too low for humans to hear. Dogs' superior sense of smell might detect subtle chemical changes in the air that warn them of calamities.

Different animals, then, have different sensory apparatuses, and many of them sense things that people cannot sense. Just how do humans sense the world around them?

Ben Cranke/The Image Bank/Getty Images

Elephants detected the tsunami before the earth started shaking. How do the senses of various species differ?

3-1 SENSATION AND PERCEPTION

Sensation is the stimulation of sensory receptors and the transmission of sensory information to the central nervous system (the spinal cord or brain). Sensory receptors are located in sensory organs such as the eyes and ears, the skin, and elsewhere in the body. Stimulation of the senses is an automatic process. It results from sources of energy, like light and sound, or from the presence of chemicals, as in smell and taste.

Perception is *not* mechanical. Perception is an *active* process in which sensations are organized and interpreted to form an inner representation of the world (Goldstein, 2013; Hafemeister et al., 2010). Perception may begin with sensation, but it also reflects our experiences and expectations as it makes sense of sensory stimuli. A person standing 15 feet away and a 12-inch-tall doll right next to you may cast similar-sized images on the back of your eye, but whether you interpret the size to be a foot-long doll or a full-grown person 15 feet away is a matter of perception that depends on your experience with dolls, people, and distance.

Truth or Fiction?

WHAT DO YOU THINK? Folklore, common sense, or nonsense? Select T for "truth" or F for "fiction," and check the accuracy of your answers as you read through the chapter.

T	F	People have only five senses.
T	F	If we could see waves of light with slightly longer wavelengths, warm-blooded animals would glow in the dark.
T	F	People sometimes hear what they want to hear.
T	F	When we mix blue light and yellow light, we obtain green light.
T	F	People can be "wide-eyed with fear."
T	F	Many people experience pain "in" limbs that have been amputated.
T	F	Some people can read other people's minds.

sensation the stimulation of sensory receptors and the transmission of sensory information to the central nervous system

perception the process by which sensations are organized into an inner representation of the world

absolute threshold the minimal amount of energy that can produce a sensation

pitch the highness or lowness of a sound, as determined by the frequency of the sound waves

In this chapter, you will see that your perception of the world of changing sights, sounds, and other sources of sensory input depends largely on the so-called five senses: vision, hearing, smell, taste, and touch. But touch is just one of several "skin senses," which also include pressure, warmth, cold, and pain. There are also senses that alert you to your own body position without your having to watch every step you take. As we explore each of these senses, we will find that similar sensations may lead to different perceptions in different people—or to different situations in the same person.

Before we begin our voyage through the senses, let's consider a number of concepts that we use to talk about the relationships between sensations and perceptions: *absolute threshold, subliminal stimulation, difference threshold, signal–detection theory, feature detectors,* and *sensory adaptation.* In doing so, we will learn why we can dim the lights gradually to near darkness without anyone noticing. We will also learn why we might become indifferent to the savory aromas of delightful dinners.

3-1a ABSOLUTE THRESHOLD

Nineteenth-century German psychologist Gustav Fechner used the term **absolute threshold** to refer to the weakest level of a stimulus that is necessary to produce a sensation. For example, the absolute threshold for light would be the minimum brightness (physical energy) required to activate the visual sensory system.

Psychophysicists look for the absolute thresholds of the senses by exposing individuals to progressively stronger stimuli until they find the minimum stimuli that the person can detect 50% of the time. These absolute thresholds are not all that absolute, however. Some people are more sensitive than others, and even the same person might have a slightly different response at different times (Rouder & Morey, 2009). Nevertheless, under ideal conditions, our ability to detect stimuli is quite sensitive. (See the nearby feature on "Absolute Thresholds of the Senses.")

How different our lives would be if the absolute thresholds for the human senses differed! If your ears were sensitive to sounds that are lower in **pitch**, you might hear the collisions among molecules of air. If you could see light with slightly longer wavelengths, you would see infrared light waves and people and other animals would glow in the dark. Your world would be transformed because heat generates infrared light.

3-1b SUBLIMINAL STIMULATION

Some television commercials contain words or sexual images that are flashed so briefly on the screen that we do not become conscious of them. But can they still influence us? Behaviorist John B. Watson was a pioneer in associating appealing stimuli with products, as auto ads frequently associate attractive women with cars. But most ads make the associations openly.

Sensory stimulation that is below a person's absolute threshold for conscious perception is termed

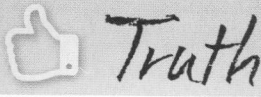

Fiction

T **F** People have only five senses.

It is not true that people have only five senses. People actually have many more than five senses.

Truth

T F If we could see waves of light with slightly longer wavelengths, warm-blooded animals would glow in the dark.

It is true that people and other animals would glow in the dark if you could see light with slightly longer wavelengths. You would then be seeing infrared light, and most of the thermal radiation given off by warm bodies—e.g., people and warm-blooded animals—is infrared.

Absolute Thresholds of the Senses

Can you see a burning candle 20 miles away on a starlit night? Can you hear a watch ticking 15 feet away in a quiet room? For most people, the answer is a resounding *yes*. Here are measures of the absolute thresholds for the human senses of vision, hearing, taste, smell, and touch:

▶ **Vision: a candle flame viewed from about 30 miles on a clear, dark night.**

▶ **Hearing: a watch ticking from about 20 feet away in a quiet room.**

▶ **Taste: 1 teaspoon of sugar dissolved in 2 gallons of water.**

▶ **Smell: about one drop of perfume diffused throughout a small house (1 part in 500 million).**

▶ **Touch: the pressure of the wing of a fly falling on a cheek from a distance of about 0.4 inch.**

Finnbarr Webster/Alamy

subliminal stimulation—and its perception is called *subliminal perception*. Visual stimuli can be flashed too briefly to enable us to process them. Auditory stimuli can be played at a volume too low to consciously hear or can be played backward.

In one experiment, Johan Karremans and his colleagues (2006) repeatedly flashed "Lipton Ice" for about 1/50th of a second—too briefly to be consciously recognized—on a computer screen that was viewed by a group of participants. They flashed a message without a brand name to a control group. Afterward, thirsty participants in the first group showed a preference for Lipton Ice.

3-1c DIFFERENCE THRESHOLD

How much of a difference in intensity between two lights is required before you will detect one as being brighter than the other? The minimum difference in *magnitude*

of two stimuli required to tell them apart is their **difference threshold**. As with the absolute threshold, psychologists agree to the standard of a difference in strength that can be detected 50% of the time.

Psychophysicist Ernst Weber discovered through laboratory research that the threshold for perceiving differences in the intensity of light is about 2% (actually closer to 1/60th) of their intensity. This fraction, 1/60th, is known as **Weber's constant** for light. A related concept is the **just noticeable difference (jnd)**—the minimum difference in stimuli that a person can detect. For example, at least 50% of the time, most people can tell if a light becomes just 1/60th brighter or dimmer. Weber's constant for light holds whether we are comparing moderately bright lights or moderately dull lights. But it becomes inaccurate when we compare extremely bright or extremely dull lights.

Weber's constant *for* noticing differences in lifted weight is 1/53rd. (Round it off to 1/50th, or 2%.) That means if you are strong enough to heft a 100-pound barbell, you would not notice that it was heavier until about two pounds were added. Yet if you are a runner who carries two-pound dumbbells, you would definitely notice if someone slipped you dumbbells even a pound heavier because the increase would be 50%.

What about sound? People are most sensitive to changes in the pitch (frequency) of sounds. The Weber constant for pitch is 1/333, meaning that on average, people can tell when a tone rises or falls in pitch by an extremely small one-third of 1%. (Even a small error in pitch makes singers sound sharp or flat.) Remember this when friends criticize your singing.

The sense of taste is much less sensitive. On average, people cannot detect differences in saltiness of less than 20%. That is why "low-salt" chips that have 15% less salt than your favorite chips do not taste so bad.

3-1d SIGNAL–DETECTION THEORY

From the discussion so far, it might seem that people are simply switched on by certain amounts of stimulation. This is not quite so. People are also influenced

subliminal stimulation sensory stimulation below a person's absolute threshold for conscious perception

difference threshold the minimal difference in intensity required between two sources of energy so that they will be perceived as being different

Weber's constant the fraction of the intensity by which a source of physical energy must be increased or decreased so that a difference in intensity will be perceived

just noticeable difference (jnd) the minimal amount by which a source of energy must be increased or decreased so that a difference in intensity will be perceived

by psychological factors. **Signal–detection theory** considers these factors.

According to signal–detection theory, the relationship between a physical stimulus and a sensory response is not fully mechanical (Gigerenzer, 2010). People's ability to detect stimuli such as blips on a radar screen depends not only on the intensity of the blips but also on their training (learning), motivation (desire to perceive blips), and psychological states such as fatigue or alertness (Berry et al., 2012; Goldstein, 2013).

The intensity of the signal is one factor that determines whether people will perceive sensory stimuli (signals) or a difference between signals. Another is the degree to which the signal can be distinguished from background noise. It is easier to hear a friend speaking in a quiet room than in a room in which people are singing and clinking glasses. The sharpness of a person's biological sensory system is still another factor. Is sensory capacity fully developed? Is it diminished by age?

We also tend to detect stimuli we are searching for. People sometimes hear what they want to hear. The place in which you are reading this book may be abuzz with signals. If you are focusing your attention on this page, the other signals recede into the background. One psychological factor in signal detection is focusing on signals one considers important.

3-1e FEATURE DETECTORS IN THE BRAIN

Imagine you are standing by the curb of a busy street as a bus approaches. When neurons in your sensory organs—in this case, your eyes—are stimulated by the approach of the bus, they relay information to the sensory cortex in the brain. Nobel Prize winners David Hubel and Torsten Wiesel (1979) discovered that various neurons in the visual cortex of the brain fire in response to particular features of the visual input. Many cells in the brain detect (i.e., fire in response to) lines presented at various angles—vertical, horizontal, and in between. Other cells fire in response to specific colors. Because they respond to different aspects or features of a scene, these brain cells are termed **feature detectors**. In the example of the bus, visual feature detectors respond to the bus's edges, depth, contours, textures, shadows, speed, and kinds of motion (up, down, forward, and back). There are also feature detectors for other senses. Auditory feature detectors, for example, respond to the pitch, loudness, and other aspects of the sounds of the bus.

3-1f SENSORY ADAPTATION

Our sensory systems are admirably suited to a changing environment. **Sensory adaptation** refers to the processes by which we become more sensitive to stimuli of low magnitude and less sensitive to stimuli that remain the same, such as the background noises outside the window (Lawless & Heymann, 2010).

Consider how the visual sense adapts to lower intensities of light. When we first walk into a darkened movie theater, we see little but the images on the screen. As we search for our seats, however, we become increasingly sensitive to the faces around us and to the features of the theater. The process of becoming more sensitive to stimulation is referred to as **sensitization**, or *positive adaptation*.

But we become less sensitive to constant stimulation. When we live in a city, for example, we become desensitized to sounds of traffic except, perhaps, for the occasional backfire or siren. The process of becoming less sensitive to stimulation is referred to as **desensitization**, or *negative adaptation*.

> I think I can hear a watch ticking on an page 65

Michael Haegele/Comet/Corbis

signal–detection theory the view that the perception of sensory stimuli involves the interaction of physical, biological, and psychological factors

feature detectors neurons in the sensory cortex that fire in response to specific features of sensory information such as lines or edges of objects

sensory adaptation the processes by which organisms become more sensitive to stimuli that are low in magnitude and less sensitive to stimuli that are constant or ongoing in magnitude

sensitization the type of sensory adaptation in which we become more sensitive to stimuli that are low in magnitude. Also called *positive adaptation*

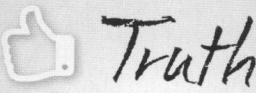

Truth

T F People sometimes hear what they want to hear.

It is true that people do sometimes hear what they want to hear. After all, that is what they are paying attention to.

Our sensitivities to stimulation provide our brains with information that we use to understand and influence the world outside. Therefore, it is not surprising that psychologists study the ways in which we sense and perceive this information—through vision, hearing, the chemical senses, and still other senses, as we see throughout the remainder of the chapter.

3-2 VISION

Our eyes are literally our "windows on the world." Because vision is our dominant sense, blindness is considered by many to be the most debilitating sensory loss. To understand vision, let's first "look" at light.

3-2a LIGHT

Light is fascinating stuff. It radiates. It illuminates. It dazzles. In almost all cultures, light is a symbol of goodness and knowledge. We speak of genius as "brilliance." People who aren't in the know are said to be "in the dark."

It is **visible light** that triggers visual sensations. Yet visible light is just one small part of a spectrum of electromagnetic energy that surrounds us (see Figure 3.1). All forms of electromagnetic energy

desensitization the type of sensory adaptation in which we become less sensitive to constant stimuli. Also called *negative adaptation*

visible light the part of the electromagnetic spectrum that stimulates the eye and produces visual sensations

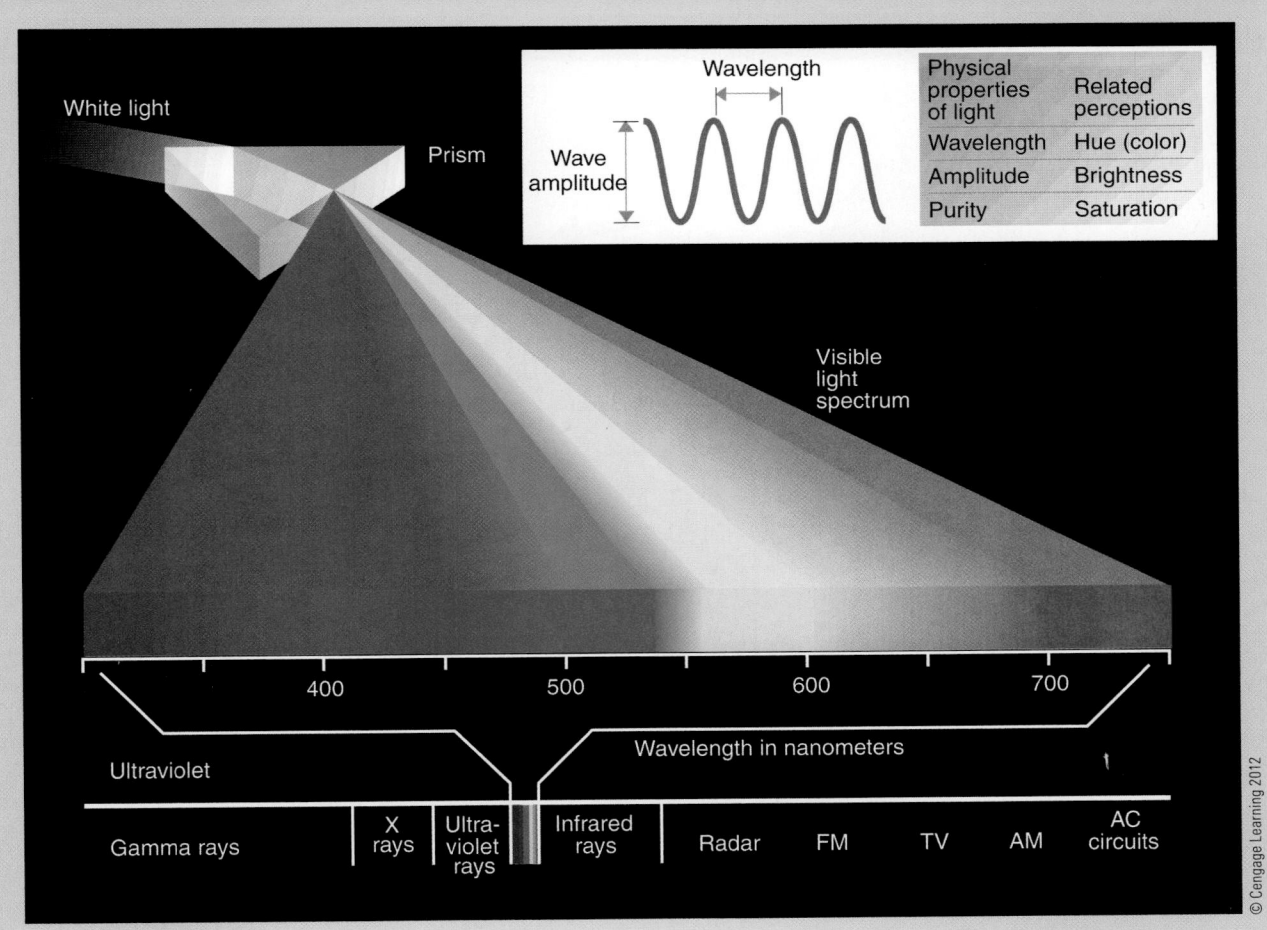

FIG.3.1 THE VISIBLE SPECTRUM

Physical properties of light	Related perceptions
Wavelength	Hue (color)
Amplitude	Brightness
Purity	Saturation

© Cengage Learning 2012

Did you know that the millions of colors that you can see make up just a tiny part of the spectrum of electromagnetic energy? Visible light shares the electromagnetic spectrum with X-rays, radio waves—both AM and FM, cosmic rays, radar, infrared, ultraviolet, and microwaves. By passing a source of white light, such as sunlight, through a prism, we break it down into the colors of the visible spectrum. Different forms of electromagnetic energy have wavelengths that vary from a few trillionths of a meter to thousands of miles. Visible light varies in wavelength from about 400 to 700 *billionths* of a meter. (One meter = 39.37 inches.)

move in waves, and different kinds of electromagnetic energy have signature wavelengths:

▶ Cosmic rays: The wavelengths of these rays from outer space are only a few *trillionths* of an inch long.

▶ Radio waves: Some radio signals extend for miles.

▶ Visible light: Roses are red, and violets are blue. Why? Different colors have different wavelengths, with violet the shortest at about 400 *billionths* of a meter in length and red the longest at 700 billionths of a meter.

Sir Isaac Newton, the British scientist, discovered that sunlight could be broken down into dif-ferent colors by means of a triangular solid of glass called a *prism* (see Figure 3.1). You can remember the colors of the spectrum, from longest to shortest wavelengths, by using the mnemonic device *Roy G. Biv* (red, orange, yellow, green, blue, indigo, violet). The wavelength of visible light determines its color, or **hue**. The wavelength for red is longer than the wavelength for orange, and so on through the spectrum.

3-2b THE EYE

Consider the major parts of the eye, as shown in Figure 3.2. As with a camera, light enters through a narrow opening and is projected onto a sensitive surface. Light first passes through the transparent **cornea**, which covers the front of the eye's surface. (The "white" of the eye, or *sclera*, is composed of hard protective

hue the color of light, as determined by its wavelength

cornea transparent tissue forming the outer surface of the eyeball

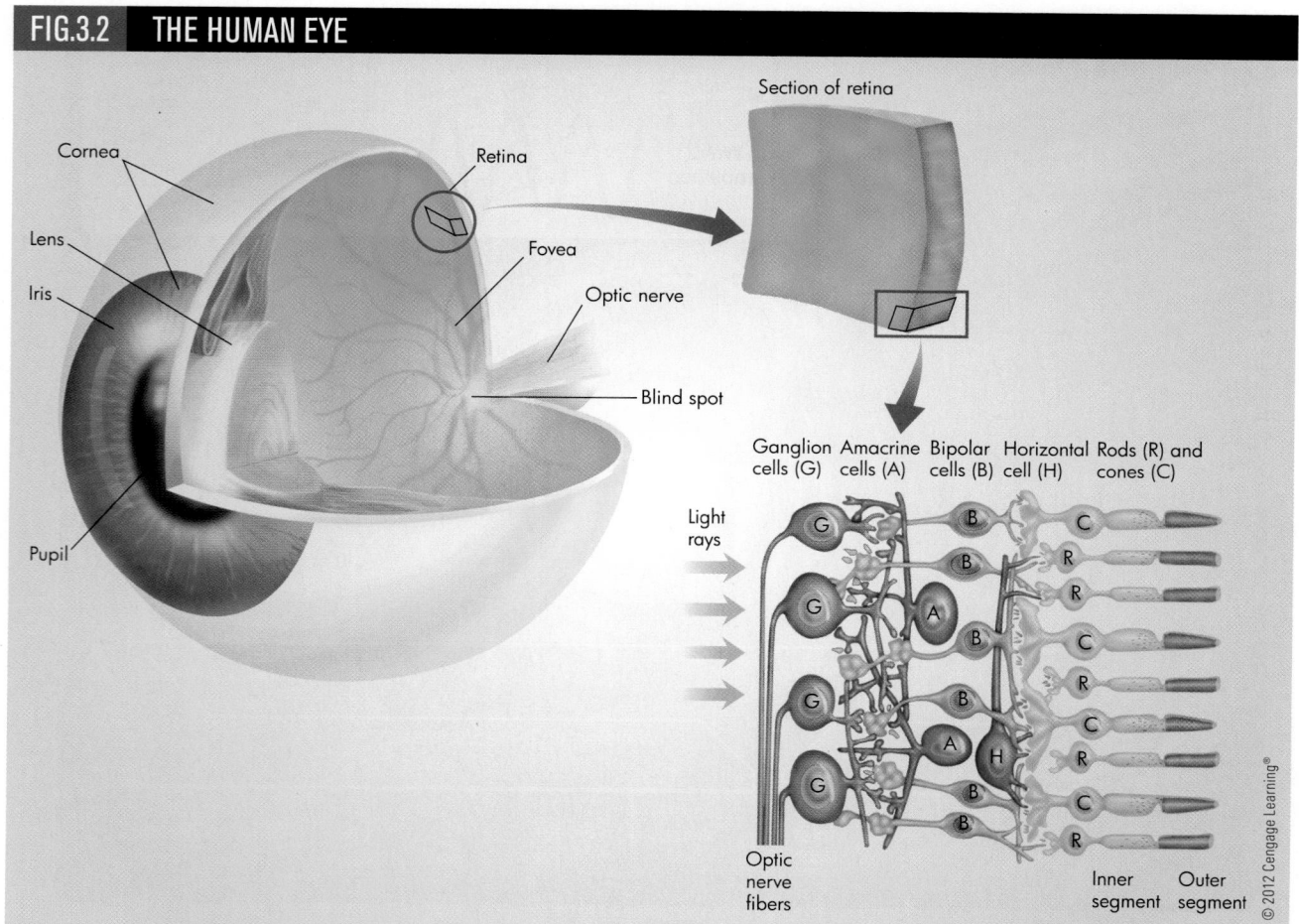

FIG.3.2   THE HUMAN EYE

Section of retina

Cornea
Retina
Lens
Fovea
Iris
Optic nerve
Blind spot
Pupil

Ganglion Amacrine Bipolar Horizontal Rods (R) and
cells (G) cells (A) cells (B) cell (H)   cones (C)

Light rays

Optic nerve fibers

Inner segment   Outer segment

© 2012 Cengage Learning®

Our eyes are our cameras on the world. In both the eye and a camera, light enters through a narrow opening and is projected onto a sensitive surface. In the eye, the photosensitive surface is called the retina, and information concerning the changing images on the retina is transmitted to the brain. The retina contains photoreceptors called rods and cones. Rods and cones transmit sensory input back through the bipolar neurons to the ganglion neurons. The axons of the ganglion neurons form the optic nerve, which transmits sensory stimulation through the brain to the visual cortex of the occipital lobe.

tissue.) The amount of light that passes through the cornea is determined by the size of the opening of the muscle called the **iris**, which is the colored part of the eye. The opening in the iris is the **pupil**. The size of the pupil adjusts automatically to the amount of light present. Therefore, you do not have to purposely open your eyes wider to see better in low lighting—the more intense the light, the smaller the opening. Pupil size is also sensitive to your emotions: Fear is associated with sympathetic nervous system arousal. Sympathetic arousal dilates the pupils. Therefore, we can be truly "wide-eyed with fear."

Once light passes through the iris, it encounters the **lens**. The lens adjusts or accommodates to the image by changing its thickness. Changes in thickness permit a clear image of the object to be projected onto the retina. These changes focus the light according to the distance of the object from the viewer. If you hold a finger at arm's length and slowly bring it toward your nose, you will feel tension in the eye as the thickness of the lens accommodates to keep the retinal image in focus. When people squint to bring an object into focus, they are adjusting the thickness of the lens.

The **retina** consists of cells called **photoreceptors** that are sensitive to light (photosensitive). There are two

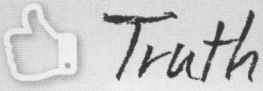

👍 Truth

| T | F | People can be "wide-eyed with fear." |

It is true that people can be "wide-eyed with fear." Fear is connected with arousal of the sympathetic nervous system, and sympathetic arousal dilates the pupils of the eyes.

types of photoreceptors: *rods* and *cones*. The retina (see Figure 3.2) contains several layers of cells: the rods and cones, **bipolar cells**, and **ganglion cells**. All of these cells are neurons. The rods and cones respond to light with chemical changes that create neural impulses that are picked up by the bipolar cells. These then activate the ganglion cells. The axons of the million or so ganglion cells in our retina converge to form the **optic nerve**. The optic nerve conducts sensory input to the brain, where it is relayed to the visual area of the occipital lobe.

As if this were not enough, the eye has additional neurons to enhance this process. Amacrine cells and horizontal cells make sideways connections at a level near the rods and cones and at another level near the ganglion cells. As a result, single bipolar cells can pick up signals from many rods and cones, and, in turn, a single ganglion cell is able to funnel information from multiple bipolar cells. In fact, rods and cones outnumber ganglion cells by more than 100 to one.

RODS AND CONES

Rods and **cones** are the photoreceptors in the retina (see Figure 3.2). About 125 million rods and 6.4 million cones are distributed across the retina. The cones are most densely packed in a small spot at the center of the retina called the **fovea**. Visual acuity (sharpness and detail) is greatest at this spot. The fovea is composed almost exclusively of cones. Rods are most dense just outside the fovea and thin out toward the periphery of the retina.

Rods allow us to see in black and white. Cones provide color vision. Rods are more sensitive to dim light than cones are. Therefore, as light grows dim during the evening hours, objects appear to lose their color before their outlines fade from view.

iris a muscular membrane whose dilation regulates the amount of light that enters the eye

pupil the black-looking opening in the center of the iris, through which light enters the eye

lens a transparent body behind the iris that focuses an image on the retina

retina the area of the inner surface of the eye that contains rods and cones

photoreceptors cells that respond to light

bipolar cells neurons that conduct neural impulses from rods and cones to ganglion cells

ganglion cells neurons whose axons form the optic nerve

optic nerve the nerve that transmits sensory information from the eye to the brain

rods rod-shaped photoreceptors that are sensitive only to the intensity of light

cones cone-shaped photo-receptors that transmit sensations of color

fovea an area near the center of the retina that is dense with cones and where vision is consequently most acute

In contrast to the visual acuity of the fovea is the **blind spot**, which is insensitive to visual stimulation. It is the part of the retina where the axons of the ganglion cells converge to form the optic nerve (see Figure 3.2). Figure 3.3 will help you find your blind spot.

Visual acuity (sharpness of vision) is connected with the shape of the eye. People who have to be unusually close to an object to discriminate its details are *nearsighted*. People who see distant objects unusually clearly but have difficulty focusing on nearby objects are *farsighted*. Nearsightedness can result when the eyeball is elongated such that the images of distant objects are focused in front of the retina. When the eyeball is too short, the images of nearby objects are focused behind the retina, causing farsightedness. Eyeglasses or contact lenses help nearsighted people focus distant objects on their retinas. Laser surgery can correct vision by changing the shape of the cornea. Farsighted people usually see well enough without eyeglasses until they reach their middle years, when they may need glasses for reading.

Beginning in their late 30s to the mid-40s, people's lenses start to grow brittle, making it more difficult to accommodate to, or focus on, objects. This condition is called **presbyopia**, from the Greek words for "old man" and "eyes." Presbyopia makes it difficult to perceive nearby visual stimuli. People who had normal visual acuity in their youth often require corrective lenses to read in middle adulthood.

LIGHT ADAPTATION When we walk out onto a dark street, we may at first not be able to see people, trees, and cars clearly. But as time goes on, we are better able to discriminate the features of people and objects. The process of adjusting to lower lighting is called **dark adaptation**.

The amount of light needed for detection is a function of the amount of time spent in the dark. The cones and rods adapt at different rates. The cones, which permit perception of color, reach their maximum adaptation to darkness in about 10 minutes. The rods, which allow perception of light and dark only, are more sensitive to dim light and continue to adapt for 45 minutes or so.

Adaptation to brighter lighting conditions takes place more rapidly. For instance, when you emerge from the theater into the brilliance of the afternoon, you may at first be painfully surprised by the featureless blaze around you. But within a minute or so of entering the street, the brightness of the scene dims and objects regain their edges.

blind spot the area of the retina where axons from ganglion cells meet to form the optic nerve

visual acuity sharpness of vision

presbyopia a condition characterized by brittleness of the lens

dark adaptation the process of adjusting to conditions of lower lighting by increasing the sensitivity of rods and cones

FIG.3.3   THE BLIND SPOT

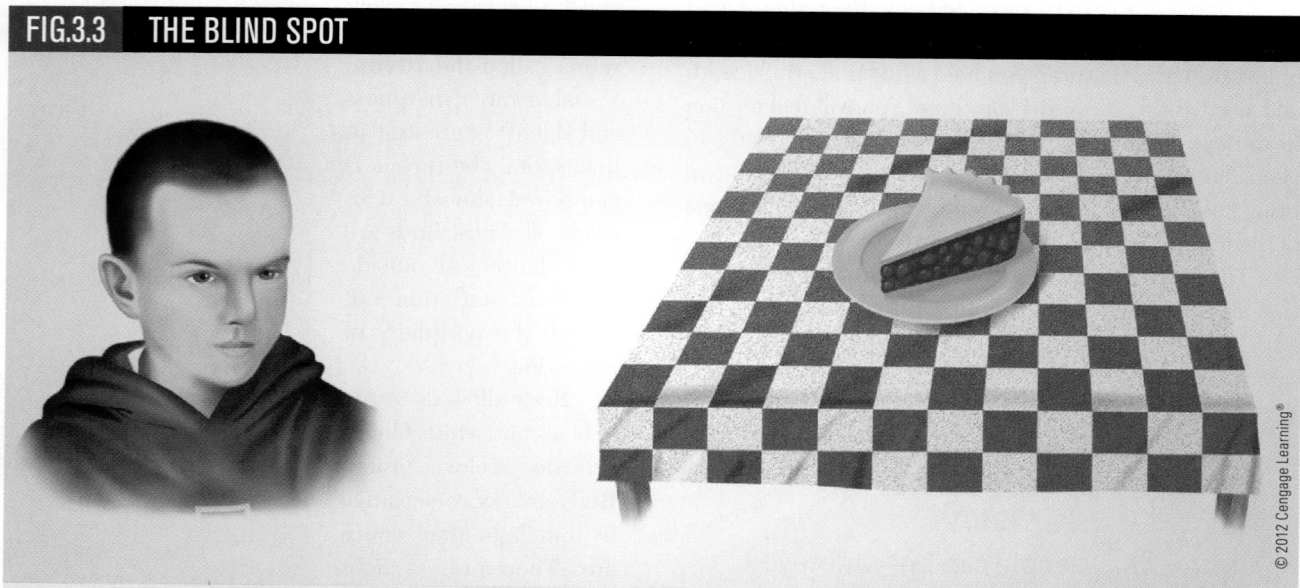

© 2012 Cengage Learning®

Try a "disappearing act." No, don't go away! Instead, close your left eye, hold the book close to your face, and look at the boy with your right eye. Slowly move the book away until the pie disappears. The pie disappears because it is being projected onto the blind spot of your retina, the point at which the axons of ganglion neurons collect to form the optic nerve. Note that when the pie disappears, your brain "fills in" the missing checkerboard pattern, which is one reason that you're not usually aware that you have blind spots.

3-2c COLOR VISION

For most of us, the world is a place of brilliant colors. Color is an emotional and aesthetic part of our everyday lives. In this section, we explore some of the dimensions of color and then examine theories about how we manage to convert different wavelengths of light into perceptions of color. The perceptual dimensions of color include hue, *value*, and *saturation*.

The wavelength of light determines its color, or hue. The *value* of a color is its degree of brightness or darkness. The *saturation* refers to how intense a color appears to us. A fire-engine red is more saturated than a pale pinkish-red.

Colors also have psychological associations within various cultural settings. For example, in the United States a bride may be dressed in white as a sign of purity. In traditional India, the guests would be shocked, because white is the color for funerals. Here we mourn in black.

WARM AND COOL COLORS If we bend the colors of the spectrum into a circle, we create a color wheel, as shown in Figure 3.4. Psychologically, the colors on the green–blue part of the color wheel are considered to be cool in temperature. You might prefer a green or blue room on a sweltering day. Those colors in the yellow–orange–red area are considered to be warm. You might prefer a room of these colors in the depths of winter.

COMPLEMENTARY COLORS The colors across from one another on the color wheel are labeled **complementary**.

FIG.3.4 THE COLOR WHEEL

COOL COLORS

Red
Orange
Orange yellow
Reddish purple
Yellow
Bluish purple
Gray
Yellow green
Violet blue
Green
Blue
Green blue
Blue green
WARM COLORS

© 2012 Cengage Learning®

The color wheel bends the colors of the visible spectrum into a circle. Colors across from one another on the wheel are called complementary. When we mix them, as in mixing blue and orange–yellow, they dissolve into gray. (Remember that we are mixing lights, not crayon colors or paints.)

Red–green and blue–yellow are the major complementary pairs. If we mix complementary colors together, they dissolve into gray.

"But wait!" you say. "Blue and yellow cannot be complementary because by mixing pigments of blue and yellow we create green, not gray." True enough, but we have been talking about mixing *lights*, not *pigments*. Light is the source of all color. Pigments reflect and absorb different wavelengths of light selectively. The mixture of lights is an *additive* process. The mixture of pigments is *subtractive*. Figure 3.5 shows mixtures of lights and pigments of various colors.

Pigments gain their colors by absorbing light from certain segments of the spectrum and reflecting the rest. For example, we see most plant life as green because the pigment in chlorophyll absorbs most of the red, blue, and violet wavelengths of light. The remaining green is reflected. A red pigment absorbs most of the spectrum but reflects red. White pigments reflect all colors equally. Black pigments reflect very little light.

AFTERIMAGES Try this experiment: Look at the strangely colored American flag on the next page for at least half a minute. Try not to blink as you are doing so. Then look at a sheet of white or light-gray paper. What has happened to the flag? If your color vision is working properly, and if you looked at the flag long enough, you should see a flag composed of the familiar red, white, and blue. The flag you perceive on the white sheet of paper is an **afterimage** of the first. (If you didn't look at the green, black, and

"IT IS A TERRIBLE THING TO SEE AND HAVE NO VISION."

HELEN KELLER, 1880–1968, AMERICAN AUTHOR, POLITICAL ACTIVIST, AND LECTURER

"Art Archive, The/SuperStock"

complementary descriptive of colors of the spectrum that when combined produce white or nearly white light

afterimage the lingering visual impression made by a stimulus that has been removed

FIG.3.5 **THE DIFFERENCE BETWEEN MIXING LIGHTS AND MIXING PIGMENTS**

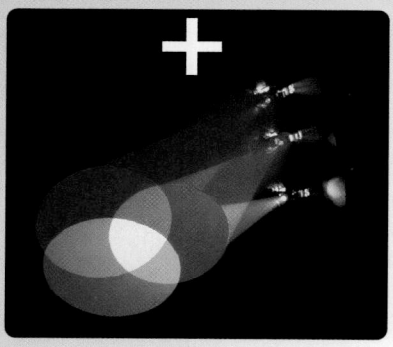

Mixing Lights—An Additive Process. When you mix lights of different colors, you obtain lighter colors. When you mix red and blue, you get magenta, an "off-red." When you mix blue and green, you get cyan, a lighter blue. When you mix green and red, you get yellow. When you mix red, green, and blue lights, you get white light. This may sound strange, but remember that when you add more light, things become brighter, not darker.

Source: Fritz Goro/Time & Life Pictures/Getty Images

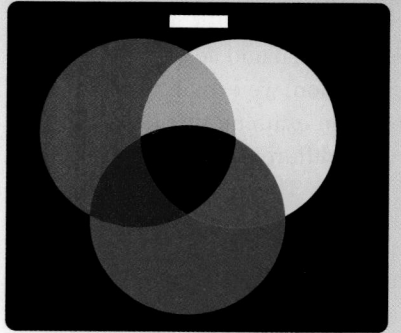

Mixing Pigments—A Subtractive Process. Here we obtain the results familiar to every child with a box of crayons. Mixing red and blue yields purple; blue and yellow yields green; and red and yellow gets orange. Mixing all colors yields black—the absence of color. Why? Because in mixing pigments, you are subtracting light, and when you subtract all light, things get black—as in a shuttered room without a source of light.

yellow flag long enough the first time, try it again.) In afterimages, persistent sensations of color are followed by perception of the complementary color when the first color is removed. The same holds true for black and white. Staring at one will create an afterimage of the other. The phenomenon of afterimages has contributed to one of the theories of color vision, as we will see.

3-2d **THEORIES OF COLOR VISION**

Adults with normal color vision can discriminate many thousands of colors—perhaps millions of colors—across the visible spectrum. Different colors have different wavelengths. Although we can vary the physical wavelengths of light in a continuous manner from shorter to longer, many changes in color are discontinuous. Our perception of a color shifts suddenly from blue to green, even though the change in wavelength may be smaller than that between two blues.

Our perception of color depends on the physical properties of an object and on the eye's transmission of different

trichromatic theory the theory that color vision is made possible by three types of cones, some of which respond to red light, some to green, and some to blue

opponent–process theory the theory that color vision is made possible by three types of cones, some of which respond to red or green light, some to blue or yellow, and some to the intensity of light

messages to the brain when lights with different wavelengths stimulate the cones in the retina. There are two main theories of color vision: the *trichromatic theory* and the *opponent–process theory* (Goldstein, 2013).

Trichromatic theory is based on an experiment conducted by the British scientist Thomas Young in the early 1800s. As in Figure 3.5, Young projected red, green, and blue–violet lights onto a screen so that they partly overlapped. He found that he could create any color in the visible spectrum by varying the intensities of the three lights. When all three lights fell on the same spot, they created white light, or the appearance of no color at all.

The German physiologist Hermann von Helmholtz saw in Young's discovery an explanation of color vision. Helmholtz suggested that the retina in the eye must have three different types of color photoreceptors or cones. Some cones must be sensitive to red light, some to green, and some to blue. We see other colors when various color receptors are stimulated simultaneously. For example, we perceive yellow when the receptors for red and green are firing.

In 1870, another German physiologist, Ewald Hering, proposed the **opponent–process theory** of color vision: There are three types of color receptors, but they are not sensitive only to red, green, and blue, as Helmholtz had claimed. Hering suggested instead that afterimages (such as that of the American flag shown in Figure 3.6) are made possible by three types of color receptors: red–green, blue–yellow, and a type that perceives differences in brightness. According to Hering, a red–green cone cannot transmit messages for red and green at the same time. Therefore, staring at the green, black, and yellow flag for 30 seconds will disturb the balance of neural activity. The afterimage of red, white, and blue would represent the eye's attempt to reestablish a balance.

Research suggests that each theory of color vision is partially correct. For example, research shows that some cones are sensitive to blue, some to green, and some to red (Horiguchi et al., 2013). However, cones appear to be connected by bipolar and ganglion neurons such that the messages produced by the cones are transmitted to the brain in an opponent–process fashion (Reichenbach & Bringmann, 2013).

A neural rebound effect apparently helps explain the occurrence of afterimages. That is, a green-sensitive ganglion that had been excited by green light for half a minute or so might switch briefly to inhibitory activity when the light is shut off. The effect is to perceive red even though no red light is present (Hornstein et al., 2004).

3-2e COLOR BLINDNESS

If you can discriminate among the colors of the visible spectrum, you have normal color vision and are labeled a **trichromat**. This means that you are sensitive to red–green, blue–yellow, and light–dark. People who are totally color–blind, called **monochromats**, are sensitive only to lightness and darkness. Total color blindness is rare. Fully color–blind individuals see the world as trichromats would in a black-and-white movie.

Partial color blindness is a sex-linked trait that affects mostly males. Partially colorblind people are called **dichromats**. They can discriminate only between two colors—red and green or blue and yellow—and the colors that are derived from mixing these colors (Baraas et al., 2010). Figure 3.7 shows the types of tests that are used to diagnose color blindness.

A dichromat might put on one red sock and one green sock, but would not mix red and blue socks. Monochromats might put on socks

> **trichromat** a person with normal color vision
>
> **monochromat** a person who is sensitive to black and white only and hence color–blind
>
> **dichromat** a person who is sensitive to black–white and either red–green or blue–yellow and hence is partially color–blind

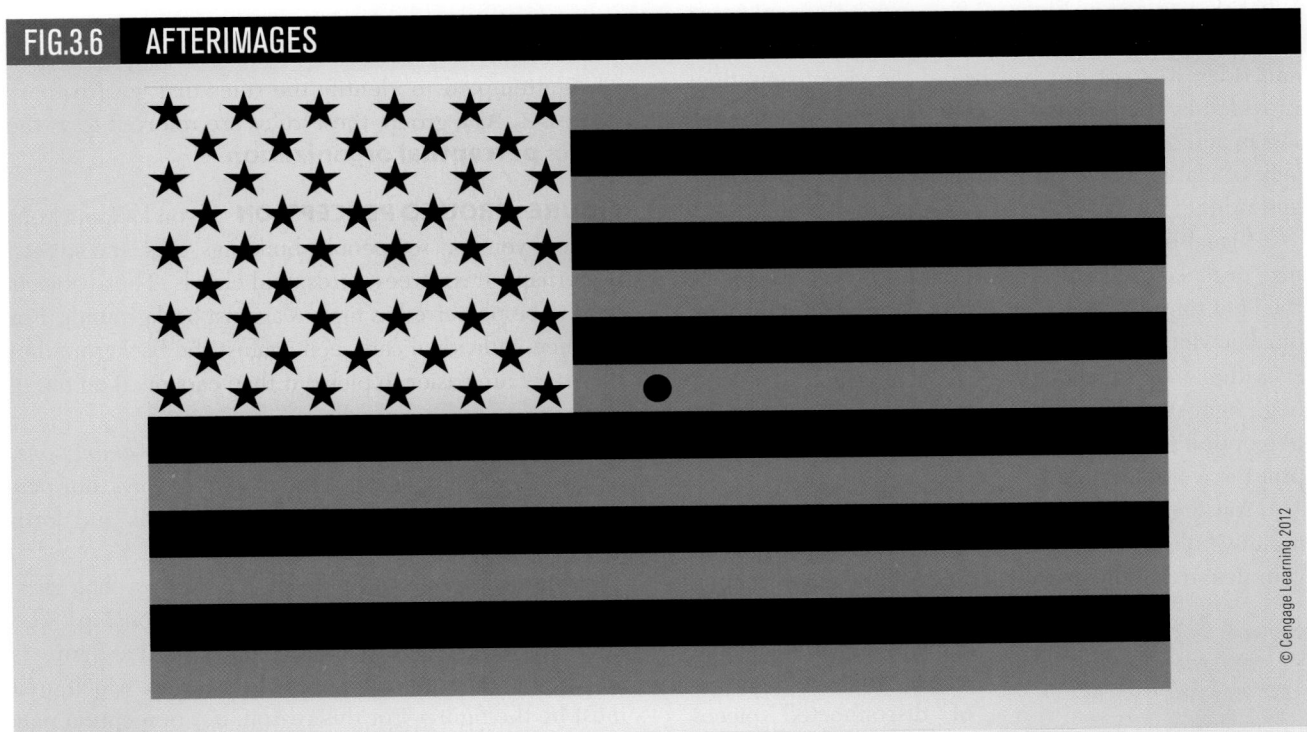

FIG.3.6 AFTERIMAGES

© Cengage Learning 2012

What is wrong with this flag and how can you fix it? Hold a sheet of white paper close to the the image. Focus on the black dot in the center of the flag for at least 30 seconds. Now move your focus to the sheet of paper. The afterimage on the paper beneath will look familiar.

FIG.3.7   TESTING FOR COLOR BLINDNESS

Can you see the numbers in these plates from a test for color blindness? A person with red–green color blindness would not be able to see the 6, and a person with blue–yellow color blindness would probably not discern the 12. (Caution: These reproductions cannot be used for actual testing of color blindness.)

of any color. They would not notice a difference as long as the socks' colors did not differ in intensity—that is, brightness.

3-3   VISUAL PERCEPTION

What do you see in Figure 3.8—meaningless splotches of ink or a rider on horseback? If you perceive a horse and rider, it is not just because of the visual sensations provided by the drawing. Each of the blobs is meaningless in and of itself, and the pattern is vague. Despite the lack of clarity, however, you may still perceive a horse and rider.

Visual perception is the process by which we organize or make sense of the sensory impressions caused by the light that strikes our eyes. Visual perception involves our knowledge, expectations, and motivations. Whereas sensation may be thought of as a mechanical process (e.g., light stimulating the rods and cones of our retina), perception is an active process through which we interpret the world around us.

You organize bits of visual information into meaningful wholes by means of your general knowledge and your desire to fit incoming bits and pieces of information into familiar patterns. In the case of the horse and rider, your integration of disconnected pieces of information into a meaningful whole also reflects the principle of **closure**—that is, the

closure the tendency to perceive a broken figure as being complete or whole

perceptual organization the tendency to integrate perceptual elements into meaningful patterns

FIG.3.8   THE PRINCIPLE OF CLOSURE

Do you see meaningless splotches of ink, or do you see a horse and rider? This figure illustrates the Gestalt principle of closure.

tendency to perceive a complete or whole figure even when there are gaps in the sensory input.

3-3a   PERCEPTUAL ORGANIZATION

Early in the 20th century, Gestalt psychologists noted certain consistencies in the way we integrate bits and pieces of sensory stimulation into meaningful wholes. They attempted to identify the rules that govern these processes. As a group, these rules are referred to as the laws of **perceptual organization**.

FIGURE–GROUND PERCEPTION If you look out your window, you may see people, buildings, cars, and streets, or perhaps grass, trees, birds, and clouds. These objects tend to be perceived as figures against backgrounds. For instance, individual cars seen against the background of the street are easier to pick out than cars piled on top of one another in a junkyard.

When figure–ground relationships are *ambiguous*, or capable of being interpreted in various ways, our perceptions tend to be unstable and shift back and forth (Bull et al., 2003).

Figure 3.9 shows a Rubin vase, one of psychologists' favorite illustrations of figure–ground relationships. The figure–ground relationship in part A of the figure is ambiguous. There are no cues that suggest which area must be the figure. For this reason, our perception may shift from seeing the vase to seeing two profiles. There is no such problem in part B. Because it seems that a blue vase has been brought forward against a colored ground, we are more likely to perceive the vase than the profiles.

FIG.3.9 **THE RUBIN VASE**

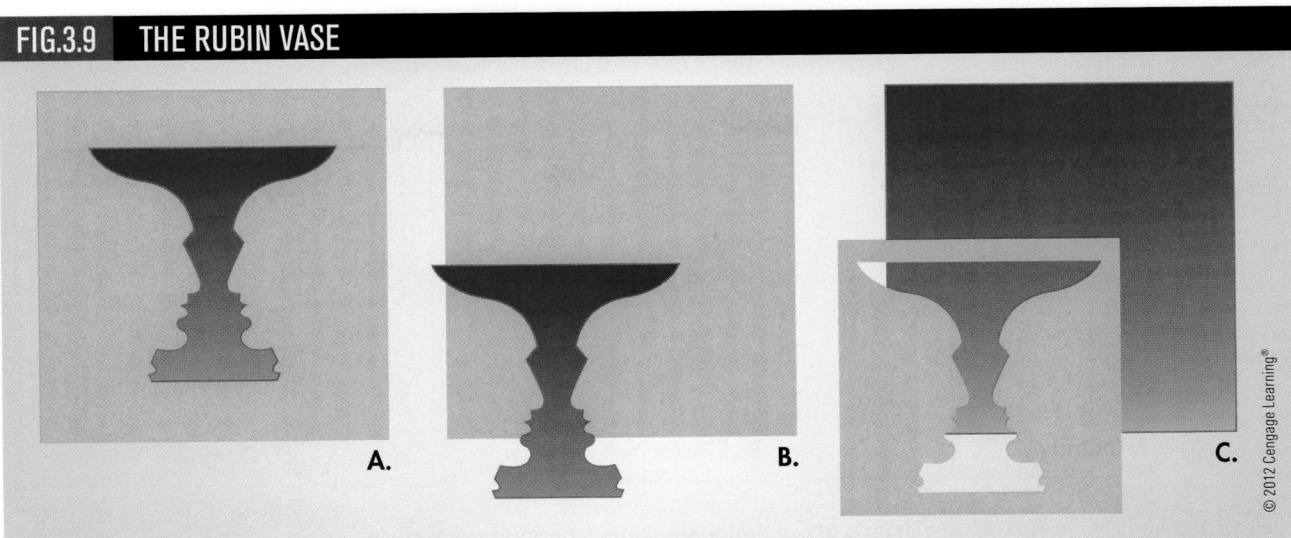

A.　　B.　　C.

© 2012 Cengage Learning®

When looking at part A, your perception is likely to switch back and forth between profiles and a vase. When looking at part B, you are more likely to perceive the vase. Why? Which are you more likely to perceive in part C—the vase or the profiles? Why?

In part C, we are more likely to perceive the profiles than the vase, because the profiles are complete and the vase is broken against the background. Of course, if we wish to, we can still perceive the vase in part C, because experience has shown us where it is.

OTHER GESTALT RULES FOR ORGANIZATION

Gestalt psychologists have noted that our perceptions are also guided by rules or laws of *proximity, similarity, continuity,* and *common fate.*

Let's try a mini-experiment. Without reading further, describe part A of Figure 3.10. Did you say it consists of six lines or of three groups of two parallel lines? If you said three sets of lines, you were influenced by the **proximity**, or nearness, of some of the lines. There is no other reason for perceiving them in pairs or subgroups: All lines are parallel and equal in length.

Now describe part B of Figure 3.10. Did you perceive the figure as a six-by-six grid, or as three columns of **X**'s and three columns of **O**'s? According to the law of **similarity**, we perceive similar objects as belonging together. For this reason, you may have been more likely to describe part B in terms of columns than in terms of rows or a grid.

What of part C? Is it a circle with two lines stemming from it, or is it a (broken) line that goes through a circle? If you saw it as a single (broken) line, you were probably organizing your perceptions according to the rule of **continuity**. That is, we perceive a series of points or a broken line as having unity.

According to the law of **common fate**, elements seen moving together are perceived as belonging together.

A group of people running in the same direction appears unified in purpose. Part D of Figure 3.10 provides another example of the law of closure. The arcs tend to be perceived as a circle (or a circle with gaps) rather than as just a series of arcs.

TOP-DOWN VERSUS BOTTOM-UP PROCESSING

Imagine that you are trying to put together a thousand-piece jigsaw puzzle. Now imagine that you are trying to accomplish it after someone has walked off with the box showing the picture formed by the completed puzzle.

If you use the picture on the box, you're engaging in **top-down processing**—that is, you are using the completed image to search for the proper pieces. Similarly, we may form more lasting relationships when we search with an idea of the qualities we will find compatible in another person. Or we may make better investments when we have a retirement financial goal and date in mind. With **bottom-up processing**, we begin with bits and pieces of

proximity nearness; the perceptual tendency to group together objects that are near one another

similarity the perceptual tendency to group together objects that are similar in appearance

continuity the tendency to perceive a series of points or lines as having unity

common fate the tendency to perceive elements that move together as belonging together

top-down processing the use of contextual information or knowledge of a pattern in order to organize parts of the pattern

bottom-up processing the organization of the parts of a pattern to recognize, or form an image of, the pattern they compose

FIG.3.10 SOME GESTALT LAWS OF PERCEPTUAL ORGANIZATION

A. Proximity

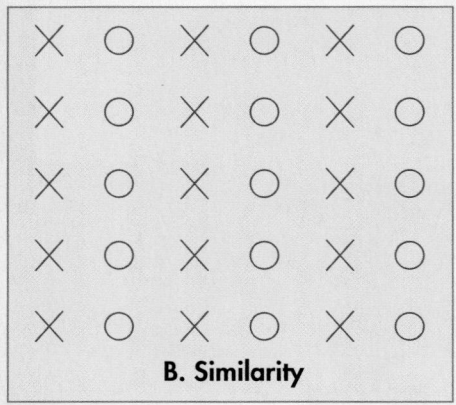

B. Similarity

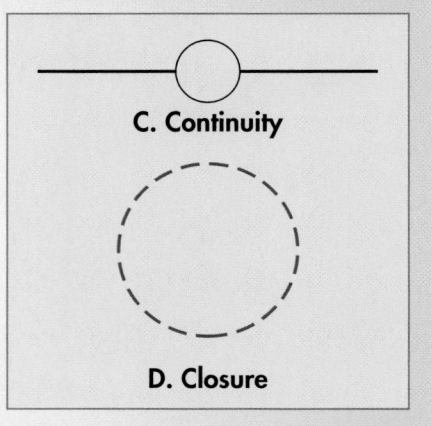

C. Continuity

D. Closure

© 2012 Cengage Learning®

These drawings illustrate the Gestalt laws of proximity, similarity, continuity, and closure

information and try to assemble them in a pattern—in jigsaw puzzles and, perhaps, by being thrown into a social or vocational situation. In bottom-up processing, we do not have a clear idea of where we are going, and perhaps we try to make the best of things.

3-3b PERCEPTION OF MOTION

Imagine yourself on a train that has begun to pull out of the station while the train on the next track stays still. If your own train does not lurch as it accelerates, it might seem that the other train is moving. Or you might not be sure whether your train is moving forward or the other train is moving back.

The visual perception of movement is based on change of position relative to other objects. To early scientists, whose only tool for visual observation was the naked eye, it seemed logical that the sun circled the earth. You have to be able to imagine the movement of the earth around the sun as seen from a theoretical point in outer space; you cannot observe it directly.

How, then, can you be certain which train is moving? One way is to look for objects that you know are still, such as platform columns, houses, signs, or trees. If your position does not change in relation to them, your train is not moving. You might also try to sense the motion of the train in your body. You probably know from experience how to do these things quite well.

illusions sensations that give rise to misperceptions

stroboscopic motion a visual illusion in which the perception of motion is generated by a series of stationary images that are presented in rapid succession

monocular cues stimuli suggestive of depth that can be perceived with only one eye

We have been considering the perception of real movement. Psychologists have also studied several types of apparent movement, or **illusions** of movement. One of these illusions is stroboscopic motion.

STROBOSCOPIC MOTION So-called motion pictures do not really consist of images that move. Rather, the audience is shown 16 to 22 pictures, or *frames,* per second. Each frame differs slightly from the preceding one. Showing the frames in rapid succession provides the illusion of movement. This illusion of motion is termed **stroboscopic motion** (Figure 3.11).

At the rate of at least 16 frames per second, the "motion" in a film seems smooth and natural. With fewer than 16 or so frames per second, the movement looks jumpy and unnatural. That is why slow motion is usually achieved by filming 100 or more frames per second. When they are played back at about 22 frames per second, the movement seems slowed down, but still smooth and natural.

3-3c DEPTH PERCEPTION

Monocular and *binocular cues* help us perceive the depth of objects—that is, their distance from us.

MONOCULAR CUES Artists use **monocular cues** called pictorial cues to create an illusion of depth. These cues can be perceived by one eye (*mono* means "one"). They include perspective, relative size, clearness, overlapping, shadows, and texture gradient, and they cause some objects to seem more distant than others even though they are all drawn or painted on a flat surface.

Distant objects stimulate smaller areas on the retina than nearby ones, even though they may be the same

FIG.3.11 STROBOSCOPIC MOTION

Abe Rezny/The Image Works

In a motion picture, viewing a series of stationary images at the rate of about 22 frames per second provides an illusion of movement termed stroboscopic motion. The actual movement that is occurring is the rapid switching of stationary images.

size. The distances between far-off objects also appear to be smaller than equivalent distances between nearby objects. For this reason, the phenomenon known as **perspective** occurs. That is, we tend to perceive parallel lines as coming closer together, or converging, as they recede from us. As we will see when we discuss *size constancy,* however, experience teaches us that distant objects that look small are larger when they are close. In this way, their relative size also becomes a cue to their distance.

Artists normally use *relative size*—the fact that distant objects look smaller than nearby objects of the same size—to suggest depth in their works.

The *clearness* of an object suggests its distance. Experience teaches us that we sense more details of nearby objects. For this reason, artists can suggest that objects are closer to the viewer by depicting them in greater detail.

We also learn that nearby objects can block our view of more distant objects. *Overlapping* is the placing of one object in front of another. Experience teaches us that partly covered objects are farther away than the objects that obscure them (see Figure 3.12).

Additional information about depth is provided by *shadowing* and is based on the fact that opaque objects block light and produce shadows. Shadows and highlights give us information about an object's three-dimensional shape and its relationship to the source of light. For example, in the right part of Figure 3.12, the left circle is perceived as a two-dimensional circle, but the right circle tends to be perceived as a three-dimensional sphere because of the highlight on its surface and the shadow underneath. In the "sphere," the highlighted central area is perceived as closest to us, with the surface receding to the edges.

Another monocular cue is **texture gradient**. (A gradient is a progressive change.) Closer objects are perceived as having rougher textures.

Motion cues are another kind of monocular cue. If you have ever driven in the country, you have probably noticed that distant objects such as mountains and stars appear to move along with you. Objects at an intermediate distance seem to be stationary, but nearby objects such as roadside markers, rocks, and trees seem to go by quite rapidly. The tendency of objects to seem to move backward or forward as a function of their distance is known as **motion parallax**. We learn to perceive objects that appear to move with us as being at greater distances.

We noted that nearby objects cause the lens of the eye to accommodate or bend more in order to bring them into focus. The sensations of tension in the eye muscles also provide a monocular cue to depth, especially when we are within about four feet of the objects.

BINOCULAR CUES

Binocular cues, or cues that involve both eyes, also help us perceive depth. Two binocular cues are *retinal disparity* and *convergence.*

Try an experiment. Hold your right index finger at arm's length.

perspective a monocular cue for depth based on the convergence (coming together) of parallel lines as they recede into the distance

texture gradient a monocular cue for depth based on the perception that closer objects appear to have rougher (more detailed) surfaces

motion parallax a monocular cue for depth based on the perception that nearby objects appear to move more rapidly in relation to our own motion

binocular cues stimuli suggestive of depth that involve simultaneous perception by both eyes

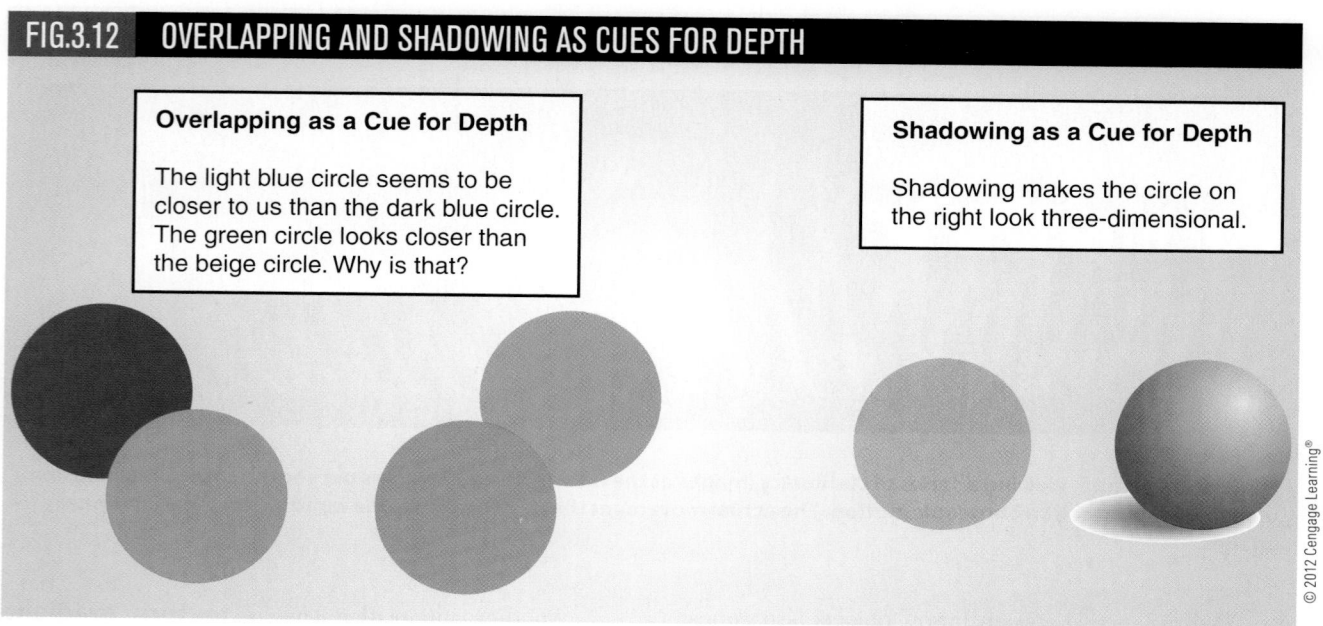

FIG.3.12   OVERLAPPING AND SHADOWING AS CUES FOR DEPTH

Overlapping as a Cue for Depth

The light blue circle seems to be closer to us than the dark blue circle. The green circle looks closer than the beige circle. Why is that?

Shadowing as a Cue for Depth

Shadowing makes the circle on the right look three-dimensional.

Now hold your left index finger about a foot closer, but in a direct line. If you keep your eyes relaxed as you do so, you will see first one finger and then the other. An image of each finger will be projected onto the retina of each eye, and each image will be slightly different because the finger will be seen from different angles. The difference between the projected images is referred to as **retinal disparity** and serves as a binocular cue for depth perception. Note that in the case of the closer finger, the "two fingers" appear to be farther apart. Closer objects have greater retinal disparity.

If we try to maintain a single image of the closer finger, our eyes must turn inward, or converge on it, making us cross-eyed. **Convergence** causes feelings of tension in the eye muscles and provides another binocular cue for depth. (After convergence occurs, try looking at the finger first with one eye closed, then the other. You will readily see how different the images are in each eye.) The binocular cues of retinal disparity and convergence are strongest when objects are close.

retinal disparity a binocular cue for depth based on the difference in the image cast by an object on the retinas of the eyes as the object moves closer or farther away

convergence a binocular cue for depth based on the inward movement of the eyes as they attempt to focus on an object that is drawing nearer

size constancy the tendency to perceive an object as being the same size even as the size of its retinal image changes according to the object's distance

color constancy the tendency to perceive an object as being the same color even though lighting conditions change its appearance

3-3d PERCEPTUAL CONSTANCIES

Have a look at the woman in Figure 3.13. Is her thumb really as long as her head? Is her hand really as large as her upper body? If you answered these questions "No," it is because of your knowledge of *size constancy*—even if you haven't heard the term before. Perceptual constancies enable us to recognize the characteristics of objects even when their apparent size, color, brightness, and shape differ from the norm.

SIZE CONSTANCY There are a number of perceptual constancies, including that of **size constancy**. The image of a dog seen from 20 feet away occupies about the same amount of space on your retina as an inch-long insect crawling on your hand. Yet you do not perceive the dog to be as small as the insect. Through your visual experiences you have acquired size constancy—that is, the tendency to *perceive* an object as the same size even though the size of its image on your retina varies as a function of its distance. Experience teaches us about perspective—that the same object seen at a distance appears to be smaller than when it is nearby.

COLOR CONSTANCY Color constancy is the tendency to perceive objects as retaining their color even though lighting conditions may alter their appearance. Your bright yellow car may edge toward gray as the hours wend their way through twilight. But when you finally locate the car in the parking lot, you may still think of it as yellow. You expect to find a yellow car and still judge it to be "more yellow" than the (twilight-faded) red and green cars on either side of it.

FIG.3.13 SIZE CONSTANCY

Enamul Hoque/Getty Images

Is this woman's hand really twice the size of her head? Due to our awareness of size constancy—whether or not we would use that term in everyday speech—we recognize that the apparent size of her hand is an illusion created by the fact that it is closer to us than her head.

BRIGHTNESS CONSTANCY

Brightness constancy is similar to color constancy. Consider Figure 3.14. The yellow–orange squares within the blue squares are equally bright, yet the one within the dark blue square is perceived as brighter. Why? Again, consider the role of experience. If it were nighttime, we would expect yellows and oranges to fade to gray. The fact that the yellow–orange within the dark square stimulates the eye

FIG.3.14 BRIGHTNESS CONSTANCY

© 2012 Cengage Learning®

The orange squares within the blue squares are the same hue, yet the orange within the dark blue square is perceived as brighter. Why?

with equal intensity suggests that it must be much brighter than the orange within the lighter square.

SHAPE CONSTANCY

Shape constancy is the tendency to perceive objects as maintaining their shape, even if we look at them from different angles so that the shape of their image on the retina changes dramatically. You perceive the top of a coffee cup or a glass to be a circle even though it is a circle only when seen from above. When seen from an angle, it is an ellipse (see Figure 3.15). When the cup or glass is seen on edge, its retinal image is the same as that of a straight line. So why do you still describe the rim of the cup or glass as a circle? Perhaps for two reasons: First, experience has taught you that the cup will look circular when seen from above. Second, you may have labeled the cup as circular or round.

Think of a door to a room. The door is a rectangle only when viewed straight on. When we move to the side or we open it, the left or right edge comes closer and appears to be larger, changing the retinal image to a trapezoid. Yet we continue to think of doors as rectangles. Why is that?

3-3e VISUAL ILLUSIONS

The principles of perceptual organization make it possible for our eyes to "play tricks" on us. That is, the perceptual constancies trick the eye through *visual illusions*.

The *Hering–Helmholtz* and *Müller–Lyer illusions* (see Figure 3.16) are named after the people who devised them. In the Hering–Helmholtz illusion (part A), the horizontal lines are straight and parallel. However, the radiating lines cause them to appear to be bent outward near the center. The two lines in the Müller–Lyer illusion (part B) are the same length, but the line on the right, with its reversed arrowheads, looks longer.

Let's try to explain these illusions. Because of our experience and lifelong use of perceptual cues, we tend to perceive the Hering–Helmholtz drawing as three-dimensional. Because of our tendency

brightness constancy the tendency to perceive an object as being just as bright even though lighting conditions change its intensity

shape constancy the tendency to perceive an object as being the same shape although the retinal image varies in shape as it rotates

FIG.3.15 SHAPE CONSTANCY

What is the shape of the cover of this coffee cup? Did you think you were looking at a "circle" even though you were actually looking at an ellipse? If so, it's because of the principle of shape constancy.

to perceive bits of sensory information as figures against grounds, we perceive the blue area in the center as a circle in front of a series of radiating lines, all of which lie in front of a blue ground. Next, because of our experience with perspective, we perceive the radiating lines as parallel. We perceive the two horizontal lines as intersecting the "receding" lines, and we know that they would have to appear bent out at the center if they were to be equidistant at all points from the center of the circle.

Experience probably compels us to perceive the vertical lines in the Müller–Lyer illusion as the corners of a building (see

> **hertz (Hz)** a unit expressing the frequency of sound waves. One hertz equals one cycle per second

Figure 3.16, part B). We interpret the length of the lines based on our experience with corners of buildings.

3-4 HEARING

Consider the advertising slogan for the classic science fiction film *Alien*: "In space, no one can hear you scream." It's true. Space is an almost perfect vacuum. Hearing requires a medium through which sound can travel, such as air or water.

Sound, or *auditory stimulation,* is the vibration of molecules in a medium such as air or water. Sound travels through the medium like waves, or like ripples in a pond when you toss in a pebble. The molecules of the medium are alternately compressed and expanded like the movements of an accordion. If you were listening under water, you would also hear the splash because of changes in the pressure of the water. In either case, the changes in pressure are vibrations that approach your ears in waves. These vibrations—sound waves—can also be created by a ringing bell, your vocal cords, guitar strings, or the slam of a book thrown down on a desk. A single cycle of compression and expansion is one wave of sound. Sound waves can occur many times in one second. The human ear is sensitive to sound waves with frequencies of from 20 to 20,000 cycles per second.

3-4a PITCH AND LOUDNESS

Pitch and loudness are two psychological dimensions of sound. The pitch of a sound is determined by its frequency, or the number of cycles per second as expressed in the unit **hertz (Hz)**. One cycle per second is 1 Hz.

FIG.3.16 THE HERING–HELMHOLTZ AND MÜLLER–LYER ILLUSIONS

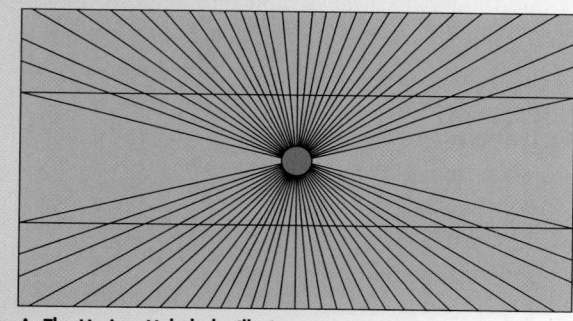

A. The Hering–Helmholtz Illusion

B. The Müller–Lyer Illusion

In the Hering–Helmholtz illusion, are the horizontal lines straight or curved? In the Müller–Lyer illusion, are the vertical lines equal in length?

The greater the number of cycles per second (Hz), the higher the pitch of the sound.

The pitch of women's voices is usually higher than that of men's voices because women's vocal cords are usually shorter and therefore vibrate at a greater frequency. Also, the strings of a violin are shorter than those of a viola or double bass. Pitch detectors in the brain allow us to tell differences in pitch.

The loudness of a sound roughly corresponds to the height, or amplitude, of sound waves. Figure 3.17 shows records of sound waves that vary in frequency and amplitude. Frequency and amplitude are independent. That is, both high- and low-pitched sounds can be either high or low in loudness. The loudness of a sound is expressed in **decibels (dB)**. Zero dB is equivalent to the threshold of hearing—the lowest sound that the typical person can hear. How loud is that? It's about as loud as the ticking of a watch 20 feet away in a very quiet room.

The decibel equivalents of familiar sounds are shown in Figure 3.18. Twenty-five dB is equivalent in loudness to a whisper at five feet. Thirty dB is roughly the limit of loudness at which your librarian would like to keep your college library. You may suffer hearing damage if you are exposed to sounds of 85 to 90 dB for long periods.

3-4b THE EAR

The ear is shaped and structured to capture sound waves, vibrate in sympathy with them, and transmit them to the brain. In this way, you not only hear

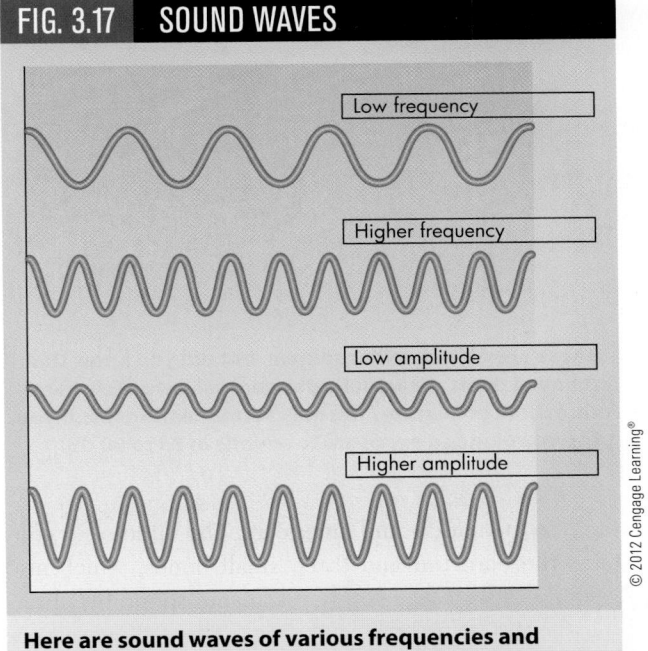

FIG. 3.17 SOUND WAVES

Low frequency

Higher frequency

Low amplitude

Higher amplitude

© 2012 Cengage Learning®

Here are sound waves of various frequencies and amplitudes. Which sounds have the highest pitch? Which are loudest?

something, you can also figure out what it is. The ear has three parts: the outer ear, the middle ear, and the inner ear (see Figure 3.19).

The outer ear is shaped to funnel sound waves to the *eardrum*, a thin membrane that vibrates in response to sound waves, and thereby transmits

decibel (dB) a unit expressing the loudness of a sound

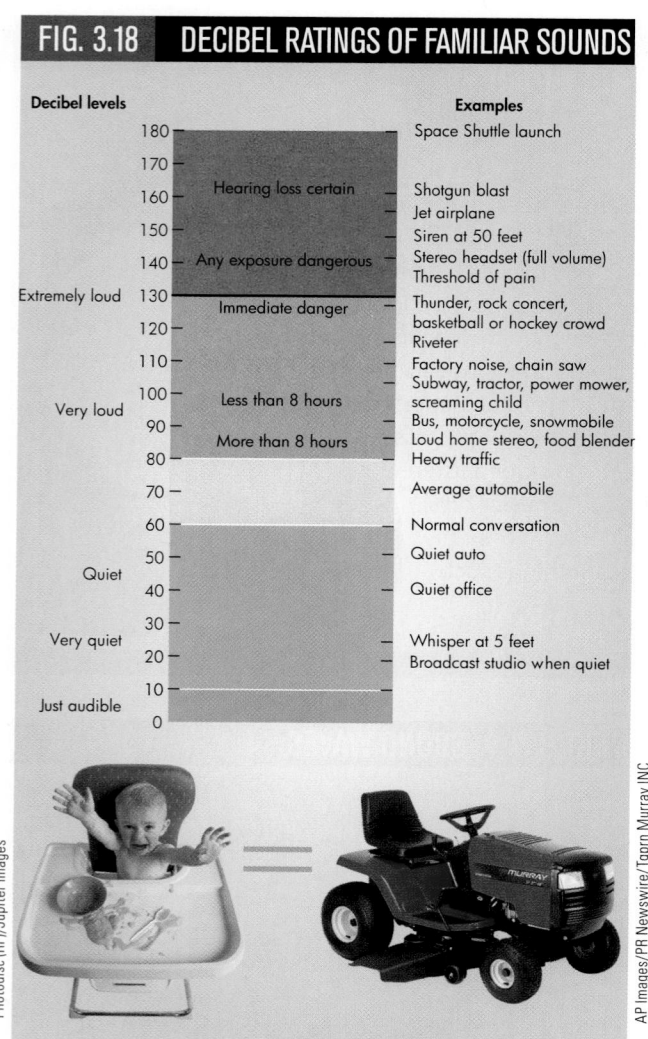

FIG. 3.18 DECIBEL RATINGS OF FAMILIAR SOUNDS

Decibel levels		Examples
	180	Space Shuttle launch
	170	
Hearing loss certain	160	Shotgun blast
	150	Jet airplane
		Siren at 50 feet
Any exposure dangerous	140	Stereo headset (full volume)
		Threshold of pain
Extremely loud	130	Thunder, rock concert,
Immediate danger	120	basketball or hockey crowd
		Riveter
	110	Factory noise, chain saw
	100	Subway, tractor, power mower,
Very loud	Less than 8 hours	screaming child
	90	Bus, motorcycle, snowmobile
More than 8 hours		Loud home stereo, food blender
	80	Heavy traffic
	70	Average automobile
	60	Normal conversation
Quiet	50	Quiet auto
	40	Quiet office
	30	
Very quiet	20	Whisper at 5 feet
	10	Broadcast studio when quiet
Just audible	0	

Photodisc (RF)/Jupiter Images

AP Images/PR Newswire/Tgprn Murray INC

These are quite familiar sounds, but did you know that many of them are actually dangerous? Zero dB is the threshold of hearing. You may suffer hearing loss if you incur prolonged exposure to sounds of 85 to 90 dB.

The stirrup is attached to another vibrating membrane, the *oval window*. The oval window works in conjunction with the round window, which balances the pressure in the inner ear (see Figure 3.19). The round window pushes outward when the oval window pushes in, and is pulled inward when the oval window vibrates outward.

The oval window transmits vibrations into the inner ear, the bony tube called the **cochlea** (from the Greek word for "snail"). The cochlea, which is shaped like a snail shell, contains two longitudinal membranes that divide it into three fluid-filled chambers. One of the membranes that lies coiled within the cochlea is called the **basilar membrane**. Vibrations in the fluids within the chambers of the inner ear press against the basilar membrane.

The **organ of Corti**, sometimes referred to as the "command post" of hearing, is attached to the basilar membrane. Some 16,000 receptor cells—called *hair cells* because they project like hair from the organ of Corti—are found in each ear. Hair cells "dance" in response to the vibrations of the basilar membrane (Hwang et al., 2010). Their movements generate neural impulses, which are transmitted to the brain via the **auditory nerve**. Auditory input is then projected onto the hearing areas of the temporal lobes of the cerebral cortex.

3-4c LOCATING SOUNDS

There is a resemblance between balancing a set of stereo speakers and locating sounds. A sound that is louder in the right ear is perceived as coming from the right. A sound coming from the right also reaches the right ear first. Both loudness and the sequence in which the sounds reach the ears provide directional cues.

But it may not be easy to locate a sound coming from in front or in back of you or above. Such sounds are equally distant from each ear and equally loud. So what do we do? Simple—we turn our head slightly to determine in which ear the sound increases. If you turn your head to the right and the loudness increases in your left ear, the sound is likely coming from in front.

3-4d PERCEPTION OF LOUDNESS AND PITCH

Sounds are heard because they cause vibration in parts of the ear and information about these vibrations is transmitted to the brain. The loudness and pitch of sounds appear to be

them to the middle and inner ears. The middle ear contains the eardrum and three small bones, which also transmit sound by vibrating. These bones were given their Latin names (*malleus, incus,* and *stapes* [pronounced *STAY-peas*], which translate as "hammer," "anvil," and "stirrup") because of their shapes. The middle ear functions as an amplifier, increasing the pressure of the air entering the ear.

cochlea the inner ear; the bony tube that contains the basilar membrane and the organ of Corti

basilar membrane a membrane that lies coiled within the cochlea

organ of Corti the receptor for hearing that lies on the basilar membrane in the cochlea

auditory nerve the axon bundle that transmits neural impulses from the organ of Corti to the brain

FIG.3.19   THE HUMAN EAR

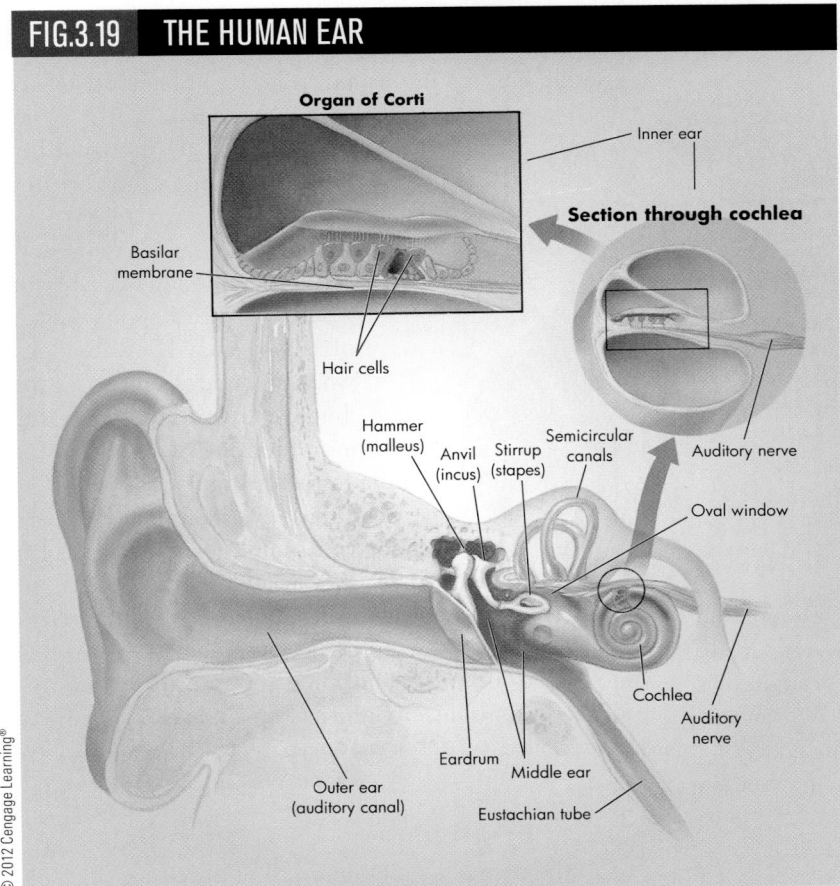

Organ of Corti

Inner ear

Section through cochlea

Basilar membrane

Hair cells

Hammer (malleus)
Anvil (incus)
Stirrup (stapes)
Semicircular canals

Auditory nerve

Oval window

Cochlea
Auditory nerve

Eardrum
Middle ear

Outer ear (auditory canal)

Eustachian tube

© 2012 Cengage Learning®

You think of your ear as the fleshy protuberance on the side of your head, but most of the ear is actually inside your head.

related to the number of receptor neurons on the organ of Corti that fire and how often they fire. Psychologists generally agree that sounds are perceived as louder when more of these sensory neurons fire.

As discussed earlier, it takes two processes to explain perception of color: *trichromatic theory* and *opponent–process theory*. Explaining pitch perception—that is, perception of sound waves that vary in frequency from 20 to 20,000 cycles per second—apparently takes three processes: *place theory, frequency theory*, and the *volley principle*.

Hermann von Helmholtz helped develop the place theory of pitch discrimination as well as the trichromatic theory of color vision. **Place theory** holds that the pitch of a sound is sensed according to the place along the basilar membrane that vibrates in response to it. In research that led to the award of a Nobel Prize, Georg von Békésy (1957) found that receptors at different sites along the membrane fire in response to tones of differing frequencies. Receptor neurons appear to be lined up along the basilar membrane like piano keys. The higher the pitch of a sound, the closer the responsive neurons lie to the

oval window. However, place theory appears to apply only to pitches that are at least 4,000 Hz. But what about lower pitches? That's where frequency theory comes in.

Frequency theory notes that for us to perceive lower pitches, we need to match the frequency of the sound waves with our neural impulses. That is, in response to low pitches—say 20 to 1,000 cycles per second—hair cells on the basilar membrane fire at the same frequencies as the sound waves. However, neurons cannot fire more than 1,000 times per second. Therefore, frequency theory best explains perception of pitches between 20 and 1,000 cycles per second. In actuality, frequency theory appears to account only for pitch perception between 20 and a few hundred cycles per second.

The *volley principle* accounts for pitch discrimination between a few hundred and 4,000 cycles per second (Machery & Carlyon, 2010; Martignoli et al., 2013). In response to sound waves of these frequencies, groups of neurons take turns firing in the way that one row of soldiers used to fire rifles while another row knelt to reload. Alternating firing—that is, volleying—appears to transmit sensory information about pitches in the intermediate range.

3-4e DEAFNESS

More than 1 in 10 Americans have a hearing impairment, and 1 in 100 cannot hear at all. Two major types of deafness are *conductive deafness* and *sensorineural deafness*. *Conductive deafness* stems from damage to the structures of the middle ear—either to the eardrum or to the bones that conduct (and amplify) sound waves from the outer ear to the inner ear (Daud et al., 2010). This is the hearing impairment often found among older people. Hearing aids amplify sound and often help people with conductive deafness.

Sensorineural deafness usually stems from damage to the structures of the inner ear, most often the loss of hair cells.

place theory the theory that the pitch of a sound is determined by the section of the basilar membrane that vibrates in response to the sound

frequency theory the theory that the pitch of a sound is reflected in the frequency of the neural impulses that are generated in response to the sound

Sensorineural deafness can also stem from damage to the auditory nerve, caused by such factors as disease or exposure to very loud sounds. In sensorineural deafness, people tend to be more sensitive to some pitches than others. In so-called Hunter's notch, the loss is limited to the frequencies of the sound waves generated by a gun firing. Prolonged exposure to 85 dB can cause hearing loss. People who attend rock concerts, where sounds may reach 140 dB, risk damaging their ears, as do workers who run pneumatic drills or drive noisy vehicles. The ringing sensation that often follows exposure to loud sounds probably means that hair cells in the inner ear have been damaged.

Cochlear implants, or "artificial ears," contain microphones that sense sounds and electronic equipment that transmits sounds past damaged hair cells to stimulate the auditory nerve. Such implants have helped many people with sensorineural deafness (Tait et al., 2010). However, they cannot assume the functions of damaged auditory nerves.

3-5 THE CHEMICAL SENSES: SMELL AND TASTE

Smell and taste are the chemical senses. In vision and hearing, physical energy strikes our sensory receptors. In smell and taste, we sample molecules of substances.

flavor a complex quality of food and other substances that is based on their odor, texture, and temperature as well their taste

olfactory nerve the nerve that transmits information concerning odors from olfactory receptors to the brain

taste cells receptor cells that are sensitive to taste

taste buds the sensory organs for taste; they contain taste cells and are located mostly on the tongue

Mark Wragg/Polka Dot (RF)/Jupiter Images

3-5a SMELL

Smell has an important role in human behavior. It contributes to the **flavor** of foods, for example. If you did not have a sense of smell, an onion and an apple might taste the same to you. People's sense of smell may be deficient when compared with that of a dog, but we can detect the odor of 1 one-millionth of a milligram of vanilla in a liter of air.

What's that SCENT you're wearing?

The sense of smell detects odors. An odor is a sample of molecules of a substance in the air. Odors trigger firing of receptor neurons in the *olfactory membrane* high in each nostril. Receptor neurons can detect even a few molecules of the substance in gaseous form. The receptor neurons transmit information about odors to the brain via the **olfactory nerve**.

Mike Kemp/Rubberball/Jupiter Images

3-5b TASTE

As in the case of smell, the sense of taste samples molecules of a substance. Taste is sensed through **taste cells**—receptor neurons located on **taste buds**. You have about 10,000 taste buds, most of which are located near the edges and back of your tongue. Some taste buds are more responsive to sweetness, whereas others react to several tastes. Other taste receptors are found in the roof, sides, and back of the mouth, and in the throat. Buds in the mouth are evolutionarily adaptive because they can warn of bad food before it is swallowed (Brand, 2000).

Researchers historically agreed on four primary taste qualities: sweet, sour, salty, and bitter. They have recently added a new basic taste to the list: *umami*, which is pronounced *ooh-mommy* in Japanese and means "meaty" or "savory" (Rolls, 2009; Yamamoto et al., 2009).

Believe it or not, apples and onions are quite similar in taste, but their flavors differ greatly. What is the difference between a taste and a flavor?

Comstock/Stockbyte (RF)/Jupiter Images

Regardless of the number of basic tastes, the flavor of a food is more complex than taste alone. *Flavor* depends on odor, texture, and temperature as well as on taste. Apples and onions are similar in taste, but their flavors differ greatly.

Just as some people have better vision than others, some people are more sensitive to tastes than others—but their superiority may be limited to one or more basic tastes. Those of us with low sensitivity for sweetness may require twice the sugar to sweeten our food as those who are more sensitive. Those of us who claim to enjoy bitter foods may actually be taste-blind to them. Sensitivities to various tastes have a genetic component (Knaapila et al., 2012; Feeney & Hayes, 2014).

3-6 THE SKIN SENSES

The skin senses include touch, pressure, warmth, cold, and pain. We have distinct sensory receptors for pressure, temperature, and pain, but some nerve endings may receive more than one type of sensory input. Let's focus on touch, pressure, temperature, and pain.

3-6a TOUCH AND PRESSURE

Sensory receptors embedded in the skin fire when the surface of the skin is touched. There may be several kinds of receptors for touch, some that respond to constant pressure, some that respond to intermittent pressure, as in tapping the skin. *Active touching* means continuously moving your hand along the surface of an object so that you continue to receive sensory input from the object. If you are trying to "get the feel of" a fabric or the texture of a friend's hair, you must move your hand over it. Otherwise, the sensations quickly fade. If you pass your hand over the fabric or hair and then hold it still, the sensations of touching will fade. Active touching receives information concerning pressure, temperature, texture, and feedback from the muscles involved in movements of our hands.

Different parts of the body are more sensitive to touch and pressure than others. The parts of the body that "cover" more than their fair share of somatosensory cortex are most sensitive to

touch. These parts include the hands, face, and some other regions of the body. Our fingertips, lips, noses, and cheeks are more sensitive than our shoulders, thighs, and calves. Why the difference in sensitivity? First, nerve endings are more densely packed in the fingertips and face than in other locations. Second, more sensory cortex is devoted to the perception of sensations in the fingertips and face (see Figure 2.10 on page 50).

3-6b TEMPERATURE

The receptors for temperature are neurons located just beneath the skin. When skin temperature increases, the receptors for warmth fire. Decreases in skin temperature cause receptors for cold to fire.

Sensations of temperature are relative. When we are at normal body temperature, we might perceive another person's skin as warm. When we are feverish, though, the other person's skin might seem cool. We also adapt to differences in temperature. When we enter a swimming pool, the water may seem cold because it is below body temperature. Yet after a few moments an 80°F pool may seem quite warm. In fact, we may chide a newcomer for not diving right in.

3-6c PAIN

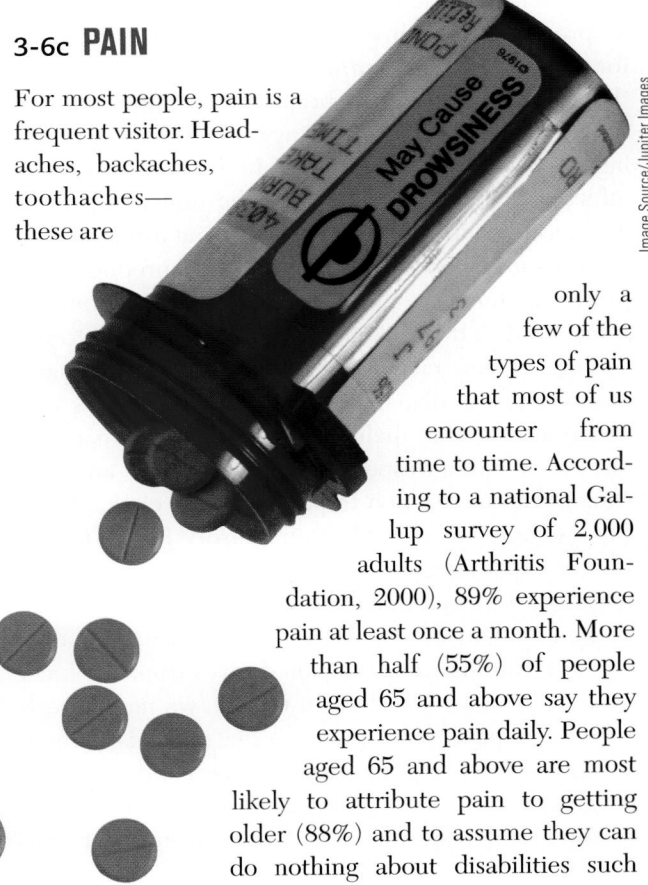

For most people, pain is a frequent visitor. Headaches, backaches, toothaches— these are

only a few of the types of pain that most of us encounter from time to time. According to a national Gallup survey of 2,000 adults (Arthritis Foundation, 2000), 89% experience pain at least once a month. More than half (55%) of people aged 65 and above say they experience pain daily. People aged 65 and above are most likely to attribute pain to getting older (88%) and to assume they can do nothing about disabilities such as arthritis. By contrast, people aged 18 to 34 are more likely to attribute pain to tension or stress (73%), overwork (64%), or their lifestyle (51%). When we assume that there is nothing we can do about pain, we are less likely to try. Yet 43% of Americans say that pain curtails their activities, and 50% say that pain puts them in a bad mood.

Pain results when neurons called *nociceptors* in the skin are stimulated. Evolutionary psychologists would point out that pain is adaptive, if unpleasant, because it motivates us to do something about it. For some of us, however, chronic pain—pain that lasts once injuries or illnesses have cleared—saps our vitality and interferes with the pleasures of everyday life (Fenton, 2010; Gatchel & Kishino, 2010).

We can sense pain throughout most of the body, but pain is usually sharpest where nerve endings are densely packed, as in the fingers and face. Pain can also be felt deep within the body, as in the cases of abdominal pain and back pain. Even though headaches may seem to originate deep inside the head, there are no nerve endings for pain in the brain.

Pain usually originates at the point of contact, as when you bang a knee. But it reverberates throughout the nervous system. The pain message to the brain is facilitated by the release of chemicals such as prostaglandins, bradykinin, and P (yes, P stands for "pain"). *Prostaglandins* facilitate transmission of the pain message to the brain and heighten circulation to the injured area, causing the redness and swelling that we call inflammation. Inflammation attracts infection-fighting blood cells to the injury to protect it against invading germs. Pain-relieving drugs such as aspirin and ibuprofen help by inhibiting production of prostaglandins. The pain message is relayed from the spinal cord to the thalamus and then projected to the cerebral cortex, making us aware of the location and intensity of the damage. Ronald Melzack speaks of a "neuromatrix" that includes these chemical reactions but involves other aspects of our physiology and psychology in our reaction to pain (Gatchel et al., 2012). For example, visual and other sensory inputs tell us what is happening and affect our interpretation of the situation. Our emotional response affects the degree of pain, and so do the ways in which we respond to stress. If, for instance, the pain derives from an object we fear, perhaps a knife or a needle, we may experience more pain. If we perceive that there is nothing we can do to change the situation, perception of pain may increase. If we have self-confidence and a history of successful response to stress, perception of pain may diminish.

PHANTOM LIMB PAIN One of the more intriguing topics in the study of pain is phantom limb pain. About two out of three combat veterans with amputated limbs report feeling pain in such missing, or "phantom," limbs (Foell & Flor, 2012). Although the pain occurs in the absence of the limb, it is real enough. The pain sometimes involves activation of nerves in the stump of the missing limb, but local anesthesia does not always eliminate the pain.

Researchers have found that many people who experience phantom limb pain have also undergone reorganization of the motor and somatosensory cortex that is consistent with the pain (Flor et al., 2013).

GATE THEORY Simple remedies like rubbing a banged knee frequently help relieve pain. Why? According to the *gate theory* of pain originated by Ronald Melzack and Patrick Wall, the nervous system can process only a limited amount of stimulation at a time. Rubbing the knee transmits sensations to the brain that "compete" for the attention of neurons. Many nerves are thus prevented from transmitting pain messages to the brain. It is like shutting down a "gate" in the spinal cord, or like a switchboard being flooded with calls.

ACUPUNCTURE Thousands of years ago, the Chinese began mapping the body to learn where pins might be placed to deaden pain. This practice is termed acupuncture. Traditional acupuncturists believe that the practice balances the body's flow of energy, but research has shown that it stimulates nerves that reach the hypothalamus and may also cause the release of endorphins and cortisol (Stener-Victorin, 2013). Endorphins are neurotransmitters that are similar in effect to the narcotic morphine. Cortisol is a stress hormone.

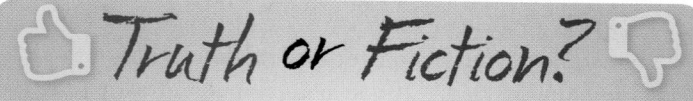

Truth or Fiction?

| T | F | Many people experience pain "in" limbs that have been amputated. |

This statement has no perfectly clear truth or fiction answer. Many people feel *as though* they experience pain in limbs that have been amputated (this phenomenon is called *phantom limb pain*). However, the limbs are gone, so that pain cannot actually be "in" the limb.

3-7 KINESTHESIS AND THE VESTIBULAR SENSE

Try an experiment. Close your eyes and then touch your nose with your finger. If you weren't right on target, I'm sure you came close. But how? You didn't see your hand moving, and you didn't hear your arm swishing through the air. Humans and many other animals have senses that alert them to their movements and body position without relying on vision, including *kinesthesis* and the *vestibular sense*.

3-7a KINESTHESIS

Kinesthesis is the sense that informs you about the position and motion of parts of the body. The term is derived from the ancient Greek words for "motion" (kinesis) and "perception" (aisthesis). In kinesthesis, sensory information is fed back to the brain from sensory organs in the joints, tendons, and muscles. You were able to bring your finger to your nose easily by employing your kinesthetic sense. When you make a muscle in your arm, the sensations of tightness and hardness are also provided by kinesthesis.

Imagine going for a walk without kinesthesis. You would have to watch the forward motion of each leg to be certain you

Good gymnasts and dancers can sense the location and movement of nearly every part of their body.

had raised it high enough to clear the curb. And if you had tried the brief nose-to-finger experiment without the kinesthetic sense, you would have had no sensory feedback until you felt the pressure of your finger against your nose (or cheek, or eye, or forehead), and you probably would have missed dozens of times.

3-7b THE VESTIBULAR SENSE

It is your **vestibular sense** that provides your brain with information as to whether or not you are physically upright. Sensory organs located in the semicircular canals and elsewhere in the ears monitor your body's motion and position in relation to gravity. They tell you whether you are falling and provide cues to whether your body is changing speed, such as when you are in an accelerating airplane or automobile.

3-8 ESP: IS THERE PERCEPTION WITHOUT SENSATION?

Imagine the wealth you could amass if you had *precognition*, that is, if you were able to perceive future events in advance. Perhaps you would check the next week's stock market reports and know what to buy or sell. Or you could bet with confidence on who would win the next Super Bowl or World Series. Or think of the power you would have if you were capable of *psychokinesis*, that is, mentally manipulating or moving objects. Precognition and psychokinesis are two concepts associated with extrasensory perception (ESP). Two other theoretical forms of ESP are *telepathy*, or direct transmission of thoughts or ideas from one person to another, and *clairvoyance*, or the perception of objects that do not stimulate the known sensory organs. An example of clairvoyance is "seeing" what card will be dealt next, even though it is still in the deck and unseen even by the dealer.

ESP—also referred to as *parapsychological* or *psi phenomena*—refers to the perception of objects or events through means other than the known sensory organs. *Parapsychological* (psi) means standing alongside psychology, not being a part of psychology. Psychological communication occurs verbally or by means of body language. *Psi communication* refers to the transfer of information through an irregular or unusual process—not through the usual senses.

Many psychologists do not believe ESP is an appropriate area for scientific inquiry. Psychologist Ray Hyman (2011) argues that "It's craziness, pure craziness." Scientists study natural events, but ESP smacks of the supernatural, even the occult.

kinesthesis the sense that informs us about the positions and motion of parts of our bodies

vestibular sense the sense of equilibrium that informs us about our bodies' positions relative to gravity

extrasensory perception (ESP) perception of objects or events through means other than the recognized sensory organs

Extrasensory perception also has the flavor of a nightclub act in which a blindfolded "clairvoyant" calls out the contents of an audience member's pocketbook. Other psychologists, however, believe that there is nothing wrong with investigating ESP. The issue for them is not whether ESP is sensationalistic but whether its existence can be demonstrated in the laboratory.

Perhaps the best known of the ESP researchers was Joseph Banks Rhine, who studied ESP for several decades beginning in the late 1920s (Viulli, 2008). In a typical experiment in clairvoyance, Rhine would use a pack of 25 Zener cards, which contained five sets of simple symbols. Pigeons' pecking randomly to indicate which one was about to be turned up would be "correct" 20% of the time. Rhine found that some people guessed correctly significantly more often than the 20% chance rate. He concluded that these individuals might have some degree of ESP.

A more current method for studying *telepathy* (direct communication between minds) is the *ganzfeld procedure* (Howard et al., 2009). In this method, one person acts as a "sender" and the other as a "receiver." The sender views randomly selected visual stimuli such as photographs or videotapes, while the receiver, who is in another room and whose eyes are covered and ears are blocked, tries to mentally tune in to the sender. After a session, the receiver is shown four visual stimuli and asked to select the one transmitted by the sender. A person guessing which stimulus was "transmitted" would be correct 25% of the time (1 time in 4) by chance alone. An analysis of 28 experiments using the ganzfeld procedure, however, found that receivers correctly identified the visual stimulus 38% of the time (Honorton, 1985), a percentage unlikely to be due to chance.

An article by Daryl Bern (2011) reported the results of several experiments with more than 1,000 participants. In one experiment, the researchers showed 100 Cornell University students photos of erotic or nonerotic scenes. They were then shown the photos again, in random order, but asked to predict whether the next photo would have erotic or nonerotic content. Since half were erotic and half were not, a chance result would be 50–50. Participants correctly predicted the erotic photos 53.1% of the time, whereas their hit rate on predicting nonerotic photos was just 50-50, a chance result. The chances that the 53.1% success rate was due to chance alone were less than one in 20. However, no single individual was correct every time.

Overall, there are many reasons for skepticism of ESP. First is the *file-drawer problem* (Howard et al., 2009). Buyers of supermarket magazines tend to forget "psychics'" predictions when they fail to come true (i.e., they have "filed" them away). Similarly, ESP researchers are less likely to report research results that show failure. Therefore, we would expect unusual findings (e.g., a subject with a high success rate at psi-communication tasks over a period of several days) to appear in the research literature. In other words, if you flip a coin

indefinitely, eventually you will flip 10 heads in a row. The odds against it are high, but if you report only your success and not the weeks of failure, you appear to have unique coin-flipping ability.

Then, too, people who appear to have demonstrated ESP with one researcher have failed to do so with another researcher or have refused to participate in other studies (Howard et al., 2009). Moreover, in all of these studies, *not one person has emerged who can reliably show ESP from one occasion to another and from one researcher to another.* In sum, most psychologists do not grant ESP research much credibility. They prefer to study perception that involves sensation. After all, what is life without sensation?

Fiction 👎

T F Some people can read other people's minds.

It is not true that some people can read other people's minds. We may be sensitive to other people's facial expressions, postures, and tone of voice, but there is no scientific evidence that people can actually read other people's minds.

STUDY TOOLS 3

IN THE BOOK, YOU CAN:

☐ Check your understanding of what you've read with the quizzes that follow.

☐ Rip out the chapter review card at the back of the book to have a summary of the chapter and the key terms handy.

ONLINE AT CENGAGEBRAIN.COM YOU CAN:

☐ Learn more about the major structures and functions of the eye and ear in learning modules.

☐ Practice retrieving what you've learned using the interactive figures on the human eye and ear.

☐ Explore dreaming in a short video.

☐ Prepare for tests with quizzes

☐ Review the key terms with Flash Cards.

☐ Play games to master concepts.

FILL-INS

Answers can be found in the back of the book, starting.

1. _____ is the organization of sensations into an inner representation of the world; it reflects learning and expectations as well as sensations.

2. The _____ threshold for a stimulus, such as light, is the lowest intensity at which it can be detected.

3. The retina is made up of photoreceptors called _____ and _____.

4. The axons of ganglion cells make up the _____ nerve, which conducts visual information to the brain.

5. We perceive movement by sensing motion across the _____ of the eye and change of position in relation to other objects.

6. Odors are detected by the _____ membrane in each nostril.

7. The receptor neurons for taste are called _____ cells, which are located in taste buds on the tongue.

8. Kinesthesis is the sensing of bodily _____ and movement.

9. The vestibular sense is housed mainly in the _____ canals of the ears.

10. One reason for skepticism about ESP is the _____ - _____ problem; that is, researchers are less likely to report research results that show failure.

MULTIPLE CHOICE

1. _____ is to mechanical stimulation as perception is to mental representation.
   a. Adaptation
   b. Organization
   c. Sensation
   d. Cognition

2. Which of the following accommodates to an image by changing thickness and focusing light onto the retina?
   a. sclera
   b. lens
   c. iris
   d. cornea

3. Which of the following colors is longest in wavelength?
   a. red
   b. yellow
   c. violet
   d. green

4. The Gestalt rule describing the perceptual tendency to see objects that are near each other as belonging to a set is termed_____; while the tendency to see like objects as belonging together is termed _____.
   a. proximity; continuity
   b. closure; constancy
   c. continuity; similarity
   d. proximity; similarity

5. The normal human ear can hear sounds varying in frequency from _____ to _____ cycles per second (Hz).
   a. 2 to 2,000
   b. 20 to 2,000
   c. 20 to 20,000
   d. 200 to 20,000

6. Which of the following is *not* involved in explaining the perception of pitch?
   a. place theory
   b. the volley principle
   c. opponent–process theory
   d. frequency theory

7. The following are considered to be basic tastes, with the exception of
   a. savory.
   b. sweet.
   c. sour.
   d. salty.

8. Because one odor can mask another, people use _____.
   a. air fresheners
   b. perfumes
   c. incense burners
   d. all of the above

9. The sensory receptors for kinesthesis are located in the
   a. tendons, muscles, and joints.
   b. semicircular canals.
   c. bony frame of the body.
   d. skin and hair.

10. Most psychologists do not believe in extrasensory perception because
    a. scientists have not defined what is meant by extrasensory perception.
    b. there is no evidence to support the existence of extrasensory perception.
    c. extrasensory perception would give those who have it unfair advantages.
    d. it is a sensationalistic concept.

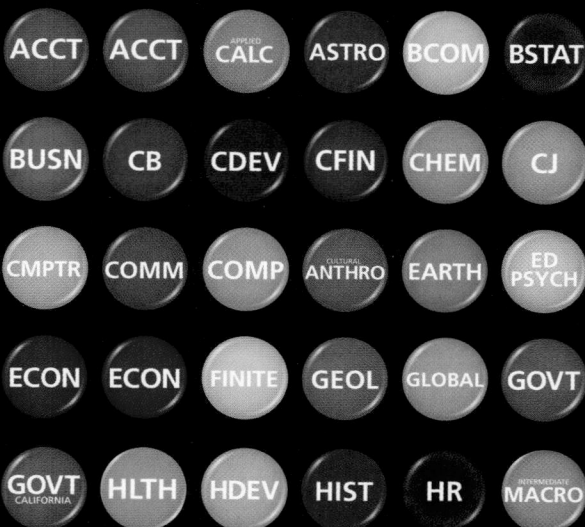

ONE APPROACH.
70 UNIQUE SOLUTIONS.

4 | Consciousness

LEARNING OUTCOMES

After studying this chapter, you will be able to…

4-1 Define consciousness

4-2 Explain the nature of sleep and various sleep disorders

4-3 Explain the natures and uses of hypnosis, meditation, and biofeedback in altering consciousness

4-4 Define substance use disorders, identify categories of psychoactive drugs, and explain their allures and dangers

After you finish this chapter, go to **PAGE 116** for **STUDY TOOLS**

When you talk to yourself, who talks, and who listens?

This is the type of question posed by philosophers and scientists who study consciousness. Although it might seem that psychologists, who study the brain and mental processes, are best equipped to look into consciousness, they banished this topic from their field for many years. In 1904, for example, William James wrote an article with the intriguing title "Does Consciousness Exist?" James did not think consciousness was a proper area of study for psychologists because scientific methods could not directly observe or measure another person's consciousness.

> When you **talk** to yourself, who talks, and who listens?

John Watson, the "father of modern behaviorism," agreed. Watson insisted that only observable, measurable behavior is the province of psychology: "The time seems to have come when psychology must discard all references to consciousness" (1913, p. 163). When Watson became the president of the

American Psychological Association in 1914, his view was further cemented in the minds of many psychologists.

But the past few decades have seen a cognitive revolution, and thousands of psychologists now believe we cannot capture the richness of human experience without referring to consciousness (Kriegel, 2014; Sternberg, 2009). We are flooded with studies of consciousness by psychologists, biologists, neuroscientists, physicists, even computer scientists. Yet we still cannot directly observe the consciousness of another person, and so we rely on self-reports of consciousness as we observe events such as neural activity in the brain.

4-1 WHAT IS CONSCIOUSNESS?

Mental concepts such as consciousness acquire scientific status by being tied to observable behavior whenever possible. The concept of consciousness has various meanings, and psychologists use it in many ways.

4-1a CONSCIOUSNESS AS AWARENESS

One meaning of **consciousness** is *sensory awareness* of the environment. The sense of vision enables us to see, or be *conscious* of, the sun gleaming on the snow. The sense of hearing allows us to hear, or be conscious of, a concert. Yet sometimes we are not aware of sensory stimulation. We may be unaware, or unconscious, of sensory stimulation when we do not pay attention to it. The world is abuzz with signals, yet you are conscious of or focusing on only the words on this page (I hope).

Therefore, another aspect of consciousness is **selective attention**. Selective attention means focusing one's consciousness on a particular stimulus. Selective attention is a key to self-control. To keep your car on the road, you must pay more attention to driving conditions than to your hunger pangs or a cellphone call.

Adaptation to our environment involves learning which stimuli must be attended to and which can be safely ignored. Selective attention makes our senses

keener (Kerlin et al., 2010; McLachlan & Wilson, 2010). This is why we can pick out the speech of a single person across a room at a cocktail party, a phenomenon aptly termed the *cocktail party effect* (L. Miller, 2013). Selective attention also plays a role in the advertisements and marketing ploys we notice.

 Truth or Fiction?

WHAT DO YOU THINK? Folklore, common sense, or nonsense? Select T for "truth" or F for "fiction," and check the accuracy of your answers as you read through the chapter.

T	F	We act out our forbidden fantasies in our dreams.
T	F	Insomnia can be caused by trying too hard to fall asleep.
T	F	It is dangerous to awaken a sleepwalker.
T	F	You can be hypnotized against your will.
T	F	You can teach a rat to raise or lower its heart rate.
T	F	Heroin was once used as a cure for addiction to morphine.
T	F	Many health professionals calm down hyperactive children by giving them a stimulant.
T	F	Coca-Cola once "added life" to its signature drink through the use of a powerful—but now illegal—stimulant.
T	F	The number of people who die from smoking-related causes is greater than the number lost to motor vehicle accidents, abuse of alcohol and all other drugs, suicide, homicide, and aids *combined*.

How do advertisers of running shoes, automobiles, or beer use these facts to get "into" our consciousness and, they hope, our pocketbooks? Think of some television commercials that captured your attention. What kinds of stimuli made them front and center in your awareness?

Yet another meaning of consciousness is that of **direct inner awareness**. Close your eyes and imagine spilling a can of bright, red paint across a black tabletop. Watch it spread across the black, shiny surface and then spill onto the floor. Although this image may be vivid, you did not "see" it literally. Neither your eyes nor any other sensory organs were involved. You were conscious of the image through direct inner awareness.

We are conscious of—or have direct inner awareness of—our own thoughts, images, emotions, and memories. However, we may not be able to measure direct inner awareness scientifically. Nevertheless, many psychologists would argue that if you have it, you know it. Self-awareness is connected with the firing of billions of neurons hundreds of times per second. Even so, we detect psychological processes but not neural events (Roth, 2000).

information conscious by directing your attention to them.

According to Freud, still other mental events are **unconscious**, or

We know that we have consciousness, but how do we define it? We can look inward, but psychologists have labored to answer the question: How do we study the consciousness of another person?

---

consciousness a concept with many meanings, including sensory awareness of the world outside, direct inner awareness of one's thoughts and feelings, personal unity, and the waking state

selective attention the focus of one's consciousness on a particular stimulus

direct inner awareness knowledge of one's own thoughts, feelings, and memories without the use of sensory organs

preconscious in psychodynamic theory, descriptive of material that is not in awareness but can be brought into awareness by focusing one's attention

unconscious in psychodynamic theory, descriptive of ideas and feelings that are not available to awareness; also: without consciousness

repression in psychodynamic theory, the automatic (unconscious) ejection of anxiety-evoking ideas, impulses, or images from awareness

4-1b CONSCIOUS, PRECONSCIOUS, UNCONSCIOUS, AND NONCONSCIOUS

Sigmund Freud, the founder of psychoanalysis, differentiated between thoughts and feelings of which we are conscious and those that are preconscious and unconscious.

Preconscious material is not currently in awareness but is readily available. For example, if you answer the following questions, you will summon up "preconscious" information: What did you eat for breakfast? What is your phone number? You can make these preconscious bits of

unavailable to awareness under most circumstances. Freud believed that some painful memories and sexual and aggressive impulses are unacceptable to us, so we *automatically* (unconsciously) eject them from awareness. That is, we *repress* them. **Repression** of

✳ May I Have Your Attention Please

Although we can decide where and when we will focus our attention, various kinds of stimuli also tend to capture our attention. These include:

▶ **sudden changes,** such as when a cool breeze enters a sweltering room or we receive a particularly high grade on an exam.

▶ **novel stimuli,** such as when a dog enters the classroom.

▶ **intense stimuli,** such as bright colors or sharp pain.

▶ **repetitive stimuli,** such as when the same commercial is aired a dozen times throughout a football game.

Courtesy of Michael Gazzaniga

The Flavors of Consciousness

"Consciousness comes in many flavors. Anyone who has taught an introductory psychology class, or attended one at eight o'clock Friday morning, has seen them all. There may be a couple of party-hearty frat boys in the back row, dozing after a long night spent celebrating the upcoming weekend. These two are not conscious. Up a couple of rows is the scammer checking out [someone] across the aisle and wondering if he can get a date. He is conscious, but not

> Consciousness comes in many **flavors**.

of you; nor are the three girls down the way who are passing notes to each other and suppressing their merriment. Another student has a tape recorder going and is finishing up a paper for another class, and he will be conscious of you later. The front-row kids are sippin' their coffee, taking notes furiously and occasionally nodding in agreement; at least they are conscious of you."

—MICHAEL S. GAZZANIGA, 2008, P. 277.

these memories and impulses allows us to avoid feelings of anxiety, guilt, or shame.

Related, non-Freudian concepts include *suppression* and *nonconscious* processes. When people choose to stop thinking about unacceptable ideas or distractions, they are using **suppression**. When we consciously eject unwanted mental events from awareness, we are using suppression. We may, for example, suppress thoughts of an upcoming

One of the meanings of consciousness is the continuing sense of self in the world.

Dex Image /Getty images

party when we need to study for a test. We may also try to suppress thoughts of the test while we are at the party!

Some bodily processes, such as the firing of neurons, are **nonconscious**. They cannot be experienced through sensory awareness or direct inner awareness. Growing hair and carrying oxygen in the blood are nonconscious processes. We can see that our hair has grown, but we have no sense receptors that provide sensations of growing. We feel the need to breathe but do not experience the exchange of carbon dioxide and oxygen.

4-1c CONSCIOUSNESS AS PERSONAL UNITY

As we develop, we differentiate ourselves from that which is not us. We develop a sense of being persons, individuals. There is a totality to our impressions, thoughts, and feelings that makes up our consciousness—our continuing sense of self in the world. That self forms intentions and guides behavior. In this usage of the word, consciousness *is* self.

suppression the deliberate, or conscious, placing of certain ideas, impulses, or images out of awareness

nonconscious descriptive of bodily processes, such as growing hair, of which we cannot become conscious; we may "recognize" that our hair is growing, but we cannot directly experience the biological process

4-1d CONSCIOUSNESS AS THE WAKING STATE

The word *conscious* also refers to the waking state as opposed, for example, to sleep. From this perspective, sleep, meditation, the hypnotic "trance," and the distorted perceptions that can accompany use of consciousness-altering drugs are considered *altered states of consciousness.*

The remainder of the chapter explores various altered states of consciousness, including sleep and dreams; hypnosis, meditation, and biofeedback; and, finally, the effects of psycho-active drugs.

4-2 SLEEP AND DREAMS

Sleep is a fascinating topic. After all, we spend about one-third of our adult lives asleep. Sleep experts recommend that adults get seven to nine hours of sleep a night, but according to the National Sleep Foundation (2013), adults in the United States typically get about 6.8 hours of sleep. About one-third get six hours or less of sleep a night during the workweek. One-third admit that lack of sleep impairs their ability to function during the day, and nearly one in five admits to falling asleep at the wheel.

Yes, we spend one-third of our lives in sleep—or would if we could. As you can see in Figure 4.1, some animals get much more sleep than we do, and some obtain much less. Why? It might have something to do with evolutionary forces. Animals that are most at risk of being hunted by predators tend to sleep less—an adaptive response to the realities of life and death.

4-2a BIOLOGICAL AND CIRCADIAN RHYTHMS

We and other animals are subject to rhythms, and they are related to the rotation and revolutions of the planet. Many birds (and people who can afford it!) migrate south in the fall and north in the spring. A number of

> **circadian rhythm** a cycle that is connected with the 24-hour period of the earth's rotation

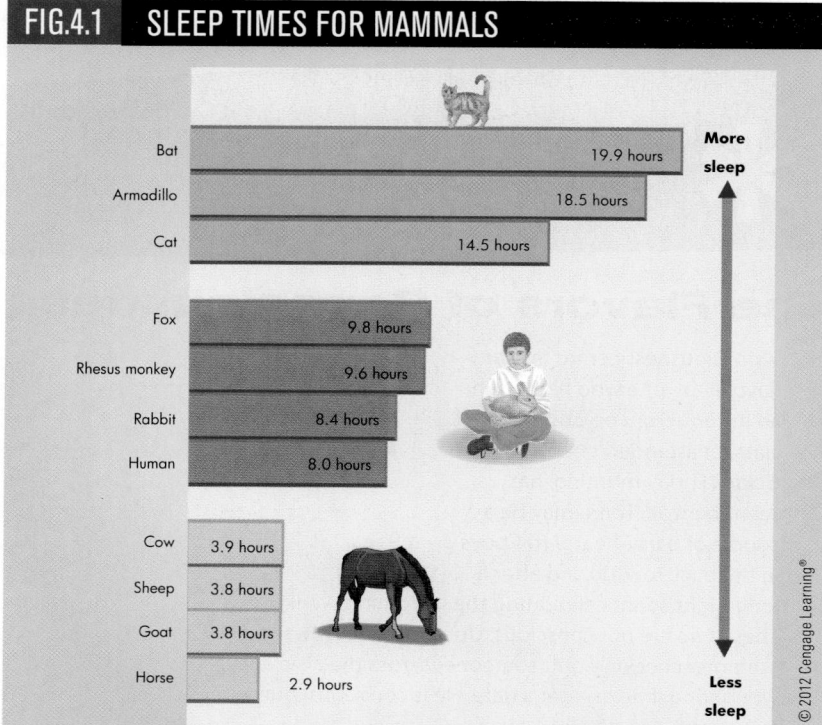

FIG.4.1 SLEEP TIMES FOR MAMMALS

Bat	19.9 hours
Armadillo	18.5 hours
Cat	14.5 hours
Fox	9.8 hours
Rhesus monkey	9.6 hours
Rabbit	8.4 hours
Human	8.0 hours
Cow	3.9 hours
Sheep	3.8 hours
Goat	3.8 hours
Horse	2.9 hours

More sleep ← → Less sleep

© 2012 Cengage Learning®

Different mammals require different amounts of sleep. Reasons remain uncertain, but evolution apparently plays a role: Animals more prone to being attacked by predators sleep less.

animals hibernate for the winter and emerge when buds are once again about to blossom.

Alternating periods of wakefulness and sleep reflect an internally generated *circadian rhythm.* A **circadian rhythm** is a cycle that is connected with the 24-hour period of the earth's rotation. A cycle of wakefulness and sleep is normally 24 hours long. When people are removed from cues that signal day or night, however, a cycle tends to become extended to about 25 hours, and people sleep nearly 10 of them (National Sleep Foundation, 2009). Why? We do not know. And during a night of sleep, we typically undergo a series of 90-minute cycles in which we run through the stages of sleep. In the morning, the shining sun adjusts the timing of the circadian clock by activating proteins in the retinas of the eyes. The proteins then signal tiny structures in the hypothalamus called the *suprachiasmatic nucleus (SCN).* In turn, the SCN stimulates the pineal gland to decrease its output of the hormone melatonin, which promotes sleep.

Some of us, known as "morning people," function best in the morning; others function best in the afternoon. Some of us are "night owls," who are at our best when most neighbors are sound asleep.

Why do we sleep? Why do we dream? Let's explore the nature of sleep, dreams, and sleep disorders.

4-2b THE STAGES OF SLEEP

When we sleep, we slip from consciousness to unconsciousness. When we are conscious, our brains emit waves characterized by certain *frequencies* (numbers of waves per second) and *amplitudes* (heights—an index of strength). Brain waves are rough indicators of the activity of large numbers of neurons. The strength, or energy, of brain waves is expressed in volts (an electrical unit). When we sleep, our brain waves differ from those emitted when we are conscious. The electroencephalograph (EEG; see Figure 2.6 on page 42) has enabled researchers to measure brain waves. Figure 4.2 shows EEG patterns that reflect the frequency and strength of brain waves during the waking state, when we are relaxed, and when we are in the various stages of sleep. Brain waves, like other waves, are cyclical. The printouts in Figure 4.2 show what happens during a period of 15 seconds or so.

High-frequency brain waves are associated with wakefulness. As we move deeper into sleep, their frequency decreases and their amplitude (strength) increases. When we close our eyes and begin to relax before going to sleep, our brains emit **alpha waves**—low-amplitude brain waves of about 8 to 13 cycles per second.

Figure 4.2 shows five stages of sleep. The first four sleep stages are considered **non-rapid eye movement (NREM) sleep**. These contrast with the fifth stage, **rapid eye movement (REM) sleep**, so called because our eyes dart back and forth beneath our eyelids.

As we enter stage 1 sleep, our brain waves slow down from the alpha rhythm and enter a pattern of **theta waves**. Theta waves, with a frequency of about 6 to 8 cycles per second, are

alpha waves rapid low-amplitude brain waves that have been linked to feelings of relaxation

non-rapid eye movement (NREM) sleep the first four stages of sleep

rapid eye movement (REM) sleep a stage of sleep characterized by rapid eye movements, which have been linked to dreaming

theta waves slow brain waves produced during the hypnagogic state

FIG.4.2   THE STAGES OF SLEEP

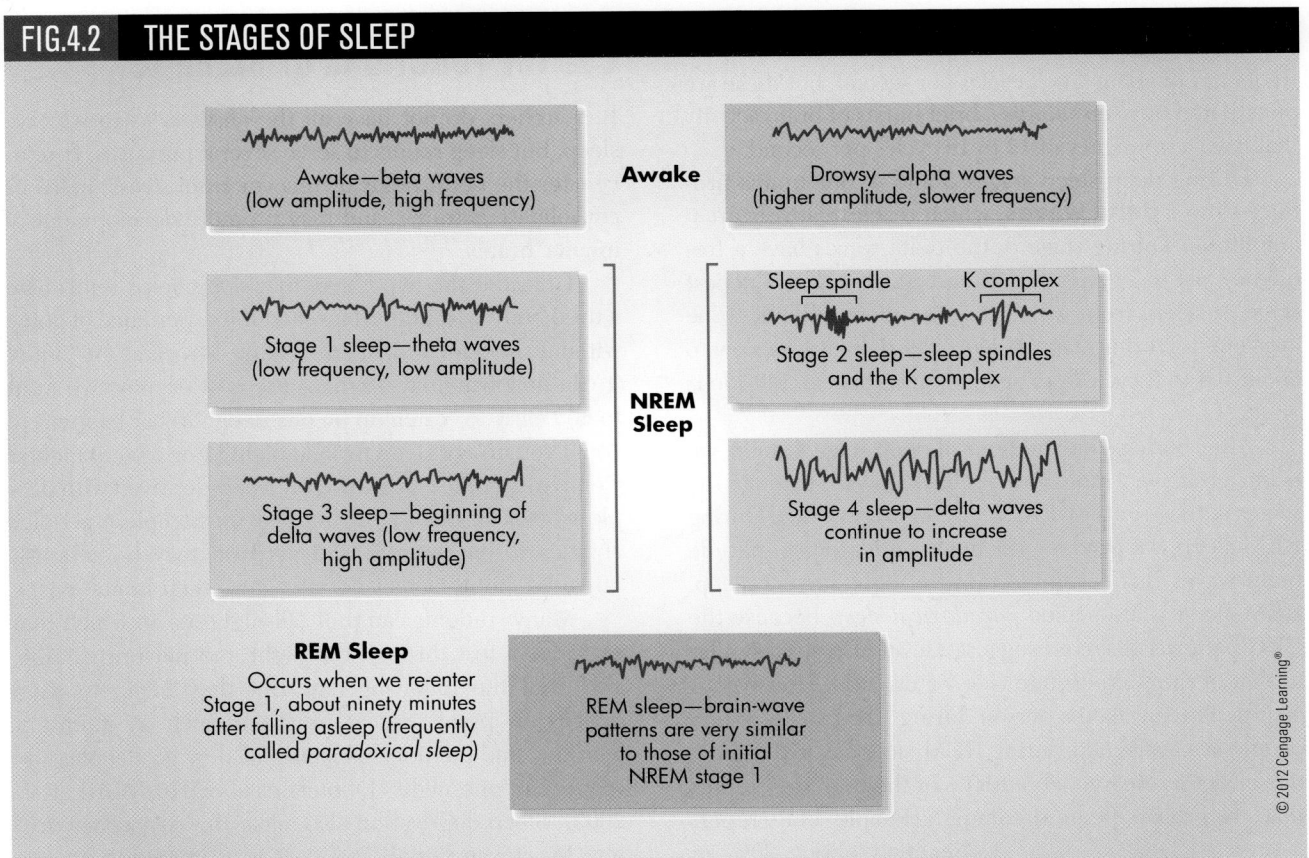

Awake—beta waves
(low amplitude, high frequency)

Awake

Drowsy—alpha waves
(higher amplitude, slower frequency)

Stage 1 sleep—theta waves
(low frequency, low amplitude)

NREM Sleep

Sleep spindle   K complex

Stage 2 sleep—sleep spindles
and the K complex

Stage 3 sleep—beginning of
delta waves (low frequency,
high amplitude)

Stage 4 sleep—delta waves
continue to increase
in amplitude

REM Sleep
Occurs when we re-enter
Stage 1, about ninety minutes
after falling asleep (frequently
called *paradoxical sleep*)

REM sleep—brain-wave
patterns are very similar
to those of initial
NREM stage 1

© 2012 Cengage Learning®

This figure illustrates typical EEG patterns for the stages of sleep. During REM sleep, EEG patterns resemble those of the waking state. For this reason, REM sleep is often termed *paradoxical sleep*. As sleep progresses from stage 1 to stage 4, brain waves become slower, and their amplitude increases. Dreams, including normal nightmares, are most vivid during REM sleep. More disturbing sleep terrors tend to occur during deep stage 4 sleep.

FIG.4.3 SLEEP CYCLES

| Sleep stage | A | 1 | 2 | 3 | 4 | 3 | 2 | REM | 1 | 2 | 3 | 4 | 3 | 2 | 3 | 2 | REM | 1 |

11 PM   12 AM   1 AM   2 AM

This figure illustrates the alternation of REM sleep and NREM sleep (stages 1-4) for the typical sleeper. There are about five periods of REM sleep during an eight-hour night. Sleep is deeper earlier in the night, and REM sleep tends to become prolonged toward morning.

accompanied by slow, rolling eye movements. The transition from alpha waves to theta waves may be accompanied by a *hypnagogic state* during which we may experience brief but vivid dreamlike images. Stage 1 sleep is the lightest stage of sleep. If we are awakened from stage 1 sleep, we may feel we were not sleeping at all.

After 30 to 40 minutes of stage 1 sleep, we undergo a steep descent into stages 2, 3, and 4 (see Figure 4.3). During stage 2, brain waves are medium in amplitude with a frequency of about 4 to 7 cycles per second, but these are punctuated by *sleep spindles*, brief bursts of brain activity that have a frequency of 12 to 16 cycles per second.

During deep sleep stages 3 and 4, our brains produce slower **delta waves**, which reach relatively great amplitude. During stage 3, the delta waves have a frequency of 1 to 3 cycles per second. Stage 4 is the deepest stage of sleep, from which it is the most difficult to be awakened. During stage 4 sleep, the delta waves slow to about 0.5 to 2 cycles per second, and their amplitude is greatest.

After perhaps half an hour of deep stage 4 sleep, we begin a relatively rapid journey back upward through the stages until we enter REM sleep (see Figure 4.3). During REM sleep, we produce relatively rapid, low-amplitude brain waves that resemble those of light stage 1 sleep. REM sleep is also called *paradoxical sleep* because the EEG patterns observed suggest a level of arousal similar to that of the waking state (see Figure 4.2). However, it is difficult to awaken a person during REM sleep. When people are awakened during REM sleep, as is the practice in sleep research, about 80% of the time they report that they have been dreaming. (People only report dreaming about 20% of the time when awakened during NREM sleep.)

Each night we tend to undergo five cycles through the stages of sleep (see Figure 4.3). Five cycles include five periods of REM sleep. Our first journey through stage 4 sleep is usually the longest. Sleep tends to become lighter as the night wears on; periods of REM sleep lengthen, and we may not enter the deepest stages of sleep. Toward morning our last period of REM sleep may last about half an hour.

4-2c THE FUNCTIONS OF SLEEP

Researchers do not have all the answers as to why we sleep, but sleep seems to serve several purposes: It rejuvenates the body, helps us recover from stress, helps us consolidate learning, and may promote development of infants' brains.

Consider the hypothesis that sleep helps rejuvenate a tired body. Most of us have had the experience of going without sleep for a night and feeling "wrecked" or "out of it" the following day. Perhaps the next evening we went to bed early to "catch up on our sleep." What happens to you if you do not sleep for one night? For several nights? Compare people who are highly sleep-deprived with people who have been drinking heavily. Sleepless people's abilities to concentrate and perform may be seriously impaired, but they may not recognize their limitations.

Many students can pull "all-nighters" in which they cram for a test through the night and perform reasonably well the following day. But they begin to show deficits in psychological functions such as attention, learning, and memory, especially if they go sleepless for more than one night (Dubiela et al., 2010; Ward et al., 2009). Sleep deprivation also makes for dangerous driving (M. Howard et al., 2013). It is estimated to be connected with 100,000 vehicular crashes and 1,500 deaths each year (S. Clark, 2009). To combat sleep deprivation during the week, many people sleep late or nap on their days off (National Sleep Foundation, 2013).

delta waves strong, slow brain waves usually emitted during stage 4 sleep

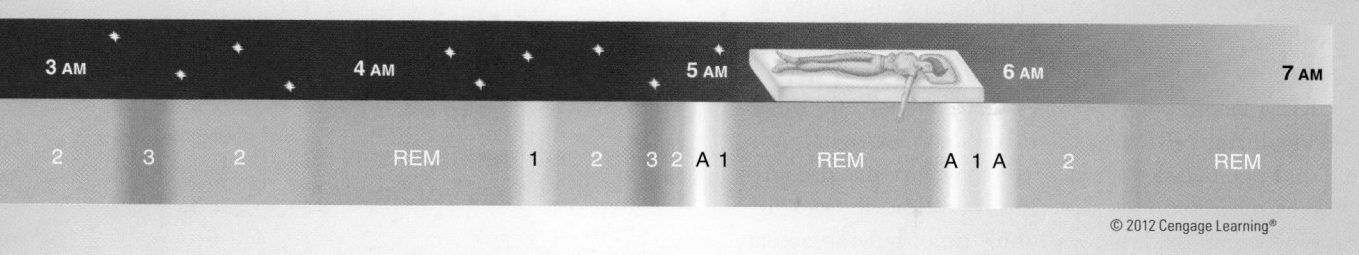

3 AM		4 AM		5 AM		6 AM	7 AM
2	3	2	REM	1 2 3 2 A 1	REM	A 1 A 2	REM

© 2012 Cengage Learning®

Sleep deprivation is connected with 100,000 vehicular crashes and 1,500 deaths each year.

WHY DO YOU NEED THE AMOUNT OF SLEEP YOU NEED? The amount of sleep we need seems to be in part genetically determined (Shaw et al., 2013). People also need more sleep when they are under stress, as caused by a change of job (Mayers et al., 2009; Rosekind et al., 2010). Sleep seems to help us recover from stress, and lack of sleep can lead to depression (de Wild-Hartmann et al. 2013).

Newborn babies may sleep 16 hours a day, and teenagers may sleep 12 hours or more (National Sleep Association, 2013). It is widely believed that older people need less sleep than younger adults do, but sleep in older people is often interrupted by physical discomfort or the need to go to the bathroom. To make up for sleep lost at night, older people may "nod off" during the day.

SLEEP, LEARNING, AND MEMORY REM sleep and deep sleep are both connected with the consolidation of learning and memory (Dubiela et al., 2010; Ward et al., 2009). In fact, fetuses have periods of waking and sleeping, and REM sleep may foster the development of the brain before birth (Rurak et al., 2011; Uhlhaas et al., 2010). In some studies, animals or people have been deprived of REM sleep. Under deprivation of REM sleep, animals and people learn more slowly and forget what they have learned more quickly. REM-sleep-deprived people and animals tend to show *REM rebound,* meaning that they spend more time in REM sleep during subsequent sleep periods. They "catch up."

4-2d DREAMS

A few facts about dreams (Bulkeley, 2013):

▶ Artists are more likely than other people to have nightmares.

▶ Children are more likely than adults to dream about animals.

▶ Younger people are more likely to have dreams in which they know they are dreaming.

▶ Non-religious people have more dreams than highly religious people.

Dreams produce imagery in the absence of external stimulation and can seem real. In college, I often had "anxiety dreams" the night before a test. I would dream that I had taken the test and it was all over. (Imagine my disappointment when I awakened and realized the test still lay before me!)

Many college students report anxiety dreams of one kind or another (Nielsen et al., 2003):

▶ 82% dream of being chased

▶ 74% dream of falling

▶ 60% dream that they are too late to do something such as catch a train

On the other hand:

▶ 77% dream of sex

▶ 48% dream of flying (which Sigmund Freud believed symbolized sexual intercourse)

▶ 37% dream of being a child again (ah, to be free?)

The psychoanalyst Sigmund Freud, as a matter of fact, believed that nearly all dreams had something to do with sex—a view with which most modern psychologists, as we will see, disagree (Hobson, 2013).

In any event, dreams are most likely to be vivid during REM sleep, whereas images are vaguer and more fleeting during NREM sleep. If you sleep for eight hours and undergo five sleep cycles, you may have five dreams. Dreams may compress time the way a movie does, by skipping hours or days to a future time, but the actual action tends to take place in "real time." Fifteen minutes of events fills about 15 minutes of dreaming. Furthermore, your dream theater is quite flexible. You can dream in black and white or in full color.

Some dreams are nightmares. We saw that one common nightmare is that you are falling. Another is that you are trying to run away from a threat but cannot gain your footing or coordinate your legs. Nightmares, like most pleasant dreams, are products of REM sleep.

There are many theories about why we dream what we dream. Some are psychological, and others are more biologically oriented.

DREAMS AS "THE RESIDUE OF THE DAY" You may recall dreams involving fantastic adventures, but most dreams involve memories of the activities and problems of the day (Hobson, 2013). If we are preoccupied with illness or death, sexual or aggressive urges, or moral dilemmas, we are likely to dream about them. The characters in our dreams are more likely to be friends and neighbors than spies, monsters, and princes—subjects that have been referred to, poetically, as "the residue of the day."

Traumatic events, however, can spawn nightmares, as reported by veterans who fought in Iraq and Afghanistan and in the aftermath of the terrorist attacks on the World Trade Center and Pentagon in 2001 (Raskind et al., 2013). People with frequent nightmares are also more likely than others to have anxiety, depression, and other psychological problems (Roberts et al., 2009).

DREAMS AS THE EXPRESSION OF UNCONSCIOUS DESIRES In the Disney film *Cinderella*, a song lyric goes, "A dream is a wish your heart makes." Freud, as noted, theorized that dreams reflect unconscious wishes and urges. He argued that dreams express impulses we would censor during the day, although researchers find no evidence for this assertion. Moreover, he said that the content of dreams is symbolic of unconscious fantasized objects such as the genitals. In his method of psychoanalysis, Freud would interpret his clients' dreams.

activation–synthesis model
the view that dreams reflect activation of cognitive activity by the reticular formation and synthesis of this activity into a pattern

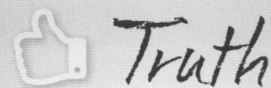

Although Freud suggested that we act out forbidden fantasies in our dreams, research does not find evidence for this view.

THE ACTIVATION–SYNTHESIS MODEL OF DREAMS
There are also biological views of the "meanings" of dreams. According to the **activation–synthesis model**, acetylcholine (a neurotransmitter) and the pons (see Figure 2.10 on page 50) stimulate responses that lead to dreaming (Hobson, 2003, 2009; Stuart & Conduit, 2009). One is *activation* of the reticular formation, which arouses us, but not to waking. During the waking state, firing of these cells is linked to movement, particularly the movements in walking, running, and other physical acts. But during REM sleep, neurotransmitters tend to inhibit activity so we usually do not thrash about as we dream (Stuart & Conduit, 2009). In this way, we save ourselves—and our bed partners—some wear and tear. But the eye muscles are stimulated and show the REM activity associated with dreaming. The reticular formation also stimulates parts of the cortex involved in memory. The cortex then *synthesizes*, or puts together, these sources of stimulation to yield the stuff of dreams. Yet research with the PET scan shows that the frontal lobes of the brain, which seem to be where we make sense of experience, are relatively inactive during sleep (Wade, 1998). Dreams are therefore more likely to be emotionally gripping than coherent in plot.

Because recent events are most likely to be reverberating in our brains, we are most likely to dream about them. With the brain cut off from the world outside, learning experiences and memories are replayed and consolidated during sleep (Siegel, 2009). It's useful to get a night of sleep between studying and test-taking, if you can.

4-2e SLEEP DISORDERS

Although nightmares are unpleasant, they do not qualify as sleep disorders. The term *sleep disorder* is reserved for other problems that can seriously interfere with our functioning. Some sleep disorders, like insomnia, are all too familiar, experienced by at least half of American adults. Others, like apnea (pauses in

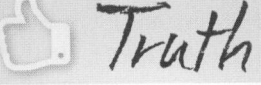

Many dreams involve memories of the day gone by, or, poetically, 'the residue of the day.'

breathing) affect fewer than 10% of us. In this section we discuss insomnia and less common sleep disorders: narcolepsy, apnea, sleep terrors, bedwetting, and sleepwalking.

INSOMNIA It appears that about 40% of American adults are affected by insomnia in any given year (LeBlanc et al., 2009). Older adults are more likely than younger adults to have insomnia because of a greater incidence of poor health and pain—factors that may make it more difficult to get comfortable in bed. Trying to get to sleep can compound sleep problems by creating autonomic activity and muscle tension. You cannot force or will yourself to go to sleep. You can only set the stage for sleep by relaxing when you are tired.

NARCOLEPSY A person with **narcolepsy** falls asleep suddenly. Narcolepsy afflicts as many as 100,000 people in the United States and seems to run in families. The "sleep attack" may last 15 minutes or so, after which the person feels refreshed. Nevertheless, sleep attacks are dangerous and upsetting. They can occur while driving or working with sharp tools. They may be accompanied by the collapse of muscle groups or the entire body—a condition called *sleep paralysis*. In sleep paralysis, the person cannot move during the transition from consciousness to sleep, and hallucinations (as of a person or object sitting on the chest) occur.

narcolepsy a "sleep attack" in which a person falls asleep suddenly and irresistibly

👍 *Truth*

T F   Insomnia can be caused by trying too hard to fall asleep.

It is true that many people do have insomnia because they try too hard to get to sleep at night. Trying to get to sleep creates anxiety, which then prevents them from sleeping.

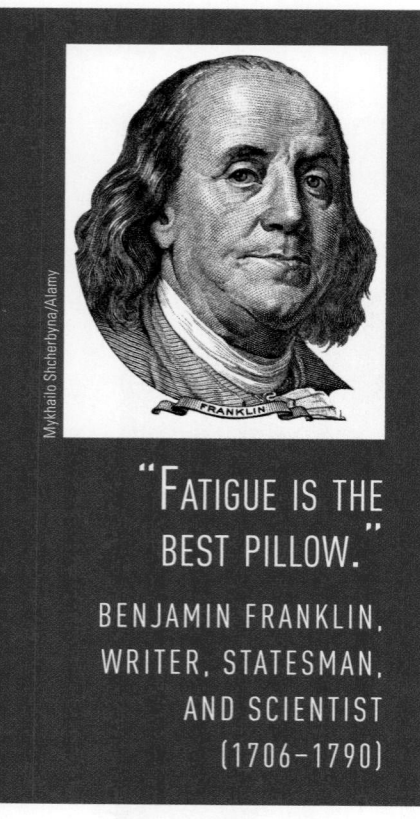

"FATIGUE IS THE BEST PILLOW."

BENJAMIN FRANKLIN, WRITER, STATESMAN, AND SCIENTIST (1706–1790)

Narcolepsy is thought to be a disorder of REM-sleep functioning. Stimulants and antidepressant drugs have helped many people with the problem (Mignot, 2012).

SLEEP APNEA Sleep **apnea** is a dangerous sleep disorder in which the air passages are obstructed. People with apnea stop breathing periodically, up to several hundred times per night. Obstruction may cause the sleeper to sit up and gasp for air before falling back asleep. People with sleep apnea are stimulated nearly, but not quite, to waking by the buildup of carbon dioxide. Sleep apnea is associated with obesity and chronic snoring. It can lead to high blood pressure, heart attacks, and strokes (Sekizuka et al., 2010).

Causes of sleep apnea include anatomical deformities that clog the air passageways, such as a thick palate, and problems in the breathing centers in the brain. Sleep apnea is treated by such measures as weight loss, surgery, and continuous positive airway pressure (CPAP), which is supplied by a mask that provides air pressure that keeps the airway open during sleep.

DEEP-SLEEP DISORDERS: SLEEP TERRORS, BEDWETTING, AND SLEEPWALKING Sleep terrors, bedwetting, and sleepwalking all occur during deep (stage 3 or 4) sleep. They are more common among children and may reflect immaturity of the nervous system (Haupt et al., 2013; Nir & Tononi, 2010). **Sleep terrors** are similar to, but more severe than, nightmares, which occur during REM sleep. Sleep terrors usually occur during the first two sleep cycles of the night, whereas nightmares are more likely to occur toward morning.

sleep apnea temporary absence or cessation of breathing while sleeping

sleep terrors frightening, dreamlike experiences that occur during the deepest stage of NREM sleep; nightmares, in contrast, occur during REM sleep

Fiction 👎

T F It is dangerous to awaken a sleepwalker.

Contrary to myth, it is not true that sleepwalkers become violent if they are awakened. However, they may be confused and upset.

Experiencing a surge in the heart and respiration rates, the person may suddenly sit up, talk incoherently, and thrash about. He or she is never fully awake, returns to sleep, and may recall a vague image as of someone pressing on his or her chest. (Memories of nightmares tend to be more detailed.) Sleep terrors are often decreased by a minor tranquilizer at bedtime, which reduces the amount of time spent in stage 4 sleep.

Bedwetting probably reflects immaturity of the nervous system. In most cases, it resolves itself before adolescence, often by age eight. Methods that condition children to awaken when they are about to urinate have been helpful (Jackson, 2009). The drug imipramine often helps. Sometimes all that is needed is reassurance that no one is to blame for bedwetting and that most children outgrow it.

Perhaps half of children talk in their sleep now and then. Adults occasionally do so, too. Surveys suggest that some 7% to 15% of children walk in their sleep—a behavior pattern that is technically termed *somnambulism* (Arya & Jain, 2013; Cotton & Richdale, 2010). Only 2% of a random sample of nearly 5,000 people aged 15 to 100 did so (Ohayon et al., 1999). Sleepwalkers may roam about nightly while their parents fret about possible accidents. Sleepwalkers typically do not remember their excursions, although they may respond to questions while they are up and about. Mild tranquilizers and maturity typically put an end to it.

4-3 ALTERING CONSCIOUSNESS: HYPNOSIS, MEDITATION, AND BIOFEEDBACK

Perhaps you have watched a fellow student try to place a friend in a "trance" after reading a book on hypnosis. Or perhaps you have seen an audience member hypnotized in a nightclub act. If so, chances are the person acted as if he or she had returned to childhood, imagined that a snake was about to have a nip, or lay rigid between two chairs for a while. In this section we deal with three altered states of consciousness: hypnosis, meditation, and biofeedback. Each of these is an *altered state of consciousness* because they involve focusing on stimuli that are not common parts of our daily lives.

4-3a HYPNOSIS

Of these altered states, the one we hear of most is hypnosis. The word **hypnosis** is derived from the Greek word for *sleep*. It is an altered state of consciousness in which people are suggestible and behave as though they are in a trance. Modern hypnosis evolves from the ideas of Franz Mesmer in the 18th century. Mesmer asserted that everything in the universe was connected by forms of magnetism—which actually may not be far off the mark. However, he also claimed that people, too, could be drawn to one another by "animal magnetism." Not so. Mesmer used bizarre props to bring people under his "spell" and managed a respectable cure rate for minor ailments. Scientists now attribute his successes to the placebo effect, not animal magnetism.

Today, hypnotism is more than a nightclub act. It is also used as an anesthetic in dentistry, childbirth, and medical procedures. Some psychologists use hypnosis to help clients reduce anxiety, overcome fears, or lessen the perception of chronic pain. A study with 241 surgery patients shows how hypnosis can help people deal with pain and anxiety. The patients underwent procedures that used only local anesthetics (Lang et al., 2000). They could use as much pain medication as they wished. Patients who were hypnotized needed less additional pain medication and experienced less anxiety as measured by blood pressure and heart rate. The hypnotized patients focused on pleasant imagery rather than the surgery.

Hypnosis as an aid in relaxation training also helps people cope with stress and enhance the functioning of their immune systems (Accardi et al., 2014; Kiecolt-Glaser et al., 2001). Research also shows that hypnosis can be a useful supplement to other forms of therapy, especially in helping people control their weight and stop smoking (Tahiri et al., 2013; Tonnesen, 2009). Police may use hypnosis to prompt the memories of witnesses.

The state of consciousness called the *hypnotic trance* has traditionally been induced by asking people to narrow their attention to a small light, a spot on the wall, an object held by the hypnotist, or the hypnotist's voice. The hypnotist usually suggests that the person's limbs are becoming warm, heavy, and relaxed. People may also be told that they are

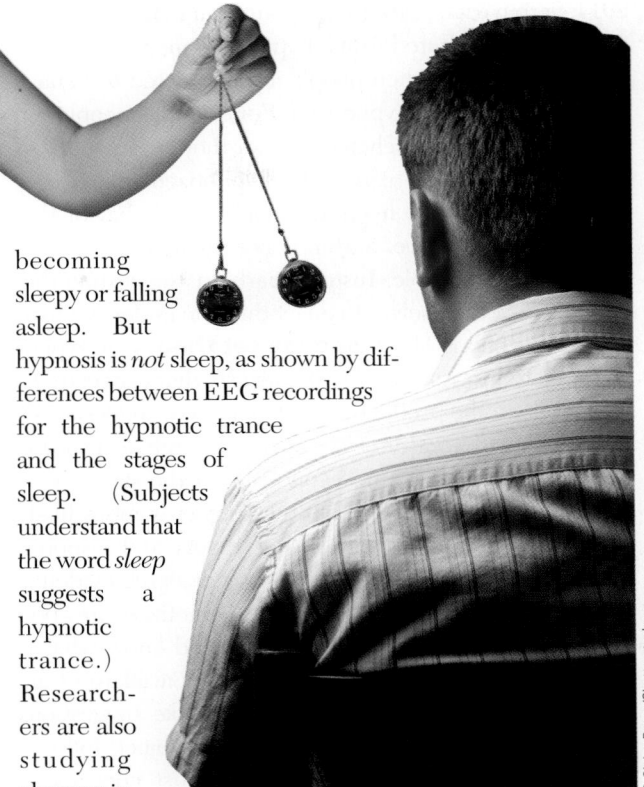

© Sinisa Botas/Shutterstock.com

becoming sleepy or falling asleep. But hypnosis is *not* sleep, as shown by differences between EEG recordings for the hypnotic trance and the stages of sleep. (Subjects understand that the word *sleep* suggests a hypnotic trance.) Researchers are also studying changes in the brain that result from hypnosis. For example, Rainville and his colleagues (2002) used PET scans on people being hypnotized and found that mental absorption and mental relaxation are associated with changes in blood flow in the cerebral cortex (absorption) and parts of the brain involved in arousal and attention (relaxation).

People who are easily hypnotized are said to have *hypnotic suggestibility.* Part of "suggestibility" is knowledge of what is expected during the "trance state." Generally speaking, suggestible people are prone to fantasy and want to cooperate with the hypnotist (Accardi et al., 2014; Dienes & Hutton, 2013). As a result, they pay close attention to the instructions.

EXPLAINING HYPNOSIS Hypnotism is no longer explained in terms of animal magnetism, but others have offered explanations. According to Freud, hypnotized adults permit themselves to return to childish modes of responding that emphasize fantasy and impulse rather than fact and logic. Modern views of hypnosis are quite different.

Theodore Sarbin offers a **role theory** view of hypnosis (Accardi et al.,

> **hypnosis** an altered state of consciousness in which people are highly suggestible and behave as though they are in a trance
>
> **role theory** a theory that explains hypnotic events in terms of the person's ability to act *as though* he or she were hypnotized

2014; Sarbin & Coe, 1972). He points out that the changes in behavior attributed to the hypnotic trance can be successfully imitated when people are instructed to behave *as though* they were hypnotized. For example, people can lie rigid between two chairs whether they are hypnotized or not. Also, people cannot be hypnotized unless they are familiar with the hypnotic "role"—the behavior that constitutes the trance. Sarbin is not saying that subjects *fake* the hypnotic role. Instead, Sarbin is suggesting that people *allow* themselves to enact this role under the hypnotist's directions. The **response set theory** of hypnosis is related to role theory. It suggests that expectations play a role in the production of experiences suggested by the hypnotist (Accardi et al., 2014). A positive response to each suggestion of the hypnotist sets the stage—creates a *response set*—in which the subject is more likely to follow further suggestions. Role theory and response set theory appear to be supported by research evidence that "suggestible" people want to be hypnotized, are good role players, have vivid imaginations, and know what is expected of them (Accardi et al., 2014; Cavallaro et al., 2010). When the hypnotist is able to make suggestions that the subject follows, the hypnotist gets his or her "foot in the door," increasing the likelihood that the subject will follow additional suggestions. The fact that the behaviors shown by hypnotized people can be mimicked by people who know what is expected of them means that we need not resort to the concept of the "hypnotic trance"—an unusual and mystifying altered state of awareness—to explain hypnotic events.

response set theory the view that response expectancies play a key role in the production of the experiences suggested by the hypnotist

transcendental meditation (TM) the simplified form of meditation brought to the United States by the Maharishi Mahesh Yogi and used as a method for coping with stress

mindfulness meditation (MM) a form of meditation that provides clients with techniques they can use to focus on the present moment rather than ruminate about problems

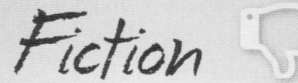

T **F** You can be hypnotized against your will.

It is extremely unlikely that someone could be hypnotized against his or her will. Becoming hypnotized requires suggestibility and cooperation on the part of the subject.

Let's now consider two other altered states of consciousness that involve different ways of focusing our attention: meditation and biofeedback.

4-3b MEDITATION

The dictionary defines *meditation* as the act or process of thinking. But the concept usually suggests thinking deeply about the universe or about one's place in the world, often within a spiritual context. As the term is commonly used by psychologists, however, meditation refers to various ways of focusing one's consciousness to alter one's relationship to the world. In this use, ironically, *meditation* can also refer to a process by which people seem to suspend thinking and allow the world to fade away.

The kinds of meditation that psychologists and other kinds of helping professionals speak of are not the first definition you find in the dictionary. Rather, they tend to refer to rituals, exercises, even passive observation—activities that alter the normal relationship between the person and the environment. They are methods of suspending problem solving, planning, worries, and awareness of the events of the day. These methods alter consciousness—the normal focus of attention—and help people cope with stress by inducing feelings of relaxation.

One common form of meditation, **transcendental meditation (TM)**, was brought to the United States by the Maharishi Mahesh Yogi in 1959. People practice TM by concentrating on *mantras*—words or sounds that are claimed to help the person achieve an altered state of consciousness. TM has some goals that cannot be assessed scientifically, such as expanding consciousness to encompass spiritual experiences, but there are also measurable goals, such as reducing anxiety and lowering blood pressure. For example, Herbert Benson (1975) found that TM lowered heart and respiration rates and produced what he labeled a *relaxation response* (Taylor et al., 2010). The blood pressure of people with hypertension—a risk factor in cardiovascular disease—decreased. Meditators produced more frequent alpha waves—brain waves associated with feelings of relaxation. Meditation has also been shown to increase nighttime concentrations of the hormone melatonin, which helps people get to sleep (Nagendra et al., 2012). Research in brain imaging has shown that meditation activates neural structures involved in attention and control of the autonomic nervous system as well, helping produce feelings of relaxation (Rubia, 2009). Psychologist Jon Kabat-Zinn, founder of the Stress Reduction Clinic at the University of Massachusetts Medical Center, has promoted the use of **mindfulness meditation (MM)** in cognitive and behavior therapy. MM, as opposed to TM, makes no pretense of achieving spiritual goals. Instead, MM provides clients with mantra-like techniques they can use to focus on the present moment rather than ruminate about problems. MM holds promise for helping clients cope with problems such as anxiety as well as reducing stress (Hoge et al., 2013).

4-3c BIOFEEDBACK

Psychologist Neal E. Miller (1909–2002) trained laboratory rats to increase or decrease their heart rates. How? His procedure was simple but ingenious. As discovered by James Olds and Peter Milner (1954), there is a "pleasure center" in the rat's hypothalamus. A small burst of electricity in this center is strongly reinforcing: Rats learn to do what they can, such as pressing a lever, to obtain this "reward."

Neal Miller (1969) implanted electrodes in the rats' pleasure centers. Some rats were then given a burst of electricity whenever their heart rates happened to increase. Other rats received the burst when their heart rates decreased. After a 90-minute training session, the rats learned to alter their heart rates by as much as 20% in the direction for which they had been rewarded. Miller's research was an example of **biofeedback training (BFT)**. Biofeedback is a system that provides, or "feeds back," information about a bodily function. Miller used electrical stimulation of the brain to feed back information to rats when they had engaged in a targeted bodily response—in this case, raised or lowered their heart rates.

Similarly, people have learned to change some bodily functions voluntarily, including heart rate, that were once considered beyond conscious control. However, electrodes are not implanted in people's brains. Rather, people hear a "blip" or receive some other signal that informs them the targeted response is being displayed.

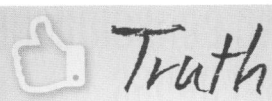

It is true that through biofeedback training, you can teach a rat to raise or lower its heart rate. (This does not mean that the rat "knows" it is changing its heart rate.)

BFT is used in many ways, including helping people combat stress, tension, and anxiety. For example, people can learn to emit alpha waves through EEG feedback and feel more relaxed. The psychologist asks the person to "make the blip go faster." A blip may blink faster whenever alpha waves are being emitted. An **electromyograph (EMG)** monitors muscle tension. The EMG can be used to help people become more aware of muscle tension in the forehead, fingers, and elsewhere and to learn to lower tension, thus decreasing the discomfort and incidence of muscle-tension headaches (Sun-Edelstein & Mauskop, 2012). Through the use of other instruments, people have learned to lower their heart rates, blood pressure, and sweating (Greenhalgh et al., 2010). Biofeedback is widely used by sports psychologists to teach athletes how to relax muscle groups that are unessential to the task at hand so that the athletes can control anxiety and tension.

biofeedback training (BFT) the systematic feeding back to an organism information about a bodily function so that the organism can gain control of that function

electromyograph (EMG) an instrument that measures muscle tension

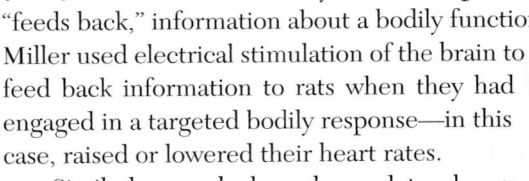

Jose Luis Pelaez Inc/Jupiterimages

4-4 ALTERING CONSCIOUSNESS THROUGH DRUGS

The world is a supermarket of **psychoactive substances**, or drugs. The United States is flooded with drugs that distort perceptions and change mood—drugs that take you up, let you down, and move you across town. Some of these drugs are legal, others illegal. Some are used recreationally, others medically. Some are safe if used correctly and dangerous if they are not. Some people use drugs because their friends do or because their parents tell them not to. Some are seeking pleasure; others are seeking inner truth or escape.

Young people often become involved with drugs that impair their ability to learn at school and are connected with reckless behavior (Pani et al., 2010). Alcohol is the most popular drug on high school and college campuses (Johnston et al., 2013a, 2013b). Nearly half of college students have smoked marijuana (Johnston et al., 2013b). Many Americans take **depressants** to get to sleep at night and **stimulants** to get going in the morning. Cocaine was once a toy of the well-to-do, but price breaks have brought it into the lockers of high school students.

4-4a SUBSTANCE USE AND SUBSTANCE USE DISORDERS

Where does substance use end and a **substance use disorder** begin? Most psychologists use the *Diagnostic and Statistical Manual of Mental Disorders* of the American Psychiatric Association (2013) in defining substance use disorders. The manual is now in its fifth edition and usually referred to simply as the DSM-5. The DSM-5 defines a **substance use disorder** in terms of behavioral, cognitive, and biological symptoms or factors. With repeated use of many substances, the DSM-5 notes that there are changes in "brain circuitry" that are connected with impaired

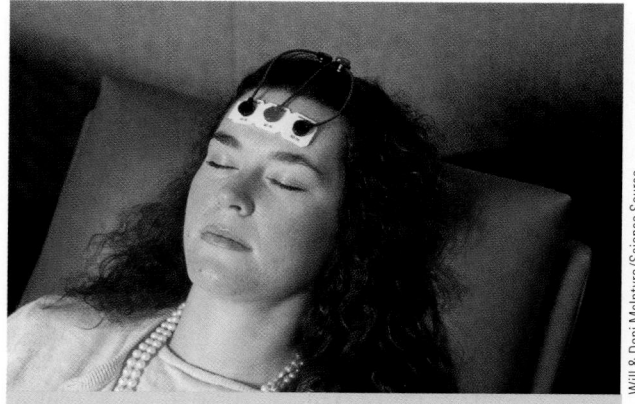

Will & Deni McIntyre/Science Source

Biofeedback is a system that provides, or "feeds back," information about a bodily function to an organism. Through biofeedback training, people have learned to gain voluntary control over a number of functions that are normally automatic, such as heart rate and blood pressure.

control over use of the substance, social problems, risky behavior (such as reckless driving or "unprotected" sex), and biological factors suggestive of addiction. People who miss school or work because they are drunk or are "sleeping it off," might have a substance use disorder. Excessive drinking may suggest a disorder because it is associated with health problems such as heart failure, traffic accidents, and interpersonal problems such as rape (McCauley et al., 2010; Zagrosek et al., 2010).

A substance use disorder is characterized by loss of control over one's use of the substance. People may organize their lives around getting and using a substance. Biological symptoms suggestive of physical addiction include tolerance, withdrawal symptoms, or both. **Tolerance** is the body's habituation to a substance so that, with regular usage, higher doses are needed to achieve similar effects. There is also an **abstinence syndrome**—that is, a characteristic group of withdrawal symptoms—when the level of usage of a substance suddenly drops off. Withdrawal symptoms for alcohol include anxiety, tremors, restlessness, rapid pulse, and high blood pressure.

When going without a substance, people with substance use disorders experience *cravings*—intense urges to use the drug, typically accompanied by signs of anxiety such as shakiness, rapid pulse, and sweating. People withdrawing from chronic alcohol use

psychoactive substances drugs that have psychological effects such as stimulation or distortion of perceptions

depressant a drug that lowers the rate of activity of the nervous system

stimulant a drug that increases activity of the nervous system

substance use disorder a problem characterized by loss of control over usage, social impairment, risky use, and tolerance and withdrawal symptoms

tolerance habituation to a drug, with the result that increasingly higher doses of the drug are needed to achieve similar effects

abstinence syndrome a characteristic cluster of withdrawal symptoms that results from sudden decease in an addictive drug's level of usage

may experience *delirium tremens* ("the DTs"), with heavy sweating, restlessness, disorientation, and frightening hallucinations—often of crawling animals.

CAUSAL FACTORS IN SUBSTANCE USE DISORDERS Substance use usually begins with experimental use in adolescence (Marlatt, 2010; Schulte et al., 2009). People experiment with drugs for various reasons, including curiosity, conformity to peer pressure, parental use, rebelliousness, escape from boredom or pressure, or to attain excitement and pleasure (T. T. Clark, 2010; Lindgren et al., 2010).

Social–cognitive theorists suggest that people often try alcohol and tranquilizers such as Valium (the generic name is diazepam) on the basis of a recommendation or observation of others. Use of a substance may be reinforced by peers or by the drug's positive effects on mood and its reduction of anxiety, fear, and stress (McCarty et al., 2012; Wolitzky-Tayloer et al., 2012). Many people use drugs as self-medication for anxiety,

depression, and even low self-esteem. Parents who use drugs may increase their children's knowledge of drugs. They also, in effect, show their children when to use them—for example, by drinking alcohol to cope with tension or to lessen the anxiety associated with meeting people at parties and other get-togethers (Power et al., 2005).

People may have a genetic predisposition toward physiological dependence on various substances, including alcohol, opioids, cocaine, and nicotine (Agrawal et al., 2010; Clarke et al., 2013; Kuo et al., 2010). For example, the biological children of alcoholics who are reared by adoptive parents seem more likely to develop alcohol-related problems than the natural children of the adoptive parents. An inherited tendency toward alcoholism may involve greater sensitivity to alcohol (i.e., greater enjoyment of it) and greater tolerance of it (Radcliffe et al., 2009). College students with alcoholic parents, exhibit better muscular control and visual-motor coordination when they drink than do college students whose parents are not alcoholics. They also feel less intoxicated when they drink (Correia et al., 2012).

Now that we have learned about substance abuse and dependence, let's consider different kinds of psychoactive drugs. Some are depressants, others stimulants, and still others hallucinogens.

4-4b DEPRESSANTS

Depressant drugs generally act by slowing the activity of the central nervous system. There are also effects specific to each depressant drug. In this section, we consider the effects of alcohol, opiates, and barbiturates.

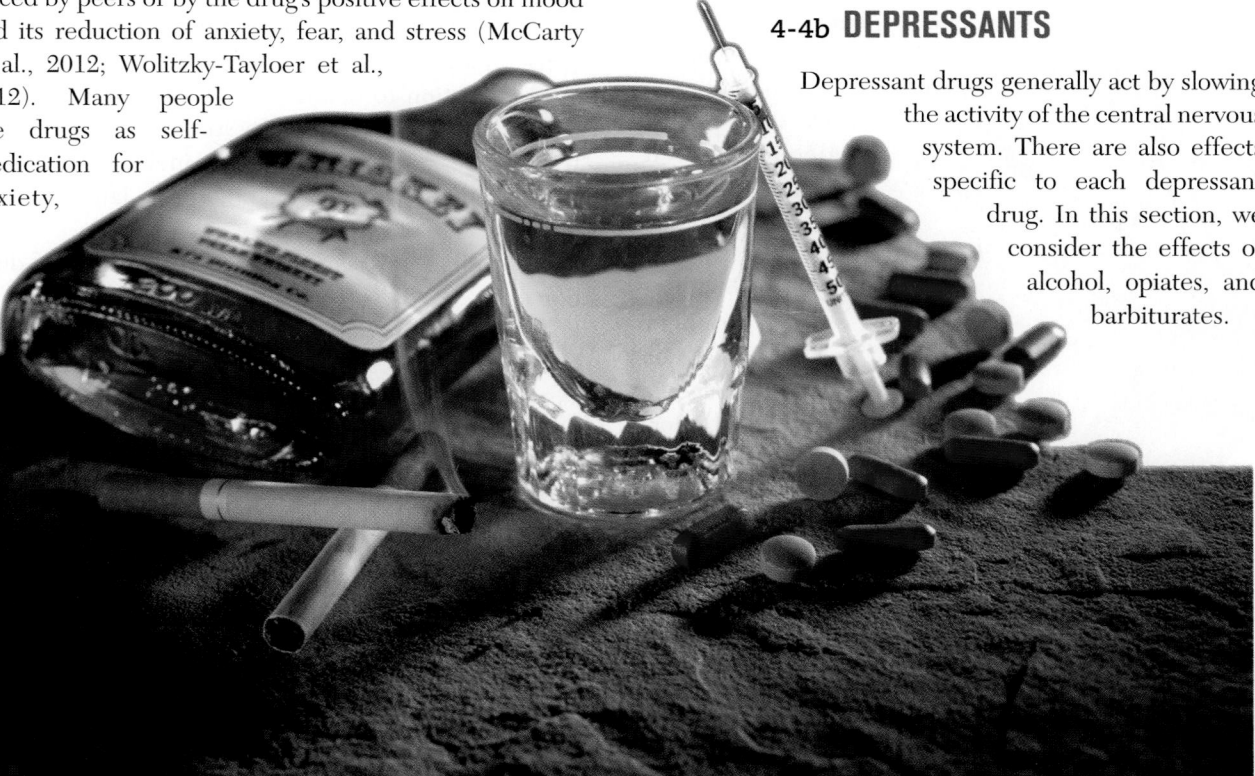

Noble Stock/Jupiterimages

ALCOHOL No drug has meant so much and to so many as alcohol. Alcohol is our dinnertime relaxant, our bedtime sedative, and our social facilitator at cocktail parties. We use alcohol to celebrate holy days, applaud our accomplishments, and express joyous wishes. The young assert their maturity with alcohol. Alcohol is used at least occasionally by the majority of high school and college students (Johnston et al., 2013). Alcohol even kills germs on surface wounds.

People use alcohol like a Swiss Army knife. It does it all. It is the all-purpose medicine you can buy without a prescription. It is the relief from anxiety, depression, or loneliness that you can swallow in public without criticism or stigma. A man who takes a Valium tablet may look weak. A man who downs a bottle of beer may be perceived as "macho."

But the army knife also has a sharp blade. No drug has been so abused as alcohol. Ten million to 20 million Americans are alcoholics. In contrast, 750,000 to 1 million use heroin regularly, and about 800,000 use cocaine regularly (Johnston et al., 2013). Excessive drinking has been linked to lower productivity, loss of employment, and downward movement in social status. Yet, half of all Americans use alcohol regularly.

What about alcohol on campus? About four college students die *each day* from alcohol-related causes (Correia et al., 2012). *Binge drinking*—defined as having five or more drinks in a row for a male, or four or more for a female—is connected with aggressive behavior, poor grades, sexual promiscuity, and accidents (McCauley et al., 2010; Randolph et al., 2009; Swartout &

About four college students die from alcohol-related causes every day.

Alcohol can be thought of as the Swiss Army Knife of psychoactive substances.

White, 2010). Nevertheless, nearly half of college men and three in ten college women binge at least twice a month (Johnston et al., 2010). The media pay more attention to deaths due to heroin and cocaine overdoses, but more college students die each year from causes related to drinking, including accidents and overdoses (Correia et al., 2012; Hustad et al., 2010).

The effects of alcohol vary with the dose and duration of use. Low doses may be stimulating because alcohol dilates blood vessels, which ferry sugar through the body. Higher doses have a sedative effect, which is why alcohol is classified as a depressant. Alcohol relaxes people and deadens minor aches and pains. Alcohol impairs cognitive functioning, slurs the speech, and impairs coordination.

Alcohol lowers inhibitions. Drinkers may do things they would not do if they were sober, such as having unprotected sex (Collins et al., 2010; Tumwesigye et al., 2012). When drunk, people may be less able to foresee the consequences of their behavior. They may also be less likely to summon up their moral beliefs. Then, too, alcohol induces feelings of elation and euphoria that may wash away doubts. Alcohol is also associated with a liberated social role in our culture. Drinkers may place the blame on alcohol ("It's the alcohol, not me"), even though they choose to drink.

Men are more likely than women to become alcoholics. Why? A cultural explanation is that tighter social constraints are usually placed on women. A biological explanation is that alcohol hits women harder, discouraging them from overindulging. If you have the impression that alcohol "goes to women's heads" more quickly than to men's, you are probably right. Women seem more affected by alcohol because they have less of an enzyme—*aldehyde dehydrogenase*—that metabolizes alcohol in the stomach than men do (Petrosino et al., 2014; Shimizu et al., 2012). Thus, alcohol reaches women's bloodstream and brain relatively intact.

Levels of aldehyde dehydrogenase are also associated with levels of drinking in some ethnic groups. Asians and Asian Americans, who have lower levels of aldehyde dehydrogenase than Europeans do, are more likely than Europeans and European Americans to show a "flushing response" to alcohol, as evidenced by redness of the face,

Blend Images Photography/Veer

Women have less of an enzyme—aldehyde dehydrogenase—that metabolizes alcohol in the stomach than women do. Therefore, alcohol "goes to women's heads" more quickly. Asians also have less of the enzyme than Europeans do, placing them at greater risk of a "flushing response" when they drink.

rapid heart rate, dizziness, and headaches (Kawano, 2010). Such sensitivity to alcohol may inhibit immoderate drinking among Asian Americans as well as women in general.

Regardless of how or why one starts drinking, regular drinking can lead to physiological dependence. People are then motivated to drink to avoid withdrawal symptoms. Still, even when alcoholics have "dried out"—withdrawn from alcohol—many return to drinking. Perhaps they still want to use alcohol as a way of coping with stress or as an excuse for failure.

OPIATES Opiates are a group of **narcotics** derived from the opium poppy, from which they obtain their name. The ancient Sumerians gave the opium poppy its

opiates a group of narcotics derived from the opium poppy that provide a euphoric rush and depress the nervous system

narcotics drugs used to relieve pain and induce sleep; the term is usually reserved for opiates

name: It means "plant of joy." **Opioids** are similar in chemical structure but made in a laboratory. Opiates include morphine, heroin, codeine, Demerol, and similar drugs. The major medical application of opiates is relief from pain.

Heroin can provide a strong euphoric "rush." Users claim that it is so pleasurable it can eradicate thoughts of food or sex. High doses can cause drowsiness and stupor, alter time perception, and impair judgment. With regular use of opiates, the brain stops producing neurotransmitters that are chemically similar to opiates—the pain-relieving endorphins.

As a result, people can become physiologically dependent on opiates, such that going without them can be agonizing. Withdrawal syndromes may begin with flu-like symptoms and progress through tremors, cramps, chills alternating with sweating, rapid pulse, high blood pressure, insomnia, vomiting, and diarrhea. This information seems to have gotten through to high school students; most disapprove of using heroin (Johnston et al., 2010).

Heroin was once used as a cure for addiction to morphine. Now we have methadone, a synthetic opioid that is used to treat physiological dependence on heroin. Methadone is slower acting than heroin and does not provide the thrilling rush, but it does prevent withdrawal symptoms.

BARBITURATES Barbiturates like Nembutal and Seconal are depressants with several medical uses, including relief from anxiety, tension, and pain, and treatment of epilepsy, high blood pressure, and insomnia. With regular use, barbiturates lead rapidly to physiological and psychological dependence. Physicians therefore provide them with caution.

Barbiturates are popular as street drugs because they are relaxing and produce mild euphoria. High doses result in drowsiness, motor impairment, slurred speech, irritability, and poor judgment. A highly physiologically dependent person who is withdrawn abruptly from barbiturates may experience convulsions and die. Because of additive effects, it is dangerous to mix alcohol and other depressants.

opioids chemicals that act on opiate receptors but are not derived from the opium poppy

barbiturate an addictive depressant used to relieve anxiety or induce sleep

amphetamines stimulants derived from *alpha-methyl-beta-phenyl-ethylamine*, a colorless liquid consisting of carbon, hydrogen, and nitrogen

4-4c STIMULANTS

Stimulants increase the activity of the nervous system. Some of their effects

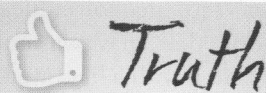

can be positive. For example, amphetamines stimulate cognitive activity and apparently help people control impulses (Wilner et al., 2009). Some stimulants are appealing as street drugs because they contribute to feelings of euphoria and self-confidence. But they also have their risks. In this section, we discuss amphetamines, cocaine, and nicotine.

AMPHETAMINES AND RELATED STIMULANTS Amphetamines are a group of stimulants that were first used by soldiers during World War II to help them stay alert at night. Truck drivers have also used them to drive through the night. Students sometimes use amphetamines for all-night cram sessions, whereas dieters sometimes use them because they reduce hunger.

Amphetamines are often abused for the euphoric rush that high doses can produce. Some people swallow amphetamines in pill form or inject liquid Methedrine, the strongest form, into their veins. As a result, they may stay awake and high for days on end. But such highs must end. People who have been on prolonged highs sometimes "crash," or fall into a deep sleep or depression. Some commit suicide when crashing.

On the other hand, physicians frequently prescribe stimulants in an effort to help hyperactive children control their behavior. Stimulants such as Ritalin and Adderall are widely used to treat attention-deficit/hyperactivity disorder (ADHD) in children. They have been shown to increase the attention span, decrease aggressive and disruptive behavior, and lead to academic gains (May & Kratochvil, 2010; Wanchoo et al., 2010). Why should these stimulants calm children? Hyperactivity may be connected with immaturity of the cerebral cortex, and these drugs may stimulate the cortex to exercise control over more primitive parts of the brain. On the other hand, these stimulants place children—and adults who may continue to use them—at increased risk for sleep disorders and loss of appetite (Meijer et al., 2009).

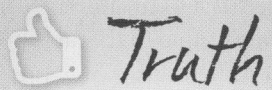

Tolerance for amphetamines develops quickly, and users can become dependent on them, especially when they use them to medicate themselves for depression. Whether these stimulants cause physical addiction has been a subject of controversy. It is widely accepted, however, that high doses can cause restlessness, insomnia, loss of appetite, hallucinations, paranoid delusions (e.g., false ideas that others are eavesdropping or intend them harm), and irritability.

COCAINE Cocaine is derived from coca leaves—the plant from which the soft drink took its name. Do you recall commercials claiming that "Coke adds life"? Given its caffeine and sugar content, "Coke"—Coca-Cola, that is—should provide quite a lift. It is true that Coca-Cola once "added life" through the use of cocaine—legal then but illegal today. But Coca-Cola hasn't been "the real thing" since 1906, when the company stopped using cocaine in its formula.

Cocaine is a stimulant that produces euphoria, reduces hunger, deadens pain, and boosts self-confidence. As shown in Figure 4.4, cocaine apparently works by binding to sites on sending neurons that normally reuptake molecules of the neurotransmitters norepinephrine, dopamine, and serotonin. As a result, molecules of these transmitters remain longer in the synaptic cleft, enhancing their mood-altering effects and producing a "rush." But when cocaine levels drop, lower absorption of neurotransmitters by receiving neurons causes the user's mood to "crash."

Cocaine may be brewed from coca leaves as a "tea," snorted in powder form, or injected in liquid form. Repeated snorting constricts blood vessels in the nose, drying the skin and sometimes exposing cartilage and perforating the nasal septum. These problems require cosmetic surgery. The potent cocaine derivatives known

FIG.4.4 HOW COCAINE PRODUCES EUPHORIA AND WHY PEOPLE "CRASH"

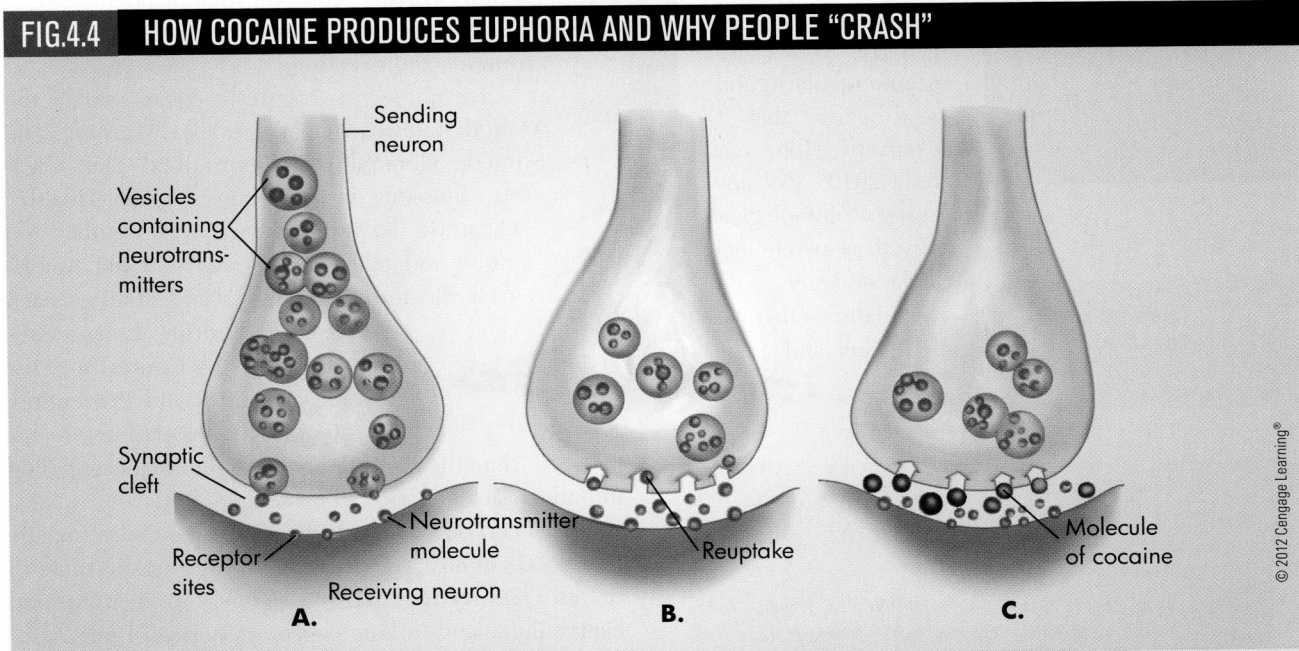

© 2012 Cengage Learning®

A. In the normal functioning of the nervous system, neurotransmitters are released into the synaptic cleft by vesicles in terminal buttons of sending neurons. Many are taken up by receptor sites in receiving neurons. B. In the process called reuptake, sending neurons typically reabsorb excess molecules of neurotransmitters. C. Molecules of cocaine bind to the sites on sending neurons that normally reuptake molecules of neurotransmitters. As a result, molecules of norepinephrine, dopamine, and serotonin remain longer in the synaptic cleft, increasing their typical mood-altering effects and providing a euphoric "rush." When the person stops using cocaine, the lessened absorption of neurotransmitters by receiving neurons causes his or her mood to "crash."

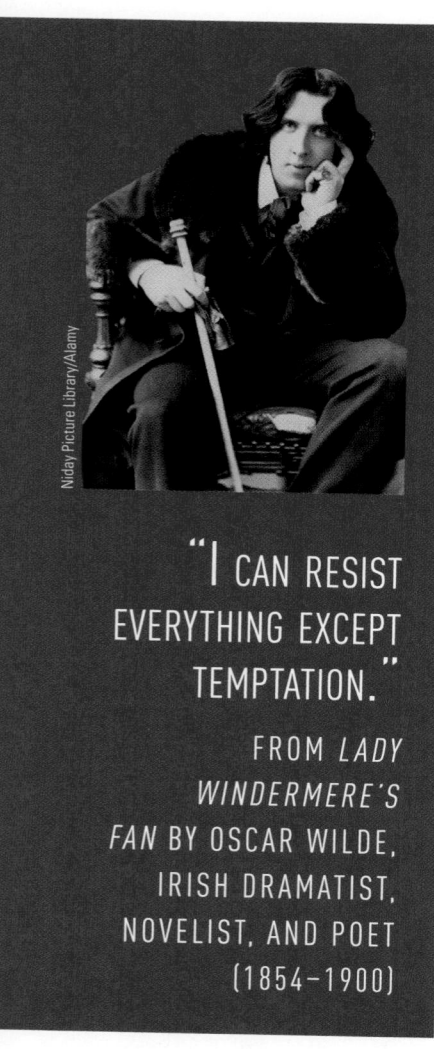

Niday Picture Library/Alamy

hydrocarbons chemical compounds consisting of hydrogen and carbon

as "crack" and "bazooka" are inexpensive because they are unrefined.

Physical dangers include sudden rises in blood pressure, which constricts the coronary arteries and decreases the oxygen supply to the heart, and quickens the heart rate, events that can lead to respiratory and cardiovascular collapse, as in the sudden deaths of some young athletes (Lange & Hillis, 2010). Overdoses can cause restlessness and insomnia, tremors, headaches, nausea, convulsions, hallucinations, and delusions. Use of crack has been connected with strokes. Only about 4% of adolescents aged 15 to 19 use cocaine regularly, and most believe that it is harmful (Johnston et al., 2010). Cocaine causes physiological as well as psychological dependence.

Cocaine—also called *snow* and *coke*—has been used as a local anesthetic since the early 1800s. In 1884 cocaine came to the attention of Sigmund Freud, who used it to fight his own depression and published an article about it: "Song of Praise." Freud's early ardor was tempered when he learned that cocaine is habit-forming and can cause hallucinations and delusions.

NICOTINE Nicotine is the stimulant in tobacco smoke. Nicotine stimulates discharge of the hormone adrenaline and the release of neurotransmitters, including dopamine, acetylcholine, GABA, and endorphins (Herman et al., 2014). Adrenaline creates a burst of autonomic activity that accelerates the heart rate and pours sugar into the blood. Acetylcholine is vital in memory formation, and nicotine appears to enhance memory and attention; improve performance on simple, repetitive tasks; and enhance the mood (Levin, 2013). Although it is a stimulant, because of GABA and endorphins, nicotine has a relaxing effect (Bricker et al., 2012). It depresses the appetite and raises the metabolic rate. Thus, some people smoke cigarettes to control their weight.

Nicotine is the agent that creates physiological dependence on tobacco products (Small et al., 2010). Symptoms of withdrawal include nervousness, drowsiness, loss of energy, headaches, irregular bowel movements, lightheadedness, insomnia, dizziness, cramps, palpitations, tremors, and sweating.

It's no secret. Cigarette packs sold in the United States carry messages like "Warning: The Surgeon General Has Determined That Cigarette Smoking Is Dangerous to Your Health". Cigarette advertising has been banned on radio and television. Nearly 440,000 Americans die from smoking-related illnesses each year (American Lung Association, 2013; Centers for Disease Control and Prevention, 2013). This number is greater than the equivalent of two jumbo jets colliding in midair each day with all passengers lost.

The carbon monoxide in cigarette smoke impairs the blood's ability to carry oxygen, causing shortness of breath. The **hydrocarbons** ("tars") in cigarette and cigar smoke lead to lung cancer (American Lung Association, 2013). Cigarette smoking also stiffens arteries (Campbell et al., 2010) and is linked to death from heart disease, chronic lung and respiratory diseases, and other health problems. Women who smoke show reduced bone density, increasing the risk of fracture of the hip and back (American Lung Association, 2013). Pregnant women who smoke have a higher risk of miscarriage,

ian nolan/Alamy

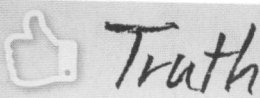

👍 *Truth*

| **T** | F | Coca-Cola once "added life" to its signature drink through the use of a powerful—but now illegal—stimulant. |

It is true that Coca-Cola once numbered cocaine among its ingredients, but it was not illegal at the time. Nor were people yet aware of cocaine's hazards.

What Would Happen If Two Jumbo Jets Crashed Every Day?

Stockbyte/Getty Images

The perils of cigarette smoking are widely known today. One surgeon general declared that cigarette smoking is the chief preventable cause of death in the United States. The number of Americans who die from smoking are comparable to the number of lives that would be lost if two jumbo jets crashed every day. If flying were that unsafe, would the government ground all flights? Would the public continue to make airline reservations?

preterm births, stillborn babies, and children with learning problems (American Lung Association, 2013).

Secondhand smoke—smoke inhaled from other people's tobacco products—is also connected with respiratory illnesses, asthma, and other health problems. Prolonged exposure to secondhand smoke (also referred to as *passive smoking*) during childhood is a risk factor for lung cancer (American Cancer Society, 2013). Because of the effects of second-hand smoke, smoking has been banished from many airplanes, restaurants, and other public spaces.

The incidence of smoking is connected with gender and level of education (see Table 4.1). Better-educated people are less likely to smoke and more likely to quit if they do smoke.

Electronic cigarettes (e-cigarettes) allow smokers to obtain their nicotine without also inhaling cancer-causing hydrocarbons. E-cigarettes looks like cigarettes but have no tobacco. Liquid nicotine is heated into a vapor that users inhale and exhale, but they are not "smoking" because no material is burned. E-cigarettes do keep smokers hooked on nicotine, which is the addictive stimulant found in tobacco smoke. Research trials are underway to determine how safe e-cigarettes are. In the meantime, the numbers of middle and high school students who are using e-cigarettes is mushrooming (Simon, 2013).

secondhand smoke smoke from the tobacco products and exhalations of other people; also referred to as *passive smoking*

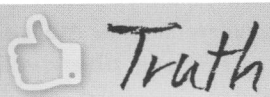 Truth

| T | F | The number of people who die from smoking-related causes is greater than the number lost to motor vehicle accidents, abuse of alcohol and all other drugs, suicide, homicide, and aids *combined*. |

It is true that there are more smoking-related deaths than deaths from motor vehicle accidents, alcohol and drug abuse, suicide, homicide, and AIDS combined.

TABLE 4.1	SNAPSHOT, U.S.A.: GENDER, LEVEL OF EDUCATION, AND SMOKING	
Factor	**Group**	**Percent Who Smoke**
Gender	Women	18.3
	Men	23.1
Level of education	Fewer than 12 years	27.5
	College graduate and above	10.6

Data based on reports of persons aged 18 and above.

Source: Dube, S. R., Asman, K., Malarcher, A., & Carabollo, R. (2009). Cigarette smoking among adults and trends in smoking cessation—United States. *Morbidity and Mortality Weekly Report*, 58(44), 1227–1232.

4-4d HALLUCINOGENICS

Hallucinogenics are so named because they produce hallucinations—that is, sensations and perceptions in the absence of external stimulation. Hallucinogenics may also have additional effects such as relaxation, euphoria, or, in some cases, panic. In this section, we discuss marijuana, LSD, and other hallucinogenics.

MARIJUANA Marijuana is a substance that is produced from the *Cannabis sativa* plant, which grows wild in many parts of the world. Marijuana helps some people relax and can elevate their mood. It also sometimes produces mild hallucinations, which is why we discuss it as a hallucinogen. The major psychedelic substance in marijuana is delta-9-tetrahydrocannabinol, or THC. THC is found in the branches and leaves of the plant, but it is highly concentrated in the resin. *Hashish*, or "hash," is derived from the resin and is more potent than marijuana.

Some users report that marijuana helps them socialize. Moderate to strong intoxication is linked to reports of sharpened perceptions, increases in self-insight, creative thinking, and empathy for others. Time seems to slow. A song might seem to last an hour rather than minutes. There is increased awareness of bodily sensations such as heartbeat. Marijuana users also report that strong intoxication heightens sexual sensations. Visual hallucinations may occur, and strong intoxication may cause disorientation. If the smoker's mood is euphoric, disorientation may be interpreted as "harmony" with the universe, but some users find disorientation threatening and fear they will not regain their identity (Bonn-Miller et al., 2007).

Marijuana carries a number of health risks. For example, it impairs the perceptual–motor coordination used in driving and operating machines. It is connected with an impulsivity that impairs short-term memory and slows learning (Dougherty et al., 2013). Strong intoxication can cause nausea and vomiting. Regular users may experience tolerance and withdrawal symptoms (Gorelick et al., 2013; Gonzalex & Swanson, 2012). Brain-imaging studies suggest that males who begin using marijuana in adolescence may have smaller brains and less gray matter than other males (Ashtari et al., 2009). Both males and females who started marijuana use early may be generally smaller in height and weight than other people. These differences may reflect the effect of marijuana on pituitary and sex hormones.

LSD AND OTHER HALLUCINOGENICS LSD is the abbreviation for lysergic acid diethylamide, a synthetic hallucinogen. Users of "acid" claim that it "expands consciousness" and opens up new worlds to them. Sometimes people say they have achieved great insights while using LSD, but when it wears off they cannot apply or recall them. LSD produces vivid, colorful hallucinations.

Some LSD users have **flashbacks**—distorted perceptions or hallucinations that mimic the LSD "trip" but occur days, weeks, or longer after usage. The experiencing of flashbacks is more technically termed *hallucinogen persisting perception disorder* (HPPD) by the American Psychiatric Association (2013). The psychological explanation of "flashbacks" is that people who would use LSD regularly are also more likely to allow flights of fancy. Yet research with 38 people with HPPD suggests that following extensive use of LSD, the brain may fail to inhibit certain internal sources of vision-like experiences, especially when the eyes are closed (Catts & Catts, 2009).

Other hallucinogens include **mescaline** (derived from the peyote cactus) and **phencyclidine (PCP)**. PCP was developed as an anesthetic and an animal tranquilizer. It goes by the street names "angel dust," "ozone," "wack," and "rocket fuel." The street terms "killer joints" and "crystal super grass" refer to PCP combined with marijuana.

Regular use of hallucinogens may lead to tolerance and psychological dependence, but hallucinogens are not known to create physiological dependence. High doses may impair coordination, cloud judgment, change the mood, and cause frightening hallucinations and paranoid delusions. Table 4.2 summarizes the effects of various psychoactive drugs.

> "AS AN EXAMPLE TO OTHERS, AND NOT THAT I CARE FOR MODERATION MYSELF, IT HAS ALWAYS BEEN MY RULE NEVER TO SMOKE WHEN ASLEEP, AND NEVER TO REFRAIN FROM SMOKING WHEN AWAKE"
>
> MARK TWAIN, AMERICAN AUTHOR AND HUMORIST (1835-1910)

hallucinogenic a substance that causes hallucinations

marijuana the dried vegetable matter of the *Cannabis sativa* plant

LSD lysergic acid diethylamide; a hallucinogen

flashbacks distorted perceptions or hallucinations that occur days or weeks after LSD usage but mimic the LSD experience

mescaline a hallucinogen derived from the mescal (peyote) cactus

phencyclidine (PCP) another hallucinogen whose name is an acronym for its chemical structure

TABLE 4.2   PSYCHOACTIVE DRUGS AND THEIR EFFECTS

Drug	Type	How Taken	Desired Effects	Tolerance	Abstinence Syndrome	Side Effects
Alcohol	Depressant	By mouth	Relaxation, euphoria, lowered inhibitions	Yes	Yes	Impaired coordination, poor judgment, hangover
Opiates	Depressant	Injected, smoked, by mouth	Relaxation, euphoria, relief from anxiety and pain	Yes	Yes	Impaired coordination and mental functioning, drowsiness, lethargy
Barbiturates	Depressant	By mouth, injected	Relaxation, sleep, euphoria, lowered inhibitions	Yes	Yes	Impaired coordination and mental functioning, drowsiness, lethargy
Amphetamines	Stimulant	By mouth, injected	Alertness, euphoria	Yes	?	Restlessness, loss of appetite, psychotic symptoms
Cocaine	Stimulant	By mouth, snorted, injected	Euphoria, self-confidence	Yes	Yes	Restlessness, loss of appetite, convulsions, strokes, psychotic symptoms
Nicotine	Stimulant	By tobacco (smoked, chewed, or sniffed)	Relaxation, stimulation, weight control	Yes	Yes	Cancer, heart disease, lung and respiratory diseases
Marijuana	Hallucinogenic	Smoked, by mouth	Relaxation, perceptual distortions, enhancement of experience	?	?	Impaired coordination and learning, respiratory problems, panic
LSD, Mescaline, PCP	Hallucinogenic	By mouth	Perceptual distortions, vivid hallucinations	Yes	No	Impaired coordination, psychotic symptoms, panic

STUDY TOOLS 4

IN THE BOOK, YOU CAN:

☐ Check your understanding of what you've read with the quizzes that follow.

☐ Rip out the chapter review card at the back of the book to have a summary of the chapter and the key terms handy.

ONLINE AT CENGAGEBRAIN.COM YOU CAN:

☐ Explore dream science or learn about research on addiction in short videos.

☐ Prepare for tests with quizzes

☐ Review the key terms with Flash Cards.

☐ Play games to master concepts.

 **FILL-INS**

Answers can be found in the back of the book, starting on page XXX.

1. *Consciousness* has several meanings, including sensory awareness, the selective aspect of attention, direct inner _____, personal unity, and the waking state.

2. Because EEG patterns during REM sleep resemble those of the waking state, REM sleep is also called _____ sleep.

3. During a typical eight-hour night, we undergo (how many?) _____ trips through the different stages of sleep.

4. According to the _____ –synthesis model, dreams reflect neural activity.

5. Hypnosis is an altered state of consciousness in which people are suggestible and behave as though they are in a _____.

6. In meditation, one focuses on a _____ to alter the normal person-environment relationship.

7. A substance use disorder is characterized by loss of _____ over the use of the substance.

8. Biological or physiological symptoms of a substance use disorder include tolerance and an(a) _____ syndrome when one discontinues use of the substance.

9. _____ is a stimulant that boosts self-confidence but also triggers rises in blood pressure and constricts the coronary arteries.

10. _____ substances distort perceptions.

MULTIPLE CHOICE

1. When we say that we are "conscious of" seeing something or hearing a sound, we are referring to consciousness as
   a. a stream.
   b. a behavioral concept.
   c. the sense of personal unity.
   d. sensory awareness.

2. The notion that animals that are most at risk from predators sleep less is taken from which of the following perspectives?
   a. behaviorist
   b. environmental
   c. evolutionary
   d. developmental

3. Which of the following statements is correct concerning brain waves and the sleep cycle?
   a. Low-frequency brains waves are associated with being awake.
   b. High-frequency brains waves are associated with being awake.
   c. There are no recordable brain waves when we sleep.
   d. It is difficult to tell the difference between "sleep" brain waves and "awake" brain waves.

4. Allegra is said to have hypnotic suggestibility. She is likely to
   a. be prone to fantasy.
   b. have no idea as to what is expected in the trance state.
   c. attend to her own internal feelings rather than the instructions of the hypnotist.
   d. all of the above.

5. In his classic study of transcendental meditation, Benson found that meditation leads to
   a. spiritual awakening.
   b. expanded consciousness.
   c. a relaxation response.
   d. more intense hypnagogic states.

6. Which of the following are children most likely to "outgrow"?
   a. insomnia
   b. bedwetting
   c. sleep apnea
   d. narcolepsy

7. When Clay joined AA in order to stop drinking, he received a pamphlet that described the symptoms of alcohol withdrawal. These included
   a. high blood pressure and rapid pulse.
   b. restlessness and tremors.
   c. anxiety and weakness.
   d. all of the above.

8. The most popular drug on college campuses is
   a. alcohol.
   b. marijuana.
   c. cocaine.
   d. LSD.

9. Elyse is a college student who has developed a tolerance to heroin and experiences withdrawal symptoms whenever she doesn't have a "fix" at least every eight hours. She feels that she has lost control and has to organize her life around her habit. She would be classified as having
   a. substance intoxication.
   b. a substance use disorder.
   c. poor judgment.
   d. an anxiety disorder.

10. Which of the following is most likely to be prescribed for use with hyperactive children?
    a. Ritalin
    b. morphine
    c. dopamine
    d. tranquilizers

5 | Learning

Eric Audras/Onoky (RF)/Jupiter Imgaes

LEARNING OUTCOMES

After studying this chapter, you will be able to…

5-1 Define learning

5-2 Describe principles and methods of classical conditioning

5-3 Describe principles and methods of operant conditioning

5-4 Discuss cognitive factors in learning

After you finish this chapter, go to **PAGE 142** for **STUDY TOOLS**

was showing my daughter how to teach our new dog, Phoebe, to fetch. I bought a soft, yellow ball for the dog that squeaked when she bit into it. She enjoyed playing with it, and I assumed she would want to run after it. (Wrong!) I waved it under her nose. She sniffed at it, barked, and wagged her tail excitedly.

As my daughter watched, I tossed the ball about 20 feet away. "Fetch!" I said to Phoebe as the ball bounced invitingly in the grass.

Phoebe just stared. My daughter scoffed. I ran after the ball, picked it up, and waved it under Phoebe's nose again. She barked and wagged her tail rapidly like a reed in a brisk wind.

"Fetch!" I said and tossed the ball again.

Again Phoebe refused to run. She barked and snapped at my legs again. "This is ridiculous," I muttered, and I went to get the ball. As I brought it back to Phoebe, my daughter said, "Don't you see what's happening?"

"What?"

"Phoebe's teaching you to fetch."

Must a dog learn to fetch balls and other toys, or is fetching a 'built-in' instinctive response in some dogs, as the building of a nest is instinctive in birds?

Jessica Peterson/RubberBall/Alamy

5-1 LEARNING, EXPERIENCE, AND CHANGE

One could say that Phoebe was teaching me what to do by showing excitement when I did the "right" thing—that is, fetch the ball. She was teaching, and I was learning. Learning is a key area in psychology.

Learning is defined in psychology as more than listening to teachers, honing skateboard jumps, or mastering the use of a tablet computer. From the behaviorist point of view, **learning** is a relatively permanent change in behavior that arises from practice or experience. The behaviorist perspective plays down the roles of cognition and choice. It suggests that psychologists learn to run after balls because they have been rewarded or reinforced for doing so.

Cognitive psychologists define learning as the process by which organisms change the way they represent the environment because of experience. These changes influence the organism's behavior but do not fully determine it. From this perspective, I learned that I would earn Phoebe's attention by running after the ball, but I could have chosen not to do it. Learning, for cognitive psychologists, may be *shown* by changes in behavior, but learning itself is a mental process. Cognitive psychologists suggest that people choose whether or not to imitate the aggressive and other behaviors they observe, and that people are most likely to imitate behaviors that are consistent with their values.

Sometimes learning experiences are direct, as when we are praised for doing something properly. But we can also learn from the experiences of others—by watching their behavior and hearing their life stories.

learning (1) according to behaviorists, a relatively permanent change in behavior that results from experience; (2) according to cognitive theorists, the process by which organisms make relatively permanent changes in the way they represent the environment because of experience

WHAT DO YOU THINK? Folklore, common sense, or nonsense? Select T for "truth" or F for "fiction," and then check the accuracy of your answers as you read through the chapter.

T	F	A single nauseating meal can give rise to a taste aversion that lasts for years.
T	F	Psychologists helped a young boy overcome his fear of rabbits by having him eat cookies while a rabbit was brought closer and closer.
T	F	During World War II, psychologist B. F. Skinner proposed that pigeons be trained to guide missiles to their targets.
T	F	Slot-machine players pop coins into the machines most rapidly when they have no idea when they might win.
T	F	You can train a rat to climb a ramp, cross a bridge, climb a ladder, pedal a toy car, and do several other tasks—all in proper sequence.
T	F	You have to make mistakes in order to learn.
T	F	Despite all the media hoopla, no scientific connection has been established between violence in the media and real-life aggression.

Ivan Pavlov and His Associates at the Russian Institute for Experimental Medicine. Does his name 'ring a bell'? What is the importance of Pavlov's experiments to the science of psychology?

Bettmann/CORBIS

We learn, too, from books and audiovisual media. In this chapter, we consider various kinds of learning, including conditioning and learning in which cognition plays a more central role.

CLASSICAL CONDITIONING: LEARNING WHAT IS LINKED TO WHAT

Classical conditioning involves ways in which we learn to associate events with other events. It is involuntary, automatic learning. For example, we generally prefer grades of A to grades of F and are more likely to stop for red lights than green lights. Why? A's are associated with the approval of our teachers and caregivers. Because of experience in crossing streets or riding in cars, we associate green lights with the word "go" and red lights with "stop."

Classical conditioning is a simple form of learning in which organisms come to anticipate or associate events with one another.

If the name Ivan Pavlov rings a bell with us, it is most likely because of his research in learning with dogs. Ivan Pavlov (1927) made his great contribution to the psychology of learning by

> We are not born with instinctive attitudes toward letter grades or stoplights.

classical conditioning a simple form of learning in which a neutral stimulus comes to evoke the response usually evoked by another stimulus by being paired repeatedly with the other stimulus

reflex a simple unlearned response to a stimulus

stimulus an environmental condition that elicits a response

accident. Pavlov was actually attempting to identify neural receptors in the mouth that triggered a response from the salivary glands. But his efforts were hampered by the dogs' annoying tendency to salivate at undesired times, such as when a laboratory assistant was clumsy and banged the metal food trays.

Just as you salivate after you've taken a bite of cake, a dog salivates if meat powder is placed on its tongue. Pavlov was dosing his dogs with meat powder for his research because he knew that salivation in response to meat powder is a **reflex**. Reflexes are unlearned and evoked by certain **stimuli**. Pavlov discovered that reflexes can also be learned, or *conditioned*, by association. His dogs began salivating in response to clanging food trays because clanging, in the past, had been repeatedly paired with arrival of food. The dogs would also salivate when an assistant entered the laboratory. Why? In the past, the assistant had brought food.

Pavlov at first viewed the extra salivation of his dogs as a hindrance to his research. But then it dawned on him that this "problem" might be worth looking into. He found out that he could train, or condition, his dogs to salivate in response to any stimulus.

In his initial experiments, Pavlov trained dogs to salivate when he sounded a tone or a bell. Pavlov termed these trained salivary responses *conditional reflexes*. The reflexes were conditional on the repeated pairing of a previously neutral stimulus (such as the clanging of a food tray) and a stimulus (in this case, food) that evoked the target response (in this case, salivation). Today, conditional reflexes are generally referred to as *conditioned responses.*

Pavlov demonstrated conditioned responses by showing that when meat powder was placed on a dog's tongue, the dog salivated. Pavlov repeated the process several times, with one difference. He preceded the meat powder by half a second or so with the sounding of a tone on each occasion. After several pairings of the meat powder and the tone, Pavlov sounded the tone but did *not* follow it with the meat powder. Still the dog salivated. It had learned to salivate in response to the tone.

5-2a EXPLAINING CLASSICAL CONDITIONING

Behaviorists explain the outcome of *classical conditioning* in terms of the publicly observable conditions of learning. For them, classical conditioning is a simple form of learning in which one stimulus comes to evoke the response usually evoked by another stimulus. Why? Because the stimuli are paired repeatedly. In Pavlov's demonstration, the dog learned to salivate in response to the tone because the tone had been paired with meat powder. Behaviorists do not say that the dog "knew" food was on the way. How can we guess what a dog "knows," they ask. We can only outline the conditions under which targeted behaviors occur.

Cognitive psychologists view classical conditioning as the learning of relationships among events. The relationships allow organisms to mentally represent their environments and make predictions (De Houwer et al., 2013; Pickens & Holland, 2004). In Pavlov's demonstration, the dog salivated in response to the tone because the tone became mentally connected with the meat. The cognitive focus is on the information learned by the organism. Organisms are seen as seekers of information that generate and test rules about relationships among events.

5-2b STIMULI AND RESPONSES IN CLASSICAL CONDITIONING

In Pavlov's experiment, the meat powder is an **unconditioned stimulus (UCS)**. Salivation in response to the meat powder is an unlearned or **unconditioned response (UCR)**. The tone was at first a meaningless or neutral stimulus. It might have caused the dog to look in the direction of the sound—an **orienting reflex**.

But the tone was not yet associated with food. Then, through repeated association with the meat powder, the tone became a learned or **conditioned stimulus (CS)** for the salivation response. Salivation in response to the tone (or conditioned stimulus) is a learned or **conditioned response (CR)**. Therefore, salivation can be either a conditioned response or an unconditioned response, depending on the method used to evoke the response (see Figure 5.1).

unconditioned stimulus (UCS) a stimulus that elicits a response from an organism prior to conditioning

unconditioned response (UCR) an unlearned response to an unconditioned stimulus

FIG.5.1   HOW CLASSICAL CONDITIONING WORKS

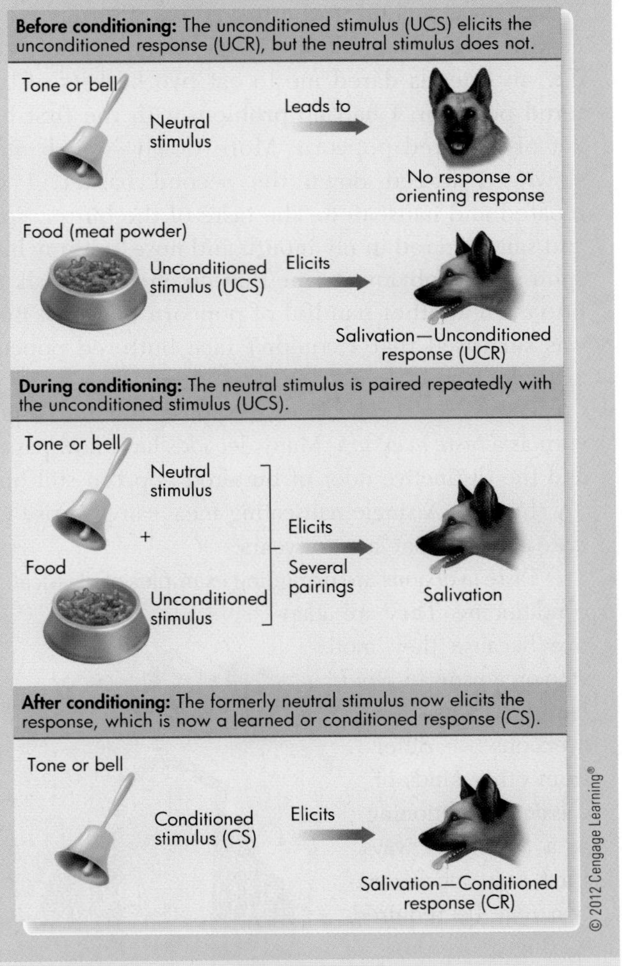

Before conditioning: The unconditioned stimulus (UCS) elicits the unconditioned response (UCR), but the neutral stimulus does not.

Tone or bell — Neutral stimulus — Leads to — No response or orienting response

Food (meat powder) — Unconditioned stimulus (UCS) — Elicits — Salivation—Unconditioned response (UCR)

During conditioning: The neutral stimulus is paired repeatedly with the unconditioned stimulus (UCS).

Tone or bell — Neutral stimulus + Food — Unconditioned stimulus — Elicits / Several pairings — Salivation

After conditioning: The formerly neutral stimulus now elicits the response, which is now a learned or conditioned response (CS).

Tone or bell — Conditioned stimulus (CS) — Elicits — Salivation—Conditioned response (CR)

© 2012 Cengage Learning®

Prior to conditioning, food elicits salivation. The tone, a neutral stimulus, elicits either no response or an orienting response. During conditioning, the tone is rung just before meat powder is placed on the dog's tongue. After several repetitions, the tone, now a CS, elicits salivation, the CR.

orienting reflex an unlearned response in which an organism attends to a stimulus

conditioned stimulus (CS) a previously neutral stimulus that elicits a conditioned response because it has been paired repeatedly with a stimulus that already elicited that response

conditioned response (CR) a learned response to a conditioned stimulus

Here is a mini-experiment that many adults have tried. They smile at infants, say something like "kitchie-coo," and then tickle the infant's foot. Perhaps the infant laughs and perhaps she or he curls or retracts the foot. After a few repetitions—which psychologists call "trials"—the adult's simply saying "kitchie-coo" is likely to be enough to cause the infant to laugh and retract its foot.

5-2c TASTE AVERSION

When I was a child in the Bronx, on Saturday mornings my friends and I would go to the movies. One day my friends dared me to eat two baskets of buttered popcorn. I had no problem with the first basket of buttered popcorn. More slowly—much more slowly—I forced down the second basket. I felt bloated and nauseated. The taste of the butter, corn, and salt lingered in my mouth and nose, and my head spun. It was obvious to me that no one could talk me into even another handful of popcorn that day. But I was surprised that I couldn't face buttered popcorn again for a year.

Psychologists refer to my response to buttered popcorn as a *taste aversion*. Many decades have now passed, and the distinctive odor of buttered popcorn still turns my stomach. A single nauseating meal can give rise to a taste aversion that lasts for years.

Taste aversions are intriguing examples of classical conditioning. They are adaptive because they motivate organisms to avoid harmful foods. Taste aversions differ from other kinds of classical conditioning in a couple of ways. First, only one association may be required. A single overdose of popcorn left me with a lifetime aversion.

Jupiter Images

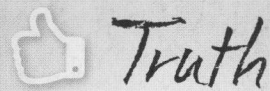
Second, whereas most kinds of classical conditioning require that the unconditioned stimulus and conditioned stimulus be close together in time, in taste aversion the unconditioned stimulus (in this case, nausea) can occur hours after the conditioned stimulus (in this case, the flavor of food).

THE EVOLUTION OF TASTE AVERSION Research on taste aversion also challenges the view that organisms learn to associate any stimuli that are linked in time. In reality, not all stimuli are created equal. The evolutionary perspective suggests that animals (and humans) are

Psychologists are interested in the development of taste aversions because they can be learned on the basis of one bad experience—that is, they can be acquired by a single pairing of the US (unconditioned stimulus) and the CS (conditioned stimulus). Evolutionary psychologists point out that the rapid acquisition of a taste aversion makes it more likely that a human or a nonhuman animal will survive and reproduce.

© Gelpi JM/Shutterstock.com

biologically prepared to develop aversions that are adaptive in their environments (Mallan et al., 2013; Öhman & Mineka, 2001). Those of us who acquire taste aversions quickly are less likely to eat poisonous food, more likely to survive, and more likely to contribute our genes to future generations.

In a classic study, Garcia and Koelling (1966) conditioned two groups of rats. Each group was exposed to the same three-part conditioned stimulus: a taste of sweetened water, a light, and a clicker. Afterward, one group of rats was induced to experience nausea by radiation or poison, and the other group received electric shock.

After conditioning, the rats that had been nauseated showed an aversion for sweetened water but not to the light or clicker. Although all three stimuli had been presented at the same time, the rats had acquired only the taste aversion. After conditioning, the rats that had been shocked avoided both the light and the clicker, but they did not show a taste aversion to the sweetened water. For each group of rats, the conditioning that took place was adaptive. In the natural scheme of things, nausea is more likely to stem from poisoned food than from lights or sounds. So, for nauseated rats, acquiring the taste aversion was appropriate. Sharp pain, in contrast, is more likely to stem from natural events involving lights (e.g., fire, lightning) and sharp sounds (e.g., twigs snapping, things falling). Therefore, it was more appropriate for the shocked animals to develop an aversion to the light and the clicker than the sweetened water.

In classical conditioning, organisms learn to connect stimuli, such as the sound of a tone with food. Now let's consider various factors in classical conditioning, beginning with what happens when the connection between stimuli is broken.

5-2d EXTINCTION AND SPONTANEOUS RECOVERY

Extinction and *spontaneous recovery* are aspects of conditioning that help us adapt by updating our expectations or revising our thinking about (representations of) the changing environment. For example, a child may learn to connect hearing a car pull into the driveway (a conditioned stimulus) with the arrival of his or her parents (an unconditioned stimulus). Thus, the child may squeal with delight (squealing is a conditioned response) when he or she hears the car.

Extinction enters the picture when times—and the relationships between events—change. After moving to a new house, the child's parents may commute by public transportation. The sound of a car in a nearby driveway may signal a neighbor's, not a parent's, homecoming. When a conditioned stimulus (such as the sound of a car) is no longer followed by an unconditioned stimulus (a parent's homecoming), the conditioned stimulus loses its ability to elicit a conditioned response. In this way, the organism adapts to a changing environment.

In classical conditioning, **extinction** is the process by which conditioned stimuli lose the ability to elicit conditioned responses because the conditioned stimuli are no longer associated with unconditioned stimuli. That is, the toddler is no longer gleeful at the sounds of the car in the driveway. From the cognitive perspective, extinction changes the child's mental representation of its environment because the conditioned stimulus no longer allows the child to make the same prediction.

In experiments on the extinction of conditioned responses, Pavlov found that repeated presentations of the conditioned stimulus (in this case, the tone) without the unconditioned stimulus (in this case, meat powder) led to extinction of the conditioned response (salivation in response to the tone). Basically, the dog stopped salivating at the sound of the tone. Interestingly, Figure 5.2 shows that after the initial conditioning, a dog's responsive salivation increased for a while and then leveled off. The dog was conditioned to begin to salivate in response to a tone after two or three pairings of the tone with meat powder. Continued pairings of the stimuli led to increased salivation (measured in number of drops of saliva). After seven or eight trials, salivation leveled off at 11 to 12 drops.

In the next series of experiments, salivation in response to the tone was extinguished through several trials in which the tone was presented without the meat powder. After about 10 extinction trials, the animal no longer salivated. That is, it no longer showed the conditioned response when the tone was sounded.

What would happen if we were to allow a day or two to pass after we had extinguished salivation in Pavlov's dog and then again sounded the tone? Where would you place your bet? Would the dog salivate or not?

If you bet that the dog would again show the conditioned response (in this case, salivation in response to the tone), you were correct. Organisms tend to show **spontaneous recovery** of extinguished conditioned responses as a function of the passage of time. For this reason, the term *extinction* may be a bit misleading. When

extinction the process by which stimuli lose their ability to evoke learned responses because the events that had followed the stimuli no longer occur (The learned responses are said to be *extinguished*.)

spontaneous recovery the recurrence of an extinguished response as a function of the passage of time

Acquisition
The researcher repeatedly pairs the CS (a tone) and the US (meat).

*Actual data from Pavlov (1927) is illustrated by the dots, and the curved lines are idealized.

Extinction
Now the researcher repeatedly presents the CS (tone) alone, in the absence of the US (meat).

Time is allowed to pass after extinction has occurred.

Spontaneous recovery
Initially, the dog shows greater salivation in response to the CS (tone) than at the end of the round of extinction trials, but the second round of extinction trials extinguishes the CR (salivation) more rapidly.

Drops of saliva elicited by CS

Trial

Time interval

Trial

© 2012 Cengage Learning®

a species of animal becomes extinct, all members of that species capable of reproducing have died. The species vanishes. But the experimental extinction of conditioned responses does not lead to their permanent

© Hedrus/Shutterstock.com

A Case Study in Successful Spontaneous Recovery. Water holes dry up at times and then may again be filled with water as the seasons change. Evolution would favor the survival of animals which continue to associate a waterhole with the thirst drive as time passes, because they will then return to the waterhole from time to time and may succeed at finding water.

eradication. Rather, extinction inhibits the response. The response remains available for the future under the "right" conditions.

Evolutionary psychologists note that spontaneous recovery, like extinction, is adaptive. In the wild, a water hole may contain water for only a couple of months during the year. But evolution would favor the survival of animals that associate the water hole with the thirst drive from time to time so that they return to it when it again holds water. As time passes and the seasons change, things sometimes follow circular paths and arrive where they were before. Spontaneous recovery helps organisms adapt to situations that recur from time to time.

5-2e GENERALIZATION AND DISCRIMINATION

No two things are exactly alike. Traffic lights are hung at slightly different heights, and shades of red and green differ a little. The barking of two dogs differs, and the sound of the same animal differs slightly from one bark to the next. Rustling sounds in the undergrowth differ, but evolution would favor the survival of rabbits and deer that flee when they perceive any rustling sound. Adaptation requires us to respond similarly (or *generalize*) to stimuli that are equivalent in function and to respond differently to (or *discriminate* between) stimuli that are not.

Pavlov noted that responding to different stimuli as though they were functionally equivalent—*generalizing*—is adaptive for animals. **Generalization** is the tendency for a conditioned response to be evoked by stimuli that are similar to the stimulus to which the response was conditioned. For example, Pavlov demonstrated generalization by getting his dog to salivate when it was shown a circle. Then later the dog salivated in response to being shown closed geometric figures—even squares. The more closely the figure resembled a circle, however, the greater the strength of the response (as measured by drops of saliva).

But what happens if food follows the presentation of a circle but not a square? Organisms must also learn that (1) many stimuli perceived as being similar are functionally different, and (2) they must respond adaptively to each. During the first couple of months of life, for example, babies can discriminate their mother's voice from those of other women. They often stop crying when they hear their mother but not when they hear a stranger.

Pavlov showed that a dog conditioned to salivate in response to circles could be trained not to salivate in response to ellipses. After a while, the dog no longer salivated in response to the ellipses. Instead, it showed **discrimination**: it salivated only in response to circles. Pavlov found that increasing the difficulty of the discrimination task apparently tormented the dog. After the dog was trained to salivate in response to circles but not ellipses, Pavlov showed it a series of progressively rounder ellipses. Eventually the dog could no longer distinguish the ellipses from circles. The animal was so stressed that it urinated, defecated, barked profusely, and snapped at laboratory personnel.

How do we explain the dog's belligerent behavior? In *Frustration and Aggression*, a classic work written more than 70 years ago, a group of behaviorally oriented psychologists suggested that frustration induces aggression (Dollard et al., 1939). Why is failure to discriminate circles from ellipses frustrating? For one thing, in

Mike Kemp/Rubberball/Getty Images

such experiments, rewards—such as food—are usually contingent on correct discrimination. That is, if the dog errs, it doesn't eat. Cognitive theorists, however, disagree (Hilton, 2012; Rescorla, 1988). They would say that in Pavlov's experiment, the dog lost its ability to adjust its mental map of the environment as the ellipses grew more circular. Thus, it was frustrated.

Daily life requires generalization and discrimination. No two hotels are alike, but when we travel from one city to another, it is adaptive to expect to stay in a hotel. It is encouraging that a green light in Washington has the same meaning as a green light in Paris. But returning home in the evening requires the ability to discriminate between our home and those of others. Imagine the confusion that would occur if we could not discriminate among our friends, mates, or coworkers from other people.

5-2f HIGHER-ORDER CONDITIONING

Consider a child who is burned by touching a hot stove. After this experience, the sight of the stove may evoke fear. And because hearing the word *stove* may evoke a mental image of the stove, just hearing the word may evoke fear.

Recall the mini-experiment in which an adult smiles, says "kitchie-coo," and then tickles an infant's foot. After a few repetitions, just smiling at the infant may cause the infant to retract its foot. In fact, just walking into the room may have the same effect! The experiences with touching the hot stove and tickling the infant's foot are examples of *higher-order conditioning*.

In **higher-order conditioning**, a previously neutral stimulus (e.g., hearing the word *stove* or seeing the adult who had done the tickling enter the room) comes to serve as a learned or conditioned stimulus after being paired repeatedly with a stimulus that has already become a learned or conditioned stimulus (e.g., seeing the stove or hearing the phrase "kitchie-coo"). Pavlov demonstrated higher-order conditioning by first conditioning a dog to salivate in response to a tone. He then repeatedly paired the shining

generalization in conditioning, the tendency for a conditioned response to be evoked by stimuli that are similar to the stimulus to which the response was conditioned

discrimination in conditioning, the tendency for an organism to distinguish between a conditioned stimulus and similar stimuli that do not forecast an unconditioned stimulus

higher-order conditioning a classical conditioning procedure in which a previously neutral stimulus comes to elicit the response brought forth by a *conditioned* stimulus by being paired repeatedly with that conditioned stimulus

of a light with the sounding of the tone. After several pairings, shining the light (the higher-order conditioned stimulus) came to evoke the response (salivation) that had been elicited by the tone (the first-order conditioned stimulus).

5-2g APPLICATIONS OF CLASSICAL CONDITIONING

Some of the most important applications of classical conditioning involve the conditioning of fear and the counterconditioning or extinction of fear. The fear-reduction methods we discuss are part of behavior therapy and are elaborated in Chapter 13.

"LITTLE ALBERT": CLASSICAL CONDITIONING OF EMOTIONAL RESPONSES

In 1920, John B. Watson and his future wife, Rosalie Rayner, published an article describing their demonstration that emotional reactions such as fears can be acquired through principles of classical conditioning. The subject of their demonstration was a lad known in psychological literature by the name of Little Albert. Albert was a phlegmatic fellow at the age of 11 months, not given to ready displays of emotion. But prior to the study, the infant did enjoy playing with a laboratory rat.

Using a method that some psychologists have criticized as unethical, Watson startled Little Albert by clanging steel bars behind his head when he played with the rat. After seven pairings, Albert showed fear of the rat even though clanging was suspended. Albert's fear was also generalized to objects similar in appearance to the rat, such as a rabbit and the fur collar on his mother's coat. Albert's conditioned fear of rats may never have become extinguished because extinction would have required perceiving rats (the conditioned stimuli) without painful consequences (in the absence of the unconditioned stimuli). But Albert's mother removed him from the laboratory before Watson and Rayner could attempt to countercondition the boy's acquired fear. And once outside the laboratory, fear might have prevented Albert from facing furry animals. And as we shall see in the section on operant conditioning, avoiding furry animals might have been reinforced by reduction of fear.

PREPAREDNESS AND THE CONDITIONING OF FEAR

Little Albert developed his fear of rats

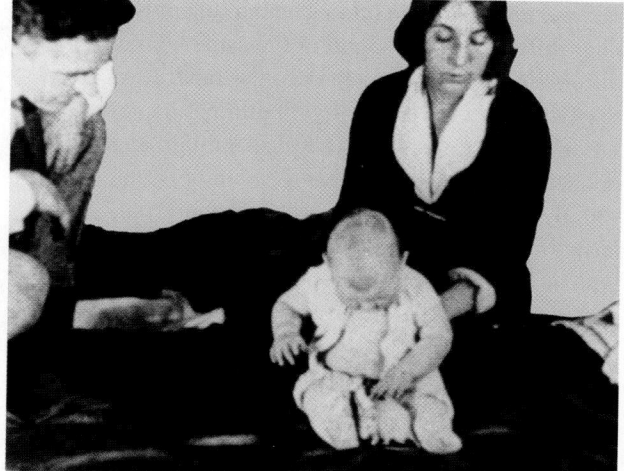

In a landmark experiment in the history of psychology, John B. Watson and Rosalie Rayner, shown here with 'Little Albert', conditioned the boy to fear rats by clanging steel bars behind his head when he played with the animal. Many psychologists have argued that their experiment was unethical because it was painful and they never counterconditioned the boy's acquired fear.

easily enough, but would Watson and Rayner have been able to condition him to fear flowers or potted plants? Perhaps not. As suggested by Arne Öhman and Susan Mineka (2003), humans (and other primates) may be **biologically prepared** by evolutionary forces to rapidly develop fears of certain animals, including snakes, that could do them harm. People also seem to be prepared to fear thunder, threatening faces, sharp objects, darkness, and heights—all of which would have been sources of danger to our ancestors and which, to some degree, may still threaten us (Mineka & Oehlberg, 2008; Starratt & Shackelford, 2010).

COUNTERCONDITIONING

In **counterconditioning**, an organism learns to respond to a stimulus in a way that is incompatible with a response that was conditioned earlier. For example, relaxation is incompatible with a fear response. The reasoning behind counterconditioning is this: if fears, as Watson had shown, could be conditioned by painful experiences like a clanging noise, perhaps fears could be counterconditioned by substituting pleasant experiences. In 1924, Watson's protégé Mary Cover

biological preparedness readiness to acquire a certain kind of conditioned response due to the biological makeup of the organism

counterconditioning a fear-reduction technique in which pleasant stimuli are associated with fear-evoking stimuli so that the fear-evoking stimuli lose their aversive qualities

Jones attempted to countercondition fear in a 2-year-old boy named Peter.

Peter had an intense fear of rabbits. Jones had a rabbit gradually brought closer to Peter while he munched candy and cookies. Jones first placed the rabbit in a far corner of the room while Peter munched and crunched. Peter cast a wary eye, but he continued to consume the treats. Over a couple of months, the animal was brought closer until Peter simultaneously ate and touched the rabbit. Jones theorized that the joy of eating was incompatible with fear and thus counterconditioned it.

FLOODING AND SYSTEMATIC DESENSITIZATION

If Mary Cover Jones had simply plopped the rabbit on Peter's lap rather than bring it gradually closer, she would have been using the method of **flooding**. Flooding, like counterconditioning, is a behavior therapy method for reducing fears. It is based on the classical conditioning principle of extinction (Ehlers, 2013). In flooding, the client is exposed to the fear-evoking stimulus until fear is extinguished. Little Albert, for example, might have been placed in close contact with a rat until his fear had become extinguished. In extinction, the conditioned stimulus (in this case, the rat) is presented repeatedly in the absence of the unconditioned stimulus (the clanging of the steel bars) until the conditioned response (fear) is no longer evoked.

Although flooding is usually effective, it is unpleasant. (When you are fearful of rats, being placed in a room with one is no picnic.) For this reason, behavior therapists frequently prefer to use **systematic desensitization**, in which the client is gradually exposed to fear-evoking stimuli under circumstances in which he or she remains relaxed. For example, while feeling relaxed, Little Albert might have been given an opportunity to look at photos of rats or to see rats from a distance before they were brought closer. Systematic desensitization takes longer than flooding but is not as unpleasant.

In any event, people can learn by means of simple association. In terms of the evolutionary perspective, organisms that can learn by several routes—including conditioning and conscious reflection—would stand a greater chance of survival than organisms whose learning is limited to conditioning.

As a follow-up to Watson and Rayner's experiment with Little Albert, Mary Cover Jones showed that fears could be counterconditioned by associating the feared object with pleasant experiences. She famously fed a 2-year-old boy cookies and candy while a feared rabbit was brought gradually closer.

© jsolpietro/Shutterstock.com

👍 *Truth*

| **T** | F | Psychologists helped a young boy overcome his fear of rabbits by having him eat cookies while a rabbit was brought closer and closer. |

It is true that psychologists helped a young boy overcome his fear of rabbits by having him eat cookies while a rabbit was brought closer and closer. They believe that the pleasure of eating the cookie counterconditioned the fear.

---

flooding a behavioral fear-reduction technique based on principles of classical conditioning; fear-evoking stimuli (CSs) are presented continuously in the absence of actual harm so that fear responses (CRs) are extinguished

systematic desensitization a behavioral fear-reduction technique in which a hierarchy of fear-evoking stimuli is presented while the person remains relaxed

OPERANT CONDITIONING: LEARNING WHAT DOES WHAT TO WHAT

Through classical conditioning, we learn to associate stimuli. As a result, a simple, usually passive response made to one stimulus is then made in response to the other. In the case of Little Albert, clanging noises were associated with a rat. As a result, the rat came to elicit the fear caused by the clanging. However, classical conditioning is only one kind of learning that occurs in these situations. After Little Albert acquired his fear of the rat, his voluntary behavior changed: he tried to avoid the rat as a way of reducing his fear. Thus, Little Albert engaged in another kind of learning—*operant conditioning*.

In operant conditioning, organisms learn to do things—or not to do things—because of the consequences of their behavior. For example, I avoided buttered popcorn to prevent nausea. But we also seek fluids when we are thirsty, sex when we are aroused, and an ambient temperature of 68° to 70°F when we feel too hot or too cold. *Classical conditioning* focuses on how organisms form anticipations about their environments. *Operant conditioning* focuses on what they do about them. Let's look at the contributions of Edward L. Thorndike and B. F. Skinner to operant conditioning.

law of effect Thorndike's view that pleasant events stamp in responses, and unpleasant events stamp them out

reinforce to follow a response with a stimulus that increases the frequency of the response

FIG.5.3 PROJECT PIGEON

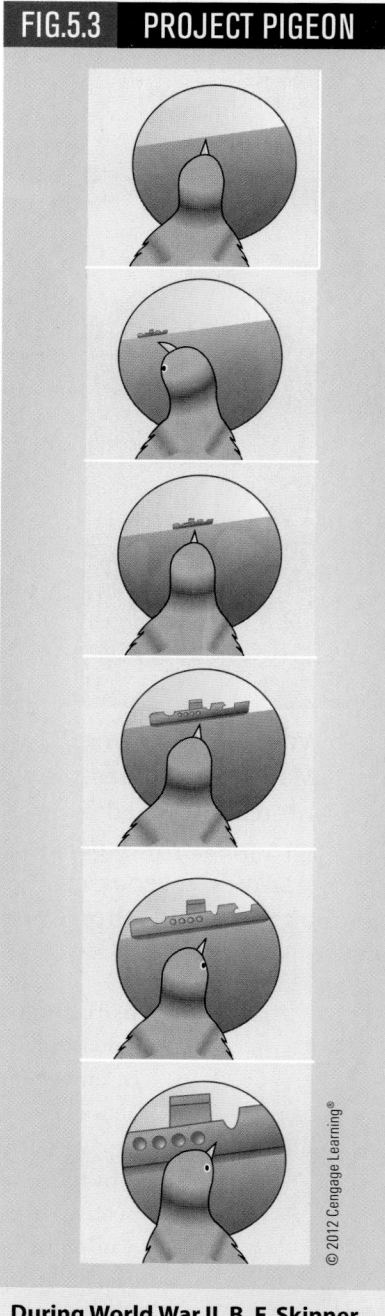

© 2012 Cengage Learning®

During World War II, B. F. Skinner proposed the use of pigeons that had been trained to peck at images of military targets to guide missiles to them. It never happened.

5-3a EDWARD L. THORNDIKE AND THE LAW OF EFFECT

In the 1890s, stray cats were mysteriously disappearing from the alleyways of Harlem. Some of them, it turned out, were being brought to the quarters of Columbia University doctoral student Edward L. Thorndike. Thorndike was using them as subjects in experiments on the effects of rewards and punishments on learning.

Thorndike placed a cat in a "puzzle box." If it pulled a dangling string, a latch would be released, allowing it to jump out and reach a bowl of food. When first placed in a puzzle box, a cat would claw and bite at the bars and wire. Through such random behavior, it might take 3 to 4 minutes for the cat to chance upon the response of pulling the string. When placed back in the cage, it might again take several minutes for the cat to pull the string. But with repetition, it took less time, and after seven or eight tries, the cat might pull the string immediately.

Thorndike explained the cat's learning to pull the string in terms of his **law of effect**: a response (such as string pulling) would be—to use Thorndike's term—"stamped in" (i.e., strengthened) in a particular situation (such as being inside a puzzle box) by a reward (escaping from the box and eating). But punishments—using Thorndike's terminology once again—"stamp out" response. That is, organisms would learn not to behave in ways that bring on punishment. Later, we shall see that the effects of punishment on learning are not so certain.

5-3b B. F. SKINNER AND REINFORCEMENT

When it comes to unusual war stories, few will top that of B. F. Skinner. One of Skinner's wartime efforts was "Project Pigeon." During World War II, Skinner proposed that pigeons be trained to guide missiles to their targets. In their training, the pigeons would be **reinforced** with food pellets for pecking at targets projected onto a screen (see Figure 5.3). Once trained,

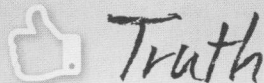

the pigeons would be placed in missiles. Their pecking at similar targets displayed on a screen would correct the missile's flight path, resulting in a "hit" and a sacrificed pigeon. However, plans for building the necessary missile—for some reason called the *Pelican* and not the *Pigeon*—were scrapped. The pigeon equipment was too bulky, and Skinner's suggestion was not taken seriously.

Project Pigeon may have been scrapped, but the principles of learning Skinner applied to the project have found wide application. Skinner taught pigeons and other animals to engage in **operant behavior**, behavior that operates on, or manipulates, the environment. In classical conditioning, involuntary responses such as salivation or eyeblinks are often conditioned. In operant conditioning, voluntary responses such as pecking at a target, pressing a lever, or skills required for playing tennis are acquired, or conditioned.

Operant conditioning is therefore defined as a simple form of learning in which an organism learns to engage in certain behavior because of the effects of that behavior. In operant conditioning, we learn to engage in operant behaviors, also known simply as **operants**, that result in presumably desirable outcomes such as food, a hug, an A on a test, attention, or social approval. For example, some children learn to conform to social rules to earn the attention and approval of their parents and teachers. Ironically, other children may learn to "misbehave" because misbehavior also gets attention. In particular, children may learn to be "bad" when their "good" behavior is routinely ignored. Some children who do not do well in school seek the approval of deviant peers (Patterson et al., 2000).

5-3c METHODS OF OPERANT CONDITIONING

Skinner (1938) made many theoretical and technological innovations. Among them was his focus on discrete behaviors, such as lever pressing, as the unit, or type, of behav-

ior to be studied. Other psychologists might focus on how organisms think or "feel." Skinner focused on measurable things they do. Many psychologists have found these kinds of behavior inconsequential, especially when it comes to explaining and predicting human behavior. But Skinner's supporters point out that focusing on discrete behavior creates the potential for helpful changes. For example, in helping people combat depression, one psychologist might focus on their "feelings." A Skinnerian would focus on cataloging (and modifying) the types of things that "depressed people" do. Directly modifying depressive behavior might also brighten clients' self-reports about their "feelings of depression."

To study operant behavior, Skinner devised an animal cage (or "operant chamber") that has been dubbed the *Skinner box*. (Skinner himself repeatedly requested that his operant chamber not be called a Skinner box, but history has thus far failed to honor his wishes.) Such a box is shown in Figure 5.4. The cage is ideal for laboratory experimentation because experimental conditions can be carefully introduced and removed, and their effects on laboratory animals can be observed.

> **operant behavior** behavior that operates on, or manipulates, the environment
>
> **operant conditioning** a simple form of learning in which an organism learns to engage in behavior because it is reinforced
>
> **operant** the same as an operant behavior

FIG.5.4 A RAT IN A "SKINNER BOX"

Skinner used the conditioning of rats and pigeons as "models" for much human learning. His boxes allowed him to control the environments of the animals and demonstrate how the environments determined the animals' behavior. Skinner's approach left no roles for thinking and decision making.

© Cengage Learning 2012

The rat in Figure 5.4 was deprived of food and placed in a Skinner box with a lever at one end. At first it sniffed its way around the cage and engaged in random behavior. The rat's first pressing of the lever was accidental. However, because of this action, a food pellet dropped into the cage. The arrival of the food pellet increased the probability that the rat would press the lever again. The pellet is thus said to have reinforced lever pressing.

In operant conditioning, it matters little why or how the first "correct" response is made. The animal can happen on it by chance or be physically guided to make the response. You may command your dog to "Sit!" and then press its backside down until it is sitting. Finally, you reinforce sitting with food or a pat on the head and a kind word. Animal trainers use physical guiding or coaxing to bring about the first "correct" response. Can you imagine how long it would take to train your dog if you waited for it to sit or roll over and then seized the opportunity to command it to sit or roll over?

People, of course, can be verbally guided into desired responses when they are learning tasks such as spelling, adding numbers, or operating a machine. But they need to be informed when they have made the correct response. Often, knowledge of results is all the reinforcement people need to learn new skills.

5-3d TYPES OF REINFORCERS

Any stimulus that increases the probability that responses preceding it—whether pecking a button in a Skinner box or studying for a quiz—will be repeated serves as a reinforcer. Reinforcers include food pellets when an animal has been deprived of food, water when it has been deprived of liquid, the opportunity to mate, and the sound of a tone that has previously been associated with eating. Skinner distinguished between *positive* and *negative* reinforcers and *primary* and *secondary* reinforcers.

POSITIVE AND NEGATIVE REINFORCERS Positive **reinforcers** increase the

Skinner himself repeatedly requested that his operant chamber not be called a Skinner box, but history has thus far failed to honor his wishes.

Nina Leen/Time Life Pictures/Getty Images

probability that a behavior will occur when they are applied. Food and approval usually serve as positive reinforcers. **Negative reinforcers** increase the probability that a behavior will occur when the reinforcers are removed (see Figure 5.5). People often learn to plan

FIG.5.5 POSITIVE VERSUS NEGATIVE REINFORCERS

Procedure	Behavior	Consequence	Change in behavior
Use of positive reinforcement	Behavior (studying)	Positive reinforcer (teacher approval) is *presented* when student studies	Frequency of behavior *increases* (student studies more)
Use of negative reinforcement	Behavior (studying)	Negative reinforcer (teacher disapproval) is *removed* when student studies	Frequency of behavior *increases* (student studies more)

© 2012 Cengage Learning®

ahead so that they need not fear that things will go wrong. In such cases, fear acts as a negative reinforcer because removal of fear increases the probability that the behaviors preceding it (such as planning ahead) will be repeated.

IMMEDIATE VERSUS DELAYED REINFORCERS Immediate reinforcers are more effective than delayed reinforcers. Therefore, the short-term consequences of behavior often provide more of an incentive than the long-term consequences.

For example, some students socialize when they should be studying because the pleasure of socializing is immediate. Studying may not pay off until the final exam or graduation. (This is why younger students do better with frequent tests.) It is difficult to quit smoking cigarettes because the reinforcement of nicotine is immediate and the health hazards of smoking are more distant. Focusing on short-term reinforcement is also connected with risky sex, such as engaging in sexual activity with a stranger or failing to prevent pregnancy (Castor et al., 2010; Shuper et al., 2010). One of the aspects of being human is the ability to foresee the long-range consequences of one's behavior and to make choices. But immediate reinforcers—such as those cookies staring in the face of the would-be dieter—can be powerful temptations indeed.

PRIMARY AND SECONDARY REINFORCERS We can also distinguish between primary and secondary, or conditioned, reinforcers. **Primary reinforcers** are effective because of the organism's biological makeup. For example, food, water, warmth (positive reinforcers), and pain (a negative reinforcer) all serve as primary reinforcers. **Secondary reinforcers** acquire their value through being associated with established reinforcers. For this reason they are also termed **conditioned reinforcers**. We may seek money because we have learned that it may be exchanged for primary reinforcers.

5-3e EXTINCTION AND SPONTANEOUS RECOVERY IN OPERANT CONDITIONING

Keisha's teacher writes "Good" on all of her homework assignments before returning them. One day, her teacher no longer writes anything on the assignments—

Nicotine Creates Short-Term Reinforcement. One of the difficulties in quitting smoking cigarettes is that the reinforcement of nicotine is strong and immediate, whereas the health hazards of smoking are a distant and uncertain punishment or threat.

primary reinforcer an unlearned reinforcer whose effectiveness is based on the biological makeup of the organism and not on learning

secondary reinforcer a stimulus that gains reinforcement value through association with established reinforcers

conditioned reinforcer another term for a secondary reinforcer

the reinforcement ends. Reinforcers are used to strengthen responses. What happens when reinforcement stops?

In Pavlov's experiment, the meat powder was the event that followed and confirmed the appropriateness of salivation. In operant conditioning, the ensuing events are reinforcers. The extinction of learned responses results from the repeated performance of operant behavior without reinforcement. Keisha might stop doing her homework if she is not reinforced for completing it. In other words, reinforcers maintain operant behavior or strengthen habitual behavior in operant conditioning. With humans, fortunately, people can reinforce themselves for desired behavior by telling themselves they did a good job—or in Keisha's case, she may tell herself that she is doing the right thing regardless of whether her teacher recognizes it.

Spontaneous recovery of learned responses occurs in operant conditioning as well as in classical conditioning. Spontaneous recovery is adaptive in operant conditioning as well as in classical conditioning. Reinforcers may once again become available after time elapses, just as there are new tender sprouts on twigs when the spring arrives.

"YOUR MOST UNHAPPY CUSTOMERS ARE YOUR GREATEST SOURCE OF LEARNING."

BILL GATES, FOUNDER OF MICROSOFT (BORN 1955)

5-3f REINFORCERS VERSUS REWARDS AND PUNISHMENTS

Reinforcers are defined as stimuli that increase the frequency of behavior. Skinner distinguished between reinforcers, on the one hand, and rewards and punishments, on the other. Reinforcers are known by their effects, whereas rewards and punishments are more known by how they feel. It may be that most reinforcers—food, hugs, having the other person admit to starting the argument, and so on—feel good, or are pleasant events. Yet things that we might assume would feel bad, such as a slap on the hand, disapproval from a teacher, even suspensions and detention may be positively reinforcing to some people—perhaps because such experiences confirm negative feelings toward teachers or one's belonging within a deviant subculture (Atkins et al., 2002).

Skinner preferred the concept of reinforcement to that of reward because reinforcement does not suggest trying to "get inside the head" of an organism (whether a human or lower animal) to guess what it would find pleasant or unpleasant. A list of reinforcers is arrived at scientifically and empirically—that is, by observing what sorts of stimuli increase the frequency of the behavior.

Whereas reinforcers—even negative reinforcers—increase the frequency of the behavior they follow, punishments decrease it (see Figure 5.6). Punishment can rapidly suppress undesirable behavior (Marchant et al., 2013) and may be warranted in "emergencies," such as when a child tries to run into the street.

> **discriminative stimulus** in operant conditioning, a stimulus that indicates that reinforcement is available

Psychologists distinguish between *positive punishments* and *negative punishments*. Both kinds of punishments are aversive events, and both decrease the frequency of the behavior they follow. *Positive punishment* is the application of an aversive stimulus to decrease unwanted behavior, such as spanking, scolding, or a parking ticket. *Negative punishment* is the removal of a pleasant stimulus, such as removing a student's opportunity to talk with friends in class by seating them apart, or removing a student's opportunity to mentally escape from class by taking his or her smart phone or tablet computer. "Time out" is a form of negative punishment because it places a misbehaving child in an environment in which she or he cannot experience rewards.

5-3g DISCRIMINATIVE STIMULI

Skinner might not have succeeded in getting his pigeons into the drivers' seats of missiles, but he had no problem training them to respond to traffic lights. Imagine yourself trying the following experiment: place a pigeon in a Skinner box with a button on the wall. Deprive it of food for a while. Drop a food pellet into the cage whenever it pecks the button. Soon it will learn to peck the button. Now you place a small green light in the cage and turn it on and off intermittently throughout the day. Reinforce button pecking with food whenever the green light is on, but not when the light is off. It will not take long for the pigeon to learn that it will gain as much by grooming itself or cooing and flapping around as it will by pecking the button when the light is off.

The green light has become a discriminative stimulus. **Discriminative stimuli**, such as green or red lights, indicate whether behavior (in the case of the pigeon, pecking a button) will be reinforced (by a food pellet being dropped into the cage). Behaviors (or operants) that are not reinforced tend to be extinguished. For the pigeon in our experiment, the behavior of pecking the button when the light is off is extinguished.

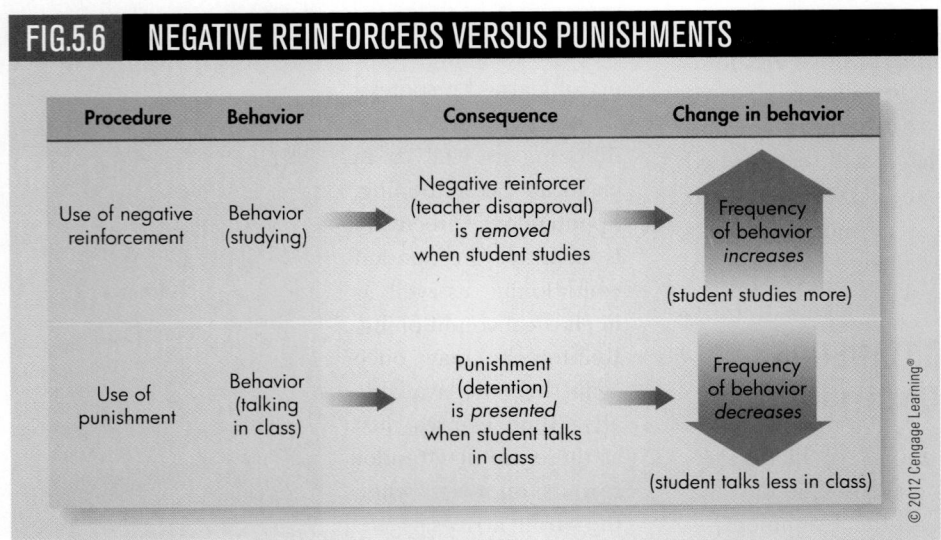

FIG.5.6 NEGATIVE REINFORCERS VERSUS PUNISHMENTS

Procedure	Behavior	Consequence	Change in behavior
Use of negative reinforcement	Behavior (studying)	Negative reinforcer (teacher disapproval) is *removed* when student studies	Frequency of behavior *increases* (student studies more)
Use of punishment	Behavior (talking in class)	Punishment (detention) is *presented* when student talks in class	Frequency of behavior *decreases* (student talks less in class)

© 2012 Cengage Learning®

A moment's reflection will suggest many ways in which discriminative stimuli influence our behavior. Isn't it more efficient to answer the telephone when it is ringing? Do you think it is wise to ask someone for a favor when she or he is displaying anger and disapproval toward you?

We noted that a pigeon learns to peck a button if food drops into its cage when it does so. What if you want the pigeon to continue to peck the button, but you're running out of food? Do not despair. As we see in the following section, you can keep that bird pecking away indefinitely, even as you hold up on most of the food.

5-3h SCHEDULES OF REINFORCEMENT

In operant conditioning, some responses are maintained by means of **continuous reinforcement**. You probably become warmer every time you put on heavy clothing. You probably become less thirsty every time you drink water. Yet if you have ever watched people toss their money down the maws of slot machines, you know that behavior can also be maintained by means of **partial reinforcement**.

Folklore about gambling is based on solid learning theory. You can get a person "hooked" on gambling by fixing the game to allow heavy winnings at first. Then you gradually space out the winnings (reinforcements) until gambling is maintained by infrequent winning—or even no winning at all. Partial reinforcement schedules can maintain gambling, like other behavior, for a great deal of time, even though it goes unreinforced (Pulley, 1998).

Responses that have been maintained by partial reinforcement are more resistant to extinction than responses that have been maintained by continuous reinforcement (Yeung et al., 2014). From the cognitive perspective, we could suggest that organisms that have experienced partial reinforcement do not expect reinforcement every time they engage in a response. Therefore, they are more likely to persist in the absence of reinforcement.

There are four basic reinforcement schedules: *fixed-interval, variable-interval, fixed-ratio,* and *variable-ratio.*

INTERVAL SCHEDULES In a **fixed-interval schedule**, a fixed amount of time—say, a minute—must elapse before the correct response will result in a reinforcer. With a fixed-interval schedule, an organism's response rate falls off after each reinforcement and then picks up again as the time when reinforcement will occur approaches. For example, in a 1-minute fixed-interval schedule, a rat is reinforced with, say, a food pellet for the first operant—for example, the first pressing of a lever—that occurs after 1 minute has elapsed.

The rat's rate of lever pressing slows down after each reinforcement, but as the end of the 1-minute interval draws near, lever pressing increases in frequency, as suggested in Figure 5.7. It is as if the rat has learned that it must

continuous reinforcement a schedule of reinforcement in which every correct response is reinforced

partial reinforcement one of several reinforcement schedules in which not every correct response is reinforced

fixed-interval schedule a schedule in which a fixed amount of time must elapse between the previous and subsequent times that reinforcement is available

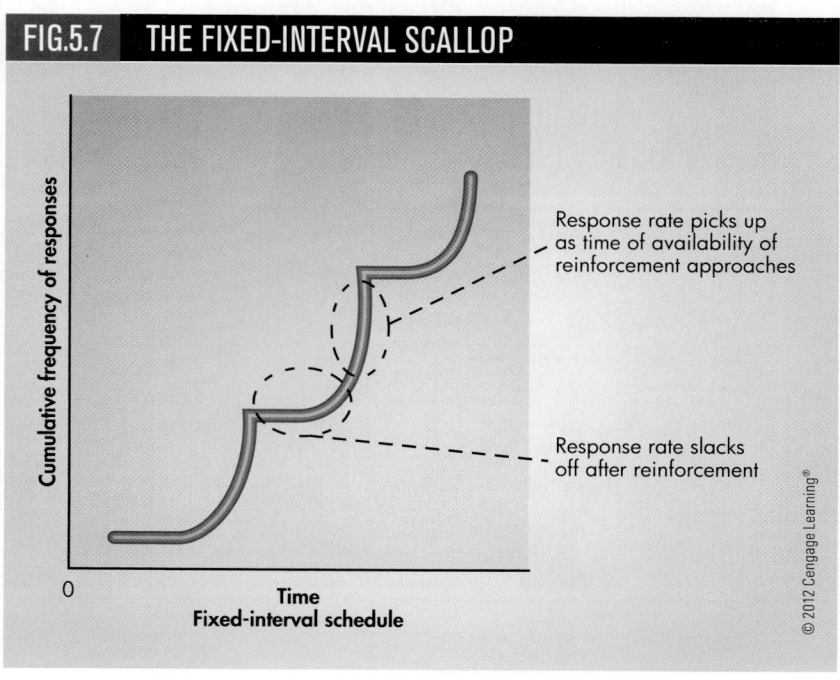

FIG.5.7 THE FIXED-INTERVAL SCALLOP

Cumulative frequency of responses

Response rate picks up as time of availability of reinforcement approaches

Response rate slacks off after reinforcement

0   Time
Fixed-interval schedule

© 2012 Cengage Learning®

wait awhile before it is reinforced. The resultant record on the cumulative recorder shows a typical series of upward waves, or scallops, which are called *fixed-interval scallops.*

Car dealers use fixed-interval reinforcement schedules when they offer incentives for buying up the remainder of the year's line in summer and fall. In a sense, they are suppressing buying at other times, except for consumers whose current cars are in their death throes or those with little self-control. Similarly, you learn to check your email only at a certain time of day if your correspondent writes at that time each day.

Reinforcement is more unpredictable in a **variable-interval schedule**. Therefore, the response rate is lower, but it is also steadier. If the boss calls us in for a weekly report, we probably work hard to pull things together just before the report is to be given, just as we might cram the night before a weekly quiz. But if we know that the boss might call us in for a report on the progress of a certain project at any time (variable-interval), we are likely to keep things in a state of reasonable readiness at all times. However, our efforts are unlikely to have the intensity they would in a fixed-interval schedule (e.g., a weekly report). Similarly, we are less likely to cram for unpredictable pop quizzes than to study for regularly scheduled quizzes. But we are likely to do at least some studying on a regular basis in preparation for pop quizzes. Likewise, if you receive email from your correspondent irregularly,

 The Four Basic Reinforcement Schedules in Real Life.

Commuter trains are usually planned to arrive at a fixed interval. Fish will bite at variable intervals. The piece worker will be paid on a per-shirt basis. Gamblers at slot machines win on a variable-ratio schedule.

	FIXED	VARIABLE
INTERVAL	 IS-200710/Image Source Plus/Getty Images	 Alaska Stock/Alamy
RATIO	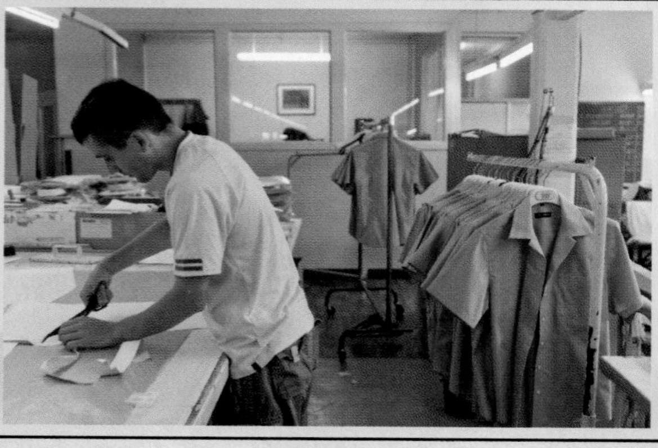 Jasmin Brutus/Alamy	 ERproductions Ltd/Blend Images/Alamy

you are likely to check your email regularly for his or her communication, but with less eagerness.

RATIO SCHEDULES In a **fixed-ratio schedule**, reinforcement is provided after a *fixed* number of correct responses have been made. In a **variable-ratio schedule**, reinforcement is provided after a variable number of correct responses have been made. In a 10:1 ratio schedule, the mean number of correct responses that would have to be made before a subsequent correct response would be reinforced is 10, but the ratio of correct responses to reinforcements might be allowed to vary from, say, 1:1 to 20:1 on a random basis.

Fixed- and variable-ratio schedules both maintain a high response rate. With a fixed-ratio schedule, it is as if the organism learns that it must make several responses before being reinforced. It then "gets them out of the way" as rapidly as possible. Consider the example of piecework. If a worker must sew five shirts to receive $10, he or she is on a fixed-ratio (5:1) schedule and is likely to sew at a uniformly high rate, although after each reinforcement there might be a brief pause. With a variable-ratio schedule, reinforcement can come at any time. This unpredictability also maintains a high response rate. Slot machines tend to pay off on variable-ratio schedules, and players can be seen popping coins into them and yanking their "arms" with barely a pause. For gamblers, the unpredictability of winning maintains a high

Stockbyte (RF)/Jupiter Images

response rate. I have seen players who do not even stop to pick up their winnings. Instead, they continue to pop in the coins, either from their original stack or from the winnings tray.

5-3i SHAPING

If you are teaching hip-hop dancing to people who have never danced, do not wait until they have performed it precisely before telling them they're on the right track. The foxtrot will be back in style before they have learned a thing.

We can teach complex behaviors by **shaping**. Shaping reinforces progressive steps toward the behavioral goal. At first, for example, it may be wise to smile and say, "Good," when a reluctant newcomer gathers the courage to get out on the dance floor, even if your feet are flattened by his initial clumsiness. If you are teaching someone to drive a car with a standard shift, at first generously reinforce the learner simply for shifting gears without stalling.

But as training proceeds, we come to expect more before we are willing to provide reinforcement. We reinforce **successive approximations** of the goal. If you want to train a rat to climb a ladder, first reinforce it with a food pellet when it turns toward the ladder. Then wait until it approaches the ladder before giving it a pellet. Then do not drop a pellet into the cage until the rat touches the ladder. In this way, the rat will reach the top of the ladder more quickly than if you had waited for the target behavior to occur at random.

Have you ever driven home and suddenly realized that you couldn't recall exactly how you got there? Your entire trip may seem "lost." Were you in great danger? How could you allow such a thing to happen? Actually, your driving and your responses to the demands of the route may have become so habitual that you did not have to focus on

fixed-ratio schedule a schedule in which reinforcement is provided after a fixed number of correct responses

variable-ratio schedule a schedule in which reinforcement is provided after a variable number of correct responses

shaping a procedure for teaching complex behaviors that at first reinforces approximations of the target behavior

successive approximations behaviors which are progressively closer to a target behavior

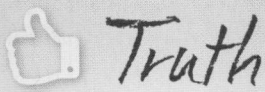

them. As you drove, you were able to think about dinner, work, or the weekend. But if something unusual had occurred on the way, such as an engine problem or a rainstorm, you would have devoted as much attention to your driving as was needed to arrive home. Your trip was probably quite safe after all.

5-3j APPLICATIONS OF OPERANT CONDITIONING

Operant conditioning, like classical conditioning, is not just an exotic laboratory procedure. We use it every day in our efforts to influence other people. Parents and peers induce children to acquire so-called gender-appropriate behavior patterns through rewards and punishments. Peers influence peers by playing with those who are generous and nonaggressive and by avoiding those who are not (Warman & Cohen, 2000).

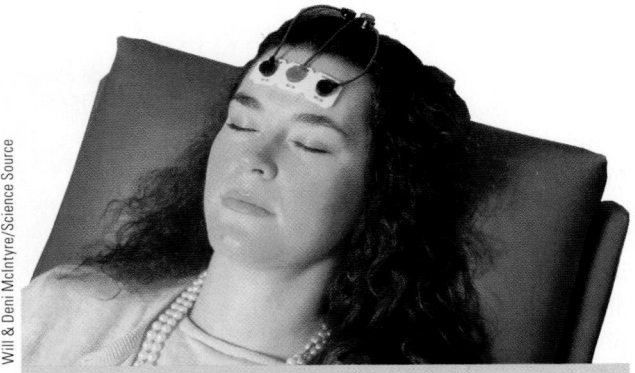

This woman is using biofeedback training to relax muscles in her forehead, which, in turn, will reduce anxiety.

Operant conditioning also plays a role in attitude formation. Adults often reward children for expressing attitudes that coincide with their own and punish or ignore them for expressing contradictory attitudes. Let's now consider some specific applications of operant conditioning.

BIOFEEDBACK TRAINING *Biofeedback training (BFT)* is based on operant conditioning. It has enabled people and lower animals to learn to control autonomic responses to attain reinforcement (N. E. Miller, 1969; Vernon et al., 2003). In BFT, people receive reinforcement in the form of information. For example, we can learn to emit alpha waves—the kind of brain wave associated with relaxation—through feedback from an electroencephalograph, which measures brain waves. People use other instruments to learn to lower muscle tension, heart rates, and blood pressure.

BEHAVIOR MODIFICATION Remember that reinforcers are not defined as pleasant events but rather as stimuli that increase the frequency of behavior. Ironically, adults frequently reinforce undesirable behavior in children by paying attention to them, or punishing them, when they misbehave but ignoring them when they behave in desirable ways. Similarly, teachers who raise their voices when children misbehave may be unintentionally conferring hero status on those pupils in the eyes of their peers. To the teacher's surprise, some children may then go out of their way to earn disapproval. But teachers can learn to use *behavior modification* to reinforce children when they are behaving appropriately and, when possible, to extinguish misbehavior by ignoring it.

Teachers also frequently use time out from positive reinforcement to discourage misbehavior. In this method, children are placed in a drab, restrictive environment for a specified period, usually about 10 minutes, when they behave disruptively. While isolated, they cannot earn the attention of peers or teachers, and no reinforcers are present.

PROGRAMMED LEARNING B. F. Skinner developed an educational method called *programmed learning* that is based on operant conditioning. This method assumes that any complex task can be broken down into a number of small steps. These steps can be shaped individually and then combined in sequence to form the correct behavioral chain.

Programmed learning does not punish errors. Instead, correct responses are reinforced, usually with immediate feedback. Every child earns a 100, but at her or his own pace. Programmed learning also assumes it is the task of the teacher (or program) to structure the learning experience in such a way that errors will not be made. In programmed learning, one can learn without making mistakes.

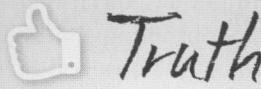

5-4 COGNITIVE FACTORS IN LEARNING

Classical and operant conditioning were originally conceived of as relatively simple forms of learning. Much of conditioning's appeal is that it can be said to meet the behaviorist objective of explaining behavior in terms of observable events—in this case, laboratory conditions. Building on this theoretical base, some psychologists have suggested that the most complex human behavior involves the summation of a series of instances of conditioning. Many psychologists believe, however, that conditioning is too mechanical a process to explain all instances of learned behavior, even in laboratory rats (Weiner, 2006). They turn to cognitive factors to describe and explain additional findings in the psychology of learning.

In addition to concepts such as *association* and *reinforcement*, cognitive psychologists use concepts such as *mental structures*, *schemas*, *templates*, and *information processing*. Cognitive psychologists see people as searching for information, weighing evidence, and making decisions. Let's consider some classic research which points to cognitive factors in learning, as opposed to mechanical associations. These cognitive factors are not limited to humans—although, of course, humans are the only species that can talk about them.

5-4a LATENT LEARNING: FORMING COGNITIVE MAPS

Many behaviorists argue that organisms acquire only responses, or operants, for which they are reinforced. E. C. Tolman, however, showed that rats also learn about their environment in the absence of reinforcement. In doing so, he showed that rats must form **cognitive maps** of their surroundings.

Tolman trained some rats to run through mazes for standard food goals. Other rats were allowed to explore the same mazes for several days without food goals or other rewards. After the unrewarded rats had been allowed to explore the mazes for 10 days, food rewards were placed in a box at the far end of the maze. The previously unrewarded rats reached the food box as quickly as the rewarded rats after only one or two trials (Tolman & Honzik, 1930).

Tolman concluded that the rats had learned about the mazes by exploring them even when they were unrewarded for doing so. He distinguished between *learning* and *performance*. Rats apparently created a cognitive map of a maze. Even though they were not externally motivated to follow a rapid route through the maze, they would learn fast routes just by exploring it. Yet this learning might remain hidden, or be considered **latent learning**, until food motivated them to take the rapid routes.

5-4b CONTINGENCY THEORY

Behaviorists and cognitive psychologists interpret classical conditioning in different ways. Behaviorists explain it in terms of the pairing of stimuli. Cognitive psychologists explain classical conditioning in terms of the ways in which stimuli provide information that allows organisms to form or revise mental representations of their environment. Robert Rescorla conducted research in an effort to demonstrate which view is more accurate. His viewpoint, **contingency theory**, suggests that learning occurs only when the conditioned stimulus (CS) provides information about the unconditioned stimulus (US).

In classical conditioning of dogs, Rescorla (1967) obtained some results that are difficult to explain without reference to cognitive concepts. Each phase of his work paired a tone (a CS) with an electric shock (a US), but in different ways. With one group of animals, the shock was consistently presented after the tone. That is, the unconditioned stimulus followed on the heels

cognitive map a mental representation of the layout of one's environment

latent learning learning that is hidden or concealed

contingency theory the view that learning occurs when stimuli provide information about the likelihood of the occurrence of other stimuli

of the conditioned stimulus, as in Pavlov's studies. The dogs in this group learned to show a fear response when the tone was presented.

A second group of dogs heard an equal number of tones and received an equal number of electric shocks, but the shock never immediately followed the tone. In other words, the tone and the shock were not paired. Now, from the behaviorist perspective, the dogs should not have learned to associate the tone and the shock because one did not predict the other. Actually, the dogs learned quite a lot: they learned that they had nothing to fear when the tone was sounded! They showed vigilance and fear when the laboratory was quiet—for the shock might come at any time—but they were calm in the presence of the tone.

The third group of dogs also received equal numbers of tones and shocks, but the stimuli were presented at random intervals. Occasionally, they were paired, but most often, they were not. According to Rescorla, behaviorists might argue that intermittent pairing of the tones and shocks should have brought about some learning. Yet it did not. The animals showed no fear in response to the tone. Rescorla suggests that the animals in this group learned nothing because the tones did not allow them to make predictions about electric shock. Rescorla concluded that learning occurs only when the CS (in this case, the tone) provides information about the US (in this case, the shock).

5-4c OBSERVATIONAL LEARNING

How many things have you learned from watching other people in real life, in films, and on television? From films and television, you may have gathered vague ideas about how to skydive, ride a surfboard, and dust

observational learning the acquisition of knowledge and skills through the observation of others (who are called *models*) rather than by means of direct experience

model an organism that engages in a response that is then imitated by another organism

© First Light

"Boys Will Be Boys? Perhaps. But the question is, how much of being a boy—or a girl—is inborn or biologically influenced, and how much is learned by observation?"

for fingerprints, even if you have never tried them yourself. How do people learn by observing others?

In experiments on **observational learning**, Albert Bandura and his colleagues conducted experiments (e.g., Bandura et al., 1963) that show that we can acquire skills by observing the behavior of others. In the terminology of observational learning, a person who engages in a response that is imitated is a **model**. When we see modeled behavior being reinforced, we are said to be vicariously reinforced. Engaging in the behavior thus becomes more likely for us as well as for the model. Observational learning occurs when, as children, we watch our parents cook or clean. Observational learning takes place when we watch teachers solve problems on the blackboard or hear them speak in a foreign language. Observational learning is not acquired through reinforcement. We can learn through observation without engaging in overt responses at all. It appears sufficient to pay attention to the behavior. We may need some practice to refine the skills we acquire. We may also allow these skills to lie dormant or latent. For example, we may not imitate aggressive behavior unless we are provoked and believe that we are more likely to be rewarded than punished for it.

MIRROR NEURONS It is clear that we can learn from observing others, but, is there something in us (and monkeys and apes) that leads us to automatically imitate the behavior of others? The answer is apparently yes. We are referring to *mirror neurons*—neurons that fire when an animal observes the behavior of another and that tend to stimulate imitative behavior (Bonini et al., 2012). Mirror neurons are apparently involved when newborn babies return the favor if their caregivers stick out their tongues at them, but as babies develop, this particular type of automatic imitation tends to drop out (Meltzoff & Prinz, 2002). Nevertheless, mirror neurons also allow us to anticipate other people's intentions when they reach for things. Mirror neurons are also apparently involved when we yawn because people around us are yawning (Haker et al., 2013), and that may be why laughter can be "contagious" (Davila-Ross et al., 2011).

5-4d VIOLENCE IN THE MEDIA AND AGGRESSION

Adam Lanza shot himself to death in 2012 at the age of 20. Before he did so, he shot and killed his mother in her bed. Then he shot and killed 26 people at the Sandy Hook Elementary School in Newtown, Connecticut, including 20 elementary school children and 6 adults.

We don't know why Lanza did these things, but we do know that he lived with his mother, who supported him, and that his windows were covered with trash bags. Not only was he a loner; he communicated with his mother by email only. He hated birthdays and holidays and wouldn't eat unless his food was arranged on his plate in a precise arrangement. He also kept a spreadsheet describing some of the worst mass killings in American history.

And, like Dylan Klebold and Eric Harris, who committed the Columbine High School killings in 1999; Evan Ramsey, who in 1997 shot four people on a rampage in a school in Alaska; and Seung-Hui Cho, who killed 32 people in the "Virginia Tech massacre" in 2007—he played violent video games.

The debate as to whether violence in media such as films, television, and video games fuels violence in the real world has been going on for more than 50 years. However, research strongly suggests that media violence is a risk factor for increasing emotional arousal, aggressive behavior, and violent thoughts (Huesmann et al., 2013).

It seems that violent video games create the greatest risk because they require audience participation (Lin, 2013). Players don't just watch; they participate. Some games reward players for killing police, prostitutes, or bystanders. Virtual weapons include guns, knives, flamethrowers, swords, clubs, cars, hands, and feet. Sometimes, the player assumes the role of a hero, but it is also common for the player to assume the role of a criminal.

Television is also a risk factor. It is one of our major sources of informal observational learning. Children are routinely exposed to murders, beatings, and sexual assaults—just by turning on the television (Huesmann et al., 2013). If children watch 2 to 4 hours of television a day, they will have seen 8,000 murders and another 100,000 acts of violence by the time they have finished elementary school (Eron, 1993). Are kids less likely to be exposed to violence by going to the movies? No. One study found that virtually all G-rated animated films have scenes of violence (Yokota & Thompson, 2000). Another study found that gun violence in PG-13 rated movies has more than tripled over the past 30 years, containing as much or more violence as R-rated movies (Bushman et al., 2013). Violent PG-13 movies are especially popular among adolescent males. Music, music videos, advertisements, and comic books are also brimming with violence.

Why all this violence? Simple: violence sells. But does violence do more than sell? That is, does media violence cause real violence? If so, what can parents and educators do to prevent the fictional from spilling over into the real?

bananastock/Jupiter Images

What do we learn from violence in video games and other media? The research suggests that we learn a great deal—not only aggressive skills, but also the idea that violence is the normal state of affairs.

CONSENSUS ON THE EFFECTS OF VIOLENCE IN THE MEDIA? In any event, most organizations of health professionals agree that media violence does contribute to aggression (Huesmann et al., 2013) even if it does not directly cause it. After all, most people who watch violent television shows and movies and who play violent video games do not go on murderous rampages. Still, a connection between media violence and real-life aggression has been found for girls and boys of different ages, social classes, ethnic groups, and cultures (Huesmann et al., 2003). Consider a number of ways that depictions of violence make such a contribution (Anderson et al., 2010; Huesmann et al., 2013):

▶ *Observational learning*: Children learn from observation. Television violence supplies models of aggressive "skills," which children may acquire. In fact, children are more likely to imitate what others do than to heed what they say.

▶ *Disinhibition*: Punishment inhibits or discourages behavior. Conversely, media violence may *disinhibit* aggressive behavior, especially when media characters "get away" with violence or are rewarded for it.

▶ *Increased emotional arousal*: Media violence and aggressive video games increase viewers' level of emotional arousal. It "works them up." We are more likely to be aggressive when we are highly aroused.

▶ *Priming of aggressive thoughts and memories*: Media violence triggers aggressive ideas and memories.

▶ *Habituation*: We become used to repeated stimuli. Repeated exposure to media violence may decrease viewers' sensitivity to real violence. If children perceive violence as the norm, they may be more tolerant of it and place less value on restraining aggressive urges.

▶ *Provision of aggressive scripts*: Media violence provides aggressive scripts—or roles—as ways to manage various social situations.

Violent video games are also connected with aggressive behavior, including juvenile delinquency (DeLisi et al., 2013; Lin, 2013) and dating violence (Friedlander et al., 2013). Playing violent video games increases aggressive thoughts and behavior in the laboratory (Anderson et al., 2010). However, males are relatively more likely than females to act aggressively after playing violent video games and are more likely to see the world as a hostile place. Students who obtain higher grades are also less likely to behave aggressively following exposure to violent video games. Thus, cultural stereotyping of males and females, possible biological sex differences, and moderating variables such as social connectedness and academic achievement also figure into the effects of media violence.

There seems to be a circular relationship between exposure to media violence and aggressive behavior (Anderson et al., 2010). Yes, media violence and violent video games contribute to aggressive behavior, but aggressive youngsters are also more likely to seek it out. Figure 5.8 explores the possible connections between media violence and aggressive behavior.

The family also affects the likelihood that children will imitate media violence. Studies find that parental substance abuse, paternal physical punishments, and single parenting contribute to the likelihood of aggression in early childhood (Brook et al., 2001; Ferguson, 2012). Parental rejection and use of physical punishment further increase the likelihood of aggression in children (Bradshaw et al., 2013; Eron, 1982). These family factors suggest that the parents of aggressive children may be absent or unlikely to help young children understand that the kinds of socially inappropriate behaviors they see in the media are not for them. A harsh home life may also confirm the television viewer's or game player's vision of the world as a violent place.

If children believe violence to be inappropriate for them, they will be less likely to act aggressively, even if they have acquired aggressive skills from exposure to the media or other sources. It would be of little use to talk about learning if we couldn't remember what we learn from second to second or from day to day. In the next chapter, we turn our attention to memory. In Chapter 8, we see how learning is intertwined with thinking, language, and intelligence.

TEACHING CHILDREN NOT TO IMITATE MEDIA VIOLENCE Children are going to be exposed to media violence—if not in Saturday-morning cartoon shows, then in evening dramas and in the news. Or they'll hear about violence from friends, watch other children get into fights, or read about violence in the newspapers. If all those sources of violence were somehow hidden from view, they would learn about violence in *Hamlet*, *Macbeth*,

FIG.5.8

WHAT ARE THE CONNECTIONS BETWEEN MEDIA VIOLENCE AND AGGRESSIVE BEHAVIOR?

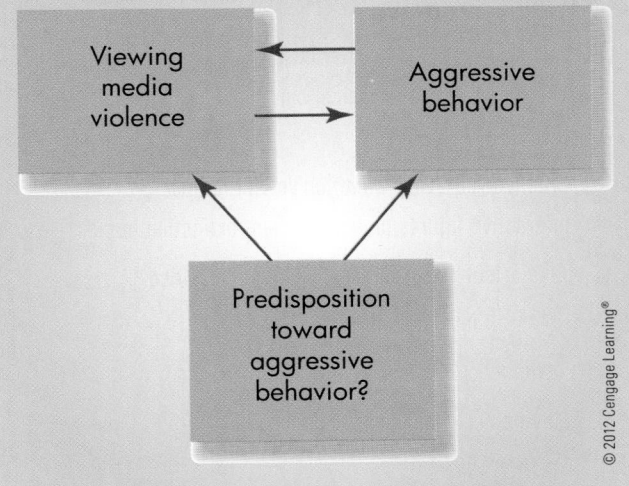

© 2012 Cengage Learning®

Does media violence cause aggressive behavior? Do aggressive children prefer to tune in to violent shows? Or do other factors, such as personality traits that create a disposition toward aggression, contribute both to aggressive behavior and the interest in media violence?

and the Bible. The notion of preventing children from being exposed to violent models may be impractical.

What, then, should be done? Parents and educators can do many things to tone down the impact of media violence. Children who watch violent shows may act less aggressively when they are informed that:

▶ The violent behavior they observe in the media does not represent the behavior of most people.

▶ The apparently aggressive behaviors they watch are not real. They reflect camera tricks, special effects, and stunts.

▶ Most people resolve conflicts by nonviolent means.

▶ The real-life consequences of violence are harmful to the victim and often to the aggressor.

Despite our history of evolutionary forces, and despite the fact that in most species, successful aggression usually wins individuals the right to transmit their genes to future generations, humans are thinking beings. If children consider violence to be inappropriate for them, they will be less likely to act aggressively, even when they have acquired aggressive skills from exposure to the media or other sources.

✳ Albert Bandura's Classic Study of the Imitation of Aggressive Models

Half a century ago, Albert Bandura and his colleagues (1963) applied his views on observational learning to the question as to whether viewing aggressive behavior in the media would stimulate children to behave aggressively. They found that children frequently imitate the aggressive behavior that they observe. In the top row, an adult model attacks a clown doll as children watch. The lower rows show a boy and a girl imitating the aggressive behavior.

Stanford University

STUDY TOOLS 5

READY TO STUDY? IN THE BOOK, YOU CAN:

☐ Check your understanding of what you've read with the quizzes below.

☐ Rip out the chapter review card at the back of the book to have a summary of the chapter and the key terms handy.

ONLINE AT CENGAGEBRAIN.COM YOU CAN:

☐ Learn more about classical conditioning in learning modules.

☐ Practice retrieving what you've learned using the interactive figures on learning and extinction curves.

☐ Take a tour of a Skinner box in a short video.

☐ Prepare for tests with quizzes.

☐ Review the key terms with Flash Cards.

☐ Play games to master concepts.

FILL-INS

Answers can be found in the back of the book, starting on page XXX.

1. A response to an unconditioned stimulus is called a(n) _____ response.

2. A response to a conditioned stimulus is termed a(n) _____ response.

3. Repeated presentation of a CS (such as a tone) without the UCS (such as meat) will _____ the CR (salivation).

4. Extinguished responses often show _____ recovery as a function of the passage of time.

5. John B. Watson and Rosalie Rayner used conditioning to teach a boy who is known as "Little _____" to fear rats.

6. In the behavior-therapy method of _____, a client is continuously exposed to a fear-evoking stimulus until the fear response is extinguished.

7. _____ reinforcers increase the probability that operants will occur when they are removed.

8. In a _____-_____ schedule, a specific amount of time must elapse since a previous correct response before reinforcement again becomes available.

9. _____ learning breaks down learning tasks into small steps and reinforces correct performance of each step.

10. According to _____ theory, learning occurs because a CS indicates that the UCS is likely to follow.

MULTIPLE CHOICE

1. According to behaviorists, _____ is a relatively permanent change in an organism's behavior that occurs because of experience.
   a. extinction
   b. learning
   c. acquisition
   d. higher-order conditioning

2. While attempting to identify neural receptors that trigger salivary glands, Ivan Pavlov inadvertently found that responses can be learned through
   a. operant conditioning.
   b. observation.
   c. instinct.
   d. association.

3. Roberto kept seeing signs on the highway advertising Pizza Hut. He started to salivate at the possibility of having a pizza. The signs were
   a. unconditioned stimuli.
   b. unconditioned responses.
   c. conditioned stimuli.
   d. conditioned responses.

4. Johnny was tormented in the schoolyard every day by a bully with bright red frizzy hair. One day, Johnny's father brought his boss, Mr. Dale, home. The boss had bright, red frizzy hair, and Johnny ran to his room, crying. Mr. Dale's hair functioned as a _____, and Johnny's fear was a _____.
   a. US; CR
   b. US; UR
   c. CS; CR
   d. CR; CS

5. Spotted zebras learn to stop going to a particular water hole after approaching it several times and finding that it is dry. However, after a month or two passes, they may return to the water hole. Learning to stop going to the water hole because it is dry, but then returning to it after time passes, is an example of _____ followed by _____.
   a. extinction, spontaneous recovery
   b. shaping, successive approximations
   c. discrimination training, generalization
   d. contingency theory, latent learning

6. Which of the following best illustrates operant conditioning according to Skinner?
   a. A dog salivates at the sound of a dinner bell
   b. A cat comes running when it hears the sound of the can opener
   c. A dolphin is given a fish every time it jumps through a hoop
   d. The mating behavior of salmon

7. When a behavior is followed by negative reinforcement, the behavior is likely to
   a. be extinguished.
   b. be suppressed.
   c. decrease.
   d. increase.

8. Slot machines tend to keep gamblers playing by using a _____ schedule of reinforcement.
   a. fixed-interval
   b. variable-interval
   c. fixed-ratio
   d. variable-ratio

9. Professor Fournier gives a quiz every Monday. His students would then tend to _____ because they are on a _____ schedule of reinforcement.
   a. start studying immediately after the quiz; fixed-ratio
   b. study regularly through the week; fixed-interval
   c. study on Sunday nights; fixed-interval
   d. pay attention in class; variable-interval

10. Johnny watches television violence for an hour or two a day, but he is not violent outside the home. Then one day Billy attacks him on the way home from school, and Johnny imitates the behavior he saw on television to fight Billy off and teach Billy never to attack him again. Although Johnny had not shown violent behavior until he was attacked, we can assume that when watching television, he was engaging in
    a. latent learning.
    b. shaping.
    c. discrimination training.
    d. operant conditioning.

6 | Memory: Remembrance of Things Past—and Future

AsiaTravelCollection/Alamy

LEARNING OUTCOMES

After studying this chapter, you will be able to…

6-1 Define memory and differentiate between types of memories

6-2 Explain the processes of memory

6-3 Explain the stages of memory

6-4 Identify contributors to forgetting

6-5 Describe the biological aspects of memory

After you finish this chapter, go to **PAGE 169** for **STUDY TOOLS**

Jeff would never forget his sudden loss of memory. He watched in horror as his cellphone slipped from his pocket and fell to the floor of the Blockbuster store in Boston. Before he could grab it, it shattered into pieces. A New York college student, Jeff experienced the trauma of phone loss on his winter break.

Why was the loss traumatic? Why was it a memory problem? Simple: There was no way for Jeff to retrieve his phone book. "I was at the store and it was snowing out, and I suddenly realized that I had no way of getting in touch with anyone," he explains (Metz, 2005). Jeff now copies every cellphone entry in a little black book—made of paper. Other people back up their phone books—and their pictures and downloads—on servers provided by cellular telephone operating companies or cellphone manufacturers. For example, smart phones have backups available. Verizon's method is called Backup Assistant. Most people transfer their memories from their old cellphone to the new one when they make a change.

What's the problem with remembering all those phone numbers? The answer lies partly in their length. Psychologist George Miller (1956) researched the amount of information people can keep in mind at once, and he found that the average person is comfortable with digesting about seven digits at a time. Most people have little trouble recalling five pieces of information, as in a zip code. Some can remember nine, which is, for most, an upper limit. So seven pieces of information, plus or minus one or two, is the "magic" number.

This chapter is all about the "backup assistant" in your brain—your memory. Without memory, there is no past. Without memory, experience is trivial and learning is lost. Let's see what psychologists have learned about the ways in which we remember things—other than keying them into a cellphone's memory chip.

> Without memory, there is no past.

6-1 KINDS OF MEMORY

Jeff remembered a thing he had personally done, like drop his cellphone in Boston on a blustery day in January. Remembering dropping one's cellphone is an *episodic memory*—a memory of an event in one's life. And when I learned of Jeff's experience, I tried to remind myself repeatedly not to forget to jot down notes about it and write it up as soon as I could. (I was trying to jog my *prospective memory*—remembering to do something in the future.) Let's consider several memory systems.

6-1a EXPLICIT MEMORY

Explicit memory—also referred to as *declarative memory*—is memory for specific information. Things that are *explicit* are clear, or clearly stated or explained. The use of the term *declarative* indicates that these memories state or reveal (i.e., *declare*) specific information. The information may be autobiographical or refer to general knowledge.

There are two kinds of explicit memories: episodic and semantic (Martin-Ordas et al., 2012). They are identified according to the type of information they hold.

EPISODIC MEMORY (I REMEMBER...) Episodic memories are memories of the things that happen to us or take place in our presence (Grillon et al., 2010).

Episodic memory is also referred to as *autobiographical memory*. Your memories of what you ate for breakfast and of what your professor said in class today are episodic memories. We tend to use the phrase "I remember…" when we are referring to episodic memories, as in "I remember the blizzard of 2004."

SEMANTIC MEMORY (I KNOW…) General knowledge is referred to as **semantic memory**—another kind of explicit memory. *Semantics* concerns meanings. You can "know" that the United States has 50 states without visiting them and personally adding them up. You "know" who authored *Hamlet*, although you were not looking over Shakespeare's shoulder as he did so. These are examples of semantic memory.

Your future recollection that there are several memory systems is more likely to be semantic than episodic. That is, you are more likely to "know" that there are several types of memory than to recall where you were and how you were sitting. We are more likely to say "I know…" in reference to semantic memories, as in "I know about—" (or "I heard about—") "—the blizzard of 1898." Put another way, you may *remember* that you emailed a friend, but you *know* that Shakespeare wrote *Hamlet*.

6-1b IMPLICIT MEMORY

Implicit memory—also referred to as *nondeclarative memory*—is memory of how to perform a task. It is the act itself, doing something, like riding a bike, accessing your cellphone contacts list, and texting a message. Implicit memories are suggested (or implied) but not plainly stated or verbally expressed. Implicit memories are illustrated by the things that people do but not by the things they state clearly. Implicit memories involve procedures and skills, cognitive and physical, and are also referred to as *procedural* or *skill memories*.

Implicit memories can endure even when we have not used them for years. Getting to class "by habit"—without paying attention to landmarks or directions—is another instance of implicit memory. If someone asked you what 2 times 2 is, the number 4 would probably "pop" into mind without conscious calculation. After

explicit memory memory that clearly and distinctly expresses (explicates) specific information

episodic memory memories of events that happen to a person or that take place in the person's presence

semantic memory general knowledge, as opposed to episodic memory

implicit memory memory that is suggested (implied) but not plainly expressed, as illustrated in the things that people do but do not state clearly

Five Challenges to Your Memory

Let's challenge your memory. This is not an actual memory test of the sort used by psychologists to determine whether people's memory functioning is within normal limits. Instead, it will provide you with some insight into how your memory works and may also be fun.

Directions: Find four sheets of blank paper and number them 1 through 4. Also use a watch with a second hand. Then follow these instructions:

1. Following are 10 letters. Look at them for 15 seconds. Later in the chapter I will ask you if you can write them on sheet number 1. (No cheating! Don't do it now.)

THUNSTOFAM

2. Look at these nine figures for 30 seconds. Then try to draw them in the proper sequence on sheet number 2, right after you have finished looking at them. (We'll talk about your drawings later.)

3. Look at the following list of 17 letters for 60 seconds and then see whether you can reproduce it on sheet number 3.

GMC-BSI-BMA-TTC-IAF-BI

4. Which of these pennies is an accurate reproduction of the Lincoln penny you see every day? This time there's nothing to draw on another sheet; just circle or put a checkmark by the penny that you think resembles the ones you throw in the back of the drawer.

A   B   C   D   E   F

5. Examine the following drawings for 1 minute. Then copy the names of the figures on sheet number 4. When you're finished, just keep reading. Soon I'll be asking you to draw those figures.

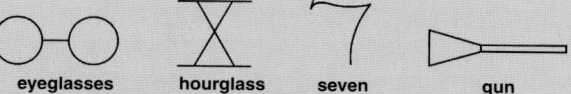

eyeglasses   hourglass   seven   gun

That's it. You'll find out about the results of these memory challenges as you read through the chapter.

going over the alphabet or multiplication tables hundreds of times, our memory of them becomes automatic or implicit. We need not focus on them to use them.

Your memory of the alphabet or the multiplication tables is the result of a great deal of repetition that makes associations automatic, a phenomenon that psychologists refer to as **priming**. Studies involving brain imaging reveal that priming makes it possible for people to carry out mental tasks with less neural activity (Cabeza & Moscovitch, 2013; Koenig & VanRullen, 2013). Years of priming help people make complete words out of the following word fragments (Radel et al., 2013; Schacter et al., 2007). Even though the cues in the following fragments are limited, you might make them into words:

PYGY.....TXT.....BUFL

Sample answers are "pygmy," "text," and "buffalo." Can you think of others?

Daniel Schacter (1992) illustrates implicit memory with the story of a woman with amnesia who was wandering the streets. The police picked her up and found that she could not remember who she was and that she had no identification. After fruitless interviewing, the police hit on the idea of asking her to dial phone numbers—just any number at all. When asked for the phone numbers of people she knew, she had no answer. She could not declare her mother's

phone number. She could not make the number explicit. She could not even remember her mother's name, or whether she had a mother. But dialing her mother's phone number was a habit, and she did it "on automatic pilot." We can assume that she had been *primed* for this task by dialing the number hundreds of times. Implicit memory reveals the effects of experience when we are not specifically trying to recall information.

6-1c RETROSPECTIVE MEMORY VERSUS PROSPECTIVE MEMORY

Do you ever forget how to ride a bicycle?

Retrospective memory is the recalling of information that has been previously learned. Episodic, semantic, and implicit memories involve remembering things that were learned. **Prospective memory** refers to remembering to do things in the future, such as remembering to pay your bills or to withdraw some cash.

Most of us have had failures of prospective memory in which we felt we were supposed to do something but couldn't remember what. Prospective memory may fail when we are preoccupied, distracted, or "stressed out" about time (Cook et al., 2014; Zogg et al., 2012).

There are various kinds of prospective memory tasks. For example, *habit tasks* such as getting to class on time are easier to remember than occasional tasks such as meeting someone for coffee at an arbitrary time (Squire, 2004). But motivation also plays a role. You are more likely to remember the coffee date if the person you are meeting excites you. Psychologists also distinguish between event-based and time-based prospective memory tasks (Gonneaud et al., 2013). *Event-based tasks* are triggered by events,

Ocean/Corbis

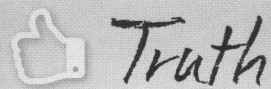
priming the activation of specific associations in memory, often as a result of repetition and without making a conscious effort to access the memory

retrospective memory memory for past events, activities, and learning experiences, as shown by explicit (episodic and semantic) and implicit memories

prospective memory memory to perform an act in the future, as at a certain time or when a certain event occurs such as remembering to take one's medicine at breakfast or to brush one's teeth after eating. *Time-based tasks* are to be performed at a certain time or after a certain amount of time has elapsed between occurrences, such as tuning in to a favorite news program at 7:30 p.m. or taking a pill every four hours (Cook et al., 2014).

An age-related decline takes place in retrospective and prospective memories (Mattll et al., 2013). Generally speaking, the decline in older adults may be related to their speed of cognitive processing rather than the "loss" of information per se. In the case of prospective memory, older adults appear about equally aware of specific cues or reminders as young adults; however, it takes them longer to respond to the cues or reminders (Mattll et al., 2013). That is, if they meet with a friend, they are likely to remember that they were supposed to ask something, but it may take longer for them to remember the particular question.

Moods and attitudes affect prospective memory (Clasen et al., 2013). For example, depressed people are less likely to push to remind themselves to do what they intend to do (Clasen et al., 2013).

Before moving to the next section, why don't you turn to the piece of paper on which you wrote the names of the four figures you first saw in the challenges to memory section—that is, sheet 4—and draw them from memory as exactly as you can. Hold on to the drawings. We'll talk about them soon.

6-2 PROCESSES OF MEMORY

Psychologists as well as computer scientists speak of processing information. Think of using a computer to write a term paper. Once the system is up and operating, you begin to enter information. You can enter information into the computer's memory by, for example, typing alphanumeric characters on a keyboard, scanning images, or—in the case of voice recognition technology—speaking. But if you were to do some major surgery on your computer and open up its memory, you wouldn't find these characters, images, or sounds inside it. This is because the computer is programmed to change the characters, images, and sounds you enter into a form that can be placed in its electronic memory. Similarly, when we perceive information, we must change it into a form that can be remembered if we are to place it in our memory— that is, by encoding it.

encode modifies information so that it can be placed in memory; encoding is the first stage of information processing

6-2a ENCODING

Information about the outside world reaches our senses in the form of physical and chemical stimuli. The first stage of information processing **encodes** these stimuli so that we can place them in memory. When transform sensory input and our own ideas into psychological formats that can be represented mentally. To do so, we commonly use visual, acoustic, and semantic codes.

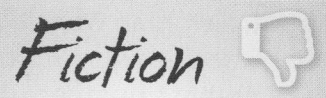

Let's illustrate the uses of coding by referring to the list of letters you first saw in the section on challenges to memory. Try to write the letters on sheet number 1. Go on, take a minute, and then come back.

If you had used a *visual code* to try to remember the list, you would have mentally represented it as a picture. That is, you would have maintained—or attempted to maintain—a mental image of the letters.

You may also have decided to read the list of letters to yourself—that is, to silently say them in sequence: "t," "h," "u," and so on. By so doing, you would have been using an *acoustic code,* or representing the stimuli as a sequence of sounds. You may also have read the list as a three-syllable word, "thun-sto-fam." This is an acoustic code, but it also involves the "meaning" of the letters, in the sense that you are interpreting the list as a word. This approach has elements of a semantic code.

Semantic codes represent stimuli in terms of their meaning. Our 10 letters were meaningless in and of themselves. However, they can also serve as an acronym—a term made up of the first letters of a phrase that is pronounced as a word—for the familiar phrase "THe UNited STates OF AMerica." This observation lends them meaning.

Fiction 👎

T | **F** | Learning must be meaningful if we are to remember it.

It is not true that learning must be meaningful if we are to remember it. Maintenance rehearsal often works as well.

6-2b STORAGE

The second memory process is *storage*. **Storage** means maintaining information over time. If you were given the task of storing the list of letters—that is, told to remember it—how would you attempt to place it in storage? One way would be by **maintenance rehearsal**—by mentally repeating the list, or saying it to yourself.

You could also encode the list of letters by relating it to something that you already know. This coding is called **elaborative rehearsal**. You are "elaborating" or extending the semantic meaning of the letters you are trying to remember. For example, as mentioned above, the list of 10 letters is an acronym for "The United States of America." That is, you take the first two letters of each of the words in the phrase and string them together to make up the 10 letters of THUNSTOFAM. If you had recognized this, storage of the list of letters might have been almost instantaneous, and it would probably have been permanent. But enough maintenance rehearsal can also often do the job.

6-2c RETRIEVAL

The third memory process is *retrieval*. **Retrieval** of stored information means locating it and returning it to consciousness. With well-known information such as our names and occupations, retrieval is effortless and rapid. But when we are trying to remember large amounts of information, or information that is not perfectly understood, retrieval can be difficult or fail. It is easiest to retrieve information stored in a computer by using the name of the file. Similarly, retrieval of information from our memories requires knowledge of the proper *retrieval cues*.

If you had encoded THUNSTOFAM as a three-syllable word, your retrieval strategy would involve recollection of the word and rules for decoding. In other words, you would say the "word" *thun-sto-fam* and then decode it by spelling it out. You might err in that "thun" sounds like "thumb" and "sto" could also be spelled "stow." However, using the semantic code, or recognition of the acronym for "The United States of America," would allow you to derive the correct list of letters every time, as follows: To "remember" the 10 letters, you envision the phrase ("The United States of America") and read off the first two letters of each word. You are actually reconstructing the list of 10 letters.

But what if you were not able to remember the list of 10 letters? What would have gone wrong? In terms of the three processes of memory, it could be that you had (a) not encoded the list in a useful way, (b) not entered the encoded information into storage, or (c) stored the information but forgotten the cues for remembering it—such as the phrase "The United States of America" or the rule for decoding the phrase.

You may have noticed that we have come a long way into this chapter, but I have not yet *defined* memory. No apologies—we weren't ready. Now that we have explored

storage the maintenance of information over time; the second stage of information processing

maintenance rehearsal mental repetition of information to keep it in memory

elaborative rehearsal the kind of coding in which new information is related to information that is already known

retrieval the location of stored information and its return to consciousness; the third stage of information processing

David Noton Photography/Alamy

THE STREAM OF THOUGHT FLOWS ON, BUT MOST OF ITS ELEMENTS FALL INTO THE BOTTOMLESS PIT OF OBLIVION. OF SOME, NO ELEMENT SURVIVES THE INSTANT OF THEIR PASSAGE. OF OTHERS, IT IS CONFINED TO A FEW MOMENTS, HOURS, OR DAYS. OTHERS, AGAIN, LEAVE VESTIGES WHICH ARE INDESTRUCTIBLE, AND BY MEANS OF WHICH THEY MAY BE RECALLED AS LONG AS LIFE ENDURES.

WILLIAM JAMES, AMERICAN PHILOSOPHER AND PSYCHOLOGIST (1842–1910)

some basic concepts, let's give it a try: **Memory** is the processes by which information is encoded, stored, and retrieved.

6-3 STAGES OF MEMORY

William James (1890) was intrigued by the fact that some memories are unreliable. They would "go in one ear and out the other," while other memories stuck for a lifetime. The world is a dazzling array of sights and sounds and other sources of sensory information, but only some of

it is remembered. Psychologists Richard Atkinson and Richard Shiffrin (1968) suggested a model for how some information is lost immediately, other information is held briefly, and still other information is held for a lifetime. As shown in Figure 6.1, they proposed three stages of memory that determine whether (and how long) information is retained: *sensory memory, short-term memory (STM),* and *long-term memory (LTM).*

6-3a SENSORY MEMORY

When we look at a visual stimulus, our impressions may seem fluid enough. Actually, however, they consist of a series of eye fixations referred to as *saccadic eye*

FIG. 6.1 STAGES OF MEMORY: SENSORY, SHORT-TERM, AND LONG-TERM

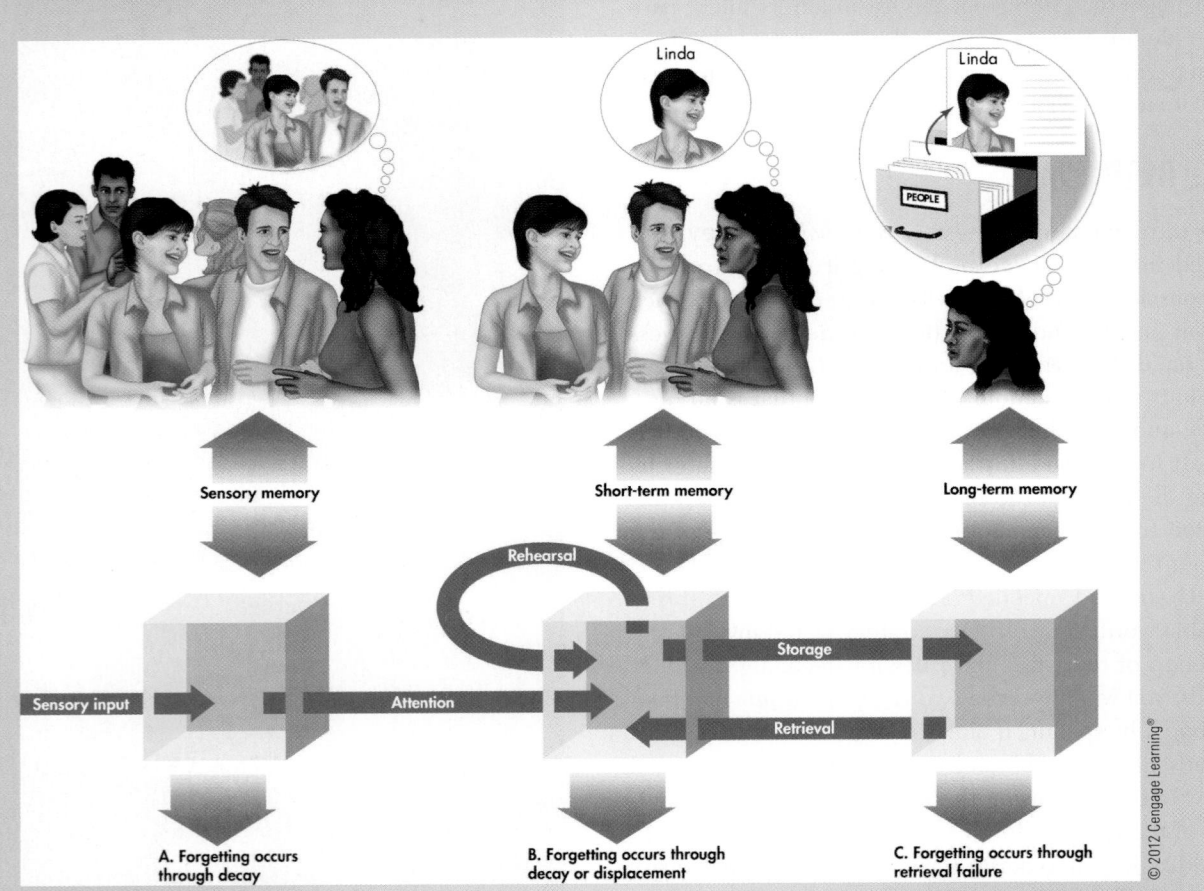

The Atkinson–Shiffrin model proposes that there are three stages of memory: (a) sensory memory, (b) short-term memory, and (c) long-term memory. Part A shows that sensory information impacts on the registers of the sensory memory. Memory traces are held briefly in sensory memory before decaying. If we attend to the information, much of it can be transferred to short-term memory (STM). Part B: Information may be maintained in STM through maintenance rehearsal or elaborative rehearsal. Otherwise, it may decay or be displaced. Part C: Once information is transferred to long-term memory (LTM), it may be filed away indefinitely. However, if the information in LTM is organized poorly, or if we cannot find cues to retrieve it, it can be lost.

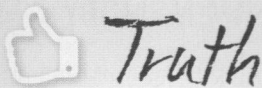
movements. These movements jump from one point to another about four times each second. Yet the visual sensations seem continuous, or stream like, because of **sensory memory**. Sensory memory is the type or stage of memory that is first encountered by a stimulus. Although sensory memory holds impressions briefly, it is long enough so that a series of perceptions seem to be connected.

To understand the functioning of sensory memory, let's return to our list of letters: THUNSTOFAM. If the list were flashed on a screen for a fraction of a second, the visual impression, or **memory trace**, of the stimulus would also last for only a fraction of a second afterward. Psychologists speak of the memory trace of the list as being held in a visual *sensory register*.

If the letters had been flashed on a screen for, say, one-tenth of a second, your ability to remember them on the basis of sensory memory alone would be limited. Your memory would be based on a single eye fixation, and the trace of the image would vanish before a single second had passed. A century ago, psychologist William McDougall (1904) engaged in research in which he showed people one to 12 letters arranged in rows—just long enough to allow a single eye fixation. Under these conditions, people could typically remember only four or five letters. Thus, recollection of THUNSTOFAM, a list of 10 letters arranged in a single row, would probably depend on whether one had encoded it so that it could be processed further.

George Sperling (1960) modified McDougall's experimental method and showed that there is a difference between what people can see and what they can report. McDougall had used a *whole-report procedure*, in which people were asked to report every letter they saw in the array. Sperling used a modified *partial-report procedure*, in which people were asked to report the contents of one of three rows of letters. In a typical procedure, Sperling flashed three rows of letters like the following on a screen for 50 milliseconds (one-twentieth of a second):

<table>
<tr><td>A</td><td>G</td><td>R</td><td>E</td></tr>
<tr><td>V</td><td>L</td><td>S</td><td>B</td></tr>
<tr><td>N</td><td>K</td><td>B</td><td>T</td></tr>
</table>

Using the whole-report procedure, people could report an average of four letters from the entire display (one out of three). But if immediately after presenting the display Sperling pointed an arrow at a row he wanted viewers to report, they usually reported most of the letters in the row successfully.

If Sperling presented six letters arrayed in two rows, people could usually report either row without error. If people were flashed three rows of four letters each—a total of 12—they reported correctly an average of three of four letters in the designated row, suggesting that about nine of the 12 letters had been perceived.

Sperling found that the amount of time that elapsed before he pointed to the row to be reported affected people's memory. If he delayed pointing for a few fractions of a second after showing the letters, people were less successful in reporting the letters in the row. If he allowed a full second to elapse, the arrow did not help people remember at all. Sperling concluded that the memory trace of visual stimuli *decays* within a second (see Figure 6.1). With a single eye fixation, people can *see* most of a display of 12 letters clearly, as shown by their ability to immediately read off most of the letters in a designated row. Yet as fractions of a second are elapsing, the memory trace of the letters is fading. By the time a full second elapses, the trace is gone.

ICONIC MEMORY

Psychologists believe we possess a sensory register for each sense. The mental representations of visual stimuli are referred to as **icons**. The sensory register that holds icons is labeled **iconic memory**. Iconic

> # THE TRUE ART OF MEMORY IS THE ART OF ATTENTION.
>
> DR. SAMUEL JOHNSON, ENGLISH POET, EDITOR, AND LEXICOGRAPHER (1709–1784)

sensory memory the type or stage of memory first encountered by a stimulus; sensory memory holds impressions briefly, but long enough so that series of perceptions are psychologically continuous

memory trace an assumed change in the nervous system that reflects the impression made by a stimulus

icon a mental representation of a visual stimulus that is held briefly in sensory memory

iconic memory the sensory register that briefly holds mental representations of visual stimuli

memories are accurate, photographic memories. If you can see and are not neurologically impaired, you have a "photographic memory." But such memories are brief. What most of us usually think of as a photographic memory—the ability to retain exact mental representations of visual stimuli over long periods—is technically termed **eidetic imagery**. Only a few people are capable of eidetic imagery.

ICONIC MEMORY AND SACCADIC EYE MOVEMENTS Saccadic eye movements occur about four times a second, but iconic memory holds icons for up to a second. For this reason, the flow of visual information seems smooth and continuous. Your impression that the words you are reading flow across the page, rather than jumping across in spurts, is a product of your iconic memory. Similarly, motion pictures present 16 to 22 separate frames, or still images, each second, but iconic memory allows you to perceive the imagery in the film as being seamless (Murphy & Andalis, 2013).

ECHOIC MEMORY Mental representations of sounds, or auditory stimuli, are called **echoes**. **Echoic memory** is the sensory register that holds echoes.

The memory traces of auditory stimuli—echoes—can last for several seconds, many times longer than the traces of visual stimuli (icons). This difference is one of the reasons that acoustic codes aid in the retention of information that has been presented visually—or why saying the letters or syllables of THUNSTOFAM makes the list easier to remember.

6-3b SHORT-TERM MEMORY

Imagine you are completing a writing assignment, and you key or speak words and phrases into your word-processing program. They appear on your monitor as a sign that your computer has them in *memory*. Your word-processing program allows you to add words, delete words, check whether they are spelled correctly, add images, and move paragraphs from place to place. Although you can manipulate the information in your computer's memory, it isn't saved. It hasn't been entered into storage. If the program or the computer crashes, the information is gone. The computer's memory is a short-term affair. To maintain a long-term connection with the information, you have to save it. Saving it means giving it a name—hopefully, a name that you will remember so that you can later find and retrieve the information—and instructing your computer to save it (keep it in storage until told otherwise).

If you focus on a stimulus in the sensory register, you will tend to retain it in your own **short-term memory**—also referred to as **working memory**—for a minute or so after the trace of the stimulus decays. As Goldman-Rakic put it, "Working memory is the mental glue that links a thought through time from its beginning to its end" (1995).

Comstock/Stockbyte/Getty Images

These actors are memorizing a script by rehearsing echoic memories. As actors work on memorizing scripts, they first encode visual information (printed words) as echoes (their corresponding sounds within the brain). Then they commit the echoes to memory by rehearsing (repeating) them, referring back to the visual information as necessary. Eventually, the lines of other actors become cues that trigger memory of an actor's own lines.

When you are given a new phone number and write it down or immediately dial the number, you are retaining the number in your short-term memory. When you are told the name of someone at a party and then use that name immediately in addressing that person, you are retaining the name in short-term memory. In short-term memory, the image tends to fade significantly after 10 to 12 seconds if it is not repeated or rehearsed. It is possible to focus on maintaining a visual image in the short-term memory, but it is more common to encode visual stimuli as sounds, or auditory stimuli. Then the sounds can be rehearsed, or repeated.

Once information is in our short-term memories, we can work on it. Like the information in the word-processing program, we can manipulate it. But it isn't necessarily saved. If we don't do something to save—such as write down a new telephone number or key it into your cellphone's contact list—it can be gone forever. You need to rehearse new information to "save" it, but you may need only the proper cue to retrieve information from long-term memory.

Let's now return to the task of remembering the first list of letters in the challenges to memory at the beginning of the chapter. If you had encoded the letters as the three-syllable "word" THUN-STO-FAM, you would probably have recalled them by mentally rehearsing (saying to yourself) the three-syllable "word" and then spelling it out from the sounds. A few minutes later, if someone asked whether the letters had been uppercase (THUNSTOFAM) or lowercase (thunstofam), you might not have been able to answer with confidence. You used an acoustic code to help recall the list, and uppercase and lowercase letters sound alike.

Because it can be pronounced, THUNSTOFAM is not too difficult to retain in short-term memory. But what if the list of letters had been TBXLFNTSDK? This list of letters cannot be pronounced as it is. You would have to find a complex acronym to code these letters, and do so within a fraction of a second—most likely an impossible task. To aid recall, you would probably choose to try to repeat the letters rapidly—to read each one as many times as possible before the memory trace fades. You might visualize each letter as you say it and try to get back to it (i.e., to run through the entire list) before it decays.

Let's assume that you encoded the letters as sounds and then rehearsed the sounds. When asked to report the list, you might mistakenly say T-V-X-L-F-N-T-S-T-K. This would be an understandable error because the incorrect V and T sounds are similar, respectively, to the correct B and D sounds.

THE SERIAL-POSITION EFFECT If asked to recall the list of letters TBXLFNTSDK, you would be likely

to recall the first and last letters in the series, T and K, more accurately than the others. The tendency to recall the first and last items in a series is known as the **serial-position effect**. This effect may occur because we pay more attention to the first and last stimuli in a series. They serve as the visual or auditory boundaries for the other stimuli. In addition, the first items are likely to be rehearsed more frequently (repeated more times) than other items. The last items are likely to have been rehearsed most recently and hence are most likely to be retained in short-term memory.

CHUNKING Rapidly rehearsing 10 meaningless letters is not an easy task. With TBXLFNTSDK there are 10 discrete elements, or **chunks**, of information that must be kept in short-term memory. When we encode THUNSTOFAM as three syllables, there are only three chunks to memorize at once—a memory task that is much easier on the digestion.

Psychologist George Miller (1956), as we noted earlier, found that the average person is comfortable with remembering about seven integers at a time, the number of integers in a telephone number. Businesses pay the phone company hefty premiums so that they can attain numbers with two or three zeroes or repeated digits—for example, 592-2000 or 272-3333. These numbers include fewer chunks of information and so are easier to remember. Customer recollection of business phone numbers increases sales. A financial services company might use the toll-free number CALL-IRA, which reduces the task to two chunks of information that also happen to be meaningfully related (semantically coded) to the nature of the business.

Return to the third challenge to memory presented earlier. Were you able to remember the six groups of letters (GMC-BSI-BMA-TTC-IAF-BI)? Would your task have been simpler if you had grouped them differently? How about moving the dashes forward by a letter, so that they read GM-CBS-IBM-ATT-CIA-FBI? If we do this, we have the same list of letters, but we also have six chunks of information that can be coded semantically (according to what they mean). You may have also been able to generate the list by remembering a rule, such as "big corporations and government agencies."

Reconsider the second challenge to memory presented earlier. You were asked to remember nine chunks of visual information. Perhaps you could have used the acoustic codes "L" and

serial-position effect the tendency to recall more accurately the first and last items in a series

chunk a stimulus or group of stimuli that are perceived as a discrete piece of information

FIG.6.2 A FAMILIAR GRID

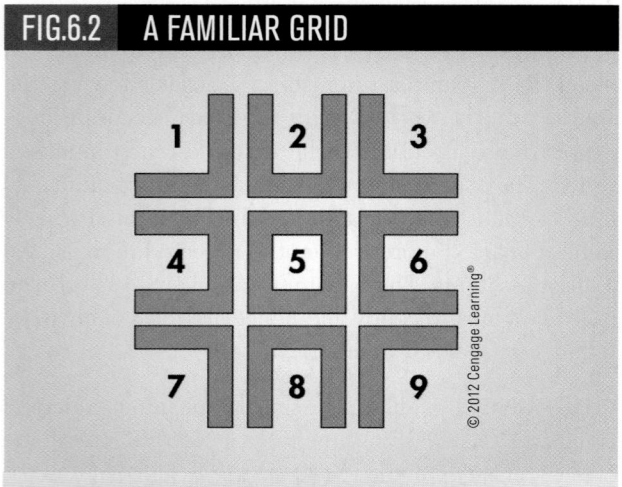

The nine drawings in the second challenge to memory form this familiar tic-tac-toe grid when the numbers are placed inside them and they are arranged in order. This method for recalling the shapes collapses nine chunks of information into two. One is the tic-tac-toe grid. The second is the rule for decoding the drawings from the grid.

displace in memory theory, to cause information to be lost from short-term memory by adding new information

long-term memory the type or stage of memory capable of relatively permanent storage

"Square" for chunks three and five, but no obvious codes are available for the seven other chunks. Now look at Figure 6.2. If you had recognized that the elements in the challenge could be arranged as the familiar tic-tac-toe grid, remembering the nine elements might have required two chunks of information. The first would have been the mental image of the grid, and the second would have been the rule for decoding: Each element corresponds to the shape of a section of the grid if read like words on a page (from upper left to lower right). The number sequence 1 through 9 would not in itself present a

problem, because you learned this series by rote many years ago and have rehearsed it in countless calculations since then.

INTERFERENCE IN SHORT-TERM MEMORY In a classic experiment with college students, Lloyd and Margaret Peterson (1959) demonstrated how prevention of rehearsal can wreak havoc with short-term memory. They asked students to remember three-letter combinations such as HGB—normally, three easy chunks of information. They then had the students count backward from an arbitrary number, such as 181, by threes (i.e., 181, 178, 175, 172, and so on). The students were told to stop counting and to report the letter sequence after the intervals of time shown in Figure 6.3. The percentage of correctly recalled letter combinations fell dramatically within seconds. Counting backward for 18 seconds had dislodged the letter sequences in almost all of these bright students' memories.

Psychologists say that the appearance of new information in short-term memory **displaces** the old information. Remember: only a few bits of information can be retained in short-term memory at the same time (Farrell, 2012).

6-3c LONG-TERM MEMORY

Long-term memory is the third stage of information processing (refer back to Figure 6.1). Think of your long-term memory as a vast storehouse of information

FIG.6.3 THE EFFECT OF INTERFERENCE ON SHORT-TERM MEMORY

In this experiment, college students were asked to remember a series of three letters while they counted backward by threes. After just three seconds, retention was cut by half. Ability to recall the words was almost completely lost by 15 seconds.

containing names, dates, places, what Johnny did to you in second grade, and what Susan said about you when you were 12.

Some psychologists (Freud was one) believed that nearly all of our perceptions and ideas are stored permanently. We might not be able to retrieve all of them, however. Some memories might be "lost" because of lack of proper cues. Still others might be kept unconscious by the forces of **repression**. Adherents to this view often pointed to the work of neurosurgeon Wilder Penfield (1969). When parts of their brains were electrically stimulated, many of Penfield's patients reported the appearance of images that had something of the feel of memories.

Today, most psychologists view this notion as exaggerated. Memory researcher Elizabeth Loftus, for example, notes that the "memories" stimulated by Penfield's probes lacked detail and were sometimes incorrect (e.g., Bernstein & Loftus, 2009). Therefore, it has *not* been shown that all of our experiences are permanently imprinted on the brain. Now let's consider some other questions about long-term memory.

HOW ACCURATE ARE LONG-TERM MEMORIES?
Psychologist Elizabeth Loftus notes that memories are distorted by our biases and needs—by the ways in which we conceptualize our worlds. We represent much of our world in the form of **schemas**. A *schema* is a way of mentally representing the world, such as a belief or expectation, which can influence our perception of persons, objects, and situations.

Now, retrieve sheet number 4. You drew the figures "from memory" according to instructions on page 000. Now look at Figure 6.4. Are your drawings closer in form to those in group 1 or to those in group 2? I wouldn't be surprised if they were more like those in group 1—if, for example, your first drawing looked more like eyeglasses than a dumbbell. After all, they were labeled like the drawings in group 1. The labels serve as *schemas* for the drawings—ways of organizing your knowledge of them—and these schemas may have influenced your recollections. By the way, take out a penny and look at it. Did you pick the correct penny when you answered the challenges to memory?

HOW MUCH INFORMATION CAN BE STORED IN LONG-TERM MEMORY? How many terabytes of storage are there in your most personal computer—your brain? Unlike a computer, the human ability to

repression in Freud's psychodynamic theory, the ejection of anxiety-evoking ideas from conscious awareness

schema a way of mentally representing the world, such as a belief or an expectation, that can influence perception of persons, objects, and situations

FIG.6.4 MEMORY AS RECONSTRUCTIVE

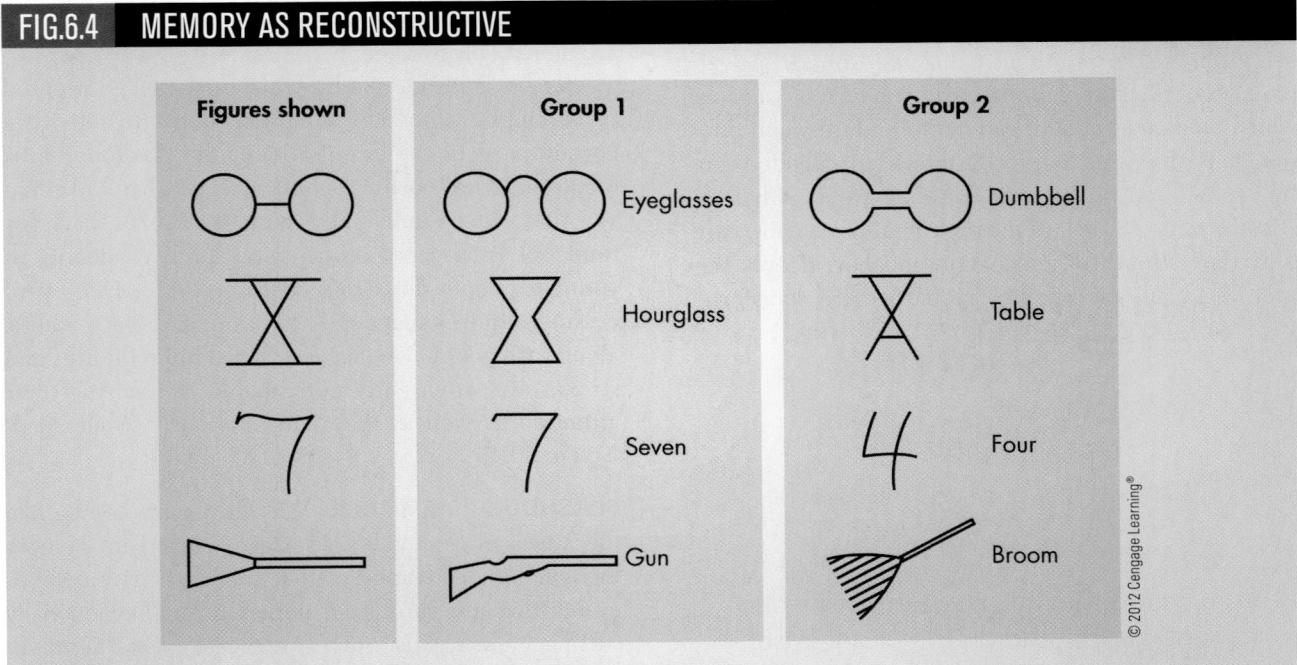

In their classic experiment, Carmichael, Hogan, and Walter (1932) showed people the figures in the left box and made remarks as suggested in the other boxes. For example, the experimenter might say, "This drawing looks like eyeglasses [or a dumbbell]." When people later reconstructed the drawings, they were influenced by the labels.

© 2012 Cengage Learning®

store information is, for all practical purposes, unlimited (Voss, 2009; Y. Wang et al., 2009). Even the largest hard drives fill up when we save Web pages, pictures, or videos. Yet how many "movies" of the past have you saved in your own long-term memory? How many thousands of scenes and stories can you rerun at will? And, assuming that you have an intact sensory system, the movies in your personal storage bins not only have color and sound but also aromas, tactile sensations, and more. *Your long-term memory is a biochemical "hard drive" with no known limits on the amount of information it can store.*

New information may replace older information in short-term memory, but there is no evidence that long-term memories—those in "storage"—are lost by displacement. Long-term memories may endure a lifetime. Now and then, it may seem that we have forgotten, or "lost," a long-term memory such as the names of elementary-school classmates, yet it may be that we cannot find the proper cues to retrieve them. However, if you drive by your elementary school (a cue) you might suddenly recall the long-lost names of schoolteachers.

LEVELS OF PROCESSING INFORMATION People who use elaborative rehearsal (the kind of coding in which new information is related to information that is already known) to remember things are processing information at a deeper level than people who use maintenance rehearsal (mental repetition of information to keep it in memory). Fergus Craik and Robert Lockhart pioneered the *levels-of-processing model of memory,* which holds that memories tend to endure when information is processed *deeply*—attended to, encoded carefully, pondered, and related to things we already know (Rose & Craik, 2012). Remembering relies on how carefully they attend to information and how deeply they process it, not on whether memories are transferred

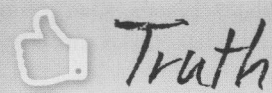
Truth

T F It may be easier for you to recall the name of your first-grade teacher than the name of someone you just met at a party.

It is true that it may be easier to recall the name of your first grade teacher than those of people you have just met. The learning of additional names may interfere with remembering a name learned a few minutes ago. In addition, you probably had countless meaningful interactions with your first grade teacher.

from one stage of memory to another (Rose & Craik, 2012). If you are bombarded by one name after another at a cocktail party, it may be easier for you to recall the name of your first-grade teacher—someone with whom you had countless interactions—than the name of someone you just met.

Think of all the math problems we solved in high school. Each problem is an application of a procedure and, perhaps, of certain formulas. By repeatedly applying the procedures and formulas in slightly different contexts, we rehearse them elaboratively. As a result, we are more likely to remember them.

There is also a good deal of biologically oriented research that connects deep processing with activity in certain parts of the brain, notably the prefrontal area of the cerebral cortex (Schott et al., 2013). One reason that older adults show memory loss is that they tend not to process information quite as deeply as younger people do (Craik & Rose, 2013). Deep processing requires sustained attention, and older adults, along with people who have suffered brain injuries and strokes, are apparently not capable of focusing their attention as well as they had previously (Sherratt & Bryan, 2012).

FLASHBULB MEMORIES Why are some events, like the attack of September 11, 2001, etched in memory for a lifetime? It appears that we tend to remember events that are surprising, important, and emotionally stirring more clearly. Such events can create *flashbulb memories,* which preserve experiences in detail (Tinti et al., 2013). Why is the memory etched when the "flashbulb" goes off? One factor is the distinctness of the memory. It is easier to discriminate stimuli that stand out.

Fiction

T F All of our experiences are permanently imprinted on the brain, so the proper stimulus can cause us to remember them exactly.

It is not true that all experiences are permanently imprinted on the brain. Experiences are more likely to be remembered when we pay attention to them and encode them in a useful way.

Such events are striking in themselves. The feelings caused by them are also special. It is thus relatively easy to pick them out from the storehouse of memories. Major events such as the assassination of a president or the loss of a close relative also tend to have important effects on our lives. We are likely to dwell on them and form networks of associations. That is, we are likely to rehearse them elaboratively. Our rehearsal may include great expectations, or deep fears, for the future. Therefore, you may always recall where you were and what you were doing on the morning of September 11, 2001, when terrorists attacked the World Trade Center and the Pentagon.

Biology is intimately connected with psychology. Strong feelings are connected with the secretion of stress hormones, and stress hormones help carve events into memory— "as almost to leave a scar upon the cerebral tissues," as noted by William James.

ORGANIZATION IN LONG-TERM MEMORY The storehouse of long-term memory is usually well organized. Items are not just piled on the floor or thrown into closets. We tend to gather information about rats and cats into a certain section of the storehouse, perhaps the animal or mammal section. We put information about oaks, maples, and eucalyptus into the tree section. Such categorization of stimuli is a basic cognitive function. It allows us to make predictions about specific instances and to store information efficiently.

Why is it that some events, such as the terrorist attack of September 11, 2001, can be etched in memory for a lifetime?

AP Images/Carmen Taylor

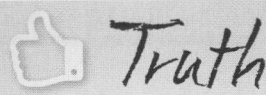

T F You may always recall where you were and what you were doing on the morning of September 11, 2001.

It is true that the "flashbulb" in your memory probably went off on September 11, 2001, even though you were quite a bit younger than you are now and that event occurred more than 10 years ago. You may recall where you were and what you were doing at the time for decades to come.

We tend to organize information according to a *hierarchical structure*, as shown in Figure 6.5. A *hierarchy* is an arrangement of items (or chunks of information) into groups or classes according to common or distinct features. As we work our way up the hierarchy shown in the figure, we find more encompassing, or *superordinate*, classes to which the items below them belong. For example, all mammals are animals, but there are many types of animals other than mammals.

When items are correctly organized in long-term memory, you are more likely to recall—or know—accurate information about them. For example, do you "remember" whether whales breathe underwater? If you did not know that whales are mammals (or in Figure 6.5, *subordinate* to mammals), or if you knew nothing about mammals, a correct answer might depend on some remote instance of rote learning. That is, you might be depending on chancy episodic memory rather than on reliable semantic memory. For example, you might recall some details from a TV documentary on whales. If you *did* know that whales are mammals, however, you would also know—or remember—that whales do not breathe underwater. How? You would reconstruct information about whales from knowledge about mammals, the group to which whales are subordinate. Similarly, you would know, or remember, that because they are mammals, whales are warm-blooded, nurse their young, and are a good deal more intelligent than, say, tunas and sharks, which are fish. Had you incorrectly classified whales as fish, you might have searched your memory and constructed the incorrect answer that they do breathe underwater.

FIG.6.5 THE HIERARCHICAL STRUCTURE OF LONG-TERM MEMORY

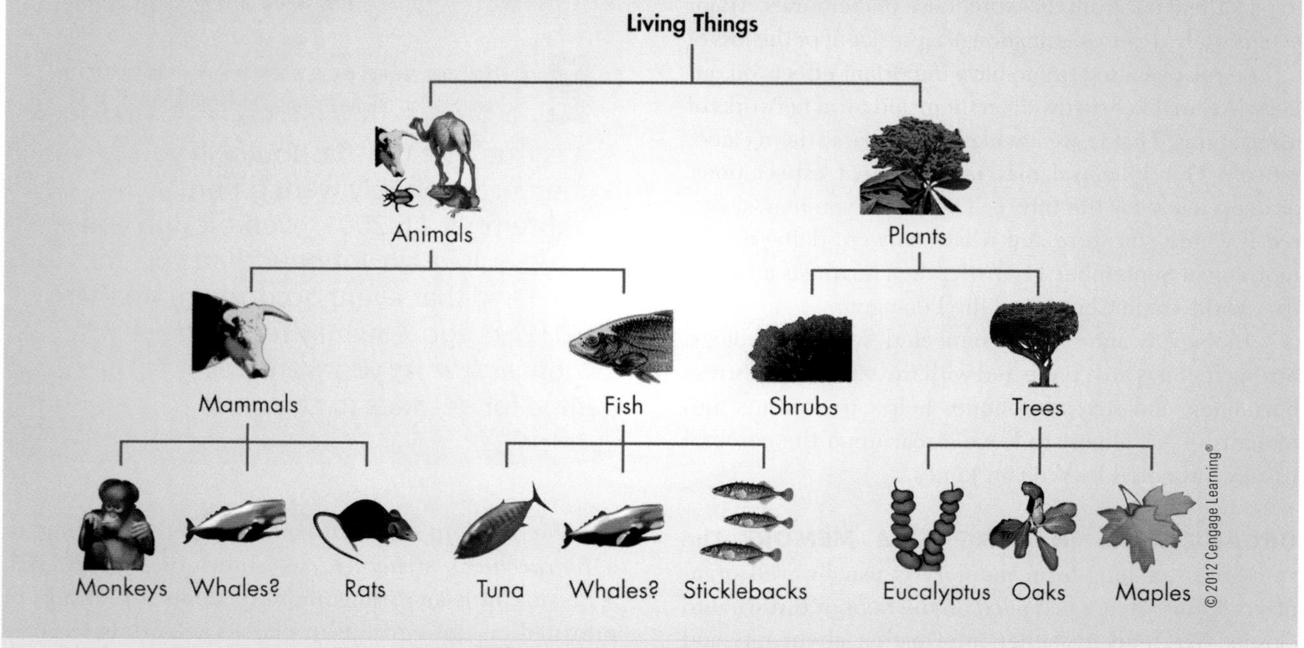

Living Things

Animals — Plants

Mammals — Fish — Shrubs — Trees

Monkeys — Whales? — Rats — Tuna — Whales? — Sticklebacks — Eucalyptus — Oaks — Maples

© 2012 Cengage Learning®

Where are whales filed in the hierarchical cabinets of your memory? Your classification of whales may influence your answers to these questions: Do whales breathe underwater? Are they warm-blooded? Do they nurse their young? A note to biological purists: This figure is not intended to represent phyla, classes, orders, and so on accurately. Rather, it shows how an individual's classification scheme might be organized.

> IT'S DÉJÀ VU ALL OVER AGAIN.
>
> YOGI BERRA, AMERICAN MAJOR LEAGUE BASEBALL PLAYER (B.1925)

Your memory is thus organized according to a remarkably complex filing system that has a certain internal logic. If you place a piece of information into the wrong file, it is probably not the fault of the filing system itself. Nevertheless, you may "lose" the information in the sense of not being able to find the best cues to retrieve it.

THE TIP-OF-THE-TONGUE PHENOMENON How often have you had something on "the tip of your tongue" and not been quite able to remember it? Having something on the tip of your tongue can be a frustrating experience. The **tip-of-the-tongue**

tip-of-the-tongue (TOT) phenomenon the feeling that information is stored in memory although it cannot be readily retrieved; also called the *feeling-of-knowing experience*

(TOT) phenomenon is also known as the *feeling-of-knowing experience*.

Research provides insight into the TOT phenomenon (Brown & McNeill, 1966; Schwartz, 2008). In classic research, Brown and McNeill (1966) defined some rather unusual words for students, such as *sampan*, a small riverboat used in China and Japan. The students were then asked to recall the words they had learned. Some of the students often had the right word "on the tip of their tongue" but reported words with similar meanings such as junk, barge, or houseboat. Still other students reported words that sounded similar, such as Saipan, Siam, sarong, and sanching. Why?

To begin with, the words were unfamiliar, so elaborative rehearsal did not take place. The students did not have an opportunity to relate the words to other things they knew. Brown and McNeill also suggested that our storage systems are indexed according to cues that include both the sounds and the meanings of words—that is, according to both acoustic and semantic codes. By scanning words similar in sound and meaning to the word on the tip of the tongue, we sometimes find a useful cue and retrieve the word for which we are searching.

Sometimes an answer seems to be on the tip of our tongue because our learning of the topic is incomplete. We may not know the exact answer, but we know something. (As a matter of fact, if we have good writing skills, we may present our incomplete knowledge so forcefully that we earn a good grade on an essay question on the topic!) At such times, the problem lies not in retrieval but in the original processes of learning and memory—that is, encoding and storage.

CONTEXT-DEPENDENT MEMORY The context in which we acquire information can also play a role in retrieval. I remember walking down the halls of the apartment building where I had lived as a child. Cooking odors triggered a sudden assault of images of playing under the staircase, of falling against a radiator, of the shrill voice of a former neighbor calling for her child at dinnertime. Odors, it turns out, are particularly likely to trigger related memories (Zucco et al., 2012).

My experience was an example of a **context-dependent memory**. My memories were particularly clear in the context in which they were formed. It could also be helpful, if possible, to study in the same room in which a test will be given. Being in the proper context—for example, studying in the exam room or under the same conditions—can dramatically enhance recall (Isarida & Isarida, 2006).

According to a study with 20 bilingual Cornell students, the "context" for memory extends to language (Marian & Neisser, 2000). The students emigrated from Russia at an average age of 14 and were an average of about 22 years old at the time of the experiment. They were asked to recall the details of experiences in Russia and the United States. When they were interviewed in Russian, they were better able to retrieve experiences from their lives in Russia. Similarly, when they were interviewed in English, they were better able to recall events that happened in the United States.

STATE-DEPENDENT MEMORY **State-dependent memory** is an extension of context-dependent memory. We sometimes retrieve information better when we are in a biological or emotional state similar to the one in which we encoded and stored the information. Feeling the rush of love may trigger other images of falling in love. The grip of anger may prompt memories of incidents of frustration. The research in this area extends to states in which we are sober or inebriated.

> **context-dependent memory** information that is better retrieved in the context in which it was encoded and stored, or learned
>
> **state-dependent memory** information that is better retrieved in the physiological or emotional state in which it was encoded and stored, or learned
>
> **nonsense syllables** meaningless sets of two consonants, with a vowel sandwiched in between, that are used to study memory

Datacraft Co Ltd/Getty Images

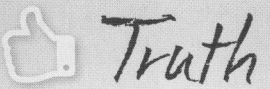

Truth

| **T** | F | If you study with the stereo on, you would probably do better to take the test with the stereo on. |

It is true that you might do better taking the test with the stereo on—as with earbuds—if you studied with the stereo on. (Of course, your professor might object to your using an MP3 player during an exam.)

6-4 FORGETTING

What do DAL, RIK, BOF, and ZEX have in common? They are all **nonsense syllables**. Nonsense syllables are meaningless sets of two consonants with a vowel sandwiched in between. They were first used by Hermann Ebbinghaus (1850–1909) to study memory and forgetting. Because nonsense syllables are intended to be meaningless, remembering them should depend on simple acoustic coding and maintenance rehearsal rather than on elaborative rehearsal, semantic coding, or other ways of making learning meaningful. They are thus well suited for use in the measurement of forgetting.

6-4a MEMORY TASKS USED IN MEASURING FORGETTING

Three basic memory tasks have been used by psychologists to measure forgetting: recognition, recall, and relearning. Nonsense syllables have been used in studying each of them. The study of these memory tasks has led to several conclusions about the nature of forgetting.

RECOGNITION One aspect of forgetting is failure to recognize something we have experienced. There are many ways of measuring *recognition*. In many studies, psychologists ask subjects to read a list of nonsense syllables. The subjects then read a second list of nonsense syllables and indicate whether they recognize any of the syllables as having appeared on the first list. Forgetting is defined as failure to recognize a syllable that has been read before.

In another kind of recognition study, Harry Bahrick and his colleagues (1975) studied high-school graduates who had been out of school for various lengths of time. They interspersed photos of the graduates' classmates with four times as many photos of strangers. Recent graduates correctly recognized former classmates 90% of the time. Those who had been out of school for 40 years, recognized former classmates 75% of the time. A chance level of recognition would have been only 20% (one photo in five was of an actual classmate). Thus, even older people showed rather solid long-term recognition ability.

Recognition is the easiest type of memory task. This is why multiple-choice tests are easier than fill-in-the-blank or essay tests. We can recognize correct answers more easily than we can recall them unaided.

RECALL In his own studies of *recall*, another memory task, Ebbinghaus would read lists of nonsense syllables aloud to the beat of a metronome and then see how many he could produce from memory. After reading through a list once, he usually would be able to recall seven syllables—the typical limit for short-term memory.

Psychologists also often use lists of pairs of nonsense syllables, called **paired associates**, to measure recall. A list of paired associates is shown in Figure 6.6. Subjects read through the lists pair by pair. Later they are shown the first member of each pair and are asked to recall the second. Recall is more difficult than recognition. In a recognition task, one simply indicates whether an item has been seen before or which of a number of items is paired with a stimulus (as in a multiple-choice

paired associates nonsense syllables presented in pairs in experiments that measure recall

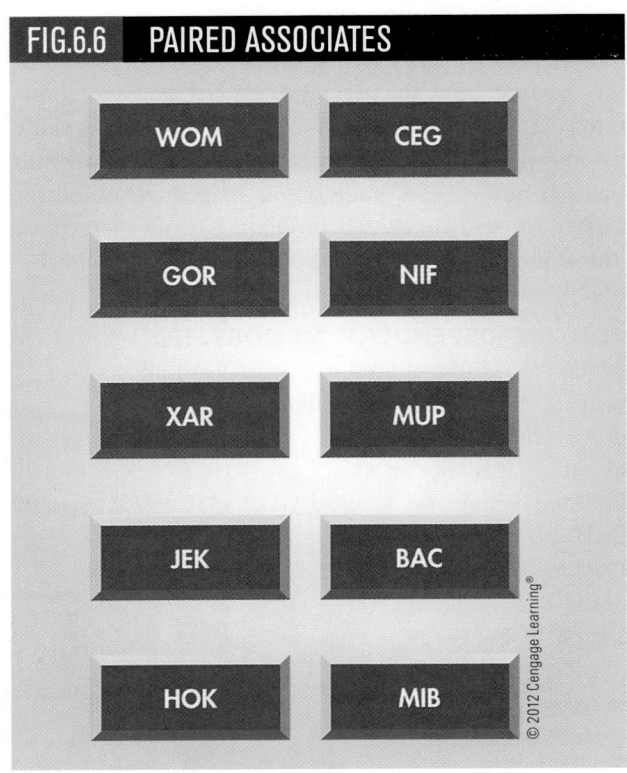

FIG.6.6 PAIRED ASSOCIATES

WOM	CEG
GOR	NIF
XAR	MUP
JEK	BAC
HOK	MIB

© 2012 Cengage Learning®

test). In a recall task, the person must retrieve a syllable, with another syllable serving as a cue.

Retrieval is made easier if the two syllables can be meaningfully linked—that is, encoded semantically—even if the "meaning" is stretched. Consider the first pair of nonsense syllables in Figure 6.6. The image of a WOMan smoking a CEG-arette may make CEG easier to retrieve when the person is presented with the cue WOM.

Harry Bahrick (Bahrick et al., 2008) conducted a study to see whether people could recall college grades from 1 to 50 years earlier. The researchers recruited 276 alumni of Ohio Wesleyan University who had graduated 1 to 50 years earlier. Participants were asked to recall their college grades, and their recollections

> I'VE LEARNED THAT PEOPLE WILL FORGET WHAT YOU SAID, PEOPLE WILL FORGET WHAT YOU DID, BUT PEOPLE WILL NEVER FORGET HOW YOU MADE THEM FEEL.
>
> MAYA ANGELOU, AMERICAN AUTHOR AND POET (1928–2014)

FIG.6.7 MEMORY FOR COLLEGE GRADES, HALF A CENTURY LATER

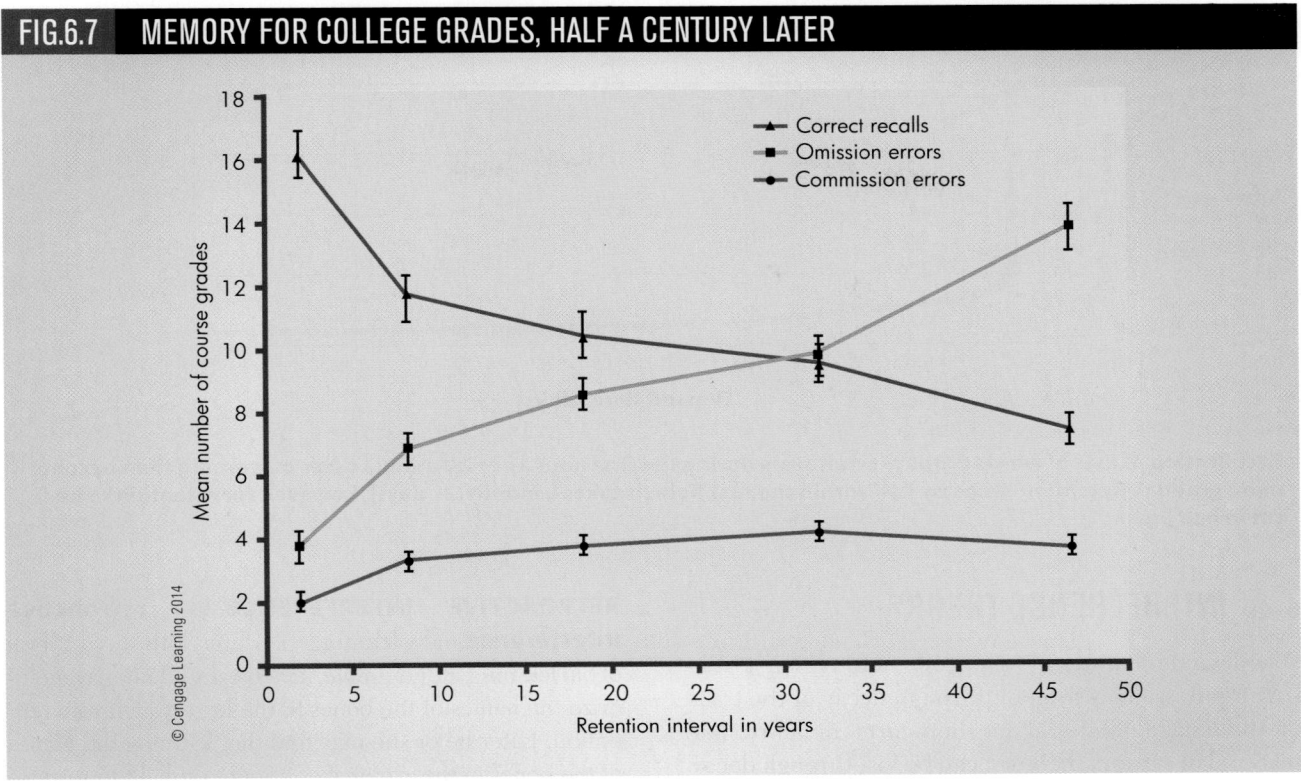

were checked against their actual grades. The alumni accurately recalled 3,025 of 3,967 college grades. As you can see in Figure 6.7, the number of correct recollections fell off with the age of the respondent, generally due to errors of omission. But graduates who were out of school more than 40 years, made no more errors of commission—that is, entered no more wrong grades—than those who were out of school about eight years. Students who received better grades made fewer errors. Eighty-one percent of wrong entries inflated the grade. The researchers suggest that we bring in relevant generic memories to fill in gaps ("I was sort of a good student; I got a B+.") after our actual episodic memory fails and that most of us distort our memories in a more emotionally gratifying fashion.

RELEARNING *Relearning* is a third method of measuring retention. Do you remember having to learn all of the state capitals in grade school? What were the capitals of Wyoming and Delaware? Even when we cannot recall or recognize material that had once been learned, such as Cheyenne for Wyoming and Dover for Delaware, we can relearn it more rapidly the second time.

To study the efficiency of relearning, Ebbinghaus devised the **method of savings**. First, he recorded the number of repetitions required to learn a list of nonsense syllables or words. Then, he recorded the number of repetitions required to relearn the list after a certain amount of time had elapsed. Next, he computed the difference in the number of repetitions to determine the **savings**. If a list had to be repeated 20 times before it was learned, and 20 times again after a year had passed, there were no savings. Relearning, that is, was as tedious as the initial learning. If the list could be learned with only 10 repetitions after a year had elapsed, however, half the number of repetitions required for learning had been saved.

Figure 6.8 shows Ebbinghaus's classic curve of forgetting. As you can see, there was no loss of memory as measured by savings immediately after a list had been learned. However, recollection dropped quite a bit, by half, during the first hour after learning a list. Losses of learning then became more gradual. It took a month (31 days) for retention to be cut in half again. That is, forgetting occurred most rapidly right after material was learned. We continue to forget material as time elapses but at a slower pace.

method of savings a measure of retention in which the difference between the number of repetitions originally required to learn a list and the number of repetitions required to re-learn the list after a certain amount of time has elapsed is calculated

savings the difference between the number of repetitions originally required to learn a list and the number of repetitions required to relearn the list after a certain amount of time has elapsed

FIG.6.8   HOW QUICKLY THEY FORGET! EBBINGHAUS'S CURVE OF FORGETTING

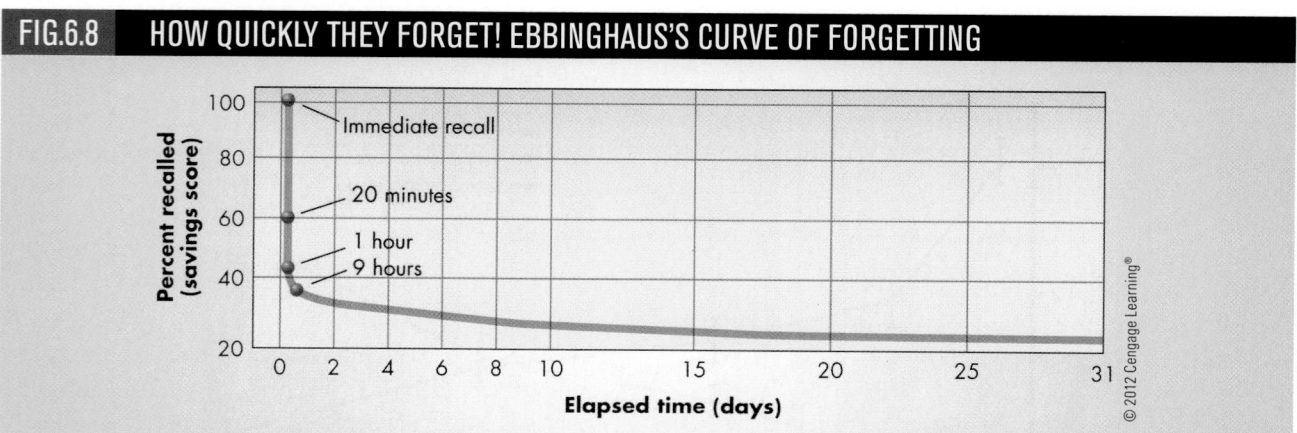

Recollection of lists of words drops precipitously during the first hour after learning. Losses of learning then become more gradual. Retention drops by half within the first hour. It takes a month (31 days), however, for retention to be cut in half again.

6-4b INTERFERENCE THEORY

When we do not attend to, encode, and rehearse sensory input, we may forget it through decay of the trace of the image. Material in short-term memory, like material in sensory memory, can be lost through decay. It can also be lost through displacement, as may happen when we try to remember several new names at a party.

Why can learning Spanish make it harder to remember French? The answer may be found in **interference theory**. According to this view, we also forget material in short-term and long-term memory because newly learned material interferes with it. The two basic types of interference are retroactive interference (also called *retroactive inhibition*) and proactive interference (also called *proactive inhibition*).

RETROACTIVE INTERFERENCE In **retroactive interference**, new learning interferes with the retrieval of old learning. For example, a medical student may memorize the names of the bones in the leg through rote repetition. Later he or she may find that learning the names of the bones in the arm makes it more difficult to retrieve the names of the leg bones, especially if the names are similar in sound or in relative location on each limb.

In retroactive interference, new learning interferes with the retrieval of old learning. In proactive interferences, older learning interferes with the capacity to retrieve more recently learned material. For example, high-school French may "pop in" when you are trying to retrieve Spanish words learned in college.

interference theory the view that we may forget stored material because other learning interferes with it

retroactive interference the interference of new learning with the ability to retrieve material learned previously

PROACTIVE INTERFERENCE In **proactive interference**, older learning interferes with the capacity to retrieve more recently learned material. High-school Spanish may pop in when you are trying to retrieve college French or Italian words. All three are Romance languages, with similar roots and spellings. Previously learned Japanese words probably would not interfere with your ability to retrieve more recently learned French or Italian, because the roots and sounds of Japanese differ considerably from those of the Romance languages.

6-4c REPRESSION

According to Freud, we are motivated to forget painful memories and unacceptable ideas because they produce anxiety, guilt, and shame. Repression, according to Freud, is the automatic ejection of painful memories and unacceptable urges from conscious awareness. It is motivated by the desire to avoid facing painful memories and emotions. Psychoanalysts believe that repression is at the heart of disorders such as **dissociative amnesia**, which is discussed in Chapter 12. There is a current controversy in psychology about whether repression (motivated forgetting) exists and, if it does, how it works.

There is much research on repression, often in the form of case studies that are found in psychoanalytic journals. Much has been made of case studies in which veterans have supposedly forgotten traumatic battlefield experiences, developed post-traumatic stress disorder (once called "battlefield neurosis"), and then "felt better" once they recalled and discussed the traumatic events. Critics argue that the evidence for such repression and recovery of memories is weak and that this kind of "memory" can be implanted by the sugges-

tions of interviewers (Loftus & Davis, 2006; McNally, 2012). The issue remains controversial, as we see next.

DO PEOPLE REALLY RECOVER REPRESSED MEMORIES OF CHILDHOOD? Despite shaky scientific support, there are cases of so-called recovered memories, especially memories of childhood sexual abuse by a relative, teacher, or friend. The question is whether these memories are induced by therapists who foster beliefs that become so deeply ingrained they seem like authentic memories. "We don't know what percent of these recovered memories are real and what percent are pseudomemories," notes psychiatrist Harold Lief (cited in Brody, 2000), one of the first to challenge such memories.

Psychologist Elizabeth Loftus (Loftus & Davis, 2006) cited numerous studies that demonstrated how easy it was to implant a false memory. In one study, researchers were able to readily convince half the subjects that they had been lost in a mall or hospitalized with severe pain as children.

6-4d INFANTILE AMNESIA

When he interviewed people about their early experiences, Freud discovered that they could not recall episodes that had happened prior to the age of three or so and that recall was cloudy through the age of five. This phenomenon is referred to as **infantile amnesia**.

Infantile amnesia has little to do with the fact that the episodes occurred in the distant past. Middle-aged and older people have vivid memories from the ages of 6 through 10, yet the events happened many decades ago. But 18-year-olds show steep declines in memory when they try to recall episodes that occurred earlier than the age of 6, even though they happened less than 18 years earlier (Wetzler & Sweeney, 1986).

Freud believed that young children have aggressive impulses and perverse lusts toward their parents. He attributed infantile amnesia to repression of these impulses. The episodes lost to infantile amnesia, however, are not weighted in the direction of such "primitive" impulses. In fact, infantile amnesia probably reflects the interaction of physiological and cognitive factors. For example, a structure of

Truth

| T | **F** | Learning Spanish can make it harder to remember French—and vice versa. |

It is true that learning a romance language such as Spanish or Italian could interfere with your learning another romance language, French later on, and vice versa. New learning can interfere with old learning, and vice versa.

proactive interference the interference by old learning with the ability to retrieve material learned recently

dissociative amnesia loss of memory of personal information that is thought to stem from psychological conflict or trauma

infantile amnesia inability to recall events that occur prior to the age of three or so; also termed *childhood amnesia*

hippocampus a structure in the limbic system that plays an important role in the formation of new memories

anterograde amnesia failure to remember events that occurred after physical trauma because of the effects of the trauma

retrograde amnesia failure to remember events that occurred prior to physical trauma because of the effects of the trauma

engram an assumed electrical circuit in the brain that corresponds to a memory trace

the limbic system (the **hippocampus**) that is involved in the storage of memories does not become mature until we are about two years old (Allene et al., 2012; Shrager et al., 2008). In addition, myelination of brain pathways is incomplete for the first few years, contributing to the inefficiency of information processing and memory formation.

There are also cognitive explanations for infantile amnesia (Cho et al., 2012; Piolino et al., 2009; Q. Wang, 2008):

▸ Infants are not particularly interested in remembering the past.

▸ Infants, in contrast to older children, tend not to weave episodes together into meaningful stories of their own lives. Information about specific episodes thus tends to be lost. Research shows that when parents reminisce about the past with children, the children's memories of being infants are strengthened.

▸ Infants do not make reliable use of language to symbolize or classify events. Their ability to *encode* sensory input—that is, to apply the auditory and semantic codes that facilitate memory formation—is therefore limited. Yet research shows that young infants can recall events throughout the period when infantile amnesia is presumed to occur if they are now and then exposed to objects they played with or photos of events.

In any event, we are unlikely to remember episodes from the first two years of life unless we are reminded of them from time to time as we develop. Many early childhood memories that seem so clear today might be reconstructed and hold many inaccuracies. They might also be memories of events that occurred later than the period to which we attribute them. Yet there is no evidence that such early memories are systematically repressed.

6-4e ANTEROGRADE AND RETROGRADE AMNESIA

Adults also experience amnesia, although usually for biological reasons, as in the cases of anterograde and retrograde amnesia. In so-called **anterograde amnesia**, there are

memory lapses for the period following a trauma such as a blow to the head, an electric shock, or an operation. In some cases the trauma seems to interfere with all the processes of memory. The ability to pay attention, the encoding of sensory input, and rehearsal are all impaired. A number of investigators have linked certain kinds of brain damage—such as damage to the hippocampus—to amnesia (Dede et al., 2013; Kikuchi et al., 2010).

In **retrograde amnesia**, the source of trauma prevents people from remembering events that took place before the accident. In one well-known case of retrograde amnesia, a man received a head injury in a motorcycle accident (Baddeley, 1982). When he regained consciousness, he had lost memory for all events that had occurred after the age of 11. In fact, he appeared to believe that he was still 11 years old. During the next few months he gradually recovered more knowledge of his past. He moved toward the present year by year, up until the critical motorcycle ride.

But he never did recover the events just prior to the accident. The accident had apparently prevented the information that was rapidly unfolding before him from being transferred to long-term memory. In terms of stages of memory, it may be that our perceptions and ideas need to consolidate, or rest undisturbed for a while, if they are to be transferred to long-term memory (Nader et al., 2000).

6-5 THE BIOLOGY OF MEMORY

Psychologists know that mental processes such as the encoding, storage, and retrieval of information—that is memory—are accompanied by changes in the brain (Kandel et al., 2014). Early in the 20th century, many psychologists used the concept of the **engram** in their study of memory. Engrams were viewed as electrical circuits in the brain that corresponded to memory traces—neurological processes that paralleled experiences. Yet biological psychologists such as Karl Lashley (1950) spent many fruitless years searching for such circuits or for the structures of the brain in which they might be housed. Much research on the biology of memory focuses today on the roles of stimulants, neurons, neurotransmitters, hormones, and structures in the brain.

6-5a NEURAL ACTIVITY AND MEMORY

Rats that are reared in stimulating environments provide some insight into the neural events that are involved in memory. The animals develop more

Forever 27

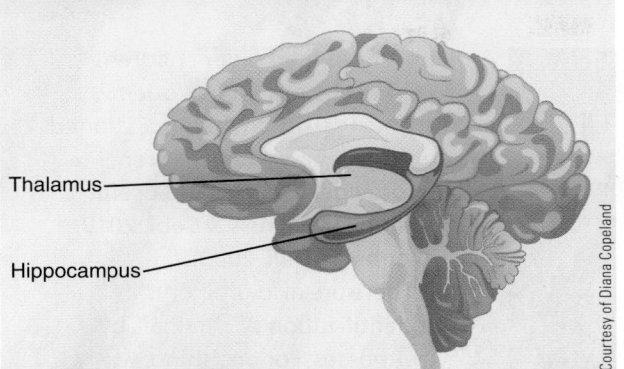

Thalamus

Hippocampus

Courtesy of Diana Copeland

The hippocampus is essential to the formation of new memories. Consider the classic case of a man called "H. M." Parts of the brain are sometimes lesioned to help people with epilepsy. In H.M.'s case, a section of the hippocampus was removed (Milner, 1966). Right after the operation, H. M.'s mental functioning appeared normal. As time went on, however, it became clear that he had problems processing new information. For example, two years after the operation, H. M. believed he was 27—his age at the time of the operation. When his family moved to a new address, H. M. could not find his new home or remember the new address. He responded with appropriate grief to the death of his uncle, yet he then began to ask about his uncle and why he did not visit. Each time he was reminded of his uncle's passing, he grieved as if he were hearing it for the first time. H. M.'s operation apparently prevented him from transferring information from short-term to long-term memory.

Experiences perceived by several senses are apparently stored in numerous parts of the cortex. The recall of sensory experiences apparently involves neural activity in related regions of the brain.

Research with sea snails such as Aplysia and Hermissenda offers more insight into the biology of memory. Aplysia has only some 20,000 neurons compared with humans' billions. As a result, researchers have been able to study how experience is reflected at the synapses of specific neurons. The sea snail will reflexively withdraw its gills when it receives electric shock, in the way a person will reflexively withdraw a hand from a hot stove or a thorn. In one kind of experiment, researchers precede the shock with a squirt of water. After a few repetitions, the sea snail becomes conditioned to withdraw its gills when squirted with the water. When sea snails are conditioned, they release more serotonin at certain synapses. As a consequence, transmission at these synapses becomes more efficient as trials (learning) progress (Kandel et al., 2014; Squire & Kandel, 2008). This greater efficiency is termed **long-term potentiation (LTP)**. As shown in Figure 6.9, dendrites can also participate in LTP by sprouting new branches that attach to the transmitting axon. Rats that are given substances that enhance LTP learn mazes with fewer errors; that is, they are less likely to turn down the wrong alley (Mayford et al., 2012; Tabassum & Frey, 2013).

FIG.6.9 ONE AVENUE TO LONG-TERM POTENTIATION (LTP)

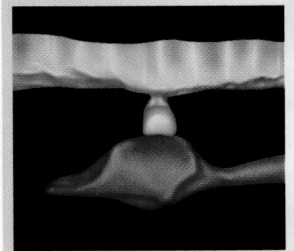
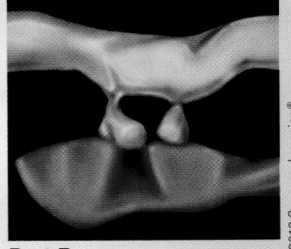

Part A Part B

© 2012 Cengage Learning®

LTP can occur via the action of neurotransmitters such as serotonin and glutamate at synapses. Structurally, LTP can also occur as shown in Parts A and B, when dendrites sprout new branches that connect with transmitting axons, increasing the amount of stimulation they receive.

dendrites and synapses in the cerebral cortex than rats reared in impoverished environments (Rojas et al., 2013). Moreover, visually stimulating rats increases the number of synapses in their visual cortex (Inaba et al., 2009). Therefore, the storage of experience does involve avenues of communication among brain cells.

Information received through other senses is just as likely to lead to corresponding changes in the cortical regions that represent them. For example, sounds may similarly cause changes in the auditory cortex.

Jean Piaget, the investigator of children's cognitive development, distinctly remembered an attempt to kidnap him from his baby carriage as he was being wheeled along the Champs Élysées. He recalled the excited throng, the abrasions on the face of the nurse who rescued him, the police officer's white baton, and the flight of the assailant. Although they were graphic, Piaget's memories were false. Years later, the nurse admitted that she had made up the tale. However, the false information provided by his nurse had been implanted in his own memory.

Can eyewitness testimony be trusted? Is there reason to believe that the statements of eyewitnesses are any more factual than Piaget's?

One problem with eyewitness testimony is that the words chosen by an experimenter—and those chosen by a lawyer interrogating a witness—have been shown to influence the reconstruction of memories (Nadel & Sinnott-Armstrong, 2012). For example, as in the experiment described earlier, an attorney for the plaintiff might ask the witness, "How fast was the defendant's car going when it *smashed* into the plaintiff's car?" In such a case, the car might be reported as going faster than if the question had been: "How fast was the defendant's car going when the accident occurred?" (Loftus & Palmer, 1974). Could the attorney for the defendant claim that the use of the word *smashed* biased the witness? What about jurors who heard the word *smashed?* Would they be biased toward assuming that the driver had been reckless?

Children tend to be more suggestible witnesses than adults, and preschoolers are more

Rubberball/Corbis

How trustworthy is eyewitness testimony? Memories are reconstructive rather than photographic. The wording of questions also influences the content of the memory. Attorneys therefore are sometimes instructed not to phrase questions in such a way that they "lead" the witness.

suggestible than older children (Klemfuss & Ceci, 2012; Cutler & Kovera, 2010). But when questioned properly, even young children may provide accurate and useful testimony (Klemfuss & Cebi, 2012; Krähenbühl et al., 2009).

There are also problems in the identification of criminals by eyewitnesses. For one thing, witnesses may pay more attention to the suspect's clothing than to more meaningful characteristics such as facial features, height, and weight. In one experiment, viewers of a videotaped crime incorrectly identified a man as the criminal because he wore the eyeglasses and T-shirt that had been worn by the perpetrator on the tape. The man who had actually committed the crime was identified less often (Sanders, 1984).

Other problems with eyewitness testimony include the following (Nadel & Sinnott-Armstrong, 2012):

▶ **Identification is less accurate when suspects belong to ethnic or racial groups that differ from that of the witness.**

▶ **Identification of suspects is compromised when interrogators make misleading suggestions.**

▶ **Witnesses are seen as more credible when they claim to be certain in their testimony, but there is little evidence that claims of certainty are accurate.**

Thus, there are many problems with eyewitness testimony. Yet even Elizabeth Loftus (e.g., Wright & Loftus, 2008), who has extensively studied the accuracy of eyewitness testimony, agrees that it is a valuable tool in the courtroom. After all, identifications made by eyewitnesses are frequently correct, and Loftus asks, what would be the alternative to the use of eyewitnesses? If we were to prevent eyewitnesses from testifying, how many criminals would go free?

Serotonin and many other naturally occurring chemical substances, including adrenaline, noradrenaline, acetylcholine, glutamate, antidiuretic hormone, even the sex hormones estrogen and testosterone have also been shown to play roles in memory.

6-5b BRAIN STRUCTURES AND MEMORY

Memory does not reside in a single structure of the brain. Memory relies on complex neural networks that draw on various parts of the brain (Kandel et al., 2014). However, some parts of the brain play more specific roles in memory. The hippocampus is vital in storing new information even if we can retrieve old information without it (Squire, 2009). But the hippocampus is not a storage bin. Rather, it is involved in relaying sensory information to parts of the cortex.

Where are the storage bins? The brain stores parts of memories in the appropriate areas of the sensory cortex. Sights are stored in the visual cortex, sounds in the auditory cortex, and so on. The limbic system is largely responsible for integrating these pieces of information when we recall an event. However, the frontal lobes apparently store information about where and when events occur (Chafee & Goldman-Rakic, 2000; C. R. E. Wilson et al., 2008).

But what of the decision to try to recall something? What of the spark of consciousness that drives us to move backward in time or to strive to remember to do something in the future? The prefrontal cortex (see Figure 6.10) is the executive center in memory (Nee et al., 2013). It appears to empower people with consciousness—the ability to mentally represent and become aware of experiences that occur in the past, present, and future. It enables people to mentally travel back in time to re-experience the personal, autobiographical past. It enables people to focus on the things they intend to do in the future, such as mail a letter on the way to class or brush their teeth before going to bed.

The hippocampus is also involved in the where and when of things (Eichenbaum & Fortin, 2003). The hippocampus does not become mature until we are about two years old. Immaturity may be connected with infantile amnesia. Adults with hippocampal damage may be able to form new procedural memories, even though they cannot form new episodic ("where and when") memories (Fields, 2005). They can develop new skills even though they cannot recall the practice sessions (Squire & Kandel, 2008).

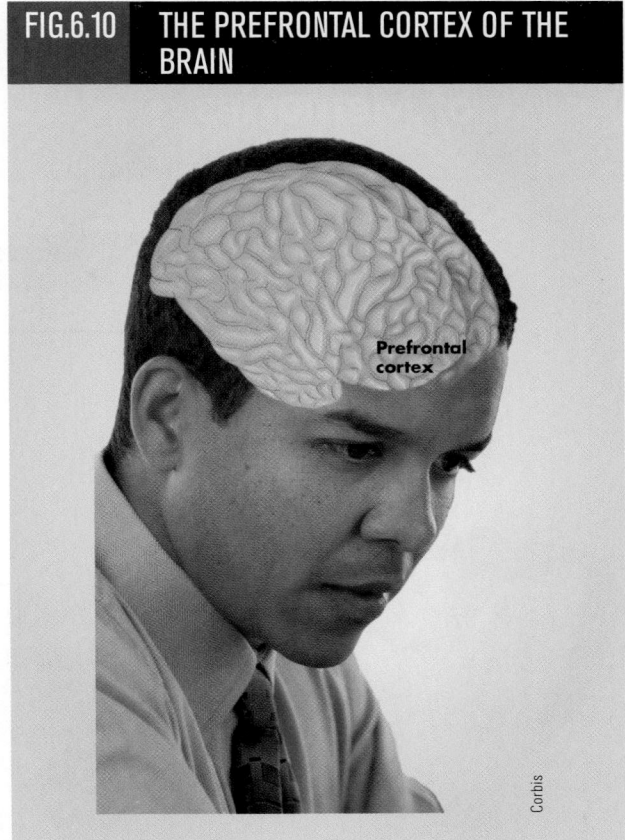

FIG.6.10 THE PREFRONTAL CORTEX OF THE BRAIN

Prefrontal cortex

Corbis

The prefrontal cortex comes in pairs. One is found in each hemisphere, a bit above the outer edge of the eyebrow. The prefrontal cortex is highly active during visual and spatial problem solving. Your sense of self—your continuous sense of being in and operating on the world—may also reside largely in the prefrontal cortex.

The thalamus is involved in the formation of verbal memories. Part of the thalamus of an Air Force cadet known as N. A. was damaged in a fencing accident. Afterward, N. A. could no longer form verbal memories, but he could form visual memories (Squire, 2004). (One might measure visual memory by showing people pictures, allowing time to pass, and then asking them to point out those they have been shown.)

The encoding, storage, and retrieval of information thus involve biological activity. As we learn, new synapses are developed, and changes occur at existing synapses. Parts of the brain are also involved in the formation of memories. In the next chapter, we see how people manipulate information they have stored to adapt to the environment or create new environments.

The Relationships Among the Various Kinds of Memories

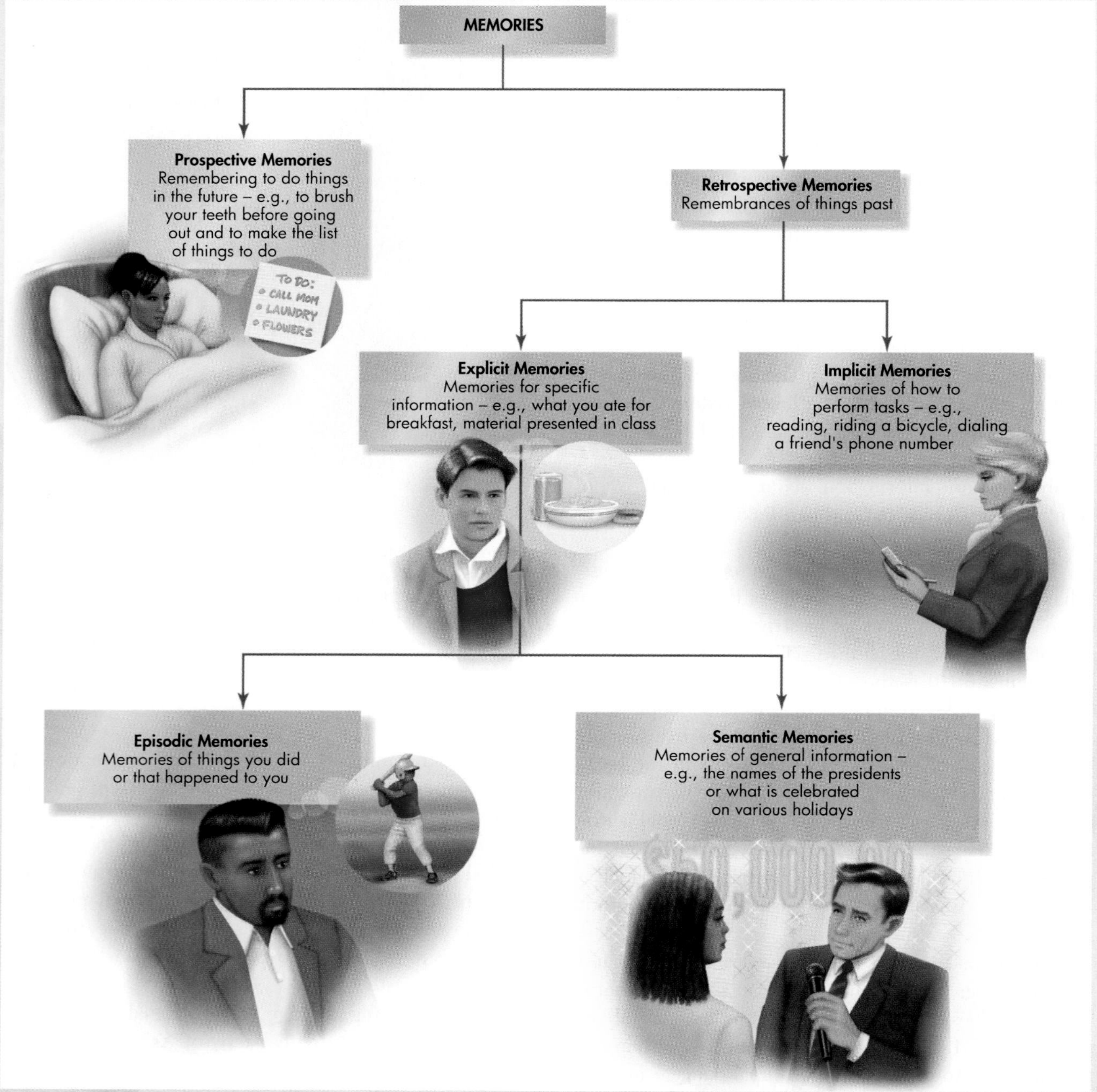

MEMORIES

Prospective Memories
Remembering to do things in the future – e.g., to brush your teeth before going out and to make the list of things to do

TO DO:
• CALL MOM
• LAUNDRY
• FLOWERS

Retrospective Memories
Remembrances of things past

Explicit Memories
Memories for specific information – e.g., what you ate for breakfast, material presented in class

Implicit Memories
Memories of how to perform tasks – e.g., reading, riding a bicycle, dialing a friend's phone number

Episodic Memories
Memories of things you did or that happened to you

Semantic Memories
Memories of general information – e.g., the names of the presidents or what is celebrated on various holidays

© Cengage Learning 2012

Memories can address past events (*retrospective memories*) or future events (*prospective memories*). Memories of the past can be *explicit* (declarative) or *implicit* (nondeclarative). Explicit memories include memories of personal episodes (which are called *episodic or autobiographical memories*) or of general information (*semantic memories*).

STUDY TOOLS 6

READY TO STUDY? IN THE BOOK, YOU CAN:

☐ Check your understanding of what you've read with the quizzes below.

☐ Rip out the chapter review card at the back of the book to have a summary of the chapter and the key terms handy.

ONLINE AT CENGAGEBRAIN.COM YOU CAN:

☐ Learn more about types of memory in learning modules.

☐ Practice retrieving what you've learned using the interactive figures on the stages of memory.

☐ Learn how psychologists use high-tech brain imaging procedures and computer simulations to better understand learning and memory in a short video.

☐ Prepare for tests with quizzes.

☐ Review the key terms with Flash Cards.

☐ Play games to master concepts.

FILL-INS

Answers can be found in the back of the book, starting on page XXX.

1. Memories of the events that happen to a person are _____ memories.

2. _____ memories concern generalized knowledge.

3. One way of storing information is by _____ rehearsal, or by mentally repeating it.

4. Another way of storing information is by _____ rehearsal, when we relate new information to things we already know.

5. The Atkinson-Shiffrin model hypothesizes three stages of memory: _____, _____-_____, and _____-_____.

6. _____ imagery is the ability to retain exact mental representations of visual stimuli over long periods of time.

7. Detailed memories of surprising, important, and emotional events are termed _____ memories.

8. In _____ interference, new learning interferes with the retrieval of old learning.

9. In _____ interference, older learning interferes with the capacity to retrieve more recently learned material.

10. Experience enhances the avenues of communication among brain cells by development of dendrites and _____.

MULTIPLE CHOICE

1. Remembering what you had for dinner is an example of ___ memory.
   a. implicit
   b. episodic
   c. dependent
   d. semantic

2. Hamilton told himself to remember to get three things at the corner deli. On the way to the store, he ran into Jason and chatted for a few minutes. Afterward, he could only remember two of the items. Chatting with Jason had apparently interfered with Hamilton's
   a. episodic memory.
   b. semantic memory.
   c. prospective memory.
   d. implicit memory.

3. You recall what you ate for breakfast this morning, but you know who wrote *Hamlet*. Your knowledge that Shakespeare wrote *Hamlet* is an example of
   a. episodic memory.
   b. prospective memory.
   c. implicit memory.
   d. semantic memory.

4. Breaking THUNSTOFAM into three syllables THUN-STO-FAM and then repeating them many times in an effort to remember the ten letters is an example of using the techniques of
   a. chunking and maintenance rehearsal.
   b. encoding and elaborative rehearsal.
   c. sensory memory and short-term memory.
   d. working memory and semantic memory.

5. Tracy took tennis lessons when she was very young but had not played tennis for years when she decided to enroll in a tennis class at college. A moment after she picked up her racket, she realized with surprise that she had shifted it to the correct forehand grip without even thinking. Tracy's ___ memory made this possible.
   a. implicit
   b. episodic

   c. psychomotor
   d. semantic

6. If you learn how to do something once, and then forget it, what is most likely to happen if you attempt to relearn it?
   a. Anxiety will interfere with your ability to relearn it.
   b. The original learning will be on the tip of your tongue.
   c. Your hippocampus will be flooded with dopamine.
   d. You will relearn it more quickly than you originally learned it.

7. The process of modifying information so that we can place it in memory is called
   a. storing.
   b. memorizing.
   c. encoding.
   d. programming.

8. Mentally repeating a list or saying it to yourself refers to
   a. metamemory.
   b. elaborative rehearsal.
   c. retrospective memory.
   d. maintenance rehearsal.

9. Evan met Lesley at a party three weeks ago. He bumps into her on the way to class. He feels as though he knows her name but he just can't retrieve the information. This experience is referred to as
   a. mnemonic failure.
   b. tip-of-the-tongue phenomenon.
   c. consolidation.
   d. déjà vu.

10. From the clinical evidence on brain injury, it appears that storage bins for long-term memories are located in
    a. the hippocampus.
    b. one specific brain area.
    c. different brain areas.
    d. the frontal lobe and thalamus.

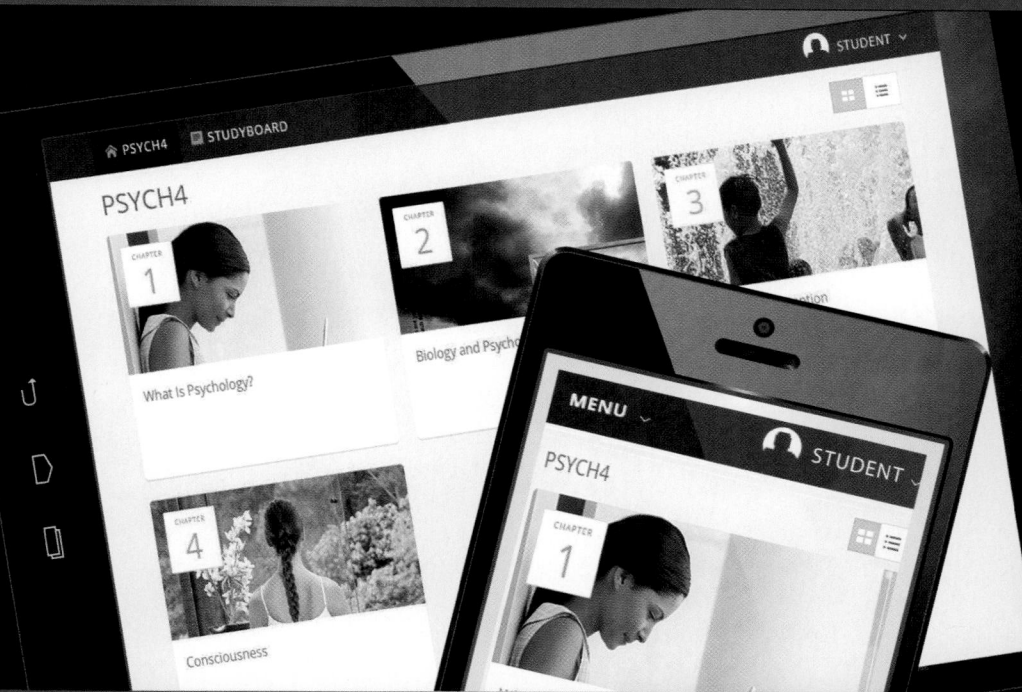

7 | Thinking, Language, and Intelligence

Lottie Davies/Photodisc/Getty Images

LEARNING OUTCOMES

After studying this chapter, you will be able to...

7-1 Define thinking and explain how thinking is used in problem solving and decision making.

7-2 Explain the nature of language.

7-3 Describe language development—the "two-year explosion."

7-4 Discuss theories about the nature of intelligence.

7-5 Discuss methods of measuring intelligence and the "testing controversy."

7-6 Discuss the roles of nature and nurture in the development of intelligence.

After you finish this chapter, go to **PAGE 200** for **STUDY TOOLS**

What form of life is so adaptive that it can survive in desert temperatures of 120°F or Arctic climes of −40°F?

What form of life can run, walk, climb, swim, live underwater for months on end, and fly to the moon and back? I won't keep you in suspense any longer. We are that form of life. Yet our unclad bodies do not allow us to adapt to these extremes in temperature. Brute strength does not allow us to live underwater or travel to the moon. Rather, it is our cognitive processes—thinking, language, and intelligence—that permit us to adapt to these conditions and surpass our physical limitations.

It is our cognitive processes that have enabled humans to survive and prosper. Other species may be stronger, run faster, smell more keenly, and even live longer, but only humans have produced literature, music, mathematics, and science. In this chapter, we look at these three related areas of **cognition:** thinking, language, and intelligence. We will see that intelligence may be the most controversial topic in psychology.

```
Intelligence
   may be the most
controversial
   topic in psychology.
```

7-1 THINKING

The Greek philosopher Aristotle argued that people differ from lower organisms in their capacity for rational thinking. *What is thinking?* **Thinking** means paying attention to information, representing it mentally, reasoning about it, and making judgments and decisions about it. Thinking refers to conscious, planned attempts to make sense of and change the world. Mental processes such as dreaming and daydreaming do not represent thinking; they may be unplanned and proceed more or less on their own. We begin with concepts, which provide many of the building blocks for thinking.

7-1a CONCEPTS

Concepts are mental categories used to group together objects, relations, events, abstractions, or qualities that have common properties. Concepts are crucial to cognition. They can represent objects, events, and activities—and visions of things that never were or cannot be measured, such as Middle Earth in *The Lord of the Rings* or the land of Oz in *The Wizard of Oz*.

Labels for objects depend on one's experience with them and on one's cultural setting (Sloman, 2011). Concepts such as *square*, *circle*, and *triangle* are not all that common in nature, and some peoples who do not construct houses with these shapes, such as the Himba of northern Namibia, have no words for them (Caparos et al., 2013; Davidoff et al., 2008). But these shapes are concepts that are basic to geometry. Much thinking has to do with categorizing new concepts and manipulating relationships among concepts, as in problems in geometry.

We tend to organize concepts in *hierarchies* (see Figure 7.1). For example, the newspaper category includes objects such as your school paper and the *Los Angeles Times*. Newspapers,

cognition mental activity involved in understanding, processing, and communicating information

thinking paying attention to information, mentally representing it, reasoning about it, and making decisions about it

concept a mental category that is used to class together objects, relations, events, abstractions, ideas, or qualities that have common properties

👍 *Truth or Fiction?* 👎

WHAT DO YOU THINK? Folklore, common sense, or nonsense? Circle the T for "truth" or the F for "fiction," and check the accuracy of your answers as you read through the chapter.

T	F	Only humans can use insight to solve problems.
T	F	Crying is a child's first use of language.
T	F	Young children say things like "daddy goed away" and "mommy sitted down" because they *do* understand rules of grammar.
T	F	"Street smarts" are a sign of intelligence.
T	F	Creative people are intelligent.
T	F	Two children can answer exactly the same items on an intelligence test correctly, yet one child can obtain an above average in IQ, and the other can obtain a below average IQ.
T	F	Intelligence tests measure many things other than intelligence.

FIG.7.1 ORGANIZATION OF CONCEPTS INTO HIERARCHIES

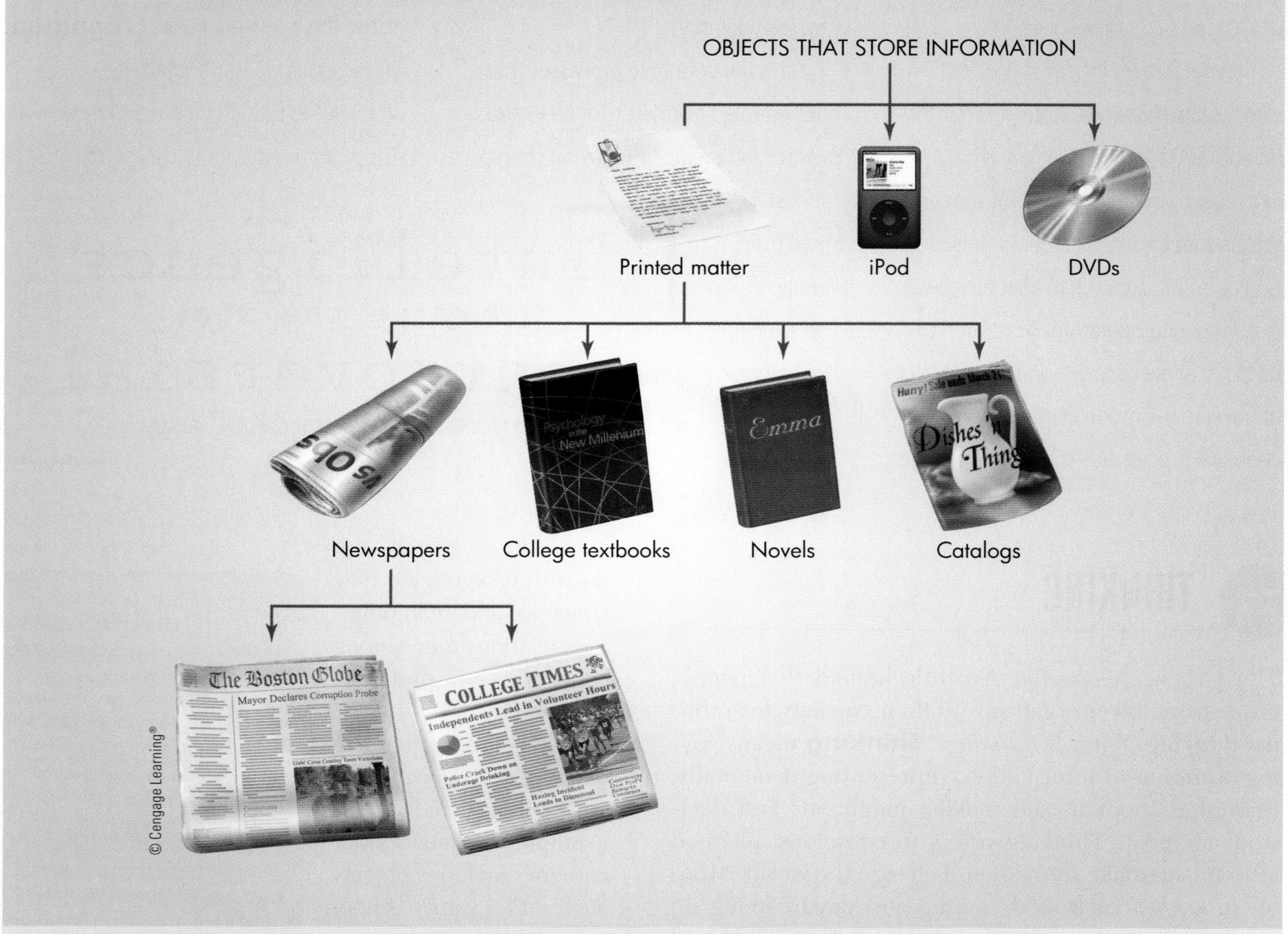

OBJECTS THAT STORE INFORMATION

Printed matter   iPod   DVDs

Newspapers   College textbooks   Novels   Catalogs

© Cengage Learning®

The Boston Globe

COLLEGE TIMES

People may have a concept, "objects that store information." This concept may include concepts such as iPod, DVD, and printed matter. Within the concept of printed matter, people may include newspapers, college textbooks (certainly the most important object that stores information!), novels, and catalogs. The concept of newspaper may include one's school newspaper and various commercial newspapers.

college textbooks, and catalogs can be combined into higher-order categories such as printed matter or printed devices that store information. If you add iPods, hard drives, and DVDs, you can create a still higher category—objects that store information. Now consider a question that requires categorical thinking: How are a newspaper and a DVD alike? Answers to such questions entail supplying the category that includes both objects. In this case, we can say that both objects store information. Their functions are alike, even if their technology differs.

Prototypes are good examples. They best match the key features of categories. Which animal seems more birdlike to

you: a robin or an ostrich? Why? Which better fits the prototype of a fish: a sea horse or a tuna? Why?

Many simple prototypes, such as dog and red, are taught by means of examples, or **exemplars**. Research suggests that it is more efficient for most of us to learn what fruits and vegetables are from experience with exemplars of each, rather than by working from definitions of them (Banaji & Gelman, 2013; Freund, 2009). We point to a dog and say to a child "dog" or "This is a dog." Dogs are *positive instances* of the dog concept. *Negative instances*—things that are *not* dogs—are then shown to the child while we say, "This is *not* a dog." Negative instances of one concept may be positive instances of another. So, in teaching a child, we may be more likely to say, "This is not a dog—it's a cat" than simply, "This is not a dog."

prototype a concept of a category of objects or events that serves as a good example of the category

exemplar a specific example

Children may at first include horses and other four-legged animals within the dog concept until the differences between dogs and horses are pointed out. In language development, such over inclusion of instances in a category (reference to horses as dogs) is labeled *overextension*. Children's prototypes become refined after they are shown positive and negative instances and given explanations. Abstract concepts such as bachelor or square root tend to be formed through explanations that involve more basic concepts.

7-1b PROBLEM SOLVING

Problem solving is an important aspect of thinking. Here's a problem for you to solve. What are the next two letters in this series?

O T T F F S S E _ _ ?

How did you try to find the answer? Did you search your personal memory banks and ask yourself what O can stand for, then T, and so on? Did you try to think of some phrase the letters might represent? Perhaps the first letters of the stars in a constellation? [If you don't resort to a search engine answer and do not arrive at the answer on your own, I'll be discussing it within a few pages.]

7-1c METHODS OF PROBLEM SOLVING

The first task in solving a problem is to understand the problem.

UNDERSTANDING THE PROBLEM Successful understanding of a problem generally requires three features:

▶ *The parts our mental representation of the problem relate to one another in a meaningful way.* If we are trying to solve a problem in geometry, our mental triangles, like actual triangles, should have angles that total 180 degrees.

▶ *The elements of our mental representation of the problem correspond to the elements of the problem in the outer world.* If we are assessing a patient in the emergency room of a hospital, we want to arrive at a diagnosis of what might be wrong before we make a treatment plan. To do so, we take the patient's vital signs, including heart rate, temperature, and blood pressure, so that our mental picture of the patient conforms to what is going on in his or her body.

> What do you do first when you're faced with a problem? What does it mean to 'understand' a problem?

▶ *We have a storehouse of background knowledge that we can apply to the problem.* We have the necessary experience or course work to solve the problem.

THE USE OF ALGORITHMS An **algorithm** is a specific procedure for solving a type of problem. An algorithm invariably leads to the solution—if it is used properly, that is. Mathematical formulas like the Pythagorean theorem are examples of algorithms. They yield correct answers to problems *as long as the right formula is used.* Finding the right formula to solve a problem may require scanning one's memory for all formulas that contain variables that represent one or more of the elements in the problem. The Pythagorean theorem concerns right triangles. Therefore, it is appropriate to consider using this formula for problems concerning right triangles, but not others.

If you are going to be meeting someone for the first time and want to make a good impression, you consider the nature of the encounter (e.g., a job interview or a blind date) and then consider how to dress and behave for the encounter. If it's a job interview, the algorithm may be to dress neatly, to be well groomed, and not to wear too much cologne or perfume. If it's a date, you may ditch the suit but hike up the cologne or perfume a notch. In either case, smile and make eye contact—it's all part of the formula.

Anagrams are scrambled words. Korc is an anagram for rock or cork. The task in anagram problems is to try to reorganize jumbles or groups of letters into words. Some anagram problems require us to use every letter from the pool of letters; others allow us to use only some of the letters. How many words can you make from the pool of letters DWARG? If you were to use the **systematic random search** algorithm, you would list every possible letter combination, using

algorithm a systematic procedure for solving a problem that works invariably when it is correctly applied

systematic random search an algorithm for solving problems in which each possible solution is tested according to a particular set of rules

from one to all five letters. You could use a dictionary or a spell-checking program to see whether each result is, in fact, a word. The method might take awhile, but it would work.

THE USE OF HEURISTIC DEVICES Sometimes people use shortcuts to "jump to conclusions"—and these are often correct conclusions. The shortcuts are called **heuristics**, or heuristic devices—rules of thumb that help us simplify and solve problems. Heuristics are often based on strategies that worked in the past (Cronin et al., 2014).

In contrast to algorithms, heuristics do not guarantee a correct solution. But when they work, they permit more rapid solutions. A heuristic device for solving the anagram problem would be to look for familiar letter combinations and then check the remaining letters for words that include these combinations. In DWARG, for example, we find some familiar combinations: *dr* and *gr*. We may then quickly find *draw*, *drag*, and *grad*. The drawback to this method is that we might miss some words.

One type of heuristic device is the **means–end analysis**. In using this heuristic device, we assess the difference between our current situation and our goals and do what we can to reduce this difference. Let's say that you are out in your car and have gotten lost. One heuristic device based on analysis of what you need to do to get to where you want to go might be to ask for directions. This approach requires no "sense of direction." An algorithm might be more complicated and require some scientific knowledge. For example, if you know your destination is west of your current location you might try driving toward the setting sun.

THE USE OF ANALOGIES An *analogy* is a partial similarity among things that are different in other ways. The analogy heuristic applies the solution of an earlier problem to the solution of a new one. We use the analogy heuristic whenever we try to solve a new problem by referring to a previous problem (Dinuta, 2013; Kujala, 2013).

Let's see whether you can use the analogy heuristic to your advantage in the following number-series problem. Look at the following series of numbers and find the rule that governs their order:

8, 5, 4, 9, 1, 7, 6, 3, 2, 0

This is rather abstract and mathematical. Actually, you use the analogy heuristic regularly. For example, when you begin a new term with a new instructor, you probably consider who the instructor reminds you of. Then, perhaps, you recall the things that helped you get along with the analogous instructor and try them on the new one. We tend to look for things—analogies—that have helped us in similar situations. When we considered OTTFFSSENT, we used the first letters of the numbers one through ten. When we consider the first 10 digits in the following order—8, 5, 4, 9, 1, 7, 6, 3, 2, and 0—we can again think of their first letters when they are spelled out. It happens that they are in alphabetical order (eight, five, four, and so on).

7-1d FACTORS THAT AFFECT PROBLEM SOLVING

The way you approach a problem is central to how effective you are at solving it. Other factors also influence your effectiveness. Three factors that can make it easier or harder to solve problems reside within you: your level of expertise, whether you fall prey to a mental set, and whether you develop insight into the problem.

EXPERTISE To appreciate the role of expertise in problem solving, unscramble the following anagrams, taken from Novick and Coté (1992). In each case use all of the letters to form an actual English word:

DNSUO

RCWDO

IASYD

How long did it take you to unscramble each anagram ("sound," "crowd," and "daisy")? Would a person whose native language is English—that is, an "expert"—unscramble each anagram more efficiently than a bilingual person who spoke another language in the home? Why or why not?

Experts solve problems more efficiently and rapidly than novices do. Generally speaking, people who are experts at solving a certain kind of problem share the following characteristics (Bassok & Novick, 2012; Bunt et al., 2013):

▶ They know the particular area well.

▶ They have a good memory for the elements in the problems.

▶ They form mental images or representations that facilitate problem solving.

▶ They relate the problem to similar problems.

▶ They are more goal-directed and have efficient methods for problem solving.

heuristics rules of thumb that help us simplify and solve problems

means–end analysis a heuristic device in which we try to solve a problem by evaluating the difference between the current situation and the goal

These factors are interrelated. Art historians, for example, acquire a database that permits them to understand the intricacies of paintings. As a result, their memory for details of paintings mushrooms.

Novick and Coté (1992) found that the solutions to the anagram problems seemed to "pop out" in under two seconds among experts. The experts apparently used more efficient methods than the novices. Experts seemed to use *parallel processing*. That is, they dealt simultaneously with two or more elements of the problems. In the case of DNSUO, for example, they may have played with the order of the vowels (CO or OU) at the same time that they tested which consonant (D, N, or S) was likely to precede them, arriving quickly at *sou* and *sound*. Novices were more likely to engage in *serial processing*—that is, to handle one element of the problem at a time.

MENTAL SETS The tendency to respond to a new problem with the same approach that helped solve similar problems is termed a **mental set**. Mental sets usually make our work easier, but they can mislead us when the similarity between problems is illusory.

INSIGHT To gain insight into the role of **insight** in problem solving, consider the following problem, posed by Metcalfe (1986):

A stranger approached a museum curator and offered him an ancient bronze coin. The coin had an authentic appearance and was marked with the date 544 BCE. The curator had happily made acquisitions from suspicious sources before, but this time he promptly called the police and had the stranger arrested. Why?

I'm not going to give you the answer to this problem. But I'll make a guarantee. When you arrive at the solution, it will hit you all at once. You'll think "Of course!" It will seem as though the pieces of information in the problem have suddenly been reorganized so that the solution leaps out—in a flash.

Bismarck, one of psychologist N. R. F. Maier's rats, appeared to suddenly reorganize the pieces of information in a problem with which he was presented, showing evidence of insight in his species (Maier & Schneirla, 1935). Bismarck had been trained to climb a ladder to a tabletop where food was placed. On one occasion, Maier used a mesh barrier to prevent the rat from reaching his goal. But, as shown in Figure 7.2, a second ladder was provided and was visible to the animal. At first Bismarck sniffed and scratched and tried to find a path through the mesh. Then he spent some time washing his face, an activity that may signal frustration in rats. Suddenly he jumped into the air, turned, ran down the familiar ladder and around to the new ladder, ran up the new ladder, and claimed his just desserts. Did Bismarck suddenly perceive the relationships between the elements of the problem so that the solution occurred by insight? He seems to have had what Gestalt psychologists have termed an "Aha! experience."

INCUBATION An incubator warms chicken eggs so that they will hatch. **Incubation** in problem solving refers to standing back from the problem for a while as some process within may continue to work on it. Later, the answer may come

mental set the tendency to respond to a new problem with an approach that was successfully used with similar problems

insight in Gestalt psychology, a sudden perception of relationships among elements of the mentally represented elements of a problem that permits its solution

incubation in problem solving, a process that may sometimes occur when we stand back from a frustrating problem for a while and the solution "suddenly" appears

FIG.7.2 BISMARCK CLAIMS HIS JUST DESSERTS IN A FLASH OF INSIGHT

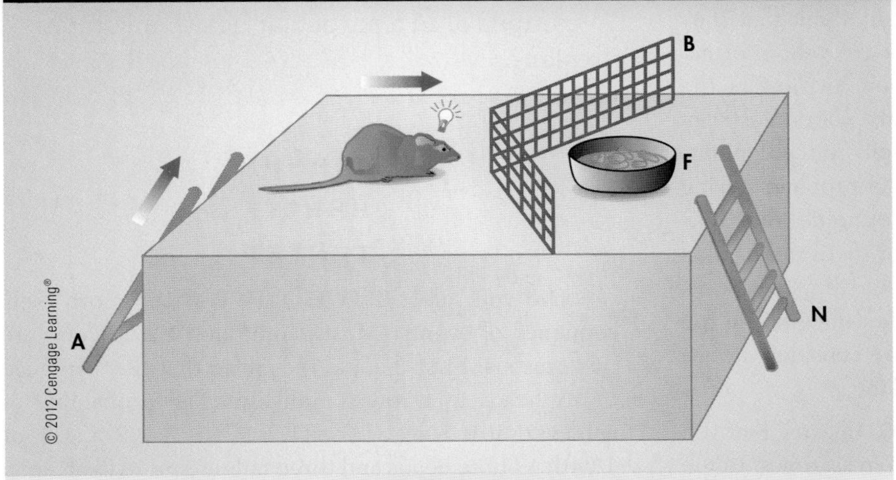

© 2012 Cengage Learning®

Bismarck has learned to reach dinner by climbing ladder A. But now the food goal (F) is blocked by a wire-mesh barrier B. Bismarck washes his face for a while, but then, in an apparent flash of insight, he runs back down ladder A and up new ladder N to reach the goal.

to us in a flash of insight. Standing back from the problem may help by distancing us from unprofitable but persistent mental sets (Gilhooly et al., 2013; Koppel & Storm, 2013).

FUNCTIONAL FIXEDNESS Functional fixedness may hinder problem solving. For example, first ask yourself what a pair of pliers is. Is it a tool for grasping, a paperweight, or a weapon?

A pair of pliers could function as any of these, but your tendency to think of it as a grasping tool is fostered by your experience with it. You have probably used pliers only for grasping things. Functional fixedness is the tendency to think of an object in terms of its name or its familiar function. It can be similar to a mental set in that it makes it difficult to use familiar objects to solve problems in novel ways.

7-1e JUDGMENT AND DECISION MAKING

You might like to think that people are so rational that they carefully weigh the pros and cons when they make judgments or decisions. Or you might think that they insist on finding and examining all the relevant information. Actually, people make most of their decisions on the basis of limited information. They take shortcuts. They use heuristic devices—rules of thumb—in judgments and decision making just as they do in problem solving (Mousavi & Gigerenzer, 2014). For example, they may let a financial advisor select stocks for them rather than research the companies themselves. Or they may see a doctor recommended by a friend rather than look at the doctor's credentials. In this section we consider various factors in judgment and decision making.

HEURISTICS IN DECISION MAKING Imagine that you flip a coin six times. In the following three possible outcomes, H stands for heads and T for tails. Circle the most likely sequence:

functional fixedness the tendency to view an object in terms of its name or familiar usage

Making a Decision: How Do You Choose a Doctor? Do you go by reputation or the advice of a friend or family member? Do you check out his or her credentials online? Or do you have no choice because you're on campus or in a particular health insurance plan?

HHHHHH

HHHTTT

THHTHT

Did you select T H H T H T as the most likely sequence of events? Most people do. Why? There are two reasons. First, people recognize that the sequence of six heads in a row is unlikely. (The probability of achieving it is $1/2 \times 1/2 \times 1/2 \times 1/2 \times 1/2 \times 1/2$, or 1/64th.) Three heads and three tails are more likely than six heads (or six tails). Second, people recognize that the sequence of heads and tails ought to appear random. T H H T H T has a random look to it, whereas H H H T T T does not.

People tend to select T H H T H T because of the **representativeness heuristic**. According to this decision-making heuristic, people make judgments about events (samples) according to the populations of events that they appear to represent (Nilsson et al., 2013). In this case, the sample of events is six coin tosses. The "population" is an infinite number of random coin tosses. But guess what? Each sequence is equally likely (or unlikely). If the question had been whether six heads or three heads and three tails had been more likely, the correct answer would have been three and three.

If the question had been whether heads and tails would be more likely to be consecutive or in random order, the correct answer would have been random order. But each of the three sequences is a *specific* sequence. What is the probability of attaining the *specific* sequence T H H T H T? The probability that the first coin toss will result in a tail is 1/2. The probability that the second will result in a head is 1/2, and so on. Thus, the probability of attaining the exact sequence T H H T H T is identical to that of achieving any other specific sequence: $1/2 \times 1/2 \times 1/2 \times 1/2 \times 1/2 \times 1/2 = 1/64$th. (Try this out on a friend.)

Another heuristic device used in decision making is the **availability heuristic**. According to this heuristic, our estimates of frequency or probability are based on how easy it is to find examples of relevant events. Let me ask you whether there are more art majors or sociology majors at your college. Unless you are familiar with the enrollment statistics, you will probably answer on the basis of the numbers of art majors and sociology majors that you know.

The **anchoring and adjustment heuristic** suggests that there can be a good deal of inertia in our judgments. In forming opinions or making estimates, we have an initial view, or presumption. This is the anchor. As we receive additional information, we make adjustments, sometimes grudgingly. That is, if you grow up believing that one religion or one political party is the "right" one, that belief serves as a cognitive anchor. When inconsistencies show up in your religion or political party, you may adjust your views of them, but perhaps not very willingly.

Let's illustrate further by means of a math problem. Write each of the following multiplication problems on a separate piece of paper:

A. $8 \times 7 \times 6 \times 5 \times 4 \times 3 \times 2 \times 1$

B. $1 \times 2 \times 3 \times 4 \times 5 \times 6 \times 7 \times 8$

Show problem A to a few friends. Give them each 5 seconds to estimate the answer. Show problem B to some other friends and give them 5 seconds to estimate the answer.

The answers to the multiplication problems are the same because the order of quantities being multiplied does not change the outcome. However, when Amos Tversky and Daniel Kahneman (1982, 2003) showed these problems to high-school students, the average estimate given by students who were shown version A was significantly higher than that given by students who were shown version B. Students who saw 8 in the first position offered an average estimate of 2,250. Students who saw 1 in the first position gave an average estimate of 512. That is, the estimate was larger when 8 served as the anchor. By the way, what is the correct answer to the multiplication problems? Can you use the anchoring and adjustment heuristic to explain why both groups were so far off?

THE FRAMING EFFECT The **framing effect** refers to the way in which wording, or the context in which information is presented, affects decision making (Takemura, 2014). Political groups, like advertisers, are aware of the framing effect and choose their words accordingly. For example, proponents of legalized abortion refer to themselves as "pro-choice" and opponents refer to themselves as "pro-life." Each group frames itself in a positive way ("pro" something) and refers to a popular value (freedom or life).

OVERCONFIDENCE Whether our decisions are correct or incorrect, most of us tend to be overconfident about them. We also tend to view our situations with 20/20 hindsight. When we are proven wrong, we frequently find a way to show that we "knew it all along." We also become overconfident that we would have known the actual outcome if we had had access to the information that became available after the event. For example, if we had known that a key player would pull a hamstring muscle, we would have predicted a different outcome for the football game. If we had known that it would be blustery on Election Day, we would have

representativeness heuristic a decision-making heuristic in which people make judgments about samples according to the populations they appear to represent

availability heuristic a decision-making heuristic in which our estimates of frequency or probability of events are based on how easy it is to find examples

anchoring and adjustment heuristic a decision-making heuristic in which a presumption or first estimate serves as a cognitive anchor; as we receive additional information, we make adjustments but tend to remain in the proximity of the anchor

framing effect the influence of wording, or the context in which information is presented, on decision making

predicted a smaller voter turnout and a different outcome. There are several reasons for overconfidence, even when our judgments are wrong:

▶ We tend to be unaware of how flimsy our assumptions may be.

▶ We tend to focus on examples that confirm our judgments and ignore those that do not.

▶ Because our working memories have limited space, we tend to forget information that runs counter to our judgments.

▶ We work to bring about the events we believe in, so they sometimes become self-fulfilling prophecies.

7-2 LANGUAGE

Oscar Wilde, the Irish playwright, wrote "It is only by language that we rise above [the lower animals]—by language, which is the parent, not the child, of thought." He gave us quite a bit to think about. Are humans the only species to use language? We'll grapple with that question in a moment. And then, which comes first: language or thinking? Can you think without using language? (Give it a try.) We'll come back to that question later too. For the moment, let's consider whether apes can use language, and also whether language is for the birds—more specifically, the African Grey Parrot.

7-2a COMMUNICATION BY NONHUMANS

In recent years, the exclusive human claim to language has been brought into question by studies of communication with various animal species. The African Grey Parrot, like many other parrots, can mimic human speech, but it is also suspected of being intelligent enough to understand some of the words it imitates. It has long been suspected that spontaneous language development occurs among many species of dolphins and whales, but we lack solid scientific evidence. Monkeys signal the peril of nearby predators with characteristic hoots. But none of these sounds contains *symbols*.

A language is a system of symbols along with rules that are used to manipulate the symbols. Symbols such as words stand for or represent other objects, events, or ideas. Because chimpanzees and gorillas have been taught to communicate by making signs with their hands, the question as to whether or not they are actu-

ally using language in the way that humans do is much more complex.

Chimpanzees are our closest genetic relatives, sharing an estimated 98.42% of their genetic code with humans (Zimmer, 2002–2003). Magnetic resonance imaging (MRI) studies with chimpanzees and gorillas show that most of them, like humans, show enlargement in the left hemisphere of the cerebral cortex, in part of Broca's area (Roth, 2013). The differences that remain between humans and chimps are at least in part associated with capabilities such as fine control of the mouth and larynx that are not found in apes (Sherwood et al., 2008). The genetic differences between chimps and humans probably explain why chimps cannot articulate speech but also apparently give chimps and other apes some meaningful ability to use language (Sherwood et al., 2008).

DO APES REALLY USE LANGUAGE? Although apes do not speak, they have been taught to use American Sign Language and other symbol systems. For example, a chimpanzee named Washoe, who was a pioneer in the effort to teach apes to use language, was using 181 signs by the age of 32 (King, 2008). Loulis, a baby chimp adopted by Washoe, gained the ability to use signs just by observing Washoe and some other chimps that had been trained in sign language. Other chimps have used plastic symbols or pressed keys on a computer keyboard to communicate.

Sue Savage-Rumbaugh and her colleagues (Segerdahl et al., 2006; Washburn et al., 2007) believe that pygmy chimpanzees can understand some of the semantic subtleties of language. She claims that one

The African Grey Parrot can mimic human speech, but does it understand any of the words it utters? Some zoologists think that it actually might do that.

Martin Harvey/Gallo Images/Getty Images

> "MAN INVENTED LANGUAGE TO SATISFY HIS DEEP NEED TO COMPLAIN."
>
> LILY TOMLIN, AMERICAN ACTRESS, COMEDIAN, AND WRITER (B. 1939)

chimp, Kanzi, picked up language from observing another chimp being trained and has the grammatical abilities of a 2½-year-old child. Kanzi also understands several words spoken by humans. Kanzi held a toy snake to a toy dog's mouth when asked to make the dog bite the snake.

Critics of the view that apes can learn to produce language, such as Herbert Terrace (Terrace & Metcalfe, 2005) and Steven Pinker (1994a, 2011), note that:

- Apes can string together signs in a given sequence to earn rewards, but animals lower on the evolutionary ladder, such as pigeons, can also peck buttons in a certain sequence to obtain a reward.

- It takes apes longer to learn new signs than it takes children to learn new words.

- Apes are unreliable in their sequencing of signs, suggesting that by and large they do not comprehend rules of grammar.

- People observing apes signing may be subject to *observer bias*—that is, they may be seeing what they want to see.

Scientists will continue to debate how well chimpanzees and gorillas understand and produce language, but there is little doubt that they have learned to use symbols to communicate (Segerdahl et al., 2006).

7-2b WHAT IS LANGUAGE?

As you can see from the discussion of apes and language, the way in which one defines language is no small matter. If we define language simply as a system of communication, many animals have language, including the birds and the bees. Through particular chirps and shrieks, birds may communicate that they have taken possession of a tree or bush. The waggle dances of bees inform other bees of the location of a food source or a predator. All of these are instinctive communication patterns but not what we mean by language.

With language, sounds or signs are symbols for objects and actions. Apes have been taught to use symbols to communicate, but is such usage an adequate definition of language? Many language experts require one more piece. They define **language** as the communication of thoughts and feelings by means of symbols *that are arranged according to rules of grammar.* Instinctive waggle dances and shrieks have no symbols and no grammar. By these rigorous rules, only humans use language. Whether apes can handle rules of grammar is under debate.

Language makes it possible for one person to communicate knowledge to another and for one generation to communicate to another. It creates a vehicle for recording experiences. It allows us to put ourselves in the shoes of other people, to learn more than we could learn from direct experience. Language also provides many units of thinking.

True language is distinguished from the communication systems of lower animals by properties such as semanticity, infinite creativity, and displacement (Hoff, 2005):

- **Semanticity:** The sounds (or signs) of a language have meaning. Words serve as symbols for actions, objects, relational concepts (*over, in, more,* and so on), and other ideas. The communication systems of the birds and the bees do not use words and symbols. Therefore, they lack semanticity.

- **Infinite creativity:** The capacity to create rather than imitate sentences.

- **Displacement:** The capacity to communicate information about events and objects in another time or place. Language makes it possible to transmit knowledge from one person to another and from one generation to another, furthering human adaptation.

7-2c LANGUAGE AND COGNITION

The relationships between language and thinking are complex and not always obvious. For example, can you think *without* using

language the communication of information by means of symbols arranged according to rules of grammar

semanticity the quality of language in which words are used as symbols for objects, events, or ideas

infinite creativity the capacity to combine words into original sentences

displacement the quality of language that permits one to communicate information about objects and events in another time and place

language? Would you be able to solve problems without using words or sentences?

Jean Piaget (Inhelder & Piaget, 1958) believed that language reflects knowledge of the world but that much knowledge can be acquired without language. For example, it is possible to understand the concepts of roundness or redness even when we do not know or use the words *round* or *red*.

7-2d LANGUAGE AND CULTURE

Different languages have different words for the same concepts, and concepts do not necessarily overlap. As noted earlier, concepts expressed in our own language (such as *square* and *triangle*) may not exist in the language of another culture—and vice versa. Is it possible for English speakers to share the thoughts experienced by people who speak other languages? The answer is probably yes in many or most cases, but in some cases, no. In any event, the question brings us to the linguistic-relativity hypothesis.

linguistic-relativity hypothesis the view that language structures the way we view the world

THE LINGUISTIC-RELATIVITY HYPOTHESIS The **linguistic-relativity hypothesis** was proposed by Benjamin Whorf (1956). Whorf believed that language structures the way we perceive the world. That is, the categories and relationships we use to understand the world are derived from our language. Therefore, speakers of various languages conceptualize the world in different ways.

Thus, most English speakers' ability to think about snow may be limited compared with that of the Inuit (Eskimos). We have only a few words for snow, whereas

Joyce Butler of Columbia University shows chimpanzee "Nim Chimpsky"—named humorously after linguist Noam Chomsky—the sign for "drink," and Nim imitates her.

Susan Kuklin/Science Source

the Inuit have many. The Inuit's words differ according to whether the snow is hard packed, falling, melting, covered by ice, and so on. When we think about snow, we have fewer words to choose from and have to search for descriptive adjectives. The Inuit, however, can readily find a single word that describes a complex weather condition. Is it therefore easier for them to think about this variety of snow? Similarly, the Hanunoo people of the Philippines use 92 words for rice depending on whether the rice is husked or unhusked and on how it is prepared. And whereas we have one word for camel, Arabs have more than 250.

In English, we have hundreds of words to describe colors. There is about a 95% overlap in perception and labeling of colors among English speakers and Chinese people (Moore et al., 2002). It has been pointed out, however, that Shona-speaking people use only three words for colors, and Bassa speakers use only two corresponding to light and dark. Nevertheless, studies of languages spoken in nonindustrialized societies find overlaps for white, black, red, green, yellow, and blue (Regier, 2005; Tohidian, 2009). Moreover, people who use only a few words to distinguish among colors seem to perceive the same color variations as people with more words. For example, the Dani of New Guinea have just two words for colors: one that refers to yellows and reds and one that refers to greens and blues. Yet performance on matching and memory tasks shows that the Dani can discriminate the many colors of the spectrum.

Most cognitive scientists no longer accept the linguistic-relativity hypothesis (Pinker, 2007, 2013). For one thing, adults use images and abstract logical propositions, as well as words, as units of thought. Infants, moreover, display considerable intelligence before they have learned to speak. Another criticism is

that a language's vocabulary suggests the range of concepts that the speakers of the language have traditionally found important, not their cognitive limits. For example, people who were magically lifted from the 19th century and placed inside an airplane probably would not think they were flying inside a bird or a large insect, even if their language lacked a word for airplane.

7-3 LANGUAGE DEVELOPMENT: THE TWO-YEAR EXPLOSION

Languages around the world develop in a specific sequence of steps, beginning with the *prelinguistic* vocalizations of crying, cooing, and babbling. These sounds are not symbols. That is, they do not represent objects or events. Therefore, they are prelinguistic, not linguistic.

7-3a PRELINGUISTIC VOCALIZATIONS

As parents are well aware, newborn children have one inborn, highly effective form of verbal expression: crying—and more crying. But crying does not represent language; it is a prelinguistic

How many words do you know for snow?

event. During the second month, babies begin *cooing,* another form of prelinguistic expression that appears to be linked to feelings of pleasure. By the fifth or sixth month, children begin to *babble.* Children babble sounds that occur in many languages, including the throaty German *ch,* the clicks of certain African languages, and rolling *r's.* Babies' babbling frequently combines consonants and vowels, as in "ba," "ga," and, sometimes, the much-valued "dada" (McCardle et al., 2009). "Dada" at first is purely coincidental (sorry, dads), despite the family's delight over its appearance.

Babbling, like crying and cooing, is inborn and prelinguistic. Deaf children babble, and children from cultures whose languages sound very different all seem to babble the same sounds (Hoff, 2005). But children single out the sounds used in the home within a few months. By the age of 9 or 10 months, they are repeating the sounds regularly, and foreign sounds are dropping out. In fact, early experience in acquiring the phonemes (i.e., meaningful units of sound) native to one's own language can make it difficult to pronounce and even discriminate the phonemes used in other languages later in life (Iverson et al., 2003).

Children tend to utter their first word at 11 to 13 months, but a range of 8 to 18 months is normal (McCardle et al., 2009; Tamis-LeMonda et al., 2014). Parents often miss the first word because it is not pronounced clearly. The growth of vocabulary is slow at first. It may take children 3 to 4 months to achieve a 10-word vocabulary after they have spoken their first word. By about 18 months, children are producing a couple of dozen words.

7-3b DEVELOPMENT OF GRAMMAR

The first linguistic utterances of children around the globe are single words that can express complex meanings. These initial utterances of children are called **holophrases.** For example, *mama* may be used by the child to

holophrase a single word used to express complex meanings

Crying communicates discomfort and, soon enough, the demand for a caregiver—now! But cries do not have symbols and are therefore prelinguistic.

Mike Kemp/Rubberball

signify meanings as varied as "There goes Mama," "Come here, Mama," and "You are my Mama." Similarly, *cat* can signify "There is a cat," "That stuffed animal looks just like my cat," or "I want you to give me my cat right now!" Most children show their parents what they intend by augmenting their holophrases with gestures and intonations. That is, they act delighted when parents do as requested and howl when they do not.

Toward the end of the second year, children begin to speak two-word sentences. These sentences are termed *telegraphic speech* because they resemble telegrams. Telegrams cut out the "unnecessary" words. "Home Tuesday" might stand for "I expect to be home on Tuesday." Two-word utterances seem to appear at about the same time in the development of all languages (Saffran, 2009; Slobin, 1983). Two-word utterances are brief but grammatically correct. The child says, "Sit chair" to tell a parent to sit in a chair, not "Chair sit." The child says, "My shoe," not "Shoe my," to show possession. "Mommy go" means Mommy is leaving. "Go Mommy" expresses the wish for Mommy to go away.

There are different kinds of two-word utterances. Some, for example, contain nouns or pronouns and verbs ("Daddy sit"). Others contain verbs and objects ("Hit ball"). The sequence of emergence of the various kinds of two-word utterances is also apparently the same in all languages—languages as diverse as English, Luo (an African tongue), German, Russian, and Turkish (Slobin, 1983). The invariance of this sequence has implications for theories of language development, as we will see.

OVERREGULARIZATION **Overregularization** is an important development for understanding the roles of nature and nurture in language development (Ambridge et al., 2013; Pinker, 2013). In English, we add *d* or *ed* to make the past tense of regular verbs and *s* or *z* sounds to make regular nouns plural. Thus, *walk* becomes *walked*, and *look* becomes *looked*. *Cat* becomes *cats,* and *doggy* becomes *doggies*. There are also irregular verbs and nouns. For example, *see* becomes *saw, sit* becomes *sat,* and *go* becomes *went. Sheep* remains *sheep* (plural) and *child* becomes *children.*

At first children learn irregular verbs and nouns by imitating older people. Two-year-olds tend to form them correctly—at first! Then they become aware of the grammatical rules for forming the past tense and plurals. As a result, they tend to make charming errors (Pinker, 2013). A three- to five-year-old, for example, may be more likely to say "I seed it" than "I saw it," and more likely to say "Mommy sitted down" than "Mommy sat down." They are likely to talk about the "gooses" and "sheeps" they "seed" on the farm and about all the "childs" they ran into at the playground. This tendency to regularize the irregular is what is meant by overregularization.

Should parents be concerned about overregularization? Not at all. Overregularization reflects knowledge of grammar, not faulty language development. In another year or two, *mouses* will be boringly transformed into *mice,* and Mommy will no longer have *sitted* down. Parents might as well enjoy overregularization while they can.

OTHER DEVELOPMENTS By the age of six, children's vocabularies have expanded to 10,000 words, give or take a few thousand. By seven to nine, most children realize that words can have more than one meaning, and they are entertained by riddles and jokes that require some sophistication with language.

Between the elementary school and high school years, language grows more complex, and children rapidly add to their vocabularies. Vocabulary, in fact, can grow for a lifetime, especially in one's fields of specialization and interest.

7-3c NATURE AND NURTURE IN LANGUAGE DEVELOPMENT

Billions of children have acquired the languages spoken by their parents and passed them down, with minor changes, from generation to generation. Language development, like many other areas of development, apparently reflects the interactions between nature and nurture.

LEARNING THEORY AND LANGUAGE DEVELOPMENT Learning theorists see language as developing according to laws of learning (Hoff, 2005). They usually refer to the concepts of imitation and reinforcement. From a social–cognitive perspective, parents serve as models. Children learn language, at least in part, through observation and imitation. Many words, especially nouns and verbs (including irregular verbs), are apparently learned by imitation.

Children initially repeat the irregular verb forms they have heard accurately, apparently as a result of modeling. Modeling, however, does not explain all of the

> "SINCE ALL NORMAL HUMANS TALK BUT NO HOUSE PETS OR HOUSE PLANTS DO, NO MATTER HOW PAMPERED, HEREDITY MUST BE INVOLVED IN LANGUAGE. BUT SINCE A CHILD GROWING UP IN JAPAN SPEAKS JAPANESE WHEREAS THE SAME CHILD BROUGHT UP IN CALIFORNIA WOULD SPEAK ENGLISH, THE ENVIRONMENT IS ALSO CRUCIAL."
>
> STEVEN PINKER, M.I.T. PSYCHOLOGIST (B. 1954)

👍 *Truth*

T F   Young children say things like "daddy goed away" and "mommy sitted down" because they do understand rules of grammar.

It is true that young children say things like "daddy goed away" and "mommy sitted down" because they understand rules of grammar. These charming errors are examples of *overregularization*.

overregularization the application of regular grammatical rules for forming inflections (e.g., past tense and plurals) to irregular verbs and nouns

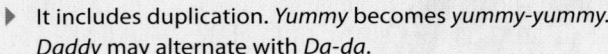
One way that adults attempt to prompt the language development of children is by using baby talk, or "motherese," referred to more technically as *infant-directed speech* (*IDS*) (Lahey & Ernestus, 2013; Meltzoff & Brooks, 2009). Motherese is a limiting term because grandparents, fathers, siblings, and unrelated people have also been observed using IDS. Moreover, women (but usually not men) often talk to their pets as if they were infants (Xu et al., 2013). Infant-directed speech is used in languages as diverse as Arabic, English, Comanche, Italian, French, German, Xhosa (an African tongue), Japanese, Mandarin Chinese, and even a Thai sign language (Broesch & Bryant, 2013; Lee et al., 2010; Nonaka, 2004).

IDS has the following characteristics (Broesch & Bryant, 2013; Meltzoff & Brooks, 2009):

▶ It is spoken more slowly, at a higher pitch, and includes pauses between ideas.

▶ Sentences are brief, and the focus is on nouns, verbs, and just a few modifiers.

▶ Keywords are placed at the ends of sentences and spoken in a higher, louder voice.

▶ The diminutive *y* is frequently added to nouns. *Dad* becomes *Daddy*; *horse* becomes *horsey*.

▶ Adults repeat sentences, sometimes using minor variations, as in "Show me your nose." "Where is your nose?"

▶ It includes duplication. *Yummy* becomes *yummy-yummy*. *Daddy* may alternate with *Da-da*.

▶ Much IDS focuses on naming objects (Meltzoff & Brooks, 2009). Vocabulary is concrete and refers to the child's environment. For example, stuffed lions may be called "kitties."

▶ Objects may be over described with compound labels. Rabbits may become "bunny rabbits," and cats may become "kitty cats." Users of IDS try to ensure they are using at least one label the child will recognize.

▶ Parents speak for the children, as in "Is baby tired?" "Oh, we're so tired." Parents seem to be helping children express themselves by offering them models of sentences they can use.

Does IDS encourage communication and foster language development? Research supports its use. Infants as two days old prefer IDS to adult talk (N. A. Smith & Trainor, 2008). The short, simple sentences and high pitch are more likely to produce a response from the child and enhance vocabulary development than complex sentences and those spoken in a lower pitch (Broesch & Bryant, 2013). Mimicking of children's vocalizations appears to encourage vocalizing.

events in language learning. As noted previously, children later overregularize irregular verb forms because they have developed an understanding of grammar. Nor can learning by imitation explain how children come to utter phrases and sentences they have not observed. Parents, for example, are unlikely to model utterances such as "Bye-bye sock" and "All gone Daddy," but children say them.

Learning theory cannot account for the unchanging sequence of language development and the spurts in children's language acquisition. Even the types of two-word utterances emerge in a consistent pattern in diverse cultures. Although timing differs from one child to another, the types of questions used, passive versus active sentences, and so on, all emerge in the same order.

THE NATIVIST APPROACH TO LANGUAGE DEVELOPMENT The nativist theory of language development holds that the innate factors—which make up children's *nature*—cause children to attend to and acquire language in certain ways. From this perspective, children bring neurological "prewiring" to language learning (A. Clark & Lappin, 2013; Pinker, 2013).

According to **psycholinguistic theory**, language acquisition involves the interaction of environmental influences—such as exposure to parental speech and reinforcement—and the inborn tendency to acquire language. Noam Chomsky (see Cherniak, 2009) refers to the inborn tendency as a **language acquisition device (LAD)**. Evidence for an LAD is found in the universality of human language abilities and in the specific sequence of language development (Cherniak, 2009; A. Clark & Lappin, 2013).

The LAD prepares the nervous system to learn grammar. On the surface, languages differ a great deal. However, the LAD serves children all over the world because languages share what Chomsky refers to as a "universal grammar"—an underlying set of rules for turning ideas into sentences (Pinker, 2013).

In the following section, we see that some aspects of language development—particularly vocabulary development—are strongly related to intelligence. Numerous researchers suggest that language learning occurs during one or more sensitive periods, which begin at about 18 to 24 months and last until puberty (Bates, 2001). During these sensitive periods, neural development (as in the differentiating of brain structures) provides plasticity that facilitates language learning.

The concept of intelligence is closely related to thinking. Whereas thinking involves the understanding and manipulating of information, **intelligence** is the underlying ability to understand the world and cope with its challenges (Cornoldi, 2006; Sternberg et al., 2005). That is, intelligence is seen as making thinking possible. Although these concepts overlap, psychologists tend to be concerned with how we think, but laypeople and psychologists are often concerned with how much intelligence we have. Although intelligence, like thinking, cannot be directly seen or touched, psychologists tie the concept to achievements such as school performance and occupational status (Nisbett, 2009).

Although psychologists have engaged in thousands of studies on intelligence, they do not quite agree on what intelligence is. Psychologists have therefore developed theories to help them understand and define intelligence.

7-4a FACTOR THEORIES

Many investigators have viewed intelligence as consisting of one or more factors. Factor theories argue that intelligence is made up of a number of mental abilities, ranging from one kind of ability to hundreds.

In 1904, British psychologist Charles Spearman suggested that the behaviors we consider intelligent have a common underlying factor that he labeled *g*, for "general intelligence" or broad reasoning and problem-solving abilities. Spearman supported his view by noting that people who excel in one area (such as vocabulary) are also likely to excel in others (such as math). But he also noted that even the most capable people are relatively superior in some areas—such as music or business or poetry. For this reason, he suggested that specific, or *s*, factors account for specific abilities.

psycholinguistic theory the view that language learning involves an interaction between environmental factors and an inborn tendency to acquire language

language acquisition device (LAD) in psycholinguistic theory, neural "prewiring" that facilitates the child's learning of grammar

intelligence a general mental capability that involves the ability to reason, plan, solve problems, think abstractly, comprehend complex ideas, learn quickly, and learn from experience

g Spearman's symbol for general intelligence, which he believed underlay more specific abilities

s Spearman's symbol for *specific* factors, or *s factors*, which he believed accounted for individual abilities

TABLE 7.1	PRIMARY MENTAL ABILITIES, ACCORDING TO THURSTONE
Ability	**Definition**
Visual and spatial abilities	Visualizing forms and spatial relationships
Perceptual speed	Grasping perceptual details rapidly, perceiving similarities and differences between stimuli
Numerical ability	Computing numbers
Verbal meaning	Knowing the meanings of words
Memory	Recalling information (e.g., words and sentences)
Word fluency	Thinking of words quickly (e.g., rhyming and doing crossword puzzles)
Deductive reasoning	Deriving examples from general rules
Inductive reasoning	Inferring general rules from examples

Contemporary psychologists continue to use the term *g* in research, speaking, for example, of the extent to which they believe a particular kind of test, such as the SATs, measure *g* (Lubinski & Benbow, 2006).

American psychologist Louis Thurstone (1938) analyzed tests of specific abilities and concluded that Spearman had oversimplified intelligence. Thurstone's data suggested the presence of eight specific factors, which he labeled **primary mental abilities** (see Table 7.1). Thurstone's primary mental abilities contain the types of items measured on the most widely used intelligence tests today. The question remains as to whether his primary mental abilities are distinct or whether they are different ways of assessing *g*.

7-4b THE THEORY OF MULTIPLE INTELLIGENCES

Thurstone wrote about various factors or components of intelligence. Howard Gardner's (1983/1993, 2009) *theory of multiple intelligences* proposes, instead, that there are a number of intelligences, not just one. Gardner refers to each kind of intelligence in his theory as "an intelligence" because they can differ so much. Two of these "intelligences" are familiar ones: language ability and logical–mathematical ability. Gardner also refers, however, to bodily–kinesthetic talents (of the sort shown by dancers and athletes), musical talent, spatial–relations skills, and two kinds of personal intelligence: awareness of one's own inner

primary mental abilities according to Thurstone, the basic abilities that make up intelligence examples include word fluency and numerical ability

feelings and sensitivity to other people's feelings. Gardner (2001) more recently added "naturalist intelligence" and "existential intelligence." Naturalist intelligence refers to the ability to look at natural events, such as kinds of animals and plants, or the stars above, and to develop insights into their nature and the laws that govern their behavior. Existential intelligence means dealing with the larger philosophical issues of life. According to Gardner, one can compose symphonies or advance mathematical theory yet be average in, say, language and personal skills.

Critics of Gardner's view agree that people function more intelligently in some aspects of life than in others. They also agree that many people have special talents, such as bodily-kinesthetic talents, even if their overall intelligence is average. But these critics question whether such talents are best thought of as "intelligences" or special talents (Neisser et al., 1996). Language skills, reasoning ability, and ability to solve math problems seem to be more closely related than musical or gymnastic talent to what most people mean by intelligence.

7-4c THE TRIARCHIC THEORY OF INTELLIGENCE

Psychologist Robert Sternberg (2000; 2006) has constructed a three-pronged or *triarchic theory of intelligence* that includes *analytical, creative,* and *practical intelligence* (see Figure 7.3).

Analytical intelligence can be defined as academic ability. It enables us to solve problems and acquire new knowledge. It is the type of intelligence measured by standard intelligence tests. Problem-solving skills include encoding information, combining and comparing bits of information, and generating a solution. Consider Sternberg's analogy problem:

Washington is to *1* as *Lincoln* is to

   (a) 5

   (b) 10

   (c) 15

   (d) 50

To solve the analogy, we must first correctly *encode* the elements—*Washington, 1,* and *Lincoln*—by identifying them and comparing them to other information. We can first encode *Washington* and *Lincoln* as the names of presidents and then try to combine *Washington* and *1* in a meaningful manner. (There are other possibilities: both are also the names of memorials and cities, for example.) If we do encode the names as presidents, two possibilities quickly come to mind. Washington was the

FIG.7.3 STERNBERG'S THEORY OF INTELLIGENCE

Analytical intelligence
(Academic ability)
Abilities to solve problems,
compare and contrast, judge,
evaluate, and criticize

Creative intelligence
(Creativity and insight)
Abilities to invent, discover,
suppose, or theorize

Practical intelligence
("Street smarts")
Abilities to adapt to the demands
of one's environment and apply
knowledge in practical situations

© 2012 Cengage Learning®

According to Robert Sternberg, there are three types of intelligence: analytical (academic ability), creative, and practical ("street smarts"). Psychologists discuss the relationships between intelligence and creativity, but within Sternberg's model, creativity is a type of intellectual functioning.

first president, and his picture is on the $1 bill. We can then generate two possible solutions and try them out. First, was Lincoln the 5th, 10th, 15th, or 50th president? Second, on what bill is Lincoln's picture found? (Do you need to consult a history book or peek into your wallet at this point?) The answer is (a) 5, because Lincoln's likeness is found on the $5 bill. (He was the nation's 16th president, not 15th president.)

Creative intelligence is defined by the ability to cope with novel situations and generate many possible solutions to problems. It is creative to quickly relate novel situations to familiar situations (i.e., to perceive similarities and differences). Psychologists who consider creativity to be separate from analytical intelligence or academic ability note that there is only a moderate relationship between academic ability and creativity (Simon-

ton, 2009). To Sternberg, however, creativity *is* a form of intelligence.

Practical intelligence ("street smarts") enables people to deal with other people, including difficult people, and to meet the demands of their environment. For example, keeping a job by adapting one's behavior to the employer's requirements is adaptive. But if the employer is making unreasonable demands, finding a more suitable job is also adaptive. Street smarts appear to help people get by in the real world, especially with other people, but are not particularly predictive of academic success (Heng, 2000).

7-4d EMOTIONAL INTELLIGENCE

Psychologists Peter Salovey and John Mayer developed the theory of emotional intelligence, which was popularized by psychologist Daniel Goleman (1995). The theory holds that social and emotional skills, like academic skills, are a form of intelligence (Salovey et al., 2008). Emotional intelligence resembles two of Gardner's "intelligences"—intrapersonal skills and interpersonal skills (including insight into the feelings of other people). It also involves self-insight and self-control—the abilities to recognize and regulate one's moods (Salovey et al., 2008). Failure to develop emotional intelligence is connected with poor ability to cope with stress, depression, and aggressive behavior (Brackett et al., 2011).

👍 *Truth*

T **F** "Street smarts" are a sign of intelligence.

It is true that street smarts are a sign of intelligence—at least according to the views of the Greek philosopher Aristotle and the psychologist Robert Sternberg.

But *is* emotional intelligence a form of intelligence? Psychologist Ulric Neisser (1997b) says that "the skills that Goleman describes ... are certainly important for determining life outcomes, but nothing is to be gained by calling them forms of intelligence."

There are thus many views of intelligence—what intelligence is and how many kinds of intelligence there may be. We do not yet have the final word on the nature of intelligence, but I would like to share psychologist Linda Gottfredson's definition: Intelligence is "a very general mental capability that, among other things, involves the ability to reason, plan, solve problems, think abstractly, comprehend complex ideas, learn quickly and learn from experience. It is not merely book learning, a narrow academic skill, or test-taking smarts. Rather it reflects a broader and deeper capability for comprehending our surroundings—'catching on,' 'making sense,' of things, or 'figuring out what to do'" (Nisbett, 2009).

creativity the ability to generate novel and useful solutions to problems

7-4e CREATIVITY AND INTELLIGENCE

Think of artists, musicians, poets, scientists and other creative individuals who innovate research methods. Like the concept of intelligence, the concept of creativity has been difficult to define. One issue is whether creativity is distinct from intelligence, or is, as Sternberg suggests, a type of intelligence. For example, we would not ask the question, "Do creative people tend to be intelligent?" unless we saw creativity as distinct from intelligence. If you consider creativity to be an aspect of intelligence, then the two concepts—intelligence and creativity—overlap. But if you think of intelligence as more closely related to academic ability, it is not always true that a highly intelligent person is creative or that a creative person is highly intelligent. Research findings suggest that the relationship between intelligence test scores and standard measures of creativity is only moderate (Simonton, 2009).

Within his triarchic theory, Sternberg defines **creativity** as the ability to do things that are novel and

TABLE 7.2	THEORIES OF INTELLIGENCE SUMMARY CHART	
Theory	**Basic Information**	**Comments**
General versus specific factors (proponent: Charles Spearman)	■ Spearman created factor analysis to study intelligence ■ There is strong evidence for the general factor (g) in intelligence. ■ s factors are specific abilities, skills, and talents	■ Concept of g remains in use today—a century later.
Primary mental abilities (proponent: Louis Thurstone)	■ Thurstone used factor analysis. ■ There are many "primary" abilities. ■ All abilities and factors are academically oriented.	■ Other researchers (e.g., Guilford) claim to have found hundreds of factors. ■ The more factors that are claimed, the more they overlap.
Triarchic theory (proponent: Robert Sternberg)	■ Intelligence is three-pronged—with analytical, creative, and practical components. ■ Analytical intelligence is analogous to academic ability.	■ The theory coincides with the views of Aristotle. ■ Critics do not view creativity as a component of intelligence.
Multiple intelligences (proponent: Howard Gardner)	■ Gardner theorized distinct "intelligences." ■ Intelligences include academic intelligences, personal and social intelligences, talents and philosophical intelligences. ■ The theory posits different bases in the brain for different intelligences	■ Proponents continue to expand the number of "intelligences." ■ Critics see little value in theorizing "intelligences" rather than aspects of intelligence. ■ Most critics consider musical and bodily skills to be special talents, not "intelligences"

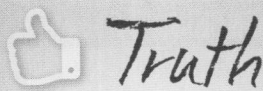
useful (Sternberg et al., 2012). Creative people can solve problems to which there are no preexisting solutions and no proven formulas. Creative people share a number of qualities (Sternberg et al., 2012): they take chances. They refuse to accept limitations. They appreciate art and music. They use common materials to make unique things. They challenge social norms and take unpopular stands. They challenge ideas that other people accept at face value.

Creative problem solving demands divergent rather than convergent thinking. In **convergent thinking,** thought is limited to present facts; the problem solver narrows his or her thinking to find the best solution. (You use convergent thinking to arrive at the right answer to a multiple-choice question.) In **divergent thinking,** the problem solver associates freely to the elements of the problem, allowing "leads" to run a nearly limitless course. (You may use divergent thinking when you are trying to generate ideas to answer an essay question on a test.) Problem solving can involve both kinds of thinking. At first, divergent thinking helps generate many possible solutions. Convergent thinking is then used to select likely solutions and reject others.

Intelligence test questions usually require analytical, convergent thinking to focus in on the one right answer. Tests of creativity determine how flexible a person's thinking is. Here is an item from a test used by Getzels and Jackson (1962) to measure associative ability, a factor in creativity: "Write as many meanings as you can for each of the following words: (a) duck; (b) sack; (c) pitch; (d) fair." Those who write several meanings for each word, rather than only one, are rated as potentially more creative.

Now that we have begun speaking of scores on intelligence tests, let's see how psychologists go about measuring intelligence. We will also see how psychologists attempt to *validate* their measures of intelligence—that is, how they try to demonstrate that they are in fact measuring intelligence.

THE MEASUREMENT OF INTELLIGENCE

Although psychologists disagree about the nature of intelligence, laypeople and educators are concerned with "how much" intelligence people have, because the issue affects educational and occupational choices. In this section we consider two of the most widely used intelligence tests.

7-5a THE STANFORD–BINET INTELLIGENCE SCALE

Many of the concepts of psychology have their origins in common sense. The commonsense notion that academic achievement depends on children's intelligence led Alfred Binet and Theodore Simon to invent measures of intelligence.

Early in the 20th century, the French public school system was looking for a test that could identify children who were unlikely to benefit from regular classroom instruction. If these children were identified, they could be given special attention. The first version of that test, the Binet–Simon scale, came into use in 1905. Since that time it has undergone extensive revision and refinement. The current version is the Stanford–Binet Intelligence Scale (SBIS).

Binet assumed that intelligence increases with age, so older children should get more items right than younger children. Binet therefore included a series of age-graded questions, as in Figure 7.4, arranged in order of difficulty.

The Binet–Simon scale yielded a score called a **mental age (MA).** The MA shows the intellectual level at which a child is functioning. For example, a child with an MA of six is functioning intellectually like the average six-year-old. In taking the test, children earned "months" of credit for each correct answer. Their MA was determined by adding up the years and months of credit they attained.

Louis Terman adapted the Binet–Simon scale for use with American children at Stanford University. The first version of the resultant Stanford–Binet Intelligence Scale was published in 1916. The SBIS included more items than the original test

convergent thinking
a thought process that narrows in on the single best solution to a problem

divergent thinking a thought process that attempts to generate multiple solutions to problems

mental age (MA) the accumulated months of credit that a person earns on the Stanford–Binet Intelligence Scale

Level (years)	Item
2	1. Children show knowledge of basic vocabulary words by identifying parts of a doll, such as the mouth, ears, and hair.
	2. Children show counting and spatial skills along with visual–motor coordination by building a tower of four blocks to match a model.
4	1. Children show word fluency and categorical thinking by filling in the missing words when they are asked questions such as: "Father is a man; mother is a ?" "Hamburgers are hot; ice cream is ?"
	2. Children show comprehension by answering correctly when they are asked questions such as: "Why do people have automobiles?" "Why do people have medicine?"
9	1. Children can point out verbal absurdities, as in this question: "In an old cemetery, scientists unearthed a skull which they think was that of George Washington when he was only five years of age. What is silly about that?"
	2. Children display fluency with words, as shown by answering these questions: "Can you tell me a number that rhymes with snore?" "Can you tell me a color that rhymes with glue?"
Adult	1. Adults show knowledge of the meanings of words and conceptual thinking by correctly explaining the differences between word pairs like "sickness and misery," "house and home," and "integrity and prestige."
	2. Adults show spatial skills by correctly answering questions like: "If a car turned to the right to head north, in what direction was it heading before it turned?"

Mike Kemp/Rubberball/Getty Images

and was used with children aged 2 to 16. The SBIS also yielded an **intelligence quotient (IQ)** rather than an MA. As a result, American educators developed interest in learning the IQs of their pupils. The SBIS is used today with children from the age of two upward and with adults.

The IQ reflects the relationship between a child's mental age and his or her actual or chronological age (CA). Use of this ratio reflects the fact that the same MA score has different implications for children of different ages. That is, an MA of 8 is an above-average score for a 6-year-old but below average for a 10-year-old. In 1912, German psychologist Wilhelm Stern suggested the IQ as a way to deal with this problem. Stern computed IQ using this formula:

$$IQ = \frac{\text{Mental age (MA)}}{\text{Chronological age (CA)}} \times 100.$$

intelligence quotient (IQ)
(a) originally, a ratio obtained by dividing a child's score (or mental age) on an intelligence test by chronological age. (b) generally, a score on an intelligence test

According to this formula, a child with an MA of 6 and a CA of 6 would have an IQ of 100. Children who can handle intellectual problems as well as older children do have IQs

above 100. For example, an 8-year-old who does as well on the SBIS as the average 10-year-old would attain an IQ of 125. Children who do not answer as many items correctly as other children of the same age attain MAs lower than their CAs. Thus, their IQ scores are below 100.

IQ scores on the SBIS today are derived by comparing their results to those of other people of the same age.

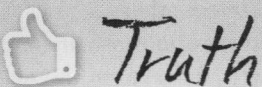

👍 *Truth*

T ~~F~~ Two children can answer exactly the same items on an intelligence test correctly, yet one child can obtain an above average in IQ, and the other can obtain a below average IQ.

It is true that two children can answer exactly the same items on an intelligence test correctly, yet one can obtain an above average IQ and the other can obtain a below average IQ. The younger of the two children would obtain the higher IQ score.

People who answer more items correctly than the average for people of the same age attain IQ scores above 100. People who answer fewer items correctly than the average for their age attain scores below 100. Therefore, two children can answer exactly the same items on an intelligence test correctly, yet one can be above average in IQ. This is because the ages of the children may differ. The more intelligent child would be the younger of the two.

7-5b THE WECHSLER SCALES

In contrast to the SBIS, David Wechsler developed a series of scales for use with children and adults. The Wechsler scales group test questions into a number of separate subtests (see Figure 7.5). Each subtest measures a different intellectual task. For this reason, the test shows how well a person does on one type of task (such as defining words) as compared with another (such as using blocks to construct geometric designs). In this way, the Wechsler scales highlight children's relative strengths and weaknesses, as well as measure overall intellectual functioning.

Wechsler described some of his scales as measuring *verbal* tasks and others as assessing *performance* tasks. In general, verbal subtests require knowledge of verbal concepts, whereas performance subtests require familiarity with spatial–relations concepts. Wechsler's scales permit the computation of verbal and performance IQs. Nontechnically oriented college students often attain higher verbal than performance IQs. Less-well-educated people often obtain higher performance than verbal IQs.

Wechsler also introduced the concept of the *deviation IQ*. Instead of dividing mental age by chronological age to compute an IQ, he based IQ scores on how a person's answers compared with those attained by people in the same age group. The average test result at any age level is defined as an IQ score of 100. Wechsler distributed IQ scores so that the middle 50% were defined as the "broad average range" of 90 to 110. As you can see in

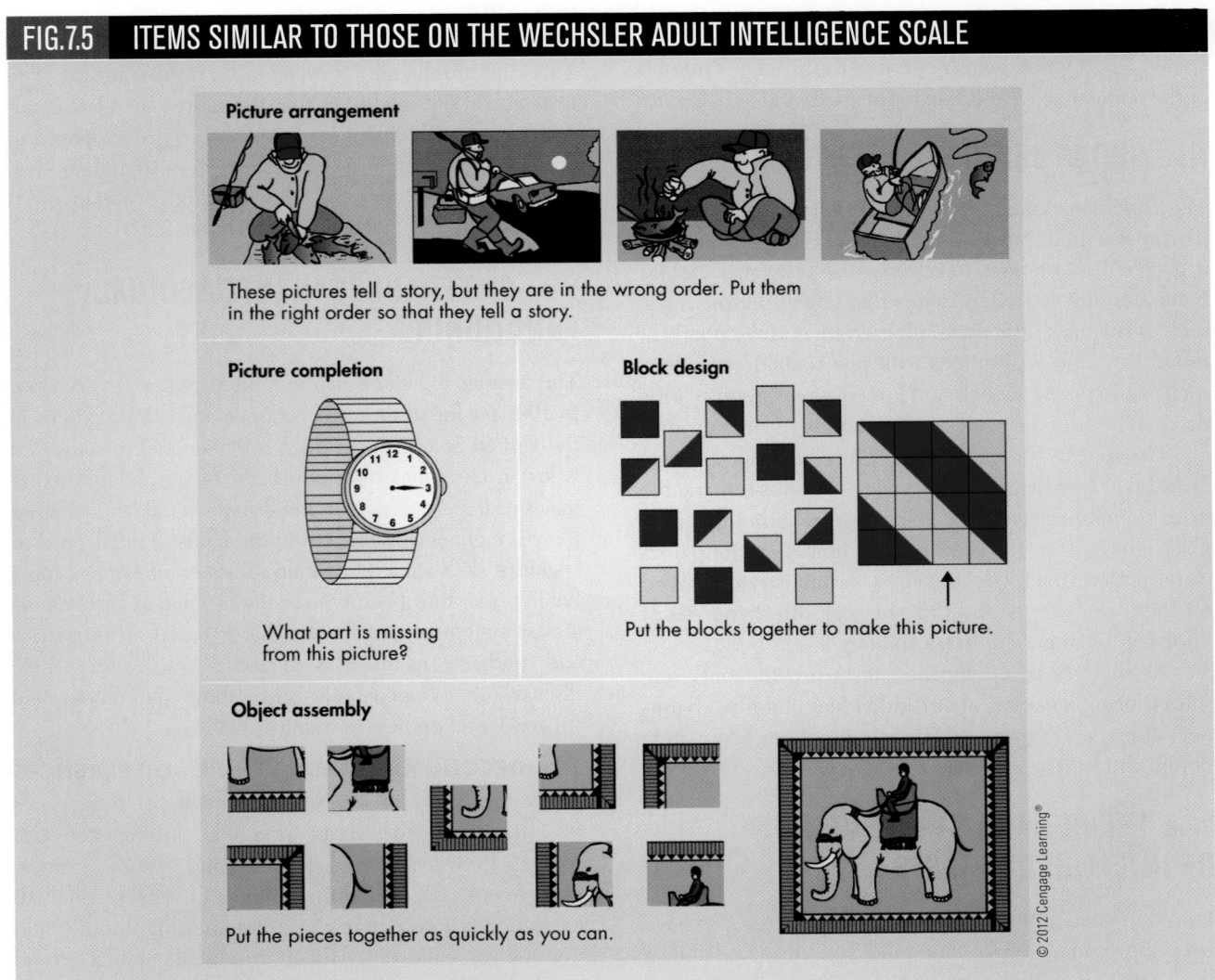

FIG.7.5   ITEMS SIMILAR TO THOSE ON THE WECHSLER ADULT INTELLIGENCE SCALE

Picture arrangement

These pictures tell a story, but they are in the wrong order. Put them in the right order so that they tell a story.

Picture completion

What part is missing from this picture?

Block design

Put the blocks together to make this picture.

Object assembly

Put the pieces together as quickly as you can.

© 2012 Cengage Learning®

FIG.7.6 **APPROXIMATE DISTRIBUTION OF IQ SCORES**

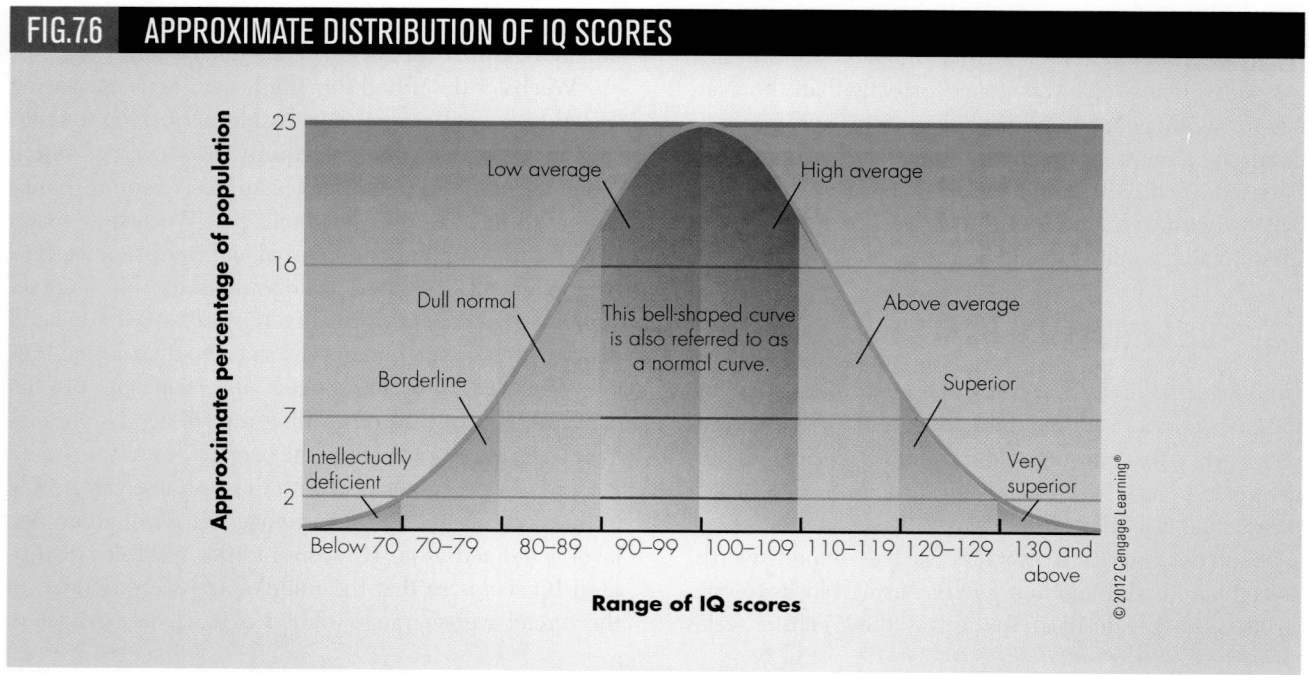

Figure 7.6, IQ scores cluster around the average. Only 4% of the population have IQ scores of above 130 or below 70.

7-5c GROUP TESTS

The SBIS and Wechsler scales are administered to one person at a time. This one-to-one ratio is optimal because it allows the examiner to observe the test taker closely. Examiners are alerted to factors that impair performance, such as language difficulties, illness, or a noisy or poorly lit room. But large institutions with few trained examiners, such as the public schools and armed forces, require tests that can be administered simultaneously to large groups.

Group tests for children were first developed during World War I. At first these tests were hailed as remarkable instruments because they helped school administrators place children. As the years passed, however, group tests came under attack because many administrators relied on them exclusively and did not seek other sources of information about children's abilities.

At their best, intelligence tests provide only one source of information about individual children. Numbers alone, and especially IQ scores, cannot adequately define children's special abilities and talents.

7-5d THE RELIABILITY AND VALIDITY OF INTELLIGENCE TESTS

Over the years, the SBIS and the Wechsler scales have been shown to be reliable and valid. In terms of reliability, the scores are rather consistent from testing to testing.

This kind of reliability is called *test–retest reliability*. The tests also show validity in that the scores correlate moderately to highly with the variables they are supposed to predict, such as school performance, even though motivation and adjustment to the school setting are also involved (Duckworth et al., 2011; Roid & Tippin, 2009).

7-5e DIFFERENCES IN INTELLECTUAL FUNCTIONING

The average IQ score in the United States is very close to 100. Yet for some socioeconomic and ethnic groups in the United States, the average is higher, and for others, it is lower. Questions have also been raised about whether males or females are more intelligent overall, and whether there are gender differences in the kinds of intellectual or cognitive skills valued in society. Tests of intellectual functioning have thus been seen as divisive and as maintaining a class system or social order that is based on prejudices and "tradition" as much as on science. In this section we discuss (a) socioeconomic and ethnic differences and (b) gender differences in cognitive skills.

SOCIOECONOMIC AND ETHNIC DIFFERENCES
There is a body of research suggestive of differences in intelligence—or, more precisely, intelligence test scores—between socioeconomic and ethnic groups. Lower-class U.S. children obtain IQ scores some 10 to 15 points lower than those obtained by middle- and upper-class children. African American children tend to obtain IQ scores some 15 points lower than those

obtained by their European American age-mates (Helms, 2006; Neisser et al., 1996). Latin American and Native American children also tend to score below the norms for European Americans (Neisser et al., 1996; Sternberg, 2007).

Many studies of IQ confuse the factors of social class and ethnicity because disproportionate numbers of African Americans, Latin Americans, and Native Americans are found among the lower socioeconomic classes (Helms, 2006; Nisbett, 2009). When we limit our observations to particular ethnic groups, we still find an effect for social class. That is, middle-class European Americans outscore poorer European Americans. Middle-class African Americans, Latin Americans, and Native Americans outscore poorer members of their own ethnic groups. *Washington Post* columnist Eugene Robinson (2011) notes that "a gap has opened up between an educated middle-class Black America and a poor, undereducated Black America." In other words, African Americans make up a very diverse group.

There may also be intellectual differences between Asians and Caucasians. Asian Americans, for example, frequently outscore European Americans on the math portion of the Scholastic Aptitude Test. Students in China (Taiwan) and Japan also outscore European Americans on achievement tests in math and science (Nisbett, 2009). In the United States, moreover, people of Asian Indian, Korean, Japanese, Filipino, and Chinese descent are more likely than European Americans, African Americans, and Latin Americans to graduate from high school and complete college (Kurtz-Costes et al., 2014; Sternberg, 2007). They are also overrepresented in competitive colleges and universities (Knapp et al., 2011; Liu, 2009). For example, Asian Americans make up 12% of the population of California, but they comprise 41% of the student population of the state's highest-ranked public university: the University of California at Berkeley.

Most psychologists believe that such ethnic differences reflect cultural attitudes toward education rather than inborn racial differences (Nisbett, 2009). That is, the Asian children may be more motivated to work in school. Research shows that Chinese and Japanese students and their mothers tend to attribute academic successes to hard work (Bae et al., 2008). European Americans are more likely to attribute their children's academic successes to "natural" ability (Bae et al., 2008).

Intelligence tests may be said to have a *cultural bias* because children reared in African American or Latin American neighborhoods are at a cultural disadvantage in intelligence testing (Dotson et al., 2009). Many psychologists, including Raymond B. Cattell (1949) and Florence Goodenough (1926) have tried to construct culture-free intelligence tests. Cattell's Culture-Fair Intelligence Test evaluates reasoning through the child's ability to understand and use the rules that govern a progression of geometric designs (see Figure 7.7). Goodenough's Draw-A-Person test is based on the premise that children from all cultural backgrounds have had the opportunity to observe people and note the relationships between the parts and the whole. Her instructions simply require children to draw a picture of a man or woman. Ironically, European American children outperform African American children on "culture-free" tests (Rushton et al., 2003), perhaps because they are more likely than disadvantaged children to have played with blocks (practice relevant to the Cattell test) and to have sketched animals, people, and things (practice relevant to the Goodenough test, which is based on test-takers' drawings). Nor do culture-free tests predict academic success as well as other intelligence tests.

GENDER DIFFERENCES It was once widely believed that males were more intelligent than females because of their greater knowledge of world affairs and their skills in science and industry. But these differences did not reflect differences in cognitive ability. Rather, they reflected exclusion of females from world affairs, science, and industry. Moreover, intelligence tests do not

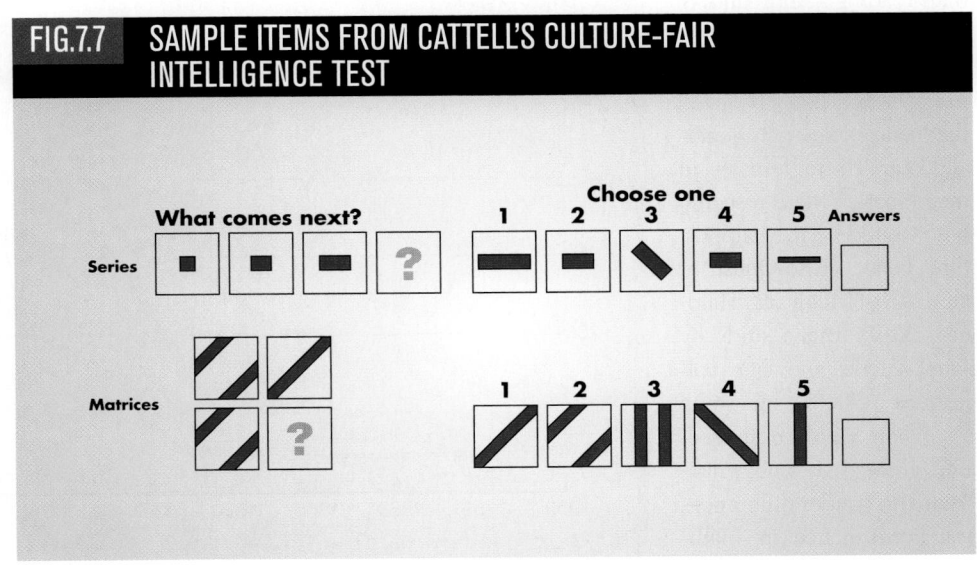

FIG.7.7   SAMPLE ITEMS FROM CATTELL'S CULTURE-FAIR INTELLIGENCE TEST

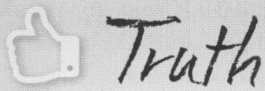
show overall gender differences in cognitive abilities (Miller & Halpern, 2014).

Reviews of the research suggest that girls are somewhat superior to boys in verbal abilities, such as vocabulary, ability to generate sentences and words that are similar in meaning to other words, spelling, knowledge of foreign languages, and pronunciation (Andreano & Cahill, 2009; Lohman & Lakin, 2009). Girls seem to acquire language somewhat faster than boys do. Also, in the United States, more boys than girls have reading problems, ranging from reading below grade level to severe disabilities (Brun et al., 2009).

Males seem to do somewhat better at manipulating visual images in working memory. Males as a group excel in visual–spatial abilities of the sort used in math, science, and map-reading (Andreano & Cahill, 2009; Yazzie, 2010).

For half a century or more, it has been believed that male adolescents generally outperform females in mathematics, and research has tended to support that belief (Else-Quest et al., 2013; Miller & Halpern, 2014). But a study by Janet Hyde and her colleagues (2008) of some 7 million children in second through eleventh grade found no gender differences for performance in math-

ematics on standardized tests. Although there are no overall gender differences in average scores on math tests in the United States, males are apparently more likely than females to perform at the extremes, as in the percentage of individuals who obtain scores under 300 or over 700 on the quantitative scale of the SAT (Else-Quest et al., 2010). Nevertheless, most Americans have different expectations for boys and girls, and these expectations may still dissuade some math-proficient girls from entering so-called STEM (science, technology, engineering, and mathematics) fields (Else-Quest et al., 2013). But note that the reported gender differences are *group* differences. There is greater variation in these skills between individuals *within* the groups than between males and females (Miller & Halpern, 2014). That is, there may be a greater difference in, say, verbal skills between two women than between the typical woman and the typical man. Millions of females outdistance the "average" male in math and spatial abilities. Men have produced their verbally adept Shakespeares. Moreover, in most cases, gender differences in cognitive skills are small (Else-Quest & Grabe, 2012). Differences in verbal, math, and visual–spatial abilities also appear to be narrowing as more females pursue course work in fields that had been typically populated by males.

While scholars sit around and debate gender differences in intellectual functioning, women are voting on the issue by flooding fields once populated almost exclusively by men (Cox & Alm, 2005). Figure 7.8 shows that women are tossing these stereotypes out the window

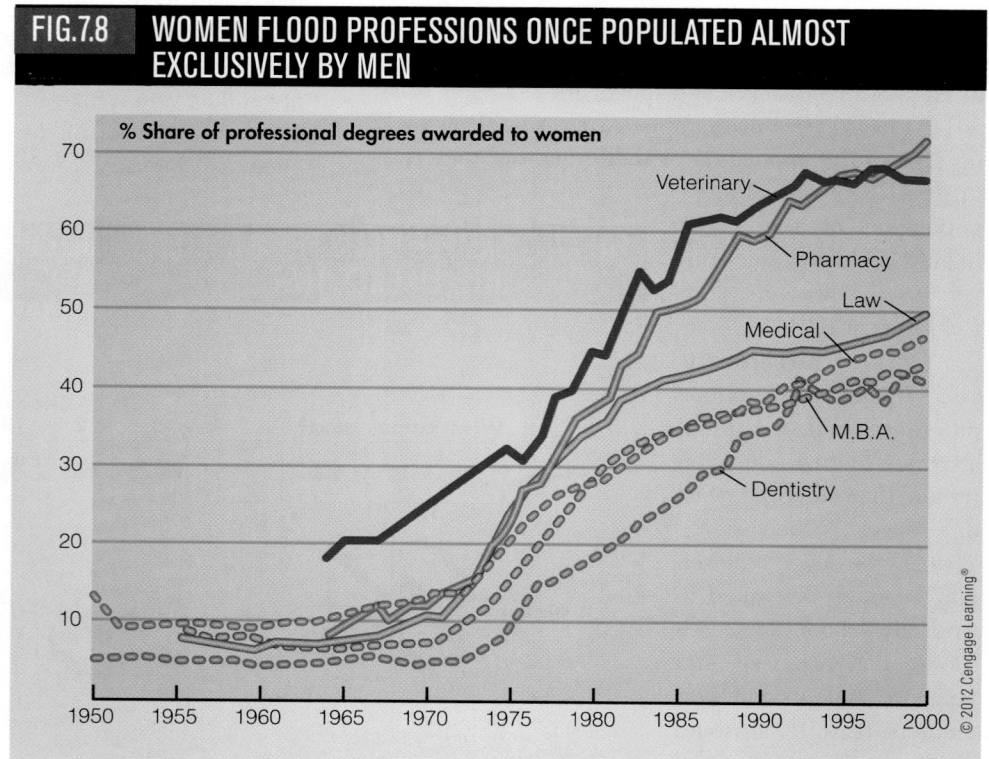

FIG. 7.8 WOMEN FLOOD PROFESSIONS ONCE POPULATED ALMOST EXCLUSIVELY BY MEN

% Share of professional degrees awarded to women

© 2012 Cengage Learning®

by entering the sciences and professional fields ranging from business to law to medicine in increasing numbers.

7-6 NATURE AND NURTURE IN INTELLIGENCE

If different ethnic groups tend to score differently on intelligence tests, psychologists—like educators and other people involved in public life—want to know why. We will see that this is one debate that can make use of key empirical findings. Psychologists can point with pride to a rich mine of research on the roles of nature (genetic influences) and nurture (environmental influences) in the development of intelligence.

7-6a GENETIC INFLUENCES ON INTELLIGENCE

Research on genetic influences has employed kinship studies, twin studies, and adoptee studies. Let's consider each of these to see whether heredity affects intellectual functioning.

We can examine the IQ scores of closely and distantly related people who have been reared together or apart. If heredity is involved in human intelligence, closely related people ought to have more similar IQs than distantly related or unrelated people, even when they are reared separately (Petrill et al., 2010).

Figure 7.9 is a composite of the results of more than a hundred studies of IQ and heredity in human beings (McGue et al., 1993; Plomin & Spinath, 2004;

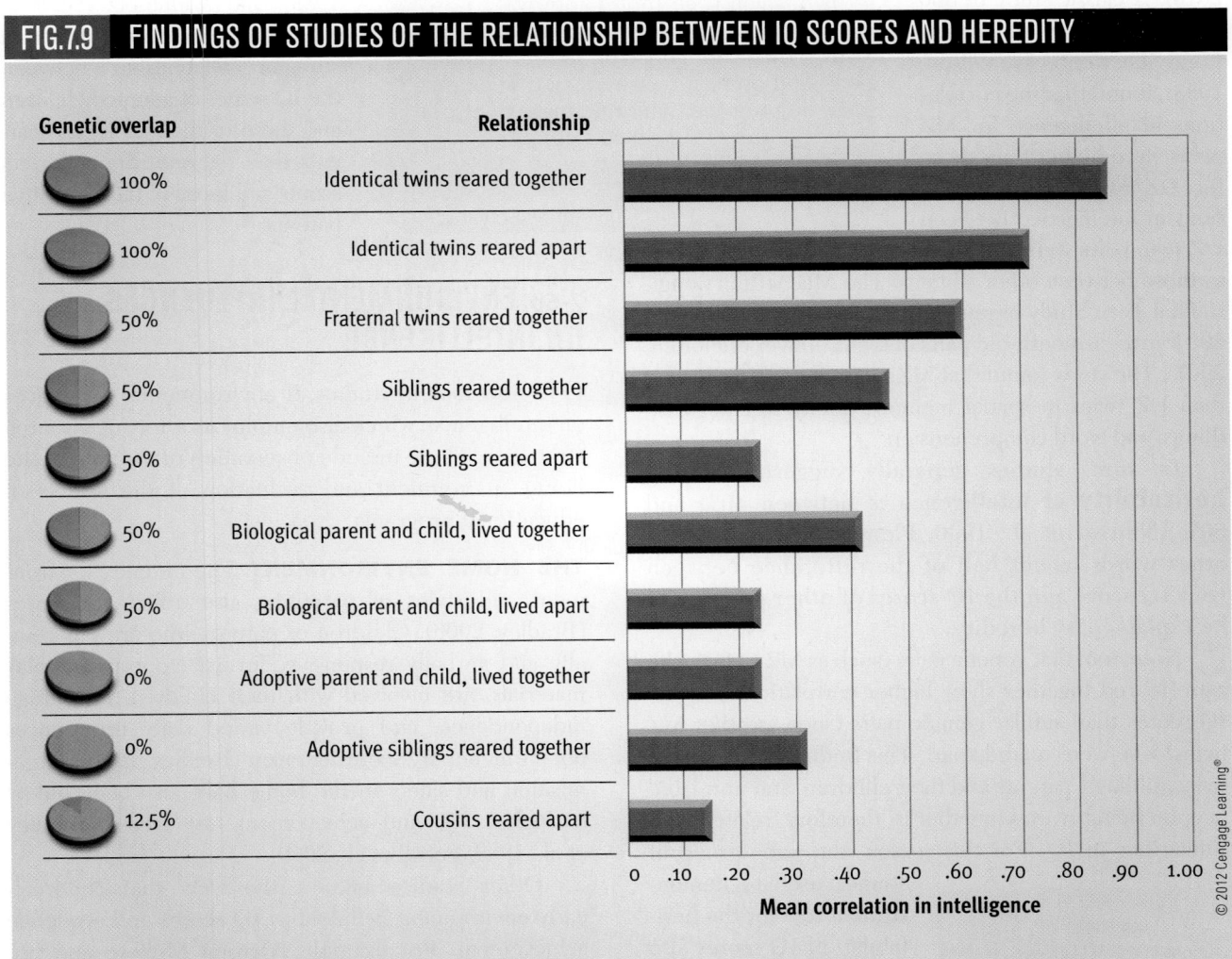

FIG.7.9 FINDINGS OF STUDIES OF THE RELATIONSHIP BETWEEN IQ SCORES AND HEREDITY

Genetic overlap	Relationship
100%	Identical twins reared together
100%	Identical twins reared apart
50%	Fraternal twins reared together
50%	Siblings reared together
50%	Siblings reared apart
50%	Biological parent and child, lived together
50%	Biological parent and child, lived apart
0%	Adoptive parent and child, lived together
0%	Adoptive siblings reared together
12.5%	Cousins reared apart

Mean correlation in intelligence

© 2012 Cengage Learning®

The data represent a composite of several studies. By and large, correlations are higher between people who are more closely related, yet people who are reared together have more similar IQ scores than people who are reared apart. Such findings suggest that both genetic and environmental factors contribute to IQ scores.

Plomin et al., 2008). The IQ scores of identical (monozygotic, or MZ) twins are more alike than scores for any other pairs, even when the twins have been reared apart. There are moderate correlations between the IQ scores of fraternal (dizygotic, or DZ) twins, between those of siblings, and between those of parents and their children. Correlations between the scores of children and their foster parents and between those of cousins are weak.

The results of large-scale twin studies are consistent with the data in Figure 7.9 (e.g., Wadsworth et al., 2014). A classic study of 500 pairs of MZ and DZ twins in Louisville, Kentucky (Wilson, 1983), found that the correlations in intelligence for MZ twins were higher than those for DZ twins. The correlations in intelligence between DZ twin pairs were the same as those between other siblings. The MacArthur Longitudinal Twin Study examined the intellectual abilities of 200 fourteen-month-old pairs of twins (Oliver & Plomin, 2007). The study found that MZ twins were more similar than DZ twins in spatial memory, ability to categorize things, and word comprehension.

In sum, studies generally suggest that the **heritability** of intelligence is between 40% and 60% (Neisser et al., 1996; Plomin et al., 2013). In other words, about half of the difference between your IQ score and the IQ scores of other people can be explained by heredity.

Note, too, that genetic pairs (such as MZ twins) who were reared together show higher correlations in their IQ scores than similar genetic pairs (such as other MZ twins) who were reared apart. This finding holds for DZ twins, siblings, parents and their children, and unrelated people. Being reared together is, therefore, related with similarities in IQ. For this reason, the same group of studies used to demonstrate a role for the heritability of IQ scores also suggests that the environment plays a role in determining IQ scores.

ALFRED BINET

"Some recent philosophers seem to have given their moral approval to these deplorable verdicts that affirm that the intelligence of an individual is a fixed quantity, a quantity that cannot be augmented. We must protest and react against this brutal pessimism; we will try to demonstrate that it is founded on nothing."

AF Fotografie/Alamy

Another strategy for exploring genetic influences on intelligence is to compare the correlations between the IQ scores of adopted children and those of their biological and adoptive parents. When children are separated from their biological parents at an early age, one can argue that strong relationships between their IQs and those of their natural parents reflect genetic influences. Strong relationships between the children's IQs and those of their adoptive parents might reflect environmental influences.

Several studies with one- and two-year-old children in Colorado (Baker et al., 1983), Texas (Horn, 1983), and Minnesota (Scarr & Weinberg, 1983) have found a stronger relationship between the IQ scores of adopted children and those of their biological parents than between the children's scores and those of their adoptive parents.

7-6b ENVIRONMENTAL INFLUENCES ON INTELLIGENCE

Let's now look at studies of environmental influences on intelligence, which also employ a variety of research strategies. These include observation of the role of the home environment and evaluation of the effects of educational programs.

THE HOME ENVIRONMENT The home environment and styles of parenting also affect IQ scores (Bradley, 2006). Children of parents who are emotionally and verbally responsive, furnish appropriate play materials, are involved with their children, encourage independence, and provide varied daily experiences obtain higher IQ scores later on (Bradley, 2006). Organization and safety in the home have also been linked to higher IQs and achievement test scores (Bradley et al., 1989; Petrill et al., 2010).

Other studies support the view that children's early environment is linked to IQ scores and academic achievement. For example, Victoria Molfese and her colleagues (1997) found that the home environment was the single most important predictor of scores on IQ tests among children aged three to eight.

heritability the degree to which the variations in a trait from one person to another can be attributed to, or explained by, genetic factors

EDUCATION Although intelligence is viewed as permitting people to profit from education, education also apparently contributes to intelligence. Government-funded efforts to provide preschoolers with enriched early environments have led to intellectual gains. Head Start programs, for example, enhance the IQ scores, achievement test scores, and academic skills of disadvantaged children (Bierman et al., 2008) by exposing them to materials and activities that middle-class children take for granted. These include letters and words, numbers, books, exercises in drawing, pegs and pegboards, puzzles, toy animals, and dolls. On the other hand, many children's IQ scores and achievements tend to decrease again in the years following the Head Start experience if they return to the less intellectually stimulating environment that preceded Head Start (Nisbett, 2009).

Later schooling also contributes to IQ. When children of about the same age start school a year apart because of admissions standards related to their date of birth, children who have been in school longer obtain higher IQ scores (Neisser et al., 1996). Moreover, test scores tend to decrease during the summer vacation (Neisser et al., 1996).

The findings on intelligence, the home environment, and educational experiences show that much indeed can be done to enhance intellectual functioning in children.

THE FLYNN EFFECT Philosopher and researcher John Flynn (2003) found that IQ scores in the Western world increased substantially between 1947 and 2002, some 18 points in the United States. Psychologist Richard Nisbett (2009) argues that our genetic codes could not possibly have changed enough in half a century to account for this enormous difference and concludes that social and cultural factors such as the effects of improved educational systems and the penetration of the mass media must be among the reasons for the change.

If such environmental factors are capable of producing changes of this magnitude over time for the entire American population, they can also produce significant differences between subpopulations, such as between African Americans and European Americans. For example, the difference in IQ scores between the two racial groups has decreased from 15 points to 9.5 points over the past 30 years (Nisbett, 2007), which is again too large a difference to reflect genetic factors. Instead, it would suggest that the educational gap between the races may be narrowing. All in all, intellectual functioning appears to reflect the interaction of a complex web of genetic, physical, personal, and sociocultural factors, as suggested in Figure 7.10.

Perhaps we need not be so concerned with whether we can sort out exactly how much of a person's intelligence is due to heredity and how much is due to environmental influences. Psychology has traditionally supported the dignity of the individual. It might be more appropriate for us to try to identify children of all ethnic groups who are at risk of failure and to do what we can to enrich their environments.

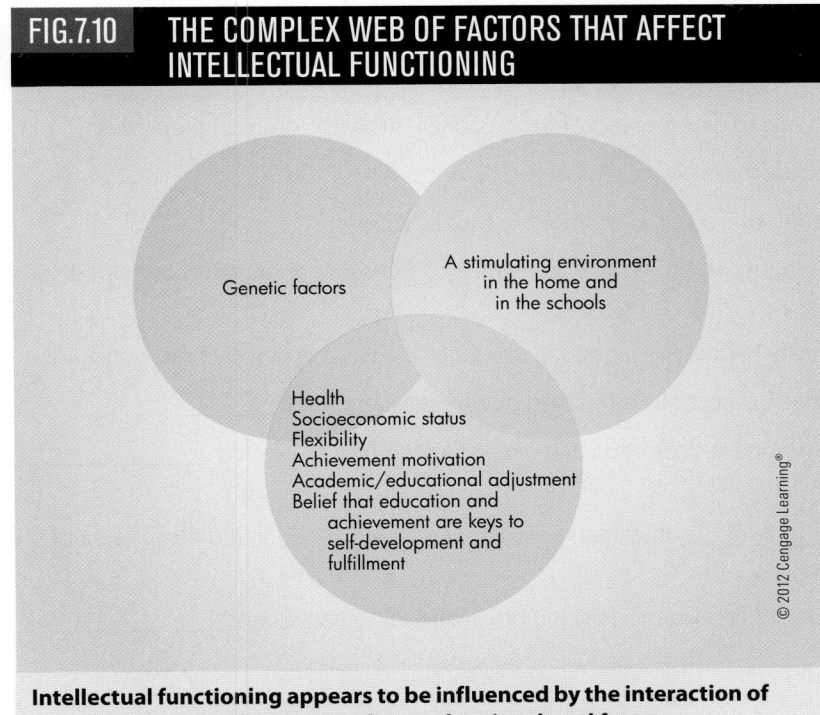

FIG. 7.10 THE COMPLEX WEB OF FACTORS THAT AFFECT INTELLECTUAL FUNCTIONING

Genetic factors

A stimulating environment in the home and in the schools

Health
Socioeconomic status
Flexibility
Achievement motivation
Academic/educational adjustment
Belief that education and achievement are keys to self-development and fulfillment

© 2012 Cengage Learning®

Intellectual functioning appears to be influenced by the interaction of genetic factors, health, personality, and sociocultural factors.

READY TO STUDY? IN THE BOOK, YOU CAN:

☐ Check your understanding of what you've read with the quizzes below.

☐ Rip out the chapter review card at the back of the book to have a summary of the chapter and the key terms handy.

ONLINE AT CENGAGEBRAIN.COM YOU CAN:

☐ Practice retrieving what you've learned using the interactive figures on the theories of intelligence.

☐ Learn about language development in early childhood, including learning strategies, vocabulary development, grammar, and common problems in a short video.

☐ Prepare for tests with quizzes.

☐ Review the key terms with Flash Cards.

☐ Play games to master concepts.

FILL-INS

Answers can be found in the back of the book, starting on page 392.

1. _____ are mental categories used to group objects, relations, or events with common properties.

2. A(n) _____ is a specific procedure for solving a type of problem.

3. _____ devices are rules of thumb that serve as shortcuts to rapid solutions.

4. A _____ set is the tendency to respond to a new problem with the same approach that helped solve similar problems.

5. According to the _____ -relativity hypothesis, language structures the way we perceive the world.

6. Children's use of sentences such as "I standed up" and "Mommy sitted down" are examples of _____.

7. Spearman suggested that intelligent behaviors have a common underlying factor, which he labeled _____, and specific factors that account for specific abilities.

8. Gardner proposes the existence of _____ intelligences, each of which is based in a different area of the brain.

9. Sternberg constructed a "triarchic" model of intelligence, including analytical, creative, and _____ intelligence.

10. The Stanford–Binet Intelligence Scale yields a score called a(n) _____ (IQ).

MULTIPLE CHOICE

1. Eight-year-old Stephanie understands that her dog Boodles is a dog and that all dogs are animals. Stephanie's concept of animal is best characterized as
   a. intuitive.
   b. ideational.
   c. overextended.
   d. hierarchical.

2. Algorithms are usually time consuming, whereas _____ provide a more rapid solution when they work.
   a. anagrams
   b. formulas
   c. systematic random searches
   d. heuristics

3. What conclusion may be drawn about problem solving from Maier's studies with Bismarck?
   a. Only humans can solve problems by means of insight.
   b. A rat has demonstrated insight under laboratory conditions.
   c. A rat has demonstrated trial-and-error learning under laboratory conditions.
   d. Rats are capable of insight under a variety of conditions.

4. One plausible explanation of the incubation effect is
   a. the tendency to allow the unconscious to free up insights.
   b. distancing problem solvers from persistent but unproductive mental sets.
   c. conscious searching for heuristic devices.
   d. spontaneous means–end analysis.

5. True language is distinguished from the communications systems of lower animals by all of the following except
   a. infinite creativity.
   b. displacement.
   c. making sounds.
   d. semanticity.

6. When reading the sentences, "The chicken is ready for dinner," and "The lion is ready for dinner," if you understand which is ready to eat and which is ready to be eaten, you are using the phrase "is ready to eat" with different _____ in each case.
   a. morphemes
   b. phonemes
   c. factors
   d. semanticity

7. Jamie's mother was concerned that her 4-year-old daughter overregularized plurals and tenses. She took Jamie to Dr. Acton, a noted learning theorist, who advised her to
   a. wait for Jamie's speech to correct itself.
   b. take her to a speech therapist.
   c. correct her grammar through imitation and repetition.
   d. begin instruction in another language.

8. According to Robert Sternberg, the three types of intelligence are
   a. logical, musical, emotional.
   b. experimental, logical, verbal.
   c. verbal, performance, problem solving.
   d. analytical, creative, practical.

9. The ability to do things that are unique and beneficial and to generate novel combinations out of existing elements describes
   a. insight.
   b. creativity.
   c. intelligence.
   d. expertise.

10. According to the text, Janet Hyde and her colleagues studied the performance of some 7 million children in second through eleventh grades in mathematics and found that
    a. boys obtained higher scores than girls.
    b. girls obtained higher scores than boys.
    c. there were no overall gender differences in scores.
    d. European Americans obtained higher scores than any other racial or ethnic group.

8 | Motivation and Emotion

John Lund/Blend Images/Alamy

LEARNING OUTCOMES

After studying this chapter, you will be able to…

8-1 Define motivation including needs, drives, and incentives.

8-2 Identify the theories of motivation.

8-3 Describe the biological and psychological contributions to hunger.

8-4 Explain the role of sex hormones and the sexual response cycle in human sexuality.

8-5 Describe achievement motivation.

8-6 Identify the theoretical explanations of emotions.

After you finish this chapter, go to **PAGE 226** for **STUDY TOOLS**

The Seekers had received word that the world was coming to an end on December 21st. A great flood would engulf their city and the rest of the Earth. Now they were gathered around their leader, Marian Keech, in her home, as she recorded messages that she said were sent to her by the Guardians from outer space. The messages were received through "automatic writing"; that is, the Guardians communicated through Ms. Keech, who wrote down their words without awareness. Another message brought good news, however. Because of their faith, the Seekers would be saved by flying saucers at the stroke of midnight on the 21st.

Why do we **eat**? Why do some of us **strive** to get ahead?

In their classic observational study, Leon Festinger and his colleagues (1956) described how they managed to be present in Ms. Keech's household at the fateful hour by pretending to belong to the group. Their purpose was to observe the behavior of the Seekers during and following the prophecy's failure. The cognitive theory of motivation that Festinger was working on—*cognitive-dissonance theory*—suggested that there would be a discrepancy or conflict between two key cognitions: (1) Ms. Keech is a prophet, and (2) Ms. Keech is wrong.

How might the conflict be resolved? One way would be for the Seekers to lose faith in Ms. Keech. But the researchers expected that according to their theory, the Seekers could also be motivated to resolve the conflict by going out to spread the word and find additional converts. Otherwise, the group would be painfully embarrassed.

Let's return to the momentous night. Many members of the group had quit their jobs and gone on spending sprees before the anticipated end. Now, as midnight approached, they fidgeted, awaiting the flying saucers. Midnight came, but there were no saucers. Anxious glances were exchanged. There was silence, and then some coughs. Minutes passed, torturously slowly. Watches were checked, more glances exchanged.

At 4:00 a.m., a bitter and frantic Ms. Keech complained that she sensed that members of the group were doubting her. At 4:45 a.m., however, she seemed suddenly relieved. Another message was arriving, and Ms. Keech was spelling it out through automatic writing! The Seekers, it turned out, had managed to save the world through their faith. The universal powers had decided to let the world travel on along its sinful way for a while longer. Why? Because of the faith of the Seekers, there was hope!

With their faith restored, the followers called wire services and newspapers to spread the word. The three psychologists from the University of Minnesota went home, weary but enlightened. They wrote a book entitled *When Prophecy Fails*, which serves as one of the key documents of their theory.

8-1 THE PSYCHOLOGY OF MOTIVATION

The psychology of **motivation** is concerned with the *why* of behavior. Why do we eat? Why do some of us strive to get ahead? Why do some of us ride motorcycles at breakneck speeds? Why are some people aggressive? Why were the Seekers in a state of discomfort when the prophecy failed?

To answer these questions, psychologists use concepts such as *motives, needs, drives,* and *incentives.* **Motives** are hypothetical states that activate behavior,

> **motivation** the state in which an organism experiences an inducement or incentive to do something
>
> **motive** a hypothetical state within an organism that propels the organism toward a goal

 Truth or Fiction?

WHAT DO YOU THINK? Folklore, common sense, or nonsense? Select T for "truth" or F for "fiction," and then check the accuracy of your answers as you read through the chapter.

T	F	Getting away from it all by going on a vacation from all sensory input for a few hours is relaxing.
T	F	People feel hunger due to contractions ("pangs") in the stomach.
T	F	Fashion magazines can contribute to eating disorders among women.
T	F	Money can't buy you happiness.
T	F	You may be able to fool a lie detector by biting your tongue or wiggling your toes.

propelling us toward goals. We call them "hypothetical states" because motives are not seen and measured directly. They are inferred from behavior. Motives may take the form of *needs*, *drives*, and *incentives*, which are also inferred from behavior.

Psychologists speak of physiological and psychological **needs**. We must meet physiological needs to survive. Examples include the needs for oxygen, food, drink, pain avoidance, proper temperature, and elimination of waste products. Some physiological needs, such as hunger and thirst, are states of physical deprivation. When we have not eaten or drunk for a while, we develop needs for food and water. The body also needs oxygen, vitamins, and so on.

Psychological needs include needs for achievement, power, self-esteem, social approval, and belonging. Psychological needs are not necessarily based on states of deprivation. A person with a need for achievement may already have a history of successful achievements. Because people's biological makeups are similar, we share similar physiological needs. But because we are influenced by our cultural settings, our needs may be expressed in different ways. We all need food, but some prefer a vegetarian diet whereas others prefer meat. Because learning enters into psychological needs, they can differ markedly from one person to another.

Needs give rise to **drives**. Depletion of food gives rise to the hunger drive, and depletion of liquids gives rise to the thirst drive. *Physiological drives* are the counterparts of physiological needs. When we have gone without food and water, our body may need these substances. However, our experience of the drives of hunger and thirst is psychological. Drives arouse us to action and tend to be stronger when we have been deprived longer. We are hungrier when we haven't eaten for 10 hours than 1 hour.

Psychological needs for approval, achievement, and belonging also give rise to drives. We can have a drive to get ahead in the business world just as we have a drive to eat. Psychologists are working to learn more about the origins of these drives. We do know that we can also be driven to obtain *incentives*. An **incentive** is an object, a person, or a situation that can satisfy a need or is desirable for its own sake. Money, food, a

sexually attractive person, social approval, and attention can all act as incentives.

THEORIES OF MOTIVATION

Although psychologists agree that it is important to understand why humans and lower animals do things, they do not agree about the precise nature of motivation. Let's consider various theoretical perspectives on motivation.

8-2a THE EVOLUTIONARY PERSPECTIVE

The evolutionary perspective notes that many animals are neurally "prewired"—that is, born with preprogrammed tendencies—to respond to certain situations in certain ways (Macedo & Machado, 2014; Shackelford & Hansen, 2014). Spiders spin webs by **instinct**. Birds build nests by instinct. Bees "dance" instinctively to communicate the location of food to other bees.

These instinctive behaviors are found in particular species. That is, they are *species-specific* and are inborn. They are genetically transmitted from generation to generation.

Psychologists have asked whether humans have instincts, and if so, what kind and how many. More than a century ago, psychologists William James (1890) and William McDougall (1908) asserted that humans have instincts that foster survival and social behavior. James numbered love, sympathy, and modesty as social instincts. McDougall compiled 12 "basic" instincts, including hunger, sex, and self-assertion. Other psychologists have made longer lists, and still others deny that people have instincts. The question of whether people have instincts—and what they might be—remains unresolved.

George Diebold/Photodisc/Getty Images

A Fixed Action Pattern In the presence of another male, Siamese fighting fish (Betta splendens) assume stereotypical threatening postures in which they extend their fins and gills and circle one another. If neither male retreats, there will be conflict.

need a state of deprivation

drive a condition of arousal in an organism that is associated with a need

incentive an object, person, or situation perceived as capable of satisfying a need or as desirable for its own sake

instinct involving an inherited disposition to activate specific behavior patterns that enable an organism to reach specific goals

What Are These Infant Monkeys Doing, and Why Are They Doing It? Do organisms have innate drives to obtain sensory stimulation, manipulate objects (like these young rhesus monkeys), and explore the environment? The monkeys appear to monkey around with gadgets just for the fun of it. No external incentives are needed. Children similarly enjoy manipulating gadgets that honk, squeak, rattle, and buzz, even though the resultant honks and squeaks to do not satisfy physiological drives such as hunger or thirst.

© Harlow Primate Lab/University of Wisconsin

8-2b DRIVE-REDUCTIONISM AND HOMEOSTASIS

Sigmund Freud believed that tension motivates us to behave in ways that restore us to a resting state. His views are similar to those of the **drive-reduction theory** of learning, as set forth by psychologist Clark Hull in the 1930s (Hergenhahn & Henley, 2013).

According to Hull, *primary drives* such as hunger, thirst, and pain trigger arousal (tension) and activate behavior. We learn to engage in behaviors that reduce the tension. We also acquire drives—called *acquired drives*—through experience. We may acquire a drive for money because money enables us to obtain food, drink, and homes, which protect us from crime and extremes of temperature. We might acquire drives for social approval and affiliation because other people, and their goodwill, help us reduce primary drives, especially when we are infants. In all cases, reduction of tension is the goal. Yet some people appear to acquire what could be considered excessive drives for money or affiliation. They gather money long after their material needs have been met, and some people find it difficult to be alone, even briefly.

Primary drives like hunger are triggered when we are in a state of deprivation. Sensations of hunger motivate us to act in ways that will restore the bodily balance. This tendency to maintain a steady state is called **homeostasis**. Homeostasis works like a thermostat. When the temperature in a room drops below the *set point*, the heating system turns on. The heat stays on until the set point is reached. Similarly, most animals eat until they are no longer hungry. But many people eat "recreationally"—as when they see an appealing dessert—suggesting there is more to eating than drive reduction.

8-2c THE SEARCH FOR STIMULATION

Physical needs give rise to drives like hunger and thirst. In such cases, we are motivated to *reduce* the tension or stimulation that impinges on us. However, in the case of *stimulus motives,* organisms seek to *increase* stimulation.

A classic study conducted at McGill University in Montreal during the 1950s suggests the importance of sensory stimulation and activity. Some "lucky" students were paid $20 a day (which, with inflation, would now be more like $200) for doing nothing—literally. Would you like to "work" by doing nothing for $200 a day? Don't answer too quickly. According to the results of this study you might not like it at all.

In this experiment, student volunteers were placed in quiet cubicles and blindfolded (Bexton et al., 1954). Their arms were bandaged so that they felt little if anything with their hands. They could hear nothing but the dull, continuous hum of air conditioning. Many slept for a while, but after a few hours of sensory-deprived wakefulness, most felt bored and irritable. As time went on, many grew more uncomfortable. Many students quit the experiment during the first day despite the financial incentive. Many of those who remained for a few days found it hard to concentrate on simple problems for days afterward. For many, the experiment did not provide a relaxing vacation. Instead, it produced boredom, discomfort, and disorientation.

Humans and other animals appear motivated to seek novel stimulation. Even when they have been deprived of food, rats may explore unfamiliar arms of mazes rather than head straight

> **drive-reduction theory** the view that organisms learn to engage in behaviors that have the effect of reducing drives
>
> **homeostasis** the tendency of the body to maintain a steady state

for the food source. Animals that have just copulated and thereby reduced their primary sex drives often show renewed interest in sex when presented with a novel sex partner. People (and nonhumans) take in more calories at buffets and smorgasbords than when fewer kinds of food are available (Wansink & Shimizu, 2013; Yip et al., 2013). Children spend hour after hour playing video games for the pleasure of zapping virtual people or monsters (Ferguson & Olson, 2013).

Stimulus motives provide an evolutionary advantage. Animals that are active and motivated to explore and manipulate their environment are more likely to survive. If you know where the nearest tall tree is, you're more likely to escape a leopard and transmit your genes to future generations.

But note that survival is more or less a question of defending oneself or one's group against dangers of one kind or another. In the following section, we see that many psychologists believe people are also motivated to develop their unique potentials, even in the absence of external threat.

8-2d HUMANISTIC THEORY

Humanistic psychologists such as Abraham Maslow (1908–1970) suggest that human behavior is not just mechanical and aimed toward survival and the reduction of tension. Maslow believed that people are also motivated by a conscious desire for personal growth. Humanists note that people tolerate pain, hunger, and many other kinds of

self-actualization according to Maslow and other humanistic psychologists, self-initiated striving to become what one is capable of being

hierarchy of needs Maslow's ordering of needs from most basic (physiological needs such as hunger and thirst) to most elaborate and sophisticated (self-actualization)

tension to obtain personal fulfillment.

Maslow believed that we are separated from other animals by our capacity for **self-actualization**, or self-initiated striving to become what we believe we are capable of being. Maslow considered self-actualization to be as important a need in humans as hunger. The need for self-actualization pushes people to strive to become concert pianists, chief executive officers, or best-selling authors—even when they have plenty of money to live on.

Maslow (1970) organized human needs into a hierarchy. Maslow's **hierarchy of needs** ranges from physiological needs such as hunger and thirst, through self-actualization (see Figure 8.1). He believed that we naturally strive to climb this hierarchy.

Critics of Maslow's theory argue that there is too much individual variation for the hierarchy of motives to apply to everyone. Some people whose physiological, safety, and love needs are met show little interest in achievement and recognition. Some artists devote themselves fully to their craft, even if they have to pass up the comforts of a warm home or alienate their families. And many children from broken and unsafe homes strive to achieve in school (Noltemeyer et al., 2012).

> "SUCH IS THE STATE OF LIFE, THAT NONE ARE HAPPY BUT BY THE ANTICIPATION OF CHANGE: THE CHANGE ITSELF IS NOTHING; WHEN WE HAVE MADE IT, THE NEXT WISH IS TO CHANGE AGAIN."
>
> DR. SAMUEL JOHNSON, ENGLISH WRITER, EDITOR, AND LEXICOGRAPHER (1735–1752)

8-2e COGNITIVE PERSPECTIVES ON MOTIVATION

Cognitive theorists note that people represent their worlds mentally. As in Piaget's cognitive developmental theory, they see people as natural scientists who strive to understand the world so that they can predict and control events. Therefore, people try to eliminate inconsistencies—or, as we saw in the case of the Seekers at the beginning of the chapter—discrepancies in information so that their ability to make sense of the world remains whole.

Children also attempt to create consistency between their own gender and what experience teaches them that boys

FIG.8.1   **MASLOW'S HIERARCHY OF NEEDS**

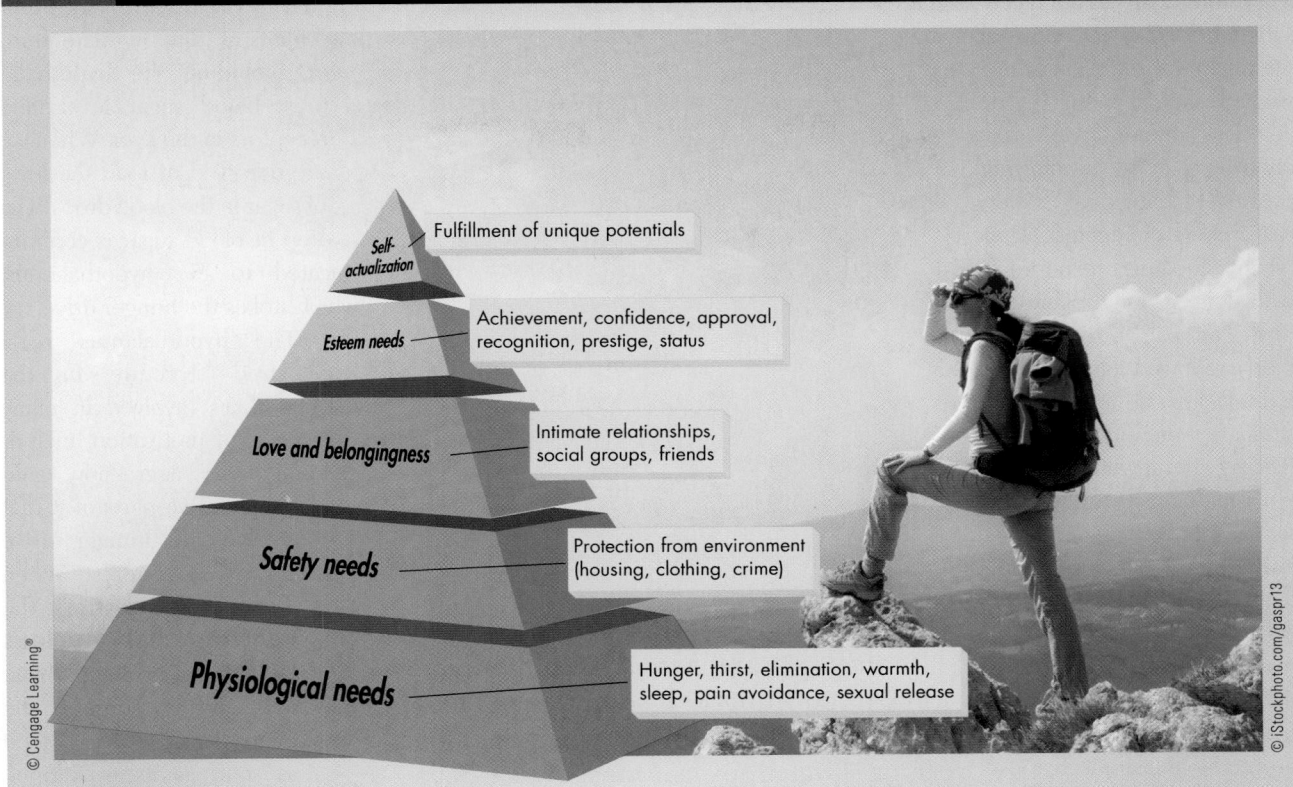

© Cengage Learning®

© iStockphoto.com/gaspr13

What do you do when you're no longer hungry? Maslow believed we progress toward higher psychological needs once basic survival needs have been met. Where do you fit in this picture?

and girls are expected to do in their cultural settings. As soon as they come to understand whether they are male or female, they begin to imitate the behavior of older people of the same gender (Halim et al., 2013; Ruble et al., 2006). According to *cognitive-dissonance theory*, people are generally motivated to hold consistent beliefs and to justify their behavior. That is why we are generally more likely to appreciate what we must work to obtain.

Each theory of motivation may have something to offer. Drive-reduction theory may explain why we drink when thirsty, but stimulus motives might explain why we go clubbing and drink alcohol. Each theory might apply to certain aspects of behavior. As the chapter progresses, we will describe research that lends support to each theory.

8-3 HUNGER

We need food to survive, but for many of us, food means more than survival. Food is a symbol of family togetherness and caring. We associate food with the nurturance of the parent–child relationship and with visits home

on holidays. Friends and relatives offer us food when we enter their homes, and saying no may be viewed as a personal rejection. Bacon and eggs, coffee with cream and sugar, meat and mashed potatoes—all seem to be part of sharing American values and abundance.

8-3a BIOLOGICAL INFLUENCES ON HUNGER

In considering the bodily mechanisms that regulate hunger, let's begin with the mouth, where we get signals of **satiety** that regulate our eating. We also get signals of satiety from the digestive tract, although it takes

"IN GENERAL MY CHILDREN REFUSE TO EAT ANYTHING THAT HASN'T DANCED ON TELEVISION."
ERMA BOMBECK, AMERICAN HUMORIST (1927–1996)

satiety the state of being satisfied; fullness

longer for these signals to reach the brain. Therefore, if we did not receive signals of satiety from chewing and swallowing, we might eat for a long time after we had taken in enough food.

To demonstrate that chewing and swallowing provide feelings of satiety, researchers conducted classic "sham feeding" experiments with dogs. They implanted a tube in the animals' throats so that any food swallowed fell out of the body. Even though no food reached the stomach, the animals stopped feeding after a while (Janowitz & Grossman, 1949). Thus, sensations of chewing and swallowing must provide some feelings of satiety. However, the dogs in the study resumed feeding sooner than animals whose food did reach the stomach. Let's proceed to the stomach, too, as we seek further regulatory factors in hunger.

An empty stomach leads to stomach contractions, which we call *hunger pangs*. Classic research suggested that stomach contractions are crucial to hunger. A man (A. L. Washburn) swallowed a balloon that was inflated in his stomach. His stomach contractions squeezed the balloon, so the contractions could be recorded by observers. Washburn also pressed a key when he felt hungry, and the researchers found a correspondence between his stomach contractions and his feelings of hunger (Cannon & Washburn, 1912).

Medical observations and classic research find that humans and nonhumans whose stomachs have been removed still regulate food intake so as to maintain a normal weight (Tsang, 1938). (Food is absorbed through their intestines.) This finding led to the discovery of other mechanisms that regulate hunger, including the hypothalamus, blood sugar level, and receptors in the liver. When we are deprived of food the level of sugar in the blood drops. The drop in blood sugar is communicated to the hypothalamus, which stokes the hunger drive.

The hypothalamus is a pea-sized structure in the brain that's involved in many aspects of motivation, including sex, aggression, and hunger. Two parts of it that involve the hunger drive are of particular interest. When a researcher destroys the **ventromedial nucleus (VMN)** of a rat's hypothalamus during surgery, the rat will grope toward food as soon as its eyes open (Berthoud & Levin, 2014). Then it eats vast quantities of Purina Rat Chow or whatever is available. Investigators have concluded that the VMN functions like a "stop-eating center" in the rat's brain. If the VMN is electrically stimulated—that is, "switched on"—the rat stops eating until the current is turned off. When the VMN is destroyed, the rat becomes **hyperphagic** (see Figure 8.2). That is, it continues to eat until it has about doubled its normal weight. Then it will level off its eating rate and maintain the higher weight. It is as if the set point

Mascarucci/Terra/Corbis

Do the Sight and Aroma of Hamburgers Make You Hungry? If so, you're not alone. Some of us may only eat when our blood sugar level drops, but most of us can be tempted by tasty, aromatic foods. What Triggers Your Hunger Drive? Are you only interested in eating when your blood sugar level falls, or do the sights and aromas of foods stimulate you to eat?

ventromedial nucleus (VMN) a central area on the underside of the hypothalamus that appears to function as a stop-eating center

hyperphagic characterized by excessive eating

lateral hypothalamus an area at the side of the hypothalamus that appears to function as a start-eating center

aphagic characterized by under-eating

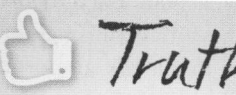

👍 *Truth*

| T | F | People feel hunger due to contractions ("pangs") in the stomach. |

It is true that pangs in the stomach are connected with feelings of hunger, but stomach contractions are not as influential as was once thought.

FIG.8.2 A HYPERPHAGIC RAT

Dr. Neal Miler/Yale University

This rodent winner of the basketball look-alike contest went on a binge after it received a lesion in the ventro-medial nucleus (VMN) of the hypothalamus. It is as if the lesion pushed the "set point" for the body weight up several notches; the rat's weight is now about five times normal. But now it eats only enough to maintain its pleasantly plump figure, so you need not be concerned that it will eventually burst. If the lesion had been made in the lateral hypothalamus, the animal might have slimmed down to an unhealthful weight.

of the stop-eating center has been raised to a higher level, like turning up the thermostat in a house from 65°F to 70°F. Some people develop tumors near the base of the brain that damage the VMN and apparently cause them to overeat and grow obese (Acs et al., 2014).

By contrast, the **lateral hypothalamus** may function like a "start-eating center." If you electrically stimulate the lateral hypothalamus, the rat starts to eat (N. E. Miller, 1995). If you destroy the lateral hypothalamus, the rat may stop eating altogether—that is, become **aphagic**. If you force-feed an aphagic rat for a while, however, it begins to eat on its own and levels off at a relatively low body weight. It is as if you have lowered the rat's set point. It is like turning down the thermostat from, say, 70°F to 40°F.

8-3b PSYCHOLOGICAL INFLUENCES ON HUNGER

Although many areas of the body work in concert to regulate the hunger drive, this is only part of the story. In human beings, the hunger drive is more complex.

Psychological as well as physiological factors play an important role. How many times have you been made hungry by the sight or aroma of food? How many times have you eaten not because you were hungry but because you were at a relative's home or hanging around a cafeteria or coffee shop? Or because you felt anxious or depressed? Or simply because you were bored?

Research has confirmed what most of us already assumed—that sitting around watching television increases the amount of food we eat (Higgs & Woodward, 2009). Watching television can distract us from bodily changes that signal fullness and from cognitive awareness of how much we have already eaten. The same seems to hold true for gorging on popcorn, candy, and soft drinks at the movies. The more time we spend sitting rather than moving, the more weight we tend to gain (Bond et al., 2013; Owen & Hamilton, 2014).

8-3c BEING OVERWEIGHT: A SERIOUS AND PERVASIVE PROBLEM

Consider some facts about being overweight (Bray & Bouchard, 2014):

▶ More than two out of three adult Americans are overweight, according to the national *body mass index (BMI)* guidelines, and one in three are obese.

▶ Problems with unhealthy weight gain have been on the upswing in the United States; for example, 68% of Americans were overweight in 2013 as compared with 60% in 1988–1994.

▶ More than 78% of African American women and 81% of Latina Americans, age 40 and older, are overweight, and about half are obese.

▶ Obesity is a risk in various chronic medical conditions including type 2 diabetes, hypertension (high blood pressure), high cholesterol levels, stroke, heart disease, some cancers, and arthritis (Bray & Bouchard, 2014).

▶ Weight control is elusive for most people, who regain most of the weight they have lost, even when they have dieted "successfully."

Studies using data obtained by the federal government find that extremely obese people,

> "THERE IS NO SINCERER LOVE THAN THE LOVE OF FOOD."
>
> GEORGE BERNARD SHAW, IRISH PLAYWRIGHT (1856–1950)

whose BMIs are greater than or equal to 40, live shorter lives than people who are normal in weight (Finkelstein et al., 2010; see Table 8.1). With all the health problems connected to obesity, why are so many people obese?

FACTORS IN BECOMING OVERWEIGHT Many biological and psychological factors are involved in obesity. Being overweight runs in families. A study of Scandinavian adoptees by Albert Stunkard and his colleagues (1990) found that children bear a closer resemblance in weight to their biological parents than to their adoptive parents. Today, it is widely accepted that heredity plays a role in obesity in humans and other animals, including monkeys and rats (Hansen, 2014; Perusse et al., 2014).

The efforts of overweight people to maintain a slender profile may be sabotaged by an adaptive mechanism that would help preserve life in times of famine—*adaptive thermogenesis*. This mechanism causes the body to produce less energy (burn fewer calories) when someone goes on a diet (Bray & Bouchard, 2014; Schutz & Dullou, 2014). This does not mean that overweight people will not lose weight by dieting; it means that it might take longer than expected.

Fatty tissue in the body also metabolizes (burns) food more slowly than muscle does. For this reason, a person with a high fat-to-muscle ratio metabolizes food more slowly than a person of the same weight with more muscle (Langin & Lafontan, 2014). That is, two people of the same weight may metabolize food at different rates, depending on their distribution of muscle and fat. Meanwhile, the normal distribution of fat cells is different for men and women. The average man is 40% muscle and 15% fat. The average woman is 23% muscle and 25% fat. If a man and a woman with typical distributions of muscle and fat are of equal weight, therefore, the woman—who has more fat cells—must eat less to maintain that weight.

We also live in an "obesogenic environment" (Mattes & Tan, 2014). Foods high in sugar and fat are everywhere. Children in the United States are exposed to an average of 10,000 food commercials a year. More than nine of ten of these commercials are for fast foods, sugared cereals, candy, and soft drinks (Harris et al., 2009; Sixsmith & Furnham, 2010). Situations contribute as well. Family celebrations, watching television, arguments, and tension at work can all lead to overeating or going off a diet. Efforts to diet may also be impeded by negative emotions such as depression and anxiety, which can lead to binge eating (Rosenbaum & White, 2013).

8-3d EATING DISORDERS

Consider some facts about eating and eating disorders in the United States, as reported by the National Eating Disorders Association (2010):

▶ More than half of teenage girls and nearly one third of teenage boys use unhealthful methods to try to control their weight, including fasting, skipping meals, smoking cigarettes, vomiting, and using laxatives.

▶ About two out of five first- through third-grade girls would like to be thinner.

▶ More than four out of five 10-year-old girls report fear of being fat.

▶ Nearly half of 9- to 11-year-old girls are "sometimes" or "very often" dieting.

▶ More than 90% of college women have dieted at some time.

Eating disorders are characterized by persistent, gross disturbances in eating patterns. In this section, we focus on an eating disorder in which individuals are too thin, *anorexia nervosa*, and one in which the person may be normal in weight, but certainly not in the methods used to maintain that weight—*bulimia nervosa*.

Mike Kemp/Rubberball/Getty Images

TABLE 8.1	YEARS OF LIFE LOST BY AN EXTREMELY OBESE, NON-SMOKING 40-YEAR-OLD, COMPARED WITH A NORMAL-WEIGHT PERSON OF THE SAME AGE	
	European American	African American
Male	9	8
Female	7	5

Source: Finkelstein, E. A., Brown, D. S., Wrage, L. A., Allaire, B. T., & Hoerger, T. J. (2010). Individual and aggregate years-of-life-lost associated with overweight and obesity. *Obesity, 18*(2), 333–339.

ANOREXIA NERVOSA Anorexia nervosa is a life-threatening eating disorder characterized by extreme fear of being too heavy, dramatic weight loss, a distorted body image, and resistance to eating enough to reach or maintain a healthful weight.

Anorexia nervosa mostly afflicts women during adolescence and young adulthood (Stice et al., 2013a). Affluent females may be at greater risk because they have greater access to fitness centers and health clubs. They are also more likely to subscribe to magazines that idealize slender bodies and shop in boutiques that cater to svelte women. American women are regularly confronted with unrealistic standards of slimness that make them dissatisfied with their own figures (Harrison, 2013). Female athletes are also at risk. The **female athlete triad** describes women who have low availability of energy (as from eating poorly), menstrual problems, and lessened bone density, a cluster of health problems that usually afflicts people in late adulthood (House et al., 2013). Females with anorexia nervosa can drop 25% or more of their weight within a year, also leading to respiratory and cardiovascular problems (Papadopoulos et al., 2009). Given these health issues, the mortality rate for females with anorexia nervosa is approximately 5%.

In one common pattern, the girl sees that she has gained some weight after reaching puberty, and she resolves that she must lose it. But even after the weight is gone, she continues to diet and, in many cases, exercises at a fever pitch. This pattern continues as her weight plunges. Girls with the disorder are in denial about health problems; some point to feverish exercise routines as evidence of strength. Distortion of the body image—seeing oneself as overweight—is a feature of anorexia (Harrison, 2013).

BULIMIA NERVOSA Bulimia nervosa entails repeated cycles of binge eating and purging. Like anorexia, it tends to afflict women during adolescence and young adulthood (Bravender et al., 2010). Binge eating often follows on the heels of food restriction—as in dieting (Osborn et al., 2013). There are various methods of purging. Some people vomit. Other avenues include strict dieting or fasting, the use of laxatives, and engaging in demanding, prolonged exercise regimens. Individuals with eating disorders tend to be perfectionists about their bodies. They will not settle for less than their idealized body shape and

anorexia nervosa a life-threatening eating disorder characterized by dramatic weight loss and a distorted body image

female athlete triad a problem affecting female athletes, especially in college, involving (1) low energy, (2) menstrual problems, and (3) loss of bone density.

bulimia nervosa an eating disorder characterized by repeated cycles of binge eating and purging

Kristian Dowling/Getty Images

The Model Figure for the 2010s? The great majority of women who compare themselves to the idealized embodiment of the tall, slender model are likely to be disappointed. Their body mass index (BMI) is about 17, and nearly two of three American women have a BMI in excess of 25.

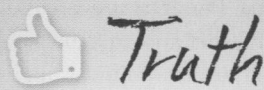
weight (Chang et al., 2013; Watson et al., 2010). Bulimia, like anorexia, triggers hormonal imbalances: many women with bulimia nervosa have irregular menstrual cycles (Mendelsohn, & Warren, 2010). Eating disorders are upsetting and dangerous in themselves, of course, but they are also often connected with deep depression (Stice et al., 2013b).

ORIGINS OF THE EATING DISORDERS Health professionals have done a great deal of research into the origins of eating disorders, but they admit that many questions about them remain unanswered.

Many parents are obsessed with getting their children—especially their infants—to eat. Thus, some psychologists suggest that children now and then refuse to eat as a way of engaging in warfare with their parents. ("You have to eat something!" "I'm not hungry!") It often seems that warfare does occur in the families of adolescents with eating disorders. Parents in such families are often unhappy with the family's functioning. They frequently have issues with eating and dieting themselves. They also "act out" against their daughters—letting them know that they consider them unattractive and, prior to the development of the eating disorder, letting them know that they think they should lose weight (Cooper et al., 2001; Crittenden & Dallos, 2009). Another disturbing risk factor for eating disorders in adolescent females is a history of child abuse, particularly sexual abuse, although the numbers of eating disorders that are reported as attributable to abuse and neglect are variable (Leung et al., 2010; Mitchell & Bulik, 2013). The sociocultural climate also affects eating behavior. Slimness is idealized in the United States. When you check out current fashion magazines and catalogs, you are looking at models who, on average, are 9% taller and 16% thinner than the typical female—and who still manage to have ample bust lines. Miss America, the annually renewed American role model, has also been slenderizing across the years. Over the past 80 years, the winner has added only 2% in height but has lost 12 pounds in weight. In the 1920s, Miss America's weight relative to her height yielded a body mass index (BMI) of 20 to 25, which is considered normal by the World Health Organization (WHO). The WHO labels people as malnourished when their BMIs are lower than 18.5. Recent Miss Americas, however, come in at a BMI near 17 (Shick et al., 2009). As the cultural ideal slenderizes, women with average body weights according to the health charts feel overweight, and more-than-average women feel gargantuan.

8-4 SEXUAL MOTIVATION AND SEXUAL ORIENTATION

In a television comedy, a mother referred to her teenage son as "a hormone with feet." She recognized that her son had become obsessed with sex, which is normal enough for adolescents in our culture. It is also now widely understood that the adolescent preoccupation with sex is strongly related to the surge in sex hormones that occurs at puberty. The phrase "a hormone with feet" implies movement as well as motivation, and movement means direction. We will see that sex hormones tend to propel us in certain directions as well as provide the driving force.

8-4a HORMONES AND SEXUAL MOTIVATION

Sex hormones can be said to fuel the sex drive. Research with men who produce little testosterone—due to age or health problems—shows that their sex drive increases when they receive testosterone replacement therapy (Koch & Zitzmann, 2013). The most common sexual problem among women is lack of sexual desire

Walter Lockwood/Photolibrary/Getty Images

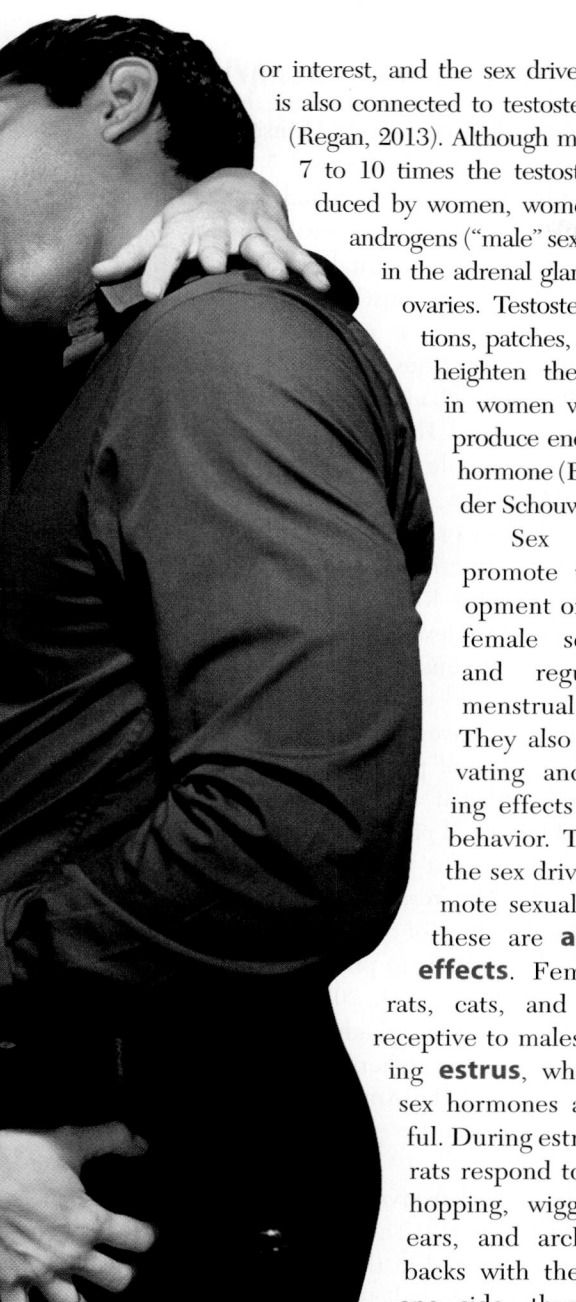

or interest, and the sex drive in women is also connected to testosterone levels (Regan, 2013). Although men produce 7 to 10 times the testosterone produced by women, women produce androgens ("male" sex hormones) in the adrenal glands and the ovaries. Testosterone injections, patches, or pills can heighten the sex drive in women who do not produce enough of the hormone (Brand & van der Schouw, 2010).

Sex hormones promote the development of male and female sex organs and regulate the menstrual cycle. They also have activating and organizing effects on sexual behavior. They affect the sex drive and promote sexual response; these are **activating effects**. Female mice, rats, cats, and dogs are receptive to males only during **estrus**, when female sex hormones are plentiful. During estrus, female rats respond to males by hopping, wiggling their ears, and arching their backs with their tails to one side, thus enabling males to penetrate them.

8-4b SEXUAL RESPONSE AND SEXUAL BEHAVIOR

Men show more interest in sex than women do (Masters et al., 2013). A survey of more than 1,000 undergraduates found that men reported being more interested than women in casual sex and multiple sex partners (Schmitt et al., 2001). Women are more likely to want to combine sex with a romantic relationship (Treger et al., 2013).

Although we may be more culturally attuned to focus on sex differences rather than similarities, William Masters and Virginia Johnson (1966) found that the biological responses of males and females to sexual stimulation are quite similar. Masters and Johnson use the term **sexual response cycle** to describe the changes that occur in the body as men and women become sexually aroused. They divide the sexual response cycle into four phases: *excitement, plateau, orgasm,* and *resolution.*

The sexual response cycle is characterized by *vasocongestion* and *myotonia*. **Vasocongestion** is the swelling of the genital tissues with blood, causing erection of the penis and swelling of the area surrounding the vaginal opening. The testes and the nipples swell as blood vessels dilate in these areas. **Myotonia** is muscle tension, which causes grimaces, spasms in the hands and feet, and the spasms of orgasm.

Erection, vaginal lubrication, and orgasm are all reflexes. That is, they occur automatically in response to adequate sexual stimulation.

EXCITEMENT PHASE Vasocongestion during the **excitement phase** causes erection in men. The scrotal skin thickens, becoming less baggy. The testes increase in size and become elevated.

In the female, excitement is characterized by vaginal lubrication, which may start 10 to 30 seconds after sexual stimulation begins. Vasocongestion swells the clitoris, flattens and spreads the vaginal lips, and expands the inner part of the vagina. The breasts enlarge, and blood vessels near the surface become more prominent. The nipples may erect in both men and women. Heart rate and blood pressure increase.

PLATEAU PHASE The level of sexual arousal remains somewhat stable

---

activating effect the arousal-producing effects of sex hormones that increase the likelihood of sexual behavior

estrus the periodic sexual excitement of many female mammals as governed by levels of sex hormones

sexual response cycle Masters and Johnson's model of sexual response, which consists of four stages or phases: excitement, plateau, orgasm, and resolution

vasocongestion engorgement of blood vessels with blood, which swells the genitals and breasts during sexual arousal

myotonia muscle tension

excitement phase the first phase of the sexual response cycle, which is characterized by muscle tension, increases in the heart rate, and erection in the male and vaginal lubrication in the female during the **plateau phase** of the cycle. Because of vasocongestion, the circumference of the head of the penis increases somewhat. The testes are elevated into position for **ejaculation** and may reach one-and-a-half times their unaroused size.

In women, vasocongestion swells the outer part of the vagina and the inner vagina expands further. The clitoris withdraws beneath the clitoral hood and shortens. Breathing becomes rapid, like panting. Heart rate may increase to 100 to 160 beats per minute. Blood pressure continues to rise.

ORGASMIC PHASE During **orgasm** in the male, muscle contractions propel semen from the body. Sensations of pleasure tend to be related to the strength of the contractions and the amount of seminal fluid. The first three to four contractions are generally most intense and occur at 0.8-second intervals (five contractions every 4 seconds). Additional contractions occur more slowly.

Orgasm in the female is manifested by three to fifteen contractions of the pelvic muscles that surround the vaginal barrel. As with males, the contractions first occur at 0.8-second intervals. Weaker and slower contractions follow.

Blood pressure and heart rate reach a peak, with the heart beating up to 180 times per minute. Respiration may increase to 40 breaths per minute.

RESOLUTION PHASE In the **resolution phase**, after orgasm, the body returns to its unaroused state. Men enter a **refractory period** during which they cannot experience another orgasm or ejaculate. Women do not undergo a refractory period and therefore can become quickly re-aroused to the point of repeated (multiple) orgasm if they desire and receive continued sexual stimulation.

The sexual response cycle describes what happens when females and males are exposed to sexual stimulation. But what kinds of sexual experiences do people seek? How many sex partners do they have? Who are their partners? What do we know about the sex lives of people in the United States?

plateau phase the second phase of the sexual response cycle, which is characterized by increases in vasocongestion, muscle tension, heart rate, and blood pressure in preparation for orgasm

ejaculation the process of propelling seminal fluid (semen) from the penis

orgasm the height or climax of sexual excitement, involving involuntary muscle contractions, release of sexual tensions, and usually, subjective feelings of pleasure

resolution phase the fourth phase of the sexual response cycle, during which the body gradually returns to its pre-aroused state

refractory period in the sexual response cycle, a period of time following orgasm during which an individual is not responsive to sexual stimulation

8-4c SURVEYS OF SEXUAL BEHAVIOR

The well-known Kinsey reports (Kinsey et al., 1948, 1953) interviewed 5,300 males and 5,940 females in the United States between 1938 and 1949. Interviewers asked about sexual experiences including masturbation, oral sex, and premarital sex. The nation was astounded to learn that most males masturbated and had had sexual intercourse prior to marriage. Moreover, significant minorities of females reported these behaviors. But Kinsey had not obtained a random sample of the population. His samples underrepresented people of color, people in rural areas, older people, poor people, Catholics, and Jews. There is thus no way of knowing whether or not Kinsey's results accurately mirrored general American sexual behavior at the time. But the *relationships* Kinsey uncovered, such as the positive link between level of education and premarital sex, may be accurate enough.

If you're trying to report accurately on sex in the United States, you have to give everyone in the country an equal chance of participating. That never happens perfectly. What if you want to interview college students and use listed phone numbers to reach them? In doing so, you've just left out all students who use cellphones only. The researchers who published the recent National Survey of Sexual Health and Behavior (NSSHB) took measures to prevent that type of thing from happening (Reece et al., 2010). All in all, they surveyed 5,865 adolescents and adults, aged 14 to 94, and derived what most researchers believe is a reasonably accurate snapshot of the American population—or at least a reasonably accurate picture of what people are willing to report.

You'll find a quick overview of some of the researchers' results in Figure 8.3. The kinds of sexual behaviors they surveyed are listed in the first column. The ages of the respondents are indicted in the row at the top. Respondents are broken down by sex (Men and Women) as well as by age. Let's take a look at the first sexual behavior in the list, masturbation, and see what we find. For every age group, men are more likely than women to report masturbating in the past year. Why do you think that is so? Also, the incidence of masturbation generally rises through the late twenties and then begins to decline. How would you explain that?

Despite the availability of methods of contraception and disease prevention, and despite the widespread portrayal of casual sex in the media, a survey by the Centers for Disease Control and Prevention (Martinez et al., 2011) finds that fewer teenagers are having unmarried sex now than they did in the 1980s

Percentage of Americans Performing Certain Sexual Behaviors in the Past Year (N=5865)

Sexual Behaviors	Age Groups																	
	14-15		16-17		18-19		20-24		25-29		30-39		40-49		50-59		60-69		70+
	Men	Women	Men	Women	Men	Women	Men	Women	Men	Women	Men	Women	Men	Women	Men	Women	Men	Women	Men	Women
Masturbated Alone	62%	40%	75%	45%	81%	60%	83%	64%	84%	72%	80%	63%	76%	65%	72%	54%	61%	47%	46%	33%
Masturbated with Partner	5%	8%	16%	19%	42%	36%	44%	36%	49%	48%	45%	43%	38%	35%	28%	18%	17%	13%	13%	5%
Received Oral from Women	12%	1%	31%	5%	54%	4%	63%	9%	77%	3%	78%	5%	62%	2%	49%	1%	38%	1%	19%	2%
Received Oral from Men	1%	10%	3%	24%	6%	58%	6%	70%	5%	72%	6%	59%	6%	52%	8%	34%	3%	25%	2%	8%
Gave Oral to Women	8%	2%	18%	7%	51%	2%	55%	9%	74%	3%	69%	4%	57%	3%	44%	1%	34%	1%	24%	2%
Gave Oral to Men	1%	12%	2%	22%	4%	59%	7%	74%	5%	76%	5%	59%	7%	53%	8%	36%	3%	23%	3%	7%
Vaginal Intercourse	9%	11%	30%	30%	53%	62%	63%	80%	86%	87%	85%	74%	74%	70%	58%	51%	54%	42%	43%	22%
Received Penis in Anus	1%	4%	1%	5%	4%	18%	5%	23%	4%	21%	3%	22%	4%	12%	5%	6%	1%	4%	2%	1%
Inserted Penis into Anus	3%		6%		6%		11%		27%		24%		21%		11%		6%		2%	

Source: Center for Sexual Health Promotion. (2011). *National Survey of Sexual Health and Behavior (NSSHB)*. Indiana University, Bloomington: School of Health, Physical Education, and Recreation. http://www.nationalsexstudy.indiana.edu/graph.html (Accessed February 22, 2012)

and 1990s (see Figure 8.4). According to the survey, 43% of unmarried female teens and 42% of unmarried male teens have had sex at least one time in the years since 2006, whereas the percentages were 52% for girls and 60% for boys as recently as 2002. Teenage pregnancy has also been undergoing a steady decline as unmarried teens have also become more likely to use condoms.

8-4d SEXUAL ORIENTATION

Earlier we discussed that sex hormones have *activating* effects. However, they also have directional or **organizing effects**. That is, they predispose lower animals toward stereotypical masculine or feminine mating patterns. Sex hormones are thus likely candidates for influencing the development of sexual orientation (De Rooij et al., 2009).

Sexual orientation refers to the direction of a person's sexual and romantic interests—toward people of the other sex or toward people of the same sex. The great majority of people have a **heterosexual** orientation; they are sexually attracted to and interested in forming romantic relationships with people of the other sex. Some people, however, have a **homosexual** orientation; they are attracted to and interested in forming romantic

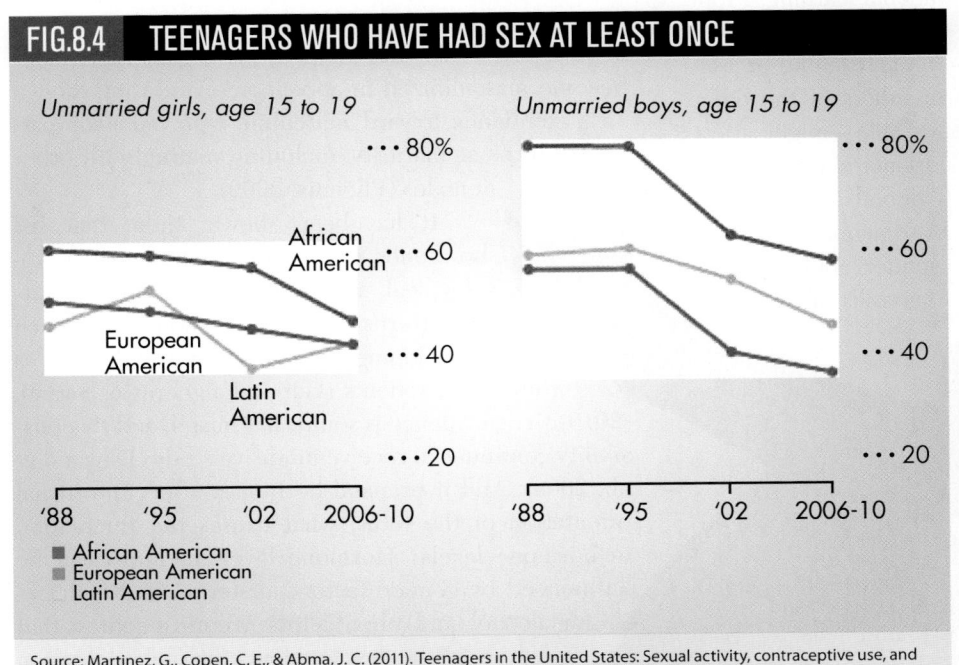

FIG.8.4 TEENAGERS WHO HAVE HAD SEX AT LEAST ONCE

Unmarried girls, age 15 to 19

African American
European American
Latin American

'88 '95 '02 2006-10

■ African American
■ European American
  Latin American

Unmarried boys, age 15 to 19

'88 '95 '02 2006-10

Source: Martinez, G., Copen, C. E., & Abma, J. C. (2011). Teenagers in the United States: Sexual activity, contraceptive use, and childbearing, 2006–2010. *National Survey of Family Growth*. National Center for Health Statistics. Vital Health Statistics, 23(31).

organizing effect the directional effect of sex hormones—for example, along typical male or female patterns of mating

sexual orientation the directionality of one's sexual and romantic interests; that is, whether one is sexually attracted to, and desires to form a romantic relationship with, members of the other gender or of one's own gender

heterosexual referring to people who are sexually aroused by, and interested in forming romantic relationships with, people of the other gender

homosexual referring to people who are sexually aroused by, and interested in forming romantic relationships with, people of the same gender

relationships with people of their own sex. Males with a homosexual orientation are referred to as *gay males.* Homosexual females are referred to as *lesbians. Bisexual* people are attracted to both females and males.

About 7% of American men and women define themselves as being "other than heterosexual," but as noted earlier, the behavior of the other 93% doesn't exactly match up with the way people label themselves. For example, nearly twice as many people—about 14%—say they have had oral sex with a person of the same gender (Herbenick et al., 2010a, 2010b, 2010c; Reece et al., 2010). Estimates of the prevalence of various sexual orientations in our culture remain somewhat speculative.

THEORIES OF THE ORIGINS OF SEXUAL ORIENTATION Theories of the origins of sexual orientation look both at nature and nurture—the biological makeup of the individual and environmental influences. Several theories bridge the two.

Social–cognitive theorists look for the roles of factors such as reinforcement and observational learning. From this perspective, reinforcement of sexual behavior with members of one's own gender—as in reaching orgasm with them when members of the other gender are unavailable—might affect one's sexual orientation. Similarly, childhood sexual abuse by someone of the same gender could lead to fantasies about sex with people of one's own gender and affect sexual orientation. Observation of others engaged in enjoyable male–male or female–female sexual encounters could also affect the development of sexual orientation. But critics point out that most individuals become aware of their sexual orientation before they have sexual contacts with other people of either gender (Savin-Williams & Cohen, 2007). Moreover, in a society that generally condemns homosexuality, young people are unlikely to believe that male–male or female–female contacts will have positive effects for them.

There is evidence for genetic factors in sexual orientation (Best & Fortenberry, 2013; Ramagopalan et al., 2010). About 52% of identical (MZ) twin pairs, whose genetic codes are completely the same, share a gay male sexual orientation as compared with 22% of fraternal (DZ) twins, whose genetic codes overlap only 50%, and 11% for adoptive brothers (Dawood et al., 2009).

In many families of animals, such as rodents, there is little room for thinking about sex and deciding whether an individual will pursue sexual relationships with males or females. Sexual motivation comes under the governance of sex hormones (Henley et al., 2010; Piffer et al., 2009). Furthermore, much sexual motivation is determined by whether the brains and sex organs of fetuses are bathed in large doses of testosterone in the uterus. In male fetuses, testosterone is normally produced by the developing testes. Yet female fetuses are exposed to testosterone when they share the uterus with many male siblings. Researchers have also injected male sex hormones into the uteruses of rodents. When they do, the sex organs of females become masculinized in appearance, and they show a tendency toward masculine-type behavior patterns at maturity, including mating with other females (Phoenix, 2009).

It has been shown, then, that sex hormones predispose nonhumans to stereotypical masculine or feminine mating patterns. Do sex hormones influence the developing human embryo and fetus as they affect rodents (Garcia-Falgueras & Swaab, 2010)? The evidence is somewhat mixed, and this possibility continues to receive intensive study (Dawood et al., 2009). And if prenatal hormones affect the sexual orientation of the fetus, what causes the fluctuation in hormone levels? Hormone levels in utero can be influenced by genetic factors, maternal stress, drinking alcohol, and other factors. We must confess that much about the development of sexual orientation remains speculative.

Ryan Pierse/The Image Bank/Getty Images

8-5 ACHIEVEMENT MOTIVATION

Many students persist in studying despite being surrounded by distractions. Many people strive relentlessly to get ahead, to "make it," to earn large sums of money, to invent, to accomplish the impossible. Psychological research has pointed to these people having something called *achievement motivation*.

Psychologist David McClelland (1958) helped pioneer the assessment of achievement motivation through evaluation of fantasies. One method involves the Thematic Apperception Test (TAT), developed by Henry Murray. The TAT contains cards with pictures and drawings that are subject to various interpretations. Individuals are shown one or more TAT cards and asked to construct stories about the pictured theme: to indicate what led up to it, what the characters are thinking and feeling, and what is likely to happen.

One TAT card is similar to that in Figure 8.5. The meaning of the card is ambiguous—unclear. Is the girl sleeping, thinking about the book, wishing she were out with friends?

Consider two stories that could be told about this card:

▶ *Story 1:* "She's upset that she's got to read the book because she's behind in her assignments and doesn't particularly like to work. She'd much rather be out with her friends, and she may very well sneak out to do just that."

▶ *Story 2:* "She's thinking, 'Someday I'll be a great scholar. I'll write books like this, and everybody will be proud of me.' She reads all the time."

The second story suggests more achievement motivation than the first. Classic studies find that people with high achievement motivation earn higher grades than people with comparable learning ability but lower achievement motivation. They are more likely to earn high salaries and be promoted than less motivated people with similar opportunities (Maurer & Chapman, 2013; Story et al., 2009).

McClelland (1965) used the TAT to sort college students into groups—students with high achievement motivation and students with low achievement motivation. He found that 83% of college graduates with high achievement motivation found jobs in occupations characterized by risk, decision-making, and the chance for great success, such as business management, sales, or self-employment. Most (70%) of the graduates who chose non-entrepreneurial positions showed low achievement motivation. People with high achievement motivation seem to prefer challenges and are willing to take moderate risks to achieve their goals.

8-5a EXTRINSIC VERSUS INTRINSIC MOTIVES

Do you want to do well in this course? If you do, why? Carol Dweck (2009) finds that achievement motivation can be driven by performance or learning goals, or both. For example, are you motivated mainly by performance goals, such as your grade in the course? If so, it may be in part because your motives concern tangible rewards such as getting into graduate school, landing a good job, reaping approval from your parents or your instructor, or avoiding criticism. Performance goals are usually met through *extrinsic rewards* such as praise and income. Parents of children who develop performance goals are likely to respond to good grades with rewards such as toys or money and to respond to poor grades with anger and removal of privileges.

Or is it learning goals that mainly motivate you to do well? That is, is your central motive the enhancing of your knowledge and skills—your ability to understand and master the subject matter? Learning goals usually lead to *intrinsic rewards*, such as self-satisfaction.

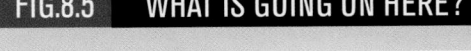
FIG.8.5 WHAT IS GOING ON HERE?

© Cengage Learning 2012

This card, like TAT cards, presents an ambiguous situation, and your interpretation of it says something about you.

Students who develop learning goals often have parents with strong achievement motivation who encourage their children to think and act independently. Parents and teachers help children develop learning goals by showing warmth and praising them for their efforts to learn, exposing them to novel and stimulating experiences, and encouraging persistence (Dweck, 2006, 2009). Children who are stimulated in this way tend to set high standards for themselves, associate their achievements with self-worth, and attribute their achievements to their own efforts rather than to chance or to the intervention of others.

Many of us strive to meet both performance and learning goals in our courses as well as in other areas of life. Grades are important because they are connected with tangible benefits, but learning for its own sake is also of value and can provide great pleasure.

8-6 EMOTION

Emotions color our lives. We are green with envy, red with anger, blue with sorrow. Positive emotions such as love and desire can fill our days with pleasure. Negative emotions such as fear, depression, and anger can fill us with dread and make each day a chore. Sometimes our emotions "lurk in the background." Sometimes they seize control of the day. And *emotion* can be hard to define.

An emotion can be a response to a situation, in the way that fear is a response to a threat. An emotion can motivate behavior, as anger can motivate aggression. An emotion can also be a goal in itself. We may behave in ways that will lead us to experience happiness or love. Emotions are thus intertwined with motivation. We are driven by emotions, and meeting—or failing to meet—our needs can have powerful emotional results.

Emotions are defined as feeling states with physiological, cognitive, and behavioral components. Strong emotions are associated with arousal of the **autonomic nervous system (ANS)**. The greater the arousal, the more intense the emotion. It also appears that the type of arousal affects the emotion being experienced. Although the word *emotion* might seem to be about feeling and not about thinking, cognitions—particularly interpretations of the meanings of events—are important aspects of emotions. *Fear*, which usually occurs in response to a threat, involves cognitions that one is in danger as well as arousal of the **sympathetic nervous system** (e.g., rapid heartbeat and breathing, sweating, muscle tension).

Emotions also involve behavioral tendencies. Fear is connected with behavioral tendencies to avoid or escape a situation (see Table 8.2). As a response to a social provocation, *anger* involves cognitions that the provocateur should be paid back, arousal of both the sympathetic and **parasympathetic nervous systems**, and tendencies to attack (Carver & Harmon-Jones, 2009). *Depression* usually involves cognitions of helplessness and hopelessness, parasympathetic arousal, and tendencies toward inactivity—or sometimes self-destruction. *Happiness, grief, jealousy, disgust, embarrassment, liking*—all have cognitive, physiological, and behavioral components.

8-6a The Expression of Emotions

Happiness and sadness are found in all cultures, but do people around the world express emotions in the same way? It turns out that the expression of many emotions may

emotion a state of feeling that has cognitive, physiological, and behavioral components

autonomic nervous system (ANS) the division of the peripheral nervous system that regulates glands and activities such as heartbeat, respiration, digestion, and dilation of the pupils

sympathetic nervous system the branch of the autonomic nervous system that is most active during processes that spend body energy from stored reserves, such as in a fight-or-flight reaction to a predator or when you are anxious about a big test

parasympathetic nervous system the branch of the autonomic nervous system that is most active during processes that restore reserves of energy to the body, such as relaxing and eating

TABLE 8.2	COMPONENTS OF EMOTIONS		
Emotion	**Physiological**	**Cognitive**	**Behavioral**
Fear	Sympathetic arousal	Belief that one is in danger	Avoidance tendencies
Anger	Sympathetic and parasympathetic arousal	Frustration or belief that one is being mistreated	Attack tendencies
Depression	Parasympathetic arousal	Thoughts of helplessness, hopelessness, worthlessness	Inactivity, possible selfdestructive tendencies

© Cengage Learning 2012

be universal (Ekman, 2003). Smiling is apparently a universal sign of friendliness and approval. Baring the teeth, as noted by Charles Darwin (1872) in the 19th century, may be a universal sign of anger. As the originator of the theory of evolution, Darwin believed that the universal recognition of facial expressions would have survival value. For example, in the absence of language, facial expressions could signal the approach of enemies (or friends).

Most investigators agree that certain facial expressions suggest the same emotions in people who are reared in diverse cultures (Farb et al., 2013). Moreover, people in diverse cultures recognize the emotions indicated by certain facial expressions. Paul Ekman (1980) took photographs of people exhibiting anger, disgust, fear, happiness, sadness, and surprise (see Figure 8.6). He then asked people around the world to say what emotions were being depicted. Those queried ranged from European college students to members of the Fore, a tribe that dwells in the New Guinea highlands.

All groups, including the Fore, who had almost no contact with Western culture, agreed on the emotions. The Fore also displayed familiar facial expressions when asked how they would respond if they were the characters in stories that called for basic emotional responses.

```
Happy people
• believe in
  their ability
  to effect
  change
• are open to
  new experience
• are willing
  to risk
  developing new
  relationships
```

Ekman and his colleagues (1987) obtained similar results in a study of 10 cultures.

On the other hand, there is no perfect one-to-one relationship between facial expressions and emotions (Farb et al., 2013). Facial expressions sometimes occur in the absence of the emotion they are thought to accompany (Porter & ten Brinke, 2008). The voice, posture, and gestures also provide clues to what people are feeling and are about to do.

8-6b POSITIVE PSYCHOLOGY

Ted Lewis, the Great Depression–era bandleader, used to begin his act by asking, "Is evvvvrybody happy?" Well, everybody is not happy, but surveys do suggest that most people in developed nations are reasonably satisfied with their lives (Cummins & Nistico, 2002). Many people might think that psychologists are interested only in negative emotions such as anxiety, depression, and anger. Not at all. An area of psychology called **positive psychology** deals with positive emotions such

positive psychology the field of psychology that is about personal well-being and satisfaction; joy, sensual pleasure, and happiness; and optimism and hope for the future

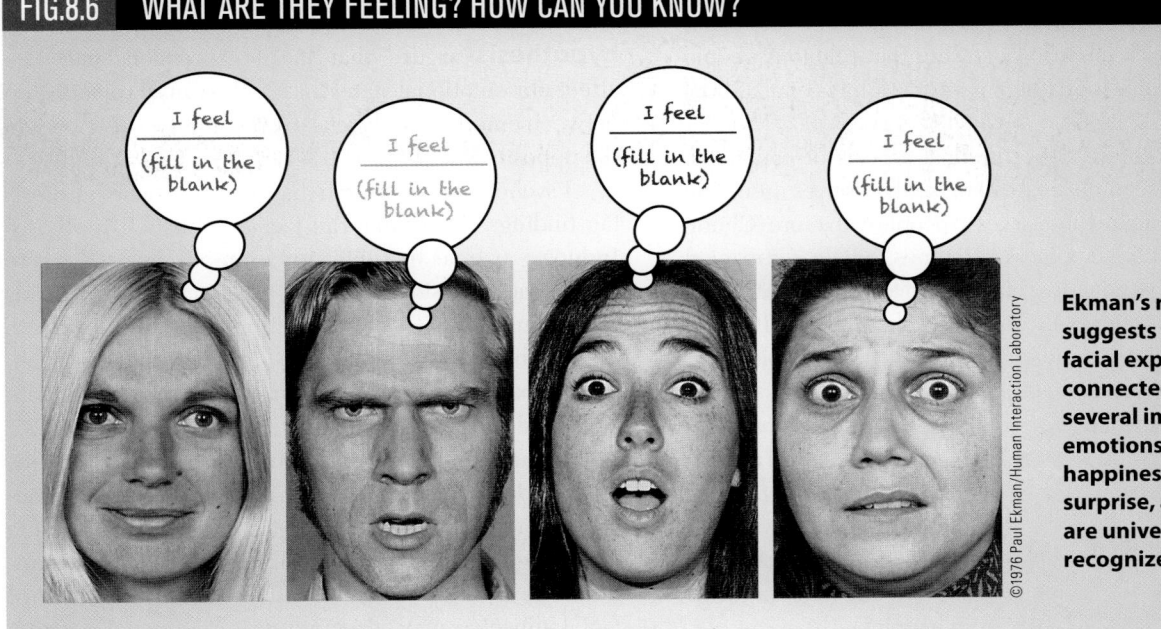

FIG.8.6 WHAT ARE THEY FEELING? HOW CAN YOU KNOW?

I feel ___ (fill in the blank)

I feel ___ (fill in the blank)

I feel ___ (fill in the blank)

I feel ___ (fill in the blank)

©1976 Paul Ekman/Human Interaction Laboratory

Ekman's research suggests that the facial expressions connected with several important emotions such as happiness, anger, surprise, and fear are universally recognized.

as happiness and love, optimism and hope, and joy and sensual pleasures.

Are some people just "born happy," or do life experiences determine happiness? What factors interfere with happiness? Some psychologists believe that genetic factors play a powerful role in happiness (Compton & Hoffman, 2013). They note that happiness tends to run in families and that we tend to have a more or less stable level of happiness throughout much of our lives (W. Johnson & Krueger, 2006). Positive events such as learning that the person we love also loves us or receiving recognition for our work can certainly raise our level of happiness at the moment. Similarly, negative life events, such as the loss of a loved one, financial reverses, or injuries can depress us—and understandably so. Yet we may tend to bounce back to a more or less characteristic level of happiness, as did the actor Christopher Reeve following the accident—being thrown from a horse—that paralyzed him.

Which life experiences contribute to happiness? Despite the saying "Money can't buy you happiness," people tend to be happier when they live in affluent societies and earn decent incomes (W. Johnson & Krueger, 2006). Perhaps money doesn't make people happy in itself, but people who have it at least do not have to worry about money. Money aside, Chinese students tend to think of happiness in terms of feelings of contentment, inner harmony, personal achievement, physical wellness, spiritual enhancement, hopefulness about the future, generosity, and self-development (Lu, 2001). People who are married or in enduring relationships tend to be happier than loners (Waite et al., 2009; Wienke & Hill, 2009). Happy people are also more open to new experiences and new relationships (Demir & Weitekamp, 2007). Research has also suggested that religious people are happier than those who are not (Francis et al., 2004; Swinyard et al., 2001).

Then there are the attitudinal aspects of happiness. People at any income level can make themselves miserable when they compare themselves to people with more (Chung & Leung, 2008). Happiness also tends to be accompanied by optimism—a cognitive bias toward assuming that things will work out (Ho et al., 2010; Wilhelm et al., 2010). But the "bias" is not groundless, because happy people often believe in their ability to effect change and then try harder. They are also willing to pat themselves on the back for their successes and are not quick to blame themselves when things go wrong—attitudes that contribute to self-esteem, another factor in happiness.

facial-feedback hypothesis the view that stereotypical facial expressions can contribute to stereotypical emotions

8-6c THE FACIAL-FEEDBACK HYPOTHESIS

The face has a special place among visual stimuli. Social animals, like humans, need to be able to differentiate and recognize members of their group, and in people, the face is the most distinctive key to identity (Parr et al., 2000). Faces are also a key to social communication. Facial expressions reflect emotional states, and our ability to "read" these expressions enables us to interact appropriately with other people.

Emotional states can give rise to certain patterns of electrical activity in the facial muscles and in the brain (Porter & ten Brinke, 2008; Price et al., 2013). But can it work the other way around? The **facial-feedback hypothesis** argues that facial expressions can also affect our emotional state; that is, the causal relationship between emotions and facial expressions can also work in the opposite direction.

Psychological research has yielded some interesting findings concerning the facial-feedback hypothesis. Inducing people to smile, for example, leads them to report more positive feelings and to rate cartoons as more humorous (Soussignan, 2002). When induced to frown, they rate cartoons as more aggressive. When people exhibit pain through facial expressions, they rate electric shocks as more painful.

What are the possible links between facial feedback and emotion? One is arousal. Intense contraction of facial muscles such as those used in signifying fear heightens arousal, which, in turn, boosts emotional response. Feedback from the contraction of facial muscles may also induce emotions. Engaging

Smiling is usually a response to feeling good within, but experimental research into the facial-feedback hypothesis suggests that the act of smiling can also enhance our moods.

in the "Duchenne smile," characterized by "crow's feet wrinkles around the eyes and a subtle drop in the eye cover fold so that the skin above the eye moves down slightly toward the eyeball" can induce pleasant feelings (Price et al., 2013; Soussignan, 2002; see Figure 8.7).

You may have heard the British expression "Keep a stiff upper lip" as a recommendation for handling stress. It might be that a "stiff" lip suppresses emotional response—as long as the lip is relaxed rather than quivering with fear or tension. But when the lip is stiffened through strong muscle tension, facial feedback may heighten emotional response.

8-6d THEORIES OF EMOTION

David, 32, is not sleeping well. He wakes before dawn and cannot get back to sleep. His appetite is off, his energy level is low, and he has started smoking again. He has a couple of drinks at lunch and muses that it's lucky that any more alcohol makes him sick to his stomach—otherwise, he'd probably be drinking too much, too. Then he thinks, "So what difference would it make?" Sometimes he is sexually frustrated; at other times he wonders whether he has any sex drive left. Although he's awake, each day it's getting harder to drag himself out of bed in the morning. This week he missed one day of work and was late twice. His supervisor has suggested in a nonthreatening way that he "do something about it." David knows that her next warning will not be

---

FIG.8.7 — WE MAY SMILE WHEN WE FEEL GOOD, BUT DOES SMILING MAKE US FEEL GOOD?

A.

B.

According to the facial-feedback hypothesis, smiling just might have that effect. When people are compelled to smile because they are holding a pen between their teeth, they are more likely to rate comic strips as funny (see photo A). Holding the pen between their lips forces a frown, and the rating of the cartoons plummets (photo B).

nonthreatening. It's been going downhill since Sue walked out. Suicide has even crossed David's mind. He wonders if he's going crazy.

David is experiencing the emotion of depression, and seriously so. Depression is to be expected following a loss, such as the end of a relationship, but David's feelings have lingered. His friends tell him that he should get out and things, but David is so down that he hasn't the motivation to do much at all. After much prompting by family and friends, David consults a psychologist who ironically also pushes him to get out and do things—the things he used to enjoy. The psychologist also shows David that part of his problem is that he sees himself as a failure who cannot make meaningful changes.

The "commonsense theory" of emotions is that something happens (a situation) that is cognitively appraised (interpreted) by the person, and the feeling state (a combination of arousal and thoughts) follows. For example, you meet someone new, you appraise that person as delightful, and feelings of attraction follow. Or, as in the case of David, a social relationship comes to an end, you recognize your loss, feel powerless to change it, and feel down in the dumps.

However, both historic and contemporary theories of how the components of emotions interact are at variance with this commonsense view. Let's consider a number of theories and see whether we can arrive at some useful conclusions.

THE JAMES–LANGE THEORY A century ago, William James suggested that our emotions follow, rather than cause, our behavioral responses to events. At about the same time this view was also proposed by the Danish physiologist Karl G. Lange. It is therefore termed the *James–Lange theory of emotion.*

According to James and Lange, certain external stimuli instinctively trigger specific patterns of arousal and action, such as fighting or fleeing (see Figure 8.8, part A). We then become angry *because* we are acting aggressively or become afraid *because* we are running away. Emotions are simply the cognitive representations (or by-products) of automatic physiological and behavioral responses.

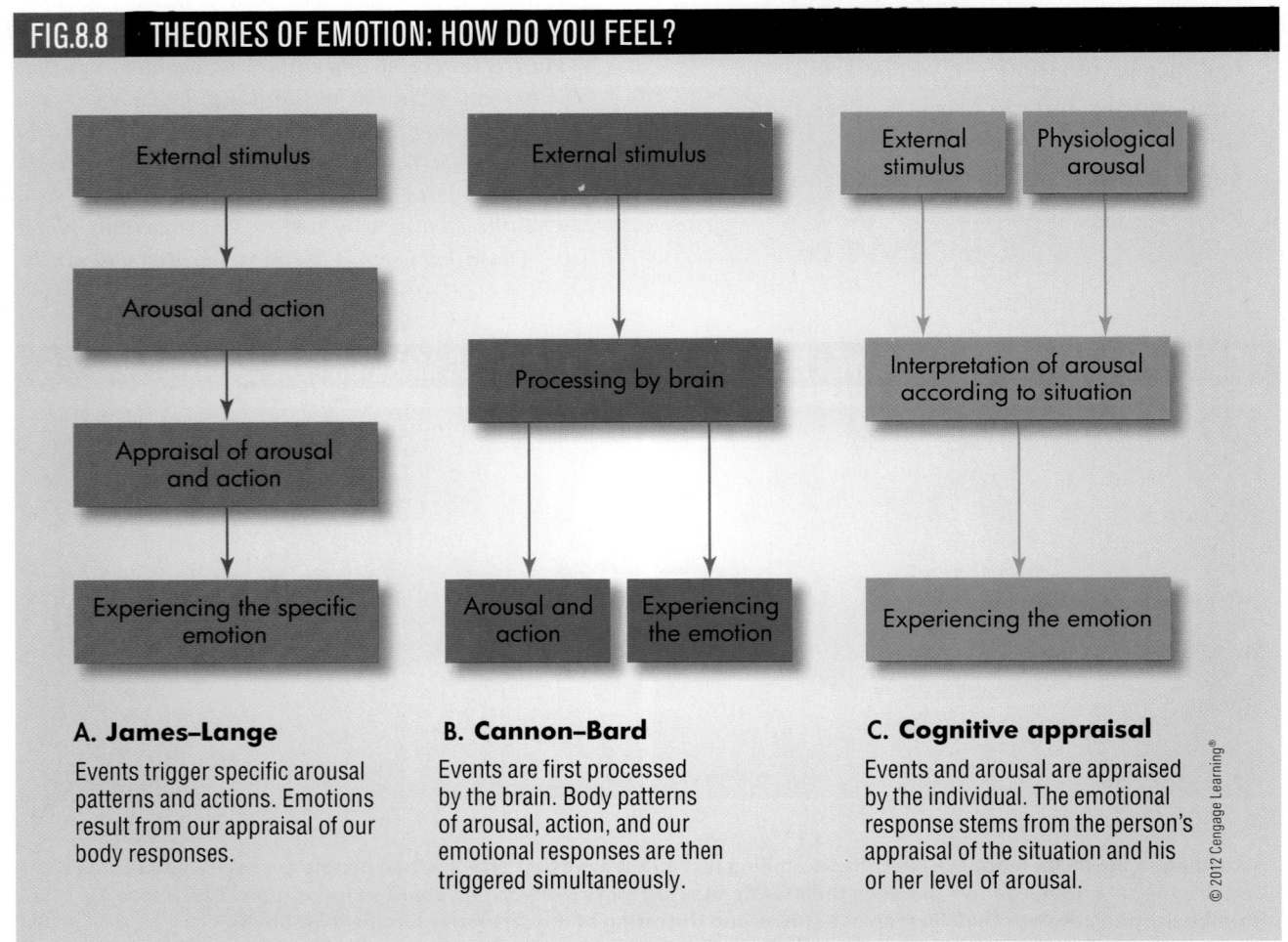

FIG.8.8 THEORIES OF EMOTION: HOW DO YOU FEEL?

A. James–Lange

Events trigger specific arousal patterns and actions. Emotions result from our appraisal of our body responses.

B. Cannon–Bard

Events are first processed by the brain. Body patterns of arousal, action, and our emotional responses are then triggered simultaneously.

C. Cognitive appraisal

Events and arousal are appraised by the individual. The emotional response stems from the person's appraisal of the situation and his or her level of arousal.

© 2012 Cengage Learning®

The James–Lange theory is consistent with the facial-feedback hypothesis. That is, smiling apparently can induce pleasant feelings, even if the effect may not be strong enough to overcome deep feelings of sadness. The theory also suggests that we may be able to change our feelings by changing our behavior. Changing one's behavior to change one's feelings is one aspect of behavior therapy. When David's psychologist urges him to get out and do things, she is assuming that by changing his behavior, David can have a positive effect on the way he feels.

Walter Cannon (1927) criticized the James–Lange assertion that each emotion has distinct physiological correlates. He argued that the physiological arousal associated with emotion A is not as distinct from the arousal associated with emotion B as the theory asserts. Note that the James–Lange view downplays the importance of human cognition; it denies the roles of cognitive appraisal, personal values, and personal choice in our behavioral and emotional responses to events.

THE CANNON–BARD THEORY Walter Cannon (1927) and Philip Bard (1934) suggested that an event might simultaneously trigger bodily responses (arousal and action) and the experience of an emotion. As shown in Figure 8.8 (part B), when an event is perceived (processed by the brain), the brain stimulates autonomic and muscular activity (arousal and action) and cognitive activity (experience of the emotion). Thus, according to the *Cannon–Bard theory of emotion*, emotions accompany bodily responses. They are not produced by bodily changes, as in the James–Lange theory.

The central criticism of the Cannon–Bard theory focuses on whether bodily responses (arousal and action) and emotions are in fact stimulated simultaneously. For example, pain or the perception of danger may trigger arousal before we begin to feel distress or fear. Also, many of us have had the experience of having a "narrow escape" and becoming aroused and shaky afterward, when we have had time to consider the damage that might have occurred. What is needed is a theory that allows for an ongoing interaction of external events, physiological changes (such as autonomic arousal and muscular activity), and cognitive activities.

THE THEORY OF COGNITIVE APPRAISAL More recent theoretical approaches to emotion stress cognitive factors. For example, Stanley Schachter asserts that many emotions have similar patterns of bodily arousal but that the labels we give them depend largely on our cognitive appraisal of our situations. Cognitive appraisal is based on many factors, including our perception of events and the ways other people respond to those events (see Figure 8.8, part C). When other people are present, we engage in social comparison to arrive at a response.

In a classic experiment, Schachter and Singer (1962) showed that arousal can be labeled quite differently, depending on the situation. The investigators told participants they wanted to determine the effects of a vitamin on vision. Half the participants received an injection of adrenaline, a hormone that stimulates the sympathetic branch of the autonomic nervous system. A control group received an injection of a placebo. Those who had been given adrenaline received one of three "cognitive manipulations." Group 1 was told nothing about possible emotional effects of the "vitamin." Group 2 was deliberately misinformed; members of this group were led to expect itching, numbness, or other irrelevant symptoms. Group 3 was informed accurately about the increased arousal they would experience. Group 4 was a control group injected with a placebo and given no information about its effects.

After receiving injections and cognitive manipulations, the participants were asked to wait in pairs while the experimental apparatus was being set up. The participants did not know that the person with whom they were waiting was a confederate of the experimenter. The confederate's purpose was to respond in a way that the participant would believe was caused by the injection.

Some participants waited with a confederate who acted happy-go-lucky. He flew paper airplanes about the room and tossed paper balls into a wastebasket. Other participants waited with a confederate who acted angry. He complained about the experiment, tore up a questionnaire, and stormed out of the room. As the confederates worked for their Oscar awards, the real participants were observed through a one-way mirror.

ANGER

JOY

LOVE

FEAR

SADNESS

PRIDE

SHAME

GUILT

Dimitri Otis/Digital Vision/Getty Images

The people in groups 1 and 2 were likely to imitate the behavior of the confederate. Those who were exposed to the happy-go-lucky confederate acted jovial and content. Those who were exposed to the angry confederate imitated that person's complaining, aggressive behavior. But those in groups 3 and 4 were less influenced by the confederate's behavior.

Schachter and Singer concluded that participants in groups 1 and 2 were in an ambiguous situation. Members of these groups felt arousal from the adrenaline injection but couldn't label it as a specific emotion. Social comparison with a confederate led them to attribute their arousal either to happiness or to anger. Members of Group 3 expected arousal from the injection, but no particular emotional consequences. These participants did not imitate the confederate's display of happiness or anger because they were not in an ambiguous situation; they knew their arousal was caused by adrenaline. Members of Group 4 had no arousal for which they needed an attribution, except perhaps for some arousal induced by observing the confederate. Nor did they imitate the behavior of the confederate.

arent emotions. Yet Schachter and Singer suggest that the bodily differences between these two emotions are slight enough that different views of the situation can lead one person to label arousal as happiness and another person to label it as anger. The Schachter–Singer view could not be further removed from the James–Lange theory, which holds that each emotion is associated with specific and readily recognized body sensations. The truth, it happens, may lie somewhere in between.

In science, it must be possible to replicate experiments and attain identical or similar results; otherwise, a theory cannot be considered valid. The Schachter and Singer study has been replicated, but with different results (Friedman, 2010). For example, some studies found that participants were less likely to imitate the behavior of the confederate and were likely to perceive unexplained arousal negatively, attributing it to nervousness or anger (Zimbardo et al., 1993).

The connections between arousal and emotions have led to the development of many kinds of lie detection, as we see in the following section.

THE POLYGRAPH: JUST WHAT DO LIE DETECTORS DETECT? Lying, for better or worse, is a part of life. People admit to lying in 14% of their emails, 27% of their face-to-face interactions, and 37% of their phone calls (Hancock, 2007). Political leaders lie to get elected.

When people communicate with online "matches," men are most likely to lie about their personal assets and their goals for a relationship (Hall et al., 2010). Women are most likely to lie about their weight (Hall et al., 2010). Most people lie to their lovers, usually about other relationships (Toma et al., 2008). People also lie about their qualifications to get jobs, and of course, some people lie about whether or not they have committed a crime.

Facial expressions often offer clues to deceit, but some people can lie with a straight face—or a smile. As Shakespeare points out in Hamlet, "One may smile, and smile, and be a villain." The use of devices to detect lies has a long if not laudable history:

> *The Bedouins of Arabia … until quite recently required conflicting witnesses to lick a hot iron; the one whose tongue was burned was thought to be lying.*

One way to fool a lie detector is to bite your tongue—less obviously than this, perhaps.

The Chinese, it is said, had a similar method for detecting lying: suspects were forced to chew rice powder and spit it out; if the powder was dry, the suspect was guilty (Kleinmuntz & Szucko, 1984, pp. 766–767).

These methods may sound primitive, even bizarre, but they are broadly consistent with modern psychological knowledge. Anxiety about being caught in a lie is linked to arousal of the sympathetic division of the autonomic nervous system. One sign of sympathetic arousal is lack of saliva, or dryness in the mouth. The emotions of fear and guilt are also linked to sympathetic arousal and hence to dryness in the mouth.

Polygraphs, or lie detectors, monitor indicators of sympathetic arousal during an interrogation: heart rate, blood pressure, respiration rate, and electrodermal response (sweating). But questions have been raised about the validity of assessing truth or fiction by means of polygraphs (Iacono, 2008).

The American Polygraph Association claims that use of the polygraph is 85% to 95% accurate. Critics find polygraph testing to be less accurate and claim that it is sensitive to more than lies (Iacono, 2008). Factors such as tense muscles, drugs, and previous experience with polygraph tests can significantly reduce their accuracy rate. In one experiment, people were able to reduce the accuracy of polygraph-based judgments to about 50% by biting their tongues (to produce pain) or pressing their toes against the floor (to tense muscles) while being interrogated (Fiske & Borgida, 2008; Honts et al., 1985). You might thus give the examiner the impression that you are lying even when you are telling the truth, throwing off the test's results.

It appears that no specific pattern of bodily responses pinpoints lying (Iacono, 2008). Because of validity problems, results of polygraph examinations are no longer admitted as evidence in many courts.

EVALUATION What can we make of all this? Research suggests that the patterns of arousal connected with various emotions are more specific than suggested by Schachter and Singer—although less so than suggested by James and Lange (Larsen et al., 2008). Research

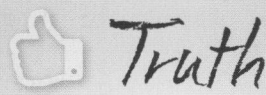

T F You may be able to fool a lie detector by biting your tongue or wiggling your toes.

It is true that you might be able to fool a lie detector by biting your tongue or wiggling your toes. These measures can distract your body from emitting the signals generally associated with lying.

with brain imaging suggests that different emotions, such as happiness and sadness, involve different structures in the brain (Lane et al., 2009; Suslow at al., 2010). Even so, researchers have not found brain cells that respond to but a single emotion. The emotion of disgust apparently has the most specific location, the primary taste cortex. It makes sense that an emotion related to "distasteful" experiences would be centered here.

Regarding the Schachter and Singer study, Zimbardo and his colleagues (1993) note that a lack of control over our feelings and a lack of understanding of what is going on are disturbing experiences. Thus, our cognitive appraisal of situations does affect our emotional responses, but perhaps not as Schachter and Singer believed.

In sum, various components of an experience—cognitive, physiological, and behavioral—contribute to our emotional responses. Our bodies may become aroused in a given situation, but people also appraise those situations; arousal in itself does not appear to directly cause one emotion or another. The fact that none of the theories of emotion we have discussed applies to all people in all situations is comforting. Apparently our emotions are not quite as easily understood, manipulated, or—as in the case of the polygraph—even detected, as some theorists have suggested.

STUDY TOOLS 8

READY TO STUDY? IN THE BOOK, YOU CAN:

☐ Check your understanding of what you've read with the quizzes below.

☐ Rip out the chapter review card at the back of the book to have a summary of the chapter and the key terms handy.

ONLINE AT CENGAGEBRAIN.COM YOU CAN:

☐ Practice retrieving what you've learned using the interactive figures on Maslow's Hierarchy of Needs.

☐ Learn how man and machine might work together to help make better clinical decisions and improve our nation's security in a short video.

☐ Prepare for tests with quizzes.

☐ Review the key terms with Flash Cards.

☐ Play games to master concepts.

FILL-INS

Answers can be found in the back of the book, starting on page XXX.

1. _____ are hypothetical states that activate behavior and direct organisms toward goals.

2. A(n) _____ is an object, person, or situation that is perceived as capable of satisfying a need.

3. Drives help the body maintain a steady state, a tendency that is called _____.

4. Maslow argued that people have a hierarchy of needs, the highest of which is the need for _____.

5. _____ nervosa is a life-threatening eating disorder characterized by dramatic weight loss and a distorted body image.

6. Masters and Johnson divide the sexual response cycle into four phases: the _____, plateau, orgasm, and resolution phases.

7. Sex hormones have activating and _____ effects on sexual behavior.

8. McClelland used the Thematic _____ Test to measure achievement motivation.

9. Students with _____ goals are mainly motivated by factors such as good grades, rewards from parents, and the prospect of landing a good job.

10. According to the James–Lange theory, emotions have specific patterns of arousal and _____.

MULTIPLE CHOICE

1. **Money, food, and a sexually attractive person can all be viewed as**
   a. drives.
   b. physiological.
   c. incentives.
   d. psychological.

2. **Drive-reduction theory defines hunger, pain, and thirst as**
   a. primary drives.
   b. instincts.
   c. secondary drives.
   d. acquired motives.

3. **The _____ is signaled when there is a drop in blood sugar due to food deprivation.**
   a. hypothalamus
   b. basilar membrane
   c. corpus callosum
   d. medulla

4. **Whenever Farah eats, she immediately excuses herself and goes to the rest room and vomits. Farah is most likely to be diagnosed with**
   a. anorexia nervosa.
   b. bulimia nervosa.
   c. aphagia.
   d. a disorder in the thyroid gland.

5. **Performance goals are to _____ rewards as learning goals are to _____ rewards.**
   a. intrinsic; extrinsic
   b. satisfaction with self; prestige
   c. extrinsic; intrinsic
   d. none of these

6. **According to the text, which of the following hormones is most strongly connected with the sex drive in women?**
   a. Estrogen
   b. Prolactin
   c. Oxytocin
   d. Testosterone

7. **Identical (MZ) twins have the same sexual orientation about _____ percent of the time.**
   a. 12
   b. 32
   c. 52
   d. 72

8. **Fear involves activation of the _____ nervous system, but depression involves activation of the _____ nervous system.**
   a. peripheral; somatic
   b. somatic; peripheral
   c. parasympathetic; sympathetic
   d. sympathetic; parasympathetic

9. **Which of the following quotes supports the research regarding socioeconomic factors and happiness?**
   a. "Money can't buy you love."
   b. "Good nature is worth more than money."
   c. "Happiness is a warm puppy."
   d. "Having money is better than poverty if only for financial reasons."

10. **Which of the following is correct concerning relationships and happiness?**
   a. People who are married or in enduring relationships report the highest level of happiness.
   b. People who are divorced or separated are happiest.
   c. People who are single are happiest.
   d. People who have a series of casual sexual relationships are happiest.

9 | The Voyage through the Life Span

LEARNING OUTCOMES

After studying this chapter, you will be able to …

9-1 Describe the events of prenatal development and the role that sex hormones play.

9-2 Explain the physical, cognitive, moral, social, and emotional development of children.

9-3 Explain the physical, cognitive, moral, social, and emotional development of adolescents.

9-4 Explain the features of emerging adulthood.

9-5 Explain the physical, cognitive, moral, social, and emotional development of adults.

After you finish this chapter, go to **PAGE 254** for STUDY TOOLS

Billions make the **voyage**, yet each is unique.

We have a story to tell. An important story. A fascinating story about the remarkable voyage you have already taken through childhood and adolescence. It is about the unfolding of your adult life. Billions have made this voyage before. Yet you are unique, and things will happen to you that have never happened before.

Developmental psychologists are interested in studying our voyage through the life span for several reasons. The discovery of early influences and developmental sequences helps psychologists understand adults. Psychologists are also interested in the effects of genetic factors, early interactions with parents and siblings, and the school and community on traits such as aggressiveness and intelligence.

Developmental psychologists also seek to learn the causes of developmental abnormalities. For example, should pregnant women abstain from smoking and drinking? (Yes.) What factors contribute to child abuse? Other developmental psychologists focus on adult development. For example, what can we expect as we voyage through our 30s, 40s, 50s, and beyond? The information developmental psychologists acquire can help us make decisions about how we rear our children and lead our own lives. Let's now turn to prenatal developments—the changes that occur between conception and birth. They are spectacular, but they occur "out of sight."

9-1 PRENATAL DEVELOPMENT

The most dramatic gains in height and weight occur during prenatal development. Within nine months, the newly conceived organism develops from a nearly microscopic cell to a *neonate* (newborn) about 20 inches long. Its weight increases a billion fold!

During the months following conception, the single cell formed by the union of sperm and egg—the **zygote**—multiplies, becoming two cells, then four, then eight, and so on. Following conception (which takes place in the fallopian tube), the zygote divides repeatedly as it proceeds on its three- to four-day voyage to the uterus. The ball-like mass of multiplying cells wanders about the uterus for another three to four days before beginning to implant in the uterine wall. Implantation takes another week or so. The period from conception to implantation is called the **germinal stage**.

The *embryonic stage* lasts from implantation until about the eighth week of development. During this stage, the major body organ systems take form. As you can see from Figure 9.1,

> "THERE IS NO CURE FOR LIFE OR DEATH SAVE TO ENJOY THE INTERVAL."
>
> GEORGE SANTAYANA, PHILOSOPHER, POET, AND NOVELIST (1863–1952)

zygote a fertilized ovum (egg cell)

germinal stage the first stage of prenatal development, during which the dividing mass of cells has not become implanted in the uterine wall

Truth or Fiction?

WHAT DO YOU THINK? Folklore, common sense, or nonsense? Select T for "truth" or F for "fiction," and then check the accuracy of your answers as you read through the chapter.

T	F	Your heart started beating when you were only one-fifth of an inch long and weighed a fraction of an ounce.
T	F	Prior to six months or so of age, "out of sight" is literally "out of mind."
T	F	"Because mommy wants me to" may be a perfectly good explanation for a 3-year-old."
T	F	It is normal for male adolescents to think of themselves as action heroes and to act as though they are made of steel.
T	F	The architect Frank Lloyd Wright designed New York's innovative spiral-shaped Guggenheim Museum when he was 65 years old.
T	F	Alzheimer's disease is a normal part of aging.
T	F	Most parents suffer from the "empty-nest syndrome" when their youngest child leaves home.

FIG.9.1 DRAMATIC EVENTS IN THE WOMB

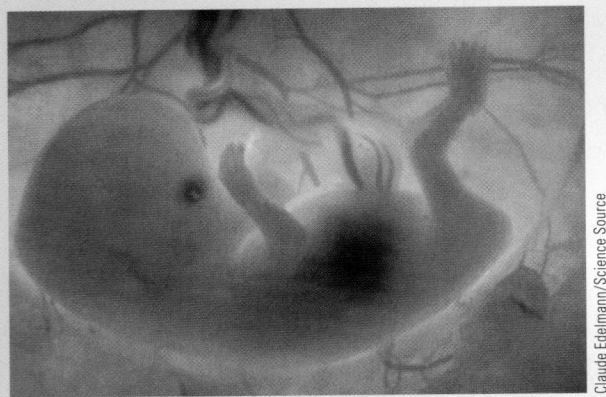

Claude Edelmann/Science Source

By the end of the first trimester, formation of all the major organ systems is complete. Fingers and toes are fully formed, and the sex of the fetus can be determined visually.

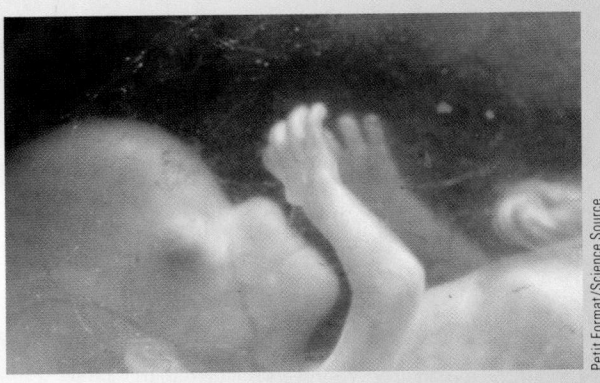

Petit Format/Science Source

At this midway point between conception and birth, the fetus is covered with fine, downy hair, called _lanugo_.

the growth of the head precedes that of other parts of the body. The growth of the organs—heart, lungs, and so on—also precedes the growth of the extremities. The relatively early _maturation_ of the brain and the organ systems allows them to participate in the nourishment and further development of the embryo. The heart will continue to beat without rest every minute of every day for most of a century, perhaps longer.

During the second month, the nervous system begins to transmit messages. By five to six weeks, the embryo is only a quarter-inch to a half-inch long, yet nondescript sex organs have formed. By about the seventh week, the genetic code (XY or XX) begins to assert itself, causing the sex organs to differentiate. If a Y sex chromosome is present, testes form and begin to produce _androgens_ (male sex hormones), which further masculinize the sex organs. In the absence of these hormones, the embryo develops sex organs typical of the female, regardless of its genetic code.

By the end of the second month, the head has become rounded and the facial features distinct—all in an embryo that is about one-inch long and weighs one thirtieth of an ounce.

As it develops, the embryo is suspended within a protective **amniotic sac** in the mother's uterus. The sac is surrounded by a clear membrane and contains amniotic fluid. The fluid

serves as a natural air bag, allowing the child to move around without injury. It also helps maintain an even temperature.

From now until birth, the embryo exchanges nutrients and wastes with the mother through the **placenta**. The embryo is connected to the placenta by the **umbilical cord**. The placenta is connected to the mother by blood vessels in the uterine wall.

The _fetal stage_ lasts from the beginning of the third month until birth. By the end of the third month, the major organ systems and the fingers and toes have formed. In the middle of the fourth month, the mother usually detects the first fetal movements. By the end of the sixth month, the fetus moves its limbs so vigorously that mothers often feel that they are being kicked. The fetus opens and shuts its eyes, sucks its thumb, and alternates between periods of wakefulness and sleep.

During the three months prior to birth, the organ systems of the fetus continue to mature. The heart and lungs become increasingly capable of sustaining independent life. The fetus gains about 5½ pounds and doubles

amniotic sac a sac within the uterus that contains the embryo or fetus

placenta a membrane that permits the exchange of nutrients and waste products between the mother and her developing child but does not allow the maternal and fetal bloodstreams to mix

umbilical cord a tube between the mother and her developing child through which nutrients and waste products are conducted

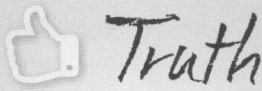

👍 _Truth_

| T | F | Your heart started beating when you were only one-fifth of an inch long and weighed a fraction of an ounce. |

It is true that your heart started beating when you were only one-fifth of an inch long and weighed a fraction of an ounce. Key organ systems develop early.

in length. Newborn boys average about 7½ pounds and newborn girls about 7 pounds.

9-2 CHILDHOOD

Childhood begins with birth. When my children are enjoying themselves, I kid them and say, "Stop having fun. You're a child, and childhood is the worst time of life." I get a laugh because they know that childhood is supposed to be the best time of life—a time for play and learning and endless possibilities. In this section, we see that childhood is an exciting time of physical, cognitive, and social and emotional developments.

9-2a PHYSICAL DEVELOPMENT

During infancy—the first two years of childhood—dramatic gains in height and weight continue. Babies usually double their birth weight in about five months and triple it by their first birthday (World Health Organization, 2010a, 2010b). Their height increases by about 10 inches in the first year. Children grow another four to six inches during the second year and gain some four to seven pounds. After that, they gain about two to three inches a year until they reach the adolescent growth spurt. Weight gains also remain fairly even at about four to six pounds per year until the spurt. Other aspects of physical development in childhood include reflexes and perceptual development.

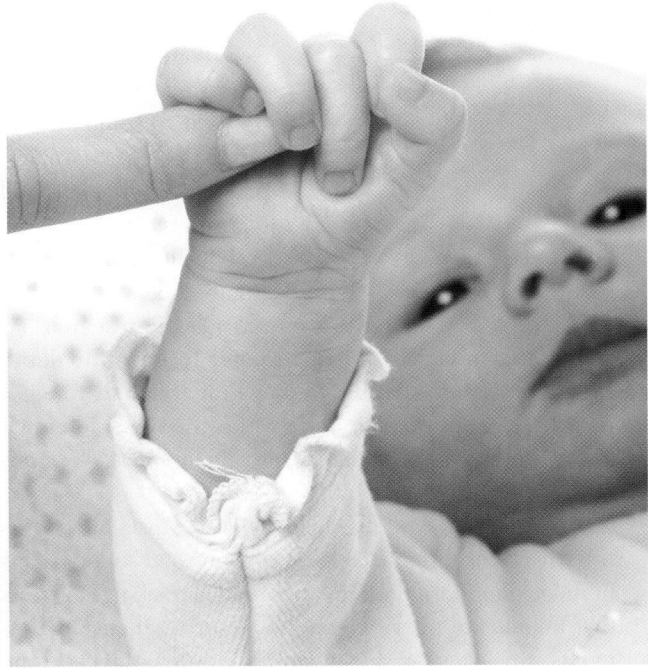

©Juriah Mosin/Shutterstock.com

REFLEXES Soon after you were born, a doctor or nurse probably pressed her fingers against the palms of your hands. Most likely you grasped the fingers firmly—so firmly that you could have been lifted from your cradle! Grasping at birth is inborn, an example of the importance of nature in human development. Grasping is one of the baby's reflexes. **Reflexes** are simple, inborn responses elicited by specific stimuli. Reflexes are essential to survival and occur automatically—that is, without thinking about them.

Newborn children do not know that it is necessary to eat to survive. Fortunately, rooting and sucking reflexes cause them to eat. They turn their head toward stimuli that prod or stroke the cheek, chin, or corner of the mouth. This is termed **rooting**. They also automatically suck objects that touch their lips.

Newborns use the *withdrawal reflex* to avoid painful stimuli. In the *startle*, or *Moro*, *reflex*, they draw up their legs and arch their backs in response to sudden noises, bumps, or loss of support while being held. They grasp objects that press against the palms of their hands (the *grasp*, or *palmar*, *reflex*). They fan their toes when the soles of their feet are stimulated (the *Babinski reflex*). Pediatricians test these reflexes to assess babies' neural functioning. Babies also breathe, sneeze, cough, yawn, blink, defecate, and urinate reflexively.

MOTOR DEVELOPMENT The motor development of the child refers to the progression from simple acts like lifting the head to running around. Maturation and experience both play key roles in motor development. Maturation of the brain is a key to motor development. Motor development provides some of the most fascinating changes in infants, in part because so much seems to happen so quickly—and so much of it during the first year. Children go through a sequence that includes rolling over, sitting up, crawling, creeping, walking, and running. The ages at which infants first engage in these activities vary, but the sequence generally remains the same (see Figure 9.2). Invariant sequences suggest an unfolding of the genetic code (maturation).

The role of maturation in areas such as physical development (for example, gains in height and weight and the effects of puberty), language development, and motor development is clear. But environmental factors are also involved. Children may have certain genetic potentials for body size and growth

reflex a simple inborn response to a stimulus

rooting the turning of an infant's head toward a touch, such as by the mother's nipple

Age (weeks)

Turns from stomach to side

Turns from stomach to back

Turns from back to stomach

Sits up

Crawls

Kneels up

Creeps

Stands up

Starts walking

Full walking

© 2012 Cengage Learning®

PERCEPTUAL DEVELOPMENT Newborn children spend about 16 hours a day sleeping and do not have much opportunity to learn about the world. Yet they perceive the world reasonably well soon after birth. Within a couple of days, infants can follow, or "track," a moving light with their eyes. By three months, they can discriminate most colors. Newborns are nearsighted (that is, they focus better on nearby than distant objects), but by about four months, infants focus on distant objects about as well as adults do (S. P. Johnson, 2011).

The visual preferences of infants are measured by the amount of time, termed **fixation time**, they spend looking at one stimulus instead of another. In classic research by Robert Fantz (1961), two-month-old infants preferred visual stimuli that resembled the human face to newsprint, a bull's-eye, and featureless red, white, and yellow disks (see Figure 9.3).

Classic research has shown that infants tend to respond to cues for depth by the time they are able to crawl (at about six to eight months). Most also have the good sense to avoid crawling off ledges and tabletops into open space (Campos et al., 1978; Dahl et al., 2013).

Normal newborns hear well. Most newborns reflexively turn their heads toward unusual sounds. This finding, along with findings about visual tracking, suggests that infants are preprogrammed to survey their environments. Speaking or singing softly in a low-pitched tone

rates, but they do not reach them unless environmental factors such as nutrition, relatively clean air, and so on are available. Children do not understand or produce language until their genetic codes spark the development of certain structures and processes in the brain. But the environment is also involved. Children learn the languages used in their homes and communities. They do not speak foreign tongues without being exposed to them.

fixation time the amount of time spent looking at a visual stimulus

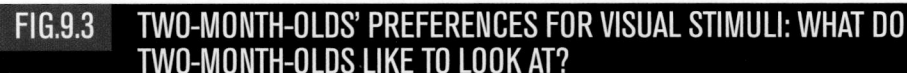

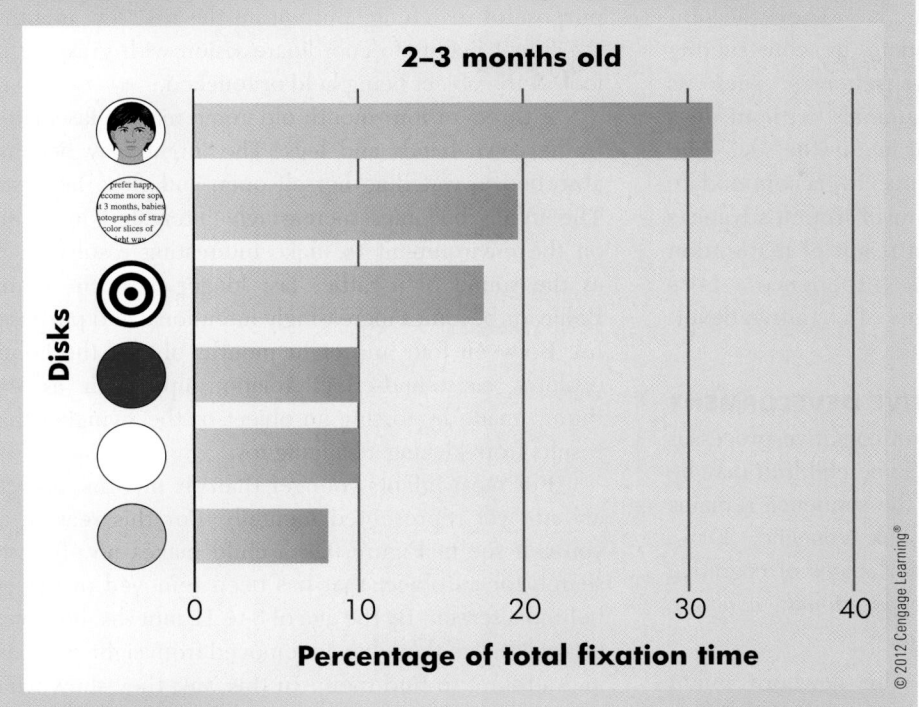

© 2012 Cengage Learning®

the Russian psychologist Lev Semenovich Vygotsky. Then we focus on Lawrence Kohlberg's theory of moral development.

JEAN PIAGET'S COGNITIVE-DEVELOPMENTAL THEORY

Jean Piaget (1896–1980) earned his Ph.D. in biology. In 1920, he obtained a job at the Binet Institute in Paris, where work on intelligence tests was being conducted. His first task was to adapt English verbal reasoning items for use with French children. To do so, he had to try out the items on children in various age groups and see whether they could arrive at correct answers. The task was boring until Piaget became intrigued by the children's *wrong* answers. Another investigator might have shrugged them off, but Piaget perceived patterns in the children's "mistakes." The wrong answers reflected consistent, if illogical, cognitive processes. Piaget's observations led to his theory of cognitive development.

ASSIMILATION Piaget described human thought, or intelligence, in terms of the concepts of assimilation and accommodation. **Assimilation** means responding to a new stimulus through existing cognitive structures.

Infants, for example, usually try to place new objects in their mouth to suck, feel, or explore. Piaget would say that the child is assimilating a new toy to the sucking schema. A **schema** is a pattern of action or a "mental structure" involved in acquiring or organizing knowledge.

ACCOMMODATION Accommodation is the creation of new ways of responding to objects or looking at the world. With accommodation, children transform existing schemas to incorporate new events. For example, children

assimilation according to Piaget, the inclusion of a new event into an existing schema

schema according to Piaget, a hypothetical mental structure that permits the classification and organization of new information

accommodation according to Piaget, the modification of schemas so that information inconsistent with existing schemas can be integrated or understood

soothes infants. This is why lullabies help infants fall asleep.

Research indicates that neonates prefer their mother's voice to those of other women, but they do not show a preference for their father's voice (DeCasper & Prescott, 1984; Freeman et al., 1993). Babies, of course, have had months of "experience" in the uterus. For at least two or three months before birth, they have been able to hear. Because they are predominantly exposed to sounds produced by their mother, learning may contribute to newborn preferences. Neonates can also discriminate distinct odors, and their preferences are quite similar to those of older children and adults (Werner & Bernstein, 2001).

9-2b COGNITIVE DEVELOPMENT

This section explores the ways in which children mentally represent and think about the world—that is, their *cognitive development*. Because cognitive functioning develops over many years, young children have ideas about the world that differ considerably from those of adults. Many of these ideas are charming but illogical—at least to adults. Let's consider three views of cognitive development. We begin with Jean Piaget's stage theory of cognitive development. Next we turn to the views of

who study biology learn that whales cannot be assimilated into the "fish" schema. They accommodate by constructing new schemas, such as "mammals without legs that live in the sea." The ability to accommodate to novel stimuli advances as a result of maturation and experience. Let's apply these concepts to the stages of cognitive development.

PIAGET'S STAGES OF COGNITIVE DEVELOPMENT

Piaget hypothesized that children's cognitive processes develop in an orderly sequence. Some children may be more advanced than others, but the sequence remains the same (Taber, 2013; Tryphon & Voneche, 2013). Piaget (1963) identified four major stages of cognitive development: *sensorimotor, preoperational, concrete operational,* and *formal operational.*

THE SENSORIMOTOR STAGE The newborn infant is capable of assimilating novel stimuli only to existing reflexes (or ready-made schemas) such as the rooting and sucking reflexes. But by the time an infant reaches the age of one month, he or she already shows purposeful behavior by repeating behavior patterns that are pleasurable, such as *-m* sucking his or her hand. During the first month or so, an infant apparently does not connect stimuli perceived through different senses. Reflexive turning toward sources of auditory and olfactory stimulation cannot be considered purposeful searching. But within the first few months, the infant begins to coordinate vision with grasping to look at the object being held or touched.

A three- or four-month-old infant may be fascinated by her own hands and legs. The infant may become absorbed in watching herself open and close her fists. The infant becomes increasingly interested in acting on the environment to make interesting results (such as the sound of a rattle) last longer or occur again. Behavior becomes increasingly intentional and purposeful. Between four and eight months of age, the infant explores cause-and-effect relationships such as the thump made by tossing an object or the swinging that results from kicking a hanging toy.

For most infants younger than six months, objects are not yet represented mentally. For this reason, as you can see in Figure 9.4, a child makes no effort to search for an object that has been removed or placed behind a screen. By the age of 8 to 12 months, however, infants realize that objects removed from sight still exist and attempt to find them. In this way, they show what is known as **object permanence**, thereby making it possible to play peekaboo (Kibbe & Leslie, 2013; Lowe et al., 2013).

Between one and two years of age, children begin to show interest in how things are constructed. It may be for this reason that they persistently touch and finger their parents' faces and their own. Toward the end of the second year, children begin to engage in mental trial and error before they try out overt behaviors. For example, when they look for an object you have removed, they will no longer begin their search in the last place they saw it. Rather, they may follow you, assuming you are carrying the object even though it is not visible. It is as though they are anticipating failure in searching for the object in the place where they last saw it.

Because the first stage of development is dominated by learning to coordinate perception of the self and of the environment with motor activity, Piaget termed it the **sensorimotor stage**. This stage comes to a close with the acquisition of the basics of language at about age two.

- schemes
- adaptation
- assimilation
- accommodation
- equilibration

Piaget's early training as a biologist led him to view children as mentally assimilating and accommodating aspects of their environment.

Farrell Grehan/Historical/Corbis

FIG.9.4 OBJECT PERMANENCE, OR NOT? OUT OF SIGHT, OUT OF MIND?

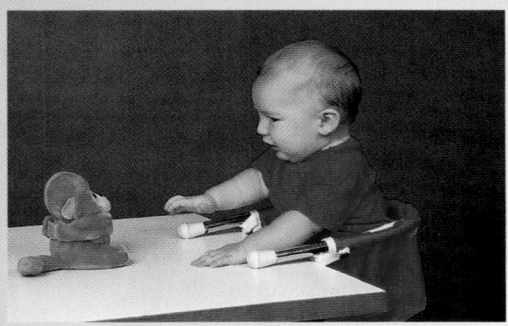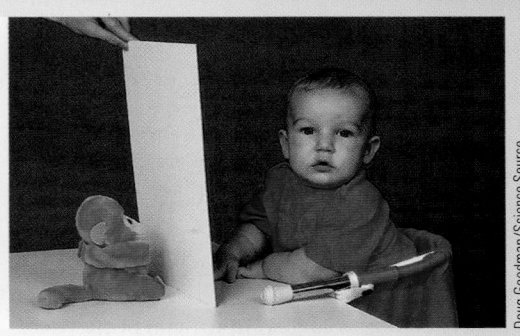

To this infant, who is in the early part of the sensorimotor stage, out of sight is truly out of mind. Once a sheet of paper is placed between the infant and the toy animal, the infant loses all interest in it. The toy is apparently not yet mentally represented.

THE PREOPERATIONAL STAGE The **preoperational stage** is characterized by the use of words and symbols to represent objects and relationships among them. But be warned—any resemblance between the logic of children between the ages of two and seven and your own logic may be coincidental. Children may use the same words as adults, but this does not mean their views of the world are the same. Preoperational children tend to think one-dimensionally—to focus on one aspect of a problem or situation at a time.

One consequence of one-dimensional thinking is **egocentrism**. Preoperational children cannot understand that other people do not see things the same way they do. When one of my daughters was 2½, I asked her to tell me about a trip to the store with her mother. "You tell me," she replied. She did not seem to understand that I could not see the world through her eyes.

To egocentric preoperational children, all the world's a stage that has been erected to meet their needs and amuse them. When asked, "What are television sets for?", they may answer, "To watch my favorite shows and cartoons." Preoperational children also show *animism.* They attribute life and consciousness to physical objects like the sun and the moon. In addition, they also show *artificialism.* They believe that environmental events like rain and thunder are human inventions. Asked what causes thunder, a four-year-old may reply "A man grumbling." Examples of egocentrism, animism, and artificialism are shown in Table 9.1.

To gain further insight into preoperational thinking, find a three- or four-year-old and try these miniexperiments:

▶ Pour water from a tall, thin glass into a low, wide glass. Now, ask the child whether the low, wide glass contains more, less, or the same amount of water that was in the tall, thin glass. If the child says that they hold the same amount of

preoperational stage the second of Piaget's stages, characterized by illogical use of words and symbols, spotty logic, and egocentrism

egocentrism according to Piaget, the assumption that others view the world as one does oneself

© Cengage Learning 2012

TABLE 9.1 EXAMPLES OF PREOPERATIONAL THOUGHT

Type of Thought	Sample Questions	Typical Answers
EGOCENTRISM	Why does it get dark out?	So I can go to sleep.
	Why does the sun shine?	To keep me warm.
	Why is there snow?	For me to play in.
ANIMISM	Why do trees have leaves?	To keep them warm.
	Why do stars twinkle?	Because they're happy and cheerful.
ARTIFICIALISM	What makes it rain?	Someone emptying a watering can.
	Why is the sky blue?	Somebody painted it.
	What is the wind?	A man blowing.

water, the child is correct. But if the child errs, why do you think this is so?

▶ Now flatten a ball of clay into a pancake, and ask the child whether you wind up with more, less, or the same amount of clay. If the child errs again, why do you think this is so?

To arrive at the correct answers to these questions, children must understand the law of **conservation**. This law holds that basic properties of substances such as mass, weight, and volume remain the same—that is, are *conserved*—when one changes superficial properties such as their shape or arrangement.

Conservation requires the ability to think about, or *center* on, two aspects of a situation at once, such as height and width. Conserving the mass, weight, or volume of a substance requires the recognition that a change in one dimension can compensate for a change in another. But the preoperational boy in Figure 9.5 focuses on only one dimension at a time. First he is shown two short, squat glasses of water and agrees that they contain the same amount of water. Then, while he watches, water is poured from a squat glass into a tall, thin glass. Now he is asked which glass contains more water.

After mulling over the problem, he points to the tall glass. Why? Because when he looks at the glasses he is "overwhelmed" by the fact that the thinner glass is taller. The preoperational child focuses on the most apparent dimension of the situation—in this case, the greater height of the thinner glass. He does not realize that the increased width of the squat glass compensates for the decreased height.

Piaget (1997) found that the moral judgment of preoperational children is also one-dimensional. Five-year-olds tend to be slaves to rules and authority. When you ask them why something should be done in a certain way, they may insist, "Because that's the way to do it!" or "Because Mommy says so!" Right is right and wrong is wrong. Why? "Because!"—that's why.

According to most older children and adults, an act is a crime only when there is criminal intent. Accidents may be hurtful, but the perpetrators are usually seen as blameless. But in the court of the one-dimensional, preoperational child, there is **objective responsibility**. People are sentenced (and harshly!) on the basis of the amount of damage they have done, not their motives or intentions. To demonstrate objective responsibility, Piaget would tell children stories and ask them which character was naughtier and why. John, for example, accidentally breaks 15 cups when he opens a door. Henry breaks one cup when he sneaks into a kitchen cabinet to find forbidden jam. The preoperational child usually judges John to be naughtier. Why? Because he broke more cups.

conservation according to Piaget, recognition that basic properties of substances such as weight and mass remain the same when superficial features change

objective responsibility according to Piaget, the assignment of blame according to the amount of damage done rather than the motives of the actor

FIG.9.5 CONSERVATION: IS IT THE SAME OR IS IT DIFFERENT?

© Cengage Learning 2012

A.

B.

C.

(a) The boy in this illustration agreed that the amount of water in two identical containers is equal. (b) He then watched as water from one container was poured into a tall, thin container. (c) When asked whether the amounts of water in the two containers are now the same, he says no.

THE CONCRETE OPERATIONAL STAGE By about age seven, the typical child is entering the **concrete operational stage**. In this stage, which lasts until about age 12, children show the beginnings of the capacity for adult logic. However, their logical thoughts, or *operations,* generally involve tangible objects rather than abstract ideas. Concrete operational children are capable of **decentration**; they can center on two dimensions of a problem at once. This attainment has implications for moral judgments, conservation, and other intellectual undertakings.

Children now show **subjective moral judgments**. When assigning guilt, they center on the motives of wrongdoers as well as on the amount of damage done. Concrete operational children judge Henry more harshly than John because John's misdeed was an accident.

Concrete operational children understand the laws of conservation. The boy in Figure 9.5, now a few years older, would say that the squat glass still contains the same amount of juice. If asked why, he might reply, "Because you can pour it back into the other one." Such an answer also suggests awareness of the concept of *reversibility*— the recognition that many processes can be reversed or undone so that things are restored to their previous condition. Centering simultaneously on the height and the width of the glasses,

To a preoperational child, right is right and wrong is wrong. Why? "Because!"—that's why.

the boy recognizes that the loss in height compensates for the gain in width.

Children in this stage are less egocentric. They are able to take on the roles of others and to view the world, and themselves, from other people's perspectives. They recognize that people see things in different ways because of different situations and sets of values.

During the concrete operational stage, children's own sets of values begin to emerge and acquire stability. Children come to understand that feelings of love between them and their parents can endure even when someone is temporarily angry or disappointed. We continue our discussion of Piaget's theory—his stage of *formal operations*—later in the chapter in the section on adolescence.

EVALUATION OF PIAGET'S THEORY A number of questions have been raised concerning the accuracy of Piaget's views. Among them are these:

▶ *Was Piaget's timing accurate?* Some critics argue that Piaget's methods led him to underestimate children's abilities (Meltzoff et al., 2013; Reed, 2013). Other researchers using different methods have found, for example, that preschoolers are less egocentric and that children are capable of conservation at earlier ages than Piaget thought.

▶ *Does cognitive development occur in stages?* Cognitive events such as egocentrism and conservation appear to develop more continuously than Piaget thought—that is, they may not occur in stages (Fuller, 2011; Reed, 2013). Although cognitive developments appear to build on previous cognitive developments, the process may be more gradual than stage like.

▶ *Are developmental sequences always the same?* Here, Piaget's views have fared better. It seems there is no variation in the sequence in which cognitive developments occur.

concrete operational stage Piaget's third stage, characterized by logical thought concerning tangible objects, conservation, and subjective morality

decentration simultaneous focusing on more than one dimension of a problem, so that flexible, reversible thought becomes possible

subjective moral judgment according to Piaget, moral judgment that is based on the motives of the perpetrator

Comstock/Stockbyte/Getty Images

In sum, Piaget's theoretical edifice has been rocked, but it has not been reduced to rubble. Now let's consider the views of Lev Vygotsky (1896–1934), a Russian psychologist whose work was banned in communist Russia. Unlike Piaget, Vygotsky was not a stage theorist. Instead, he saw the transmission of knowledge from generation to generation as cumulative, and focused on the ways in which children's interactions with their elders enhance their cognitive development.

LEV VYGOTSKY'S SOCIOCULTURAL THEORY The term *sociocultural theory* has different meanings. For example, the term can refer to the roles of factors such as ethnicity and gender in behavior and mental processes. But Vygotsky's sociocultural theory focuses instead on the ways in which children's cognitive development is influenced by the cultures in which they are reared and the people who teach them.

Vygotsky's theory (1978) focuses on the transmission of information and cognitive skills from generation to generation. The transmission of skills involves teaching and learning, but Vygotsky did not view learning as a mechanical process that can be described in terms of conditioning. Rather, he focused more generally on how the child's social interaction with adults, largely in the home, organized a child's learning experiences in such a way that the child can obtain cognitive skills—such as computation or reading skills—and use them to acquire information. Like Piaget, Vygotsky saw the child's functioning as adaptive (Piaget & Smith, 2000), and the child adapts to his or her social and cultural interactions.

Key concepts in Vygotsky's theory include the *zone of proximal development* and *scaffolding*. The word *proximal* means "nearby" or "close," as in the words *approximate* and *proximity*. The

zone of proximal development (ZPD) refers to a range of tasks that a child can carry out with the help of someone who is more skilled (Haenen, 2001). The "zone" refers to the relationship between the child's abilities and what she or he can do with help from others. Adults or older children best guide the child through this zone by gearing their assistance to the child's capabilities (Flavell et al., 2002).

Within the zone, the child works with and learns from others (Meijer & Elshout, 2001). When learning with others, the child tends to internalize—or bring inward—the conversations and explanations that help him or her gain skills (Murata & Fuson, 2006; Umek et al., 2005). Children not only learn the meanings of words from teachers but also learn ways of talking to themselves about solving problems within a cultural context. Outer speech becomes inner speech. What was the teacher's becomes the child's. What was a social and cultural context becomes embedded within the child; thus we have the term, *sociocultural theory.*

A *scaffold* is a temporary skeletal structure that enables workers to fabricate a building, bridge, or other, more permanent, structure. Cognitive **scaffolding** refers to the temporary support provided by a parent or teacher to a child who is learning to perform a task. The amount of guidance decreases as the child becomes more skilled and self-sufficient. In Vygotsky's theory, teachers and parents provide children with problem-solving methods that serve as cognitive scaffolding while the child gains the ability to function independently.

Piaget's focus was largely maturational. It was assumed that maturation of the brain allowed the child to experience new levels of insights and suddenly develop new kinds of problem solving. Vygotsky focused on the processes in the teacher–learner relationship. To Vygotsky, cognitive development was about culture and social interaction (Fuentes-Fernandez et al., 2014; Grossman & Na, 2014). Let's now turn to another aspect of cognitive development—the ways

According to Vygotsky's theory, teachers and parents provide children with problem-solving methods that serve as cognitive scaffolding.

Brand X Pictures/Jupiter Images

in which children (and adults) arrive at judgments about what is right and what is wrong.

LAWRENCE KOHLBERG'S THEORY OF MORAL DEVELOPMENT Cognitive-developmental theorist Lawrence Kohlberg (1981) used the following tale in his research into children's moral reasoning:

> *In Europe a woman was near death from a special kind of cancer. There was one drug that the doctors thought might save her. It was a form of radium that a druggist in the same town had recently discovered. The drug was expensive to make, but the druggist was charging 10 times what the drug cost him to make. He paid $200 for the radium and charged $2,000 for a small dose of the drug. The sick woman's husband, Heinz, went to everyone he knew to borrow the money, but he could only get together about $1,000, which was half of what it cost. He told the druggist that his wife was dying and asked him to sell it cheaper or let him pay later. But the druggist said: "No, I discovered the drug, and I'm going to make money from it." So Heinz got desperate and broke into the man's store to steal the drug for his wife (Kohlberg, 1969).*

Heinz is caught in a moral dilemma. A legal or social rule (in this case, the law forbidding stealing) is pitted against a strong human need (his desire to save his wife). Children and adults arrive at yes or no answers for different reasons. According to Kohlberg, the reasons can be classified according to their level of moral development.

> "WE FIND DELIGHT IN THE BEAUTY AND HAPPINESS OF CHILDREN THAT MAKES THE HEART TOO BIG FOR THE BODY."
>
> RALPH WALDO EMERSON, ESSAYIST, LECTURER, AND POET (1803–1882)

As a stage theorist, Kohlberg argues that the stages of moral reasoning follow a specific sequence. Children progress at different rates, and not all children (or adults) reach the highest stage. But the sequence is always the same: Children must go through stage 1 before they enter stage 2, and so on. According to Kohlberg, there are three levels of moral development and two stages within each level.

When it comes to the dilemma of Heinz, Kohlberg believed that people could justify Heinz's theft of the drug or his decision not to steal it by the reasoning of any level or stage of moral development. In other words, Kohlberg was not as interested in the eventual "yes" or "no" as he was in *how a person reasoned* to arrive at yes or no.

THE PRECONVENTIONAL LEVEL The **preconventional level** applies to most children through about the age of nine. Children at this level base their moral judgments on the consequences of behavior. For example, stage 1 is oriented toward obedience and punishment. Good behavior is obedient and allows one to avoid punishment. However, a child in stage 1 can decide that Heinz should or should not steal the drug.

In stage 2, good behavior allows people to satisfy their needs and those of others. (Heinz's wife needs the drug; therefore, stealing it—the only way of obtaining it—is not wrong.)

THE CONVENTIONAL LEVEL In the **conventional level** of moral reasoning, right and wrong are judged by conformity to conventional (familial, religious, societal) standards of right and wrong. According to the stage 3 "good-boy orientation," moral behavior is that which meets the needs and expectations of others. Moral behavior is what is "normal"—what the majority does. (Heinz should steal the drug because that is what a "good husband" would do. It is "natural" or "normal" to try to help one's wife. *Or* Heinz should *not* steal the drug because "good people do not steal.")

In stage 4, moral judgments are based on rules that maintain the social order. Showing respect for authority and doing one's duty are valued highly. (Heinz *must* steal the drug; it would be his fault if he let his wife die. He would pay the druggist later, when he had the money.) Many people do not mature beyond the conventional level.

THE POSTCONVENTIONAL LEVEL Postconventional moral reasoning is more complex and focuses on dilemmas in which individual needs are pitted against the need to maintain the social order and on personal conscience. We discuss the postconventional level later in the chapter in the section on adolescence.

EVALUATION OF KOHLBERG'S THEORY As Kohlberg's theory predicts, evidence supports

preconventional level according to Kohlberg, a period during which moral judgments are based largely on expectation of rewards or punishments

conventional level according to Kohlberg, a period during which moral judgments largely reflect social conventions; a "law and order" approach to morality

the view that the moral judgments of children develop in an upward sequence (Boom et al., 2007). Postconventional thought, if found at all, first occurs in adolescence. Formal-operational thinking is apparently a prerequisite, and education is likely to play a role (Moshman, 2011). Postconventional reasoning involves understanding of abstract moral principles and empathy with the views and feelings of others.

Kohlberg believed that the stages of moral development were universal, but he may have underestimated the influence of social, cultural, and educational institutions (Nather, 2013). Parents are also important. Using reason in discipline and discussing the feelings of others advance moral reasoning (Nather, 2013).

9-2c SOCIAL AND EMOTIONAL DEVELOPMENT

Social relationships are crucial to us as children. When we are infants, our very survival depends on them. Later in life, they contribute to our feelings of happiness and satisfaction. In this section, we discuss social development in childhood.

ERIK ERIKSON'S STAGES OF PSYCHOSOCIAL DEVELOPMENT According to Erik Erikson, we undergo several stages of psychosocial development. During Erikson's first stage, *trust versus mistrust,* we depend on our primary care-givers (usually our parents) and come to expect that our environments will—or will not—meet our needs. Toddlers through about the age of three are said to be in the stage of *autonomy versus shame and doubt.* During this period, their relationships with parents and friends can encourage the development of self-direction and initiative, or feelings of shame and guilt. Children in this stage need to develop feelings of self-control over physical functions—such as toileting—and a sense of independence. One of the ways that many children demonstrate their growing autonomy, much to the dismay of their parents, is by refusing to comply with parental requests or commands.

Erikson believed that children are in the stage of *initiative versus guilt* through about the age of five, in which they begin to assert control over the environment and strive to master adult skills. Erikson labeled the

attachment the enduring affectional tie that binds one person to another

Mary D. Salter Ainsworth— attached to a cat?

years of about 6 to 12 the stage of *industry versus inferiority,* during which children meet academic and social challenges in school. A positive outcome contributes to a sense of industry, whereas setbacks can lead to feelings of inferiority. Later we will see that Erikson's theory includes four more stages and straddles the life span.

ATTACHMENT Psychologist Mary D. Salter Ainsworth (1913–1999) defined **attachment** as an emotional tie that is formed between one animal or person and another specific individual. Attachment keeps organisms together—it is vital to the survival of the infant— and it tends to endure. The behaviors that define attachment include (1) attempts to maintain contact or nearness, and (2) shows of anxiety when separated. Babies and children try to maintain contact with caregivers to whom they are attached. They engage in eye contact, pull and tug at them, ask to be picked up, and may even jump in front of them in such a way that they will be "run over" if they are not picked up.

© Robert S. Marvin

THE STRANGE SITUATION AND PATTERNS OF ATTACHMENT The ways in which infants behave in strange situations are connected with their bonds of attachment with their caregivers. Given this fact, Ainsworth and her colleagues (1978) innovated the *strange situation method* to learn how infants respond to separations and reunions with a caregiver (usually the mother) and a stranger. Using this method, Ainsworth and her colleagues identified three major types of attachment, including secure attachment and two types of insecure attachment:

1. *Secure attachment.* Securely attached infants mildly protest their mother's departure, seek interaction upon reunion, and are readily comforted by her.

2. *Avoidant attachment.* Infants who show avoidant attachment are least distressed by their mother's departure. They play by themselves without fuss and ignore their mothers when they return.

3. *Ambivalent/resistant attachment.* Infants with ambivalent/resistant attachment are the most emotional. They show severe signs of distress when their mother leaves and show ambivalence upon reunion by alternately clinging to and pushing their mother away when she returns.

Attachment is connected with the quality of care that infants receive. The parents of securely attached children are more likely to be affectionate and reliable caregivers (George et al., 2010). A wealth of research literature speaks of the benefits of secure attachment. For example, secure children are happier, more sociable, and more cooperative with parents; they get along better with peers and are better adjusted in school (Borelli et al., 2010; George et al., 2010). Insecure attachment in infancy predicts psychological disorders during adolescence (Milan et al., 2013).

PHASES OF ATTACHMENT Ainsworth also identified three phases of attachment:

1. *The initial-preattachment phase,* which lasts from birth to about three months and is characterized by indiscriminate attachment. That is, they prefer being held or being with someone to being alone, but they are generally willing to be held by unfamiliar people.

2. *The attachment-in-the-making phase,* which occurs at about three or four months and is characterized by preference for familiar figures.

3. *The clear-cut-attachment phase,* which occurs at about six or seven months and is

4. characterized by intensified dependence on the primary caregiver.

John Bowlby (1988), a colleague of Ainsworth, believed that attachment is also characterized by fear of strangers ("stranger anxiety"). That is, at about 8 to 10 months of age, children may cry and cling to their parents when strangers try to befriend them. But not all children develop fear of strangers. It therefore does not seem necessary to include fear of strangers as an essential part of the process of attachment.

THEORETICAL VIEWS OF ATTACHMENT Early in the 20th century, behaviorists argued that attachment behaviors are learned through experience. Caregivers feed their infants and tend to their other physiological needs. Thus, infants associate their caregivers with gratification of needs and learn to approach them to meet their needs. The feelings of gratification associated with the meeting of basic needs generalize into feelings of security when the caregiver is present.

Classic research by psychologist Harry F. Harlow suggests that skin contact may be more important than learning experiences. Harlow noted that infant rhesus monkeys reared without mothers or companions became attached to pieces of cloth in their cages. They maintained contact with them and showed distress when separated from them. Harlow conducted a series of experiments to find out why (Harlow, 1959).

In one study, Harlow placed infant rhesus monkeys in cages with two surrogate mothers, as shown in Figure 9.6. One "mother" was made of wire mesh from which a baby bottle was extended. The other surrogate mother was made of soft, cuddly terry cloth. The infant monkeys spent most of their time clinging to the cloth mother, even though "she" did not gratify their need for food. Harlow concluded that monkeys—and perhaps

| FIG.9.6 | ATTACHMENT IN INFANT MONKEYS: WHICH "MOTHER" WOULD YOU PREFER TO HANG OUT ON? |

On Which "Mother" Would You Prefer to Hang Out? Although this rhesus monkey infant is fed by the wire "mother," it spends most of its time clinging to the soft, cuddly, terry cloth "mother." It knows where to get a meal, but contact comfort is apparently more important than food in the development of attachment in infant monkeys (and infant humans).

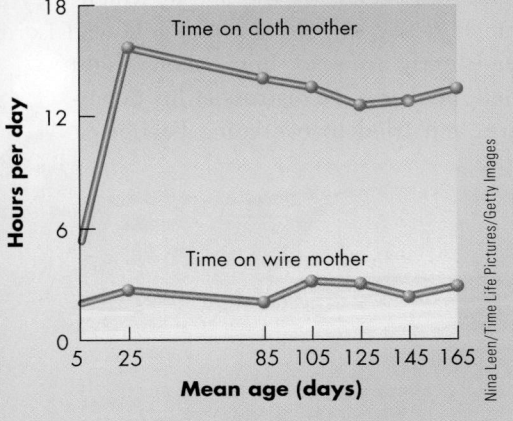

Nina Leen/Time Life Pictures/Getty Images

contact comfort a hypothesized primary drive to seek physical comfort through contact with another

ethologist a scientist who studies the characteristic behavior patterns of species of animals

critical period a period of time when an instinctive response can be elicited by a particular stimulus

imprinting a process occurring during a critical period in the development of an organism, in which that organism responds to a stimulus in a manner that will afterward be difficult to modify

authoritative parents parents who are strict and warm; authoritative parents demand mature behavior but use reason rather than force in discipline

authoritarian parents parents who are rigid in their rules and who demand obedience for the sake of obedience

humans—have an inborn need for **contact comfort** that is as basic as the need for food. Gratification of the need for contact comfort, rather than food, might be why infant monkeys (and humans) cling to their mothers.

Other researchers, such as **ethologist** Konrad Lorenz, argue that for many animals, attachment is an instinct—inborn. (Ethologists study the behavioral characteristics of various species of animals.) Attachment, like other instincts, is theorized to occur in the presence of a specific stimulus and during a **critical period** of life—that is, a period during which the animal is sensitive to the stimulus.

Some animals become attached to the first moving object they encounter. The formation of an attachment in this manner is therefore called **imprinting**. Lorenz (1981) became well known when pictures of his "family" of goslings were made public. How did Lorenz acquire his following? He was present when the goslings hatched and during their critical period, and he allowed them to follow him. The critical period for geese and some other animals is bounded, at the younger end, by the age at which they first walk and, at the older end, by the age at which they develop fear of strangers. The goslings followed Lorenz persistently, ran to him when frightened, honked with distress at his departure, and tried to overcome barriers

between them. If you substitute crying for honking, it all sounds rather human.

Ainsworth and Bowlby (1991) consider attachment to be instinctive in humans. However, among humans attachment is less related to issues such as locomotion and fear of strangers (which is not universal). Moreover, the critical period with humans is quite extended.

PARENTING STYLES Many psychologists have been concerned about the relationships between parenting styles and the personality development of the child. Diana Baumrind (1989; 2005) has been particularly interested in the connections between parental behavior and the development of children's *instrumental competence*—the ability to manipulate the environment to achieve one's goals. Baumrind has focused largely on four aspects of parental behavior: (1) restrictiveness; (2) demands for the child to achieve intellectual, emotional, and social maturity; (3) communication ability; and (4) warmth and involvement. She labeled the three parenting styles the *authoritative, authoritarian,* and *permissive* styles. Other researchers also speak of the *uninvolved* style. These four styles are defined in the following ways:

1. *Authoritative parents.* The parents of the most competent children rate high in all four areas of behavior. Such **authoritative parents** are strict (restrictive) and demand mature behavior. However, they temper their strictness with a desire to reason with their children and with love and support. They expect much, but they explain why and offer help.

2. *Authoritarian parents.* **Authoritarian parents** have strict guidelines about what is right and wrong, and they demand that their children follow those guidelines. Both authoritative and authoritarian parents adhere to strict standards of conduct, but authoritative parents explain their demands and

Nina Leen/Time & Life Pictures/Getty Images

Konrad Lorenz and His Family of Goslings

are supportive, whereas authoritarian parents rely on force and communicate poorly with their children (Larzelere et al., 2013). Authoritarian parents do not respect their children's points of view, and they may be cold and rejecting.

3. *Permissive parents.* **Permissive parents** are generally easygoing with their children. As a result, the children do pretty much what the children want. Permissive parents are warm and supportive, but poor at communicating.

4. *Uninvolved parents.* **Uninvolved parents** tend to leave their children on their own. They make few demands and show little warmth or encouragement.

Research shows that the children of warm parents are more likely to be socially and emotionally well adjusted (Gauvain et al., 2013). They are also more likely to internalize moral standards—that is, to develop a conscience.

Strictness seems to pay off, provided it is tempered with reason and warmth. Children of authoritative parents have greater self-reliance, self-esteem, social competence, and achievement motivation than other children (Gauvain et al., 2013). Children of authoritarian parents are often withdrawn or aggressive and usually do not do as well in school as children of authoritative parents (Laarzelere et al., 2013). Children of permissive parents seem to be less mature. They are often impulsive, moody, and aggressive. In adolescence, lack of parental monitoring is often linked to delinquency and poor academic performance. Children of uninvolved parents tend to obtain poorer grades than children whose parents make demands on them. The children of uninvolved parents also tend to be more likely to hang out with crowds who "party" a good deal and use drugs. The message? Children profit when parents make reasonable demands, show warmth and encouragement, and spend time with them.

9-3 ADOLESCENCE

Perhaps no other period of life is as exciting—and as bewildering— as adolescence. **Adolescence** is bounded by puberty and the assumption of adult responsibilities. Except for infancy, more changes occur during adolescence than during any other time. Like childhood, adolescence entails physical, cognitive, social, and emotional changes.

9-3a PHYSICAL DEVELOPMENT

One of the most noticeable physical developments of adolescence is a growth spurt that lasts two to three years and ends the gradual changes in height and weight that characterize most of childhood. Within this short span of years, adolescents grow some 8 to 12 inches. Most boys wind up taller and heavier than most girls.

PUBERTY: MORE THAN "JUST A PHASE"? Puberty is the period during which the body becomes sexually mature. It heralds the onset of adolescence. Puberty begins with the appearance of **secondary sex characteristics** such as body hair, deepening of the voice in males, and rounding of the breasts and hips in females. In boys, pituitary hormones stimulate the testes to increase the output of testosterone, which in turn causes enlargement of the penis and testes and the appearance of body hair. By the early teens, erections become

> "CHILDREN BEGIN BY LOVING THEIR PARENTS; AS THEY GROW OLDER THEY JUDGE THEM; SOMETIMES THEY FORGIVE THEM."
>
> OSCAR WILDE, IRISH WRITER, PLAYWRIGHT, AND POET (1854–1900)

permissive parents parents who impose few, if any, rules and who do not supervise their children closely

uninvolved parents parents who generally leave their children to themselves

adolescence the period of life bounded by puberty and the assumption of adult responsibilities

puberty the period of physical development during which sexual reproduction first becomes possible

secondary sex characteristics characteristics that distinguish females from males, such as distribution of body hair and depth of voice, but that are not directly involved in reproduction

RubberBall Photography/Veer

common, and boys may ejaculate. Ejaculatory ability usually precedes the presence of mature sperm by at least a year. Ejaculation thus is not evidence of reproductive capacity.

In girls, increases in body weight are believed to trigger a cascade of hormonal secretions in the brain that cause the ovaries to secrete higher levels of the female sex hormone, estrogen (Terasawa et al., 2012). Estrogen stimulates the growth of breast tissue and tissue in the hips and buttocks. The pelvis widens, rounding the hips. Small amounts of androgens produced by the adrenal glands, along with estrogen, spur the growth of pubic and underarm hair. Estrogen and androgens also stoke the development of female sex organs. Estrogen production becomes cyclical during puberty and regulates the menstrual cycle. The beginning of menstruation, or **menarche**, usually occurs between 11 and 14. Girls cannot become pregnant until they ovulate, however, and ovulation may begin a couple of years after menarche.

BRAIN DEVELOPMENT What happens to the brains of adolescents who spend hours a day practicing the piano or the violin? Their learning translates physically into increases in the thickness of the parts of the cerebral cortex that are being used (Ashtari & Cyckowski, 2012; Bermudez et al., 2009). The gains in thickness of the cerebral cortex represent increases in gray matter, which consists of associative neurons that transmit messages back and forth in the brain when we are engaged in thought and sensorimotor activities.

Is All She Doing Learning How to Play the Violin? This adolescent musician is not only learning to play the violin but also thickening the parts of her cerebral cortex that are being used in the effort. Associative neurons are sprouting new axon tips and dendrites, creating new synapses, and enhancing the flow of information.

Photodisc Photography/Veer

Many adolescents show poor judgment, at least from time to time, and take risks that most adults would avoid, such as excessive drinking, reckless driving, violence, disordered eating behavior, and unprotected sexual activity (Smith et al., 2013). Brain immaturity may play a role. Deborah Yurgelun-Todd and her colleagues (Sava & Yurgelun-Todd, 2008) showed pictures of people with fearful expressions to adolescents ranging in age from 11 to 17 while the adolescents' brains were scanned by functional magnetic resonance imaging (fMRI). Compared to adults, the adolescents' frontal lobes (the seat of executive functioning) were less active, and their amygdalas (a part of the limbic system involved in discriminating emotions, including fear) were more active. The adolescents often misread the facial expressions, with those younger than 14 more often inferring sadness, anger, or confusion rather than fear. The researchers suggest that one reason many adolescents fail to show the judgment, insight, and reasoning ability of adults is immaturity of the frontal lobes (Yurgelun-Todd, 2007).

9-3b COGNITIVE DEVELOPMENT

The adolescent thinker approaches problems differently from the elementary school child. A younger child sticks to the facts, to concrete reality. Speculating about abstract possibilities and what might be is very difficult. The adolescent, on the other hand, is able to deal with the abstract and the hypothetical. In this section, we explore some of the cognitive developments of adolescence by referring to the views of Piaget and Kohlberg.

THE STAGE OF FORMAL OPERATIONS According to Piaget, children undergo three stages of cognitive development prior to adolescence: sensorimotor, preoperational, and concrete operational. The **formal operational stage** is the final stage in Piaget's theory, and it represents cognitive maturity. For many children in Western societies, formal operational thought begins at about the beginning of adolescence—the age of 11 or 12. Some people enter this stage later, however, and some never do.

The major achievements of the stage of formal operations involve classification, logical thought, and the ability to hypothesize. Central features are the ability to think about ideas as well as objects and to group and classify ideas—symbols, statements, entire theories. Adolescents can generally follow arguments from premises to conclusions and back again. They can generally appreciate both the outer environment and the world of the imagination: they engage in hypothetical thinking and deductive reasoning.

Formal operational adolescents (and adults) think abstractly. They solve geometric problems about circles and squares without reference to what the circles and squares may represent in the real world. Adolescents in this stage derive rules for behavior from general principles and can focus, or center, on multiple aspects of a situation at once to solve problems.

During the stage of formal operations, adolescents become capable of dealing with hypothetical situations (Amsel, 2011). They realize that situations can have different outcomes, and they think ahead, imagining those outcomes. Adolescents also conduct social "experiments" to test their hypotheses. They may try out various tones of voice and ways of treating others to see what works best for them.

ADOLESCENT EGOCENTRISM Adolescents in the formal operational stage can reason deductively. They classify objects or people and then draw conclusions about them. Adolescents can be proud of their new logical abilities, leading to a new sort of egocentrism: they demand acceptance of their logic without recognizing the exceptions or practical problems that may be considered by adults. Consider this example: "It is

wrong to hurt people. Company A hurts people (perhaps through pollution). Therefore, Company A must be severely punished or shut down." This thinking is logical. But by impatiently demanding major changes or severe penalties, one may not fully consider various practical problems such as the thousands of workers who might be laid off if the company were shut down. Adults have often had life experiences that encourage them to see shades of gray rather than black and white.

The thought of preschoolers is characterized by egocentrism in which they cannot take another's point of view. Adolescent thought is marked by an egocentrism in which they can understand the thoughts of others, but still have trouble separating things that are of concern to others and those that are of concern only to themselves (Elkind, 1967, 1985). Adolescent egocentrism gives rise to two interesting cognitive developments: the *imaginary audience* and the *personal fable*.

The concept of the **imaginary audience** refers to the belief that other people are as concerned with

Thomas Northcut/Stone/Getty Images

imaginary audience an aspect of adolescent egocentrism; the belief that other people are as concerned with our thoughts and behaviors as we are

Adolescents can spend a great deal of time seeking imperfections—or admiring themselves—in the mirror. The concept of the imaginary audience places them on stage, but surrounded more by critics than admirers.

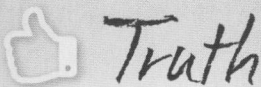
our thoughts and behavior as we are. Adolescents thus see themselves as the center of attention and assume that other people are also preoccupied with their appearance and behavior (Somerville, 2013). Adolescents may feel onstage with all eyes on them. The concept of the imaginary audience may drive the intense adolescent desire for privacy. It helps explain why adolescents are so self-conscious, why they worry about every facial blemish and spend hours grooming. Self-consciousness seems to peak at about 13 and then decline. Girls tend to be more self-conscious than boys (Johnson & Whisman, 2013).

The **personal fable** is the belief that our feelings and ideas are special, even unique, and that we are invulnerable. The personal fable seems to underlie adolescent showing off and risk taking (Alberts et al., 2007).

THE POSTCONVENTIONAL LEVEL OF MORAL REASONING Kohlberg's theory of moral reasoning involves three levels: preconventional, conventional, and postconventional. Individuals can arrive at the same decision as to whether Heinz should save his wife by taking the drug without paying for it for different reasons. Deciding not to steal the drug for fear of punishment is less cognitively complex than deciding not to because of the belief that doing could have negative consequences for the social order.

None of Kohlberg's levels is tied to a person's age. Although postconventional reasoning is the highest level, most adolescents and adults never reach it. But if postconventional reasoning emerges, it usually does so in adolescence.

postconventional level according to Kohlberg, a period during which moral judgments are derived from moral principles and people look to themselves to set moral standards

personal fable another aspect of adolescent egocentrism; the belief that our feelings and ideas are special and unique and that we are invulnerable

Kohlberg's (1969) research found postconventional moral judgments were absent among 7- to 10-year-olds. But by age 16, stage 5 reasoning is shown by about 20% of adolescents, and stage 6 reasoning by about 5%.

At the **postconventional level**, moral reasoning is based on the person's own moral standards. Moral judgments are derived from personal values, not from conventional standards or authority figures. In the contractual, legalistic orientation characteristic of stage 5, it is recognized that laws stem from agreed-upon procedures and that the rule of law is in general good for society; therefore, laws should not be violated except under pressing circumstances. (Although it is illegal for Heinz to steal the drug, in this case it is the right thing to do.) Stage 6 moral reasoning demands adherence to supposedly universal ethical principles such as the sanctity of human life, individual dignity, justice, and the Golden Rule ("Do unto others as you would have them do unto you"). If a law is unjust or contradicts the rights of the individual, it is wrong to obey it.

People at the postconventional level see their conscience as the highest moral authority. This point has created confusion. To some it suggests that it is right to break the law when it is convenient, but this interpretation is wrong. Kohlberg means that people at this level feel they must do what they think is right even if they break the law or must sacrifice themselves.

9-3c SOCIAL AND EMOTIONAL DEVELOPMENT

In terms of social and emotional development, adolescence has been associated with turbulence. In the 19th century, psychologist G. Stanley Hall described adolescence as a time of *Sturm und Drang*—storm and stress. Current views challenge the assumption that "storm and stress" is the norm (Hollenstein & Lougheed, 2013). Many adolescents experience a rather calm and joyous period of development. We need to consider individual differences and cultural variations (Arnett, 1999).

"THE BEST WAY TO KEEP CHILDREN HOME IS TO MAKE THE HOME ATMOSPHERE PLEASANT—AND LET THE AIR OUT OF THE TIRES."

DOROTHY PARKER, AUTHOR, POET, CRITIC, AND SCREENWRITER (1893–1967)

Certainly, many American teenagers abuse drugs, get pregnant, contract sexually transmitted infections, get involved in violence, fail in school, even attempt suicide (Miniño, 2010). The U.S. Centers for Disease Control and Prevention (Miniño, 2010) reported that 73% of all deaths among people aged 12 to 19 years result from three causes: motor vehicle and other accidents (48%), homicide (13%), and suicide (12%). Nevertheless, the majority of Americans make it through adolescence quite well.

RELATIONSHIPS WITH PARENTS AND PEERS

Adolescents spend much less time with their parents than they did as children (Longmore et al., 2013). Adolescents interact more with their mothers than their fathers and thus have more conflict with their mothers. But they also view their mothers as more supportive and more likely to accept their opinions (Longmore et al., 2013).

The decrease in time spent with family may reflect a striving for independence, yet most adolescents maintain love, loyalty, and respect for their parents (Smetana, 2011). And adolescents who feel close to their parents are more likely to show greater independence, higher self-esteem, better school performance, and fewer psychological problems (Flouri & Buchanan, 2003; Longmore et al., 2013).

Parent-adolescent conflict is greatest during puberty and declines in later adolescence (Smetana, 2011). Conflicts typically center on the everyday details of family life, such as chores, homework, curfews, personal appearance, finances, and dating, but parents and adolescents are usually similar in their beliefs regarding social, political, religious, and economic issues (Smetana, 2011).

Although relationships with parents generally remain positive, the role of peers as a source of activities, influence, and support increases during the teen years (Kirke, 2009). Adolescents stress the importance of acceptance, self-disclosure, mutual understanding, and loyalty in their friendships (Crosnoe, 2011). Adolescents and their friends are typically the same age and the same race (Castelli et al., 2009). Friends are also often alike in their school attitudes, educational aspirations, school achievement, and attitudes about drinking, drug use, and sexual activity (Crosnoe, 2011).

Parents often worry that their teenagers will fall in with the wrong crowd and engage in behavior that is self-destructive or goes against parental wishes. But research shows that most adolescents' friends are not bad influences (Allen & Antonishak, 2008). Many peers reinforce positive behaviors, such as academic achievement (Allen & Antonishak, 2008; Crosnoe, 2011).

EGO IDENTITY VERSUS ROLE DIFFUSION According to Erik Erikson (1963), we undergo eight stages of psychosocial development, each of which is characterized by a certain "crisis." Four of them, beginning with trust versus mistrust, occur in childhood. The fifth, that of *ego identity versus role diffusion,* occurs in adolescence. **Ego identity** is a firm sense of who one is and what one stands for. It can carry one through difficult times and lend meaning to achievements. Adolescents who do not develop ego identity may experience **role diffusion**. They spread themselves too thin, running down one blind alley after another and placing themselves at the mercy of leaders who promise to give them the sense of identity they cannot find for themselves.

In Western society, in which adolescents generally have a good deal of choice in determining what they will become, the creation of an adult identity is a key challenge. Much of this challenge involves learning about one's interests and abilities and connecting them with an occupation or a role in life. But identity also involves sexual, political, and religious beliefs and commitments. Will the individual be monogamous or sexually active with several people? Will he or she lean left or right along the political spectrum? What role will be played by religion?

9-4 EMERGING ADULTHOOD

In earlier days, adolescents made a transition directly into adulthood. Now many of them in affluent nations spend time in what some theorists consider a new period of development, roughly spanning the ages of 18 to 25: **emerging adulthood**. During this time, many young people attend college and graduate school, sort out identity issues, and create meaningful life plans. But even in the United States, of course, many people cannot afford the luxury of sojourning in emerging adulthood.

Jeffrey Arnett (2012; Tanner & Arnett, 2011) hypothesizes that five features distinguish the stage of emerging adulthood that is sandwiched between the stages of adolescence, which precedes it, and young adulthood, which follows it:

▶ *The age of identity exploration.* Many people of the ages

ego identity Erikson's term for a firm sense of who one is and what one stands for

role diffusion Erikson's term for lack of clarity in one's life roles (due to failure to develop ego identity)

emerging adulthood period of development, roughly spanning the ages of 18 to 25, during which time many young people in affluent nations attend college and graduate school, sort out identity issues, and create life plans from 18 or 20 to about 25 or 30 are on the path to making vital choices in terms of their love lives and their career lives. They are experimenting with romantic partners and career possibilities.

▶ *The age of instability.* Americans today average about seven different jobs between 20 and 29. They frequently change romantic partners—sometimes by choice, sometimes because the partner decides to move on. They may move from place to place with little if any furniture. And they frequently change educational directions, finding what they like, finding what they can do, and finding what is available.

▶ *The age of self-focus.* People are exceptionally self-focused during emerging adulthood (Arnett, 2012; Tanner & Arnett, 2011). They are freer to make decisions than they are as children or adolescents. They are more mature, more independent from parental influences, and usually have more resources.

▶ *The age of feeling in-between.* Emerging adults are similar to adolescents in one way: Whereas adolescents may feel that they exist somewhere between

childhood and adulthood, emerging adults are likely to think that they are swimming between adolescence and "real" adulthood. They are likely to be out of school—that is, high school or undergraduate college—but obtaining further training or education. They are beyond the sometimes silly flirtations of adolescence but not yet in long-term, or at least permanent, relationships. They may not be completely dependent on caregivers, but they are just as unlikely to be self-supporting. They may be between roommates or apartments. When they are asked whether they think they have become adults, Arnett (2000) found the most common answer of 18- to 25-year-olds to be something like "In some respects yes and in other respects no." Many think that they have developed beyond the conflicts and exploratory voyages of adolescence, but they may not yet have the ability—or desire—to assume the financial and interpersonal responsibilities they associate with adulthood.

▶ *The age of possibilities.* Emerging adults typically feel that the world lies open before them. Like the majority of adults, they have an optimistic bias (Arnett, 2012). They believe that things will work out. Yet some of them have a "revolving door" existence: they leave home and then return, according to the ebb and flow of financial and emotional resources.

Barry Winiker/Photodisc/Getty Images

What Now? Emerging adults tend to be self-focused. They recognize that they are freer to make decisions than they were as children and adolescents, but ... that means they need to make some.

9-5 ADULTHOOD

Development continues throughout the life span. Many theorists believe that adult concerns and involvements follow observable patterns, so that we can speak of "stages" of adult development. Others argue that there may no longer be a standard life cycle with predictable stages or phases. Age now has an "elastic quality"—being 50, 60, 70, 80, or even 90 no longer necessarily means loss of cognitive or physical ability, or even wrinkling. People are living longer than ever before and are freer than ever to choose their own destiny.

9-5a PHYSICAL DEVELOPMENT

The most obvious aspects of development during adulthood are physical. Let's consider the physical developments that take place in early adulthood, which spans the ages of 20 to 40; middle adulthood, which spans the ages of 40 to 65; and late adulthood, which begins at 65.

EARLY ADULTHOOD Physical development peaks in early adulthood. Most people are at their height of sensory sharpness, strength, reaction time, and cardiovascular fitness. Young adults are at their tallest, and height remains stable through middle adulthood, declining somewhat in late adulthood. Physical strength in both men and women peaks in the 20s and early 30s and then slowly declines (Markham, 2006). Most athletes experience a decline in their 30s, and most athletes retire by age 40. Sexually speaking, most people in early adulthood become readily aroused. They tend to attain and maintain erections as desired and to lubricate readily.

MIDDLE ADULTHOOD In our middle years, we are unlikely to possess the strength, coordination, and stamina that we had during our 20s and 30s. Still, the years between 40 and 60 are reasonably stable. There is gradual physical decline, but it is minor and likely to be of concern only if a person competes with young adults—or with idealized memories of one's self. Because the physical decline in middle adulthood is gradual, people who begin to eat more nutritious diets and to exercise may find themselves looking and feeling better than they did in early adulthood.

For women, **menopause** is usually considered to be the single most important change of life that occurs during middle adulthood. Menopause usually occurs during the late 40s or early 50s. Menopause is the final phase of the *climacteric,* which is caused by a decline in secretion of female sex hormones. Ovulation comes to an end, and there is some loss of breast tissue and skin elasticity. Loss of bone density can lead to osteoporosis (brittle bones). During the climacteric, many women experience hot flashes, loss of sleep, and some anxiety and depression. Women's experiences during and following the climacteric reflect the intensity of their physical symptoms—which vary considerably—and the extent to which their self-concept was wrapped up with their reproductive capacity (Rathus et al., 2011).

LATE ADULTHOOD *An age quake is coming.* People age 65 and older are the most rapidly growing segment of the U.S. population (National Center for Health Statistics, 2010). In 1900, only 1 person in 25 was over the

Ben Schnall/Time & Life Pictures/Getty Images

Architect Frank Lloyd Wright with a model of his Guggenheim Museum.

age of 65. Today, that figure has more than tripled to one in eight. By mid-century, more than one in five Americans will be 65 years of age or older (National Center for Health Statistics, 2010).

Various changes—some of them troublesome—do occur during the later years (see Figure 9.7). Changes in calcium metabolism increase the brittleness of the bones and heighten the risk of breaks due to falls. The skin becomes less elastic and subject to wrinkles and folds. Older people see and hear less acutely. Because of a decline in the sense of smell, they may use more spice to flavor their food. Older people need more time to respond to stimuli. Older drivers, for example, need more time to respond to changing road conditions. As we grow older, our immune system functions less effectively, leaving us more vulnerable to disease. Age-related changes impact sexual functioning, yet most people can enjoy sex for a lifetime if they remain generally healthy and adjust their expectations.

9-5b COGNITIVE DEVELOPMENT

As in the case of physical development, people are also at the height of their cognitive powers during early adulthood. Cognitive development in adulthood has many aspects—creativity, memory functioning, and intelligence.

People can be creative for a lifetime. At the age of 80, Merce Cunningham choreographed a dance that made use of computer-generated digital images (Teachout, 2000). Hans Hofmann

menopause the cessation of menstruation

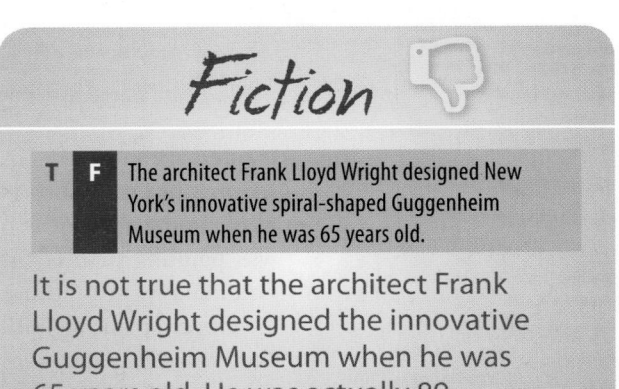

Fiction 👎

T | **F** | The architect Frank Lloyd Wright designed New York's innovative spiral-shaped Guggenheim Museum when he was 65 years old.

It is not true that the architect Frank Lloyd Wright designed the innovative Guggenheim Museum when he was 65 years old. He was actually 89.

FIG.9.7 THE RELENTLESS MARCH OF TIME

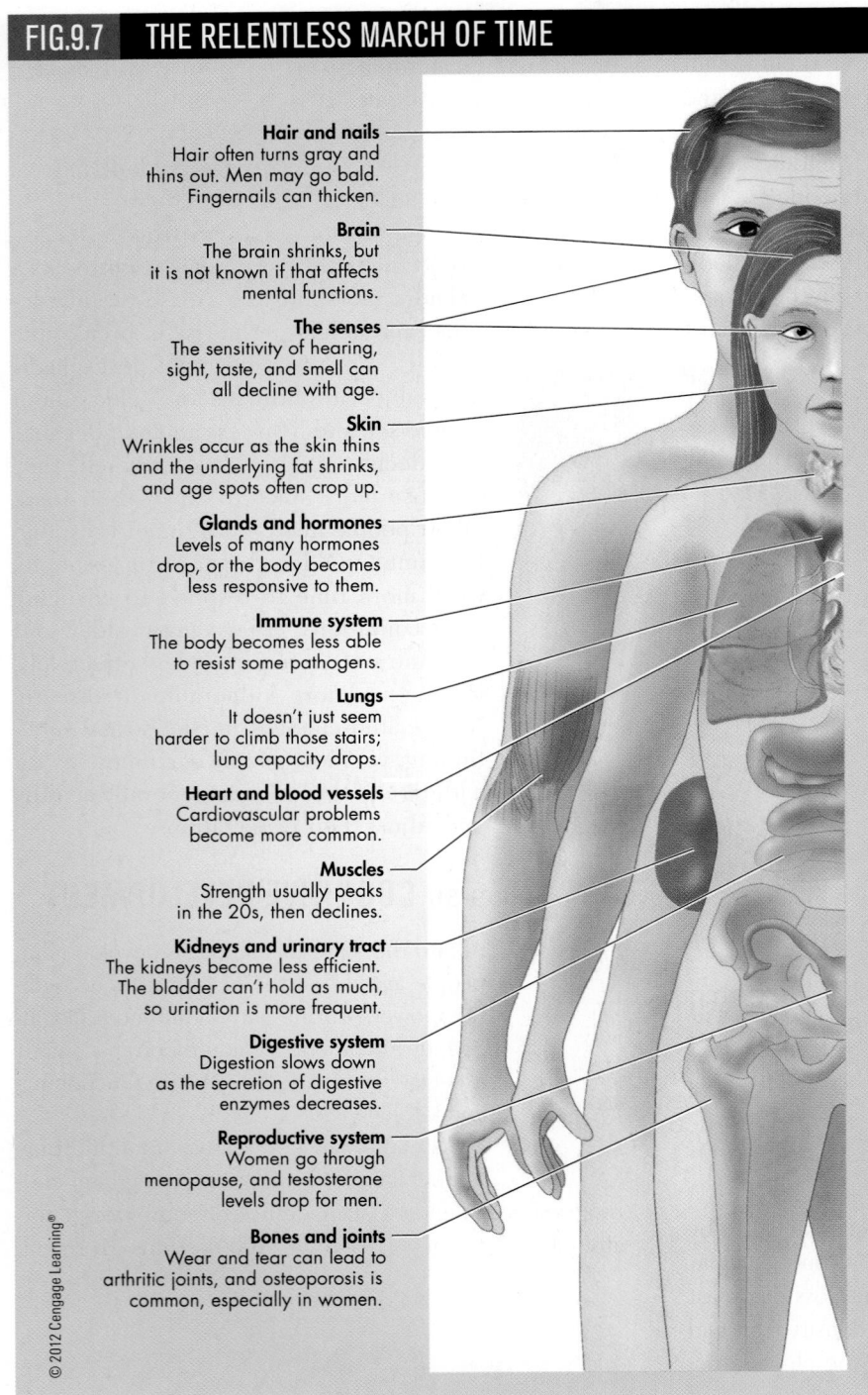

Hair and nails
Hair often turns gray and thins out. Men may go bald. Fingernails can thicken.

Brain
The brain shrinks, but it is not known if that affects mental functions.

The senses
The sensitivity of hearing, sight, taste, and smell can all decline with age.

Skin
Wrinkles occur as the skin thins and the underlying fat shrinks, and age spots often crop up.

Glands and hormones
Levels of many hormones drop, or the body becomes less responsive to them.

Immune system
The body becomes less able to resist some pathogens.

Lungs
It doesn't just seem harder to climb those stairs; lung capacity drops.

Heart and blood vessels
Cardiovascular problems become more common.

Muscles
Strength usually peaks in the 20s, then declines.

Kidneys and urinary tract
The kidneys become less efficient. The bladder can't hold as much, so urination is more frequent.

Digestive system
Digestion slows down as the secretion of digestive enzymes decreases.

Reproductive system
Women go through menopause, and testosterone levels drop for men.

Bones and joints
Wear and tear can lead to arthritic joints, and osteoporosis is common, especially in women.

© 2012 Cengage Learning®

his joyous opera *Falstaff* at the age of 79.

Memory functioning does decline with age. But declines in memory are not usually as large as people assume and are often reversible (Villa & Abeles, 2000). Memory tests usually measure ability to recall meaningless information. Older people show better memory functioning in areas in which they can apply their experience, especially their specialties, to new challenges. For example: Who would do a better job of learning and remembering how to solve problems in chemistry—a college history major or a retired professor of chemistry? You might choose the chemistry professor because of his or her *crystallized intelligence*, not his or her *fluid intelligence*.

Crystallized intelligence is defined as a cluster of knowledge and skills that depend on accumulated information and experience, awareness of social conventions, and the capacity to make good decisions. We are using the example of knowledge of chemistry, but crystallized intelligence is shown more generally by vocabulary and accumulated facts about world affairs. Therefore, crystallized intelligence can increase over the decades. **Fluid intelligence** is defined as mental flexibility, demonstrated by the ability to process information rapidly, as in learning and solving problems in new areas. It is the sort of intellectual functioning that is typically measured on intelligence tests, especially with problems that have time limits.

In the absence of senile dementias, crystallized intelligence commonly increases throughout the life span, along with scores on verbal subtests of standardized intelligence tests. The same studies that indicate

crystallized intelligence one's lifetime of intellectual achievement, as shown largely through vocabulary and knowledge of world affairs

fluid intelligence mental flexibility as shown in learning rapidly to solve new kinds of problems

created some of his most vibrant paintings at 85, and Pablo Picasso was painting in his 90s. Grandma Moses did not even begin painting until she was 78 years old. Giuseppe Verdi wrote

that crystallized intelligence tends to increase throughout adulthood tend to show a decline for fluid intelligence (Escorial et al., 2003; Salthouse, 2001).

One of the most severe assaults on intellectual functioning, especially among older people, is **Alzheimer's disease**, a progressive and irreversible brain disease affecting four to five million Americans. About one in ten Americans between the ages of 65 and 74 is diagnosed with Alzheimer's disease, jumping to more than one in two among those in the 75- to 84-year-old category (Henderson, 2009). Although Alzheimer's is connected with aging, it is a disease rather than a normal progression.

> "I'VE YET TO BE ON A CAMPUS WHERE MOST WOMEN WEREN'T WORRYING ABOUT SOME ASPECT OF COMBINING MARRIAGE, CHILDREN, AND A CAREER. I'VE YET TO FIND ONE WHERE MANY MEN WERE WORRYING ABOUT THE SAME THING."
>
> GLORIA STEINEM, WRITER AND JOURNALIST (B.1934)

9-5c SOCIAL AND EMOTIONAL DEVELOPMENT

Changes in social and emotional development during adulthood are probably the most "elastic" or fluid. These changes are affected by cultural expectations and individual behavior patterns. As a result, there is much variety. Let's look at some changes that take place at different stages of adulthood.

EARLY ADULTHOOD

Many theorists suggest that early adulthood is the period of life during which people tend to establish themselves as independent members of society. At some point during their 20s, many people become fueled by ambition. Many strive to advance in their careers. Those who seek professional careers may spend much of their 20s acquiring the skills that will enable them to succeed (Levinson et al., 1978; Levinson, 1996). It is largely during the 20s that people become generally responsible for their own support, make their own choices, and are freed from parental influences. Many young adults adopt what theorist Daniel Levinson and his colleagues (1978) call the *Dream*—the drive to "become" someone, to leave their mark on history—which serves as a tentative blueprint for life.

During young adulthood, people tend to leave their families of origin and create families of their own. Erik Erikson (1963) characterized young adulthood as the stage of *intimacy versus isolation.* Erikson saw the establishment of intimate relationships as central to young adulthood. Young adults who have evolved a firm sense of identity during adolescence are ready to "fuse" their identities with those of other people through marriage and abiding friendships. People who do not reach out to develop intimate relationships risk retreating into isolation and loneliness.

At age 30 or so, many people reassess their lives, asking themselves, "Where is my life going?" "Why am I doing this?" (Levinson et al., 1978). It is not uncommon for them to switch careers or form new intimate relationships. The later 30s are often characterized by settling down—planting roots. They become focused on career advancement, children, and long-term mortgages.

MIDDLE ADULTHOOD

Erikson (1963) labeled the life crisis of the middle years *generativity*

Alzheimer's disease a progressive form of mental deterioration characterized by loss of memory, language, problem solving, and other cognitive functions

versus stagnation. Generativity involves doing things that we believe are worthwhile, such as rearing children or producing on the job. He theorized that generativity enhances and maintains self-esteem. Generativity also involves making the world a better place through joining church or civic groups. *Stagnation* means treading water, as in keeping the same job at the same pay for 30 years or neglecting to rear one's children. Stagnation damages self-esteem.

According to Levinson and colleagues (1978), whose research involved case studies of 40 men, there is a *midlife transition* at about 40 to 45 characterized by a shift in psychological perspective from how many years one has lived to how many years one has left. Research suggests that women may undergo a midlife transition earlier than men do (Zucker et al., 2002). Why? Much of it is related to the winding down of the "biological clock"—their ability to bear children. Yet many women today are having children in their 40s and, now and then, beyond.

In both women and men, according to Levinson, the midlife transition may trigger a *midlife crisis.* The middle-level, middle-aged businessperson looking ahead to another 10 to 20 years of grinding out accounts in a cubbyhole may encounter depression. The homemaker with two teenagers and an empty house from 8 a.m. to 4 p.m. may feel that she or he is coming apart at the seams. Both feel a sense of entrapment and loss of purpose.

Yet many Americans find that these years present opportunities for new direction and fulfillment. Many people are at the height of their productive powers during this period. Many, perhaps most, of today's robust middle-aged adults can look forward to another 30 to 40 healthy years.

THE EMPTY-NEST SYNDROME? In earlier decades, psychologists placed emphasis on the so-called **empty-nest syndrome**. This concept was applied most often to women. It was assumed that women experience a sense of loss when their youngest child goes off to college, gets married, or moves out of the home (Stewart & Ostrove, 1998). However, research does not find that parents suffer from an empty-nest syndrome when the youngest child leaves home. Both parents can feel some sense of loss,

empty-nest syndrome a sense of depression and loss of purpose felt by some parents when the youngest child leaves home

sandwich generation people in middle adulthood who are responsible for meeting the needs of their children yet also responsible for aging parents

but once their children become adults, most American parents are content to "launch" their children to live on their own. In fact, many mothers report increased marital satisfaction and personal changes such as greater mellowness, self-confidence, and stability once the children have left home (Etaugh & Bridges, 2006).

MIDDLE-AGED CHILDREN AND AGING PARENTS: THE "SANDWICH GENERATION" Because of increasing life expectancy, more than half of the middle-aged people in developed nations have at least one living parent, and they frequently go on to late adulthood together (U.S. Bureau of the Census, 2011). Two-thirds of aging American parents have a residence near a child (U.S. Bureau of the Census, 2011), and there are frequent visits and phone calls. The relationships between middle-aged and older parents can grow quite close, especially as tensions and expectations from earlier years tend to slip into history. If the aging parents require assistance, the task usually falls to a middle-aged daughter, who then becomes what has been dubbed part of the **sandwich generation**. She is sandwiched between caring for or contributing to the support of her children or grandchildren at the same time she is caring for her parents (DeRigne & Ferrante, 2012). Given that she is also likely to be in the workforce, her role overload is multiplied (DeRigner & Ferrante, 2012).

LATE ADULTHOOD Generativity does not end with middle age. Research suggests that many individuals in late adulthood continue to be creative and also to maintain a firm sense of who they are and what they stand for (Webster, 2003). The Greek philosopher Plato was so optimistic about late adulthood that he argued that one could achieve great pleasure in one's later years, engage in meaningful public service, and also achieve wisdom.

According to psychologist Erik Erikson, late adulthood is the stage of *ego integrity versus despair.* The basic challenge is to maintain the belief that life is meaningful and worthwhile as one ages and faces the inevitability of death. Erikson, like Plato, spoke of the importance of wisdom. He believed that ego integrity derives from wisdom, which can be defined as expert knowledge about the meaning of life, balancing one's own needs and those of others, and pushing toward excellence in one's behavior and achievements (Baltes & Staudinger, 2000; Sternberg, 2000). Erikson also believed that wisdom enables people to accept their lifespan as occurring at a certain point in the sweep of history and as being limited. We spend most of our lives accumulating objects and relationships, and Erikson suggests that adjustment in the later years requires the ability to let go of them.

SUCCESSFUL AGING The concept of *successful aging* in some ways addresses aging from a very different perspective. Whereas Erikson focused on letting go and accepting one's place in the sweep of history, successful aging focuses on maximizing one's life experiences at any age. Researchers who study successful aging focus on factors such as overall good physical health, including the absence or control of chronic diseases such as arthritis and diabetes, engaging in physical activity, social networking, and the absence of serious cognitive impairment and depression (Baltes & Rudolph, 2013). Sexual activity remains desirable, even if some aspects of performance are not what they were (Griebling, 2011). According to researchers Margaret Baltes and Laura Carstensen, successful agers tend to seek emotional fulfillment by **selective optimization with compensation**: they reshape their lives to concentrate on what they find to be important and meaningful (Baltes & Rudolph, 2013; English & Carstensen, 2014).

Successful agers form emotional goals that bring them satisfaction (English & Carstensen, 2014). They may no longer compete in certain athletic or business activities. Instead, they focus on matters that allow them to maintain a sense of control over their own lives. Retaining social contacts and building new ones also contributes to a positive outlook, as does continuing with one's athletic activities, when possible, and one's artistic and cultural activities.

"LYING DOWN TO PLEASANT DREAMS" The American poet William Cullen Bryant is best known for his poem "Thanatopsis," which he composed at the age of 18. "Thanatopsis" expresses Erik Erikson's goal of ego integrity—optimism that we can maintain a sense of trust through life. By meeting squarely the challenges of our adult lives, perhaps we can take our leave with dignity. And when our time comes to "join the innumerable caravan"—the billions who have died before us—perhaps we can depart life with integrity as well.

The woman kissing her mother may be thought of as being in the "sandwich generation." She is "sandwiched" between the needs of her adolescent children and those of her aging parents.

"Live," wrote the poet, so that
… when thy summons comes to join
The innumerable caravan that moves
To that mysterious realm, where each shall take
His chamber in the silent halls of death,
Thou go not, like the quarry-slave at night,
Scourged to his dungeon, but, sustained and soothed
By an unfaltering trust, approach thy grave
Like one that wraps the drapery of his couch
About him, and lies down to pleasant dreams.

Bryant, of course, wrote "Thanatopsis" at age 18, not at 85, the age at which he died. At that advanced age, his feelings—and his verse—might have differed. But literature and poetry, unlike science, need not perfectly mirror reality. They can serve to inspire and warm us.

selective optimization with compensation reshaping of one's life to concentrate on what one finds to be important and meaningful in the face of physical decline and possible cognitive impairment.

STUDY TOOLS 9

READY TO STUDY? IN THE BOOK, YOU CAN:

☐ Check your understanding of what you've read with the quizzes below.

☐ Rip out the chapter review card at the back of the book to have a summary of the chapter and the key terms handy.

ONLINE AT CENGAGEBRAIN.COM YOU CAN:

☐ Learn more about on Kohlberg's Theory of Moral Development in learning modules.

☐ Learn about different types of tests for babies in the womb in a short video.

☐ Prepare for tests with quizzes.

☐ Review the key terms with Flash Cards.

☐ Play games to master concepts.

FILL-INS

Answers can be found in the back of the book, starting on page 392.

1. Neonates show_____, which are simple, unlearned, stereotypical responses elicited by specific stimuli.

2. Piaget's_____operational period is characterized by conservation and reversibility.

3. Vygotsky used the concepts of scaffolding and the _____ of proximal development to explain cognitive development.

4. Ainsworth identified three stages of attachment: The _____ phase, the attachment-in-the-making phase, and the clear-cut-attachment phase.

5. Puberty begins with the appearance of _____ sex characteristics, such as the deepening of the voice in males and rounding of the breasts and hips in females.

6. _____ operational thought is characterized by hypothetical thinking and deductive logic.

7. Adolescent egocentrism gives rise to the _____ audience and the personal fable.

8. Erik Erikson considers the life crisis of adolescence to be ego identity versus role _____.

9. _____ intelligence is mental flexibility as shown by the ability to solve new kinds of problems.

10. Research shows that most parents (do or do not?) suffer from the empty-nest syndrome.

MULTIPLE CHOICE

1. **A newborn shows a preference for his or her mother's voice rather than the father's voice. This is most likely the result of**
   a. an inability to hear until after birth.
   b. learning to recognize the mother's voice because of more exposure to these sounds before birth.
   c. an inability to hear lower pitched tones as in a male's voice.
   d. liking mom more than they like dad.

2. **Piaget's stages of cognitive development are, in order of increasing age,**
   a. sensorimotor, preoperational, concrete operational, formal operational.
   b. sensorimotor, concrete operational, formal operational, preoperational.
   c. preoperational, operational, postoperational, formal operational.
   d. assimilation, adaptation, accommodation.

3. **An adult who chooses not to park in a handicap space because they want to avoid a ticket and fine, is operating at the ___ level of Kohlberg's theory.**
   a. nonconventional
   b. postconvention
   c. preconventional
   d. conventional

4. **According to Ainsworth, babies who demonstrate proximity to their mother and separation anxiety when apart are showing indications of**
   a. socialization.
   b. neuroticism.
   c. association.
   d. attachment.

5. **Harry Harlow (1959) demonstrated that attachment in rhesus monkeys was related to**
   a. feeding only.
   b. contact comfort.
   c. learning experiences.
   d. insecurity.

6. **Menarche is the term used to describe**
   a. adolescence.
   b. the beginning of adolescent growth spurts.
   c. the first menstruation.
   d. the onset of male secondary sex characteristics.

7. **Formal operations allow adolescents to think**
   a. symbolically.
   b. in terms of cause and effect.
   c. concretely.
   d. hypothetically.

8. **An adolescent's belief that other people are as concerned with their thoughts and behavior as they are is called the**
   a. personal fable.
   b. imaginary audience.
   c. pretend view.
   d. personal fantasy.

9. **Intelligence associated with the intellectual attainments of a lifetime or acquired knowledge is called**
   a. fluid intelligence.
   b. creative intelligence.
   c. crystallized intelligence.
   d. flexible intelligence.

10. **Erikson labeled the life crisis of the middle years as**
    a. trust versus mistrust.
    b. generativity versus stagnation.
    c. identity versus stagnation.
    d. midlife transition versus despair.

10 | Personality: Theory and Measurement

© Andrew Adolphus

LEARNING OUTCOMES

After studying this chapter, you will be able to…

10-1 Describe the psychoanalytical perspective and how it contributed to the study of personality.

10-2 Explain the trait perspective and the "Big Five" trait model.

10-3 Identify the contributions of learning theory to understanding personality.

10-4 Describe the humanistic–existential perspective on personality.

10-5 Describe the sociocultural perspective on personality.

10-6 Describe the different kinds of tests psychologists use to measure personality.

After you finish this chapter, go to **PAGE 279** for **STUDY TOOLS**

Nearly 1,000 years ago, the poet Rumi wrote of the fable of *The Blind Men and the Elephant:*

Once upon a time, a group of blind men heard that an unusual animal called an elephant had come to their country. Since they had no idea what an elephant looked like and had never even heard its name, they resolved that they would obtain a "picture" of sorts, and the knowledge they sought, by

Can there ever be one **true portrait** of human personality?

feeling the animal. After all, that was the only possibility available to them. They sought out the elephant, and its handler kindly permitted them to touch the beast. One blind man stroked its leg, the other a tusk, the third an ear, and believing that they now had knowledge of the elephant, they returned home satisfied. But when they were questioned by others, they provided very different descriptions. The one who had felt the leg said that the elephant was firm, strong, and upright, like a pillar.

The one who had felt the tusk disagreed. He described the elephant as hard and smooth, clearly not as stout as a pillar, and sharp at the end. Now spoke the third blind man, who had held the ear of the elephant. "By my faith," he asserted, "the elephant is soft and rough." It was neither pillar-like nor hard and smooth. It was broad, thick, and leathery. And so the three argued about the true nature of the beast. Each was right in part, but none grasped the real nature of the elephant. Yet each was fervent in his belief that he knew the animal.

Each of the blind men had come to know the elephant from a different angle. Each was bound by his first experience and blind to the beliefs of his fellows and to the real nature of the beast—not just because of his physical limitations, but also because his initial encounter led him to think of the elephant in a certain way.

Our own conceptions about people, and about ourselves, may be similarly bound up with our own perspectives and initial beliefs. Some think of personality as consisting of the person's most striking traits, as in "This person has an outgoing personality" or "That person has an agreeable personality."

Truth or Fiction?

WHAT DO YOU THINK? Folklore, common sense, or nonsense? Select T for "truth" or F for "fiction," and then check the accuracy of your answers as you read through the chapter.

T F Biting one's fingernails or smoking cigarettes is a sign of conflict experienced during early childhood.

T F Twenty-five hundred years ago, a Greek physician devised a way of looking at personality that remains in use today.

T F Bloodletting and vomiting were once recommended as ways of coping with depression.

T F Actually, there are no basic personality traits. We are all conditioned by society to behave in certain ways.

T F The most well-adjusted immigrants are those who abandon the language and customs of their country of origin and become like members of the dominant culture in their new host country.

T F Psychologists can determine whether a person has told the truth on a personality test.

T F There is a psychological test made up of inkblots, and test-takers are asked to say what the blots look like to them.

But many psychological theorists look deeper. Those schooled in the Freudian tradition look at personality as consisting of underlying mental structures that jockey for supremacy outside the range of our ordinary awareness. Other theorists focus on how personality is shaped by learning. And to the humanistic theorists, personality is not something people *have* but rather something they *create* to give meaning and direction to their lives. Then, too, sociocultural theorists remind us that we must always consider the influences of culture, race, and ethnicity on personality.

Sometimes even psychologists prefer the first theory of personality they learn about. The Islamic theologian taught his pupils the legend of the blind men and the elephant to illustrate that no person can have a complete view of religious truths; we must therefore remain flexible in our thinking and open to new ideas. It may also be that none of the views of personality presented in this chapter will offer the one true portrait of human personality, but each may have something to contribute to our understanding. So let's approach our

study with an open mind, because years from now psychologists may well be teaching new ideas about personality.

While the blind men could touch the elephant, researchers cannot touch a personality; therefore, personality is even harder to describe and understand. Before we discuss psychologists' various approaches to personality, let's define our subject matter: psychologists define **personality** as the reasonably stable patterns of emotions, motives, and behavior that distinguish one person from another.

10-1 THE PSYCHODYNAMIC PERSPECTIVE

There are several **psychodynamic theories** of personality, each of which owes its origin to Sigmund Freud. Each teaches that personality is characterized by conflict. At first the conflict is external: drives like sex, aggression, and the need for superiority come into conflict with laws, social rules, and moral codes. But at some point laws and social rules are brought inward—that is, *internalized.* The conflict is then between opposing *inner* forces. At any given moment our behavior, our thoughts, and our emotions represent the outcome of these inner contests.

10-1a SIGMUND FREUD'S THEORY OF PSYCHOSEXUAL DEVELOPMENT

personality the reasonably stable patterns of emotions, motives, and behavior that distinguish one person from another

psychodynamic theory Sigmund Freud's perspective, which emphasizes the importance of unconscious motives and conflicts as forces that determine behavior

Sigmund Freud (1856–1939) was a mass of contradictions. Some have lauded him as one of the greatest thinkers of the 20th century. Others have criticized him as overrated. He preached liberal views on sexuality but

was himself a model of sexual restraint. He invented a popular form of psychotherapy but experienced lifelong psychologically related problems such as migraine headaches, fainting under stress, and hatred of the telephone. He smoked 20 cigars a day and could not break the habit even after he developed cancer of the jaw.

Freud was trained as a physician. Early in his practice, he was surprised to find that some people apparently experienced loss of feeling in a hand or paralysis of the legs even though they had no medical disorder. These odd symptoms often disappeared once the person recalled and discussed stressful events and feelings of guilt or anxiety that seemed to be related to the symptoms. Although these events and feelings lay hidden beneath the surface of awareness, they could influence behavior.

From this sort of clinical evidence, Freud concluded that the human mind is like an iceberg. Only the tip of an iceberg rises above the surface of the water; the great mass of it lies hidden in the depths (see Figure 10.1). Freud came to believe that people, similarly, are aware of only a small part of the ideas and impulses that dwell within their minds. He argued that a much greater portion of the mind—one that contained our deepest images, thoughts, fears, and urges—remains beneath the surface of conscious awareness, where little light illumines them.

Freud labeled the region that pokes into the light of awareness the *conscious* part of the mind. He called

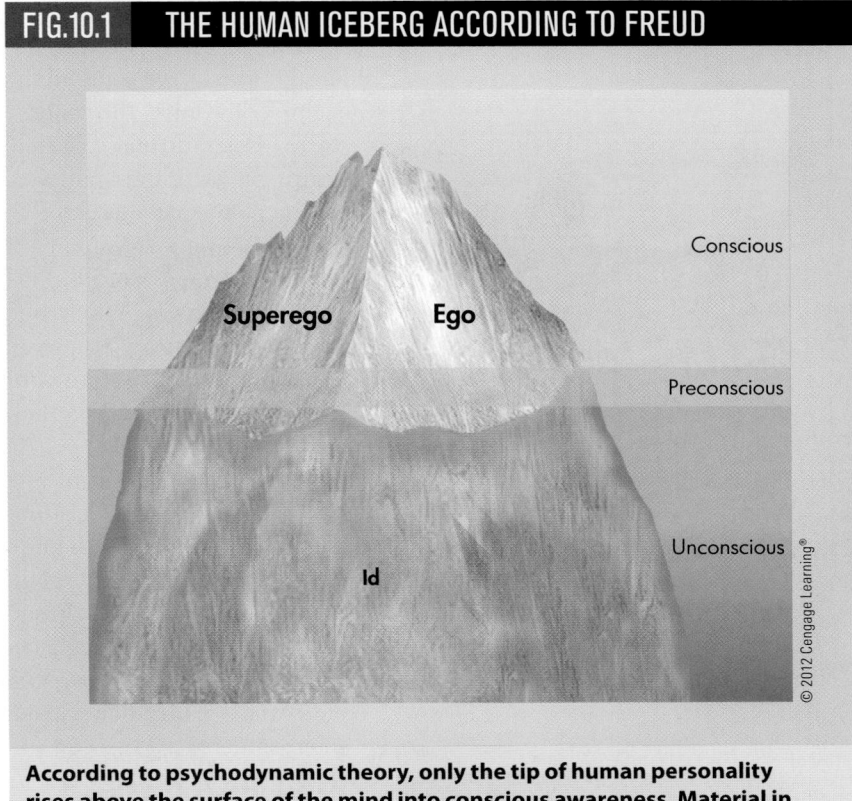

FIG.10.1 THE HUMAN ICEBERG ACCORDING TO FREUD

Conscious

Preconscious

Unconscious

Superego

Ego

Id

© 2012 Cengage Learning®

According to psychodynamic theory, only the tip of human personality rises above the surface of the mind into conscious awareness. Material in the preconscious can become conscious if we direct our attention to it. Unconscious material tends to remain shrouded in mystery.

work called *psychoanalysis*. For this reason, his theory of personality is also referred to as *psychoanalytic theory*. In psychoanalysis, people are encouraged to talk about anything that pops into their mind while they remain comfortable and relaxed.

THE STRUCTURE OF PERSONALITY

Freud spoke of mental or *psychic structures* to describe the clashing forces of personality. Psychic structures cannot be seen or measured directly, but their presence is suggested by behavior, expressed thoughts, and emotions. Freud believed that there are three psychic structures: the *id*, the *ego*, and the *superego*.

The **id** is present at birth. It represents biological drives and is entirely unconscious. Freud described the id as "a chaos, a cauldron of seething excitations" (1927/1964, p. 73). The conscious mind might find it inconsistent to love and hate the same person, but such conflicting emotions can dwell side by side in the id. In the id, one can hate one's mother for failing to gratify immediately all of one's needs while also loving her. The id follows what Freud termed the *pleasure principle*. It demands instant gratification without consideration for law, social custom, or other people.

The **ego** begins to develop during the first year of life, largely because a child's demands for gratification cannot all be met immediately. The ego stands for reason and good sense, for rational ways of coping with frustration. The ego is guided by the *reality principle*. It curbs the appetites of the id and seeks ways to find gratification yet avoid social disapproval. The id informs you that you are hungry, but the ego decides to microwave enchiladas. The ego takes into account what is practical

the regions below the surface the *preconscious* and the *unconscious*. The preconscious mind contains ideas that are out of awareness but can be made conscious by focusing on them. The unconscious mind is shrouded in mystery. It contains primitive instincts such as sex and aggression. Some unconscious urges cannot be experienced consciously because mental images and words cannot portray them in all their color and fury. Other unconscious urges may be kept below the surface by repression because they would create anxiety.

Repression is defined as the automatic ejection of anxiety-evoking ideas from awareness. People forget many ugly experiences, and some research evidence suggests that people might repress them (Mund & Mitte, 2012). Other investigators allow that forgetting and distortion of memory occurs, but view the Freudian concept of repression as little more than a myth (Hayne, 2013).

In the unconscious mind, primitive drives seek expression, while learned values try to keep them in check. The conflict can arouse emotional outbursts and psychological problems. To explore the unconscious mind, Freud used a form of mental detective

along with what is urged by the id. The ego also provides the conscious sense of self.

Although most of the ego is conscious, some of its business is carried out unconsciously. For example, the ego also

id the psychic structure, present at birth, that represents physiological drives and is fully unconscious

ego the second psychic structure to develop, characterized by self-awareness, planning, and delay of gratification acts as a censor that screens the impulses of the id. When the ego senses that improper impulses are rising into awareness, it may use psychological defenses to prevent them from surfacing. Repression is one such psychological defense, or *defense mechanism.*

The **superego** develops as the child incorporates the moral standards and values of parents and other members of the community. The child does so through *identification,* by trying to become like these people. The superego functions according to the *moral principle.* It holds up shining models of an ideal self and monitors the intentions of the ego, handing out judgments of right and wrong. It floods the ego with feelings of guilt and shame when the verdict is negative.

Freud believed that a healthy personality has found ways to gratify most of the id's demands without seriously offending the superego. Most of these demands are contained or repressed. If the ego is not a good problem solver, or if the superego is too stern, the ego will have a hard time of it.

STAGES OF PSYCHOSEXUAL DEVELOPMENT

Freud stirred controversy by arguing that sexual impulses are a central factor in personality development, even among children. He believed that sexual feelings are closely linked to children's basic ways of relating to the world, such as nursing and moving their bowels.

Freud believed that a major instinct, *eros,* aims to preserve and perpetuate life. Eros is fueled by psychological, or psychic, energy, which Freud labeled

SIGMUND FREUD

Stages of Psychosexual Development

▸ **Oral**

▸ **Anal**

▸ **Phallic**

▸ **Latency**

▸ **Genital**

Imagno/Hulton Archive/Getty Images

libido. Libidinal energy involves sexual impulses, so Freud considered it to be *psychosexual.* As the child develops, this energy is expressed through sexual feelings in different parts of the body, or *erogenous zones.* To Freud, human development involves the transfer of libidinal energy from one erogenous zone to another. He hypothesized five periods of **psychosexual development**: oral, anal, phallic, latency, and genital.

During the first year of life, a child experiences much of her or his world through the mouth. If it fits, into the mouth it goes. This is the **oral stage**. Freud argued that oral activities such as sucking and biting give the child sexual gratification as well as nourishment.

Freud believed that children encounter conflict during each stage of psychosexual development. During the oral stage, conflict centers on the nature and extent of oral gratification. Early weaning (cessation of breastfeeding) can lead to frustration. Excessive gratification, on the other hand, can lead an infant to expect that it will routinely get anything it wants. Insufficient or excessive gratification in any stage could lead to *fixation* in that stage and to the development of traits that are characteristic of the stage. Oral traits include dependency, gullibility, and excessive optimism or pessimism (depending on the child's experiences with gratification).

Freud theorized that adults with an *oral fixation* could experience exaggerated desires for "oral activities," such as smoking, overeating, alcohol abuse, and nail biting. Like the infant whose survival depends on the mercy of an adult, adults with oral fixations may desire clinging, dependent relationships.

The anal stage begins in the second year. During the **anal stage**, gratification is attained through contraction and relaxation of the muscles that control elimination of waste products. Elimination, which is reflexive during most of the first year, comes under voluntary muscular control, even if such control is not reliable

superego the third psychic structure, which functions as a moral guardian and sets forth high standards for behavior

psychosexual development in psychodynamic theory, the process by which libidinal energy is expressed through different erogenous zones during different stages of development

oral stage the first stage of psychosexual development, during which gratification is hypothesized to be attained primarily through oral activities

anal stage the second stage of psychosexual development, when gratification is attained through anal activities

If It Fits, into the Mouth It Goes! Freud labeled the first year of life the oral stage of development because of the infant's use of the mouth in relating to nursing and objects—and, in this case, toes.

at first. During the anal stage, children learn to delay the gratification that comes from eliminating whenever they feel the urge. The general issue of self-control may bring conflict between parent and child. *Anal fixations* may stem from this conflict and lead to either of two sets of traits in adulthood. *Anal-retentive* traits involve excessive use of self-control: perfectionism, a strong need for order, and exaggerated neatness and cleanliness. *Anal-expulsive* traits, on the other hand, "let it all hang out": they include carelessness, messiness, even sadism.

Children enter the **phallic stage** during the third year. The major erogenous zone is the phallic region (the penis in boys and the clitoris in girls). Parent–child conflict is likely to develop over masturbation, to which parents may respond with threats or punishment. During this stage children may develop strong sexual attachments to the parent of the other gender and begin to view the parent of the same gender as a rival for the other parent's affections.

Children have difficulty dealing with feelings of lust and jealousy. These feelings, therefore, remain unconscious, but their influence is felt through fantasies about marriage with the parent of the other gender and hostility toward the parent of the same gender. In boys, this conflict is labeled the **Oedipus complex**, after the legendary Greek king who unwittingly killed his father and married his mother. Similar feelings in girls give rise to the **Electra complex**. According to Greek legend, Electra was the daughter

of the King Agamemnon. She longed for him after his death and sought revenge against his slayers—her mother and her mother's lover.

The Oedipus and Electra complexes are resolved by about the ages of 5 or 6. Children repress their hostilities toward the parent of the same gender and begin to identify with her or him. In psychoanalytic theory, identification is the key to gender-typing: It leads children to play the gender roles of the parent of the same gender and to internalize his or her values. Sexual feelings toward the parent of the other gender are repressed for several years. When the feelings reemerge during adolescence, they are displaced, or transferred, to socially appropriate members of the other gender.

Freud believed that by the age of 5 or 6, children have been in conflict with their parents over sexual feelings for several years. The pressures of the Oedipus and Electra complexes cause them to repress all sexual urges. In so doing, they enter a period of **latency**, during which their sexual feelings remain unconscious, they prefer playmates of their own gender, and they focus on schoolwork.

Freud believed that we enter the final stage of psychosexual development, the **genital stage**, at puberty. Adolescent males again experience sexual urges toward their mother, and adolescent females experience such urges toward their father. However, the *incest taboo* causes them to repress these impulses and displace them onto other adults or adolescents of the other gender. Boys might seek girls "just like the girl that married dear old Dad." Girls might be attracted to boys who resemble their fathers.

People in the genital stage prefer to find sexual gratification through intercourse with a member of the other gender. In Freud's view, oral or anal stimulation, masturbation, and sexual activity with people of the same gender all represent *pregenital* fixations and immature forms of sexual conduct.

phallic stage the third stage of psychosexual development, characterized by a shift of libido to the phallic region

Oedipus complex a conflict of the phallic stage in which the boy wishes to possess his mother sexually and perceives his father as a rival in love

Electra complex a conflict of the phallic stage in which the girl longs for her father and resents her mother

latency a phase of psychosexual development characterized by repression of sexual impulses

genital stage the mature stage of psychosexual development, characterized by preferred expression of libido through intercourse with an adult of the other gender

10-1b NEO-FREUDIANS

Several personality theorists—*neo-Freudians*—are among Freud's intellectual heirs. Their theories, like his, include conflict and defense mechanisms. In other respects, they differ considerably.

CARL JUNG Carl Jung (1875–1961) was a Swiss psychiatrist who had been a member of Freud's inner circle. He fell into disfavor with Freud when he developed his own psychodynamic theory—**analytical psychology**. In contrast to Freud, Jung downplayed the importance of sex, which he saw as just one of several important instincts.

Jung, like Freud, was intrigued by unconscious processes. He believed that we not only have a *personal* unconscious that contains repressed memories and impulses, but also a **collective unconscious** containing primitive images, or *archetypes*, that reflect the history of our species. Examples of archetypes are the all-powerful God, the young hero, the fertile and nurturing mother, the wise old man, the hostile brother—even fairy godmothers, wicked witches, and themes of rebirth or resurrection. Archetypes themselves remain unconscious, but Jung believed they affect our thoughts and feelings and cause us to respond to cultural themes in the media.

ALFRED ADLER Alfred Adler (1870–1937), another follower of Freud, also felt that Freud had placed too much emphasis on sex. Adler believed that people are basically motivated by an **inferiority complex**. In some people, feelings of inferiority may be based on physical problems and the need to compensate for them. Adler believed, however, that all of us encounter some feelings of inferiority because of our small size as children, and that these feelings give rise to a *drive for superiority*. As a child, Adler was crippled by rickets and suffered from pneumonia, and it may be that his theory developed in part from his own striving to overcome bouts of illness.

Adler believed that self-awareness plays a major role in the formation of personality. He spoke of a **creative self**, a self-aware aspect of personality that strives to overcome obstacles and develop the person's potential. Because each person's potential is unique, Adler's views have been termed **individual psychology**.

KAREN HORNEY Karen Horney (1885–1952) was criticized by the New York Psychoanalytic Institute because she took issue with the way in which psychoanalytic theory portrayed women. Early in the 20th century, psychoanalytic theory taught that a woman's place was in the home. Women who sought to compete with men in the business world were assumed to be suffering from unconscious *penis envy*. Psychoanalytic theory taught that little girls feel inferior to boys when they learn that boys have a penis and they do not. But Horney argued that little girls do *not* feel inferior to boys and that these views were founded on Western cultural prejudice, not scientific evidence.

Horney agreed with Freud that childhood experiences are important in psychological development. Like other neo-Freudians, however, she asserted that unconscious sexual and aggressive impulses are less important than social relationships. She also believed that genuine and consistent love can alleviate the effects of a traumatic childhood.

ERIK ERIKSON Like many other modern psychoanalysts, Erik Erikson (1902–1994) believed that Freud had placed undue emphasis on sex. Like Horney, he believed that social relationships (such as that between a parent and child) are more important determinants of personality than sexual urges. Erikson also believed that to a large

KAREN HORNEY

▸ Agreed with Freud that childhood experiences are important

▸ Believed that social relationships are more important than sexual and aggressive impulses

▸ Denied that girls feel inferior to boys

analytical psychology Jung's psychodynamic theory, which emphasizes the collective unconscious and archetypes

collective unconscious Jung's hypothesized store of vague memories that represent the history of humankind

inferiority complex feelings of inferiority hypothesized by Adler to serve as a central motivating force

creative self according to Adler, the self-aware aspect of personality that strives to achieve its full potential

individual psychology Adler's psychoanalytic theory, which emphasizes feelings of inferiority and the creative self

psychosocial development Erikson's theory of personality and development, which emphasizes social relationships and eight stages of growth

ego identity a firm sense of who one is and what one stands for

What have psychologists learned about the appeal of celebrities, and especially sports celebrities? Many people form deep and enduring bonds of attachment with athletes and sports teams. Once they identify with a team, their self-esteem rises and falls with the team's wins and losses (Wann et al., 2011a, 2011b). Wins lead to a surge of testosterone in males (P. Miller et al., 2013; Wood & Stanton, 2011), which is connected with aggressiveness and self-confidence. Wins increase the optimism of both males and females.

Psychodynamic theory suggests that children identify with parents and other "big" people in their lives because big people seem to hold the keys to the resources they need for sustenance and stimulation or excitement. Athletes and entertainers—the rich and famous—have their fan clubs, filled with people who tie their own lights to the brilliant suns of their stars.

Teams and sports heroes provide both entertainment and the kind of gutsy competition that evolutionary psychologists believe whispers to us from our genes, pushing us toward aggression and dominance. If we can't do it on our own, we can do it through someone else. In some kind of psychological sense, we can be someone who is more effective at climbing the heap of humankind into the sun.

Michael Regan/Getty Images Sport/Getty Images

---

extent we are the conscious architects of our own personalities.

Erikson, like Freud, is known for devising a comprehensive theory of personality development. But whereas Freud proposed stages of psycho*sexual* development, Erikson proposed stages of psycho*social* development. Rather than label stages for various erogenous zones, Erikson labeled them for the traits that might be developed during the stages. The first stage of **psychosocial development** is labeled the stage of trust versus mistrust because two outcomes are possible: (1) a warm, loving relationship with the mother and others during infancy might lead to a sense of basic trust in people and the world; or (2) a cold, ungratifying relationship with the mother and others might generate a general sense

Ted Streshinsky/Time Life Pictures/Getty Images

ERIK ERIKSON

▶ Believed Freud placed too much emphasis on sex

▶ Spoke of psychosocial development, not psychosexual development

▶ Labeled stages of development according to traits, not erogenous zones

▶ Argued that ego identity, not genital sexuality, was key goal of adolescence

of mistrust. For Erikson, the goal of adolescence is the attainment of **ego identity**, not genital sexuality. The focus is on whom we see ourselves as being and what we stand for, not on sexual interests.

10-1c EVALUATION OF THE PSYCHODYNAMIC PERSPECTIVE

Psychodynamic theories have tremendous appeal. They are rich in concepts and seem to explain many human traits. Today, concepts such as the *id* and *libido* strike many psychologists as unscientific, but Freud was fighting for the idea that human personality and behavior are subject to scientific analysis. He developed his theory at a time when many people viewed psychological problems as signs of possession by the devil or evil spirits. Freud argued that psychological disorders stem from psychological problems—not evil spirits. His views contributed to the development of compassion for people with psychological disorders and to methods of psychotherapy.

Psychodynamic theory also focused attention on the far-reaching effects of childhood events and suggested that parents respond to the emotional needs of their children. Freud has helped us recognize that sexual and aggressive urges are common, and that recognizing them is not the same as acting on them. On the other hand, his views of girls and women have been seen as sexist, as noted by Karen Horney.

> "FREUD FOUND SEX AN OUTCAST IN THE OUTHOUSE, AND LEFT IT IN THE LIVING ROOM AN HONORED GUEST."
>
> W. BERTRAM WOLFE, AMERICAN SCHOLAR (1896–1977)

Critics note that "psychic structures"—id, ego, and superego—are too vague to measure scientifically (Hergenhahn & Henley, 2013). Nor can they be used to predict behavior. Nor have the stages of psychosexual development escaped criticism. Children begin to masturbate as early as the first year, not in the phallic stage. As parents know from discovering their children playing "doctor," the latency stage is not as sexually latent as Freud believed. Much of Freud's thinking about the Oedipus and Electra complexes remains little more than speculation.

The evidence for Erikson's developmental views seems sturdier. For example, people who fail to develop ego identity in adolescence seem to have problems with intimate relationships later on.

Freud's clinical method of gathering evidence is also suspect (Hergenhahn & Henley, 2013). Therapists may subtly guide clients into producing memories and feelings they expect to find. Also, most psychodynamic theorists restricted their evidence gathering to case studies with individuals who sought help, particularly people from the middle and upper classes. People who seek therapy differ from the general population.

Psychoanalytic theory focused on reasons that people develop certain traits. We next

trait a relatively stable aspect of personality that is inferred from behavior and assumed to give rise to consistent behavior

discuss trait theory, which is not so much concerned with the origins of traits as with their description and categorization.

10-2 THE TRAIT PERSPECTIVE

The notion of *traits* is familiar enough. If I asked you to describe yourself, you would probably do so in terms of traits such as bright, sophisticated, and witty. (That is you, is it not?) We also describe other people in terms of traits.

Traits are reasonably stable elements of personality that are inferred from behavior. If you describe a friend as "shy," it may be because you have observed anxiety or withdrawal in that person's social encounters. Traits are assumed to account for consistent behavior in different situations. You probably expect your "shy" friend to be retiring in most social confrontations. The concept of traits is also found in other approaches to personality. Freud linked the development of certain traits to children's experiences in each stage of psychosexual development.

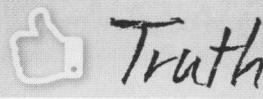

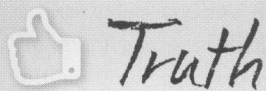
It is true that bloodletting and vomiting were once recommended as ways of coping with depression. It was believed that they would restore the balance of bodily humors.

10-2a FROM HIPPOCRATES TO THE PRESENT

The trait perspective dates at least to the Greek physician Hippocrates (ca. 460–377 BCE). Hippocrates believed that traits were embedded in bodily fluids. In his view, a person's personality depends on the balance of four basic fluids, or "humors," in the body. Yellow bile is associated with a choleric (quick-tempered) disposition; blood with a sanguine (warm, cheerful) one; phlegm with a phlegmatic (sluggish, calm, cool) disposition; and black bile with a melancholic (gloomy, pensive) temperament. Disease was believed to reflect an imbalance among the humors. Depression, for example, represented an excess of black bile. Methods such as bloodletting and vomiting were recommended to restore the balance (Ahonen, 2014). Although Hippocrates' theory was speculative, the terms *choleric, sanguine,* and so on are still used in descriptions of personality.

More contemporary trait theories assume that traits are heritable and are embedded in the nervous system. These theories rely on the mathematical technique of *factor analysis,* developed by Charles Spearman to study intelligence, to determine which traits are basic to others.

Early in the 20th century, Gordon Allport and a colleague (Allport & Oddbert, 1936) catalogued some 18,000 human traits from a search through word lists like dictionaries. Some were physical traits such as short, weak, and brunette. Others were behavioral traits such as shy and emotional. Still others were moral traits such as honest. This exhaustive list has served as the basis for personality research by many other psychologists.

10-2b HANS EYSENCK'S TRAIT THEORY

British psychologist Hans J. Eysenck (1916–1997) focused much of his research on the relationships between two personality traits: **introversion–extraversion** and emotional stability–instability (Eysenck & Eysenck, 1985). (Emotional instability is also called *neuroticism.*) Carl Jung was the first to distinguish between introverts and extraverts. Eysenck added the dimension of emotional stability–instability to introversion–extraversion. He catalogued various personality traits according to where they are situated along these dimensions (see Figure 10.2). For example, an anxious person would be high in both introversion and neuroticism—that is, preoccupied with his or her own thoughts and emotionally unstable.

Eysenck acknowledged that his scheme is similar to Hippocrates'. According to Eysenck's dimensions, the choleric type would be extraverted and unstable; the sanguine type, extraverted and stable; the phlegmatic type, introverted and stable; and the melancholic type, introverted and unstable.

10-2c THE "BIG FIVE": THE FIVE-FACTOR MODEL

More recent research suggests that there may be five basic personality factors, not two. These include the two found by Eysenck—*extraversion* and *neuroticism*—along with *conscientiousness, agreeableness,* and *openness to experience* (see Table 10.1).

Many personality theorists, especially Robert McCrae and Paul T. Costa, Jr. (2013), played a role in the development of the five-factor model. Cross-cultural research has found that these five factors appear to define the personality structure of American, German, Portuguese, Israeli, Chinese, Korean, Japanese, and Philippine people (Katigbak et al., 2002; McCrae & Costa, 1997). A study of more than 5,000 German, British, Spanish, Czech, and Turkish people suggests that the factors are related to people's basic temperaments, which are considered to be largely

> "IN MOST OF US BY THE AGE OF THIRTY, THE CHARACTER HAS SET LIKE PLASTER, AND WILL NEVER SOFTEN AGAIN."
>
> WILLIAM JAMES, AMERICAN PHILOSOPHER AND PSYCHOLOGIST (1842–1910)

introversion a trait characterized by intense imagination and the tendency to inhibit impulses

extraversion a trait characterized by tendencies to be socially outgoing and to express feelings and impulses freely

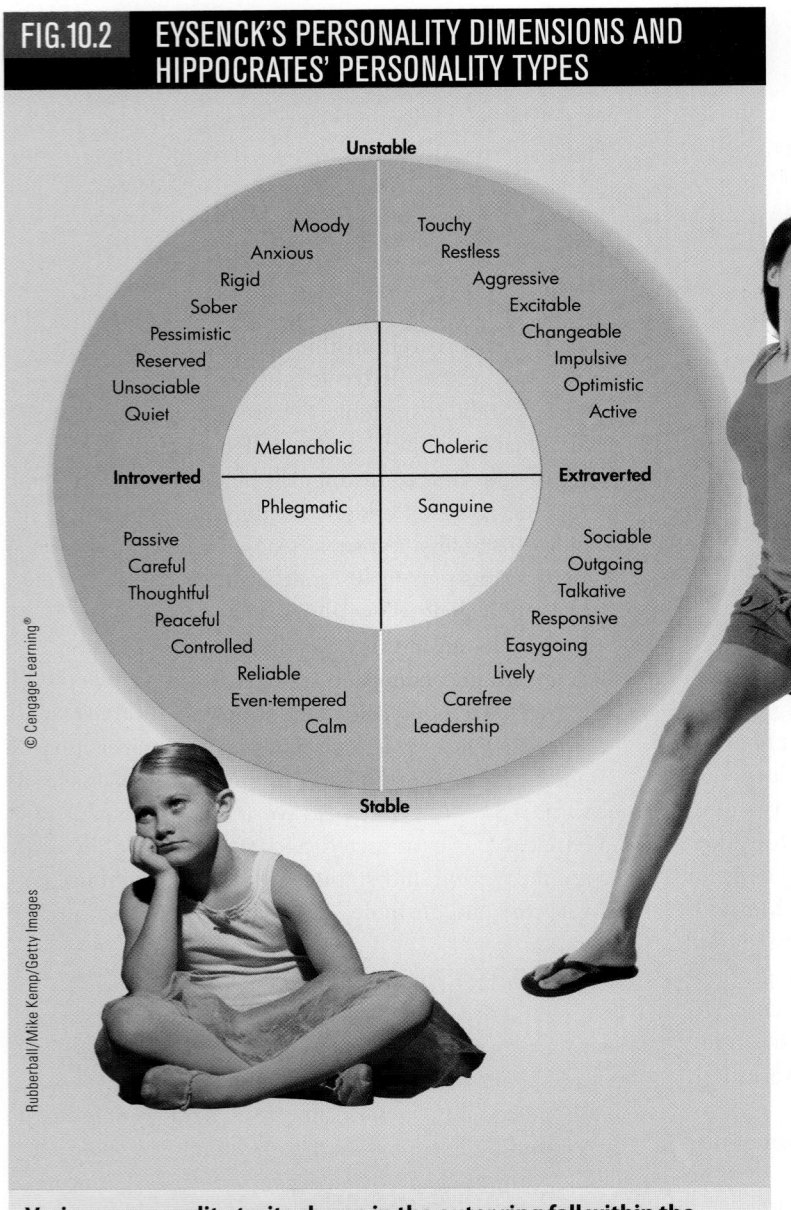

Unstable

Moody
Anxious
Rigid
Sober
Pessimistic
Reserved
Unsociable
Quiet

Touchy
Restless
Aggressive
Excitable
Changeable
Impulsive
Optimistic
Active

Melancholic | Choleric

Introverted

Extraverted

Phlegmatic | Sanguine

Passive
Careful
Thoughtful
Peaceful
Controlled
Reliable
Even-tempered
Calm

Sociable
Outgoing
Talkative
Responsive
Easygoing
Lively
Carefree
Leadership

Stable

© Cengage Learning®

Rubberball/Mike Kemp/Getty Images

Rubberball/Getty Images

Various personality traits shown in the outer ring fall within the two major dimensions of personality suggested by Hans Eysenck, The inner circle shows how Hippocrates' four major personality types—choleric, sanguine, phlegmatic, and melancholic—fit within Eysenck's dimensions.

tors with various behavior patterns, psychological disorders, and kinds of "personalities." Consider driving. Significant negative correlations have been found between the numbers of traffic citations people receive and the accidents they get into, on the one hand, and the factor of agreeableness on the other (Pearson et al., 2013; Simons-Morton et al., 2013). In other words, it's safer to share the freeway with agreeable people. People who are not judgmental—who will put up with your every whim—tend to score low on conscientiousness (they don't examine you closely) and high on agreeableness (you can be yourself) (Bernardin et al., 2000). Despite the stereotype that older people, especially men, are "crotchety," assessments of 65- to 100-year-olds suggest that people, especially men, become more agreeable as they grow older (Weiss et al., 2005). Numerous studies find that political liberals tend to score higher on openness to experience, whereas political conservatives tend to score higher on conscientiousness (Cooper et al., 2013). People who have reported greater feelings of happiness and well-being are likely to score more highly than other people on scales that measure emotional stability, agreeableness, conscientiousness, and extraversion (Soto, 2014). The author of the study suggests that happiness may be good for your personality.

10-2d BIOLOGY AND TRAITS

Researchers have also been investigating biological factors that are connected with, and may give rise to, personality traits. For example, researchers estimate

inborn (McCrae et al., 2000). The researchers interpreted the results to suggest that our personalities tend to mature over time rather than be shaped by environmental conditions, although the expression of personality traits is certainly affected by culture.

The five-factor model—also known as the "Big Five" model—is fueling a great deal of research. Costa and McCrae constructed a questionnaire to measure the factions (the *NEO Five-Factor Inventory*), and studies using the inventory are correlating scores on the five fac-

TABLE 10.1	THE "BIG FIVE": THE FIVE-FACTOR MODEL
Factor Name	**Traits**
I. Extraversion	Contrasts talkativeness, assertiveness, and activity with silence, passivity, and reserve
II. Agreeableness	Contrasts kindness, trust, and warmth with hostility, selfishness, and distrust
III. Conscientiousness	Contrasts organization, thoroughness, and reliability with carelessness, negligence, and unreliability
IV. Neuroticism	Contrasts nervousness, moodiness, and sensitivity to negative stimuli with coping ability
V. Openness to experience	Contrasts imagination, curiosity, and creativity with shallowness and lack of perceptiveness

that the heritability of the extraverted personality is 40% to 60% (Smillie et al., 2010). Research suggests that brain levels of the neurotransmitter dopamine are involved with extraversion and that levels tend to be higher in extraverts than in introverts (Smillie et al., 2010).

Jerome Kagan and other researchers (Kagan & Saudino, 2001; A. K. Smith et al., 2012) have also found evidence that genetic factors are part of a child's basic temperament and are involved in shyness and behavioral inhibition. The *antisocial personality*—characterized by frequent conflict with society and lack of feelings of guilt

or anxiety—is the other side of the coin when it comes to personality. Whereas shy children readily acquire fears and are highly reactive to stress, children who are on the path to developing antisocial personalities show low responses to threats and stressors (Gao et al., 2010; Isen et al., 2010). As children, they show a pattern of deceit, callous disregard for the feelings of others, and lack of interest in conforming their behavior to social rules (Raine et al., 2014). As adults, they are likely to become involved in criminal activity.

Virtuous Traits: Positive Psychology and Trait Theory

Trait theory has found applications within positive psychology, an approach that studies character strengths and virtues such as those just listed. Psychologists are also developing psychological methods that help people increase their happiness and life satisfaction (Lyubomirsky et al., 2011; Shyrack et al., 2010). Psychologists list six major virtues (see the table below) that were found in countries as different as Azerbaijan and Venezuela, along with the United States and other developed nations (Peterson & Seligman, 2004; Snyder et al., 2010).

The Character Strengths and Virtues inventory (CSV) was partly developed as a counterpoint to the *DSM*, which is the *Diagnostic and Statistical Manual of the Mental Disorders* of the American Psychiatric Association (2013). Whereas the *DSM* is a catalogue

of (nearly) everything that can go wrong with people, the *CSV* is a catalogue of things that go right. Fortunately, there are many of them.

Virtue	Corresponding Character Strengths
Wisdom and knowledge	Creativity, curiosity, open-mindedness, love of learning, perspective (ability to provide other people with sound advice)
Courage	Authenticity (speaking one's mind), bravery, persistence, zest
Humanity	Kindness, love, social intelligence
Justice	Fairness, leadership, teamwork
Temperance	Forgiveness, modesty, prudence, self-regulation
Transcendence	Appreciation of beauty and excellence, gratitude (when appropriate), hope, humor, religiosity (having a belief system about the meaning of life)

Source: Peterson and Seligman (2004).

Adrian Raine (2008; Raine et al., 2014) has extensively studied the intersection of biology and the antisocial personality. In a review of the literature, he found a number of brain impairments that are related to the development of an antisocial personality in the ventral prefrontal cortex (part of the so-called executive center of the brain) and the amygdala (a part of the limbic system involved in emotional reactivity).

10-2e EVALUATION OF THE TRAIT PERSPECTIVE

Trait theorists have focused much attention on the development of personality tests. They have also given rise to theories about the fit between personality and certain kinds of jobs. The qualities that suit a person for various kinds of work can be expressed in terms of abilities, personality traits, and interests.

One limitation of trait theory is that it has tended to be more descriptive than explanatory. It has historically focused on describing traits rather than on tracing their origins or seeking ways to modify maladaptive personality traits and behavior.

10-3 LEARNING-THEORY PERSPECTIVES

Trait theory focused on enduring personality characteristics that were generally presumed to be embedded in the nervous system. Learning theorists tend not to theorize in terms of traits. They focus instead on behaviors and presume that those behaviors are largely learned.

That which is learned is also, in principle, capable of being unlearned. As a result, learning theory and personality theory may not be a perfect fit. Nevertheless, learning theorists—both behaviorists and social cognitive theorists—have contributed to the discussion of personality.

10-3a BEHAVIORISM

At Johns Hopkins University in 1924, John B. Watson sounded the battle cry of the behaviorist movement:

social cognitive theory a cognitively oriented learning theory in which observational learning and person variables such as values and expectancies play major roles in individual differences

Give me a dozen healthy infants, well-formed, and my own specified world to bring them up in, and I'll guarantee to take any one at random and train him to become any type of specialist I might suggest—doctor, lawyer, merchant-chief and, yes, even beggar-man and thief, regardless of his talents, penchants, tendencies, abilities, vocations, and the race of his ancestors.

This proclamation underscores the behaviorist view that personality is plastic—that situational or environmental influences, not internal, individual variables, are the key shapers of personality. In contrast to the psychoanalysts and structuralists of his day, Watson argued that unseen, undetectable mental structures must be rejected in favor of that which can be seen and measured. In the 1930s, Watson's flag was carried onward by B. F. Skinner, who agreed that psychologists should avoid trying to see into the "black box" of the organism and instead emphasize the effects of reinforcements on behavior.

The views of Watson and Skinner largely ignored the notions of personal freedom, choice, and self-direction. Most of us assume that our wants originate within us. Watson and Skinner suggested that environmental influences such as parental approval and social customs shape us into *wanting* certain things and *not wanting* others.

In his novel *Walden Two*, Skinner (1948) described a Utopian society in which people are happy and content because they are allowed to do as they please. From early childhood, however, they have been trained or conditioned to be cooperative. Because of their reinforcement histories, they want to behave in decent, kind, and unselfish ways. They see themselves as free because society makes no effort to force them to behave in particular ways. The American poet Robert Frost wrote, "You have freedom when you're easy in your harness." Society in Skinner's *Walden Two* made children "easy" in their "harnesses," but the harnesses were very real.

Some object to behaviorist notions because they play down the importance of consciousness and choice. Others argue that humans are not blindly ruled by reinforcers (that is, rewards and punishments). In some circumstances, people have rebelled against the so-called necessity of survival by choosing pain and hardship over pleasure, or death over life. Many people have sacrificed their own lives to save those of others. The behaviorist "defense" might be that the apparent choice of pain or death is forced on some just as conformity to social custom is forced on others.

10-3b SOCIAL COGNITIVE THEORY

Social cognitive theory was developed by Albert Bandura (1986, 2012) and other psychologists. In contrast to behaviorism, which focuses on observable behavior and the situations in which behavior occurs, social cognitive theory focuses on learning by observation and on the cognitive processes that underlie personal differences. Social cognitive theorists differ from behaviorists in that they see people as influencing their environment just as their environment affects them. Social cognitive theorists agree with behaviorists that discussions of human nature should be tied to observable behavior, but they assert that variables within people—*person variables*—must also be considered if we are to understand people. *Situational variables* include rewards and punishments. Person variables include knowledge and skills, ways of interpreting experience, expectancies, emotions, and self-regulatory systems and plans (Bandura, 2012). See Figure 10.3.

We cannot predict behavior from situational variables alone. Whether a person will behave in a certain way also depends on the person's *expectancies* about the outcomes of that behavior and the perceived or *subjective values* of those outcomes. There are various kinds of expectancies. Some are predictions about what will follow what. For example, people might predict other people's behavior on the basis of body language such as "tight lips" or "shifty eyes." *Self-efficacy expectations* are beliefs that we can accomplish certain things, such as doing a backflip into a swimming pool or solving math problems. People with positive self-efficacy expectations

tend to have high self-esteem and achievement motivation (Zuffiano et al., 2013). Psychotherapy often motivates people to try new things by changing their self-efficacy expectations from "I can't" to "Perhaps I can" (Bandura, 1999, 2008).

OBSERVATIONAL LEARNING Observational learning (also termed *modeling* or *cognitive learning*) is one of the foundations of social cognitive theory. It refers to acquiring knowledge by observing others. For operant conditioning to occur, an organism must first engage in a response, and that response must be reinforced. However, observational learning occurs even when the learner does not perform the observed behavior. Direct reinforcement is not required either. Observing others extends to reading about them or seeing what they do and what happens to them in books, TV, film, and the Internet.

10-3c EVALUATION OF THE LEARNING PERSPECTIVE

Learning theorists have contributed to the scientific understanding of behavior, but they have left some psychologists dissatisfied. Psychodynamic theorists and trait theorists propose the existence of psychological structures that cannot be seen and measured directly. Learning theorists—particularly behaviorists—have dramatized the importance of referring to

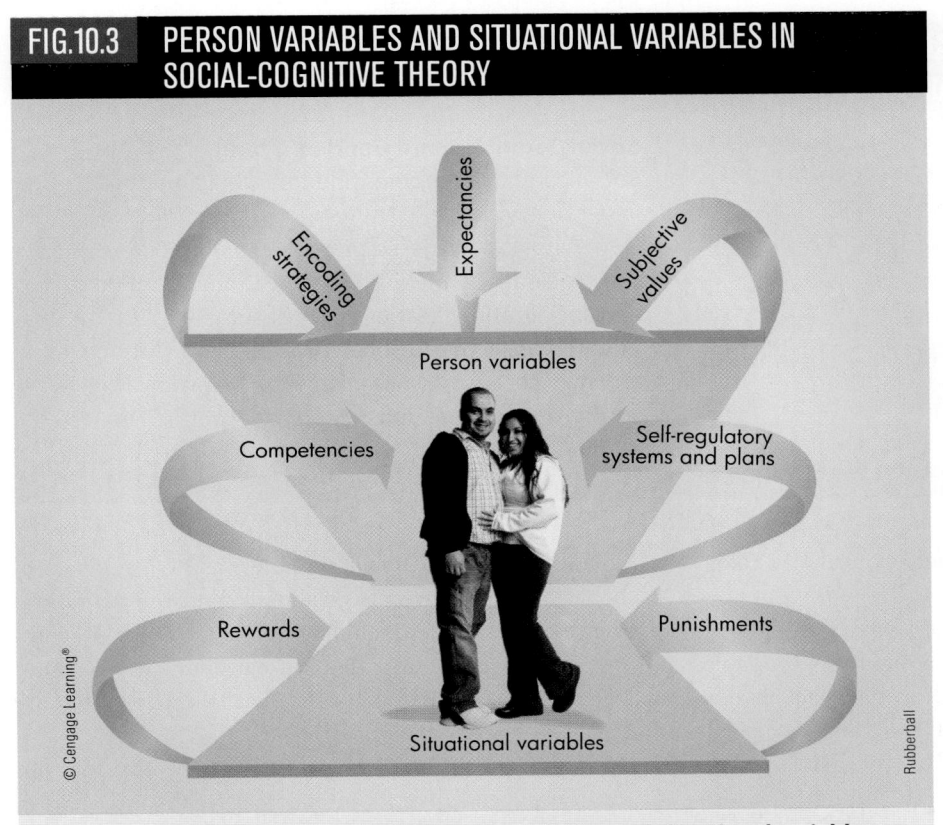

FIG. 10.3 PERSON VARIABLES AND SITUATIONAL VARIABLES IN SOCIAL-COGNITIVE THEORY

Expectancies

Encoding strategies

Subjective values

Person variables

Competencies

Self-regulatory systems and plans

Rewards

Punishments

Situational variables

© Cengage Learning®

Rubberball

According to social-cognitive theory, person variables and situational variables interact to influence behavior.

Biology, Social Cognition, and Gender-Typing

Gender-typing is the process by which males and females come to develop personality traits and behavior patterns that society considers to be consistent with their gender, male or female—at least most of the time. Researchers who investigate people's perceptions of gender differences in personality traits tend to find groups of "masculine" and "feminine" traits, such as those shown in Table 10.2. According to evolutionary psychologists, gender differences were fashioned by natural selection in response to problems in adaptation that were repeatedly encountered over thousands of generations (Buss, 2009; Leaper, 2013). Men, who have generally been the hunters, breadwinners, and warriors, are more likely to be seen as *adventurous, aggressive,* and *assertive*. Women, who have more often been the homemakers and caretakers, are more likely to be seen as *affectionate, agreeable,* and *emotional* (Leaper, 2013; Lippa, 2010).

Biology and Gender-Typing

Other researchers suggest that the development of gender differences in personality, along with the development of anatomic gender differences, may be related to prenatal levels of sex hormones. A number of studies have correlated prenatal sex hormone levels with subsequent gender-typed play. For example, a study of 212 pregnant women conducted by Bonnie Auyeung and her colleagues (2009) found that higher-than-normal levels of testosterone in the fetal environment, due to maternal stress, were related to more masculine-typed play among girls at the age of 8½ years. Emily Barrett and her colleagues (2014) found that exposure to the prenatal environments of stressed mothers can boost masculine-typed play in girls and decrease it in boys. Other studies show that children display gender-typed preferences—with boys preferring transportation toys and girls preferring dolls—as early as the age of 13 months (Knickmeyer et al., 2005). Another study investigated the gender-typed visual preferences of 30 human infants at the early ages of 3 to 8 months (Alexander et al., 2009). The researchers assessed interest in a toy truck and a doll by using eye-tracking technology to indicate the direction of visual attention. Girls showed a visual preference for the doll over the truck (that is, they made a greater number of visual fixations on the doll), and boys showed a visual preference for the truck.

TABLE 10.2	STEREOTYPICAL MASCULINE AND FEMININE TRAITS		
Masculine		**Feminine**	
Adventurous	Hardheaded	Affectionate	Fickle
Aggressive	Independent	Agreeable	Gentle
Assertive	Intelligent	Cautious	Kind
Capable	Pleasure-seeking	Dependent	Patient
Confident	Scientific	Emotional	Sensitive
Courageous	Rational	Fearful	Talkative
Determined			

Sources: Leaper (2013); Lippa (2010).

Social Cognition and Gender-Typing

Social cognitive theorists find roles for learning in gender-typing, and they suggest that children learn what is considered masculine or feminine in their societies by means of observational learning and socialization (Leaper, 2013; Zosuls et al., 2009). Children observe the behavior of adult role models and may come to assume that their behavior should conform to that of adults of the same gender.

publicly observable variables, or behaviors, if psychology is to be accepted as a science.

Similarly, psychodynamic theorists and trait theorists focus on internal variables such as unconscious conflict and traits to explain and predict behavior. Learning theorists emphasize the importance of environmental conditions, or situational variables, as determinants of behavior. They have also elaborated on the conditions that foster learning, including automatic kinds of learning. They have shown that we can learn to do things because of reinforcements and that many behaviors are learned by observing others.

Social cognitive theory does not account for self-awareness, and, like its intellectual forebear, behaviorism, it may not pay enough attention to genetic variation in explaining individual differences in behavior.

gender-typing the process by which males and females come to display behavior patterns consistent with stereotypical masculine and feminine gender roles

She's Going to Have Twins! A boy and a girl. Do you think she will raise them in the same way? Why?

In social-cognitive theory, rewards and punishments influence children to imitate adult models of the same gender. The child not only imitates the behavior of the model but also tries to become broadly like the model—that is, she or he *identifies* with the model.

Almost from the moment a baby comes into the world, she or he is treated in ways that are consistent with gender stereotypes. Parents tend to talk more to baby girls, and fathers especially engage in more roughhousing with boys. When children are old enough to speak, caregivers and even other children begin to tell them how they are expected to behave. Parents may reward children for behavior they consider gender appropriate and punish (or fail to reinforce) them for behavior they consider inappropriate. Girls are encouraged to practice caregiving, which is intended to prepare them for traditional feminine adult roles. Boys are handed Legos or doctor sets to help prepare them for traditional masculine adult roles.

The Gender-Schema Theory of Gender-Typing
Gender-schema theory emphasizes the role of cognition in gender-typing (Liben et al., 2014; Martin & Ruble, 2004). Gender-schema theory proposes that children develop a **gender schema** as a means of organizing their perceptions of the world. A gender schema is a cluster of ideas about masculine and feminine physical traits (Dinella et al., 2014). Gender becomes important because of society's emphasis on it. According to gender-schema theory, once children come to see themselves as female or male, they begin to seek information concerning gender-typed traits and try to live up to them (Liben et al., 2014; Tenenbaum et al., 2010). Jack will retaliate when provoked because boys are expected to do so. Jill will be "sugary and sweet" if such is expected of little girls.

Today, most scholars would agree that both biology and social cognition interact to affect most areas of behavior and mental processes—including the complex processes involved in gender-typing.

10-4 THE HUMANISTIC–EXISTENTIAL PERSPECTIVE

Humanists and existentialists dwell on the meaning of life. Self-awareness is the hub of the humanistic–existential search for meaning. The term **humanism** has a long history and many meanings. As a counterpoint (or "third force") to the predominant psychodynamic and behavioral models, it puts self-awareness at the center of consideration and argues that people are capable of free choice, self-fulfillment, and ethical behavior. Humanism also has represented a reaction to the "rat race" spawned by industrialization and

gender-schema theory a cognitive view of gender-typing that proposes that once girls and boys become aware of their anatomic sex, they begin to blend their self-expectations and self-esteem with the ways in which they fit the gender roles prescribed in a given culture

humanism the view that people are capable of free choice, self-fulfillment, and ethical behavior

automation. The humanistic views of Abraham Maslow and Carl Rogers emerged from these concerns.

Existentialism in part reflects the horrors of mass destruction of human life through war and genocide, frequent events in the 20th century. The European existentialist philosophers Jean-Paul Sartre and Martin Heidegger saw human life as trivial in the grand scheme of things. But psychiatrists like Viktor Frankl, Ludwig Binswanger, and Medard Boss argued that seeing human existence as meaningless could give rise to withdrawal and apathy—even suicide. Psychological salvation therefore requires giving personal meaning to things and making personal choices.

10-4a ABRAHAM MASLOW AND THE CHALLENGE OF SELF-ACTUALIZATION

Freud wrote that people are basically motivated to gratify biological drives and that their perceptions are distorted by their psychological needs. The humanistic psychologist Abraham Maslow—whose hierarchy of needs we described in Chapter 8—argued that people also have a conscious need for **self-actualization**, or to become all that they can be. Because people are unique, they must follow unique paths to self-actualization. People are not at the mercy of unconscious, primitive impulses. Rather, the main threat to individual personality development is control by other people. We must each be free to get in touch with and actualize our selves. But self-actualization requires taking risks. Many people are more comfortable with the familiar. But people who adhere to the "tried and true" may find their lives slipping into monotony and mediocrity.

10-4b CARL ROGERS'S SELF THEORY

The humanistic psychologist Carl Rogers (1902–1987) wrote that people shape themselves through free choice and action. Rogers defined the *self* as the center of experience. Your self is your ongoing sense of who and what you are, your sense of how and why you react to the environment and how you choose to act on the environment. Your choices are made on the basis of your values, and your values are also part of your self. Rogers's self theory focuses on the nature of the self and the conditions that allow the self to develop freely. Two of his major concerns are the self-concept and self-esteem.

THE SELF-CONCEPT AND FRAMES OF REFERENCE Our *self-concepts* consist of our impressions of ourselves and our evaluations of our adequacy. Rogers believed that we all have unique ways of looking at ourselves and the world—that is, unique *frames of reference*. It may be that we each use a different set of dimensions in defining ourselves and that we judge ourselves according to different sets of values. To one person, achievement–failure may be the most important dimension. To another person, the most important dimension may be decency–indecency. A third person may not even think in these terms.

SELF-ESTEEM AND POSITIVE REGARD Rogers assumed that we all develop a need for self-regard, or self-esteem. At first, self-esteem reflects the esteem in which others hold us. Parents help children develop self-esteem when they

> "ALWAYS REMEMBER THAT YOU ARE ABSOLUTELY UNIQUE. JUST LIKE EVERYONE ELSE."
>
> MARGARET MEAD, AMERICAN CULTURAL ANTHROPOLOGIST (1901–1978)

Many males tie their self-esteem to prowess in athletics. What are the sources of your self-esteem?

Pierre Tostee/ASP/Getty Images

You are unique, and if that is not fulfilled, then something has been lost. -Martha Graham

children may come to think that they have merit only if they behave as their parents wish them to behave.

Because each individual has a unique potential, children who develop conditions of worth must be somewhat disappointed in themselves. They cannot fully live up to the wishes of others and be true to themselves. Children in some families learn that it is bad to have ideas of their own, especially about sexual, political, or religious matters. When they perceive their caregivers' disapproval, they may come to see themselves as rebels and label their feelings as selfish, wrong, or evil. If they wish to retain a consistent self-concept and self-esteem, they may have to deny their feelings or disown parts of themselves. In this way, their self-concept becomes distorted. According to Rogers, anxiety often stems from recognition that people have feelings and desires that are inconsistent with their distorted self-concept. Because anxiety is unpleasant, people may deny the existence of their genuine feelings and desires.

Rogers believed that the path to self-actualization requires getting in touch with our genuine feelings, accepting them, and acting on them. This is the goal of Rogers's method of psychotherapy, *client-centered therapy*. Rogers also believed that we have mental images of what we are capable of becoming. These are termed *self-ideals*. We are motivated to reduce the difference between our self-concepts and our self-ideals.

10-4c EVALUATION OF THE HUMANISTIC-EXISTENTIAL PERSPECTIVE

Humanistic–existential theories have tremendous appeal for college students because of their focus on the importance of personal experience. We tend to treasure our conscious experiences (our "selves"). For most nonhumans, to live is to move, to process food, to exchange oxygen and carbon dioxide, and to reproduce. But for humans, an essential aspect of life is conscious experience—the sense of oneself as progressing through space and time.

Ironically, the primary strength of the humanistic–existential approaches—their focus on conscious experience—is also their main weakness. Conscious experience is private and

show them **unconditional positive regard**—that is, when they accept them as having intrinsic merit regardless of their behavior at the moment. Rogers was optimistic about human nature. He believed that people are basically good, and that when they develop in an atmosphere of unconditional positive regard, they will become generous and loving—not selfish. But when parents show children **conditional positive regard**—that is, when they accept them only when they behave in a desired manner—children may develop **conditions of worth**. Therefore,

existentialism the view that people are completely free and responsible for their own behavior

self-actualization in humanistic theory, the innate tendency to strive to realize one's potential

unconditional positive regard a persistent expression of esteem for the value of a person, but not necessarily an unqualified acceptance of all of the person's behaviors

conditional positive regard judgment of another person's value on the basis of the acceptability of that person's behaviors

conditions of worth standards by which the value of a person is judged

subjective. Therefore, the validity of formulating theories in terms of consciousness has been questioned.

Humanistic–existential theories, like learning theories, have little to say about the development of traits and personality types. They assume that we are all unique, but they do not predict the sorts of traits, abilities, and interests we will develop.

10-5 THE SOCIOCULTURAL PERSPECTIVE

Thirteen-year-old Hannah brought her lunch tray to the table in the cafeteria. Her mother, Julie, eyed with horror the French fries, the plate of mashed potatoes in gravy, the bag of potato chips, and the large paper cup brimming with soda. "You can't eat that!" she said. "It's garbage!"

"Oh come on, Mom! Chill, okay?" Hannah rejoined before taking her tray to sit with some friends rather than with us.

I used to spend Saturdays with my children at the Manhattan School of Music. Not only did they study voice and piano, they—and I—widened our cultural perspective by relating to families and students from all parts of the world.

Julie and Hannah are Korean Americans. Flustered, Julie shook her head and said, "I've now been in the United States longer than I was in Korea, and I still can't get used to the way children act here. When she talks that way, it's embarrassing." I vaguely recall making some unhelpful comments about the ketchup on the French fries having antioxidants and some slightly helpful comments about what is typical of teenagers in the United States. But as I thought about Hannah, I realized that in our multicultural society, personality cannot be understood without reference to the **sociocultural perspective**. Different ethnic groups within the United States have different attitudes, beliefs,

sociocultural perspective the view that focuses on the roles of ethnicity, gender, culture, and socioeconomic status in personality formation, behavior, and mental processes

individualist a person who defines herself or himself in terms of personal traits and gives priority to her or his own goals

collectivist a person who defines herself or himself in terms of relationships to other people and groups and gives priority to group goals

acculturation the process of adaptation in which immigrants and native groups identify with a new, dominant culture by learning about that culture and making behavioral and attitudinal changes

norms, self-definitions, and values (Phinney & Baledelomar, 2011; Schwartz et al., 2010).

Hannah was strongly influenced by her peers—she was completely at home with blue jeans and French fries. She was also a daughter in an Asian American immigrant group that views education as the key to success in our culture (Chen & Fouad, 2013; Magno, 2010). Belonging to this ethnic group had contributed to her ambition and her hard work in school and on her violin, but it had not prevented her from becoming an outspoken American teenager. Behavior that struck me as typical and inoffensive had struck her mother as brazen and inappropriate.

Let's consider how sociocultural factors can affect one's sense of self.

10-5a INDIVIDUALISM VERSUS COLLECTIVISM: WHO AM I (IN THIS CULTURAL SETTING)?

One could say that Julie's complaint was that Hannah saw herself as an individual and an artist to a greater extent than as a family member and a Korean girl. Cross-cultural research reveals that people in the United States and many northern European nations tend to be individualistic. **Individualists** tend to define themselves in terms of their personal identities and to give priority to their personal goals (Ching et al., 2014; Triandis, 2006). When asked to complete the statement "I am . . . ," they are likely to respond in terms of their personality traits ("I am outgoing," "I am artistic") or their occupations ("I am a nurse," "I am a systems analyst") (Triandis & Suh, 2005).

In contrast, many people from cultures in Africa, Asia, and Central and South America tend to be collectivistic (Ching et al., 2014; Triandis, 2006). **Collectivists** tend to define themselves in terms of the groups to which they belong and to give priority to the group's goals (Triandis, 2006). They feel complete in terms of their relationships with others (see Figure 10.4). They are more likely than individualists to conform to group norms and judgments (Triandis & Suh, 2002). When asked to complete the statement "I am . . . ," collectivists are more likely to respond in terms of their families, gender, or nation ("I am a father," "I am a Buddhist," "I am Japanese") (Triandis, 2001).

The seeds of individualism and collectivism are found in the culture in which a person grows up. The capitalist system fosters individualism to some degree. The traditional writings of the East have exalted people who resist personal temptations to do their duty and promote the welfare of the group. However, Asians in

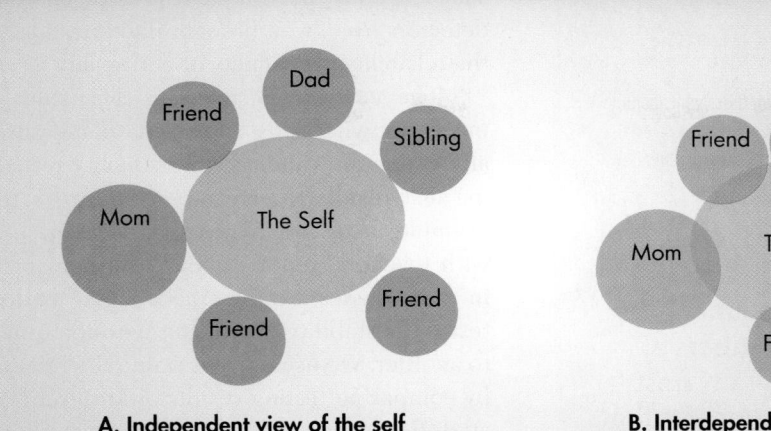

A. Independent view of the self

B. Interdependent view of the self

To an individualist, the self is separate from other people (part A). To a collectivist, the self is complete only in terms of relationships to other people (part B). (Based on Markus and Kitayama, 1991.)

burgeoning urban centers and in the United States tend to be more individualistic and achievement-oriented (Lee & Zhou, 2014).

Another issue from the sociocultural perspective is *acculturation*. Just how much acculturation is good for you?

10-5b ACCULTURATION, ADJUSTMENT, AND SELF-ESTEEM

Self-esteem is connected with patterns of **acculturation** among immigrants (Phinney & Baldelomar, 2011). Those patterns take various forms. Some immigrants are completely assimilated by the dominant culture. They lose the language and customs of their country of origin and identify with the dominant culture in the new host country. Others maintain almost complete separation. They retain the language and customs of their country of origin and never acclimate to those of the new country. Still others become bicultural. They remain fluent in the language of their country of origin but also become conversant in the language of their new country. They blend the customs and values of both cultures (Schwartz et al., 2010). They can switch "mental gears"; they apply the values of one culture under some circumstances and apply the values of the other culture

under others (Phinney & Baldelomar, 2011). Perhaps they relate to other people in one way at work or in school, and in another way at home or in the neighborhood.

Research evidence suggests that people who do not fully surrender their traditional backgrounds have relatively higher self-esteem than those who do (David et al., 2009; Leong et al., 2013). On the other hand, Latin American and Asian American immigrants who are more proficient in English are less likely to be anxious and depressed as they navigate within their new cultures (Leong et al., 2013).

10-5c EVALUATION OF THE SOCIOCULTURAL PERSPECTIVE

The sociocultural perspective provides valuable insights into the roles of ethnicity, gender, culture, and socioeconomic status in personality formation. It enhances our sensitivity to cultural differences and expectations and allows us to appreciate the richness of human behavior and mental processes.

10-6 MEASUREMENT OF PERSONALITY

Physicians have an easy time of it measuring heart rate and blood pressure. Psychologists, biologists, and neuroscientists find it easier to measure electricity in the brain or substances in the blood than to measure psychological concepts such as intelligence, depression, extraversion, or emotional stability. It may take time, money, and expertise to develop and operate the proper instruments, but once you have them, the measurements tend to be accurate enough.

In Chapter 7, we saw that many critics argue that intelligence tests measure many things other than intelligence, including motivation and familiarity with European American middle-class culture. In Chapter 8, we saw that lie detectors measure four physiological variables and detect much more than lies. The reliability and validity of intelligence tests and lie detectors have been brought into question. So too have the reliability and validity of personality tests.

The **validity** of a test is the extent to which it measures what it is supposed to measure. We usually assess the validity of personality tests by comparing test results to external criteria or standards. For example, a test of hyperactivity might be compared with teachers' reports about whether or not children in their classes are hyperactive. The **reliability** of a test is the stability of one's test results from one testing to another. We usually determine the reliability of tests by comparing testing results on different occasions or at different ages. A reliable IQ test should provide scores during childhood that remain reasonably similar in adolescence and adulthood. Test **standardization** is a process that checks out the scores, validity, and reliability of a test with people of various ages and from various groups. We cannot assess the intellectual functioning of an individual without relating it to other people in the same age group. Such information is made available when tests are professionally developed and scored.

Behavior-rating scales assess behavior in settings such as classrooms or mental hospitals. With behavior-rating scales, trained observers usually check off each occurrence of a specific behavior within a certain time frame—say, 15 minutes. However, standardized objective and projective tests are used more frequently, and we focus on them in this section.

Measures of personality are used to make important decisions, such as whether a person is suited for a certain type of work, a particular class in school, or a drug to reduce agitation. As part of their admissions process, graduate schools often ask professors to rate prospective students on scales that assess traits such as intelligence, emotional stability, and cooperation. Students may take tests to measure their *aptitudes* and interests to gain insight into whether they are suited for certain occupations. It is assumed that students who share the aptitudes and interests of people who function well in certain positions are also likely to function well in those positions.

Let's consider the two most widely used types of personality tests: objective tests and projective tests.

10-6a OBJECTIVE TESTS

Objective tests present respondents with a standardized group of test items in the form of a questionnaire. Respondents are limited to a specific range of

validity in psychological testing, the degree to which a test measures what it is supposed to measure

reliability in psychological testing, the consistency or stability of test scores from one testing to another

standardization in psychological testing, the process by which one obtains and organizes test scores from various population groups, so that the results of a person's completing a test can be compared to those of others of his or her gender, in his or her age group, and so on

objective tests tests whose items must be answered in a specified, limited manner; tests whose items have concrete answers that are considered correct

projective test a psychological test that presents ambiguous stimuli onto which the test-taker projects his or her own personality in making a response

answers. One test might ask respondents to indicate whether items are true or false for them. Another might ask respondents to select the preferred activity from groups of three.

Some tests have a *forced-choice format*, in which respondents are asked to indicate which of two or more statements is more true for them or which of several activities they prefer. The respondents are not usually given the option of answering "none of the above." Forced-choice formats are frequently used in interest inventories, which help predict whether the person would function well in a certain occupation. They are typically the only means of responding to online assessments because the test-taker is usually required to "click" the chosen answer. The following item is similar to those found in occupational interest inventories:

I would rather

  a. be a forest ranger.
  b. work in a busy office.
  c. play a musical instrument.

The Minnesota Multiphasic Personality Inventory (MMPI)[1] contains hundreds of items presented in a true–false format. The MMPI is designed for use by clinical and counseling psychologists to help diagnose psychological disorders. Accurate measurement of an individual's problems should point to appropriate treatment. The MMPI is the most widely used psychological test in clinical work and is widely used in psychological research.

The MMPI scales were constructed *empirically*—that is, on the basis of actual clinical data rather than psy-

---

[1] Currently the updated MMPI-2.

T	F	My father was a good man.
T	F	I am very seldom troubled by headaches.
T	F	My hands and feet are usually warm enough.
T	F	I have never done anything dangerous for the thrill of it.
T	F	I work under a great deal of tension.

chological theory. A test-item bank of several hundred items was derived from questions that are often asked in clinical interviews. Here are some examples of the kinds of items that were used:

The items were administered to people with previously identified symptoms, such as depressive or schizophrenic symptoms. Items that successfully set these people apart were included on scales named for these conditions. Confidence in the MMPI has developed because of its extensive use.

10-6b PROJECTIVE TESTS

Projective tests have no clear specified answers. People are shown ambiguous stimuli such as inkblots or ambiguous drawings and asked to say what they look like or to tell stories about them. Or they are asked to complete sentences or to draw pictures of persons. There is no one correct response. It is assumed that people *project* their own personalities into their responses. The meanings they attribute to these stimuli are assumed to reflect their personalities as well as the drawings or blots themselves.

THE RORSCHACH INKBLOT TEST There are a number of psychological tests made up of inkblots, and test-takers are asked to say what the blots look like to them. The best known of these is the Rorschach inkblot test, named after its originator, Hermann Rorschach.

In the Rorschach test, people are given the inkblots, one by one, and are asked what they look like or what they could be. A response that reflects the shape

 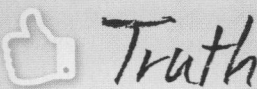

"What Does This Look Like? What Could It Be?" People taking the Rorschach Inkblot Test are given a series of cards and asked what they see on each one. Because the contents of the cards do not show actual objects, animals, or people, test-takers are believed to reveal something about themselves in their answers.

of the blot is considered a sign of adequate *reality testing*. A response that richly integrates several features of the blot is considered a sign of high intellectual functioning. Supporters of the Rorschach believe that it provides insight into a person's intelligence, interests, and perceptual processes (Mihura et al., 2013). There is less support for the test's ability to pinpoint psychological disorders and childhood conflicts (Garb et al., 2005). Even when the Rorschach is being severely challenged as a method of obtaining diagnoses of psychological disorders, researchers continue to claim that it has uses in many other areas, including the hiring and selection of personnel in organizations (Del Giudice, 2010), determination of whether individuals are suitable to have child custody (Weiner, 2006), even in the assessment of children in schools (Hojnoski et al., 2006).

Although there is no single "correct" response to the inkblot, some responses are not in keeping with the features of the blots and reveal to the examiner that the test-taker is projecting his or her personality onto the

test stimuli. The shape of the inkblot might commonly suggest a butterfly, a flower, or many other things—even pelvic bones. A test-taker who makes unusual or uncommon responses to the features of the blot may be revealing personality problems or individuality—depending on the responses.

THE THEMATIC APPERCEPTION TEST The Thematic Apperception Test (TAT) was developed in the 1930s by Henry Murray and Christiana Morgan. It consists of drawings, like the one shown in Figure 8.5 (see p. 217), that are open to various interpretations. Individuals are given the cards one at a time and asked to make up stories about them.

The TAT is widely used in research on motivation and in clinical practice. The assumption is that we are likely to project our own needs into our responses to ambiguous situations, even if we are unaware of them or reluctant to talk about them. The TAT is also widely used to assess attitudes toward other people, especially parents and intimate partners.

STUDY TOOLS 10

READY TO STUDY? IN THE BOOK, YOU CAN:

☐ Check your understanding of what you've read with the quizzes below.

☐ Rip out the chapter review card at the back of the book to have a summary of the chapter and the key terms handy.

ONLINE AT CENGAGEBRAIN.COM YOU CAN:

☐ Find out about the situation model of personality in a short video.

☐ Prepare for tests with quizzes.

☐ Review the key terms with Flash Cards.

☐ Play games to master concepts.

FILL-INS

Answers can be found in the back of the book, starting on page 393.

1. According to Freud, the unconscious psychic structure called the _____ is present at birth and operates according to the pleasure principle.

2. The _____ is the moral sense and develops by internalizing the standards of parents and others.

3. The stages of psychosexual development include the oral, _____, phallic, latency, and genital stages.

4. Jung believed that in addition to a personal unconscious mind, people also have a(n) _____ unconscious.

5. Adler believed that people are motivated by a(n) _____ complex.

6. Raine found brain impairments that are related to the development of a(n) _____ personality.

7. Maslow argued that people have growth-oriented needs for self-_____.

8. According to Rogers, we see the world through unique frames of _____.

9. According to sociocultural theory, _____ define themselves in terms of the groups to which they belong and give priority to group goals.

10. Projective tests present _____ stimuli and permit the respondent a broad range of answers.

MULTIPLE CHOICE

1. **Marisa is five months old and always chews her rattle. According to Freud, she is in the _____ stage.**
   a. anal
   b. oral
   c. phallic
   d. latency

2. **Which best illustrates a child undergoing the Oedipus complex?**
   a. Billy acts out to get his mother's attention whenever she is alone with his father.
   b. Kelly seeks out strangers for sexual encounters.
   c. Alan always goes shopping with his father.
   d. Maria has not had conscious sexual desires for the past year.

3. **Which of the following is an assumption of most trait theories?**
   a. Traits are flexible and change with time.
   b. Traits are generally learned from parents.
   c. Traits are somehow inherited and embedded in the nervous system.
   d. Traits are hard to categorize.

4. **The five-factor model includes which five basic personality factors?**
   a. depression, obsessiveness, conscientiousness, agreeableness, openness
   b. narcissism, neuroticism, conscientiousness, agreeableness, openness
   c. extraversion, neuroticism, conscientiousness, agreeableness, openness
   d. extraversion, psychosis, conscientiousness, agreeableness, openness

5. **The views of Watson and Skinner largely ignore the notion of**
   a. environmental variables.
   b. personal freedom.
   c. reinforcement and punishment.
   d. shaping.

6. **Social-cognitive theory differs from behaviorism in that social-cognitive theory argues that**
   a. rewards shape behaviors.
   b. the ego follows the moral principle.
   c. wants and desires are the result of our environment.
   d. people influence their environments.

7. **Lisa is studying musical theater. She is convinced that if she works hard enough, she will one day make it to Broadway. Her sense of conviction is an example of**
   a. self-efficacy expectations.
   b. competencies.
   c. modeling.
   d. encoding strategies.

8. **Carl Rogers believed that every person has his or her own unique**
   a. frame of character.
   b. grey eminence.
   c. frame of reinforcement.
   d. frame of reference.

9. **A test in the format of a questionnaire that has specific correct answers is an example of**
   a. an acculturated test.
   b. an innate test.
   c. an objective test.
   d. a projective test.

10. **The ability to give a response that accurately reflects the shape of the inkblot on the stimulus card is a sign of intact**
    a. neuroticism.
    b. reality testing.
    c. acculturation.
    d. collectivism.

LEARNING YOUR WAY

Go to **www.cengagebrain.com**
to access **PSYCH Online!**

 Follow us at
www.facebook.com/4ltrpress

11 | Stress, Health, and Coping

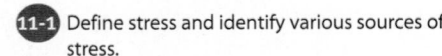

Blend Images Photography/Veer

LEARNING OUTCOMES

After studying this chapter, you will be able to…

11-1 Define stress and identify various sources of stress.

11-2 Identify the psychological moderators of stress.

11-3 Describe the impact of stress on the body.

11-4 Explain the relationships between psychology and health.

After you finish

this chapter, go

to **PAGE 299** for

STUDY TOOLS

The Earth moved. Or, a bit more precisely, in March of 2011, two immense walls of rock that had been pressing against each other for millennia finally budged. As in other places we call "faults," such as California's San Andreas Fault, they had been rubbing against each other for millions of years, trying to pass in opposite directions. Nobody saw it happen, because this particular confrontation occurred at the bottom of the ocean, off the northern coast of Japan. But the energy released caused the greatest earthquake experienced in Japan in 140 years, and it drove a wall of water 33 feet high—a tsunami—into the coast of Japan.

The earthquake and its aftershocks were felt in Tokyo, 250 miles down the coast. A 26-year-old office worker said, "I thought I was going to die when the earthquake hit. At first the shaking was not so great, but then it grew more violent and we all ducked under our desks. Ceiling tiles rained on us, and machines and reams of paper flew at us from shelves."

That was the least of it. The tsunami hit the shore and swept away boats, houses, cars, trucks, and people, turning villages and small cities into garbage heaps and graveyards. One fishing boat captain, Koji Haga, rode the tsunami inland like a rider clutching the back of some prehistoric whale, struggling to keep his pitching vessel upright. Somehow he survived, but nearly 20,000

"A fishing boat captain rode the **tsunami** inland like a rider clutching the back of some prehistoric whale."

others did not. They were swept out to sea or buried in rubble.

And some were poisoned by radiation. The tsunami also smashed six reactors at a coastal nuclear power plant. Volunteer workers braved exposure to radiation to try to keep overheated, melting fuel rods cooled with water— succeeding here, failing there. They received overdoses of radiation and face radiation poisoning and potential early demise from cancer (Bromet, 2014). Despite the workers' heroism, hundreds of thousands of people had to be evacuated for miles around the plants. Many of

them were sudden members of a new group of people in this affluent, well-organized society—the homeless.

Disasters like the tsunami take an emotional as well as a physical toll (Mason et al., 2010; Shapero et al., 2014). Studies of communities devastated by earthquakes, oil spills, fires, tsunamis, hurricanes, and other disasters suggest that most survivors eventually adjust to the stress of living with their memories and their grief. But many others have a cluster of symptoms that we call posttraumatic stress disorder: lingering nightmares, flashbacks, depression, and irritability that suggest deeper effects of stress (Weems et al., 2010).

This chapter is about stress—its origins, its psychological and physical effects, and ways of coping with it.

Truth or Fiction?

WHAT DO YOU THINK? Folklore, common sense, or nonsense? Select T for "truth" or F for "fiction," and then check the accuracy of your answers as you read through the chapter.

T	F	Some stress is good for us.
T	F	Academic success and vacations can be stressful.
T	F	Searching for social approval or perfection is an excellent way of making yourself miserable.
T	F	Type A people achieve more than Type B people, but they are less satisfied with themselves.
T	F	Humor helps us cope with stress.
T	F	At any given moment, countless microscopic warriors within our bodies are carrying out search-and-destroy missions against foreign agents.
T	F	If you have a family history of heart disease or cancer, there is little or nothing you can do to prevent developing the illness yourself.

11-1 STRESS: WHAT IT IS, WHERE IT COMES FROM

In physics, stress is defined as a pressure or force exerted on a body. Tons of rock pressing on the earth, one car smashing into another, a rubber band stretching—all are types of physical stress. Psychological forces, or stresses, also press, push, or pull. We may feel "crushed" by the weight of a big decision, "smashed" by adversity, or "stretched" to the point of snapping. In the case of the victims of the earthquake and tsunami in Japan, physical events had psychological and physical consequences. As we will see throughout the chapter, those psychological consequences can also affect our health.

Psychologists define **stress** as the demand made on an organism to adapt, cope, or adjust. Some stress is healthful and necessary to keep us alert and occupied. Stress researcher Hans Selye (1907–1982) referred to such healthful stress as **eustress** (pronounced YOU-stress). We may experience eustress when we begin a sought-after job or are trying to choose the color of an iPad. But intense or prolonged stress, such as that caused by a natural disaster or social or financial problems, can overtax our ability to adjust, affect our moods, impair our ability to experience pleasure, and harm the body (Folkman, 2011; Gotlieb & Joormann, 2010).

A study by the UCLA Higher Education Research Institute found that first-year college students are now encountering a record level of stress. Figure 11.1 shows that over the past 30 years, more and more first-year college students have been reporting that they felt overwhelmed during their senior year at high school. Either first-year students are being more open about their feelings or we have been living in increasingly stressful times—or both.

Stress is one of the key topics in health psychology. **Health psychology** studies the relationships between psychological factors and the prevention and treatment of physical health problems. Health psychologists investigate how:

▶ psychological factors such as stress, behavior patterns, and attitudes can lead to or aggravate illness;

▶ people can cope with stress;

▶ stress and **pathogens** (disease-causing organisms such as bacteria and viruses) interact to influence the immune system;

▶ people decide whether or not to seek health care; and

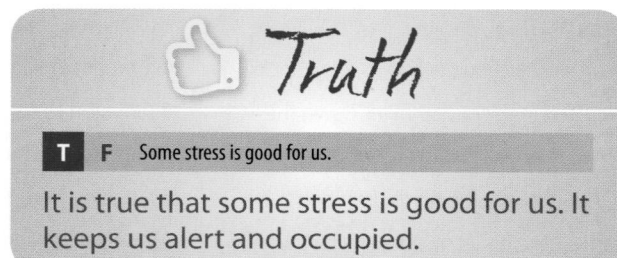

T **F** Some stress is good for us.

It is true that some stress is good for us. It keeps us alert and occupied.

stress the demand that is made on an organism to adapt

eustress (YOU-stress) stress that is healthful

health psychology the field of psychology that studies the relationships between psychological factors (e.g., attitudes, beliefs, situational influences, and behavior patterns) and the prevention and treatment of physical illness

pathogen a microscopic organism (e.g., bacterium or virus) that can cause disease

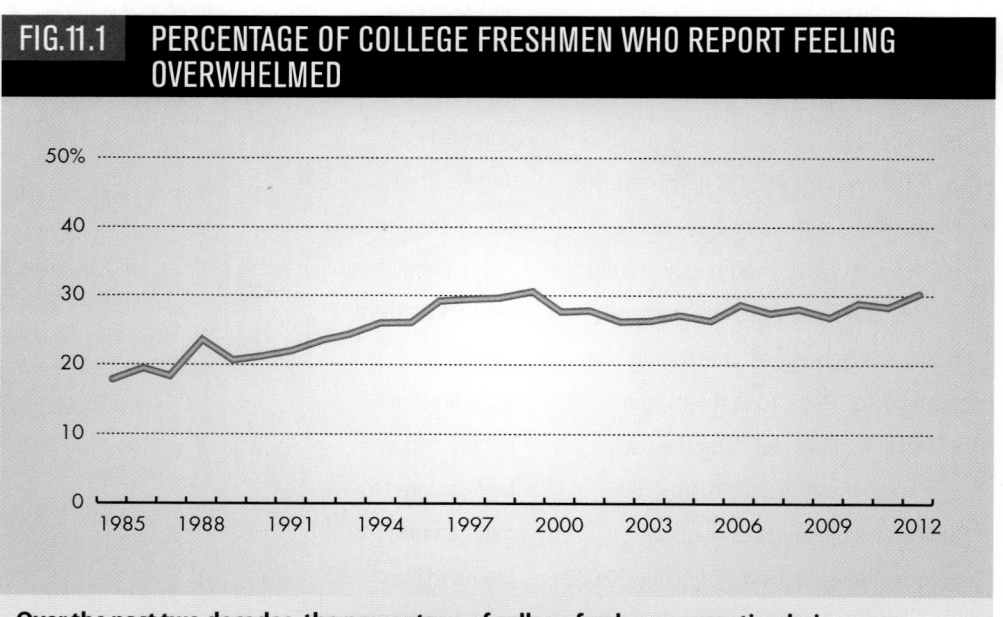

FIG.11.1 PERCENTAGE OF COLLEGE FRESHMEN WHO REPORT FEELING OVERWHELMED

Over the past two decades, the percentage of college freshmen reporting being overwhelmed during their senior year in high school has increased from about 18% to over 30%.

Source: Pryor, J. H., Eagan, K., Palucki Blake, L., Hurtado, S., Berdan, J., & Case, M. H. (2012). *The American Freshman: National Norms Fall 2012.* Los Angeles: Higher Education Research Institute, UCLA.

▶ psychological interventions such as health education (e.g., nutrition, smoking, and exercise) and behavior modification can contribute to physical health.

11-1a DAILY HASSLES AND LIFE CHANGES

Which straw will break the camel's back? The last straw, according to the saying. Similarly, stresses can pile up until we can no longer cope with them. Some of these stresses are *daily hassles*. Daily hassles are regularly occurring experiences that can harm our well-being, even our sex lives (Hamilton & Julian, 2014; Henderson et al., 2010). Lazarus and his colleagues (1985) noted the following hassles:

▶ *Household hassles:* preparing meals, shopping, and home maintenance

▶ *Health hassles:* illness, obtaining medical treatment, side effects of medication

▶ *Time-pressure hassles:* having too many things to do and not enough time

▶ *Inner concern hassles:* being socially isolated, lonely

▶ *Environmental hassles:* crime, weather, noise, pollution

▶ *Financial responsibility hassles:* not affording things, owing money

▶ *Work hassles:* job dissatisfaction, problems with coworkers

▶ *Security hassles:* job security, terrorism, investments, retirement

Life changes differ from daily hassles in two ways:

▶ Many life changes are positive, whereas all hassles are negative.

▶ Hassles occur regularly, whereas life changes occur at irregular intervals.

Peggy Blake and her colleagues (1984) constructed a scale of "life-change units" to measure the impact of life changes among college students. Surveys with students revealed that death of a spouse was considered the most stress-

TABLE 11.1	LIFE-CHANGE "UNITS" CONNECTED WITH VARIOUS EVENTS
Life Change	**Units**
Death of a spouse	94
Beginning college	84
Unwanted pregnancy	80
Academic failure	77
Graduating college	68
Prepping for a big test	65
Major financial problems	65
Academic success	54
Change of address	43
Going on vacation	30

Source: Adapted from *Self-Assessment and Behavior Change Manual* (pp. 43–47), by Peggy Blake, Robert Fry, and Michael Pesjack, 1984, McGraw-Hill. Reprinted by permission of McGraw-Hill Companies.

ful life change (94 life-change units; see Table 11.1). Academic failure (77 units) and graduating from college (68 units) were also considered highly stressful, even though graduation from college is a positive event—considering the alternative. Positive life changes such as academic success (54 units) and going on vacation (30 units) also made the list.

Daily Hassles are notable conditions and experiences that are threatening or harmful to a person's well-being. This person is apparently overworked. Perhaps he works so hard because of financial hassles. He probably has time-pressure hassles and health hassles, or given his diet, health hassles may be forthcoming. His work environment also seems to be crashing in on him.

Masterfile

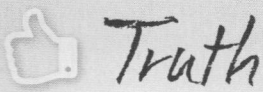

Truth

T	F	Academic success and vacations can be stressful.

It is true that academic success and vacations can be stressful. They are stressful because they are life changes, and changes—even good changes—require adjustment.

11-1b HASSLES, LIFE CHANGES, AND HEALTH PROBLEMS

Hassles and life changes—especially negative life changes—can cause us to worry and can affect our moods (McLaughlin et al., 2009; O'Drisscoll & Brough, 2010). Hassles and life changes also predict physical health problems such as heart disease and cancer, and even athletic injuries (Contrada & Baum, 2011).

STRESS IN AMERICA: The American Psychological Association Survey

Each year, the American Psychological Association (2012) commissions surveys of stress in America. Three respondents in four report that money is their major source of stress. Seventy percent mention work. When we add in the costs of housing, which are mentioned by 49% of the sample, we find another area in which finances contribute to stress. Health is another major area of concern, mentioned by more than half of the sample (53%). Intimate relationships are also a

> YOUR BODY'S STRESS WARNING SIGNS TELL YOU THAT THAT SOMETHING ISN'T RIGHT. MUCH LIKE THE GLOWING ORANGE "CHECK ENGINE" LIGHT ON YOUR CAR'S DASHBOARD, IF YOU NEGLECT THE ALERTS SENT OUT BY YOUR BODY, YOU COULD HAVE A MAJOR ENGINE MALFUNCTION.
>
> APA PSYCHOLOGY HELP CENTER WEBSITE

source of stress for more than half (58%) of the sample. One might think that intimate relationships would serve as a buffer against external sources of stress for people, *and perhaps they do.* (Life is complex.) However, these relationships can also contribute to stress.

Respondents reported many physical and psychological symptoms of stress (see Figure 11.2). Nearly half (45%) reported that stress made them irritable or angry. Stress made more than two in five (41%) tired, and more than one-third (36%) reported having headaches. More than one in four (26%) had indigestion, and almost one in four (23%) felt tense. About one-third felt depressed (34%) or as though they could cry (30%).

The most commonly reported methods of coping with stress were listening to music (49%), exercising or going for walks (48%), spending time with friends or family (46%), and reading (45%). Watching television or movies was close behind (38%). About one-third reported praying (37%) or napping (34%). One in six (16%) drank, and one in seven (13%) smoked—not a healthful choice.

FIG.11.2 WARNING SIGNS OF STRESS

- ▸ Headaches, muscle tension, neck or back pain
- ▸ Upset stomach
- ▸ Dry mouth
- ▸ Chest pains, rapid heartbeat
- ▸ Difficulty falling or staying asleep
- ▸ Fatigue
- ▸ Loss of appetite or overeating "comfort foods"
- ▸ Increased frequency of colds
- ▸ Lack of concentration or focus
- ▸ Memory problems or forgetfulness
- ▸ Jitters
- ▸ Irritability
- ▸ Short temper
- ▸ Anxiety

How do you know when you're stressed? We each react to stress somewhat differently, but the American Psychological Association lists these common responses to stress. Unchecked stress can contribute to high blood pressure, heart disease, diabetes, obesity, and suicide. We can try to tamp down sources of stress in our lives, change our reactions to stress, or seek professional help.
American Psychological Association (2014). Help Center, Signs of Stress. http://www.apa.org/helpcenter/stress-signs.aspx

Not all people report that the same events cause them stress, or course. And the stress of an event also reflects the meaning of the event to an individual (Buchanan et al., 2010; David et al., 2010). Pregnancy, for example, may seem like a blessing to a well-established couple who have been trying to have a child for years, but it may seem disastrous to a single teenager without resources. We appraise events, and our responses depend on their perceived danger, our values and goals, our beliefs in our coping ability, and our social situations.

11-1c CONFLICT

Should you eat dessert or try to stick to your diet? Should you live on campus, which is more convenient, or should you rent an apartment, where you may have more independence? Choices like these can place us in conflict. In psychology, **conflict** is the feeling of being pulled in two or more directions by opposing motives. Conflict is stressful. Psychologists often classify conflicts into four types: approach–approach, avoidance–avoidance, approach–avoidance, and multiple approach–avoidance.

Classic experimental research by Neal E. Miller (1944) and others suggests that the *approach–approach conflict* is the least stressful type of conflict. Here, each of two goals is desirable, and both are within reach. You may not be able to decide between pizza or tacos, or a trip to Nassau or Hawaii. I recently had such a conflict in which I was "forced" to choose between triple-chocolate fat-free frozen yogurt and coffee chocolate-chip fat-free frozen yogurt. Such conflicts are usually resolved by making a decision (I took the triple chocolate). Those who experience this type of conflict may vacillate until they make a decision, as shown by people who put off decisions and ruminate about conflicting goals.

Avoidance–avoidance conflict is more stressful because you are motivated to avoid each of two negative goals. However, avoiding one requires approaching the other. You may be fearful of visiting the dentist but also afraid that your teeth will decay if you do not make an appointment and go. Each potential outcome in an avoidance–avoidance conflict is undesirable. When an avoidance–avoidance conflict is highly stressful and no resolution is in sight, some people withdraw from the conflict by focusing on other matters or doing nothing.

When the same goal produces both approach and avoidance motives, we have an *approach–avoidance conflict*. People and things have their pluses and minuses, their good points and their bad points. Cheesecake may be delicious, but oh, the calories! Goals that produce mixed motives may seem more attractive from a distance but undesirable from up close (Elliot & Mapes, 2005). Many couples who repeatedly break up and reunite recall each other fondly when apart and swear that they could make the relationship work if they got together again. But after they do spend time together, they again wonder, "How could I ever have believed that this so-and-so would change?"

The most complex form of conflict is the *multiple approach–avoidance conflict*, in which each of several alternative courses of action has pluses and minuses. This sort of conflict might arise on the eve of an examination, when you are faced with the choice of studying or, say, going to a film. Each alternative has both positive and negative aspects: "Studying's a bore, but I won't have to worry about flunking. I'd love to see the movie, but I'd just be worrying about how I'll do tomorrow."

11-1d IRRATIONAL BELIEFS

Psychologist Albert Ellis (1913–2007) noted that our *beliefs* about events, not just the events themselves, can be stressors (David et al., 2010; Ellis, 2005). Consider a case in which a person is fired from a job and is anxious and depressed about it. It may seem logical that losing the job is responsible for the misery, but Ellis pointed out how the individual's beliefs about the loss compounded his or her misery (Table 11.2).

Consider this situation according to Ellis's A → B → C approach: Losing the job is an *activating event* (A). The eventual outcome, or *consequence* (C), is misery. Between the activating event (A) and the consequence (C), however, lie *beliefs* (B), such as these: "This job was the most important thing in my life," "What a no-good failure I am," "My family will starve," "I'll never find a job as good," "There's nothing I can do about it." Such beliefs compound misery, foster helplessness, and divert us from planning and deciding what to do next. The belief that

> "THE DEEPEST PRINCIPLE OF HUMAN NATURE IS THE CRAVING TO BE APPRECIATED."
> WILLIAM JAMES, AMERICAN PHILOSOPHER AND PSYCHOLOGIST (1842–1910)

conflict being torn in different directions by opposing motives; feelings produced by being in conflict

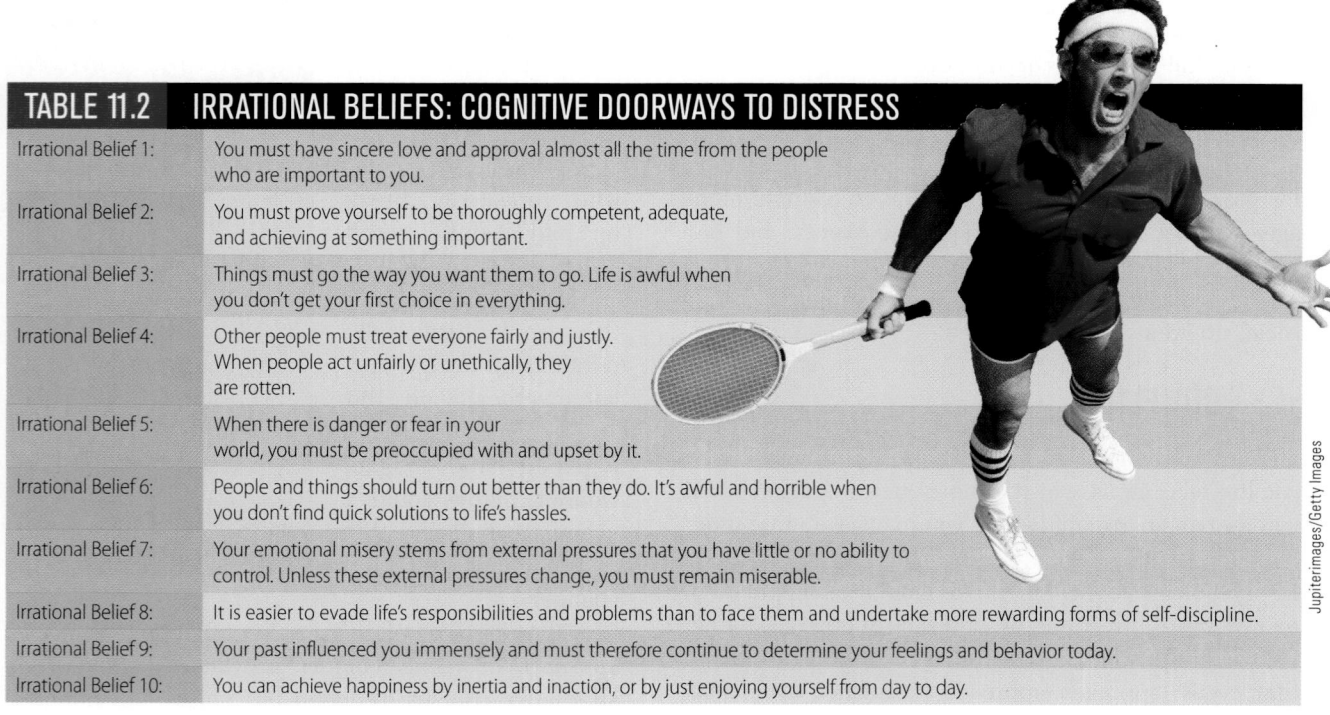

TABLE 11.2	IRRATIONAL BELIEFS: COGNITIVE DOORWAYS TO DISTRESS
Irrational Belief 1:	You must have sincere love and approval almost all the time from the people who are important to you.
Irrational Belief 2:	You must prove yourself to be thoroughly competent, adequate, and achieving at something important.
Irrational Belief 3:	Things must go the way you want them to go. Life is awful when you don't get your first choice in everything.
Irrational Belief 4:	Other people must treat everyone fairly and justly. When people act unfairly or unethically, they are rotten.
Irrational Belief 5:	When there is danger or fear in your world, you must be preoccupied with and upset by it.
Irrational Belief 6:	People and things should turn out better than they do. It's awful and horrible when you don't find quick solutions to life's hassles.
Irrational Belief 7:	Your emotional misery stems from external pressures that you have little or no ability to control. Unless these external pressures change, you must remain miserable.
Irrational Belief 8:	It is easier to evade life's responsibilities and problems than to face them and undertake more rewarding forms of self-discipline.
Irrational Belief 9:	Your past influenced you immensely and must therefore continue to determine your feelings and behavior today.
Irrational Belief 10:	You can achieve happiness by inertia and inaction, or by just enjoying yourself from day to day.

Jupiterimages/Getty Images

"There's nothing I can do about it" fosters helplessness. The belief that "I am a no-good failure" internalizes the blame and may be an exaggeration. The belief that "My family will starve" may also be an exaggeration. We can diagram the situation like this:

Activating events → Beliefs → Consequences
or A → B → C

Anxieties about the future and depression over a loss are normal and to be expected. The beliefs of the person who lost the job, however, tend to **catastrophize** the extent of the loss and contribute to anxiety and depression—and thus raise the person's blood pressure (David et al., 2010; DiGiuseppe, 2009). By heightening the individual's emotional reaction to the loss and fostering feelings of helplessness, these beliefs also impair coping ability (Pirbaglou et al., 2013; Samar et al., 2013).

Ellis proposed that many of us carry with us the irrational beliefs shown in Table 11.2. They are our personal doorways to distress. In fact, they can give rise to problems in themselves. When problems assault us from other sources, these beliefs can magnify their effect.

Ellis found it understandable that we would want the approval of others but irrational to believe that we cannot survive without it. It would be nice to be competent in everything we do, but it's unreasonable to *expect* it. Sure, it would be nice to be able to serve and volley like a tennis pro, but most of us haven't the time or natural ability to perfect the game. Demanding perfection prevents us from going out on the court on weekends and batting the ball back and forth just for fun. The belief that one must be preoccupied by threats is a prescription for perpetual emotional upheaval. Believing that we cannot overcome the influences of the past leads to feelings of helplessness and demoralization. Sure, Ellis might say, childhood experiences can explain the origins of irrational beliefs, but it is our own cognitive appraisal—here and now—that causes us to be miserable.

 **Truth**

| T | F | Searching for social approval or perfection is an excellent way of making yourself miserable. |

It is true that searching for social approval or perfection is an excellent way of making yourself miserable. Research findings confirm the connections between irrational beliefs (e.g., excessive dependence on social approval and perfectionism) and feelings of anxiety and depression.

11-1e THE TYPE A BEHAVIOR PATTERN

Some people create stress for themselves through the **Type A behavior** pattern. Type A people are highly driven, competitive, impatient, hostile, and aggressive—so much so that they are prone to getting into auto accidents (Neelakantan, 2013; Wickens et al., 2013). They feel rushed and pressured and keep one eye glued to the clock. They are not only prompt for appointments but often early. They eat, walk, and talk rapidly. They grow restless when others work slowly. They attempt to dominate group discussions. Type A people find it difficult to surrender control or share power. They are reluctant to delegate authority in the workplace and thus increase their own workloads. They watch their form,

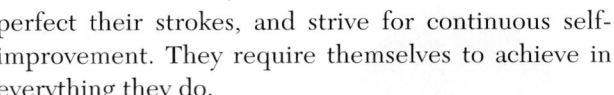

Our self-efficacy expectations affect our abilities to withstand stress and make things happen.

perfect their strokes, and strive for continuous self-improvement. They require themselves to achieve in everything they do.

Type B people, in contrast, relax more readily and focus more on the quality of life. They show lower blood pressure than Type A people in response to stressors, which is a key reason that Type A behavior is also referred to as the *coronary-prone behavior pattern.* Type B people are less ambitious and less impatient, and they pace themselves. Type A people earn higher grades and more money than Type B's who are equal in intelligence, but Type A people are more likely to continue to strive for more and more.

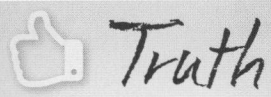

| T | F | Type A people achieve more than Type B people, but they are less satisfied with themselves. |

It is true that Type A people achieve more than Type B people but are less satisfied with themselves. They are excessively highly driven.

11-2 PSYCHOLOGICAL MODERATORS OF STRESS

Psychological factors can influence, or *moderate,* the effects that stressors have on us. In this section, we discuss several psychological moderators of stress: self-efficacy expectations, psychological hardiness, humor, predictability and control, and social support.

11-2a SELF-EFFICACY EXPECTATIONS: "THE LITTLE ENGINE THAT COULD"

Self-efficacy is the ability to make things happen. Our **self-efficacy expectations**—our beliefs that we can bring about desired changes through our own efforts—affect our ability to withstand stress (Bosmans et al., 2013).

In a classic experiment, Albert Bandura and his colleagues (1985) assessed participants' self-efficacy, exposed them to fearful stimuli, and then monitored the levels of adrenaline and noradrenaline in their bloodstreams as they did so. Adrenaline and noradrenaline are secreted when we are under stress. They arouse the body in several ways, such as accelerating the heart rate and releasing glucose from the liver. Excessive arousal can distract us from coping with the tasks at hand. Bandura and his colleagues exposed participants to fear-inducing objects and found that high self-efficacy expectations are accompanied by relatively *lower* levels of adrenaline and noradrenaline. People with higher self-efficacy expectations thus have biological as well as psychological reasons for remaining calmer.

People who have higher self-efficacy expectations are less prone to be disturbed by adverse events (Maddi, 2008). They are more likely to lose weight, quit smoking, and control their alcohol intake (Foster et al., 2014; Martinez et al., 2010). They are also better able to function in spite of pain (Howard et al., 2010).

catastrophize to interpret negative events as being disastrous; to "blow out of proportion"

Type A behavior behavior characterized by a sense of time urgency, competitiveness, and hostility

self-efficacy expectations our beliefs that we can bring about desired changes through our own efforts

Jose Luis Pelaez Inc./Blend Images/Jupiter Images

11-2b PSYCHOLOGICAL HARDINESS

Psychological hardiness also helps people resist stress (Golubovich et al., 2014; Maddi et al., 2009). Our understanding of hardiness is derived largely from the pioneering work of Suzanne Kobasa (Maddi, 2008). Kobasa and her colleagues studied business executives who seemed able to resist illness despite stress. In one phase of the research, executives completed a battery of psychological tests, and the researchers found that the psychologically hardy executives had three key characteristics. The characteristics include commitment, challenge, and control (Maddi et al., 2009).

1. *Commitment.* Psychologically hardy executives tended to involve themselves in, rather than feel alienated from, what they were doing or encountering.

2. *Challenge.* Psychologically hardy executives believed that change, rather than stability, is normal in life. They appraised change as an interesting incentive to personal growth, not a threat to security.

3. *Control.* Psychologically hardy executives were high in perceived control over their lives. Psychologically hardy people tend to have what psychologist Julian B. Rotter (1990) termed an internal **locus of control** (Weiner, 2010). The nearby Locus of Control Self-Assessment will offer you insight as to whether you see yourself as in control over your own life.

Psychologically hardy people may be more resistant to stress because they *choose* to face it (Bartone et al., 2008; Maddi et al., 2009). They also interpret stress as making life more interesting. For example, they see a conference with a supervisor as an opportunity to persuade the supervisor rather than as a risk to their position.

11-2c SENSE OF HUMOR

The idea that humor lightens the burdens of life and helps people cope with stress has been with us for millennia. Consider the biblical maxim, "A merry heart doeth good like a medicine" (Proverbs 17: 22). Research suggests that humor can moderate the effects of stress (Sultanoff, 2013). In one classic study, for example, students completed a checklist of negative life events and a measure of mood disturbance (Martin & Lefcourt, 1983). The measure of mood

psychological hardiness a cluster of traits that buffer stress and are characterized by commitment, challenge, and control

locus of control the place (locus) to which an individual attributes control over the receiving of reinforcers—either inside or outside the self

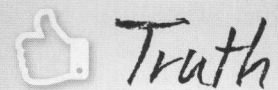
disturbance yielded a stress score. The students also rated their sense of humor. Students were asked to try to produce humor in an experimental stressful situation, and their ability to do so was rated by the researchers. Students who had a greater sense of humor and were capable of producing humor in the stressful experimental condition were less affected by the stress than other students. Later experimentation found that exposing students to humorous videotapes raised the level of immunoglobulin A (a measure of the functioning of the immune system) in their saliva (Lefcourt et al., 1997; K. L. Smith, 2009).

How does humor help people cope with stress? There are many possibilities. One is that laughter stimulates the output of endorphins, which might enhance the functioning of the immune system. Another is that the benefits of humor may be explained in terms of the positive cognitive shifts they entail and the positive emotions that accompany them.

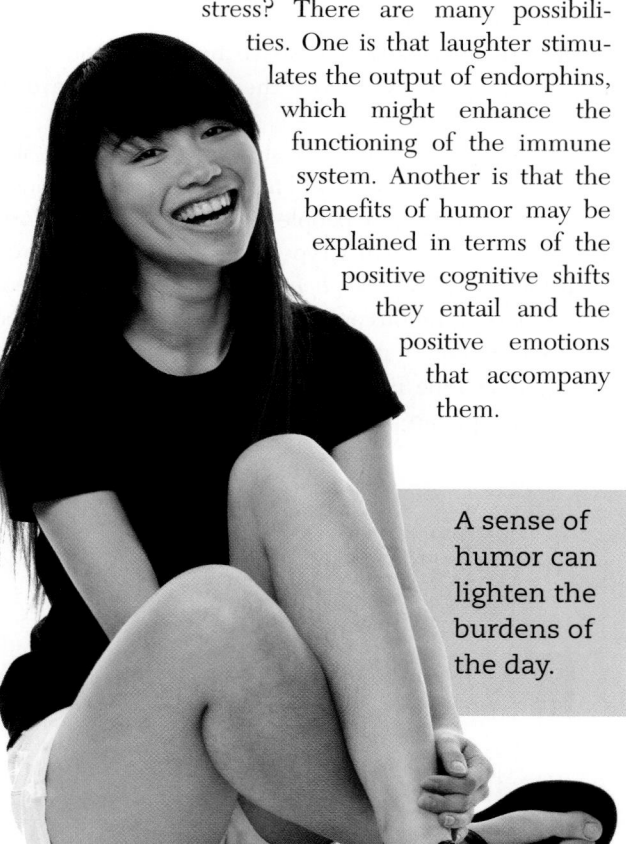

drbimages/Getty Images

A sense of humor can lighten the burdens of the day.

11-2d PREDICTABILITY AND CONTROL

The ability to predict a stressor apparently moderates its impact. Predictability allows us to brace ourselves for the inevitable and, in many cases, plan ways of coping with it. Control—even the illusion of being in control—allows us to feel that we are not at the mercy of the fates (Contrada & Baum, 2011). There is also a relationship between the desire to assume control over one's situation and the usefulness of information about impending stressors. Predictability is of greater benefit to **internals**—that is, to people who wish to exercise control over their situations—than to **externals**. People who want information about medical procedures and what they will experience cope better with pain when they undergo those procedures (Thompson, 2009; Zhang, 2013).

11-2e SOCIAL SUPPORT

People are social beings, and social support also seems to act as a buffer against the effects of stress (Contrada & Baum, 2011; Panagioti et al., 2014). Kinds of social support include:

▶ *Emotional concern:* listening to people's problems and expressing feelings of sympathy, caring, understanding, and reassurance.

▶ *Instrumental aid:* the material supports and services that facilitate adaptive behavior. For example, after a disaster, relief organizations may provide food, medicines, and temporary living quarters.

▶ *Information:* guidance and advice that enhance people's ability to cope.

▶ *Appraisal:* feedback from others about how one is doing. This kind of support involves helping people interpret, or "make sense of," what has happened to them.

▶ *Socializing:* conversation, recreation, even going shopping with someone. Socializing has beneficial effects, even when it is not oriented toward solving problems.

Research supports the value of social support. People with fewer friends, nearby family, and social skills are more prone to developing infectious diseases such as colds

> "ONE OF THE OLDEST HUMAN NEEDS IS HAVING SOMEONE TO WONDER WHERE YOU ARE WHEN YOU DON'T COME HOME AT NIGHT."
>
> MARGARET MEAD, AMERICAN CULTURAL ANTHROPOLOGIST (1901–1978)

(Cohen et al., 2012; Thompson et al., 2013). Social support helps people cope with the stresses of cancer and other health problems (Ikeda et al., 2013). Social support helps people cope with the stresses of natural disasters such as hurricanes and earthquakes (Hu et al., 2010; Kukihara et al., 2014). Social support helps women cope with the aftermath of rape (Panagioti et al., 2014). Stress is also less likely to lead to high blood pressure or alcohol abuse among people with social support (Dennis et al., 2008; Rodriguez et al., 2008).

How does stress contribute to the development of physical health problems? In the next section, we consider the effects of stress on the body.

11-3 STRESS AND THE BODY

Stress is more than a psychological event. It is more than "knowing" it is there; it is more than "feeling" pushed and pulled. Stress also has very definite effects on the body, which, as we will see, can lead to psychological and physical health problems. Stress researcher Hans Selye outlined a number of the bodily effects in his concept of the *general adaptation syndrome* (GAS).

11-3a THE GENERAL ADAPTATION SYNDROME

Selye suggested that under stress, the body is like a clock with an alarm that does not shut off until the clock shakes apart or its energy has been depleted. The body's response to different stressors shows certain similarities whether the stressor is a bacterial invasion, perceived danger, or a major life change (Selye, 1976). For this reason, Selye labeled this response the **general adaptation syndrome (GAS)**. The GAS is a group of bodily changes that occur in three stages: an alarm reaction,

internals people who perceive the ability to attain reinforcements as being largely within themselves

externals people who perceive the ability to attain reinforcements as being largely outside themselves

general adaptation syndrome (GAS) Selye's term for a hypothesized three-stage response to stress

a resistance stage, and an exhaustion stage. These changes mobilize the body for action and—like that alarm that goes on ringing—can eventually wear out the body.

THE ALARM REACTION The **alarm reaction** is triggered by perception of a stressor. This reaction mobilizes or arouses the body, biologically speaking. Early in the 20th century, physiologist Walter B. Cannon (1932) argued that this mobilization was the basis for an instinctive **fight-or-flight reaction**. The fight-or-flight response kicks the endocrine, cardiovascular, and musculoskeletal systems into action to enable survival. Short-term stress can enhance the functioning of the immune system as well, thus helping prevent infection from wounds, but chronic or long-term stress can impair the functioning of the immune system (Sizemore, 2012).

Stress has a domino effect on the endocrine system (Contrada & Baum, 2011; Hueston & Deak, 2014; see Figure 11.3). The hypothalamus secretes corticotrophin-releasing hormone (CRH). CRH causes the pituitary gland to secrete adrenocorticotrophic hormone (ACTH). ACTH then causes the adrenal cortex to secrete cortisol and other corticosteroids (steroidal hormones). Corticosteroids help protect the body by combating allergic reactions (such as difficulty in breathing) and producing inflammation. (However, corticosteroids can be harmful to the cardiovascular system, which is one reason that chronic stress can impair one's health and why athletes who use steroids to build muscle mass can experience cardiovascular problems.) Inflammation increases circulation to parts of the body that are injured. It ferries in hordes of white blood cells to fend off invading pathogens.

Two other hormones that play a major role in the alarm reaction are secreted by the adrenal medulla. The sympathetic division of the autonomic nervous system (ANS) activates the adrenal medulla, causing it to release a mixture of adrenaline and noradrenaline. This mixture arouses the body by accelerating the heart rate and causing the liver to release glucose (sugar). This provides the energy that fuels the fight-or-flight reaction, which activates the body so that it is prepared to fight or flee from a predator.

The fight-or-flight reaction stems from a period in human prehistory when many stressors were life threatening. It was triggered by the sight of a predator at the edge of a thicket or by a sudden rustling in the undergrowth. Today it may be aroused when you are caught in stop-and-go traffic or learn that your mortgage payments are going to increase. Once the threat is removed, the body returns to a lower state of arousal. Many of the bodily changes that occur in the alarm reaction are outlined in Table 11.3.

THE RESISTANCE STAGE According to Selye's theory, if the alarm reaction mobilizes the body and the stressor is not removed, we enter the adaptation or **resistance stage** of the GAS. Levels of endocrine and sympathetic

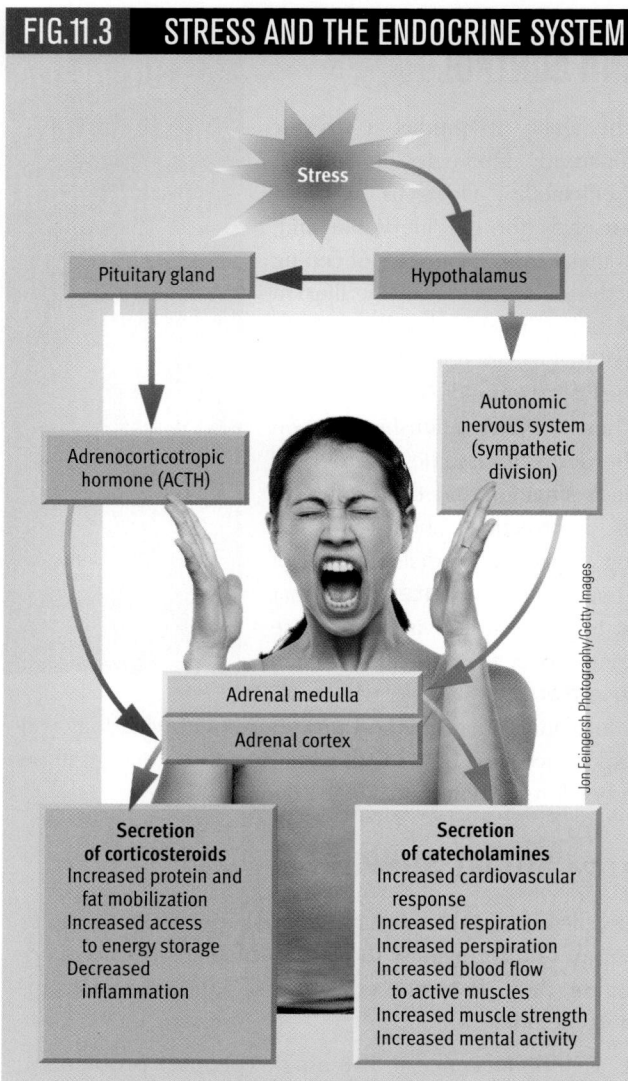

FIG. 11.3 STRESS AND THE ENDOCRINE SYSTEM

Stress

Pituitary gland → Hypothalamus

Adrenocorticotropic hormone (ACTH)

Autonomic nervous system (sympathetic division)

Adrenal medulla
Adrenal cortex

Secretion of corticosteroids
Increased protein and fat mobilization
Increased access to energy storage
Decreased inflammation

Secretion of catecholamines
Increased cardiovascular response
Increased respiration
Increased perspiration
Increased blood flow to active muscles
Increased muscle strength
Increased mental activity

Stress has a domino effect on the endocrine system, leading to the release of corticosteroids and a mixture of adrenaline and noradrenaline. Corticosteroids combat allergic reactions (such as difficulty in breathing) and cause inflammation. Adrenaline and noradrenaline arouse the body to cope by accelerating the heart rate and providing energy for the fight-or-flight reaction.

---

alarm reaction the first stage of the GAS, which is triggered by the impact of a stressor and characterized by sympathetic activity

fight-or-flight reaction an innate adaptive response to the perception of danger

resistance stage the second stage of the GAS, characterized by prolonged sympathetic activity in an effort to restore lost energy and repair damage. Also called the *adaptation stage*

TABLE 11.3 **COMPONENTS OF THE ALARM REACTION***

➤ Corticosteroids are secreted.

➤ Adrenaline is secreted.

➤ Noradrenaline is secreted.

➤ Respiration rate increases.

➤ Heart rate increases.

➤ Blood pressure increases.

➤ Muscles tense.

➤ Blood shifts from internal organs to the skeletal musculature.

➤ Digestion is inhibited.

➤ Sugar is released from the liver.

➤ Coagulability of the blood increases.

Cocoon/Photodisc/Jupiter Images

*The alarm reaction is defined by the release of corticosteroids and adrenaline and by activity of the sympathetic branch of the autonomic nervous system.

activity are lower than in the alarm reaction but still higher than normal. (It's as if the alarm is still on, but a bit softer.) But make no mistake: The person feels tense, and the body remains under a heavy burden.

THE EXHAUSTION STAGE If the stressor is still not dealt with adequately, we may enter the **exhaustion stage** of the GAS. The muscles become fatigued. The body is depleted of the resources required for combating stress. With exhaustion, the parasympathetic division of the ANS may predominate. As a result, our heartbeat and respiration rate slow down, and many aspects of sympathetic activity are reversed. It might sound as if we would profit from the respite, but remember that we are still under stress—possibly an external threat. Continued stress in the exhaustion stage may lead to what Selye terms "diseases of adaptation." These are connected with constriction of blood vessels and alteration of the heart rhythm and can range from allergies to hives and heart disease—and ultimately, death.

Discussion of the effects of stress on the immune system paves the way for understanding the links between psychological factors and physical illness.

11-3b EFFECTS OF STRESS ON THE IMMUNE SYSTEM

Psychologists, biologists, and medical researchers have combined their efforts in a field of study called *psychoneuroimmunology* that addresses the relationships among psychological factors, the nervous system, the endocrine system, the immune system, and disease. One of its major concerns is the effect of stress on the immune system. Research shows that stress suppresses the immune system, as measured by the presence of substances in the blood that make up parts of the immune system (Contrada & Baum, 2011).

THE IMMUNE SYSTEM The **immune system** combats disease in several ways (Iwasaki & Medzhitov, 2010). One way is the production of white blood cells, which engulf and kill pathogens such as bacteria, fungi, and viruses, and worn-out and cancerous body cells. The technical term for white blood cells is **leukocytes**. They engage in search-and-destroy missions in which they "recognize" and eradicate foreign agents and unhealthy cells.

Leukocytes recognize foreign substances, or antigens, by their shapes. The body reacts to **antigens** by generating specialized proteins, or **antibodies**. Antibodies

exhaustion stage the third stage of the GAS, characterized by weakened resistance and possible deterioration

immune system the system of the body that recognizes and destroys foreign agents (antigens) that invade the body

leukocytes white blood cells (derived from the Greek words *leukos*, meaning "white," and *kytos*, literally meaning "a hollow" but used to refer to cells)

antigen a substance that stimulates the body to mount an immune system response to it (short for *anti*body *gen*erator)

antibodies substances formed by white blood cells that recognize and destroy antigens

Are There Gender Differences in Response to Stress?

For a century, it has been widely believed that humans are prewired to experience what biologist Walter Cannon labeled a "fight-or-flight" reaction to stress. Cannon believed we are instinctively pumped up to fight like demons or, when advisable, to beat a hasty retreat.

Or are we? According to reviews of the literature by psychologist Shelley E. Taylor and her colleagues (Taylor, 2006, 2012; Taylor et al., 2000), women under stress are more likely to care for their children and seek social contact and support from others. The "woman's response" to stress, the "tend-and-befriend" response, involves nurturing and seeking social support rather than fighting or fleeing.

This response may be prewired in female humans and in females of other mammalian species. Evolutionary psychologists might suggest that the tend-and-befriend response may have become sealed in human genes because it promotes the survival of females who are tending their young. Females who choose to fight might die or be separated from their young—no evolutionary brass ring there.

Gender differences in behavior are frequently connected with gender differences in hormones and other biological factors. This one is no different. Taylor (2012) points to the effects of the pituitary hormone oxytocin which is connected with nurturing behaviors such as cuddling one's young. The literature shows that when oxytocin is released during stress, it tends to have a calming effect on both rats and humans. It makes them less afraid and more social.

But men also release oxytocin when they are under stress. So why the gender difference? The answer may lie in other hormones—estrogen and testosterone. Females have more estrogen than males, and estrogen appears to enhance the effects of oxytocin. Males, on the other hand, have more testosterone than females, and testosterone may mitigate the effects of oxytocin (Taylor, 2012).

It is thus possible that males are more aggressive than females under stress because of the genetic balance of hormones in their bodies. Due to such differences, suggests Taylor, women tend to outlive men.

Torff/plainpicture

---

inflammation increased blood flow to an injured area of the body, resulting in redness, warmth, and an increased supply of white blood cells

attach themselves to the antigens, deactivating them and marking them for destruction. The immune system "remembers" how to battle antigens by maintaining their antibodies in the bloodstream, often for years.[1]

Inflammation is another function of the immune system. When injury occurs, blood vessels in the area first contract (to stem bleeding) and then dilate. Dilation increases the flow of blood, cells, and natural chemicals to the damaged area, causing the redness, swelling, and warmth that characterize inflammation. The increased blood supply also floods the region with white blood cells to combat invading microscopic life-forms such as bacteria, which otherwise might use the local damage as a port of entry into the body.

---

[1]A vaccination introduces a weakened form of an antigen (usually a bacteria or a virus) into the body to stimulate the production of antibodies. Antibodies can confer immunity for many years, in some cases for a lifetime.

STRESS AND THE IMMUNE SYSTEM One of the reasons that stress eventually exhausts us is that it stimulates the production of steroids. Steroids suppress the functioning of the immune system. Suppression has negligible effects when steroids are secreted occasionally. But persistent secretion of steroids decreases inflammation and interferes with the formation of antibodies. As a consequence, we become more vulnerable to infections, including the common cold (Cohen et al., 2012; Thompson et al., 2013). By weakening the immune system, stress may also be connected with a more rapid progression of HIV infection to AIDS (Contrada & Baum, 2011; Joska et al., 2014).

Studies with college students have shown that the stress of exams depresses the immune system's response to the Epstein-Barr virus, which causes fatigue and other problems (Glaser et al., 1993). Students who were lonely showed greater suppression of the immune system than students who had more social support. The Epstein-Barr virus remains dormant in 90% of people who recover from an episode. Stress elevates blood levels of cortisol and adrenaline (epinephrine) and heightens the probability that the virus will be reactivated (Coskun et al., 2010).

Stress Tip Sheet

The American Psychological Association offers tips on how to manage your stress:

- ▶ **Identify your sources of stress.** What events or situations trigger stressful feelings? Are they related to your children, family, health, financial decisions, work, relationships, or something else?

- ▶ **Learn your own stress signals.** People experience stress in different ways. You may have a hard time concentrating or making decisions, feel angry or irritable, or experience headaches, muscle tension, or a lack of energy. Gauge your stress signals.

- ▶ **Recognize how you deal with stress.** Determine whether you are using unhealthy behaviors (such as smoking, drinking alcohol, and over- or under-eating) to cope. Is this a routine behavior, or is it specific to certain events or situations? Do you make unhealthy choices as a result of feeling stressed?

- ▶ **Find healthy ways to manage stress.** Consider healthy, stress-reducing activities such as meditation, exercising, or talking things out with friends or family. Keep in mind that unhealthy behaviors develop over time and can be difficult to change. Don't take on too much at once. Focus on changing only one behavior at a time.

- ▶ **Take care of yourself.** Eat right, get enough sleep, drink plenty of water, and engage in regular physical activity. Take regular vacations or other breaks from work. No matter how hectic life gets, make time for yourself—even if it's just reading a book or listening to music.

- ▶ **Reach out for support.** Accepting help from friends and family can improve your ability to manage stress. If you continue to feel overwhelmed, you may want to talk to a psychologist, who can help you better manage stress and change unhealthy behaviors.

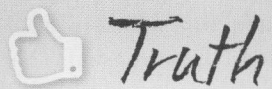

| T | F | At any given moment, countless microscopic warriors within our bodies are carrying out search-and-destroy missions against foreign agents. |

It is true that at any given moment, countless microscopic warriors within our bodies are carrying out search-and-destroy missions against foreign agents. Leukocytes continuously destroy "foreign agents" (such as germs) and internal agents, such as cancerous cells.

11-4 PSYCHOLOGY AND CHRONIC HEALTH PROBLEMS

Why do people become ill? Why do some people develop cancer? Why do others have heart attacks? Why do still others seem to be immune to these illnesses? The **biopsychosocial** approach to health recognizes that there is no single, simple answer to these questions. The likelihood of contracting an illness—be it a case of the flu or cancer—can reflect the interaction of many factors, including biological, psychological, and sociocultural factors.

Biological factors such as pathogens, injuries, age, gender, and a family history of disease may strike us as the most

> **biopsychosocial** having to do with the interactions of biological, psychological, and sociocultural factors

obvious causes of illness. Genetics, in particular, tempts some people to assume that there is little they can do about their health. It is true that there are some severe health problems that are unavoidable for people with certain genes. However, in many cases, especially with cardiovascular problems and cancer, genes only create *predispositions* toward the health problem.

Genetic predispositions interact with the environment to express themselves (Benke & Fallin, 2010; Hunter, 2005). For example, genetic factors are involved in breast cancer (Boyd, 2014). However, rates of breast cancer among women who have recently emigrated to the United States from rural Asia are similar to those in their countries of origin and nearly 80% lower than the rates among third-generation Asian American women, whose rates are similar to those of European American women (Hoover, 2000; Wu et al., 2009). Thus, one's lifestyle is also connected with the risk of breast cancer—and most other kinds of cancer.

As shown in Figure 11.4, biological factors (such as genetics and obesity), psychological factors (such as behaviors and personality), sociocultural factors (such as socioeconomic status), environmental factors, and stressors all play roles in health problems such as heart disease and cancer.

Many health problems are affected by psychological factors, such as attitudes, emotions, and behavior. Nearly one million deaths each year in the United States are preventable (Health, United States, 2010). Stopping smoking, eating right, exercising, and controlling alcohol use would prevent nearly 80% of these. Psychological states such as anxiety and depression can impair the functioning of the immune system, rendering us more vulnerable to physical disorders ranging from viral infections to cancer (Guan et al., 2014; Salovey et al., 2000).

Fiction 👎

| T | F | If you have a family history of heart disease or cancer, there is little or nothing you can do to prevent developing the illness yourself. |

It is *not* necessarily true that there is little or nothing you can do to prevent developing heart disease or cancer if you have a family history of one of these health problems. You can probably do many things to modify the risk factors in your own life.

Let's now discuss the chronic health problems of heart disease and cancer. Each involves biological, psychological, and sociocultural factors. Although these are medical problems, we also explore ways in which psychologists have contributed to their prevention and treatment.

11-4a CORONARY HEART DISEASE

Coronary heart disease (CHD) is the leading cause of death in the United States, most often from heart attacks.

RISK FACTORS The risk factors for CHD are as follow (Glynn, 2010):

▸ *Family history:* People with a family history of CHD are more likely to develop the disease themselves.

▸ *Physiological conditions:* Obesity, high *serum cholesterol* levels, and *hypertension* (high blood pressure) are risk factors for CHD. About one American in five has hypertension, which can lead to CHD. *Essential hypertension*—that is, hypertension without an identifiable cause—has a genetic component. However, blood pressure is also connected with emotions like depression and anxiety. In addition, it rises when we inhibit the expression of strong feelings or are angry or on guard against threats. When we are under stress, we may believe that we can feel our blood pressure "pounding through the roof," but most people cannot sense hypertension. Therefore, it is important to check blood pressure regularly.

▸ *Patterns of consumption:* Patterns include heavy drinking, smoking, and overeating. On the other hand, a little alcohol seems to be good for the heart.

▸ *Type A behavior:* Most studies suggest that there is at least a modest relationship between Type A behavior and CHD. Hostility seems to be the component of the Type A behavior pattern that is most harmful (Chida & Steptoe, 2009). People who are highly prone to anger are apparently more likely than other people to have heart attacks (Suls, 2013). The stress hormones connected with anger can constrict blood vessels to the heart, leading to a heart attack.

> "THE ONLY WAY TO KEEP YOUR HEALTH IS TO EAT WHAT YOU DON'T WANT, DRINK WHAT YOU DON'T LIKE, AND DO WHAT YOU'D RATHER NOT."
>
> MARK TWAIN, AMERICAN AUTHOR AND HUMORIST (1835–1910)

FIG.11.4   FACTORS IN HEART DISEASE AND CANCER

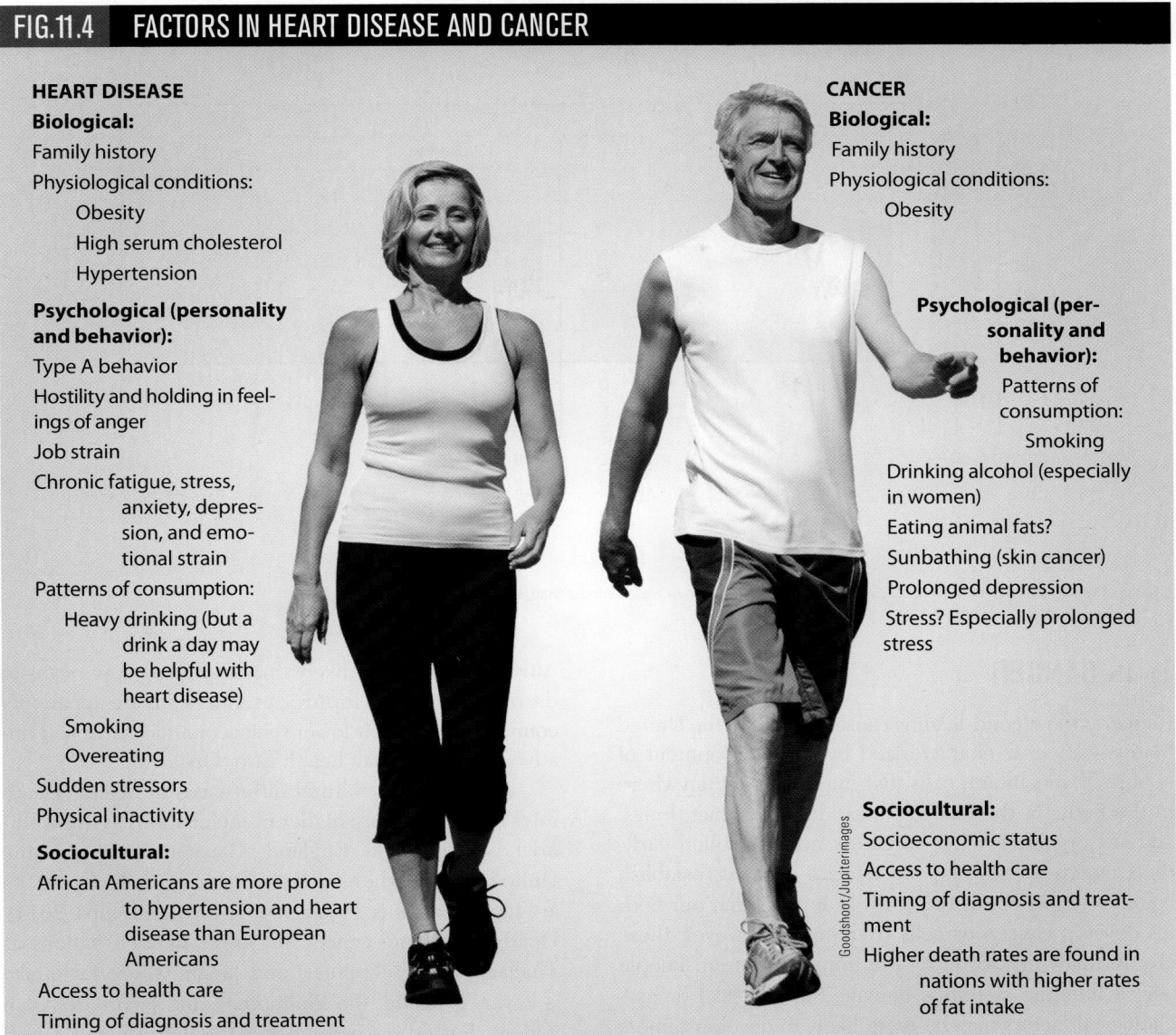

HEART DISEASE

Biological:

Family history

Physiological conditions:

   Obesity

   High serum cholesterol

   Hypertension

Psychological (personality and behavior):

Type A behavior

Hostility and holding in feelings of anger

Job strain

Chronic fatigue, stress, anxiety, depression, and emotional strain

Patterns of consumption:

   Heavy drinking (but a drink a day may be helpful with heart disease)

   Smoking

   Overeating

Sudden stressors

Physical inactivity

Sociocultural:

African Americans are more prone to hypertension and heart disease than European Americans

Access to health care

Timing of diagnosis and treatment

CANCER

Biological:

Family history

Physiological conditions:

   Obesity

Psychological (personality and behavior):

   Patterns of consumption:

   Smoking

Drinking alcohol (especially in women)

Eating animal fats?

Sunbathing (skin cancer)

Prolonged depression

Stress? Especially prolonged stress

Sociocultural:

Socioeconomic status

Access to health care

Timing of diagnosis and treatment

Higher death rates are found in nations with higher rates of fat intake

Goodshoot/Jupiterimages

▸ *Job strain:* Overtime work, assembly line labor, and exposure to conflicting demands can all contribute to CHD. High-strain work, which makes heavy demands on workers but gives them little personal control, puts workers at the highest risk (Kivimäki et al., 2012; Krantz et al., 1988).

▸ *Chronic fatigue, stress, anxiety, depression, and emotional strain.* Depression is connected with irregularities in the heart rate and may make blood platelets "sticky," which may, in turn, cause clots that lead to CHD (Mazereeuw et al., 2013).

▸ A *physically inactive lifestyle*.

African Americans are more likely than any other ethnic group in the United States to have heart attacks and to die of them (National Vital Statistics System, 2013). Figure 11.5 compares the death rates from heart disease and stroke of American men and women of various ethnic backgrounds. Asian Americans and Latin Americans are less likely than European Americans, Native Americans, or African Americans to die of heart disease or stroke. Early diagnosis and treatment might help decrease the racial gap.

REDUCING RISK Measures such as the following may help reduce the risk of CHD: stopping smoking; eating fewer saturated fats and more fruits, vegetables, and whole grains; reducing hypertension and lowering LDL (harmful) serum cholesterol, through medicine if necessary; modifying Type A behavior; managing feelings of anger; and exercising regularly (get a medical checkup first).

FIG.11.5 ANNUAL DEATHS PER 100,000 DUE TO HEART DISEASE AND STROKE

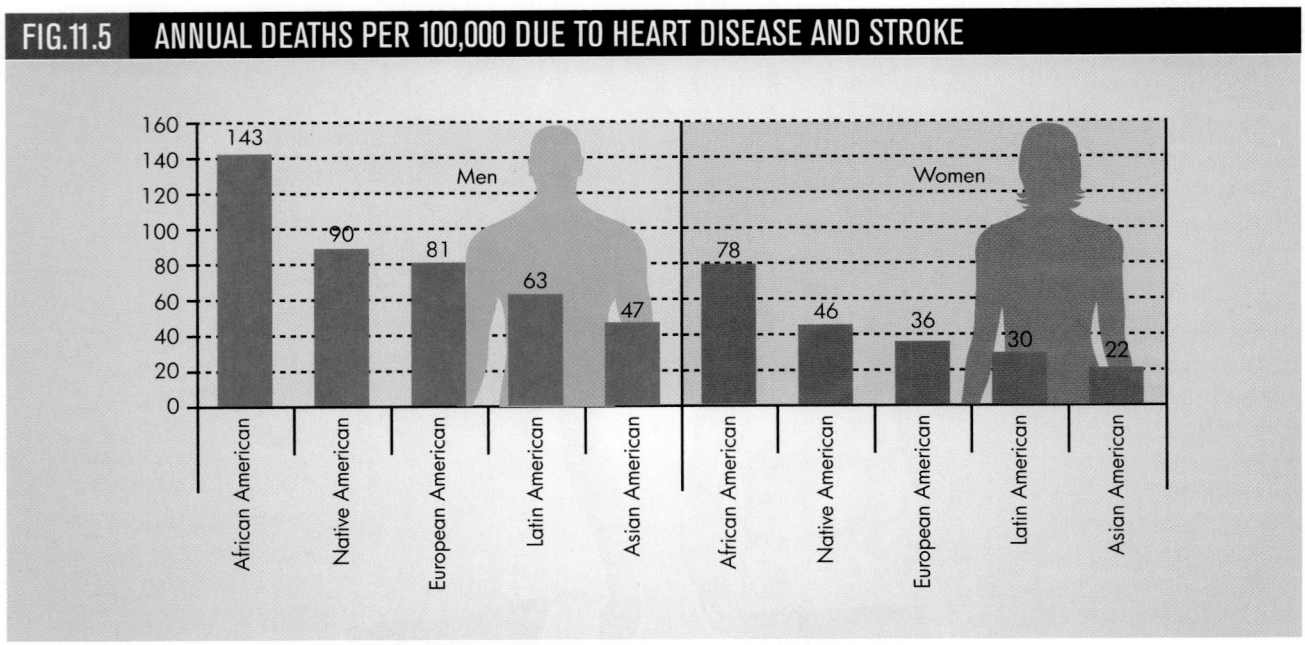

National Vital Statistics System (2013). U.S. Census Bureau, 2010. http://www.cdc.gov/dhdsp/vital_signs.htm

11-4b CANCER

Cancer is the second-leading cause of death in the United States. Cancer is characterized by the development of abnormal, or mutant, cells that may take root anywhere in the body: in the blood, bones, digestive tract, lungs, and sex organs. If their spread is not controlled early, the cancerous cells may *metastasize*—that is, establish colonies elsewhere in the body. It appears that our bodies develop cancerous cells frequently. However, these are normally destroyed by the immune system. People whose immune system is damaged by physical or psychological factors may be more likely to develop tumors (Contrada & Baum, 2011; Mantovani & Sica, 2010).

RISK FACTORS As with many other disorders, people can inherit a disposition toward cancer (Santarius et al., 2010). So-called carcinogenic genes may remove the brakes from cell division, allowing cells to multiply wildly. Or they may allow mutations to accumulate unchecked. Many behavior patterns, however, markedly heighten the risk for cancer. These include smoking, more than a drink or two a day (especially for women), eating animal fats, and sunbathing (which may cause skin cancer due to exposure to ultraviolet light). Prolonged psychological conditions such as depression or stress may heighten the risk of some kinds of cancer by depressing the functioning of the immune system (Contrada & Baum, 2011; Gross et al., 2010).

African Americans are more likely than European Americans to contract most forms of cancer (Contrada & Baum, 2011). Once they contract cancer, African Americans are more likely than European Americans to die of it. The results for African Americans are apparently connected with their lower socioeconomic status and relative lack of access to health care (Orsi et al., 2010).

Also consider cultural differences in health. Death rates from cancer are higher in such nations as the Netherlands, Denmark, England, Canada, and—yes—the United States, where average rates of daily fat intake are high (Bagchi & Preuss, 2007; Birt & Phillips, 2014). Death rates from cancer are lower in such nations as Thailand, the Philippines, and Japan, where fat intake is lower. Thailand, the Philippines, and Japan are Asian nations, but do not assume that the difference is racial! The diets of Japanese Americans are similar in fat content to those of other Americans—and so are their rates of death from cancer.

Researchers have also suggested possible links between stress and cancer (Contrada & Baum, 2011). For example, Rachel Yehuda (2003) suggests that stress sometimes lowers levels of cortisol and impairs the ability of the immune system to destroy cancer cells. But here, too, the research evidence calls these theoretical links into question.

REDUCING RISK Measures such as the following may help reduce the risk of developing or dying of cancer: getting regular medical checkups to detect cancer early; stopping smoking; eating fewer saturated fats and more fruits, vegetables, and whole grains; and exercising regularly (get a medical checkup first). Cancer is most curable when it is detected early, before it metastasizes.

STUDY TOOLS 11

READY TO STUDY? IN THE BOOK, YOU CAN:

☐ Check your understanding of what you've read with the quizzes below.

☐ Rip out the chapter review card at the back of the book to have a summary of the chapter and the key terms handy.

ONLINE AT CENGAGEBRAIN.COM YOU CAN:

☐ Find out more about the connections between mind and body in a short video.

☐ Prepare for tests with quizzes.

☐ Review the key terms with Flash Cards.

☐ Play games to master concepts.

FILL INS

Answers can be found in the back of the book, starting on page 393.

1. Daily _____ are regularly occurring conditions and experiences that threaten or harm our well-being.

2. The feeling of being pulled in two or more directions by opposing motives is called _____.

3. Albert _____ notes that our beliefs about events, as well as the events themselves, can be stressors.

4. People with (higher or lower?) self-efficacy expectations tend to cope better with stress.

5. Psychologically hardy people are high in _____, challenge, and control.

6. The GAS has three stages: _____, resistance, and exhaustion.

7. Cannon dubbed the alarm reaction the _____ or _____ reaction.

8. Women may show a tend-and-_____ response to stress rather than fight-or-flight.

9. Psychological states such as anxiety and depression impair the functioning of the _____ system, rendering us more vulnerable to health problems.

10. Risk factors for coronary heart disease include family history, obesity, hypertension, high levels of serum _____, heavy drinking, smoking, hostility, Type A behavior, and job strain.

MULTIPLE CHOICE

1. Life changes that are positive can still be stressful because _____ is required.
   a. loneliness
   b. adjustment
   c. depression
   d. none of these

2. According to Ellis, a situation like failing a test, which results in stress, is called a(n)
   a. stimulus event.
   b. causal event.
   c. initiating event.
   d. activation event.

3. Edward's professor told him that his first paper could have been shorter in length. Edward starts sweating and ruminating because he jumps to the conclusion that he does not know how to write papers and will definitely fail this class. This is an example of
   a. imbibing.
   b. imbuing.
   c. catastrophizing.
   d. impetuous behavior.

4. Which quotation best represents the Type A personality?
   a. "Do unto others as you would have them do unto you."
   b. "Winning isn't everything; it's the only thing."
   c. "Don't worry, be happy."
   d. "All for one and one for all."

5. Moderators of stress include all of the following except
   a. pretending that stressors do not exist.
   b. psychological hardiness.
   c. sense of humor.
   d. predictability and control.

6. Psychological hardiness consists of three characteristics. These include
   a. expectations, humor, and control.
   b. power, control, and commitment.
   c. commitment, challenge, and control.
   d. confidence, competence, and efficacy.

7. Randi has an internal locus of control. This means she
   a. can only control her inner emotions.
   b. can only control her outward appearance.
   c. feels she is controlled by others.
   d. feels she can control her own life.

8. The three stages of GAS (in their correct order) are
   a. alarm, snooze, rest.
   b. alarm, rest, snooze.
   c. alarm, resistance, exhaustion.
   d. resistance, alarm, exhaustion.

9. Boris has been under a great deal of stress. Which of the following is most likely true?
   a. His immune system is weakened.
   b. His immune system is strengthened.
   c. His immune system is unaffected.
   d. None of the above.

10. Clarice wants to assess her risk for coronary heart disease (CHD). Which of the following is a risk factor for CHD?
   a. Low serum cholesterol.
   b. Family history.
   c. Low blood pressure.
   d. Physically active lifestyle.

ONE APPROACH.
70 UNIQUE SOLUTIONS.

12 | Psychological Disorders

marco betti/Alamy

LEARNING OUTCOMES

After studying this chapter, you will be able to …

12-1 Define psychological disorders and describe their prevalence.

12-2 Describe the symptoms and possible origins of anxiety disorders.

12-3 Describe the symptoms and possible origins of obsessive-compulsive and related disorders.

12-4 Describe the symptoms and possible origins of trauma- and stressor-related disorders.

12-5 Describe the symptoms and possible origins of dissociative disorders.

12-6 Describe the symptoms and possible origins of somatic symptom and related disorders.

12-7 Describe the symptoms and possible origins of bipolar disorders and depressive disorders.

12-8 Describe the symptoms and possible origins of schizophrenia and other psychotic disorders.

12-9 Describe the symptoms and possible origins of personality disorders.

After you finish

this chapter, go

to **PAGE 325** for

STUDY TOOLS

"William was not the boy next door."

During one long fall semester, the Ohio State campus lived in terror. Four college women were abducted, forced to cash checks or obtain money from automatic teller machines, and then raped. A mysterious phone call led to the arrest of a 23-year-old drifter—let's call him "William"—who had been dismissed from the Navy.

William was not the boy next door.

Psychologists and psychiatrists who interviewed William concluded that 10 personalities—8 male and 2 female—resided within him (Scott, 1994). His personality had been "fractured" by an abusive childhood. His several personalities displayed distinct facial expressions, speech patterns, and memories. They even performed differently on psychological tests.

Arthur, the most rational personality, spoke with a British accent. Danny and Christopher were quiet adolescents. Christine was a 3-year-old girl. Tommy, a 16-year-old, had enlisted in the Navy. Allen was 18 and smoked. Adelena, a 19-year-old lesbian personality, had committed the rapes. Who had made the mysterious phone call? Probably David, 9, an anxious child.

The defense claimed that William's behavior was caused by a psychological disorder termed *dissociative identity disorder* (previously referred to as *multiple personality disorder*). Several distinct identities or personalities dwelled within him. Some of them were aware of the others. Some believed that they were unique. Billy, the core identity, had learned to sleep as a child to avoid his father's abuse. A psychiatrist asserted that Billy had also been "asleep," or in a "psychological coma," during the abductions. Billy should therefore be found not guilty by reason of **insanity**.

William was found not guilty. He was committed to a psychiatric institution and released six years later.

In 1982, a man named John Hinckley was also found not guilty of an assassination attempt on President Reagan's life, although the shooting was witnessed on television by millions. Expert witnesses testified that he should be diagnosed with *schizophrenia*. Hinckley, too, was committed to a psychiatric institution. William and Hinckley were diagnosed with psychological disorders, which is the topic of this chapter.

12-1 WHAT ARE PSYCHOLOGICAL DISORDERS?

Psychology is the study of behavior and mental processes. **Psychological disorders** are behaviors or mental processes that are connected with various kinds of distress or significant impairment in functioning. However, they are not predictable responses to specific events.

Some psychological disorders are characterized by anxiety, but many people are anxious now and then without being considered disordered. For example, it is appropriate to be anxious before a midterm exam. When, then, are feelings like anxiety deemed to be signs of a psychological disorder? For one thing, anxiety may suggest a disorder when it is not appropriate to the situation. For example, there is (usually) no reason to be anxious when looking out a fourth-story window. The magnitude of the problem may also suggest disorder.

Some anxiety can be expected before a job interview. However, feeling that your heart is pounding so intensely that it might leap out of your chest—and then avoiding the interview—are not usual.

> **T** F A man shot the president of the United States in front of millions of television witnesses and was found not guilty by a court of law.

It is true that a man shot the president of the United States in front of millions of television witnesses and was not found guilty in a court of law. His name is John Hinckley and he was found not guilty by reason of insanity. He was diagnosed with a psychological disorder that distorted his perception of reality.

Behaviors or mental processes are suggestive of psychological disorders when they meet some combination of the following criteria:

1. *They are unusual.* Rarity or statistical deviance may not be sufficient for behavior or mental processes to be labeled abnormal, but it helps. After all, only a few people obtain a score of 700 or more on the verbal part of the SAT, but that achievement is not considered disordered. Only a few "see things" or "hear things" as Hinckley did, and those behaviors are deemed disordered because of their bizarre quality. We must also consider the situation. Although many of us feel "panicked" when we realize that a term paper is due the next day, most of us do not have panic attacks out of the blue. Unpredictable panic attacks thus are suggestive of psychological disorder.

2. *They suggest faulty perception or interpretation of reality.* Our society considers it normal to be inspired by religious beliefs but abnormal to believe that God is literally speaking to you. "Hearing voices" and "seeing things" are considered **hallucinations.** Similarly, **ideas of persecution**, such as believing that the FBI is "out to get you," are considered signs of disorder. (Unless, of course, they *are* out to get you.) Hinckley

psychological disorders patterns of behavior or mental processes that are connected with emotional distress or significant impairment in functioning

hallucination a perception in the absence of sensory stimulation that is confused with reality

ideas of persecution erroneous beliefs that one is being victimized or persecuted

testified that he believed he would be impressing actress Jodie Foster by killing the president—an idea that was delusional.

3. *They suggest severe personal distress.* Anxiety, exaggerated fears, and other psychological states cause personal distress, and severe personal distress may be considered abnormal. William and Hinckley were in distress—although, of course, they victimized other people.

4. *They are self-defeating.* Behavior or mental processes that cause misery rather than happiness and fulfillment may suggest psychological disorder. Those who have depressive disorders suffer a great deal. We might also note that chronic drinking is deemed to be abnormal because it threatens one's health and one's social and vocational life.

> **T** F Anxiety is abnormal.

Actually, anxiety is often perfectly normal, as on the eve of a big test or on a first date.

5. *They are dangerous.* Behavior or mental processes that are hazardous to the self or others may be considered suggestive of psychological disorders. People who threaten or attempt suicide may be considered abnormal, as may people who threaten or attack others, like William and Hinckley.

6. *The individual's behavior is socially unacceptable.* We must consider the cultural context of a behavior pattern in judging whether it is normal (Matsumoto & Juang, 2013). For example, many people in the United States admire women who are self-assertive, yet some Latin American, Asian American, and "traditional" European American groups may see outspoken women as being disrespectful and having personality problems.

12-1a PERSPECTIVES ON PSYCHOLOGICAL DISORDERS

If the standards for defining psychological disorders are complex and influenced by one's culture, so too are the explanations of their origins.

THE DEMONOLOGICAL MODEL

If William and John Hinckley had lived in the 17th and 18th centuries, they might have been hanged as witches. At that time, people assumed the behaviors associated with psychological disorders were caused by possession by the Devil. So-called witches were executed for events ranging from a neighbor's infertility to a poor harvest. In fact, throughout all of recorded history, people have attributed unusual behavior and psychological disorders to demons. The ancient Greeks believed that the gods punished humans by causing madness. An exception was the physician Hippocrates, who suggested that psychological disorders are caused by brain abnormalities. The notion that biology could affect thoughts, feelings, and behavior was to lie dormant for about 2,000 years.

Exorcism This medieval woodcut represents the practice of exorcism, in which a demon is expelled from a person who has been "possessed."

THE MEDICAL MODEL The demonological model led to brutal "treatments"—from drilling holes in the skull to permit evil spirits to escape, as in prehistoric times, to burning at the stake, as practiced during the Middle Ages. During the Age of Reason, many health professionals, such as Philippe Pinel (1745–1826) in France, began to view psychological disorders as diseases of the mind, and they encouraged humane treatment. During the 1800s, it was discovered that the late stages of syphilis can distort the workings of the mind. Since that time, researchers have assumed that other physical abnormalities can have psychological effects. The so-called *medical model* assumes that illnesses have physical or biological causes that can be identified and that people afflicted by them are to be cured through treatment or therapy.

CONTEMPORARY PSYCHOLOGICAL MODELS Many contemporary psychologists have joined in the search for biological and physical contributors to psychological disorders. The *diathesis–stress model* assumes that there may be biological differences between individuals—diatheses—that explain why some people develop certain psychological disorders under stress, whereas others do not (Salomon & Jin, 2013). The *biopsychosocial model* explains psychological disorders in terms of a combination of (a) biological vulnerabilities; (b) psychological factors such as exposure to stress; and (c) sociocultural factors such as family relationships and cultural beliefs (Lane, 2014). But again, different factors take on different importance among different people. Psychologists today therefore frequently speak of the interaction between the biological *nature* of the individual and his or her life experiences, or *nurture*.

12-1b CLASSIFYING PSYCHOLOGICAL DISORDERS

Classification is at the heart of science. Without classifying psychological disorders, investigators would not be able to communicate, and scientific progress would come to a halt. The most widely used classification scheme for psychological disorders is the fifth edition of *The Diagnostic and Statistical Manual of the Mental Disorders*, compiled by the American Psychiatric Association (2013). The manual is known more simply as the *DSM-5*.

12-1c PREVALENCE OF PSYCHOLOGICAL DISORDERS

At first glance, psychological disorders might seem to affect only a few of us. Relatively few people are admitted to psychiatric hospitals. Most people will never seek the help of a psychologist or psychiatrist. Many of us have "eccentric" relatives or friends, but most of them are not considered "crazy." Nonetheless, psychological disorders affect us all in one way or another.

About half of us will meet the criteria for a *DSM* disorder at some time or another in our lives, with the disorder most often beginning in childhood or adolescence (Kessler et al., 2005a; see Table 12.1). Slightly more than a fourth of us will experience a psychological disorder in any given year (Kessler et al., 2005b; see Table 12.1). But if we include the problems of family members, friends, and coworkers, add in those who foot the bill in health insurance and taxes, and factor in increased product costs due to lost productivity, then, perhaps everyone is affected.

Let's now consider the various kinds of psychological disorders.

TABLE 12.1	PAST-YEAR AND LIFETIME PREVALENCES OF PSYCHOLOGICAL DISORDERS				
	Anxiety Disorders	Mood Disorders	Bipolar Disorders	Substance Use Disorders	Any Disorders
Prevalence during past year	18.10%	9.50%	2.80%	3.80%	26.20%
Lifetime prevalence	28.80%	20.80%	4.40%	14.60%	46.40%
Median age of onset	11 years	30 years	21 years	20 years	14 years

Source: Kessler et al., 2005; Merikangas et al., 2007.

Note: The data in this table are based on a nationally representative sample of 9,282 English-speaking U.S. residents aged 18 and above. Respondents could report symptoms of more than one type of disorder. For example, anxiety and mood disorders are often "comorbid"—that is, go together. Anxiety and mood disorders are discussed in this chapter. Substance use disorders include abuse of or dependence on alcohol or other drugs.

12-2 ANXIETY DISORDERS

Imagine allowing spiders to crawl over your body or clinging to a beam swinging hundreds of feet above the ground. These are the types of experiences to which many people are exposed on the television show *Fear Factor*. What makes the show so riveting? Possibly the fact that many of us can't imagine participating in such activities for any amount of money. Discomfort with spiders and extreme heights is common, and sensible. However, there are extreme, irrational fears of objects and situations, such as hypodermic needles and public speaking, that are examples of *phobias*—a type of anxiety disorder.

Anxiety disorders have psychological and physical symptoms. The psychological symptoms include worrying, fear of the worst happening, fear of losing control, nervousness, and inability to relax. The physical symptoms reflect arousal of the sympathetic

✳ *The Insanity Plea*

John Hinckley was found not guilty of a 1981 assassination attempt on President Ronald Reagan by reason of insanity. Hinckley was diagnosed with schizophrenia and was committed to a psychiatric institution rather than given a prison term.

What does it mean to be "insane"? What is the "insanity plea"?

In pleading insanity, lawyers use the M'Naghten rule, named after Daniel M'Naghten, who tried to assassinate British Prime Minister Robert Peel in 1843. M'Naghten had delusions that Peel was persecuting him, and he killed the minister's secretary in the attempt. The court found M'Naghten not guilty by reason of insanity. That is, the defendant did not understand what he was doing at the time of the act or did not realize it was wrong. The insanity plea is still used in much the same way (Franklin, 2014).

Many people would like to ban the insanity plea because they equate it with people's "getting away with murder." But there may not be all that much cause for concern. The insanity defense is raised in only about 1% of cases (Silver, 1994). Moreover, people found to be not guilty by reason of insanity are institutionalized for indefinite terms—supposedly until they are no longer insane.

COLORADO HIGHWAY DEPARTMENT PHOTO 01/21/81
JOHN W. HINCKLEY
SUPPLIED BY GLOBE PHOTOS, INC.

ZUMA Press, Inc. /Alamy

John W. Hinckley claimed that he shot president Ronald Reagan because he was trying to impress movie actress Jodie Foster, who had appeared in Taxi Driver. Hinckley was found not guilty of his crime by reason of insanity and committed to a psychiatric institution instead.

branch of the autonomic nervous system: trembling, sweating, a racing heart, elevated blood pressure (a flushed face), and faintness. Anxiety is an appropriate response to a real threat, but it can be abnormal when it is excessive, when it comes out of nowhere (i.e., when events do not seem to warrant it), and when it prevents us from doing important things such as going for medical exams. The anxiety disorders include *specific phobic disorders*, *social anxiety disorder*, *panic disorder*, and *generalized anxiety disorders*.

homes, especially alone. They find it difficult to hold a job or to maintain an ordinary social life.

12-2b SOCIAL ANXIETY DISORDER

Social anxiety disorder, also known as social phobia, is defined by excessive fears of social situations in which the individual is exposed to the scrutiny of others or might do something that will be humiliating or embarrassing. Excessive fear of public speaking is a common social phobia.

Stage fright, speech anxiety, and dating fears are common forms of social phobia. People with social phobias may find excuses for declining social invitations. They may eat lunch at their desks to avoid socializing with coworkers and avoid situations in which they might meet new people. Or they may find themselves in social situations and attempt a quick escape at the first sign of anxiety.

anxiety disorders disorders characterized by excessive worrying, fear of losing control, nervousness, and inability to relax

specific phobia persistent fear of a specific object or situation

claustrophobia fear of tight, small places

acrophobia fear of high places

agoraphobia fear of open, crowded places

social anxiety disorder an irrational, excessive fear of public scrutiny

panic disorder recurrent experiencing of attacks of extreme anxiety in the absence of external stimuli that usually elicit anxiety

12-2a SPECIFIC PHOBIC DISORDERS

Specific phobias are excessive, irrational fears of specific objects or situations, such as spiders, snakes, or heights. Consider fear of elevators. Some people will not enter elevators despite the hardships they incur as a result (such as walking up six flights of steps). Yes, the cable *could* break. The ventilation *could* fail. One *could* be stuck in midair waiting for repairs. These problems are uncommon, however, and it does not make sense for most people to walk up and down several flights of stairs to elude them. Similarly, some people with a specific phobia for hypodermic needles will not have injections, even to treat profound illness. Injections can be painful, but most people with a phobia for needles would gladly suffer an even more painful pinch if it would help them fight illness.

Other specific phobias include **claustrophobia** (fear of tight or enclosed places), **acrophobia** (fear of heights), and fear of mice, snakes, and other creepy crawlies. **Agoraphobia** may affect 3% to 4% of adults (Kessler et al., 2005). Agoraphobia is derived from the Greek words meaning "fear of the marketplace," or fear of being out in open, busy areas. Some people who receive this diagnosis refuse to venture out of their

12-2c PANIC DISORDER

Panic disorder is an abrupt anxiety attack that is apparently unrelated to specific objects or situations. People with panic disorder experience strong cardiac-related sensations: shortness of breath, heavy sweating, tremors, and pounding of the heart (Blechert et al., 2010). Many think they are having a heart attack (Naragon-Gainey, 2010). Levels of cortisol (a stress hormone) in the saliva are elevated during attacks (Bandelow et al., 2000).

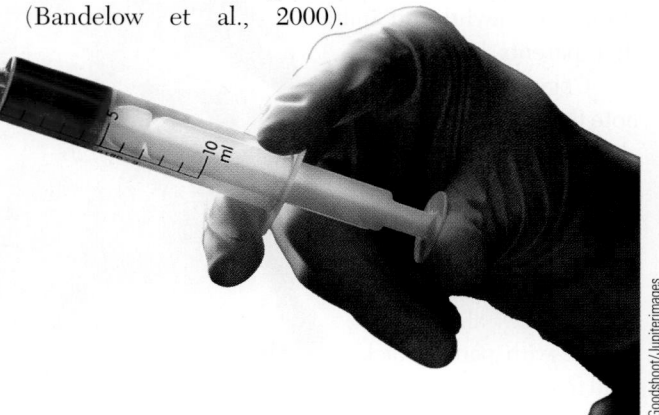

Goodshoot/Jupiterimages

Many fear suffocation. People with the disorder may also experience choking sensations, nausea, numbness or tingling, flushes or chills, and fear of going crazy or losing control. Panic attacks may last minutes or hours. Afterward, the person usually feels drained.

Many people panic now and then. The diagnosis of panic disorder is reserved for those who undergo multiple attacks or live in fear of attacks. Panic attacks seem to come from nowhere. Thus, some people who have had them stay home for fear of having an attack in public. They are diagnosed as having *panic disorder with agoraphobia* (Schmidt et al., 2010).

12-2d GENERALIZED ANXIETY DISORDER

The central symptom of **generalized anxiety disorder** is persistent anxiety that cannot be attributed to a phobic object, situation, or activity. Rather, it seems to be free floating. The core of the disorder appears to be pervasive worrying about numerous stressors (Behar et al., 2009). Symptoms include motor tension (shakiness, inability to relax, furrowed brow, fidgeting); autonomic over arousal (sweating, dry mouth, racing heart, lightheadedness, frequent urinating, diarrhea); and excessive vigilance, as shown by irritability, insomnia, and a tendency to be easily distracted.

12-2e ORIGINS OF ANXIETY DISORDERS

What is known about the origins of anxiety disorders?

PSYCHOLOGICAL VIEWS Some learning theorists—particularly behaviorists—consider phobias to be conditioned fears that were acquired in early childhood. Avoidance of feared stimuli is reinforced by the reduction of anxiety. Observational learning may also play a role in the acquisition of fears (Aktar et al., 2014). If parents squirm, grimace, and shudder at the sight of mice, blood, or dirt on the kitchen floor, children might assume that these stimuli are awful and imitate their parents' behavior.

Cognitive theorists note that people's appraisals of the magnitude of threats help determine whether they are traumatic and can lead to PTSD (Koster et al., 2009). People with panic attacks tend to misinterpret bodily cues and to view them as threats. Obsessions

and compulsions may serve to divert attention from more frightening issues, such as "What am I going to do with my life?" When anxieties are acquired at a young age, we may later interpret them as enduring traits and label ourselves as "someone who fears _____" (you fill it in). We then live up to the labels. We also entertain thoughts that heighten and perpetuate anxiety such as "I've got to get out of here" or "My heart is going to leap out of my chest." Such ideas intensify physical signs of anxiety, disrupt planning, make stimuli seem worse than they really are, motivate avoidance, and decrease self-efficacy expectations. The belief that we will not be able to handle a threat heightens anxiety. The belief that we are in control reduces anxiety (Bandura et al., 1985).

BIOLOGICAL VIEWS Genetic factors are implicated in most psychological disorders, including anxiety disorders (Hartley & Casey, 2013). Anxiety disorders tend to run in families. Identical (MZ) twins are much more likely to both have the disorder than fraternal (DZ) twins (Kendler et al., 2001). Adoptee studies show that the biological parent places the child at greater risk for anxiety and related traits than does the adoptive parent.

Evolutionary psychologists suggest that anxiety may reflect natural selection. Humans (and nonhuman primates) are genetically predisposed ("biologically prepared") to fear stimuli that may have posed a threat to their ancestors (Gerdes et al., 2009; Mineka & Oehlberg, 2008; Starratt & Shackelford, 2010). Evolutionary forces would have favored the survival of individuals who were predisposed toward acquiring fears of large animals, spiders, snakes, heights, entrapment, sharp objects, and strangers. Thus, people who fearlessly encounter potentially harmful stimuli may be at a disadvantage, evolutionarily speaking, rather than at an advantage.

Perhaps a predisposition toward anxiety—in the form of a highly reactive autonomic nervous system—can be inherited (Beesdo et al., 2010; Binder & Nemeroff, 2009). What might make a nervous system "highly reactive"? The autonomic nervous system may stimulate the production of excessive quantities of adrenaline (epinephrine) and noradrenaline (norepinephrine). These chemicals normally

Why do so many people fear spiders? Could evolutionary forces be at work?

Michael Blann/Stone/Getty Images

pump up the body in preparation for the fight-or-flight response—both sides of which can make up self-preserving responses to threats. But when their production is so intense that they flood the body, we can feel shaky and drenched with sweat and incapable of doing anything useful.

BIOPSYCHOSOCIAL VIEWS Many cases of anxiety disorders reflect the interaction of biological, psychological, and social factors. Biological imbalances may initially trigger attacks in panic disorder. But subsequent fear of attacks—and of the bodily cues that signal their onset—may heighten discomfort and give one the idea there is nothing one can do about them (Olatunji & Wolitzky-Taylor, 2009). Feelings of helplessness increase fear. People with panic disorder therefore can be helped by psychological methods that provide ways of reducing physical discomfort—including regular breathing—and show them that there are, after all, things they can do to cope with attacks (Olatunji & Wolitzky-Taylor, 2009).

12-3 OBSESSIVE–COMPULSIVE AND RELATED DISORDERS

Obsessive–compulsive and related disorders share a pattern of repetitive behavior associated with personal distress or impaired function in daily life.

12-3a OBSESSIVE–COMPULSIVE DISORDER

Obsessive–compulsive disorder (OCD) is defined by recurrent, anxiety-provoking thoughts or images that seem irrational and beyond control (*obsessions*) and seemingly irresistible urges to engage in thoughts or behaviors that tend to reduce the anxiety (*compulsions*). Obsessions are so compelling and recurrent that they disrupt daily life. They may include doubts about whether one has locked the doors and shut the windows or images such as one mother's repeated fantasy that her children had been run over on the way home from school. One woman became obsessed with the idea that she had contaminated her hands with Sani-Flush and that the chemicals were spreading to everything she touched. A 16-year-old boy complained that he was distracted by "numbers in my head" when he was about to study or take a test. The more he tried to ignore them, the louder they became.

Compulsions are seemingly irresistible urges to engage in specific acts, often repeatedly, such as elaborate washing after using the bathroom or repeatedly checking that one has locked the door or turned off the gas burners before leaving home. The impulse is recurrent and forceful, interfering with daily life.

12-3b HOARDING DISORDER

People with *hoarding disorder* feel an overpowering need to accumulate certain kinds of possessions and have difficulty discarding them. One wealthy woman bought three condominiums, two of which served as repositories for decades of accumulated newspapers and greeting cards. Her daughter, who lived in a smaller home, had difficulty discarding the remnants of meals. After a couple of years she could navigate only a narrow path in her home to reach the one place where there was still enough room to sleep: her bathtub. The board of health was called in several times to remove the festering food and other items. Neither woman recognized that she had a

A 16-year-old boy with obsessive–compulsive disorder complained that he couldn't focus on schoolwork because he could not avoid noticing "the numbers in my head."

generalized anxiety disorder feelings of dread and foreboding and sympathetic arousal of at least six months' duration

obsessive–compulsive disorder (OCD) an anxiety disorder defined by recurrent, anxiety-provoking thoughts or images that seem irrational and beyond control (obsessions) and seemingly irresistible urges to engage in thoughts or behaviors that tend to reduce the anxiety (compulsions)

psychological problem; the mother would say "You never know when you will need …" But some hoarders do have insight into their problem.

Other related disorders include body dysmorphic disorder, in which the individual is preoccupied with exaggerated or imagined physical defects; continuous hair pulling, and compulsive skin-picking.

12-4 TRAUMA- AND STRESSOR-RELATED DISORDERS

Exposure to trauma, such as natural disasters, combat, crime, terrorism, or the death of a family member can tax anyone's ability to adjust. In trauma and stressor-related disorders, the individual shows yet greater difficulty coming to terms with traumatic events. We consider posttraumatic stress disorder and acute stress disorder.

12-4a POSTTRAUMATIC STRESS DISORDER

Sharia dreamed of a man assaulting her in the night at the Superdome in New Orleans, after she had been moved to this "refuge" following Hurricane Katrina in the summer of 2005. Darla, who lives in Oregon, dreamed that she was trapped in a World Trade Center tower when it was hit by an airplane on September 11, 2001. About one in six Iraq or Afghanistan veterans has nightmares and flashbacks to buddies being killed by snipers or explosive devices (Hoge et al., 2004; Richardson et al., 2010). These all-too-real nightmarish events have caused many bad dreams. Such dreams are part of the experience of posttraumatic stress disorder.

Posttraumatic stress disorder (PTSD) is characterized by a rapid heart rate and feelings of anxiety and helplessness that are caused by a traumatic experience. Such experiences may include a natural or human-made disaster, a threat or assault, or witnessing a death. PTSD

may occur months or years after the event. It frequently occurs among firefighters, combat veterans, and people whose homes and communities have been swept away by natural disasters or who have been victims of accidents or interpersonal violence (Chard et al., 2010; McCauley et al., 2010).

The traumatic event is revisited in the form of intrusive memories, recurrent dreams, and flashbacks—the feeling that the event is recurring (McDevitt-Murphy et al., 2010). People with PTSD typically try to avoid thoughts and activities connected to the traumatic event. They may also find it more difficult to enjoy life, and they often have sleep problems, irritable outbursts, difficulty concentrating, extreme vigilance, and an intensified "startle" response. The terrorist attacks of September 11, 2001, took their toll on sleep. According to a poll taken by the National Sleep Foundation (2001) two months after the attacks, nearly half of Americans had difficulty falling asleep compared with about one-quarter of Americans before the attacks (see Figure 12.1). Women, who are more likely than men to ruminate about stressors (Nolen-Hoeksema et al., 2008), were also more likely than men to report difficulty falling asleep (50% versus 37%).

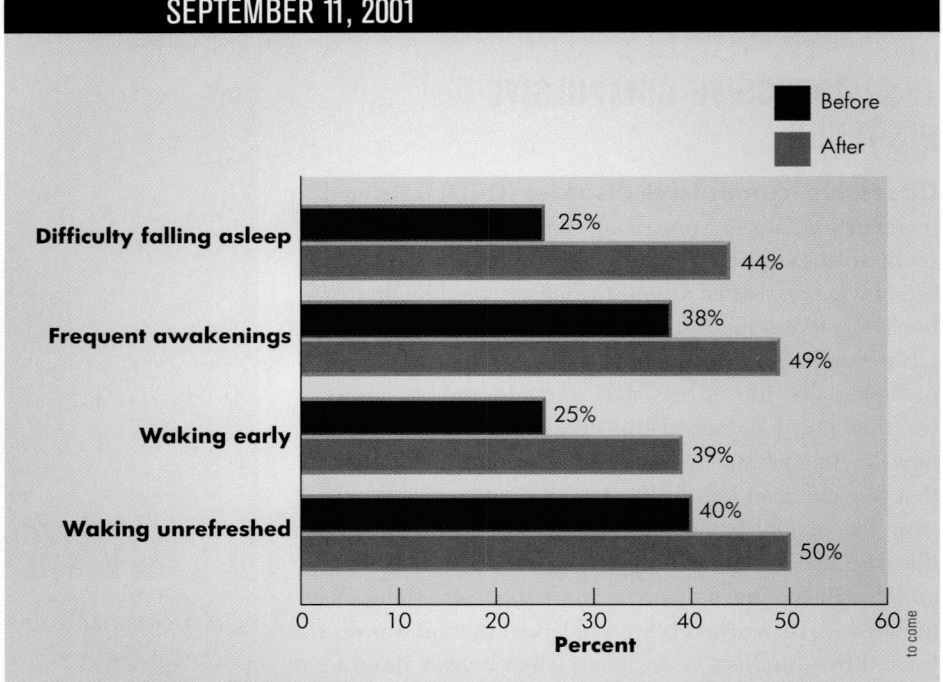

FIG.12.1 SLEEP PROBLEMS AMONG AMERICANS BEFORE AND AFTER SEPTEMBER 11, 2001

Before
After

Difficulty falling asleep — 25%, 44%
Frequent awakenings — 38%, 49%
Waking early — 25%, 39%
Waking unrefreshed — 40%, 50%

Percent (0 10 20 30 40 50 60)

Insomnia is one of the symptoms of stress disorders. A poll by the National Sleep Foundation found that Americans had a greater frequency of sleep problems after the terrorist attacks of September 11, 2001.

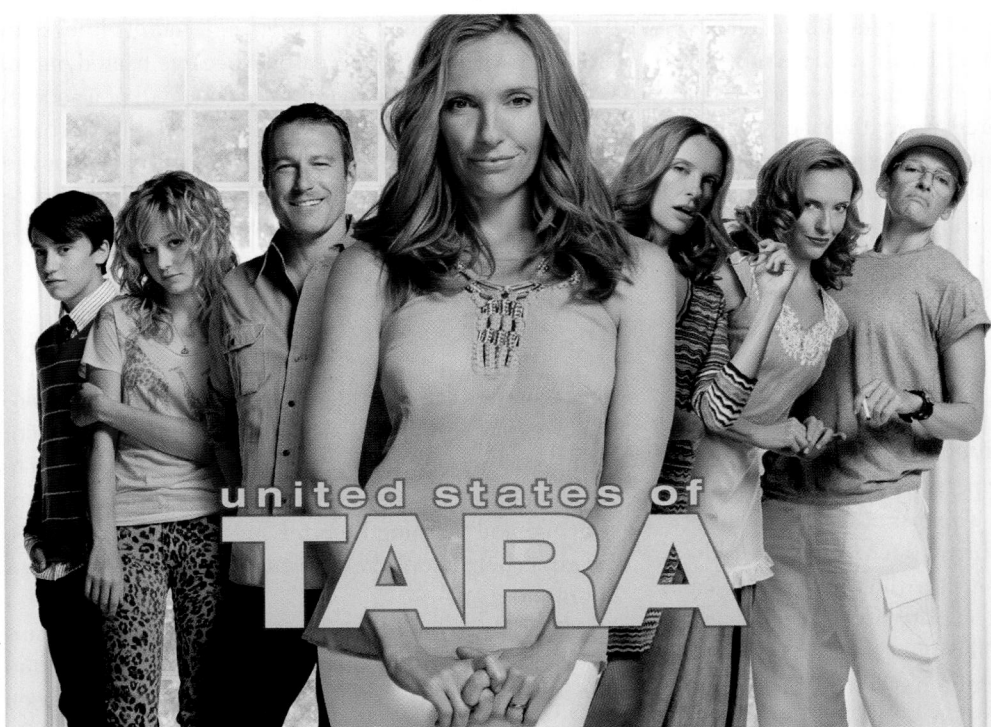

In the Showtime series *United States of Tara*, Toni Collette plays Tara Gregson, a homemaker with two children and several other personalities. Tara has dissociative identity disorder, and within her "reside" the flirty "T," a suburban housewife plucked from the 1950s, and a beer-guzzling Vietnam veteran named "Buck."

AF archive/Alamy

12-4b ACUTE STRESS DISORDER

Acute stress disorder, like PTSD, is characterized by feelings of anxiety and helplessness that are caused by a traumatic event. However, PTSD can occur six months or more after the traumatic event and tends to persist. Acute stress disorder occurs within a month of the event and lasts from two days to four weeks. Women who have been raped, for example, experience acute distress that tends to peak in severity about three weeks after the assault (Bryant, 2006). Yet the same women may go on to experience PTSD (Koss et al., 2002).

12-5 DISSOCIATIVE DISORDERS

William's disorder, described at the beginning of the chapter, was a dissociative disorder. In the **dissociative disorders**, mental processes such as thoughts, emotions, memory, consciousness, even knowledge of one's own identity—the processes that make a person feel whole—may seem to be split off from one another. The *DSM* lists several dissociative disorders. Among them are dissociative identity disorder (earlier termed multiple personality disorder), dissociative amnesia, and depersonalization disorder.

12-5a DISSOCIATIVE IDENTITY DISORDER

Dissociative identity disorder (DID) (formerly termed *multiple personality disorder*) is the name given to William's disorder. In dissociative identity disorder, two or more identities or personalities, each with distinct traits and memories, "occupy" the same person. Each identity may or may not be aware of the others or of events experienced by the others.

The identities of an individual with dissociative identity disorder might have different eyeglass prescriptions and different allergic responses (Braun, 1988). In one person, an identity named Timmy was not sensitive to orange juice. But when other

posttraumatic stress disorder (PTSD) a disorder that follows a distressing event outside the range of normal human experience and that is characterized by features such as intense fear, avoidance

acute stress disorder a disorder, like PTSD, that is characterized by feelings of anxiety and helplessness and caused by a traumatic event; acute stress disorder occurs within a month of the event and lasts from two days to four weeks

dissociative disorders disorders in which there are sudden, temporary changes in consciousness or self-identity

dissociative identity disorder (DID) (formerly termed *multiple personality disorder*) a disorder in which a person appears to have two or more distinct identities or personalities that may alternately emerge

identities gained control over him and drank orange juice, he would break out with hives. Hives would also erupt if another identity emerged while the juice was being digested. If Timmy reappeared when the allergic reaction was present, the itching of the hives would cease, and the blisters would start to subside. In other cases reported by Braun, different identities within a person might show various responses to the same medicine. Or one identity might exhibit color blindness while others have normal color vision.

12-5b DISSOCIATIVE AMNESIA

A person with **dissociative amnesia** is suddenly unable to recall important personal information (i.e., explicit episodic memories). The loss of memory cannot be attributed to organic problems such as a blow to the head or alcoholic intoxication. It is thus a psychological dissociative disorder and not an organic one. In the most common example, the person cannot recall events for a number of hours after a stressful incident, as in warfare or in the case of an uninjured survivor of an accident. In *generalized* dissociative amnesia, people forget their entire lives. Amnesia may last for hours or years.

12-5c DEPERSONALIZATION–DEREALIZATION DISORDER

People with **depersonalization–derealization disorder** experience episodes of feeling detached from themselves or feeling that the world around them is unreal. They may feel as if they are in a walking dream or as if they are going through "the motions" like a robot. Consider Richie's experience:

"We went to Disney World with the kids after school let out. We spent 3 days on the rides, and we were all wearing shirts with mice and ducks and singing Disney songs. On the third day I began to feel unreal and ill at ease while we were watching Disney characters singing and dancing in front of Cinderella's Castle. I became shaky and dizzy and sat down on the cement next to the 4-year-old's stroller.

There were strollers and kids and [adults'] legs all around me, and for some reason I became fixated on the pieces of popcorn strewn on the ground. All of a sudden it seemed that the people around me were silly mechanical creatures, like the dolls in 'It's a Small World' or the animals on the Jungle Cruise. There was this invisible wall of cotton between me and everyone else."

12-5d ORIGINS OF DISSOCIATIVE DISORDERS

According to learning theorists and cognitive psychologists, people with dissociative disorders have learned not to think about bad memories or disturbing impulses to avoid feelings of anxiety, guilt, and shame. Both psychodynamic and learning theories suggest that dissociative disorders help people keep disturbing memories or ideas out of mind.

Whereas some disorders—major depressive disorder and schizophrenia among them—are found around the world, most cases of dissociative disorders have been limited to the United States and Canada (Ross, 2006). Perhaps dissociative disorders, especially DID, are culture-bound. It might also be the case, as suggested by skeptics, that many people who claim to have multiple personalities are misrepresenting (Kong et al., 2008).

12-6 SOMATIC SYMPTOM AND RELATED DISORDERS

People with **somatoform disorders** complain of physical problems such as paralysis, pain, or a persistent belief that they have a serious disease. Yet no evidence of a physical abnormality can be found. In this section, we discuss two somatoform disorders: illness anxiety disorder and conversion disorder.

12-6a ILLNESS ANXIETY DISORDER

A more common type of somatic symptom disorder **illness anxiety disorder** (earlier called *hypochondria*). People with this disorder insist that they are suffering from a serious physical illness, even though no medical evidence of illness can be found. They become preoccupied with minor physical sensations and continue to believe that they are ill despite the reassurance of physicians that they are healthy. They may run from doctor to doctor, seeking the one who will find the causes of the sensations. Fear of illness may disrupt their work or home life.

dissociative amnesia a dissociative disorder marked by loss of memory or self-identity; skills and general knowledge are usually retained

depersonalization–derealization disorder a disorder in which one feels detached from oneself or that one's surroundings are not real

somatoform disorders disorders in which people complain of physical (somatic) problems even though no physical abnormality can be found

illness anxiety disorder a somatoform disorder characterized by persistent belief that one is ill despite lack of medical findings

12-6b CONVERSION DISORDER

Conversion disorder is characterized by a major change in, or loss of, physical functioning, although there are no medical findings to explain the loss of functioning. The behaviors are not intentionally produced. That is, the person is not faking. Conversion disorder is so named because it appears to "convert" a source of stress into a physical difficulty.

If you lost the ability to see at night or if your legs became paralyzed, you would understandably show concern. But some people with conversion disorder show indifference to their symptoms, a symptom termed **la belle indifférence** The lack of concern suggests awareness, on some level, that the physical problems have their benefits.

During World War II, some bomber pilots developed night blindness. They could not carry out their nighttime missions, although no damage to the optic nerves was found. In rare cases, women with large families have been reported to become paralyzed in the legs, again with no medical findings. More recently, a Cambodian woman who had witnessed atrocities became blind as a result.

12-6c ORIGINS OF SOMATIC SYMPTOM AND RELATED DISORDERS

The somatoform disorders offer a fascinating study in the biopsychosocial perspective. Psychologically speaking, the somatoform disorders have much to do with what one focuses on—actual social and financial problems, for example, or one's body. There is evidence that people with conversion disorder are susceptible to being hypnotized (R. J. Brown et al., 2007), and some investigators consider conversion disorder to be a form of self-hypnosis in which people focus so intently on an imaginary physical problem that they exclude conflicting information (Roelofs et al., 2002). Research evidence suggests that people who develop illness anxiety disorder are particularly sensitive to bodily sensations and tend to ruminate about them (Marcus et al., 2008).

Biologically speaking, tendencies toward perfectionism and rumination, which are found among many people with somatoform disorders, are thought to be at least partly heritable. Squeamishness about one's body may be too much of a good thing from the evolutionary perspective. That is, concern about bodily harm will presumably encourage one to avoid danger and provide advantages in survival and reproduction. But too much concern may lead to useless preoccupations.

12-7 MOOD DISORDERS

Moods are feeling states that color our psychological lives. Most of us feel elated when we have earned high grades, a promotion, or the affections of someone we care about. We feel down or depressed when we are rejected by a date, flunk a test, or suffer financial reverses. It is normal and appropriate to be happy about uplifting events. It is just as normal, and just as appropriate, to be saddened by dismal events. It might very well be abnormal if we did not feel down or depressed in the face of tragedy or disappointment. But people with mood disorders experience disturbances in mood that are unusually severe or prolonged and impair their ability to function. Some people become severely depressed when things are going well or when they encounter mildly upsetting events that others take in stride. Still others experience extreme mood swings. They ride an emotional roller coaster with dizzying heights and abysmal depths when the world around them remains largely on an even keel. We consider two mood disorders: bipolar disorder and major depressive disorder.

12-7a BIPOLAR DISORDER

People with **bipolar disorder**, earlier known as *manic–depressive disorder*, have mood swings from ecstatic elation to deep depression. The cycles seem to be unrelated to external events. In the elated, or **manic** phase, the person may show excessive excitement or silliness, carrying jokes too far. The manic person may be argumentative, show poor judgment, destroy property, make huge contributions to charity, or give away expensive possessions. People often find manic individuals abrasive and avoid them. They are often oversexed and too restless to sit still or sleep restfully. They often speak rapidly (showing *pressured speech*) and jump from topic to topic (showing **rapid flight of ideas**). It can be hard to get a word in edgewise.

conversion disorder a disorder in which anxiety or unconscious conflicts are "converted" into physical symptoms that often have the effect of helping the person cope with anxiety or conflict

la belle indifférence a French term descriptive of the lack of concern for their (imagined) medical problem sometimes shown by people with conversion disorders

bipolar disorder a disorder in which the mood alternates between two extreme poles (elation and depression); also referred to as *manic depression*

manic elated, showing excessive excitement

rapid flight of ideas rapid speech and topic changes, characteristic of manic behavior

Bipolar Disorder Actress Catherine Zeta-Jones has revealed that she sought treatment for bipolar disorder.

BEN BIRCHALL/PA Photos/Landov

Depression is the other side of the coin. People with bipolar depression often sleep more than usual and are lethargic. People with major (or unipolar) depression are more likely to have insomnia and agitation. Those with bipolar depression also exhibit social withdrawal and irritability. Some people with bipolar disorder attempt suicide when the mood shifts from the elated phase toward depression (Jamison, 2000). They will do almost anything to escape the depths of depression that lie ahead.

👍 *Truth*

| T | F | Feeling elated is not always a good thing. |

It is true that feeling "up" is not always a good thing, as in the manic phase of bipolar disorder.

Imbalances in the neurotransmitter serotonin apparently play a role in bipolar disorder (Carrard et al., 2011). Twin and adoption studies also support a role for genetic factors in bipolar disorder (Willcutt & McQueen, 2010).

12-7b DEPRESSIVE DISORDERS

People with run-of-the-mill depression may feel sad, blue, or "down in the dumps." They may complain of lack of energy, loss of self-esteem, difficulty concentrating, loss of interest in activities and other people, pessimism, crying, and thoughts of suicide.

These feelings are more intense in people with **major depressive disorder**. According to a nationally representative sample of more than 9,000 adults in the United States, major depressive disorder affects 5% to 7% of us within any given year and one person in six or seven over the course of our lives (Hasin et al., 2005; Kessler et al., 2003). About half of those with major depressive disorder experience severe symptoms such as poor appetite, serious weight loss, and agitation or **psychomotor retardation**. They may be unable to concentrate and make decisions. They may say that they "don't care" anymore and in some cases attempt suicide. A minority may display faulty perception of reality—so-called psychotic behaviors. These include delusions of unworthiness, guilt for imagined wrongdoings, even the notion that one is rotting from disease. There may also be delusions, as of the devil administering deserved punishment, or hallucinations, as of strange bodily sensations.

ORIGINS OF MAJOR DEPRESSIVE DISORDER What is known about the origins of major depressive disorder?

PSYCHOLOGICAL VIEWS Many learning theorists suggest that depressed people behave

"I DIDN'T KNOW MY MOTHER HAD IT. I THINK A LOT OF WOMEN DON'T KNOW THEIR MOTHERS HAD IT; THAT'S THE SAD THING ABOUT DEPRESSION. YOU KNOW, YOU DON'T FUNCTION ANYMORE. YOU SHUT DOWN. YOU FEEL LIKE YOU ARE IN A VOID."

MARIE OSMOND, AMERICAN SINGER AND ACTRESS (1959–)

as though they cannot obtain reinforcement. For example, they appear to be inactive and apathetic. Many people with depressive disorders have an external locus of control. That is, they do not believe they can control events so as to achieve reinforcements (Tong, 2001; Weinmann et al., 2001).

Research conducted by learning theorists has also found links between depression and **learned helplessness**. In classic research, psychologist Martin Seligman (1975) taught dogs that they were helpless to escape an electric shock. The dogs were prevented from leaving a cage in which they received repeated shocks. Later, a barrier to a safe compartment was removed, offering the animals a way out. When they were shocked again, however, the dogs made no effort to escape. They had apparently learned that they were helpless. Seligman's dogs were also, in a sense, reinforced for doing nothing. That is, the shock *eventually* stopped when the dogs were showing helpless behavior—inactivity and withdrawal. "Reinforcement" might have increased the likelihood of repeating the "successful behavior"—that is, doing nothing—in a similar situation. This helpless behavior resembles that of people who are depressed.

Cognitive factors also contribute to depression. For example, perfectionists set themselves up for depression by making irrational demands on themselves. They are likely to fall short of their (unrealistic) expectations and to feel depressed as a result (Flett et al., 2007).

Still other cognitions involve the ways people explain their failures and shortcomings to themselves. Seligman (1996) suggested that when things go wrong, we may think of the causes of failure as either *internal* or *external, stable* or *unstable, global* or *specific*. These **attributional styles** can be illustrated using the example of having a date that does not work out. An internal attribution involves self-blame (as in "I really loused it up."). An external attribution places the blame elsewhere (as in "Some couples just don't take to each other," or "She was the wrong sign for me."). A stable attribution ("It's my personality.") suggests a problem that cannot be changed. An unstable attribution ("It was because I had a head cold.") suggests a

An internal attribution involves self-blame, as in "I really loused it up." An external attribution places the blame elsewhere. Do you think this player has made an internal or external attribution for the play that led to his being benched?

temporary condition. A global attribution of failure ("I have no idea what to do when I'm with other people.") suggests that the problem is quite large. A specific attribution ("I have problems making small talk at the beginning of a relationship.") chops the problem down to a manageable size. How does this connect to depression? Research has shown that people who are depressed are more likely to attribute the causes of their failures to internal, stable, and global factors—factors that they are relatively powerless to change (Safford et al., 2007).

BIOLOGICAL VIEWS Researchers are also searching for biological factors in depression. Depression, for example, is often associated with the trait of **neuroticism**, which is heritable (Ormel et al., 2013). Anxiety is also connected with neuroticism, and depressive and anxiety disorders are frequently found in the same person (Fusar-Poli et al., 2014).

Much research into depression focuses on underutilization of the neurotransmitter serotonin in the brain (Mahar et al., 2014). Moreover, people with severe depression often respond to drugs (selective serotonin reuptake inhibitors, or SSRIs) that heighten the action of serotonin (Mahar et al., 2014).

THE BIOPSYCHOSOCIAL PERSPECTIVE Relationships between depressive disorders and biological factors are complex and under intense study. Even if people are biologically predisposed toward depression, self-efficacy expectations and attitudes—particularly attitudes about whether one can change things for the better—may play a role.

major depressive disorder a serious to severe depressive disorder in which the person may show loss of appetite, psychomotor retardation, and impaired reality testing

psychomotor retardation slowness in motor activity and (apparently) in thought

learned helplessness a possible explanation for some depressive behavior, based on findings that organisms in aversive situations learn to show inactivity when their behavior is not reinforced

attributional style the tendency to attribute one's behavior to internal or external factors, stable or unstable factors, and global or specific factors

neuroticism a personality trait characterized largely by persistent anxiety

Although depressive disorders reflect processes within the individual, many kinds of situations are also connected with depression. Depression may be a reaction to losses and stress (Pizzagalli, 2014). Stressors such as marital discord, physical discomfort, and failure or pressure at work all contribute to feelings of depression. We tend to be more depressed by things we bring on ourselves, such as academic and financial problems, unwanted pregnancy, and arguments (Greenberger et al., 2000). However, some people recover from depression less readily than others. People who remain depressed have lower self-esteem, are less likely to be able to solve social problems, and have less social support (Reinecke et al., 2001; Steiger et al., 2014).

12-7c SUICIDE

Each year about 38,000 people in the United States take their own lives (Centers for Disease Control and Prevention, 2013b). Suicide is the third leading cause of death among 15- to 24-year-olds, following accidents and assaults (Minino et al., 2010).

We discuss suicide in this section because most suicides, as in the case of the comedian and actor Robin Williams (see photo on page 317), are linked to feelings of depression and hopelessness (Bagge et al., 2014). Suicidal adolescents tend to experience confusion about who they are and where they are going, impulsiveness, emotional instability, and social problems (A. L. Miller et al., 2007). Some suicidal teenagers, like suicidal adults, are highly achieving, rigid

The Case of Women and Depression

Women are nearly twice as likely to be diagnosed with depression as men (Eaton et al., 2012). This gender difference begins to emerge in adolescence. In any given year, about 12% of women and 7% of men in the United States are diagnosed with depression. It was once assumed that depression was most likely to accompany menopause in women, because women could no longer carry out their "natural" function of childbearing. However, women are more likely to encounter depression during the childbearing years (Keyes & Goodman, 2006).

Many people assume that biological sex differences largely explain why women are more likely to become depressed (Deecher et al., 2008). Low levels of estrogen are widely seen as the culprit. Estrogen levels plummet prior to menstruation, and the deficit may trigger psychological changes. How often do we hear degrading remarks such as "It must be that time of the month" when a woman expresses feelings of anger or irritation? Some theorists suggest that women may also have a "cognitive vulnerability" to depression, connected with greater tendencies than men to ruminate about stresses and other negative events (Eaton et al., 2012; Wisco & Nolen-Hoeksema, 2009).

Some of the gender difference may also reflect the greater stresses placed on women, which tend to be maximized when they are working a triple

shift—one in the workforce and the others meeting the demands of homemaking, child rearing, and aging parents (Schwartz, 2013). Women are more likely to experience physical and sexual abuse, poverty, single parenthood, and sexism. Single mothers, in particular, have lower socioeconomic status than men, and depression and other psychological disorders are more common among poor people (Nicholson et al., 2008). A part of treatment for depressed women, then, is to modify the demands on women. The pain may lie in the individual, but the cause often lies in society.

Robin Beckham/BEEPstock/Alamy

About twice as many women as men have been diagnosed with major depressive disorder. Can you think of some reasons for this gender difference?

perfectionists who have set impossibly high expectations for themselves (A. L. Miller et al., 2007). Many people throw themselves into feelings of depression and hopelessness by comparing themselves negatively with others (Barber, 2001).

Contributors to suicidal behavior among adolescents include concerns over sexuality, sexual abuse, grades, problems at home, and substance abuse (Mustanski et al., 2014; Stone et al., 2014; Zayas et al., 2010). It is not always a stressful event itself that precipitates suicide but the individual's anxiety or fear of being "found out" about something, such as failing a course or getting arrested. People who consider suicide are apparently less capable of solving problems, especially social problems, than others (A. L. Miller et al., 2007). They are thus less likely to find productive ways of changing the stressful situation. They want a magical solution to problems that require work or else a quick way out (Shneidman, 2001).

There is a tendency for suicide to run in families (Goldston & Compton, 2010). Many suicide attempters have family members with serious psychological problems, and about one in four has family members who have taken their own lives (Petersen et al., 2014). The causal connections are unclear, however. Do people who attempt suicide inherit disorders that can lead to suicide? Does the suicide of a family member give a person the idea of committing suicide or create the impression that he or she is "fated" to commit suicide?

SOCIOCULTURAL FACTORS IN SUICIDE Suicide is connected not only with feelings of depression and stressful events but also with age, educational status, ethnicity, and gender. Suicide is more common among college students than among people of the same age who are not in college. Each year, about 10,000 college students attempt suicide. Although teenage suicides loom large in the media spotlight, older people are more likely to commit suicide (Centers for Disease Control and Prevention, 2013b). The

Comedian and Actor Robin Williams. Fans were shocked when Williams committed suicide, because he was always—in their view—bubbly and funny. Few knew that his final years were wracked with pain and despair due to illness.

Steve Granitz/WireImage/Getty Images

suicide rate among older people who are unmarried or divorced is double that of older people who are married.

Rates of suicide and suicide attempts also vary among different ethnic groups and according to gender. For example, about one in every six Native Americans (17%) has attempted suicide—a rate higher than that of other Americans (Centers for Disease Control and Prevention, 2013b). About one in eight Latin Americans has attempted suicide and three in ten have considered it. European

Andrew Bret Wallis/The Image Bank/Getty Images

Why are women more likely than men to attempt suicide? Why are men more likely to "succeed"?

Americans are next, with 8% attempting and 28% contemplating suicide. African Americans are least likely to attempt suicide (6.5%) or to think about it (20%). The actual suicide rates for African Americans are about two-thirds of those for European Americans, despite the fact that African Americans are more likely to live in poverty and experience discrimination (Centers for Disease Control and Prevention, 2013b).

About three times as many females as males attempt suicide, but about five times as many males "succeed" (Centers for Disease Control and Prevention, 2013b). Males are more likely to shoot or hang themselves; females more often use drugs, such as overdoses of tranquilizers or sleeping pills, or poisons. It takes a while for drugs to work, giving people the opportunity to find them and intervene.

MYTHS ABOUT SUICIDE You may have heard that individuals who threaten suicide are only seeking attention. Those who are serious just do it. Not so. Most people who commit suicide give warnings about their intentions or have made prior attempts (Bakst et al., 2009; Jackson & Nuttall, 2001; Waters, 2000). Contrary to widespread belief, discussing suicide with a person who is depressed does not prompt the person to attempt suicide (National Center for Injury Prevention and Control, 2005). Extracting a promise not to commit suicide before calling or visiting a helping professional seems to prevent some suicides.

Some believe that only "insane" people (meaning people who are out of touch with reality) would take their own lives. However, suicidal thinking is not necessarily a sign of psychosis, neurosis, or personality disorder. Instead, people may consider suicide when they think they have run out of options (Nock & Kazdin, 2002; Townsend et al., 2001).

positive symptoms those symptoms of schizophrenia that indicate the presence of inappropriate behavior, such as hallucinations, delusions, agitation, and inappropriate giggling

negative symptoms those symptoms of schizophrenia that reflect the absence of appropriate behavior, such as blank faces, monotonic voices, and motionless bodies

mutism refusal to talk

12-8 SCHIZOPHRENIA AND OTHER PSYCHOTIC DISORDERS

In psychotic disorders, people experience a loss of contact with reality. They may see or hear things that are not actually there (hallucinations). They may have ideas, as of people planting "radios" in their walls that have no basis in fact (delusions). We discuss schizophrenia and delusional disorder.

12-8a SCHIZOPHRENIA

Schizophrenia is a severe psychological disorder that touches every aspect of a person's life. It is characterized by disturbances in thought and language, perception and attention, motor activity, and mood, as well as withdrawal and absorption in daydreams or fantasy.

Schizophrenia has been referred to as the worst psychological disorder affecting human beings. It afflicts nearly 1% of the population worldwide. Its onset occurs relatively early in life, and its adverse effects tend to endure.

SYMPTOMS OF SCHIZOPHRENIA In schizophrenia, whatever can go wrong, psychologically, seems to go wrong. There are disturbances in thinking, language, perception, motor behavior, and social interaction. People with schizophrenia may have *positive symptoms, negative symptoms,* or both. **Positive symptoms** are the inappropriate kinds of behavior we find in afflicted people, including, for example, agitated behavior, vivid hallucinations, unshakable delusions, disorganized thinking, and nonsensical speech. **Negative symptoms** are those that reflect the absence of appropriate behavior. We see them in flat, emotionless voices, blank faces, rigid, motionless bodies, and **mutism** (refusal to talk).

PROBLEMS IN THINKING AND LANGUAGE Schizophrenia has been called a "thought disorder" because people with schizophrenia have problems in thinking, language, memory, and attention (Cellard et al., 2010). Their thinking and communication ability

> "IF YOU TALK TO GOD, YOU ARE PRAYING. IF GOD TALKS TO YOU, YOU HAVE SCHIZOPHRENIA".
>
> THOMAS SZASZ, AMERICAN PSYCHIATRIST AND ACADEMIC (1920–2012)

become unraveled. Their speech may be jumbled. They may combine parts of words into new words or make meaningless rhymes. They may jump from topic to topic, conveying little useful information. They usually do not recognize that their thoughts and behavior are abnormal.

Many people with schizophrenia have unshakeable **delusions** of grandeur, persecution, or reference. In the case of *delusions of grandeur*, a person may believe that he is a famous historical figure such as Jesus or a person on a special mission. People with *delusions of persecution* may believe that they are sought by the CIA, FBI, or some other group. Paranoid individuals tend to jump to conclusions that people intend to do them harm based on little evidence. People with *delusions of reference* erroneously believe that other people are talking about them or referring to them. For example, a woman with delusions of reference said that news stories contained coded information about her. Other people with schizophrenia have had delusions that they have committed unpardonable sins, that they were rotting away from disease, or that they or the world did not exist.

| T | F | People with schizophrenia may see and hear things that are not really there. |

It is true that people with schizophrenia may see and hear things that are not really there. Those "things" are called hallucinations.

PROBLEMS IN PERCEPTION The perceptual problems of people with schizophrenia often include hallucinations—imagery in the absence of external stimulation that the person cannot distinguish from reality. People who experience hallucinations may see colors or even obscene words spelled out in midair. Auditory hallucinations are the most common type.

PROBLEMS IN ACTIONS, EMOTIONS, AND SOCIAL INTERACTION For individuals with schizophrenia, motor activity may become wild or so slowed that the person is said to be in a **stupor**—that is, a condition in which the senses, thought, and movement are inhibited. There may be strange gestures and facial expressions. People with the condition termed **catatonia** show striking impairment in motor activity. A stupor may suddenly change into agitation. Catatonic individuals

may maintain unusual, sometimes difficult postures for hours, even as their limbs grow swollen or stiff. A striking feature of this condition is **waxy flexibility**, in which the person maintains positions into which he or she has been manipulated by others. Catatonic individuals may also show mutism, but afterward, they usually report that they heard what others were saying at the time.

The schizophrenic person's emotional responses may be flat or blunted or completely inappropriate—as in giggling upon hearing bad news. People with schizophrenia tend to withdraw from social contacts and become wrapped up in their own thoughts and fantasies (Horan et al., 2010; Mathews & Barch, 2010).

12-8b DELUSIONAL DISORDER

People with **delusional disorder** hold persistent, clearly delusional beliefs, often involving paranoid themes. The delusional beliefs typically concern events that could possibly occur, such as the infidelity of a spouse, persecution by others, or attracting the love of a famous person. The possibility of such beliefs may lead others to take them seriously and check them out before deciding that they are unfounded. Apart from the delusion, the individual does not show obviously bizarre or odd behavior. But in some there is a single bizarre delusion, such as believing that aliens have implanted electrodes in the person's head. John Nash, the character in the true story behind the film *A Beautiful Mind*, believed that the government was recruiting him to decipher coded messages sent by our Cold War enemies.

12-8c EXPLAINING SCHIZOPHRENIA

Researchers have investigated various factors that may contribute to schizophrenia, including psychological, sociocultural, and biological factors.

PSYCHOLOGICAL VIEWS
Most learning theorists have explained schizophrenia in terms of conditioning and observational learning. They have suggested that people engage in schizophrenic behavior when it is more likely to be reinforced than normal behavior. This may occur when a person is

delusions false, persistent beliefs that are unsubstantiated by sensory or objective evidence

stupor a condition in which the senses, thought, and movement are dulled

catatonia a psychotic condition characterized by striking motor impairment

waxy flexibility a feature of catatonic schizophrenia in which people can be molded into postures that they maintain for quite some time

delusional disorder a psychotic disorder characterized by persistent false beliefs.

reared in a socially unrewarding or punitive situation. Inner fantasies then become more reinforcing than social realities. Patients in a psychiatric hospital may learn what is "expected" by observing others. Hospital staff may reinforce schizophrenic behavior by paying more attention to patients who behave bizarrely. This view is consistent with folklore that the child who disrupts the class attracts more attention from the teacher than the "good" child.

SOCIOCULTURAL VIEWS Many investigators have considered whether and how social and cultural factors such as poverty, poor parenting, discrimination, and overcrowding contribute to schizophrenia—especially among people who are genetically vulnerable to the disorder. Although quality of parenting is connected with the development of schizophrenia (Buckley et al., 2000), critics note that many people who are reared in socially punitive settings are apparently immune to the disorder.

Classic research in New Haven, Connecticut, showed that the rate of schizophrenia was twice as high in the lowest socioeconomic class as in the next higher class on the socioeconomic ladder (Hollingshead & Redlich, 1958). Some sociocultural theorists therefore suggest that treatment of schizophrenia requires alleviation of poverty and other social ills rather than changing people whose behavior is deviant. But critics of this view suggest that low socioeconomic status may be a result, rather than a cause, of schizophrenia. People with schizophrenia may drift downward in social status—winding up in poor neighborhoods—because they lack the social skills and cognitive abilities to function at higher levels.

Although many researchers continue to seek psychological and social risk factors for the development of schizophrenia, research has not discovered any environmental causes that will lead to the development of schizophrenia in people who are unrelated to people with the disorder. Because of this lack of evidence, much focus today is on the biological aspects of schizophrenia—on its nature as a brain disease and on its likely biological origins. Once we have outlined the nature of the biological differences between schizophrenic people and normal people, we will turn to genetic and other biological factors that may produce schizophrenia.

BIOLOGICAL VIEWS Many studies have shown that the brains of schizophrenic people differ from those of normal people. Studies have focused on the amount of gray matter in the brain (see Figure 12.2),

---

FIG.12.2 **AVERAGE RATES OF LOSS OF GRAY MATTER AMONG NORMAL ADOLESCENTS AND ADOLESCENTS DIAGNOSED WITH SCHIZOPHRENIA**

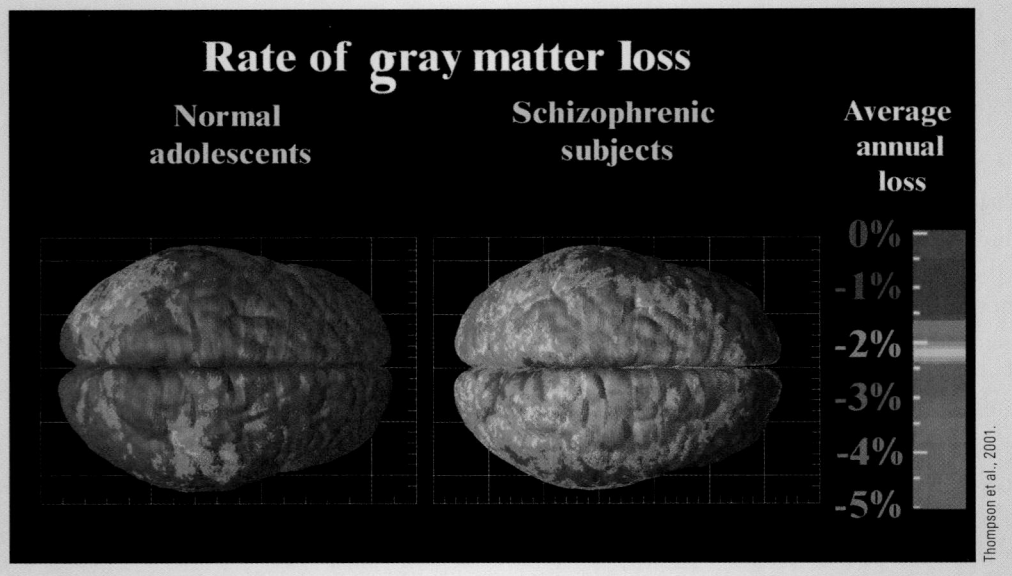

High-resolution MRI scans show rates of gray matter loss in normal 13- to 18-year-olds and among adolescents of the same age diagnosed with schizophrenia. Maps of brain changes reveal profound, progressive loss in schizophrenia (right). Loss also occurs in normal adolescents (left), but at a slower rate.

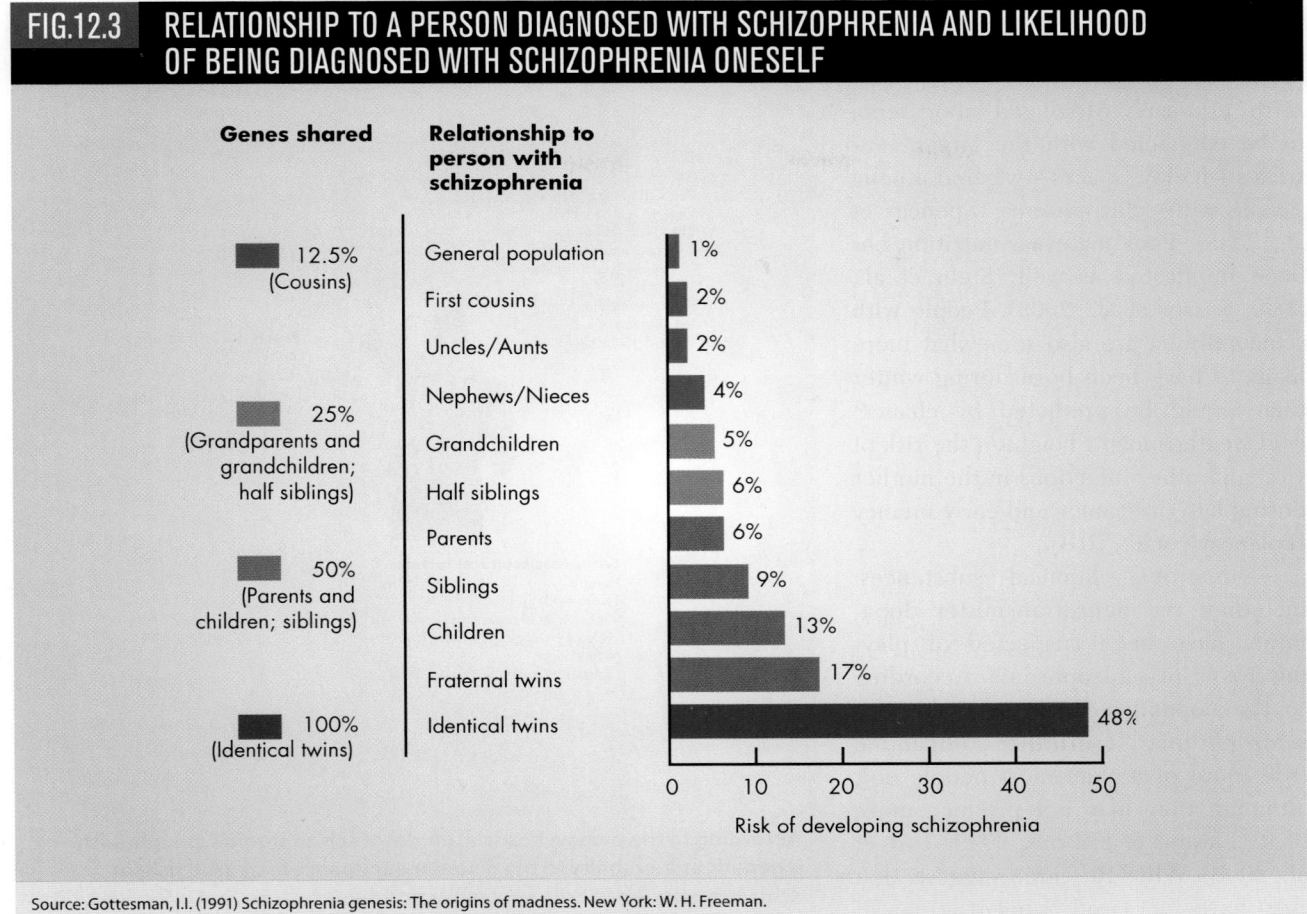

FIG.12.3 RELATIONSHIP TO A PERSON DIAGNOSED WITH SCHIZOPHRENIA AND LIKELIHOOD OF BEING DIAGNOSED WITH SCHIZOPHRENIA ONESELF

Source: Gottesman, I.I. (1991) Schizophrenia genesis: The origins of madness. New York: W. H. Freeman.

the size of ventricles (hollow spaces), activity levels in the brain, and brain chemistry (e.g., neurotransmitters).

Imaging of the brain has shown that people with schizophrenia generally have less gray matter than other people, which suggests deficiencies in attention, working memory, abstract thinking, and language (Ghohari et al., 2014; Guo et al., 2014). People with schizophrenia have smaller brains than normal people and, in particular, a smaller prefrontal region of the cortex (Shirayama et al., 2010). PET scans reveal that people with schizophrenia also tend to have a lower level of activity in the prefrontal cortex—the region responsible for planning and decision making (Farzan et al., 2010; Meyer-Lindenberg et al., 2001). Still other research connects the lower activity levels with a loss in synapses (the structures that permit communication between neurons) in the region (Glantz et al., 2010), further decreasing the likelihood that people with schizophrenia will transmit neural messages efficiently.

What might account for differences in brain structure and functioning? Schizophrenia, like many other psychological disorders, runs in families (Bolinskey & Gottesman, 2010). People with schizophrenia make up about 1% of the global population, yet children with one schizophrenic parent have about a 6% chance of being diagnosed with it (see Figure 12.3). There is about a 48% agreement rate for the diagnosis among pairs of identical twins, whose genetic codes are the same, compared with a 17% rate among pairs of fraternal twins (Gottesman, 1991). Moreover, adoptee studies find that the biological parent typically places the child at greater risk for schizophrenia than the adoptive parent (Gottesman, 1991). Many studies have been carried out to try to isolate the gene or genes involved in schizophrenia. Some studies find locations for multiple genes on several chromosomes.

In many cases of schizophrenia, a genetic vulnerability may be a necessary factor but insufficient to cause its development. The mothers of many people who develop schizophrenia have undergone complications during pregnancy and birth (Spencer et al., 2008). For example, many mothers had the flu during the sixth or seventh month of pregnancy (A. S. Brown & Sherkits, 2010; Short et al., 2010). Complications during childbirth, especially prolonged labor, seem to be connected with the larger ventricles—hollow spaces—we find among people with schizophrenia (Spencer et al., 2008). Poor maternal nutrition has been implicated as well (Stein et al., 2009; Susser et al., 2009). People with schizophrenia are also somewhat more likely to have been born during winter than would be predicted by chance; cold weather might heighten the risk of viral and other infections in the mother during late pregnancy and early infancy (Polanczyk et al., 2010).

Numerous chemical substances, including the neurotransmitter dopamine, have been suspected of playing a role in schizophrenia. According to the dopamine theory, people with schizophrenia "overutilize" dopamine (use more of it than most people do), although they may not produce more of it (Fatemi & Folsom, 2009; Tost et al., 2009). Why? Research suggests that they have increased concentrations of dopamine at the synapses in the brain and also larger numbers of dopamine receptors (Kegeles et al., 2010). It's a sort of "double-hit" of neural transmission that may be connected with the confusion that characterizes schizophrenia.

THE BIOPSYCHOSOCIAL VIEW Because biological, psychological, and sociocultural factors are implicated in schizophrenia, most investigators today favor the biopsychosocial model. According to this model, genetic factors create a predisposition toward—or vulnerability to—schizophrenia (see Figure 12.4). Genetic vulnerability to the disorder interacts with other factors, such as complications of pregnancy and birth, stress, quality of parenting, and social conditions to give rise to the disorder (Bishop, 2009; Buckley et al., 2000; Sawa & Snyder, 2002).

personality disorders
enduring patterns of maladaptive behavior that are sources of distress to the individual or others

paranoid personality disorder a personality disorder characterized by persistent suspiciousness but not involving the disorganization of paranoid schizophrenia

FIG.12.4 **THE BIOPSYCHOSOCIAL MODEL OF SCHIZOPHRENIA**

Biological factors
Genetic vulnerability
Overutilization of dopamine
Enlarged ventricles
Deficiency in gray matter
Viral infections
Birth complications
Malnutrition
 (also a sociocultural factor)

Psychological factors
Stress
Family discord
Poor quality of parenting
 (also a social factor)

Social/sociocultural factors
Poverty
Overcrowding
Poor quality of parenting
 (also a psychological factor)
Malnutrition
 (also a biological factor)

Paul Bradbury/OJO Images Ltd/Alamy

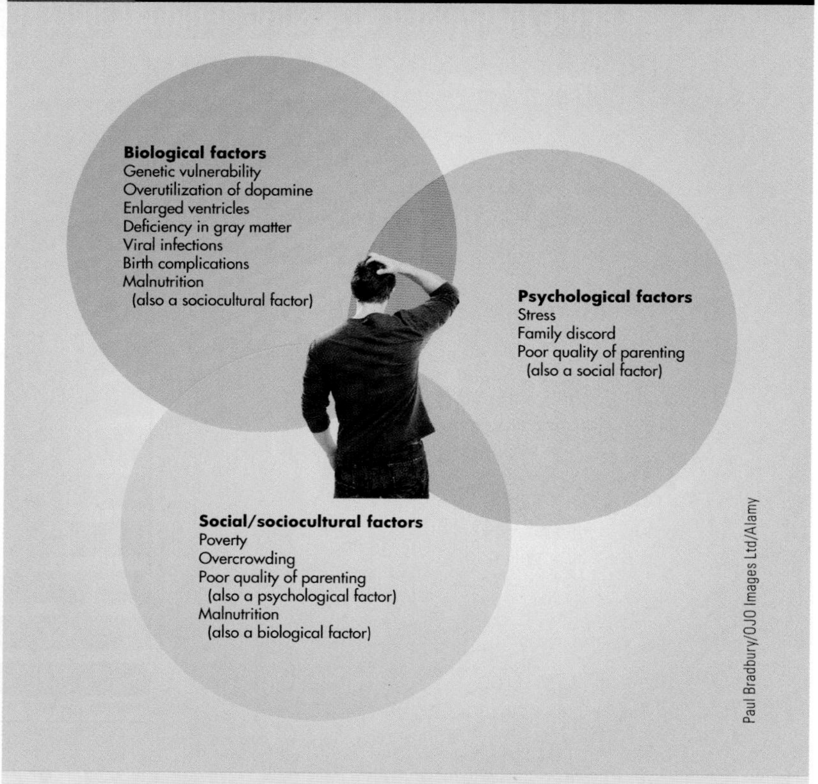

According to the biopsychosocial model of schizophrenia, people with a genetic vulnerability to the disorder experience increased risk for schizophrenia when they encounter problems such as viral infections, birth complications, stress, and poor parenting. People without the genetic vulnerability would not develop schizophrenia despite such problems.

12-9 PERSONALITY DISORDERS

Personality disorders, like personality traits, are characterized by enduring patterns of behavior. Personality disorders, however, are inflexible and maladaptive. They impair personal or social functioning and are a source of distress to the individual or to other people. There are a number of personality disorders. They include the *paranoid, schizoid, schizotypal, antisocial, borderline,* and *avoidant personality disorders*.

12-9a PARANOID PERSONALITY DISORDER

The defining trait of the **paranoid personality disorder** is a tendency to interpret other people's behavior as threatening or demeaning. They are mistrustful of others, and their relationships suffer for it. They may be suspicious of coworkers and supervisors, but they can generally hold a job.

12-9b SCHIZOID PERSONALITY DISORDER

Schizoid personality disorder is characterized by indifference to relationships and flat emotional response. People with this disorder are "loners." They do not develop warm, tender feelings for others. They have few friends and rarely maintain long-term relationships. Some people with schizoid personality disorder do very well on the job provided that continuous social interaction is not required. They do not have hallucinations or delusions.

12-9c SCHIZOTYPAL PERSONALITY DISORDER

Schizotypal personality disorder is characterized by peculiarities of thought, perception, or behavior, such as excessive fantasy and suspiciousness, feelings of being unreal, or the odd use of words. There are no complex delusions, no hallucinations, and no unusual motor activities, so this disorder is schizo*typal,* not schizophrenic.

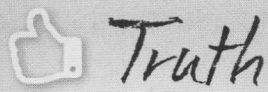 Truth

| T | F | Some people can kill or maim others without any feelings of guilt. |

It is true that some people can kill or maim others with no feelings of guilt at all. When they persistently violate the rights of others and are in repeated conflict with the law, they may be diagnosed with antisocial personality disorder.

12-9d ANTISOCIAL PERSONALITY DISORDER

People with **antisocial personality disorder** often show a superficial charm and are at least average in intelligence. They do not form strong bonds with other people. Though they are often heavily punished by their parents and rejected by peers, they continue in their impulsive, careless styles of life. Women are more likely than men to have anxiety and depressive disorders. However, antisocial personality disorder is more common among men than women (Eaton et al., 2012).

12-9e BORDERLINE PERSONALITY DISORDER

People with **borderline personality disorder** show instability in their relationships, self-image, and mood and a lack of control over impulses (Stanley & Siever, 2010). They tend to be uncertain of their values, goals, loyalties, careers, choices of friends, and sometimes even their sexual orientations (Roepke et al., 2010). Instability in self-image or identity may leave them with feelings of emptiness and boredom. Many cannot tolerate being alone and make desperate attempts to avoid feelings of abandonment. They may be clinging and demanding in social relationships, but clinging often pushes away the people on whom they depend. They alternate between extremes of adulation in their relationships (when their needs are met) and loathing (when they feel scorned). They tend to view other people as all good or all bad, shifting abruptly from one extreme to the other. As a result, they may flit from partner to partner in brief and stormy relationships. People they had idealized are treated with contempt when they feel the other person has failed them.

Instability of moods is a central characteristic of borderline personality disorder. Moods run the gamut from anger and irritability to depression and anxiety, with each lasting from a few hours to a few days. People with the disorder have difficulty controlling anger and are prone to fights or smashing things. They often act on impulse, like eloping with someone they have just met. This impulsive and unpredictable behavior is often self-destructive and linked to a risk of suicidal attempts and gestures. It may involve spending sprees, gambling, drug abuse, engaging in unsafe sexual activity, reckless driving, binge eating, or shoplifting. People with the disorder may also engage in self-mutilation, such as scratching their wrists or burning their arms with cigarettes (Zanarini et al., 2010). Self-mutilation is sometimes a means of manipulating others, particularly in times of stress. Frequent self-mutilation is also associated with suicide attempts.

schizoid personality disorder a personality disorder characterized by social withdrawal

schizotypal personality disorder a personality disorder characterized by oddities of thought and behavior but not involving bizarre psychotic behaviors

antisocial personality disorder the diagnosis given a person who is in frequent conflict with society, yet who is undeterred by punishment and experiences little or no guilt and anxiety

borderline personality disorder a personality disorder characterized by instability in relationships, self-image, mood, and lack of impulse control

12-9f AVOIDANT PERSONALITY DISORDER

People with **avoidant personality disorder** are generally unwilling to enter a relationship without some assurance of acceptance because they fear rejection and criticism. As a result, they may have few close relationships outside their immediate families. Unlike people with schizoid personality disorder, however, they have some interest in, and feelings of warmth toward, other people.

12-9g ORIGINS OF PERSONALITY DISORDERS

Numerous biological, psychological, and sociocultural factors have been implicated in the personality disorders. Cognitive psychologists find that antisocial adolescents tend to interpret other people's behavior as threatening, even when it is not (Dodge, 2006; Ellis et al., 2009). Aggressive individuals often find it difficult to solve social problems in useful ways (Fontaine et al., 2010).

BIOLOGICAL FACTORS Genetic factors are apparently involved in some personality disorders (De Fruyt & De Clercq, 2014). Personality traits are to some degree heritable, and many personality disorders seem to be extreme variations of normal personality traits. An analysis of 51 twin and adoption studies estimated that genetic factors were the greatest influences on antisocial behavior (Rhee & Waldman, 2002). Referring to the five-factor model of personality, people with schizoid personalities tend to be highly introverted (Widiger & Simonsen, 2005). People with avoidant personalities tend to be both introverted and emotionally unstable (neurotic) (Widiger & Simonsen, 2005).

Perhaps the genetics of antisocial personality involve the prefrontal cortex of the brain, which is connected with emotional responses. There is some evidence that people with antisocial personality, as a group, have less gray matter (associative neurons) in the prefrontal cortex than other people do (Glenn et al., 2013). Adrian Raine (2008) suggests that specific genes lead to this impairment and also predispose people to antisocial behavior. In addition, rapid heartbeat is a symptom of anxiety, and it may be that a lower heart rate than average is associated with less fear of consequences among children and adolescents who are contemplating antisocial behavior (Raine et al., 2014).

PSYCHOLOGICAL FACTORS Learning theorists suggest that childhood experiences can contribute to maladaptive ways of relating to others in adulthood—that is, can lead to personality disorders. Cognitive psychologists find that antisocial adolescents encode social information in ways that bolster their misdeeds. For example, they tend to interpret other people's behavior as threatening, even when it is not (Dodge, 2006). Aggressive individuals often find it difficult to solve social problems in useful ways (McMurran et al., 2002). Cognitive therapists have encouraged some antisocial male children and adolescents to view social provocations as problems to be solved rather than as threats to their "manhood," with some favorable initial results (Lochman et al., 2011).

SOCIOCULTURAL FACTORS The label of borderline personality has been applied to people as diverse as Marilyn Monroe and Lawrence of Arabia. Some theorists believe we live in fragmented and alienating times that tend to create problems in forming a stable identity and stable relationships. "Living on the edge," or border, can be seen as a metaphor for an unstable society.

Although the causes of many psychological disorders remain in dispute, various methods of therapy have been devised to deal with them. Those methods are the focus of Chapter 13.

avoidant personality disorder a personality disorder in which the person is unwilling to enter into relationships without assurance of acceptance because of fears of rejection and criticism

READY TO STUDY? IN THE BOOK, YOU CAN:

☐ Check your understanding of what you've read with the quizzes below.

☐ Rip out the chapter review card at the back of the book to have a summary of the chapter and the key terms handy.

ONLINE AT CENGAGEBRAIN.COM YOU CAN:

☐ Hear an interview with Barbara, who suffers from major depressive in a short video.

☐ Prepare for tests with quizzes.

☐ Review the key terms with Flash Cards.

☐ Play games to master concepts.

FILL-INS

Answers can be found in the back of the book, starting on page 393.

1. Behavior is labeled abnormal when it is unusual, is socially unacceptable, involves faulty _____ of reality (as with hallucinations), is dangerous, self-defeating, or distressing.

2. A(n) _____ is an irrational, excessive fear.

3. In _____ –_____ disorder, people are troubled by intrusive thoughts or impulses to repeat some activity.

4. People with dissociative _____ forget their own identities but retain general knowledge and skills.

5. In dissociative _____ disorder, the person behaves as if distinct personalities occupy the body.

6. In _____ _____ disorder, people complain of physical problems or persist in believing they have a serious disease, even though no medical problem can be found.

7. Manic people may have grand delusional schemes and show rapid _____ of ideas.

8. Depressed people are more likely than other people to make (internal or external) attributions for failures.

9. The psychotic disorder known as _____ is characterized by impaired motor activity and waxy flexibility.

10. _____ disorders are inflexible, maladaptive behavior patterns that impair personal or social functioning and are a source of distress to the individual or to others.

MULTIPLE CHOICE

1. The news just reported that a hurricane is headed toward your home. You feel anxious and can't decide what to do first to prepare. This response is indicative of
   a. unusual behavior.
   b. normal behavior.
   c. abnormal behavior.
   d. faulty behavior.

2. A man cancels an important business trip to the mountains because he cannot control his fear of heights. He goes to a psychologist to discuss the problem. What diagnosis is the psychologist likely to consider?
   a. Agoraphobia
   b. Acrophobia
   c. Conversion disorder
   d. Avoidant personality disorder

3. A woman has difficulty concentrating on her job at work because of her preoccupation with the possibility that she has left the stove on or the iron plugged in at home. She imagines that her house will catch fire because of her mistake. She confides in her doctor. What diagnosis is the doctor most likely to use to describe her behavior?
   a. Obsessive–compulsive disorder
   b. Panic disorder
   c. Specific phobia
   d. Schizophrenia

4. Dissociative disorders involve _____ that cannot be attributed to organic problems.
   a. a loss of memory
   b. lack of feelings of guilt and shame
   c. hallucinations
   d. explosive behavior

5. For as long as Shelley can remember, grandmother has always been sick. She goes from doctor to doctor even though they keep telling her she is in excellent health. Her grandmother insists the doctors don't know what they are talking about. She is sure she has some terrible disease. Shelley checks her psychology textbook and finds that her grandmother's behavior is closest to fitting the category of
   a. dissociative amnesia.
   b. panic disorder.
   c. catatonia.
   d. illness anxiety disorder.

6. Imagery in the absence of external stimulation is the definition of _____, which are often observed in people with schizophrenia.
   a. rapid flight of ideas
   b. delusions
   c. hallucinations
   d. stress disorders

7. The difference between the emotion of sadness and an episode of major depression is that the symptoms of major depression are
   a. drastically different.
   b. more intense.
   c. only observed in females.
   d. related to stressful situations.

8. According to the text, which neurotransmitter is associated with depression?
   a. Serotonin
   b. Dopamine
   c. Glutamate
   d. GABA

9. Your patient confides that the FBI and the CIA are "out to get me." He has stopped going to work. He keeps his blinds drawn and his doors and windows locked. The truth is that the FBI and CIA are not pursuing him or checking on him at all. Your patient can most likely be diagnosed with
   a. schizoid personality.
   b. dissociative identity disorder.
   c. paranoid personality.
   d. delusional disorder.

10. All of the following are symptoms of borderline personality disorder EXCEPT
    a. being a loner.
    b. unstable moods.
    c. fear of abandonment.
    d. self-mutilation.

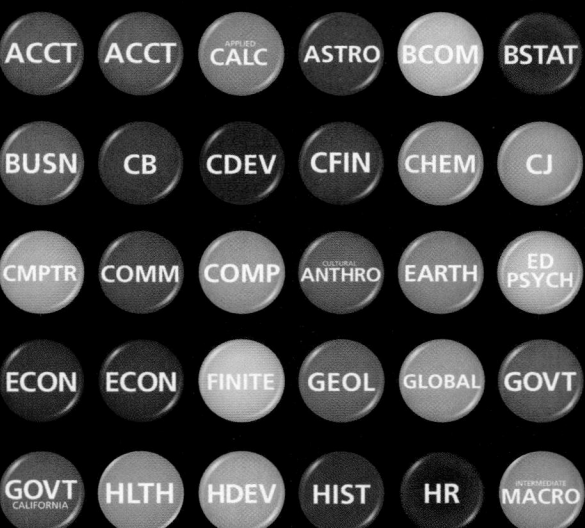

ONE APPROACH.
70 UNIQUE SOLUTIONS.

13 | Methods of Therapy

es/Laurence Mouton/PhotoAlto/Alamy

LEARNING OUTCOMES

After studying this chapter, you will be able to …

13-1 Define psychotherapy and describe the history of treatment of psychological disorders

13-2 Describe traditional psychoanalysis and short-term psychodynamic therapies

13-3 Define humanistic therapy and contrast its two main approaches

13-4 Define behavior therapy and identify various behavioral approaches to therapy

13-5 Define cognitive therapy and describe Beck's approach and REBT

13-6 Identify various types of group therapy and discuss their advantages and disadvantages

13-7 Explain whether psychotherapy works and who benefits from it

13-8 Describe methods of biological therapy—their benefits and side effects

After you finish this chapter, go to **PAGE 349** for **STUDY TOOLS**

Joanne Cartwright (dubbed "Miss Muffet" by her therapist) had a spider phobia. "I washed my truck every night before I went to work in case there were webs," she said (Robbins, 2000). "I put all my clothes in plastic bags and taped duct tape around my doors so spiders couldn't get in. I thought I was going to have a mental breakdown. I wasn't living." She checked every crack in the sidewalk for spiders—if she could push herself to go outside at all. Finally, her crippling phobia made it all but impossible for her to leave the house. After years of misery, she sought help.

Fortunately for "Miss Muffet," she wound up in the University of Washington's Human Interface Technology Laboratory, where she worked with psychologist Hunter Hoffman. Hoffman (2004) employed an elaborate virtual environment called *SpiderWorld* to help people with spider phobias overcome their aversion by gradually approaching virtual spiders and reaching out to touch them (see Figure 13.1). A toy spider and a device that tracks the patient's hand movements provide tactile sensations akin to touching a real spider.

Twelve virtual therapy desensitization sessions changed Cartwright's life. "I'm amazed," she notes, "because I am doing all this stuff I could never do," such as camping and hiking.

Joanne Cartwright received virtual therapy to learn to cope with her phobia of spiders. If she had chosen a different kind of therapist, she might have been:

▸ Lying on a couch, talking about anything that popped into awareness, trying to unearth the possible symbolic meaning of spiders.

▸ Sitting face to face with a warm, gentle therapist who expressed faith in her ability to cope with her fears.

▸ Listening to a frank, straightforward therapist assert that she was catastrophizing the awfulness of spiders and compounding her problem by ruminating about it.

▸ Taking medication.

▸ Participating in some combination of these approaches.

These methods, although different, all represent methods of therapy. In this chapter, we explore methods of psychotherapy and biological therapy.

> "To help people deal with their problems, you must get them **exposed** to what they fear most."

13-1 WHAT IS PSYCHOTHERAPY?

There are many kinds of psychotherapy, but they have certain common characteristics. **Psychotherapy** is a systematic interaction between a therapist and a client that applies psychological principles to affect the client's thoughts, feelings, or behavior in an effort to help the client overcome psychological disorders, adjust to problems in living, or develop as an individual.

Quite a mouthful? True. But note the essentials:

▸ *Systematic interaction.* Psychotherapy is a systematic interaction between a client and a therapist. The therapist's theoretical point of view interacts with the client's to determine how the therapist and client relate to each other.

▸ *Psychological principles.* Psychotherapy is based on psychological theory and research in areas such as personality, learning, motivation, and emotion.

"Miss Muffet" is the name playfully given by Hoffman to a woman with a phobia for spiders. She is wearing virtual-reality headgear and sees the scene displayed on the monitor, which shows a large and hairy—but virtual—tarantula.

▶ *Thoughts, feelings, and behavior.* Psychotherapy influences clients' thoughts, feelings, and behavior. It can be aimed at any or all of these aspects of human psychology.

▶ *Psychological disorders, adjustment problems, and personal growth.*

Psychotherapy is often used to treat people who have psychological disorders. Other people seek help in adjusting to problems such as shyness, weight problems, or loss of a life partner. Still other clients want to learn more about themselves and to reach their full potential as individuals, parents, or creative artists.

13-1a THE HISTORY OF THERAPIES

Historically speaking, "treatments" of psychological disorders often reflected the assumption that people who behaved in strange ways were possessed by demons. Because of this belief, treatment tended to involve cruel practices such as exorcism and execution. Some people who could not meet the demands of everyday life were tossed into prisons. Others begged in the streets, stole food, or became prostitutes. A few found their way to monasteries or other retreats that offered a kind word and some support. Generally speaking, they died early.

ASYLUMS Asylums originated in European monasteries. They were the first institutions intended primarily for housing people with psychological disorders. But their function was warehousing, not treatment. Their inmate populations mushroomed until the stresses created by noise, overcrowding, and disease aggravated the problems the asylums were meant to ease. Inmates were frequently chained and beaten.

The word *bedlam* derives from St. Mary's of Bethlehem, the London asylum that opened its gates in 1547. Within its walls, unfortunate people with psychological disorders were chained, whipped, and allowed to lie in their own waste.

psychotherapy a systematic interaction between a therapist and a client that brings psychological principles to bear on influencing the client's thoughts, feelings, or behavior to help the client overcome psychological disorders, adjust to problems in living, or develop as an individual

asylum an outmoded institution for the care of the mentally ill

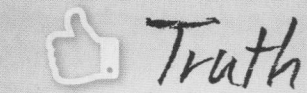

Truth

| T | **F** | Residents of London used to visit the local insane asylum for a fun night out on the town. |

It is true that the ladies and gentlemen of the British upper class might stroll by on a lazy afternoon to be amused by asylum inmates' antics. The price of admission was one penny.

The Unchaining of the Patients at La Salpêtrière Philippe Pinel sparked the humanitarian reform movement by unchaining the patients at this asylum in Paris.

Humanitarian reform movements began in the 18th century. In Paris, the physician Philippe Pinel unchained the patients at La Salpêtrière. Rather than run amok, as had been feared, most patients profited from kindness and freedom. Many eventually reentered society. Later movements to reform institutions were led by William Tuke in England and Dorothea Dix in America.

MENTAL HOSPITALS In the United States, mental hospitals gradually replaced asylums. In the mid-1950s more than a million people resided in state, county, Veterans Administration, or private facilities. The mental hospital's function is treatment, not warehousing. Still, because of high patient populations and understaffing, many patients received little attention. Even today, with somewhat improved conditions, one psychiatrist may be responsible for the welfare of several hundred residents over the weekend, when other staff are absent.

THE COMMUNITY MENTAL HEALTH MOVEMENT Since the 1960s, efforts have been made to allow people with serious psychological disorders to remain in their communities. Community mental health centers attempt to maintain new patients as outpatients and to serve patients who have been released from mental hospitals. Today, most people with chronic psychological disorders live in the community, not in the hospital. Social critics note that many people who had resided in hospitals for decades were suddenly discharged to "home" communities that seemed foreign and forbidding to them. Many do not receive adequate follow-up care. Many join the ranks of the homeless (Drake & Latimer, 2012).

13-2 PSYCHODYNAMIC THERAPIES

Psychodynamic therapies are based on the thinking of Sigmund Freud, the founder of psychodynamic theory. These therapies assume that psychological problems reflect early childhood experiences and internal conflicts. According to Freud, these conflicts involve the shifting

> **psychodynamic therapy** a type of psychotherapy that is based on Freud's thinking and assumes that psychological problems reflect early childhood experiences and internal conflicts

of psychic energy among the id, ego, and super-ego. These shifts of psychic energy determine our behavior. When primitive urges threaten to break through from the id or when the superego floods us with excessive guilt, defenses are established and distress is created. Freud's therapy method—psychoanalysis—aims to bulwark the ego against the torrents of energy loosed by the id and the superego. With impulses and feelings of guilt and shame placed under greater control, clients are freer to develop adaptive behavior.

13-2a TRADITIONAL PSYCHOANALYSIS

Imagine your therapist asking you to lie on a couch in a slightly darkened room. She or he would sit behind you and encourage you to talk about anything that comes to mind, no matter how trivial, no matter how personal. To avoid interfering with your self-exploration, she or he might say little or nothing for session after session. That would be par for the course. A traditional psychoanalysis can extend for months, even years.

Psychoanalysis is the clinical method devised by Freud. It aims to provide insight into the conflicts that are presumed to lie at the roots of a person's problems. *Insight* means many things, including knowledge of the experiences that lead to conflicts and maladaptive behavior, recognition of unconscious feelings and conflicts, and conscious evaluation of one's thoughts, feelings, and behavior.

Psychoanalysis also aims to help the client express feelings and urges that have been repressed. By so doing, Freud believed that the client spilled forth the psychic energy that had been repressed by conflicts and guilt. He called this "spilling forth" **catharsis**. Catharsis would provide relief by alleviating some of the forces assaulting the ego. Freud also sought to replace impulsive and defensive behavior with coping behavior. In this way, for example, a man with a phobia for knives might discover that he had been repressing the urge to harm someone who had taken advantage of him. He might also find ways to confront the person verbally.

A View of Freud's Consulting Room Freud would sit in a chair by the head of the couch while a client free-associated. The basic rule for free association is that no thought is censored. Freud did not believe that free association was really "free"; he assumed that significant feelings would rise to the surface and demand expression.

Early in his career as a therapist, Freud found that hypnosis allowed his clients to focus on repressed conflicts and talk about them. He also found, however, that some clients denied the accuracy of this material once they were out of the trance. Others found the memories to be brought out into the open prematurely and painfully. Freud therefore turned to **free association**, a more gradual method of breaking through the walls of defense that block a client's insight into unconscious processes. In free association, the client is made comfortable—for example, by lying on a couch—and asked to talk about any topic that comes to mind. No thought is to be censored—that is the basic rule. Psychoanalysts ask their clients to wander "freely" from topic to topic, but they do not believe that the process occurring *within* the client is fully free. Repressed impulses clamor for release.

The ego persists in trying to repress unacceptable impulses and threatening conflicts. As a result, clients might show **resistance** to recalling and discussing threatening ideas. The therapist observes the dynamic struggle between the compulsion to talk about disturbing ideas and resistance. Through discreet comments and questions, the analyst hopes to encourage the client to discuss his or her problems. Talking helps the client gain insight into his or her true wishes and explore ways of fulfilling them.

TRANSFERENCE Freud believed that clients not only responded to him as an individual but also in ways that

---

psychoanalysis Freud's method of psychotherapy

catharsis in psychoanalysis, the expression of repressed feelings and impulses to allow the release of the psychic energy associated with them

free association in psychoanalysis, the uncensored uttering of all thoughts that come to mind

resistance the tendency to block the free expression of impulses and primitive ideas—a reflection of the defense mechanism of repression

reflected their attitudes and feelings toward other people in their lives. He labeled this process **transference**. For example, a young woman client might respond to him as a father figure and displace her feelings toward her father onto Freud, perhaps seeking affection and wisdom. Analyzing and working through transference has been considered a key aspect of psychoanalysis.

DREAM ANALYSIS Freud often asked clients to jot down their dreams upon waking so they could discuss them in therapy. Freud considered dreams the "royal road to the unconscious." He believed that the content of dreams is determined by unconscious processes as well as by the events of the day. Unconscious impulses were expressed in dreams as **wish fulfillment**.

CARL ROGERS

Rogers believed that our psychological well-being is connected with our freedom to develop our unique frames of reference and potentials. Do you think you can separate your "real self" from your sociocultural experiences and religious training?

Roger Ressmeyer/Corbis

13-2b MODERN PSYCHODYNAMIC APPROACHES

Although some psychoanalysts still adhere to Freud's techniques, modern psychodynamic therapy is briefer and less intense and makes treatment available to clients who do not have the time or money for long-term therapy. Some modern psychodynamic therapies continue to focus on revealing unconscious material and breaking through psychological defenses. Nevertheless, they differ from traditional psychoanalysis in that the client and therapist usually sit face to face (i.e., the client does not lie on a couch) (Prochaska & Norcross, 2014). Modern therapists are usually directive as well. They suggest helpful behavior instead of focusing on insight alone. Finally, there is more focus on the ego as the "executive" of personality and less emphasis on the id. For this reason, many modern psychodynamic therapists are called **ego analysts**.

> "THE INTERPRETATION OF DREAMS IS THE ROYAL ROAD TO A KNOWLEDGE OF THE UNCONSCIOUS ACTIVITIES OF THE MIND."
>
> SIGMUND FREUD

13-3 HUMANISTIC THERAPIES

Psychoanalytic therapies focus on internal conflicts and unconscious processes. **Humanistic therapies** focus on the quality of the client's subjective, conscious experience. Traditional psychoanalysis focuses on early childhood experiences. Humanistic therapies are more likely to focus on what clients are experiencing here and now.

13-3a CLIENT-CENTERED THERAPY

Carl Rogers (1902–1987) believed that we are free to make choices and control our destinies, despite the burdens of the past. He also believed that we have natural tendencies toward health, growth, and fulfillment. Psychological problems arise from roadblocks placed in the path of self-actualization—that is, what Rogers believed was an inborn tendency to strive to realize one's potential. If, when we are young, other people approve of us only when we are doing what they want us to do, we may learn to disown the parts of ourselves to which they object. We may learn to be seen but not heard—not even by ourselves. As a result, we may experience stress and discomfort and the feeling that we—or the world—are not real.

Client-centered therapy aims to provide insight into the parts of us that we have disowned so that we can feel whole. It creates a warm, therapeutic atmosphere that encourages self-exploration and self-expression. The

transference responding to one person (such as a psychoanalyst) in a way similar to how one responded to another person (such as a parent) in childhood

wish fulfillment in dreams, the acting out of ideas and impulses that are repressed when one is conscious

ego analyst a psychodynamically oriented therapist who focuses on the conscious, coping behavior of the ego instead of the hypothesized, unconscious functioning of the id

humanistic therapy a form of psychotherapy that focuses on the client's subjective, conscious experience in the "here and now"

client-centered therapy Carl Rogers's method of psychotherapy, which emphasizes the creation of a warm, therapeutic atmosphere that frees clients to engage in self-exploration and self-expression

therapist's acceptance of the client is believed to foster self-acceptance and self-esteem. Self-acceptance frees the client to make choices that develop his or her unique potential.

Client-centered therapy is nondirective. An effective client-centered therapist has several qualities:

1. *Unconditional positive regard:* respect for clients as human beings with unique values and goals.

2. *Empathy:* recognition of the client's experiences and feelings. Therapists view the world through the client's *frame of reference* by setting aside their own values and listening closely.

3. *Genuineness:* Openness and honesty in responding to the client. Client-centered therapists must be able to tolerate differentness because they believe that every client is different in important ways.

The following excerpt from a therapy session shows how Carl Rogers uses empathetic understanding and paraphrases a client's (Jill's) feelings. His goal is to help her recognize feelings that she has partially disowned:

Jill: I'm having a lot of problems dealing with my daughter. She's twenty years old; she's in college; I'm having a lot of trouble letting her go…. And I have a lot of guilt feelings about her; I have a real need to hang on to her.

Wavebreak Media ltd/Alamy

By showing the qualities of unconditional positive regard, empathic understanding, and genuineness, client-centered therapists create an atmosphere in which clients can explore their feelings.

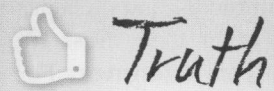
C. R.: A need to hang on so you can kind of make up for the things you feel guilty about. Is that part of it?

Jill: There's a lot of that…. Also, she's been a real friend to me, and filled my life…. And it's very hard…. a lot of empty places now that she's not with me.

C. R.: The old vacuum, sort of, when she's not there.

Jill: Yes. Yes. I also would like to be the kind of mother that could be strong and say, you know, "Go and have a good life," and this is really hard for me, to do that.

C. R.: It's very hard to give up something that's been so precious in your life, but also something that I guess has caused you pain when you mentioned guilt.

Jill: Yeah. And I'm aware that I have some anger toward her that I don't always get what I want. I have needs that are not met. And, uh, I don't feel I have a right to those needs. You know … she's a daughter; she's not my mother. Though sometimes I feel as if I'd like her to mother me … it's very difficult for me to ask for that and have a right to it.

C. R.: So, it may be unreasonable, but still, when she doesn't meet your needs, it makes you mad.

Jill: Yeah, I get very angry, very angry with her.

C. R.: (*Pauses*) You're also feeling a little tension at this point, I guess.

Jill: Yeah. Yeah. A lot of conflict…. (C. R.: M-hm.) A lot of pain.

C. R.: A lot of pain. Can you say anything more about what that's about? (Farber et al., 1996, pp. 74 –75).

Client-centered therapy is practiced widely in college and university counseling centers, not just to help students experiencing, say, anxieties or depression, but also to help them make decisions. Many college students have not yet made career choices, or wonder whether they should become involved with particular people or in sexual activity. Client-centered therapists do not tell clients what to do. Instead, they help clients arrive at their own decisions.

13-3b GESTALT THERAPY

Gestalt therapy was originated by Fritz Perls (1893–1970). Like client-centered therapy, Gestalt therapy assumes that people disown parts of themselves that might meet with social disapproval or rejection. People also don social masks, pretending to be things that they are not. Therapy aims to help individuals integrate conflicting parts of their personality. Perls used the term *Gestalt* to signify his interest in giving the conflicting parts of the personality an integrated form or shape. (The German word *Gestalt* means "unified whole.") Perls adopted the term because he wanted to help clients integrate conflicting parts of their personalities.

Although Perls's ideas about conflicting personality elements owe much to psychodynamic theory, his form of therapy, unlike psychoanalysis, focuses on the here and now. Exercises heighten clients' awareness of their current feelings and behavior. Perls (along with Rogers) also believed that people are free to make choices and to direct their personal growth. But the charismatic and forceful Perls was unlike the gentle and accepting Rogers in temperament (Prochaska & Norcross, 2014). Thus, unlike client-centered therapy, Gestalt therapy is directive. The therapist leads the client through planned experiences to heighten their awareness of inner conflict and take responsibility for their behavior.

> "I DO MY THING AND YOU DO YOURS. I AM NOT IN THIS WORLD TO LIVE UP TO YOUR EXPECTATIONS, AND YOU ARE NOT IN THIS WORLD TO MEET UP WITH MINE. YOU ARE YOU AND I AM I, AND IF BY CHANCE WE FIND EACH OTHER, THEN IT IS BEAUTIFUL. IF NOT, IT CAN'T BE HELPED."
>
> FRITZ PERLS

13-4 BEHAVIOR THERAPY

Psychodynamic and humanistic forms of therapy tend to focus on what people think and feel. Behavior therapists tend to focus on what people *do*. **Behavior therapy**—also called *behavior modification*—applies principles of learning to directly promote desired behavioral changes. Behavior therapists rely heavily on principles of conditioning and observational learning. They help clients discontinue self-defeating behavior patterns such as overeating, smoking, and phobic avoidance of harmless stimuli. They also aid clients in the acquisition of adaptive behavior patterns such as the social skills required to start social relationships or say no to insistent salespeople.

T F   Some psychotherapists tell their clients exactly what to do.

It is true that some therapists tell their clients exactly what to do. Gestalt therapists are among them, and behavior therapists may use specific procedures and homework assignments.

Behavior therapists may help clients gain "insight" into maladaptive behaviors (such as feelings of anxiety) by helping the person become aware of the circumstances in which the behaviors occur. They do not help unearth the childhood origins of problems and the symbolic meanings of maladaptive behaviors as psychoanalysts do. Behavior therapists, like other therapists, may also build warm, therapeutic relationships with clients, but they see the effectiveness of behavior therapy as deriving from specific, learning-based procedures (Lambert, 2013). They insist that their methods be established by experimentation and that results be assessed in terms of measurable behavior. In this section, we consider some frequently used behavior-therapy techniques.

Gestalt therapy Fritz Perls's form of psychotherapy, which attempts to integrate conflicting parts of the personality through directive methods designed to help clients perceive their whole selves

behavior therapy systematic application of the principles of learning to the direct modification of a client's problem behaviors

13-4a FEAR-REDUCTION METHODS

Many people seek therapy because of fears and phobias that interfere with their functioning. This is one of the areas in which behavior therapy has made great inroads. Behavior-therapy methods for reducing fears include *flooding* (see Chapter 5, page 118), *systematic desensitization*, *virtual therapy*, and *modeling*.

SYSTEMATIC DESENSITIZATION

Adam has a phobia for receiving injections. His behavior therapist treats him as he reclines in a comfortable padded chair. In a state of deep muscle relaxation, Adam observes slides projected on a screen. A slide of a nurse holding a needle has just been shown three times, 30 seconds at a time. Each time Adam has shown no anxiety. So now a slightly more discomforting slide is shown: one of the nurse aiming the needle toward someone's bare arm. After 15 seconds, our armchair adventurer notices twinges of discomfort and raises a finger as a signal (speaking might disturb his relaxation). The projector operator turns off the light, and Adam spends 2 minutes imagining his "safe scene"—lying on a beach beneath the tropical sun. Then the slide is shown again. This time Adam views it for 30 seconds before feeling anxiety.

THE AUTHOR'S FILES

Adam is undergoing **systematic desensitization**, a method for reducing phobic responses originated by psychiatrist Joseph Wolpe (1915–1997). Systematic desensitization is a gradual process in which the client learns to handle increasingly disturbing stimuli while anxiety to each one is being counterconditioned. About 10 to 20 stimuli such as slides are arranged in a sequence, or *hierarchy*, according to their capacity to trigger anxiety. In imagination or by being shown photos, the client travels gradually up through this hierarchy, counterconditioning anxiety with relaxation step by step as he or she approaches the target. In Adam's case, the target was the ability to receive an injection without undue anxiety.

VIRTUAL THERAPY Virtual therapy may use more elaborate equipment than slides, but the principle

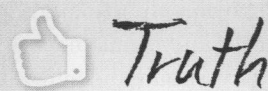
is desensitization. New York Fire Chief Stephen King was in the north tower at the World Trade Center on September 11, 2001, the first of the towers to be struck by an airplane. The experience led him to retire from the department, avoid bridges and tunnels, and stay out of Manhattan (King, 2005). "Where I was and what I saw that day—the many people that jumped, the magnitude of it—was just overwhelming."

But virtual therapy has helped King face the past—and his future. Using the technology we find in video games, programs mimic traumatic settings and events—public speaking in an auditorium, flying in an airplane, spiders, or, in King's case, images of the World Trade Center (see Figure 13.2). "The idea behind the treatment," explains Dr. JoAnn Difede (2005), "is to systematically expose the patient to aspects of their experience in a graded fashion so they can confront their fear of the trauma."

MODELING Modeling relies on observational learning. In this method, clients observe and then imitate people

FIG.13.2 A "VIRTUAL" STIMULUS USED IN VIRTUAL THERAPY

Clients in virtual therapy are exposed to virtual (not actual) stimuli that represent the sources of their anxiety and stress helping them to gradually confront and overcome their fears. In this case, a client is exposed to a stimulus that represents his experiences at the World Trade Center on 9/11, to help him overcome posttraumatic stress disorder (PTSD).

Image and Copyright by Hunter Hoffman, U.W. Virtual World Programmed by Howard Abrams.

> **systematic desensitization**
> Wolpe's method for reducing fears by associating a hierarchy of images of fear-evoking stimuli with deep muscle relaxation

who approach and cope with the objects or situations that the clients fear. Albert Bandura and his colleagues (1969) found that modeling worked as well as systematic desensitization—and more rapidly—in reducing fear of snakes. Clients observed models handling snakes. In the same session, they were able to touch the snakes, pick them up, and let them crawl on their bodies. Modeling also increases self-efficacy expectations in coping with feared stimuli.

13-4b AVERSIVE CONDITIONING

Many people also seek behavior therapy because they want to break bad habits, such as smoking, excessive drinking, nail-biting, and the like. One behavior-therapy approach

© encikepstudio/Shutterstock.com

How To Use Aversive Conditioning for a Nail-Biting Habit. Drop a coin into your "nail-biting" jar every time you slip and take a nibble. When the jar is full, count it up, make out a check in that amount to your "Most Hated Cause" and mail it.

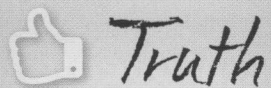

Truth

| T | F | Smoking cigarettes can be an effective method for helping people to quit smoking cigarettes. |

It is true that smoking can be used as a method to help people discontinue smoking. In the method of rapid smoking, behavior therapists use excessive smoke to make smoking aversive.

to helping people do so is **aversive conditioning**. Aversive conditioning is a controversial procedure that pairs painful or aversive stimuli with unwanted impulses in order to make the impulses less appealing. For example, to help people control alcohol intake, tastes of different alcoholic beverages can be paired with drug-induced nausea and vomiting or with electric shock.

Aversive conditioning has been used with problems as diverse as cigarette smoking and sexual abuse. *Rapid smoking* is an aversive conditioning method designed to help smokers quit. In this method, the would-be quitter inhales every 6 seconds. In another method, the hose of a hair dryer is attached to a chamber containing several lit cigarettes. Smoke is blown into the aspiring quitter's face as he or she also smokes a cigarette. A third method uses branching pipes so that the smoker draws in smoke from several cigarettes at the same time. In these methods, overexposure renders once-desirable cigarette smoke aversive. The quitter becomes motivated to avoid, rather than seek, cigarettes. Interest in aversive conditioning for quitting smoking has waned, however, because of side effects such as elevated blood pressure as well as the availability of nicotine-replacement therapies.

13-4c OPERANT CONDITIONING PROCEDURES

We tend to repeat behavior that is reinforced. Behavior that is not reinforced tends to be extinguished. Behavior therapists have used these principles of operant conditioning with psychotic patients as well as with clients with milder problems.

modeling a behavior-therapy technique in which a client observes and imitates a person who approaches and copes with feared objects or situations

aversive conditioning a behavior therapy technique in which undesired responses are inhibited by pairing repugnant or offensive stimuli with them

Helping professionals are often inspired to develop therapy methods based on their personal experiences. As Francine Shapiro (1989) paints it, she had troubling thoughts on her mind when she entered a park. But as her eyes darted about, taking in the scene, she found her troubled thoughts disappearing. Thus, she developed a therapy method called *eye-movement desensitization and reprocessing (EMDR)* to join the arsenal of therapeutic weapons against stress disorders. With this method, the client is asked to imagine a traumatic scene while the therapist moves a finger rapidly back and forth before his or her eyes for about 20–30 seconds. The client follows the finger while keeping the troubling scene in mind. The client tells the therapist what he or she was thinking and how he or she felt during the procedure. The procedure is repeated until the client's anxiety is relieved. The duration of treatment is usually around three 90-minute sessions.

BananaStock/Jupiterimages

Evidence from a number of studies suggests that EMDR helps decrease the anxiety associated with traumatic events (Engelhard et al., 2010; Van der Kolk et al., 2007). One study, for example, compared the effectiveness of EMDR with two alternative treatments: exposure therapy (as in virtual therapy for spider phobia) and relaxation training (Taylor et al., 2003). Another study looked at the effectiveness of EMDR on numerous people following September 11 (Silver et al., 2005). These studies and others suggest that EMDR is effective, but it remains unclear how effective EMDR is and why it works (Lohr et al., 2012). Research also challenges the idea that eye movements are necessary (Karatzias et al., 2011; van den Hout et al., 2011). Perhaps clients receiving EMDR profit from their relationship with the therapist and from expectations of success. Moreover, the client is to some degree exposed to the trauma that haunts him or her under circumstances in which the client believes he or she will be able to manage the trauma.

Conclusion? Exposure helps people cope with trauma. Eye movements may not be needed.

The staff at one mental hospital was at a loss about how to encourage withdrawn schizophrenic patients to eat regularly. Psychologists observed that staff members were making the problem worse by coaxing patients into the dining room and even feeding them. Staff attention apparently reinforced the patients' lack of cooperation. Some rules were changed (Dickerson et al., 2005). Patients who did not arrive at the dining hall within 30 minutes after serving were locked out. Staff could not interact with patients at mealtime. With uncooperative behavior no longer reinforced, patients quickly changed their eating habits. Then patients were required to pay one penny to enter the dining hall. Pennies were earned by interacting with other patients and showing other socially appropriate behaviors. These target behaviors also became more frequent.

Health professionals are concerned about whether people who are, or have been, dependent on alcohol can exercise control over their drink-

ing. One study showed that reinforcements for remaining abstinent from alcohol can exert a powerful effect (Alessi & Petry, 2013; Petry et al., 2000). In the study, one group of alcohol-dependent veterans was given a standard treatment while another group received the treatment *plus* the chance to win prizes for remaining alcohol-free, as measured by a Breathalyzer test. By the end of the 8-week treatment period, 84% of the veterans who could win prizes remained in the program, as compared with 22% of the standard treatment group. The prizes had an average value of $200, far less than what alcohol-related absenteeism from work and other responsibilities can cost.

THE TOKEN ECONOMY Many psychiatric wards and hospitals use **token economies** in which patients need tokens such as poker chips to purchase TV viewing time, extra visits to the canteen, or a private room (Doll et al., 2013). The tokens are dispensed as reinforcers for productive activities such as making beds, brushing teeth, and socializing. Token economies have not eliminated all symptoms of schizophrenia, but they have increased patients'

token economy a controlled environment in which people are reinforced for desired behaviors with tokens (such as poker chips) that may be exchanged for privileges

activity and cooperation. Tokens have also been used to modify the behavior of children with conduct disorders.

SUCCESSIVE APPROXIMATIONS The operant conditioning method of **successive approximations** is often used to help clients build good habits. For example: You want to study 3 hours each evening but can concentrate for only half an hour. Rather than attempting to increase your study time all at once, you could do so gradually by adding, say, 5 minutes each evening. After every hour or so of studying, you could reinforce yourself with 5 minutes of people-watching in a busy section of the library.

SOCIAL SKILLS TRAINING In **social skills training**, behavior therapists decrease social anxiety and build social skills through operant-conditioning procedures that employ *self-monitoring* (keeping a record of one's own behavior to identify problems and record successes), coaching, modeling, role-playing, *behavior rehearsal* (practicing), and *feedback* (receiving information about the effectiveness of behavior). Social skills training has been used to help formerly hospitalized mental patients maintain jobs and apartments in the community. For example, a worker can rehearse asking a supervisor for assistance or asking a landlord to fix the plumbing in an apartment. Social skills training is effective in groups. Group members can role-play key people—such as parents, spouses, or potential dates—in the lives of other members.

BIOFEEDBACK TRAINING Through **biofeedback training (BFT)**, therapists help clients become more aware of, and gain control over, various bodily functions. Therapists attach clients to devices that measure bodily functions such as heart rate. "Bleeps" or other electronic signals are used to indicate (and thereby reinforce) changes ("operants") in the desired direction—for example, a slower heart rate. (Knowledge of results is a powerful reinforcer.) One device, the electromyograph (EMG), monitors muscle tension. It has been used to increase control over muscle tension in the forehead and elsewhere, thereby alleviating insomnia, anxiety, stress, and headaches (Nestoriuc et al., 2008; Tsai, 2012).

BFT also helps clients voluntarily regulate functions once thought to be beyond conscious control, such as heart rate and blood pressure. Hypertensive clients use a blood-pressure cuff and electronic signals to gain control over their blood pressure. The electroencephalograph (EEG) monitors brain waves and can be used to teach people how to produce alpha waves, which are associated with relaxation.

Some people have overcome insomnia by learning to produce the kinds of brain waves associated with sleep.

13-5 COGNITIVE THERAPIES

What thoughts do you have when things go wrong at school or on the job? Do you tell yourself that you're facing a problem that needs a solution? That you've successfully solved problems before and will be able to create a solution this time? Or do you think, "Oh no! This is awful! It's going to get worse, and I'm going to flunk (or get fired)!" If you go the "This is awful" route, you are probably heightening your discomfort and impairing your coping ability. Cognitive therapy focuses directly on your thoughts and encourages ideas that will help you solve problems rather than blow them out of proportion and magnify your discomfort.

Cognitive therapy focuses on changing the beliefs, attitudes, and automatic types of thinking that create and compound people's problems (Beck & Haigh, 2014). Cognitive therapists, like psychoanalytic and humanistic therapists, aim to foster self-insight, but they mainly aim to help make people more aware of their *current cognitions.* Cognitive therapists also aim to directly change maladaptive thoughts in an effort to reduce negative feelings and help clients solve problems.

Many behavior therapists incorporate cognitive procedures in their methods. For example, techniques such as systematic desensitization, covert sensitization, and covert reinforcement ask clients to focus on visual imagery. Behavioral methods for treating bulimia nervosa focus on clients' irrational attitudes toward their weight and body shape as well as foster good eating habits. Let's look at the approaches and methods of the cognitive therapists Aaron Beck and Albert Ellis.

> "THERE IS NOTHING EITHER GOOD OR BAD, BUT THINKING MAKES IT SO."
>
> SHAKESPEARE, *HAMLET*

successive approximations in operant conditioning, a series of behaviors that gradually become more similar to a target behavior

social skills training a behavior-therapy method for helping people in their interpersonal relations that utilizes self-monitoring, behavior rehearsal, and feedback

biofeedback training (BFT) the systematic feeding back to an organism of information about a bodily function so that the organism can gain control of that function

cognitive therapy a form of therapy that focuses on how clients' cognitions (e.g., expectations, attitudes, beliefs) lead to distress and may be modified to relieve distress and promote adaptive behavior

13-5a AARON BECK'S COGNITIVE THERAPY

Psychiatrist Aaron Beck began his professional life as a psychoanalyst. He became impatient, however, with analysis's lengthy methods and reluctance to offer specific advice. In his own life he had successfully defeated his fear of blood by assisting in surgical operations and argued himself out of an irrational fear of driving through tunnels. Similarly, his methods of cognitive therapy focus on arguing clients out of beliefs that are making them miserable and exposing them to situations they avoid because of irrational fear (Beck & Dozois, 2011). Beck encourages clients to become their own personal scientists and challenge feelings and beliefs that make no sense.

Beck also encourages clients to see the irrationality of their ways of thinking. For example, depressed people tend to minimize their accomplishments and to assume that the worst will happen. Minimizing accomplishments and expecting the worst are (usually) distortions of reality that lead to feelings of depression. Cognitive distortions can be fleeting and automatic, difficult to detect. Beck's methods help clients become aware of such distortions and challenge them.

Beck notes a number of "cognitive errors" that contribute to clients' miseries:

1. Clients may *selectively perceive* the world as a harmful place and ignore evidence to the contrary.

2. Clients may *overgeneralize* on the basis of a few examples. For example, they may perceive themselves as worthless because they were laid off at work or as unattractive because they were refused a date.

3. Clients may *magnify,* or blow out of proportion, the importance of negative events. They may catastrophize failing a test by assuming they will flunk out of college or catastrophize losing a job by believing that they will never find another one and that serious harm will befall their family as a result.

4. Clients may engage in *absolutist thinking,* or looking at the world in black and white rather than in shades of gray.

> **rational emotive behavior therapy (REBT)** Albert Ellis's form of therapy that encourages clients to challenge and correct irrational expectations and maladaptive behaviors

In doing so, a rejection on a date takes on the meaning of a lifetime of loneliness; an uncomfortable illness takes on life-threatening proportions.

Becoming aware of cognitive errors and modifying catastrophizing thoughts help us cope with stress. Internal, stable, and global attributions of failure lead to depression and feelings of helplessness. Cognitive therapists also alert clients to cognitive errors or irrational thoughts so that the clients can change their attitudes and pave the way for more effective overt behavior.

13-5b ALBERT ELLIS'S RATIONAL EMOTIVE BEHAVIOR THERAPY

In **rational emotive behavior therapy (REBT)**, Albert Ellis (1913–2007) pointed out that our beliefs *about* events, not just the events themselves, shape our responses to them. Moreover, many of us harbor a number of irrational beliefs that can give rise to problems or magnify their impact. Two of the most important ones are the belief that we must have the love and approval of people who are important to us and the belief that we must prove ourselves to be thoroughly competent, adequate, and achieving.

Ellis, like Beck, began his career as a psychoanalyst. And, also like Beck, he became disturbed by the passive role of the analyst and by the slow rate of obtaining results—if they were obtained at all. Ellis's REBT methods are active and directive. He did not sit back like the traditional psychoanalyst and occasionally offer an interpretation. Instead,

Aaron Beck (left) and Albert Ellis (right)

Benefits of Group Therapy Group therapy is more economical than individual therapy, group members can practice social skills with one another, and members can learn from the experiences of others.

> "I GET PEOPLE TO TRULY ACCEPT THEMSELVES UNCONDITIONALLY, WHETHER OR NOT THEIR THERAPIST OR ANYONE LOVES THEM."
>
> ALBERT ELLIS, AMERICAN PSYCHOLOGIST (1913–2007)

he urged clients to seek out their irrational beliefs, which can be unconscious, though not as deeply buried as Freud believed. Nevertheless, they can be hard to pinpoint without some direction. Ellis showed clients how those beliefs lead to misery and challenged clients to change them. When Ellis saw clients behaving according to irrational beliefs, he refuted the beliefs by asking "Where is it written that you must …?" or "What evidence do you have that …?" According to Ellis, we need less misery and less blaming in our lives, and more action.

13-5c TOWARD A COGNITIVE-BEHAVIORAL THERAPY

Many theorists consider cognitive therapy to be a collection of techniques that are a part of behavior therapy. We are apparently headed toward an integration of the two approaches that is termed **cognitive-behavioral therapy (CBT)**.

Ellis straddled behavioral and cognitive therapies. He originally dubbed his method of therapy *rational-emotive therapy*, because his focus was on the cognitive—irrational beliefs and how to change them. However, Ellis also always promoted behavioral changes to cement cognitive changes. In keeping with his broad philosophy, he recently changed the name of rational-emotive therapy to rational-emotive *behavior* therapy.

13-6 GROUP THERAPIES

When a psychotherapist has several clients with similar problems—anxiety, depression, adjustment to divorce, lack of social skills—it often makes sense to treat them in a group rather than in individual sessions. The methods and characteristics of the group reflect the needs of the members and the theoretical orientation of the leader. In group psychoanalysis, clients might interpret one another's dreams. In a client-centered group, they might provide an accepting atmosphere for self-exploration. Members of behavior therapy groups might be jointly desensitized to anxiety-evoking stimuli or might practice social skills together.

Group therapy has the following advantages:

1. It is economical (Prochaska & Norcross, 2014). It allows the therapist to work with several clients at once.

2. Compared with one-to-one therapy, group therapy provides more information and life experience for clients to draw on.

3. Appropriate behavior receives group support. Clients usually appreciate an outpouring of peer approval.

cognitive-behavior therapy (CBT) an approach to therapy that uses cognitive and behavioral techniques that have been validated by research

Wavebreak Media ltd/Alamy

4. When we run into troubles, it is easy to imagine that we are different from other people or inferior to them. Affiliating with people with similar problems is reassuring.

5. Group members who show improvement provide hope for other members.

6. Many individuals seek therapy because of problems in relating to other people. People who seek therapy for other reasons also may be socially inhibited. Members of groups have the opportunity to practice social skills in a relatively nonthreatening atmosphere. In a group consisting of men and women of different ages, group members can role-play one another's employers, employees, spouses, parents, children, and friends. Members can role-play asking one another out on dates, saying no (or yes), and so on.

But group therapy is not for everyone. Some clients fare better with individual treatment. Many prefer not to disclose their problems to a group. They may be overly shy or want individual attention. It is the responsibility of the therapist to insist that group disclosures be kept confidential, to establish a supportive atmosphere, and to ensure that group members obtain the attention they need.

Many types of therapy can be conducted either individually or in groups. Couple therapy and family therapy are conducted only with groups.

13-6a COUPLE THERAPY

Couple therapy helps couples enhance their relationship by improving their communication skills and helping them manage conflict (Prochaska & Norcross, 2014). There are often power imbalances in relationships, and couple therapy helps individuals find "full membership" in the couple. Correcting power imbalances increases happiness and can decrease the incidence of domestic violence. Ironically, in situations of domestic violence, the partner with *less* power in the relationship is usually

the violent one. Violence sometimes appears to be a way of compensating for inability to share power in other ways (Salis et al., 2014).

Today the main approach to couple therapy is cognitive-behavioral. It teaches couples communications skills (such as how to listen and express feelings), ways of handling feelings such as anger, and ways of solving problems.

13-6b FAMILY THERAPY

Family therapy is a form of group therapy in which one or more families constitute the group. Family therapy may be undertaken from various theoretical viewpoints. One is the *systems approach*, in which family interaction is studied and modified to enhance the growth of individual family members and of the family unit as a whole (Prochaska & Norcross, 2014).

Family members with low self-esteem often cannot tolerate different attitudes and behaviors in other family members. Faulty communication within the family also creates problems. In addition, it is not uncommon for the family to present an "identified patient"—that is, the family member who has the problem and is causing all the trouble. Yet family therapists usually assume that the identified patient is a scapegoat for other problems among family members. It is a sort of myth: change the "bad apple," or identified patient, and the "barrel," or family, will be functional once more. The family therapist attempts to teach the family to communicate and encourages growth and autonomy in each family member.

13-6c SELF-HELP AND SUPPORT GROUPS

Millions of people in the United States and elsewhere are involved in self-help and support groups that meet in person, online, or even by telephone. Some self-help and

It is a sort of myth: Change the "bad apple," or identified patient, and the "barrel," or family, will be functional once more.

support groups enable people who have been treated for psychological disorders to reach out to others who have had similar experiences (Greidanus & Everall, 2010). These groups tend to be specific, such as groups for parents of children with autistic disorders, intellectual deficiency, or Down syndrome. Members share problems and possible solutions.

The best known of self-help and support groups is Alcoholics Anonymous (AA), whose 12-step program has been used by millions of people in the United States and around the world. Members meet regularly and call other members between meetings when they are tempted to drink. The 12 steps require admitting before the group that one's drinking is out of control, calling upon a higher power for strength, examining injurious behavior, and attempting to make amends.

Does AA work? The organization itself admits that the majority of new recruits drop out within a year. Of greater concern is a meta-analysis that concluded that AA is actually less effective than no treatment at all (Kownacki & Shadish, 1999). But most analyses suggest that AA is as effective as all forms of psychotherapy tested (Kelly, 2013). When treatments, including AA, *are* effective, it seems to be because alcoholics remain in treatment for many years, alleviate feelings of depression, and heighten their confidence that they can navigate challenges without drinking.

13-7 DOES PSYCHOTHERAPY WORK?

In 1952, the British psychologist Hans Eysenck published a review of psychotherapy research—"The Effects of Psychotherapy"—that sent shock waves through the psychotherapy community. On the basis of his review of the research, Eysenck concluded that the rate of improvement among people in psychotherapy was no greater than the rate of "spontaneous remission"—that is, the rate of improvement that would be shown by people with psychological disorders who received no treatment. Eysenck was not addressing people with schizophrenia, who typically profit from biological forms of therapy, but he argued that whether or not people with problems such as anxiety and depression received therapy, two of three reported substantial improvement within 2 years.

That was over half a century ago. Research on the effectiveness of therapy conducted since then has been encouraging (Crits-Christoph et al., 2013; Lambert, 2013). In their classic early use of meta-analysis, Mary Lee Smith and Gene Glass (1977) analyzed the results of dozens of studies and concluded that people who

Fiction 👎

T **F** There is no scientific evidence that psychotherapy helps people with psychological disorders.

It is not true that psychotherapy has never been shown to be effective. There is now a great deal of research evidence that shows that psychotherapy is in fact effective.

obtained psychodynamic therapy showed greater well-being, on average, than 70% to 75% of those who did not obtain treatment. Similar positive results were reported for client-centered therapy. More recent studies also support the effectiveness of psychodynamic psychotherapy (Driessen et al., 2010; Shedler, 2010). Psychodynamic and client-centered therapies appear to be most effective with well-educated, verbal, strongly motivated clients who report problems with anxiety, depression (of light to moderate proportions), and interpersonal relationships. Neither form of therapy appears to be effective with people with psychotic disorders such as major depression, bipolar disorder, and schizophrenia.

Studies of cognitive therapy have shown that modifying irrational beliefs of the type described by Albert Ellis helps people with problems such as anxiety and depression (David et al., 2010). Modifying self-defeating beliefs of the sort outlined by Aaron Beck also frequently alleviates anxiety and depression (Beck & Haigh, 2014). Cognitive therapy helps people with major depressive disorders which had once been thought responsive only to biological therapies (Beck & Dozois, 2011; Eisendrath et al., 2014). Cognitive therapy has also helped people with obsessive-compulsive disorder (Cuijpers et al., 2013) and personality disorders (Cummings et al., 2011; Renner et al., 2013).

Behavioral and cognitive therapies have also provided strategies for treating social skills deficits, problems in self-control, and sexual dysfunctions (DeRubeis & Crits-Christoph, 1998). These therapies have helped couples and families in distress (Baucom & Boeding, 2013). Moreover, they have modified behaviors related to health problems such as headaches, chronic pain, and substance abuse (Beck et al., 2011; Ehde et al., 2014).

13-7a EVIDENCE-BASED PRACTICES

Experimentation is the gold standard for research in psychology, and a number of methods of therapy have been shown to be effective in carefully conducted, random controlled experiments—that is, experiments in which participants are assigned at random to a specific treatment or to a control treatment. The researchers in many of these studies also rely on treatment manuals that concretely outline the treatment methods. Treatment methods that survive these grueling tests are called *evidence-based practices*. Table 13.1 shows a number of evidence-based practices and the problems for which they have been found effective. Other treatments may eventually be added as more evidence accumulates.

Many therapists argue that evidence-based practices favor cognitive-behavioral therapies because they are more readily standardized in treatment manuals and can be followed more accurately by practitioners in experiments (Kazdin, 2008; Levy & Ablon, 2009). Alternative treatments, such as psychodynamic therapy, are not so easily standardized or practiced. Therefore, they may not hold up as well in controlled trials.

Observers also note that practices common among various therapies apparently lead to positive outcomes, such as the alliance between the client and the therapist, as well as the therapist's empathy, listening skills, and positive regard for the client (Norcross & Wampold, 2011). Figure 13.3 shows that nearly one in three clinical psychologists (31%) identifies herself or himself to be a cognitive therapist. Nearly one in five (18%) sees herself or himself as following in the footsteps of Freud—that is, as being a psychodynamic therapist. About 15% consider themselves to be behavior therapists. But more than one in five (22%) draw on methods and techniques from

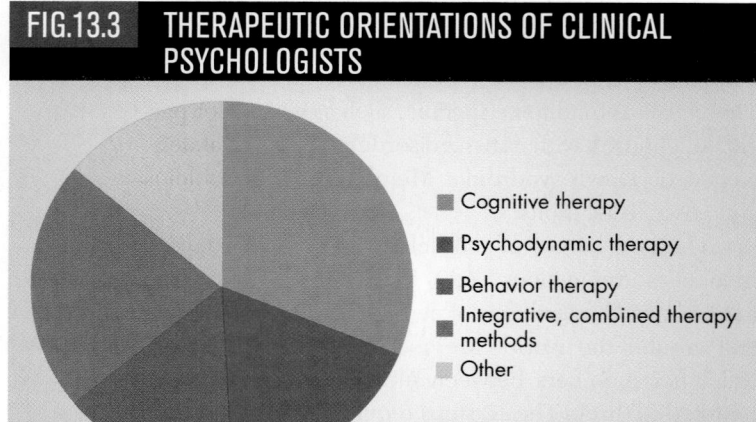

FIG.13.3 THERAPEUTIC ORIENTATIONS OF CLINICAL PSYCHOLOGISTS

- Cognitive therapy
- Psychodynamic therapy
- Behavior therapy
- Integrative, combined therapy methods
- Other

Source of data: Norcross, J. C., & Karpiak, C. P. (2012). Clinical psychologists in the 2010s: 50 years of the APA Division of Clinical Psychology. Clinical Psychology: Science and Practice, 19, 1–12.

various schools of therapy—using what they think will work best in a given situation.

As we see in the following section on ethnicity and psychotherapy, we must also consider the sociocultural features of clients in determining how to make therapy most effective.

13-7b ETHNICITY AND PSYCHOTHERAPY

Americans from ethnic minority groups are less likely than European Americans to seek therapy (Chen & Rizzo, 2010; Wang, 2013). Reasons for their lower participation rate include:

▶ Lack of awareness that therapy would help

▶ Lack of information about the availability of professional services or inability to pay for them

▶ Distrust of professionals, particularly European American professionals and (for women) male professionals

▶ Language barriers

▶ Reluctance to open up about personal matters to strangers—especially strangers who are not members of one's own ethnic group

▶ Cultural inclinations toward other approaches to problem solving, such as religious approaches and psychic healers

▶ Negative experiences with professionals and authority figures

There are thus many reasons that clinicians need to be sensitive to the cultural heritage, language, and values of their clients. That is, they need to develop

TABLE 13.1	EXAMPLES OF EVIDENCE-BASED PRACTICES
Treatment	**Condition for Which Treatment Is Effective**
Cognitive therapy	Depression Headache
Behavior therapy or behavior modification	Depression Developmental disabilities Enuresis (bed-wetting)
Cognitive-behavior therapy	Panic disorder with and without agoraphobia Generalized anxiety disorder Bulimia nervosa
Exposure treatment	Agoraphobia and specific phobia
Exposure and response prevention	Obsessive–compulsive disorder
Parent training programs	Children with oppositional behavior

Source: © Cengage Learning®

Sensitivity Psychologists need to be sensitive to the cultural heritages, languages, and values of their clients.

multicultural competence (Malgady, 2013; Wang, 2013). Let's consider some of the issues involved in conducting psychotherapy with African Americans, Asian Americans, Latin Americans, and Native Americans.

AFRICAN AMERICANS African Americans often are reluctant to seek psychological help because of cultural assumptions that people should manage their own problems (Comas-Diaz & Greene, 2013; González et al., 2010). Many African Americans are also suspicious of their therapists—especially when the therapist is a European American (Mohr et al., 2010). They may withhold personal information because of society's history of racial discrimination.

ASIAN AMERICANS Asian Americans tend to stigmatize people with psychological disorders. As a result, they may deny problems and refuse to seek help for them (Spencer et al., 2010; Wang, 2013). Asian Americans, especially recent immigrants, also may not understand or believe in Western approaches to psychotherapy. For example, Western psychotherapy typically encourages people to express their feelings. This mode of behavior may conflict with the Asian tradition of public restraint. Many Asians also experience psychological problems as physical symptoms (Wang, 2013). Rather than thinking of themselves as anxious, they may focus on physical features of anxiety such as a pounding heart and heavy sweating.

LATIN AMERICANS Therapists need to be aware of potential conflicts in reconciling the traditional Latin American values of interdependence in the family and spirituality with the typical European American belief in independence and self-reliance (Comas-Diaz & Greene, 2013; Garza & Watts, 2010). Measures like the following may help bridge the gaps between psychotherapists and Latin American clients:

▸ Interacting with clients in the language requested by them or, if this is not possible, referring them to professionals who can do so.

▸ Using methods that are consistent with the client's values and levels of acculturation, as suggested by fluency in English and level of education.

▸ Developing therapy methods that incorporate clients' cultural values. Robert Malgady (2013), for example, recommends *cuento therapy* with Puerto Ricans. This form of therapy uses traditional folktales (*cuentos*) with characters who serve as models for adaptive behavior.

NATIVE AMERICANS Many psychological disorders experienced by Native Americans involve the disruption of their traditional culture caused by European colonization (Gone & Trimble, 2012; Trimble et al., 2014). Loss of cultural identity and social disorganization have set the stage for problems such as alcoholism, substance abuse, and depression. Efforts to prevent psychological disorders may well focus on strengthening Native American cultural identity, pride, and cohesion.

Psychotherapy is most effective when therapists attend to and respect people's cultural as well as individual differences. Although it is the individual who experiences psychological anguish, the fault can often be traced to cultural issues.

13-8 BIOLOGICAL THERAPIES

The kinds of therapy we have discussed are psychological in nature—forms of *psycho*therapy. Psychotherapies apply *psychological* principles to treatment, principles based on psychological knowledge of matters such as learning and motivation. However, people with psychological disorders are also often treated with biological therapies. Biological therapies apply what is known of people's *biological* structures and processes to the amelioration of psychological disorders. For example, they may work by altering events in the nervous system, as by changing the action of neurotransmitters. In this section, we discuss three biological, or medical, approaches to treating people with psychological disorders: drug therapy, electroconvulsive therapy, and psychosurgery.

13-8a DRUG THERAPY

rebound anxiety anxiety that can occur when one discontinues use of a tranquilizer

antidepressant acting to relieve depression

selective serotonin-reuptake inhibitors (SSRIs) antidepressant drugs that work by blocking the reuptake of serotonin by presynaptic neurons, thus increasing the amount of serotonin available to the brain

Many years ago, Fats Domino popularized the song "My Blue Heaven." Fats was singing about the sky and happiness. Today, "blue heavens" is one of the street names for the 10-milligram dose of the antianxiety drug Valium. Clinicians prescribe Valium and other drugs for people with various psychological disorders.

ANTIANXIETY DRUGS Most antianxiety drugs, such as Valium and Ativan, belong to the chemical class known as *benzodiazepines*. Antianxiety drugs are usually prescribed for outpatients who complain of generalized anxiety or panic attacks, although many people also use them as sleeping pills. Valium and other antianxiety drugs depress the activity of the central nervous system (CNS). The CNS, in turn, decreases sympathetic activity, reducing the heart rate, respiration rate, and feelings of nervousness and tension. Many people come to tolerate antianxiety drugs very quickly. When tolerance occurs, dosages must be increased for the drug to remain effective.

Sedation (feeling of being tired or drowsy) is the most common side effect of antianxiety drugs. Problems associated with withdrawal from these drugs include **rebound anxiety**. That is, some people who have been using these drugs regularly report that their anxiety becomes worse than before once they discontinue them. Antianxiety drugs can induce physical dependence, as evidenced by withdrawal symptoms such as tremors, sweating, insomnia, and rapid heartbeat.

ANTIPSYCHOTIC DRUGS People with schizophrenia are often given antipsychotic drugs (also called *major tranquilizers*). In most cases, these drugs reduce agitation, delusions, and hallucinations. Many antipsychotic drugs, including phenothiazines (e.g., Thorazine) and clozapine (Clozaril) are thought to act by blocking dopamine receptors in the brain (Porsolt et al., 2010). Research along these lines supports the theory that schizophrenia is connected with overactivity of the neurotransmitter dopamine.

ANTIDEPRESSANTS People with major depression often take so-called **antidepressant** drugs. These drugs are also helpful for some people with eating disorders, panic disorder, obsessive–compulsive disorder (OCD), and social anxiety disorder (Bandelow et al., 2012). Problems in the regulation of noradrenaline and serotonin may be involved in eating and panic disorders as well as in depression. Antidepressants are believed to work by increasing levels of these neurotransmitters, which can affect both depression and the appetite (Li et al., 2012).

There are various antidepressants. Each increases the concentration of noradrenaline, serotonin, or both in the brain (Li et al., 2012). **Selective serotonin-reuptake inhibitors (SSRIs)** such as

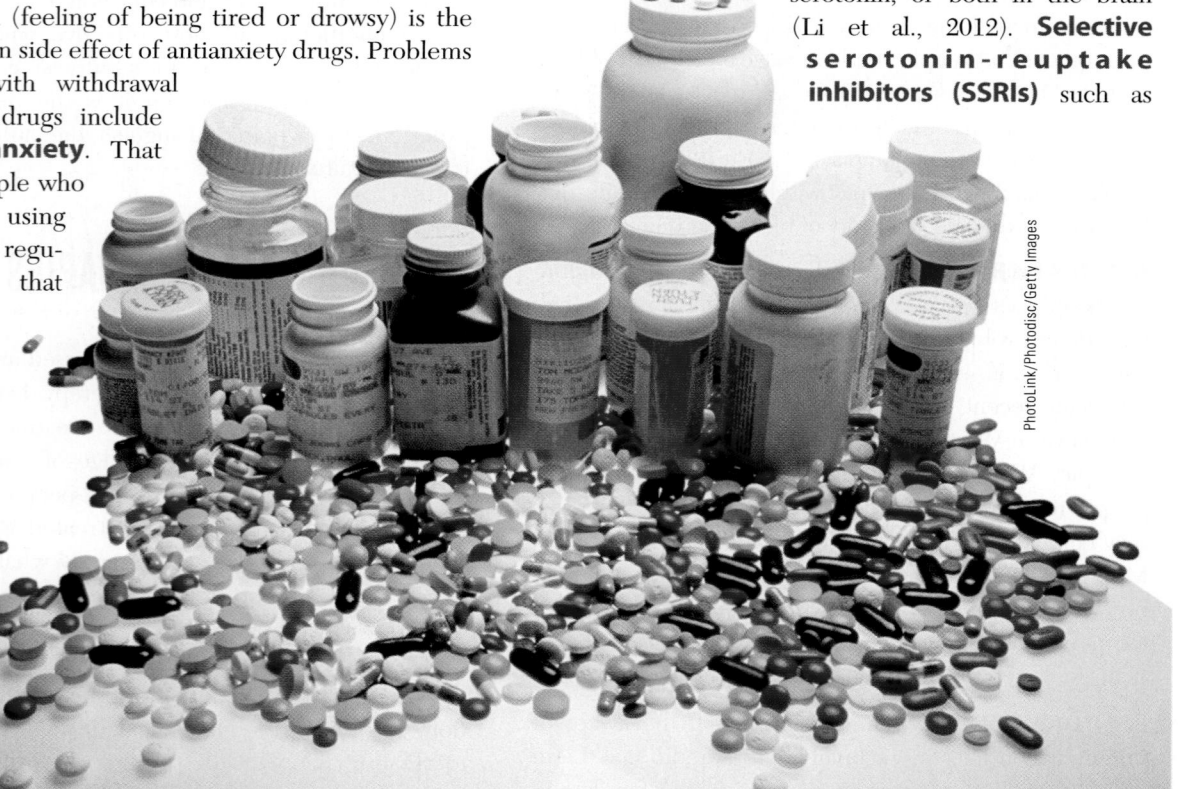

PhotoLink/Photodisc/Getty Images

Prozac and Zoloft block the reuptake of serotonin by presynaptic neurons. As a result, serotonin remains in the synaptic cleft longer, influencing receiving neurons. SSRIs appear to be more effective than other antidepressants.

MOOD STABILIZERS The ancient Greeks and Romans were among the first to use the metal lithium as a mood stabilizer. They prescribed mineral water—which contains lithium—for people with bipolar disorder. They had no inkling as to why this treatment sometimes helped. A salt found in the metal lithium (lithium carbonate), in tablet form, flattens out cycles of manic behavior and depression in most people. It is not known exactly how lithium works, although it affects the functioning of neurotransmitters. Lithium can also be used to strengthen the effects of antidepressant medication (Li et al., 2012).

People with bipolar disorder may have to use lithium indefinitely, as a person with type 1 diabetes must use insulin to control the illness. Many other drugs are also used to help stabilize the moods of patients with bipolar disorder. Among these are divalproex sodium (brand name: Depakote), lamotrigine (Lamictal), carbamazepine (Tegretol), and oxcarbazepine (Trileptal).

13-8b ELECTROCONVULSIVE THERAPY

Electroconvulsive therapy (ECT) is a biological form of therapy for psychological disorders that was introduced by the Italian psychiatrist Ugo Cerletti in 1939. Cerletti had noted that some slaughterhouses used electric shock to render animals unconscious. The shocks also produced convulsions. Along with other European researchers of the period, Cerletti erroneously believed that convulsions were incompatible with schizophrenia and other major psychological disorders.

ECT was originally used for a variety of psychological disorders. Because of the advent of antipsychotic drugs, however, it is now used mainly for people with major depression who do not respond to antidepressants (Taylor et al., 2012). People typically obtain one ECT treatment two to three times a week for up to 10 sessions. Electrodes are attached to the temples and an electrical current strong enough to produce a convulsion is induced. The shock causes unconsciousness, so the patient does not recall it. Nevertheless, patients are given a sedative (a drug that relieves nervousness or agitation or puts one to sleep) so that they are asleep during the treatment.

ECT is controversial for many reasons; most professionals are distressed by the thought of passing an electric shock through a patient's head and producing convulsions. There are also side effects, including memory problems (Rayner et al., 2009).

13-8c PSYCHOSURGERY

Psychosurgery is more controversial than ECT. The best-known modern technique, **prefrontal lobotomy**, has been used with people with severe disorders. In this method, a picklike instrument severs the nerve pathways that link the prefrontal lobes of the brain to the thalamus. It is intended to sever thought from emotion

electroconvulsive therapy (ECT) treatment of disorders like major depression by passing an electric current (that causes a convulsion) through the head

psychosurgery surgery intended to promote psychological changes or to relieve disordered behavior

prefrontal lobotomy the severing or destruction of a section of the frontal lobe of the brain

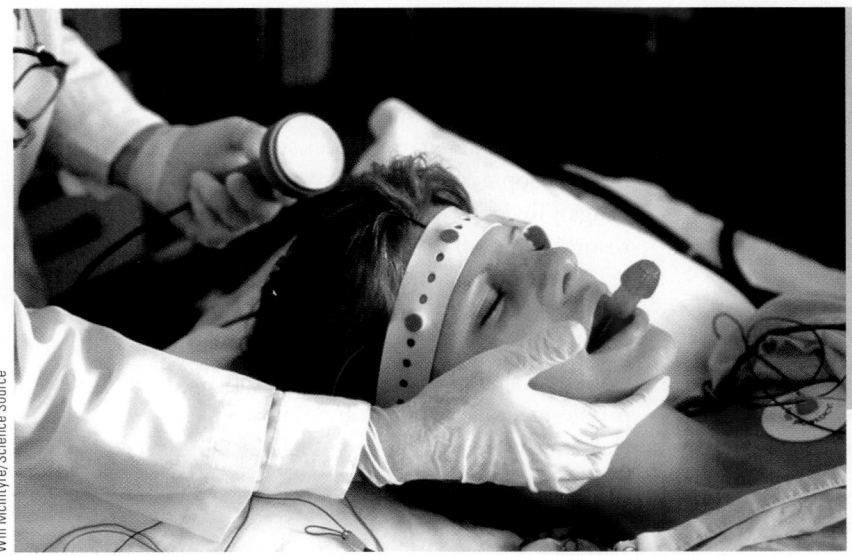

Will McIntyre/Science Source

Electroconvulsive Therapy
In ECT, electrodes are placed on each side of the patient's head and a current is passed between them, inducing a seizure. ECT is used mainly in cases of major depression when antidepressant drugs and psychotherapy are not sufficient.

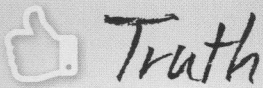

and enable severely disturbed patients to regain control. The method was pioneered by the Portuguese neurologist Antonio Egas Moniz and was brought to the United States in the 1930s. The theoretical rationale for the operation was vague and misguided, and Moniz's reports of success were exaggerated. Nevertheless, by 1950 prefrontal lobotomies had been performed on thousands of people in an effort to reduce violence and agitation. Anecdotal evidence of the method's unreliable outcomes is found in an ironic historical footnote: one of Dr. Moniz's patients returned to shoot him.

The prefrontal lobotomy also has side effects, including hyperactivity and distractibility, impaired learning ability, overeating, apathy and withdrawal, epileptic-type seizures, reduced creativity, and, occasionally, death. Because of these side effects, and because of the advent of antipsychotic drugs, the prefrontal lobotomy has been largely discontinued in the United States.

But new methods of psychosurgery are being undertaken with caution and have had mixed success in debilitating cases of OCD and phobias. They are used only when psychotherapy and drug therapy have failed and when patients are made fully aware of success rates and potential risks (Carey, 2009). In *gamma knife surgery*, for example, physicians beam streams of radiation deep into the skull, destroying spots of tissue believed to be overactive in severe OCD (Tyagi et al., 2010). Other psychosurgery procedures are also undergoing small-scale trials (Bear et al., 2010). But there are some side effects, and the treatments are not always effective.

13-8d DOES BIOLOGICAL THERAPY WORK?

There are thus a number of biological approaches to treat psychological disorders. But what do we know about the effectiveness of biological therapies?

There is little question that drug therapy has helped many people with psychological disorders. For example, antipsychotic drugs largely account for the reduced need for the use of restraint and supervision (e.g., padded cells, straitjackets, hospitalization, and so on) with people diagnosed with schizophrenia. Antipsychotic drugs have also enabled many former mental hospital residents to lead largely normal lives in the community, hold jobs, and maintain family lives. Most of the problems related to these drugs concern their side effects.

Comparisons of the effectiveness of psychotherapy and pharmacotherapy (medicine) for depression have yielded mixed results. Cognitive therapy provides coping skills that reduce the risk of recurrence of depression once treatment ends. Pim Cuijpers and his colleagues (2013) undertook a meta-analysis of randomly controlled experiments to attempt to answer the question of whether there was a difference in effectiveness of the treatment of depression when an antidepressant drug was added to a psychological treatment. They found that a treatment package that included psychotherapy and pharmacotherapy was more effective than psychological treatment alone, but it was not clear that the antidepressants offered much of an advantage.

Cognitive-behavior therapy is now a recommended treatment for schizophrenia (Jones et al., 2012). It appears to have helped relieve the positive symptoms of schizophrenia by linking people's problem behavior and distress to their underlying patterns of thinking, encouraging them to gain more control over their thinking (Gregory, 2010).

Many professionals are comfortable with the short-term use of antianxiety drugs in helping clients manage periods of unusual anxiety or tension. However, many people use antianxiety drugs routinely to dull the arousal stemming from anxiety-producing lifestyles or interpersonal problems. Rather than make the often painful decisions required to confront their problems, they take a pill.

Despite the controversies surrounding ECT, it helps many people who do not respond to antidepressant drugs (Taylor et al., 2012). ECT may be a useful "last resort" when other treatment methods offer no relief.

In sum, drug therapy and perhaps ECT seem to be effective for some disorders that do not respond to psychotherapy alone. Yet common sense and research evidence suggest that psychotherapy is preferable for problems such as anxiety and mild depression. No chemical can show a person how to change an idea or solve an interpersonal problem.

STUDY TOOLS 13

READY TO STUDY? IN THE BOOK, YOU CAN:

☐ Check your understanding of what you've read with the quizzes below.

☐ Rip out the chapter review card at the back of the book to have a summary of the chapter and the key terms handy.

ONLINE AT CENGAGEBRAIN.COM YOU CAN:

☐ Watch a demonstration of exposure therapy in a short video.

☐ Prepare for tests with quizzes.

☐ Review the key terms with Flash Cards.

☐ Play games to master concepts.

FILL-INS

Answers can be found in the back of the book, starting on page 393.

1. Psychotherapy is a systematic interaction between a therapist and a client that applies _____ principles to influence clients' thoughts, feelings, and/or behavior.

2. Freud's method of psychoanalysis attempts to shed light on _____ conflicts that are presumed to lie at the roots of clients' problems.

3. _____-conditioning methods reinforce desired responses and extinguish undesired responses.

4. The chief psychoanalytic method is _____ association.

5. _____ therapies focus on clients' subjective, conscious experience.

6. _____-_____ therapy is a nondirective method that provides clients with an accepting atmosphere that enables them to overcome roadblocks to self-actualization.

7. _____ therapists focus on the beliefs, attitudes, and automatic thoughts that create and compound their clients' problems.

8. Behavior-therapy methods for reducing fears include systematic _____, in which a client is gradually exposed to more fear-arousing stimuli.

9. Albert Ellis's form of therapy confronts clients with the ways in which _____ beliefs contribute to anxiety and depression.

10. (Minor or Major?) tranquilizers are usually prescribed for people who complain of anxiety or tension.

MULTIPLE CHOICE

1. Your therapist is accepting and warm. You are encouraged to feel good about yourself and to make choices that develop your potential. Your therapist uses a(n) _____ approach to treatment.
   a. psychoanalytic
   b. ego analytic
   c. client-centered
   d. behavioral

2. Hannah's therapist believes her anxiety is the result of unconscious impulses breaking through to the conscious level. Her therapist endorses the _____ perspective.
   a. behavioral
   b. psychodynamic
   c. cognitive
   d. humanistic

3. A client avoids talking about their relationship with their father. The psychoanalyst asks them to talk about this relationship. The client becomes restless and claims, "There is nothing to tell." This is indicative of
   a. transference.
   b. resistance.
   c. catharsis.
   d. free association.

4. Which of the following examples best represents using operant conditioning to change behavior?
   a. Using electroconvulsive therapy for depression.
   b. Withdrawing attention whenever a child has a temper tantrum.
   c. Fostering insight by using examples.
   d. Giving your sister money to see a therapist.

5. _____ therapists focus on beliefs and attitudes that create and compound their clients' psychological problems.
   a. Cognitive
   b. Psychoanalytic
   c. Learning
   d. Gestalt

6. Client-centered therapy is to _____ as Gestalt therapy is to _____.
   a. directive; nondirective
   b. nondirective; directive
   c. objective; subjective
   d. present; past

7. Family therapists usually see the "identified patient" as the
   a. cause of the family's problem.
   b. scapegoat for other problems in the family.
   c. key to the family system.
   d. black sheep of the family.

8. Social skills training is facilitated in a group setting because
   a. members of the group can practice the skills with one another.
   b. members can observe and learn from each other.
   c. members can give each other feedback.
   d. all of these

9. Dr. Schwiesow wants to use the best methods when treating her patients with depression. She should search out _____ practices.
   a. evidence-based
   b. treatment
   c. researched
   d. experimental

10. You have advised a patient to discontinue use of antianxiety drugs. After two weeks, your patient calls to complain that his anxiety symptoms are now worse than before he started to take the drug. You tell the patient that his feelings are a predictable response to discontinuing antianxiety medication. In fact, he is experiencing what is called
    a. addiction.
    b. tolerance.
    c. rebound anxiety.
    d. relapse.

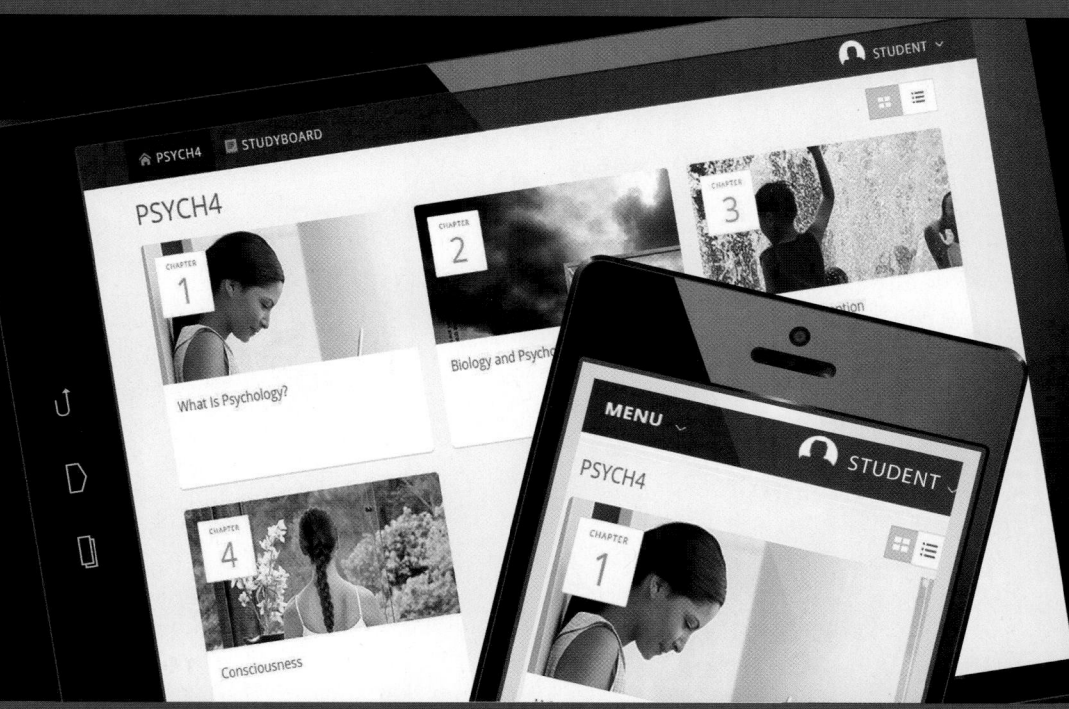

14 | Social Psychology

Steve Raymer/Encyclopedia/Corbis

Do you dan
D500
CURi
BRITNEY
A new fra

LEARNING OUTCOMES

After studying this chapter, you will be able to …

14-1 Define *attitude* and discuss factors that shape attitudes

14-2 Discuss prejudice and discrimination

14-3 Discuss factors that contribute to interpersonal attraction and love

14-4 Define *social perception* and describe factors that influence it

14-5 Explain why people obey authority figures and conform to social pressure

14-6 Discuss factors that contribute to aggression

14-7 Describe differences between the ways in which people behave as individuals and as members of a group

After you finish

this chapter, go

to **PAGE 375** for

STUDY TOOLS

> "People can be **goaded** by social influences into doing things that are not necessarily consistent with their personalities."

Consider some news items from the early years of the 21st century:

▶ 2014: ISIS militants carry out multiple suicide bombings as they try to breach Kurdish defenses in northern Iraq.

▶ 2011: A suicide bomber drives a car laden with explosives up to a Coptic Christian church in Egypt as worshipers exit a New Year's mass, killing 21 people and wounding at least 80 more.

▶ 2008: The former prime minister of Pakistan, Benazir Bhutto is assassinated in a suicide bombing.

▶ 2005: Four suicide bombers blow themselves up aboard three London commuter trains and a bus, killing more than 50 people and wounding 700.

▶ 2001: On September 11, 2001, 19 suicide terrorists in the United States use fully fueled airplanes as bombs, flying them into the World Trade Center and the Pentagon, killing nearly 3,000 people.

Although you might think of suicide terrorism as a recent development, it dates back thousands of years (Kazim et al., 2008). The word *suicide* in the phrase "suicide bomber" leads people to turn to psychologists for understanding, with the idea that something must be psychologically wrong with these terrorists. But many social scientists assert that suicide terrorists have no telltale psychological profile (Consortium of Social Science Associations, 2003; Shi & Jia, 2011). Ariel Merari and his colleagues (2010) at the University of Tel Aviv interviewed and tested would-be suicide bombers—people who had been caught in the act and arrested. They found two groups among the would-be suicide terrorists: (1) dependent types with a tendency to follow leaders and public influences, and (2) emotionally unstable and impulsive types. Among both types, some were depressed but would not be diagnosed with major depressive disorder.

Because of the difficulty in identifying suicide terrorists, social psychologist Philip Zimbardo and his colleagues (Breckenridge et al., 2010; Zimbardo, 2004) argue that we must look to the psychology of *social influence* to understand them. As we will see, social psychologist Stanley Milgram (1974), who conducted famous studies on obedience some 50 years ago, concluded, "Often, it is not so much the kind of person a man is, as the kind of situation in which he finds himself that determines how he will act."

Social psychology is the field of psychology that studies the nature and causes of behavior and mental processes in social situations. Social psychologists study the ways people can be goaded by social influences into doing things that are not necessarily consistent with their personalities. The social psychological topics we discuss in this chapter include attitudes, social perception, social influence, and group behavior. As we explore each of these, we will ask what they might offer to those of us who have difficulty imagining why people would surrender their own lives to take the lives of others. We begin with attitudes.

👍 Truth or Fiction? 👎

WHAT DO YOU THINK? Folklore, common sense, or nonsense? Select T for "truth" or F for "fiction," and check the accuracy of your answers as you read through the chapter.

T	F	People vote their consciences.
T	F	We appreciate things more when we have to work for them.
T	F	People have condemned billions of other people without ever meeting them or learning their names.
T	F	Beauty is in the eye of the beholder.
T	F	Opposites attract.
T	F	We tend to hold others responsible for their misdeeds but to see ourselves as victims of circumstances when we misbehave.
T	F	Most people will torture an innocent person if they are ordered to do so.
T	F	Seeing is believing.
T	F	Nearly 40 people stood by and did nothing while a woman was being stabbed to death.

14-1 ATTITUDES

How do you feel about abortion, same-sex marriage, and exhibiting the Ten Commandments in public buildings such as courthouses? These are hot-button topics because people have strong attitudes toward them. They each give rise to cognitive evaluations (such as approval or disapproval), feelings (such as liking, disliking, or something stronger), and behavioral tendencies (such as approach or avoidance). Although I asked you how you "feel," attitudes are not just feelings or emotions. Many psychologists view thinking—or judgment—as more basic. Feelings and behavior follow. **Attitudes** are enduring behavioral and cognitive tendencies that are expressed by evaluating particular people, places, or things with favor or disfavor (Bohner & Dickel, 2011).

Attitudes are largely learned, although we may have inborn predispositions to lean one way or another on issues (Kandler et al., 2014; Lewis & Bates, 2013). For example, if you learn that an Apple iPad is a wonderful "toy," you may feel the urge to buy one. Attitudes can foster love or hate. They can give rise to helping behavior or to mass destruction. They can lead to social conflict or to the resolution of conflicts. Attitudes can change, but not easily.

14-1a PREDICTING BEHAVIOR FROM ATTITUDES

Our definition of *attitude* implies that our behavior is consistent with our attitudes. But do people really do as they think? When we are free to do as we wish, the answer is often yes. But as indicated by the term **A–B problem**, there are exceptions. In fact, the links between attitudes (A) and behaviors (B) tend to be weak to moderate (Herr & Fazio, 2013; Petty et al., 2009a, 2009b). People do not always vote "their consciences." Moreover, research reveals that people who say that drinking alcohol, smoking, and drunken driving are serious threats to their health do not necessarily curb these activities (Kiviniemi & Rothman, 2010).

Several factors affect the likelihood that we can

social cognitive theory a cognitively oriented learning theory in which observational learning and person variables such as values and expectancies play major roles in individual differences

attitude an enduring mental representation of a person, place, or thing that typically evokes an emotional response and related behavior

A–B problem the issue of how well we can predict behavior on the basis of attitudes

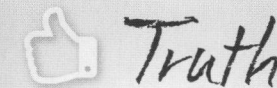
predict behavior from attitudes (Bardem & Tormala, 2014; Bohner & Dickel, 2011):

1. *Specificity.* We can better predict specific behavior from specific attitudes than from global attitudes. For example, we can better predict church attendance by knowing people's attitudes toward church attendance than by knowing whether they are Christian.

2. *Strength of attitudes.* Strong attitudes are more likely to determine behavior than weak attitudes. A person who believes that the nation's destiny depends on Democrats taking control of Congress is more likely to vote than a person who leans toward that party but does not believe that elections make much difference.

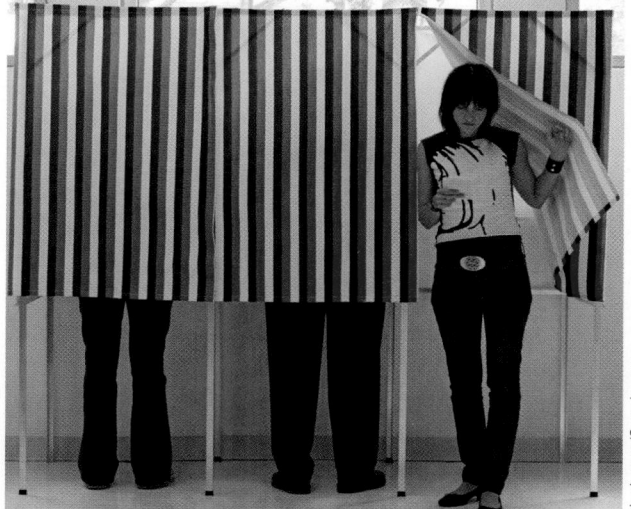

Do People Always Vote Their "Conscience"? The "A–B problem" refers to the research finding that people do not always act in accord with their attitudes.

3. *Vested interest.* People are more likely to act on their attitudes when they have a vested interest in the outcome. People are more likely to vote for (or against) unionization of their workplace when they believe that their job security depends on it.

4. *Accessibility.* People are more likely to behave in accord with their attitudes when they are accessible—that is, when they are brought to mind. This is why politicians attempt to "get out the vote" by means of media blitzes just prior to an election. Attitudes with a strong emotional impact are more accessible, which is one reason that politicians strive to get their supporters "worked up" over issues.

14-1b ATTITUDE FORMATION

Genetics may play some role in attitude formation (Chen & Li, 2014). For example, in terms of the big-five personality traits—which are believed to be partly inherited—political liberals tend to score higher on openness to experience, and political conservatives tend to score higher on conscientiousness (Cooper et al., 2013). Even so, you were not born a conservative or a liberal—although your parents and community may have supported one of these political points of view when you came along. Political, religious, and other attitudes are at least in part learned or derived from cognitive processes.

CONDITIONING AND OBSERVATIONAL LEARNING
Consider a role for conditioning (Hutter & Sweldens, 2013). Laboratory experiments have shown that attitudes toward national groups can be influenced by associating them with positive words (such as *gift* or *happy*) or negative words (such as *ugly* or *failure*) (De Houwer et al., 2001). Parents often reward children for saying and doing things that agree with their own attitudes. Patriotism is encouraged by showing children approval when they sing the national anthem or wave the flag.

Attitudes formed through direct experience may be stronger and easier to recall, but we also acquire attitudes by observing, listening to, or reading the works of other people. The approval or disapproval of peers leads adolescents to prefer short or long hair, baggy jeans, or preppy sweaters. How do the things you read in newspapers or hear on the radio influence your attitudes?

COGNITIVE APPRAISAL
Although genetics and early learning can influence attitudes, attitude formation is not fully mechanical. People are also motivated to

> "TERRORISM IS ABOUT ONE THING: PSYCHOLOGY. IT IS THE PSYCHOLOGY OF FEAR."
> PHILIP G. ZIMBARDO

understand the environment so that they can make predictions and exercise some control over it (Kuhne & Schemer, 2013). People also sometimes form or change attitudes on the basis of new information (Bohner & Dickel, 2011; Horcajo et al., 2014). For example, we may believe that a car is more reliable than we had thought if a survey by *Consumer Reports* finds that it has an excellent repair record. Even so, initial attitudes act as *cognitive anchors* (Bohner & Dickel, 2011). We often judge new ideas in terms of how much they deviate from our existing attitudes. Accepting larger deviations requires more information processing—that is, more intellectual work (Bohner & Dickel, 2011). For this reason, perhaps, great deviations—such as changes from liberal to conservative attitudes, or vice versa—are apt to be resisted.

14-1c CHANGING ATTITUDES THROUGH PERSUASION

Will Rogers's comment sounds on the mark, but he was probably wrong. It does little good to have a wonderful product if it remains a secret.

The **elaboration likelihood model** describes the ways in which people respond to persuasive messages (Bohner & Dickel, 2011). Consider two routes to persuading others to change attitudes. The *central route* inspires thoughtful consideration of arguments and evidence. The *peripheral route* associates objects with positive or negative cues. When politicians avow, "This bill is supported by liberals (or conservatives)," they are seeking predictable, knee-jerk reactions rather than careful consideration of a bill's merits. Other cues are rewards (such as a smile or a hug), punishments (such as parental disapproval), and such factors as the trustworthiness and attractiveness of the communicator.

Advertisements, which are a form of persuasive communication, also rely on central and peripheral routes. Some ads focus on the quality of the product (central route). Others attempt to associate the product with appealing images (peripheral route). For example, ads for Total cereal, which highlight its nutritional benefits, provide information about the quality of the product,

elaboration likelihood model the view that persuasive messages are evaluated (elaborated) on the basis of central and peripheral cues

but ads that show football players heading for Disney World or choosing a brand of beer offer no information about the product itself.

In this section, we look at one central factor in persuasion—the nature of the message—and three peripheral factors: the messenger, the context of the message, and the audience.

THE PERSUASIVE MESSAGE How do we respond when TV commercials are repeated until we have memorized the dimples on the actors' faces? Research suggests that familiarity breeds content, not contempt (Bohner & Dickel, 2011; Koch & Zerback, 2013). It appears that repeated exposure to people and things as diverse as political candidates, photos of college students, and abstract art enhances their appeal (Banaji & Heiphetz, 2008; Reis et al., 2011).

When trying to persuade someone, is it helpful or self-defeating to alert them to the arguments presented by the opposition? In two-sided arguments, the communicator recounts the arguments of the opposition in an effort to refute them. In research concerning a mock trial, college undergraduates were presented with two-sided arguments—those of the prosecution and those of the defendant (McKenzie et al., 2002). When one argument was weak, the college "jurors" expressed more confidence in their decision than when they did not hear the other side at all. Theologians and politicians sometimes forewarn their followers about the arguments of the opposition and then refute each one. Forewarning creates a kind of psychological immunity to them (Albarracin & Handley, 2011).

It would be nice to think that people are too sophisticated to be persuaded by emotional factors in attitude formation, but they usually aren't (Ruiter et al., 2014). Consider the **fear appeal**: women who are warned of the dire risk they run if they fail to be screened for breast cancer are more likely to obtain mammograms than women who are informed of the *benefits* of mammography

> **"ARGUMENTS ARE TO BE AVOIDED: THEY ARE ALWAYS VULGAR AND OFTEN CONVINCING."**
> OSCAR WILDE, IRISH WRITER AND POET (1854–1900)

(Ruiter et al., 2014). Interestingly, although sun tanning has been shown to increase the likelihood of skin cancer, warnings against sun tanning were shown to be more effective when students were warned of risks to their *appearance* (e.g., premature aging, wrinkling, and scarring of the skin) than when the warning dealt with the risk to their health. Fear appeals are most effective when the audience believes that the risks are serious—as in causing wrinkles!—and that the audience members can change their behavior to avert the risks—as in preventing cancer or wrinkling (Ruiter et al., 2014; Thompson et al., 2009).

Audiences also tend to believe arguments that appear to run counter to the vested interests of the communicator (Bohner & Dickel, 2011). If the president of Ford or General Motors said that Toyotas and Hondas were superior, you can bet that we would prick up our ears.

THE PERSUASIVE COMMUNICATOR Would you go to a doctor who admitted that he or she was behind the times? Research shows that persuasive communicators are characterized by expertise, trustworthiness, attractiveness, or similarity to their audiences (Petty et al., 2009a, 2009b). Because of the adoration of their fans, sports superstars such as Peyton Manning are the most valuable endorsers.

People find it painful when they are confronted with information that counters their own views. Therefore, they often show **selective avoidance** and **selective exposure** (Knobloch-Westerwick & Johnson, 2014). That is, they switch channels when the news coverage runs counter to their own

We often selectively expose ourselves to opinions with which we agree—and vice versa.

attitudes. They also seek communicators whose outlook coincides with their own. Whom would you prefer to listen to: Rush Limbaugh and Sean Hannity, or Chris Matthews and Rachel Maddow?

THE CONTEXT OF THE MESSAGE You are too shrewd to let someone persuade you by buttering you up, but perhaps someone you know would be influenced by a sip of wine, a bite of cheese, and a sincere compliment. Aspects of the immediate environment, such as music, also increase the likelihood of persuasion. When we are in a good mood, we apparently are less likely to evaluate the situation carefully (Turner et al., 2013).

It is also counterproductive to call your friends foolish when they differ with you—even though their ideas are bound to be "foolish" if they do not agree with yours. Agreement and praise are more effective ways to encourage others to embrace your views.

THE PERSUADED AUDIENCE Why can some people say no to salespeople? Why do others enrich the lives of every door-to-door salesperson? It may be that people with high self-esteem and low social anxiety are more likely to resist social pressure (Ellickson et al., 2001). Researchers have also found that people who comply with unreasonable requests are more apt to report thoughts such as (Norton, 2010):

▶ "I was worried about what the other person would think of me if I said no."

▶ "It is better to help other people than to be self-centered."

▶ "If I had said no, the other person might have been hurt or insulted."

People who refuse unreasonable requests reported thoughts like these:

▶ "It doesn't really matter what the other person thinks of me."

▶ "I am perfectly free to say no."

▶ "The request was unreasonable."

14-1d CHANGING ATTITUDES AND BEHAVIOR BY MEANS OF COGNITIVE DISSONANCE

According to **cognitive-dissonance theory**, people are thinking creatures who seek consistency

> "THE BRAIN WITHIN ITS GROOVE RUNS EVENLY AND TRUE ..."
> EMILY DICKINSON, AMERICAN POET (1830–1886)

in their behaviors and their attitudes—that is, their views of the world. People must apparently mentally represent the world accurately to predict and control events. Consistency in beliefs, attitudes, and behavior helps make the world seem like a predictable place. Therefore, if we find ourselves in the uncomfortable spot where two cherished ideas conflict, we are motivated to reduce the discrepancy.

In the first and still one of the best-known studies on cognitive dissonance, one group of participants received $1 (worth $5 to $10 today) for telling someone else that a boring task was interesting (Festinger & Carlsmith, 1959). Members of a second group received $20 (worth $100 to $200 today) to describe the chore positively. Both groups were paid to engage in **attitude-discrepant behavior**—that is, behavior that ran counter to what they actually thought. After presenting their fake enthusiasm for the boring task, the participants were asked to rate their own liking for it. Ironically, those who were paid *less* rated the task as actually more interesting than their better-paid colleagues reported. Similarly, being compelled by the law to recycle can lead to people's supporting recycling as opposed to throwing out all trash and garbage in a bundle.

Learning theorists might predict that the more we are reinforced for doing something (given more money, for example), the more we should like it (not find the task quite as boring, that is). But that is not what happened here. Cognitive-dissonance theorists rightly predicted that because the ideas (cognitions) of (a) "I was paid very little" and (b) "I told someone that this assignment was interesting" are dissonant, people will tend to engage in

cognitive-dissonance theory the view that we are motivated to make our cognitions or beliefs consistent with each other and with our behavior

attitude-discrepant behavior behavior inconsistent with an attitude that may have the effect of modifying an attitude

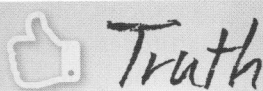

It is true that we tend to appreciate things more when we have to work for them. This is an example of effort justification.

effort justification. The discomfort of cognitive dissonance motivates people to explain their behavior to themselves in such a way that unpleasant undertakings seem worth it (Stone & Fernandez, 2008). Participants who were paid only $1 may have justified their lie by concluding that they may not have been lying in the first place.

14-2 PREJUDICE AND DISCRIMINATION

Prejudice is an attitude toward a group that leads people to evaluate members of that group negatively—even though they have never met them. On a cognitive level, prejudice is linked to expectations that members of the target group will behave poorly, say, in the workplace, or engage in criminal behavior or terrorism. On an emotional level, prejudice is associated with negative feelings such as fear, dislike, or hatred. Prejudice is the most troubling kind of attitude.

In behavioral terms, prejudice is connected with avoidance, aggression, and discrimination. **Discrimination** refers to behavior that results from prejudice. Many groups in the United States have experienced discrimination—women, gays and lesbians, older people, and ethnic groups such as African Americans, Asian Americans, Latin Americans, Irish Americans, Jewish Americans,

effort justification in cognitive-dissonance theory, the tendency to seek justification (acceptable reasons) for strenuous efforts

prejudice an attitude toward a group that leads people to evaluate members of that group negatively

discrimination hostile behavior directed against groups toward whom one is prejudiced

stereotyping erroneous assumptions that all members of a group share the same traits or characteristics

and Native Americans. Discrimination takes many forms, including denial of access to jobs, the voting booth, and housing.

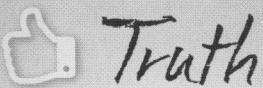

It is true that people have condemned billions of other people without ever meeting them or learning their names. Such condemnation occurs because of prejudice against groups of people. Prejudice is connected with the genocide of millions.

14-2a STEREOTYPING

Prejudice involves **stereotyping**—that is, erroneous assumptions that all members of a group share the same traits or characteristics. Have people you know characterized African Americans as superstitious and musical? What about gays and lesbians? Are they unfit for military service? Stereotypes may lead people to view members of groups in a biased fashion.

On the other hand, some stereotypes are positive, such as stereotypes about physically attractive people. By and large, we assume that "good things come in pretty packages." Attractive children and adults are judged and treated more positively than their unattractive peers (Rennels & Langlois, 2014). We expect attractive people to be poised, sociable, popular, intelligent, mentally healthy, fulfilled, persuasive, and successful in their jobs and marriages (Principe & Langlois, 2011). Attractive people are also more likely to be judged innocent of crimes in mock jury experiments, and when they are found guilty, they are given less severe sentences (Goodman-Delahunty & Sporer, 2010).

14-2b SOURCES OF PREJUDICE

The sources of prejudice are many and varied (Durlez, 2011; Stangor & Crandall, 2013):

1. *Dissimilarity.* We are apt to like people who share our attitudes. People of different religions and races often have different backgrounds, however, giving

Peter Kramer/NBC/NBC NewsWire/Getty Images

Amanda Knox Appearing on NBC's *Today* Show. In 2009 Knox was convicted in an Italian court of killing her roommate. Her conviction was overturned in 2011, but then, in 2014, she was found guilty again. Because of her beauty, many observers find it difficult to believe that Knox is actually guilty. Why, one might think, would someone this beautiful have to resort to crime to achieve her ends?

rise to dissimilar attitudes. Even when people of different races share important values, people may assume that they do not.

2. *Social conflict.* There is often social and economic conflict between people of different races and religions.

3. *Social learning.* Children acquire some attitudes from other people, especially their parents. Children tend to imitate their parents, and parents reinforce their children for doing so. In this way prejudices can be transmitted from generation to generation.

4. *Information processing.* Prejudices act as cognitive filters through which we view the social world. We tend to think of people as "familiar" or "foreign," or "good" or "bad." Our feelings and reactions toward others may be biased by these perceptions.

5. *Social categorization.* We also tend to divide our social world into "us" and "them." People usually view those who belong to their own groups—the "in-group"—more favorably than those who do not—the "out-group." Isolation from the out-group makes it easier to maintain our stereotypes.

ATTRACTION AND LOVE

Attitudes of liking and loving can lead to important, lasting relationships. They are the flip side of the coin of prejudice—positive attitudes that are associated with interpersonal **attraction** rather than avoidance. Among the factors contributing to attraction are physical appearance, similarity, and reciprocity.

14-3a PHYSICAL APPEARANCE

Physical appearance is a key factor in attraction and in the consideration of romantic partners (Sprecher et al., 2008). What determines physical allure? Are our standards subjective—that is, "in the eye of the beholder"? Or is there general agreement on what is appealing?

Many standards for beauty appear to be cross-cultural (Buss, 2009; Singh & Singh, 2011). For example, a study of people in England and Japan found that both British and Japanese men consider women with large eyes, high cheekbones, and narrow jaws to be

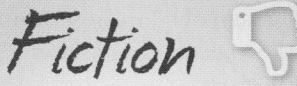

T	**F**	Beauty is in the eye of the beholder.

It turns out not to be true that standards for beauty are so flexible that they are fully "in the eye of the beholder." There are some cross-cultural commonalities in standards for attractiveness.

most attractive (Perrett, 1994). In his research, Perrett created computer composites of the faces of 60 women and, as shown in part A of Figure 14.1, of the 15 women who were rated the most attractive. He then used computer enhancement to exaggerate the differences between the composite of the 60 and the composite of the 15 most attractive women. He arrived at the image

attraction in social psychology, an attitude of liking or disliking (negative attraction)

FIG.14.1 WHAT FEATURES CONTRIBUTE TO FACIAL ATTRACTIVENESS?

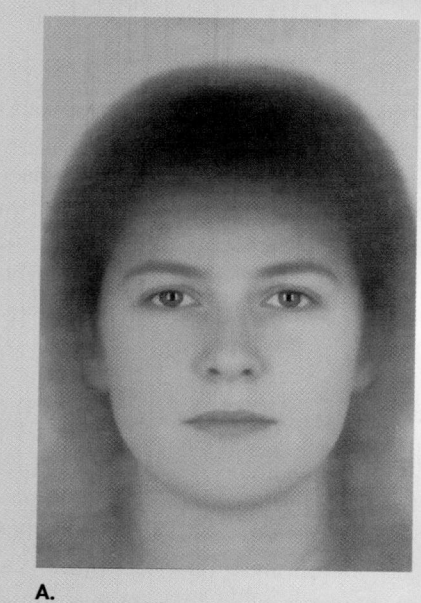
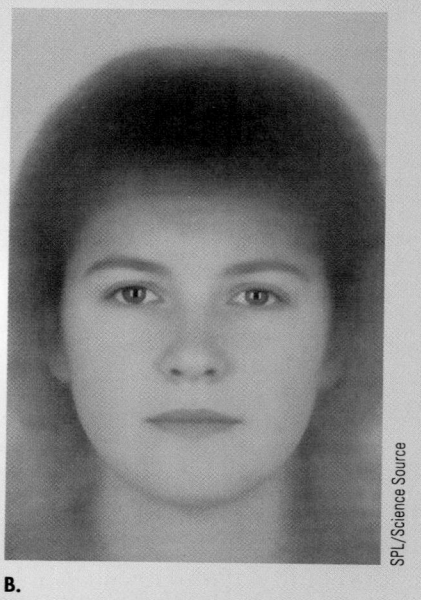

A.

B.

SPL/Science Source

In both England and Japan, features such as large eyes, high cheekbones, and narrow jaws contribute to perceptions of the attractiveness of women. Part A shows a composite of the faces of 15 women rated as the most attractive of a group of 60. Part B is a composite in which the features of these 15 women are exaggerated—that is, developed further in the direction that separates them from the average of the entire 60.

shown in part B of Figure 14.1. Part B, which shows higher cheekbones and a narrower jaw than part A, was rated as the most attractive image. Similar results were found for the image of a Japanese woman. Works of art suggest that the ancient Greeks and Egyptians favored similar facial features.

An examination of the Internet dating profiles of 5,810 Yahoo personal ads shows that "thin" is more "in" in the expressed preferences for partners of European Americans and males (Glasser et al., 2009). European American males are more likely than African and Latin American males to want to date slender and buff women. African and Latin American men are significantly more likely to be interested in women with large or thick bodies.

14-3b GENDER DIFFERENCES IN SELECTION OF A ROMANTIC PARTNER

Physical appearance may be a major factor in the selection of a romantic partner, but cross-cultural studies on mate selection find that women tend to place greater emphasis on traits such as professional status, consideration, dependability, kindness, and fondness for children. Men tend to place relatively greater emphasis

on physical allure, cooking ability, even thrift (Buss & Schmitt, 2011). U.S. women are more willing than U.S. men to marry someone who is not good-looking, but less willing to marry someone who does not hold a steady job (Sprecher & Felmlee, 2008).

Why do males tend to place relatively more emphasis than females on physical appearance in mate selection? Why do females tend to place relatively more emphasis on personal factors such as financial status and reliability? Evolutionary psychologists believe that evolutionary forces favor the survival of women who desire status in their mates and men who emphasize physical allure because these preferences provide reproductive advantages. According to the "parental investment model," a woman's appeal is more strongly connected with her age and health, both of which are markers of reproductive capacity. The value of men as reproducers, however, is more intertwined with factors that contribute to a stable environment for child rearing—such as social standing and reliability (Schmitt et al., 2012).

14-3c THE ATTRACTION–SIMILARITY HYPOTHESIS

The *attraction–similarity hypothesis* holds that people tend to develop romantic relationships with people who are similar to themselves in physical attractiveness and other traits. Apparently, opposites do *not* attract. Researchers have found that our marital and sex partners tend to be similar to us in race and ethnicity, age, level of education, and religion (Montoya & Horton, 2013). Nearly 95% of marriages and 80% to 90% of cohabiting unions were between partners of the same race at the time of the 2010 U.S. census (U.S. Census Bureau, 2011). Highly educated people are more likely than poorly educated people to marry people of other races (Qian et al., 2012).

When It Comes To Sex, Red May Mean "Go"

When you go to buy a box of Valentine's Day candy, what color will the box be? Green? Blue? The answer, of course, is red. What is the most popular color of women's lipstick? Yellow? Brown? Again, the answer is red (Elliot et al., 2013). Red has been the most popular lipstick color since the construction of the pyramids in ancient Egypt (Elliot & Niesta, 2008). At a traffic light, the color red means stop. But when it comes to sexual attraction, the color red is more likely to mean go.

Why is the color red associated with feelings of attraction? The link between red and physical attraction may be rooted in our biological heritage. Many female primates, including baboons, chimpanzees, gorillas, and rhesus monkeys, show reddened genital regions when they are nearing ovulation—the time of the month when they are fertile (Barelli et al., 2008). Reddening of the skin is caused by elevated estrogen levels, which increase the blood flow under the skin. Male primates are more likely to attempt sexual relations with females who display red (Waitt et al., 2006). Women's estrogen levels are also elevated near ovulation, slightly reddening the skin (Lynn et al., 2007). For men, as with other male primates, the reddening of a woman's skin at the time of ovulation may be a sexual signal. And women are more likely to choose to wear the color red when they wish to appear to be more sexually attractive (Elliot et al., 2013).

Experiments find that men rate the same woman as more attractive when her photograph is shown against a red background as opposed to other colors (Elliot & Niesta, 2008). Women also rate photos of men as more attractive when the photos are bordered in red or the men are wearing red clothing (Eliot et al., 2010). The male sex hormone testosterone is involved in oxygenating blood and increasing its flow to the skin—giving off a reddish hue—and to the genitals, leading to sexual excitement. Red coloration can signal good health in men because high blood levels of oxygen are maintained only by organisms in good health (Elliot et al., 2010).

Fancy Photography/Veer

Why Did They Deck Her Out in Red? Cultural conditioning and the human biological heritage provide two good answers.

Fiction 👎

| T | **F** | Opposites attract. |

Actually, it is not true that "opposites attract." People who share attitudes are more likely to be attracted to one another.

Another reason people tend to have partners from the same background is *propinquity*. Marriages are made in the neighborhood and not in heaven (Sprecher & Felmlee, 2008). We tend to live among people who are similar to us in background, and we therefore come into contact with them more often.

Reciprocity is another powerful determinant of attraction (Fehr, 2008). We tend to be more open, warm, and helpful when we are interacting with people who seem to like us (Sprecher et al., 2008).

FIG.14.2　THE TRIANGULAR MODEL OF LOVE

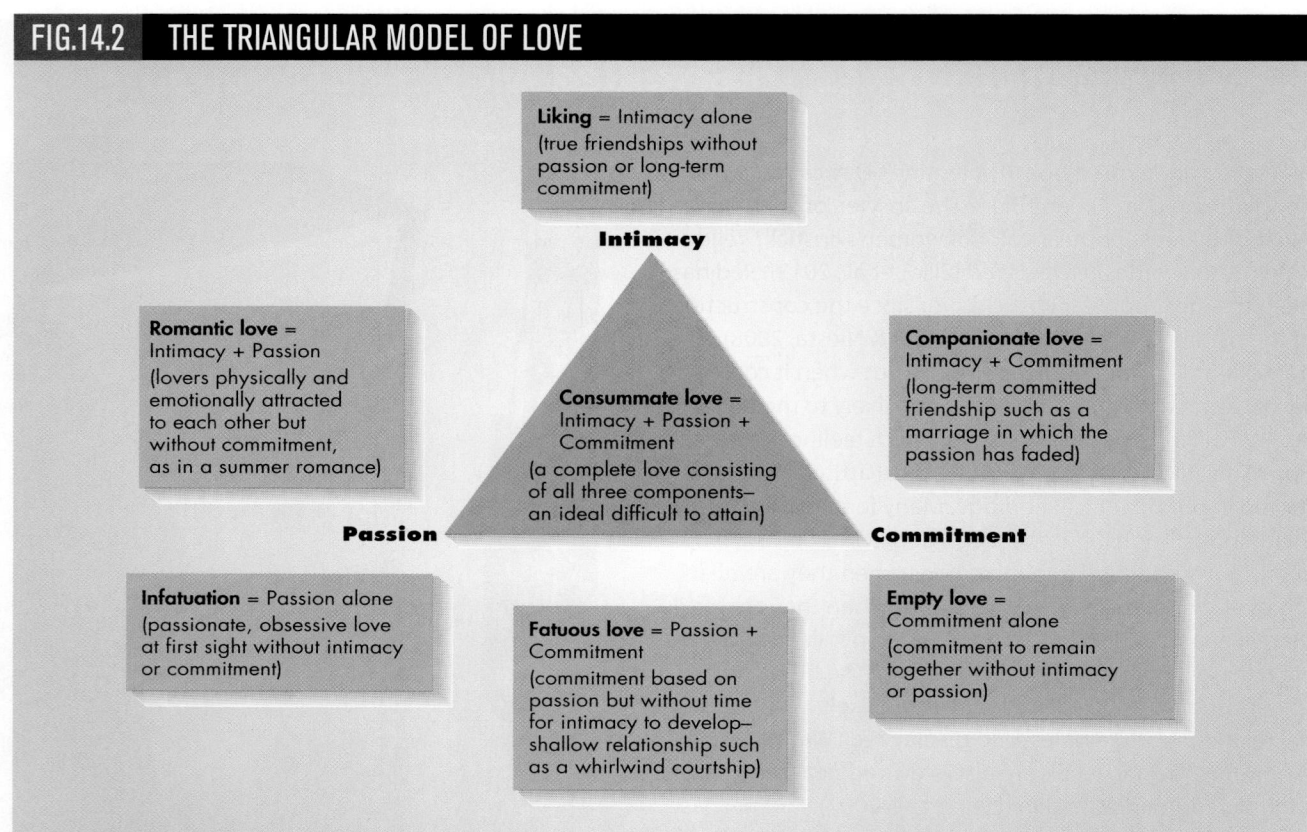

According to this model, love has three components: intimacy, passion, and commitment. The ideal of consummate love consists of romantic love plus commitment.

Source: From *The Psychology of Love* by R. J. Sternberg. Copyright 1988. Yale University Press. Reprinted by permission of the publisher.

---

triangular model of love
Sternberg's view that love involves combinations of three components: intimacy, passion, and commitment

intimacy　close acquaintance and familiarity; a characteristic of a relationship in which partners share their innermost feelings

passion　strong romantic and sexual feelings

commitment　the decision to maintain a relationship

consummate love　the ideal form of love within Sternberg's model, which combines passion, intimacy, and commitment

romantic love　an intense, positive emotion that involves sexual attraction, feelings of caring, and the belief that one is in love

14-3d LOVE

Love is a strong positive emotion. We had a look at love between children and parents in Chapter 9. Here we will focus on that most dramatic, heated, passionate love we label *romantic love.*

There are a number of theories about romantic love. One theory is Robert Sternberg's (1988, 2013) **triangular model of love**, which can be thought of as a love triangle. This love triangle does not refer to two men wooing the same woman. It refers to Sternberg's view that love involves three components: intimacy, passion, and commitment (see Figure 14.2).

Intimacy refers to a couple's closeness, to their mutual concern and sharing of feelings and resources. **Passion** means romance and sexual feelings. **Commitment** means deciding to enhance and maintain the relationship. Passion is most crucial in short-term relationships. Intimacy and commitment are more important in enduring relationships. The ideal form of love—**consummate love**—combines all three. Consummate love is made up of romantic love plus commitment.

Romantic love, in Sternberg's scheme, is characterized by passion and intimacy. Passion involves fascination (preoccupation with the loved one), sexual craving, and the desire for exclusiveness (Berscheid, 2009). Intimacy involves closeness and caring—championing the interests of the loved one, even if it entails sacrificing one's own. People are cognitively biased toward evaluating their partners positively (Acevedo et al., 2012). That is, we idealize those we love.

14-4 SOCIAL PERCEPTION

An important area of social psychology concerns the ways in which we perceive other people—for example, the importance of the first impressions they make on us. Next we explore some factors that contribute to **social perception**: the primacy and recency effects and attribution theory.

14-4a PRIMACY AND RECENCY EFFECTS

Why do you wear a suit to a job interview? Why do defense attorneys make sure that their clients dress neatly and get their hair cut before they are seen by the jury? Do first impressions really matter? Apparently they do—a great deal.

Whether we are talking about the business or social worlds, or even the relationship between a therapist and a client, first impressions are important (Bidell et al., 2002). First impressions are an example of the **primacy effect**—the tendency to evaluate others in terms of first impressions.

Participants in a classic experiment on the primacy effect read different stories about "Jim" (Luchins, 1957). The stories consisted of one or two paragraphs. The one-paragraph stories portrayed Jim as either friendly or unfriendly. These paragraphs were also used in the two-paragraph stories, but in this case the paragraphs were read in the reverse order. Of those reading only the "friendly" paragraph, 95% rated Jim as friendly. Of those who read just the "unfriendly" paragraph, 3% rated him as friendly. Seventy-eight percent of those who read two-paragraph stories in the "friendly-unfriendly" order labeled Jim as friendly. When participants read the paragraphs in the reverse order, only 18% rated Jim as friendly.

How can we encourage people to pay more attention to impressions occurring after the first encounter? Abraham Luchins accomplished this by allowing time to pass between the presentations of the two paragraphs. In this way, fading memories allowed more recent information to take precedence. The tendency to respond to the most freshly presented piece of information is known as the **recency effect**. Luchins also found a second way to counter first impressions: He simply asked participants to avoid making snap judgments and to weigh all the evidence.

14-4b ATTRIBUTION THEORY

An **attribution** is an assumption or belief about why people behave in a certain way. When you assume that one child is mistreating another child because she is "mean," you are making an attribution. This section focuses on *attribution theory*, or the processes by which people draw conclusions about the factors that influence one another's behavior. Attribution theory is important because attributions lead us to perceive others either as purposeful actors or as victims of circumstances.

DISPOSITIONAL AND SITUATIONAL ATTRIBUTIONS Social psychologists describe two types of attributions. **Dispositional attributions** ascribe a person's behavior to internal factors such as personality traits and free will. If you assume that one child is mistreating another because she is "mean," you are making a dispositional attribution. **Situational attributions** attribute a person's actions to external factors such as circumstances, social influence, or socialization. If you assume that one child is mistreating the other because her parents have given her certain attitudes toward the other child, you are making a situational attribution.

THE FUNDAMENTAL ATTRIBUTION ERROR In cultures that view the self as independent, such as ours, people tend to make dispositional attributions: they tend to attribute other people's behavior primarily to internal factors such as personality, attitudes, and free will (Reeder, 2013; Uleman et al., 2012). This bias in the attribution process is known as the **fundamental attribution error**. For example, if a teenager gets into trouble with the law, individualistic societies are more likely to blame the teenager than the social environment in which the teenager lives.

One reason for the fundamental attribution error is that we tend to infer traits from behavior. But in collectivist cultures that stress interdependence, such as Asian cultures, people are more likely to attribute another person's behavior to that person's

social perception a subfield of social psychology that studies the ways in which we form and modify impressions of others

primacy effect the tendency to evaluate others in terms of first impressions

recency effect the tendency to evaluate others in terms of the most recent impression

attribution a belief concerning why people behave in a certain way

dispositional attribution an assumption that a person's behavior is determined by internal causes such as personal traits

situational attribution an assumption that a person's behavior is determined by external circumstances such as the social pressure found in a situation

fundamental attribution error the assumption that others act predominantly on the basis of their dispositions, even when there is evidence suggesting the importance of their situations

actor–observer effect the tendency to attribute our own behavior to situational factors but to attribute the behavior of others to dispositional factors

self-serving bias the tendency to view one's successes as stemming from internal factors and one's failures as stemming from external factors

social roles and obligations (Basic Behavioral Science Task Force, 1996). For example, Japanese people might be more likely to attribute a businessperson's extreme competitiveness to the "culture of business" rather than to his or her personality.

THE ACTOR–OBSERVER EFFECT We noted that we are biased toward making dispositional attributions when we are explaining other people's behavior. When we see other people doing things that we do not like, we tend to judge them as willful actors (Baron et al., 2009). But when we find ourselves doing things that we ordinarily disapprove of, we tend to see ourselves as victims of circumstances (Baron et al., 2009). The combination of the tendency to attribute other people's behavior to dispositional factors and our own behavior to situational influences is called the **actor–observer effect**.

Consider an example. Parents and children often argue about the children's choice of friends or dates. When they do, the parents tend to infer traits from behavior and to see the children as stubborn and resistant. The children also infer traits from behavior. Thus, they may see their parents as bossy and controlling. Parents and children alike attribute the others' behavior to internal causes. That is, both make dispositional attributions about other people's behavior.

How do the parents and teenagers perceive themselves? The parents probably see themselves as being forced into combat by their children's foolishness. If they become insistent, it is in response to the teens' stubbornness. The teenagers probably see themselves as responding to peer pressures. Both parents and children make situational attributions for their own behavior.

THE SELF-SERVING BIAS There is also a **self-serving bias** in the attribution process. We are likely to ascribe our successes to internal, dispositional factors but our failures to external, situational influences

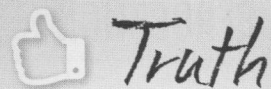
(Kestemont et al., 2014; Smith & Weber, 2005). A study of 27 college wrestlers found that they tended to attribute their wins to stable and internal conditions such as their abilities, but their losses to unstable and external conditions such as an error by a referee (De Michele et al., 1998). Sports fans fall into the same trap. They tend to attribute their team's victories to internal conditions and their losses to external conditions (Rees et al., 2005; Wallace & Hinsz, 2009).

Another interesting attribution bias is a gender difference in attributions for friendly behavior. Men are more likely than women to interpret a woman's smile or friendliness toward a man as flirting (Frisby et al., 2010).

The Actor–Observer Effect Who is at fault here? People tend to make dispositional attributions for other people's behavior, but they tend to see their own behavior as motivated by situational factors. People are aware of the external forces acting on themselves, but they tend to attribute other people's behavior to choice and will.

Blend Images Photography/Veer

14-5 SOCIAL INFLUENCE

Other people and groups can exert enormous pressure on us to behave according to their norms. **Social influence** is the area of social psychology that studies the ways in which people alter the thoughts, feelings, and behavior of others (Nolan et al., 2008). Let's examine a couple of classic experiments that demonstrate how people influence others to engage in destructive obedience or conform to social norms.

14-5a OBEDIENCE TO AUTHORITY

Throughout history, soldiers have followed orders—even when it comes to slaughtering innocent civilians. The Turkish slaughter of Armenians, the Nazi slaughter of Jews, the mutual slaughter of Hutus and Tutsis in Rwanda—these are all examples of the tragedies that can arise from simply following orders. We may say we are horrified by such crimes, and we cannot imagine why people engage in them. But how many of us would refuse to follow orders issued by authority figures?

> **social influence** the area of social psychology that studies the ways in which people influence the thoughts, feelings, and behavior of others

THE MILGRAM STUDIES Yale University psychologist Stanley Milgram also wondered how many people would resist immoral requests made by authority figures. To find out, he undertook a series of classic experiments at the university that have become known as the Milgram studies on obedience.

In an early phase of his work, Milgram (1963) placed ads in local newspapers for people who would be willing to participate in studies on learning and memory. He enlisted 40 people ranging in age from 20 to 50—teachers, engineers, laborers, salespeople, people who had not completed elementary school, and people with graduate degrees.

Let's suppose that you have answered the ad. You show up at the university in exchange for a reasonable fee ($4.50, which in the early 1960s might easily fill your gas tank) and to satisfy your own curiosity. You might be impressed. After all, Yale is a venerable institution that dominates the city. You are no less impressed by the elegant labs, where you meet a distinguished behavioral scientist dressed in a white coat and another person who

---

✳ Suicide Terrorists: Evil? Ordinary? Both?

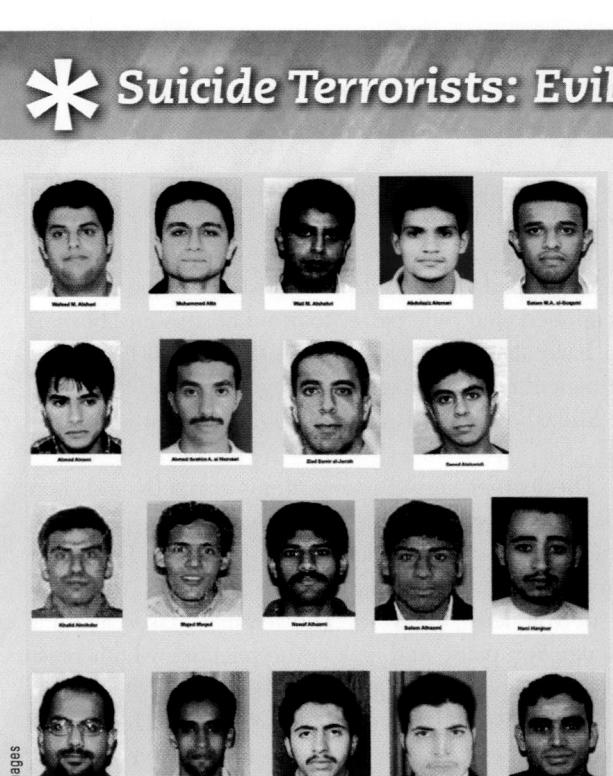

Getty Images

The Nineteen Terrorists Who Participated in the Suicide Attacks of September 11, 2001.

Why did these men fly into the World Trade Center and the Pentagon? Was it a matter of personality and personal choice? Was it a web of situational factors? Were they evil? Social psychologists who have studied the nature of evil find that many—perhaps most—perpetrators of evil are "ordinary people" (Baumeister, 1996; Berkowitz, 2004b). How can this be true? When we seek to "profile" someone, we might be making a fundamental attribution error—that is, we attribute too much of other people's behavior to internal factors such as attitude and choice (Gilovich & Eibach, 2001; Reeder, 2013). Indeed, in 2003, the Consortium of Social Science Associations (COSSA) testified to Congress that they had to conclude there was no clear profile of the suicide terrorist.

Can you also apply the social psychology concepts of polarization, groupthink, and diffusion of responsibility in the explanation of suicide terrorism?

FIG.14.3 THE EXPERIMENTAL SETUP IN THE MILGRAM STUDIES

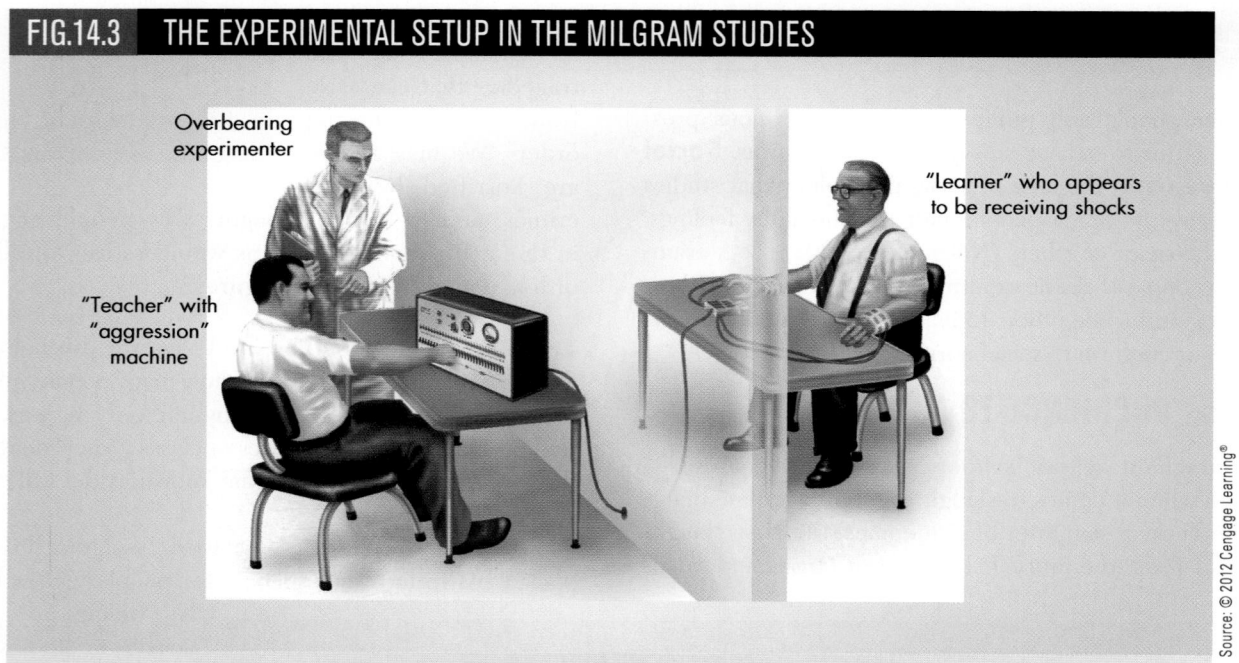

Overbearing experimenter

"Learner" who appears to be receiving shocks

"Teacher" with "aggression" machine

Source: © 2012 Cengage Learning®

When the "learner" makes an error, the experimenter prods the "teacher" to deliver a painful electric shock.

has responded to the ad. The scientist explains that the purpose of the experiment is to study the *effects of punishment on learning*. The experiment requires a "teacher" and a "learner." By chance, you are appointed the teacher and the other recruit, the learner.

You, the scientist, and the learner enter a laboratory room containing a threatening chair with dangling straps. The scientist straps the learner in. The learner expresses some concern, but this is, after all, for the sake of science. And this is Yale, isn't it? What could happen to a person at Yale?

You follow the scientist to an adjacent room, from which you are to do your "teaching." This teaching promises to have an impact. You are to punish the learner's errors by pressing levers marked from 15 to 450 volts on a fearsome-looking console. Labels describe 28 of the 30 levers as running the gamut from "Slight Shock" to "Danger: Severe Shock." The last two levers are simply labeled "XXX." Just in case you have no idea what electric shock feels like, the scientist gives you a sample 45-volt shock. It stings. You pity the person who might receive more.

Your learner is expected to learn pairs of words, which are to be read from a list. After hearing the list once, the learner is to produce the word that pairs with the stimulus word from a list of four alternatives. This is done by pressing a switch that lights one of four panels in your room. If it is the correct panel, you proceed to the next stimulus word. If not, you are to deliver an electric

shock. With each error, you are to increase the voltage of the shock (see Figure 14.3).

You probably have some misgivings. Electrodes have been strapped to the learner's wrists, and the scientist has applied electrode paste "to avoid blisters and burns." You have also been told that the shocks will cause "no permanent tissue damage," although they might be painful. Still, the learner is going along. And after all, this is Yale.

The learner answers some items correctly and then makes some errors. With mild concern you press the levers up through 45 volts. You've tolerated that much yourself. Then a few more mistakes are made. You press the 60-volt lever, then 75. The learner makes another mistake. You pause and look at the scientist, who is reassuring: "Although the shocks may be painful, there is no permanent tissue damage, so please go on." The learner makes more errors, and soon you are up to a shock of 300 volts. But now the learner is pounding on the other side of the wall! Your chest tightens, and you begin to perspire. "Damn science and the $4.50!" you think. You hesitate and the scientist says, "The experiment requires that you continue." After the delivery of the next stimulus word, the learner chooses no answer at all. What are you to do? "Wait for 5 to 10 seconds," the scientist instructs, "and then treat no answer as a wrong answer." But after the next shock the pounding on the wall resumes! Now your heart is racing, and you are convinced you are causing extreme pain and discomfort. Is it possible that no lasting damage is being done? Is the experiment that important, after all? What to do? You hesitate again, and the scientist says, "It is absolutely essential that you continue." His voice is very convincing. "You have no other choice," he says, "you *must* go on." You can barely think straight, and for some unaccountable reason you feel laughter rising in your throat. Your finger shakes above the lever. *What are you to do?*

Milgram had foreseen that some "teachers" in his experiment would hesitate. He had therefore conceived standardized statements that his assistants would use when participants balked—for example: "Although the shocks may be painful, there is no permanent tissue damage, so please go on." "The experiment requires that you continue." "It is absolutely essential that you continue." "You have no other choice: you *must* go on."

To repeat: If you are a teacher in the Milgram study, what do you do? Milgram (1963, 1974) found out what most people in his sample would do. The sample was a cross-section of the male population of New Haven. Of the 40 men in this phase of his research, only 5 refused to go beyond the 300-volt level, the level at which the learner first pounded the wall. Nine other "teachers" defied the scientist within the 300-volt range. But 65% of the participants complied with the scientist throughout the series, believing they were delivering 450-volt, XXX-rated shocks.

Were these participants unfeeling? Not at all. Milgram was impressed by their signs of stress. They trembled, they stuttered, they bit their lips. They groaned, they sweated, they dug their fingernails into their flesh. Some had fits of laughter, although laughter was inappropriate. One salesperson's laughter was so convulsive that he could not continue with the experiment.

Milgram's initial research on obedience was limited to a sample of New Haven men. Could he generalize his findings to other men or to women? Would college students, who are considered to be independent thinkers, show more defiance? A replication of Milgram's study with a sample of Yale men yielded similar results. What about women, who are supposedly less aggressive than men? In subsequent research, women, too, administered shocks to the learners. All this took place in a nation that values independence and free will.

ON DECEPTION AND TRUTH I have said that the "teachers" in the Milgram studies *believed* that they were shocking other people when they pressed the levers on the console. They weren't. The only real shock in this experiment was the 45-volt sample given to the teachers. Its purpose was to make the procedure believable.

The learners in the experiment were actually *confederates* of the experimenter. They had not answered

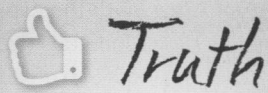

Truth

| T | F | Most people will torture an innocent person if they are ordered to do so. |

It appears to be true that most people will torture an innocent person, just because they are ordered to do so.

the newspaper ads but were in on the truth from the start. The "teachers" were the only real participants. They were led to believe they had been chosen at random for the teacher role, but the choice was rigged so that newspaper recruits would always become teachers.

Milgram debriefed his participants after the experiment was complete. He explained the purpose and methods of his research in detail. He emphasized the fact that they had not actually harmed anyone. But of course the participants did believe that they were hurting other people as the experiment was being carried out. As you can imagine, the ethics of the Milgram studies have been debated by psychologists for decades. College and university review committees might prevent similar experiments from being conducted today.

WHY DID PEOPLE IN THE MILGRAM STUDIES OBEY THE EXPERIMENTERS? Many people obey the commands of others even when they are required to perform immoral tasks. But *why?* Why did Germans "just follow orders" during the Holocaust? Why did "teachers" obey the experimenter in Milgram's study? We do not have all the answers, but we can offer a number of hypotheses:

1. *Socialization.* Despite the expressed American ideal of independence, we are socialized from early childhood to obey authority figures such as parents and teachers (Blass, 2009; Perlstadt, 2013).

2. *Lack of social comparison.* In Milgram's experimental settings, experimenters displayed command of the situation, but "teachers" (participants) did not have the opportunity to compare their ideas and feelings with those of other people in the same situation.

3. *Perception of legitimate authority.* An experimenter at Yale might have appeared to be a highly legitimate authority figure—as might a government official or a high-ranking officer in the military (Blass, 2009). The percentage of individuals who complied

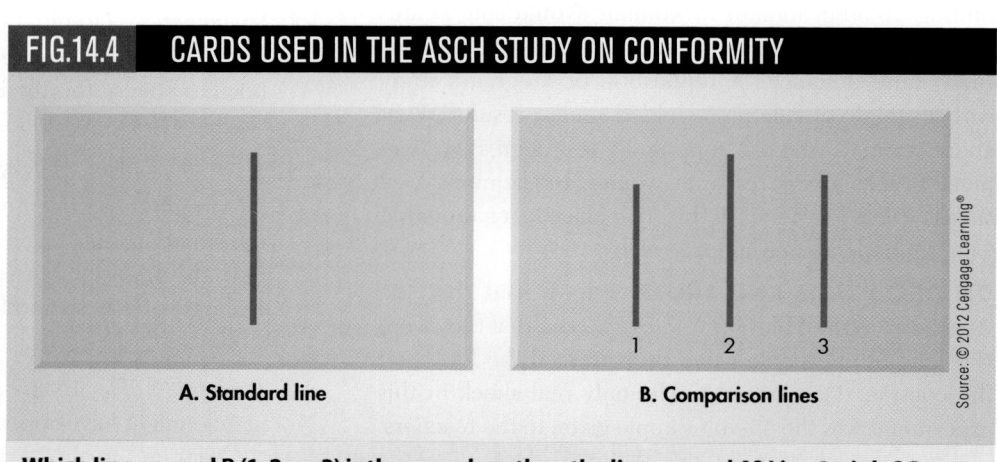

foot-in-the-door technique
a method for inducing compliance in which a small request is followed by a larger request

with the experimenter's demands dropped from 65% to 48% when Milgram (1974) replicated the study in a dingy storefront in a nearby town.

Even in that setting, many people are willing to engage in morally reprehensible acts at the behest of a legitimate-looking authority figure. Hitler and his henchmen were authority figures in Nazi Germany. "Science" and Yale University legitimized the authority of the experimenters in the Milgram studies.

4. *The foot-in-the-door technique.* The **foot-in-the-door technique** might also have contributed to the obedience of the teachers (Burger, 2009). Once they had begun to deliver shocks to learners, they might have found it progressively more difficult to extricate themselves from the situation.

5. *Inaccessibility of values.* People are more likely to act in accordance with their attitudes when their attitudes are readily available, or accessible. Most people believe it is wrong to harm innocent people, but strong emotions impair clear thinking. As the teachers in the Milgram experiments became more emotionally involved, their attitudes might thus have become less "accessible."

6. *Buffers between the perpetrator and the victim.* Several buffers decreased the effect of the learners' pain on the teachers. For example, the "learners" were in another room. When they were in the same room with the teachers, their compliance rate dropped from 65% to 40%. Moreover, when the teacher held the learner's hand on the shock plate, the compliance rate dropped to 30%.

14-5b CONFORMITY

We are said to *conform* when we change our behavior to adhere to *social norms*. Social norms are widely accepted expectations concerning social behavior.

Explicit social norms are often made into rules and laws such as those that require us to whisper in libraries and to slow down when driving past a school. There are also unspoken or implicit social norms, such as those that cause us to face the front in an elevator or to be "fashionably late" for social gatherings. Can you think of some instances in which you have conformed to social pressure?

The tendency to conform to social norms is often good. Many norms have evolved because they promote comfort and survival. Group pressure can also promote maladaptive behavior, as when people engage in risky behavior because "everyone is doing it." Why do so many people tend to follow the crowd? To answer this question, let us look at a classic experiment on conformity conducted by Solomon Asch in the early 1950s.

THE ASCH STUDY Can you believe what you see with your own eyes? Seeing is believing, isn't it? Not if you were a participant in Asch's (1952) study.

Let's say you entered a laboratory room with seven other subjects, supposedly taking part in an experiment on visual discrimination. At the front of the room stood a man holding cards with lines drawn on them.

The eight of you were seated in a series. You were given the seventh seat, a minor fact at the time. The man explained the task. There was a single line on the card on the left. Three lines were drawn on the card at the right (see Figure 14.4). One line on the right card was the same length as the line on the left card. You and the other participants were to call out, one at a time, which of the three lines—1, 2, or 3—was the same length as the one on the card on the left. Simple.

The participants to your right spoke out in order: "3," "3," "3," "3," "3," "3." Now it was your turn. Line 3

FIG.14.4   CARDS USED IN THE ASCH STUDY ON CONFORMITY

A. Standard line   B. Comparison lines

Source: © 2012 Cengage Learning®

Which line on card B (1, 2, or 3) is the same length as the line on card A? Line 2, right? But would you say "2" if you were a member of a group and six people answering ahead of you all said "3"? Are you sure?

was clearly the same length as the line on the first card, so you said "3." The fellow after you then chimed in: "3." That's all there was to it. Then two other cards were set up at the front of the room. This time line 2 was clearly the same length as the line on the first card. The answers were "2," "2," "2," "2," "2," "2." Again it was your turn. You said "2," and perhaps your mind began to wander. Your stomach was gurgling a bit. The fellow after you said "2."

Another pair of cards was held up. Line 3 was clearly the correct answer. The people on your right spoke in turn: "1," "1 … " Wait a second! "… 1," "1." You forgot about dinner and studied the lines briefly. No, line 1 was too short by a good half-inch. But the next two participants said "1" and suddenly it was your turn. Your hands had become sweaty, and there was a lump in your throat. You wanted to say "3," but was it right? There was really no time, and you had already paused noticeably. You said "1," and so did the last fellow.

Now your attention was riveted on the task. Much of the time you agreed with the other judges, but sometimes you did not. And for some reason beyond your understanding, they were in perfect agreement even when they were wrong—assuming you could trust your eyes. The experiment was becoming an uncomfortable experience, and you began to doubt your judgment.

The discomfort in the Asch study was caused by the pressure to conform. Actually, the other seven recruits were confederates of the experimenter. They prearranged a number of incorrect responses. The sole purpose of the study was to see whether you would conform to the erroneous group judgments.

How many people in Asch's study caved in? How many went along with the crowd rather than give what they thought to be the right answer? Seventy-five percent. *Three out of four agreed with the majority's wrong answer at least once.*

Fiction 👎

T **F** Seeing is believing.

It is not true that seeing is always believing—especially when the group sees things differently. When we are "all alone," we may begin to wonder about our own judgment.

14-5c FACTORS THAT INFLUENCE CONFORMITY

Several factors increase the tendency to conform, including belonging to a collectivist rather than an individualistic society (Fukushima et al., 2009), the desire to be liked by other members of the group (but valuing being right over being liked *decreases* the tendency to conform), low self-esteem, social shyness (Ecker & Buckner, 2014), and lack of familiarity with the task (Phalet & Schoenpflug, 2001; Santee & Maslach, 1982). Other factors in conformity include group size and social support. The likelihood of conformity, even to incorrect group judgments, increases rapidly as group size grows to five members; it then rises more slowly as the group grows to about eight members. At about that point, the maximum chance of conformity is reached. Yet finding just one other person who supports your minority opinion apparently is enough to encourage you to stick to your guns (Jetten & Hornsey, 2014; Mesoudi, 2009).

14-6 AGGRESSION

One could argue that humans are among the most aggressive species on Earth. There are armed conflicts of one kind or another on nearly every continent of the planet. There is murder, and there is battering, often directed at batterers' most intimate partners. There is rape. And we praise "controlled" aggression in football and hockey games. Psychologists ask why we are aggressive.

14-6a BIOLOGY, CHEMISTRY, AND AGGRESSION

Evolutionary psychologists believe that "genetic whisperings" influence aggression to some degree (Buss, 2009; Confer et al., 2010). Numerous biological structures and chemicals are involved in aggression. In response to certain stimuli, many nonhumans show instinctive aggressive reactions (Archer, 2009). This behavior is automatic. For example, the male robin responds aggressively to the red breast of another robin. The hypothalamus appears to be involved in this inborn reaction pattern. Electrical stimulation of part of the hypothalamus triggers stereotypical aggressive behaviors in many lower animals, including monkeys. However, in humans, whose brains are more complex, other brain structures apparently moderate possible aggressive instincts.

Chemistry is also involved in aggression, especially in the form of the male sex hormone testosterone.

Dennis Frates/Alamy

Social Facilitation Do we pedal faster when we are by ourselves or when we are members of a group?

Sigmund Freud, the originator of psychodynamic theory, believed that aggression is a natural and instinctive reaction to the frustrations of daily life. Children (and adults) seek to vent aggressive impulses on other people, including parents, because even the most attentive parents cannot gratify all of their demands immediately. Yet children also fear punishment and loss of love, so they repress most aggressive impulses and store them in the unconscious recesses of the mind.

Cognitive psychologists assert that our behavior is influenced by our values, by how we interpret situations, and by choice. People who believe that aggression is sometimes necessary and justified—as during wartime—are likely to act aggressively. People who believe that a particular war or act of aggression is unjust, or who oppose aggression under all circumstances, are less likely to behave aggressively (Hurka, 2010; Maxwell et al., 2009).

People also decide—sometimes making split-second decisions—whether they will lash out or not on the basis of their interpretation of the other person's motives. But many individuals who act aggressively distort other people's motives. For example, they assume that other people wish them harm when they actually do not (Dodge & Godwin, 2013). We are more likely to respond aggressively to a provocation when we magnify the importance of the "insult" or otherwise stir up feelings of anger (Ellis et al., 2009). How do you respond when someone bumps into you? If you view it as an intentional insult to your honor, you may respond with aggression.

From the behavioral perspective, learning is acquired through reinforcement. Organisms that are reinforced for aggressive behavior are more likely to behave aggressively in situations similar to those in which reinforcement occurs. Strong, agile organisms are likely to be reinforced for aggressive behavior.

Among nonhumans reinforcement is usually physical—for example, food, mating, or escaping a predator. Humans respond to such reinforcements but also to other reinforcers, such as social approval.

Testosterone appears to affect the tendencies to dominate and control other people. Men have higher testosterone levels than women do and are also (usually) more aggressive than women, especially with male strangers (Crofoot & Wrangham, 2010; Pradhan et al., 2010). Aggressive male adolescents and army veterans are likely to have higher testosterone levels than their less aggressive peers (Mazur & Booth, 2014; Popma et al., 2007). James Dabbs and his colleagues (1996) found that members of so-called rambunctious fraternities had higher testosterone levels, on average, than members of more "well-behaved" fraternities. Testosterone levels also vary with the occasion: men's testosterone levels tend to be higher when they are "winning"—whether in athletic competitions such as football or in the stock market (Apicella et al., 2014; Carré & Putnam, 2010).

14-6b PSYCHOLOGICAL ASPECTS OF AGGRESSION

Another reason that males are more likely than females to behave aggressively is that females are more likely to empathize with the victim—to put themselves in the victim's place (Proverbio et al., 2010; Yamasue et al., 2008). Empathy encourages helping behavior, not aggression.

Children are less likely to act aggressively when teachers and classmates communicate strong disapproval of aggressive behavior (Henry, 2008; Simon et al., 2009). From the social–cognitive perspective, aggressive skills are mainly acquired by observation of other people acting aggressively. However, social–cognitive theorists—like other cognitive theorists—believe that consciousness and choice play key roles in aggressive behavior among humans. Social–cognitive theorists believe that we are not likely to act aggressively unless we believe that aggression is appropriate under the circumstances and likely to be reinforced.

Situational factors also contribute to aggression. The Milgram studies showed us that the majority of "normal" people will act aggressively when they are influenced by other people to do so. In the section on group behavior, we will see that people may also act more aggressively when they are members of a mob.

14-7 GROUP BEHAVIOR

To be human is to belong to groups. Groups help us satisfy our needs for affection, attention, and belonging. They empower us to do things we could not manage by ourselves. But groups can also pressure us into doing things we might not do if we were acting alone. This section considers ways in which people behave differently as group members than they would as individuals. We begin with social facilitation.

14-7a SOCIAL FACILITATION

When you are given a group assignment, do you work harder or less hard than you would alone? Why? One effect of groups on individual behavior is **social facilitation**, the process by which a person's performance is increased when other members of a group engage in similar behavior. Research suggests that the presence of other people increases our levels of arousal, or motivation (Platania & Moran, 2001; Thomas et al., 2002). At high levels of arousal, our performance of simple tasks is facilitated. Our performance of complex responses may be impaired, however. For this reason, a well-rehearsed speech may be delivered masterfully before a larger audience, while an impromptu speech may be hampered by a large audience.

Social facilitation may be influenced by **evaluation apprehension** as well as arousal—that is, by concern that we are being evaluated (Park & Kitayama, 2014). When giving a speech, we may "lose our thread" if we are distracted by the audience and focus too much on its apparent reaction. If we believe that we have begun to flounder, evaluation apprehension may skyrocket. As a result, our performance may falter even more.

The presence of others can also impair performance—not when we are acting *before* a group but when we are anonymous members *of* a group. Workers, for example, may "goof off" or engage in *social loafing*—that is, failure to make a significant effort because others have made or are making such an effort—when they believe they will not be found out

social facilitation the process by which a person's performance is increased when other members of a group engage in similar behavior

evaluation apprehension concern that others are evaluating our behavior

Social Facilitation: How do juries make decisions? What kinds of "social decision schemes" do they use?

© bikeriderlondon/Shutterstock.com

and held accountable. Under these group conditions there is no evaluation apprehension, but rather there may be **diffusion of responsibility** in groups. Each person may feel less obligation to help because others are present, especially if the others are perceived as being capable of doing the job (Greitemeyer & Mugge, 2013; Maiden & Perry, 2010). Group members may also reduce their efforts if an apparently capable member makes no contribution but "rides free" on the efforts of others.

14-7b GROUP DECISION MAKING

Organizations use groups such as committees or juries to make decisions in the belief that group decisions are more accurate than individual decisions (Van Swol, 2008). Social psychologists have discovered a number of "rules," or **social decision schemes**, that govern much of group decision making (Stasser, 1999). Here are some examples:

1. *The majority-wins scheme.* In this commonly used scheme, the group arrives at the decision that was initially supported by the majority. This scheme appears to guide decision making most often when there is no single objectively correct decision. An example is a decision about which car models to build when their popularity has not been tested in the court of public opinion.

2. *The truth-wins scheme.* In this scheme, as more information is provided and opinions are discussed, the group comes to recognize that one approach is objectively correct. For example, a group deciding whether to use SAT scores in admitting students to college would profit from information about whether the scores predict college success.

3. *The two-thirds majority scheme.* Juries tend to convict defendants when two-thirds of the jury initially favors conviction.

4. *The first-shift rule.* In this scheme, the group tends to adopt the decision that reflects the first shift in opinion expressed by any group member. If a jury is deadlocked, the members may eventually follow the lead of the first juror to switch his or her position.

diffusion of responsibility the spreading or sharing of responsibility for a decision or behavior within a group

social decision schemes rules for predicting the final outcome of group decision making on the basis of the members' initial positions

groupthink a process in which group members are influenced by cohesiveness and a dynamic leader to ignore external realities as they make decisions

14-7c POLARIZATION AND THE "RISKY SHIFT"

We might assume that a group decision would be more conservative than an individual decision. After all, shouldn't there be an effort to compromise, to "split the difference"? We might also expect that a few mature individuals would be able to balance the opinions of daredevils.

Groups do not always appear to work as we might expect, however. Consider the *polarization* effect. As an individual, you might recommend that your company risk an investment of $500,000 to develop or market a new product. Other company executives, polled individually, might risk similar amounts. If you were gathered together to make a group decision, however, you would probably recommend either an amount well above this figure or nothing at all (Viscusi et al., 2011). This group effect is called *polarization*, or the taking of an extreme position. If you had to gamble on which way the decision would go, however, you would do better to place your money on movement toward the higher sum—that is, to bet on a *risky shift*. Why?

One possibility is that one member of the group may reveal information that the others were not aware of. This information may clearly point in one direction or the other. With doubts removed, the group moves decisively in the appropriate direction. It is also possible that social facilitation occurs in the group setting and that the resulting greater motivation prompts more extreme decisions.

Why, however, do groups tend to take *greater* risks than those their members would take as individuals? One answer is diffusion of responsibility (A. S. Brown, 2007; Viscusi et al., 2011). If the venture flops, the blame will not be placed on you alone.

14-7d GROUPTHINK

Groupthink, a concept originated by Irving Janis (1982), is a problem that may arise in group decision making when group members are swayed more by group cohesiveness and a dynamic leader than by the realities of the situation (Esser & Lindoerfer, 2006; Packer, 2009). Group problem solving may degenerate into groupthink when a group senses an external threat (Underhill, 2008). Groupthink is usually fueled by a dynamic group leader. The threat heightens the cohesiveness of the group and is a source of stress. Under stress, group members tend not to consider all their options carefully and frequently make flawed decisions.

Groupthink has been connected with historic fiascos such as the invasion of Iraq, the botched Bay of Pigs invasion of Cuba, the Watergate scandal in which members of the Nixon administration believed they could cover up a theft, and NASA's decision to launch the *Challenger* space shuttle despite engineers' warnings about the dangers created by unusually cold weather (Brownstein, 2003; Esser & Lindoerfer, 2006). Janis and other researchers (Tsintsadze-Maass & Maass, 2014) note characteristics of groupthink that contribute to flawed decisions:

1. *Feelings of invulnerability.* In the Watergate Affair, the decision-making group might have believed that it was beyond the reach of critics or the law because they were powerful people who were close to the president of the United States.

2. *The group's belief in its rightness.* Groups of terrorists apparently believe in the rightness of what they are doing. Although they are killing civilians and often committing suicide in the process, terrorists frequently believe that their actions are the only way to draw attention to their cause.

3. *Discrediting information contrary to the group's decision.* Members of terrorist groups often discredit arguments to the effect that their religions do not support the harm of innocent civilians.

4. *Pressures on group members to conform.* Striving for unanimity overrides the quest for realism, and authority can trump expertise. After the disastrous invasion of the Bay of Pigs in Cuba, President John F. Kennedy is reported to have said, "How could we have been so stupid?"

5. *Stereotyping members of the out-group.* In the cases of the invasions of the Bay of Pigs and Iraq, pro-invasion group members stereotyped members of the out-group as being out of touch with reality.

Groupthink can be averted if group leaders encourage members to remain skeptical about options and to feel free to ask probing questions and disagree with one another.

14-7e MOB BEHAVIOR AND DEINDIVIDUATION

Have you ever done something as a member of a group that you would not have done as an individual? What was it? What motivated you? How do you feel about it? The Frenchman Gustave Le Bon (1895–1960) branded mobs and crowds as irrational, resembling a "beast with many heads." Mob actions such as race riots and lynchings sometimes seem to operate on a psychology of their own. Do mobs "bring out the beast in us"?

When people act as individuals, fear of consequences and self-evaluation tend to prevent them from engaging in antisocial behavior. But in a mob, they may experience **deindividuation**, a state in which they are willing to follow a norm that emerges in a specific situation, even if it means ignoring their own values (Lan & Zuo, 2009; Postmes & Spears, 1998). Many factors lead to deindividuation, including anonymity, diffusion of responsibility, arousal due to

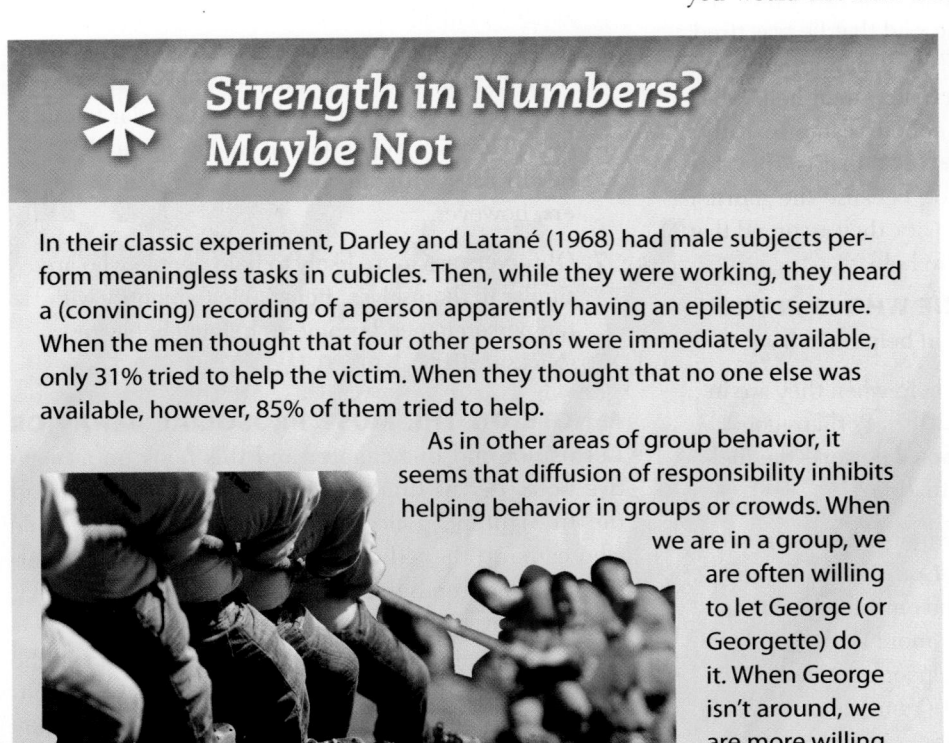

Strength in Numbers? Maybe Not

In their classic experiment, Darley and Latané (1968) had male subjects perform meaningless tasks in cubicles. Then, while they were working, they heard a (convincing) recording of a person apparently having an epileptic seizure. When the men thought that four other persons were immediately available, only 31% tried to help the victim. When they thought that no one else was available, however, 85% of them tried to help.

As in other areas of group behavior, it seems that diffusion of responsibility inhibits helping behavior in groups or crowds. When we are in a group, we are often willing to let George (or Georgette) do it. When George isn't around, we are more willing to help others ourselves.

AC Images/Alamy

noise and crowding, and a focus on emerging group norms rather than on one's own values (S. L. Taylor et al., 2006). Under these circumstances, crowd members behave more aggressively than they would as individuals.

14-7f ALTRUISM AND THE BYSTANDER EFFECT

Altruism—selfless concern for the welfare of others—is connected with some heroic behavior. Humans have sacrificed themselves to ensure the survival of their children or of comrades in battle. So how, one might ask, could the murder of 28-year-old Kitty Genovese have happened? It took place in New York City more than 40 years ago. Murder was not unheard of in the Big Apple, but Kitty had screamed for help as her killer stalked her for more than half an hour and stabbed her in three separate attacks (Manning et al., 2007; Nicksa, 2014). Thirty-eight neighbors heard the commotion. Twice, the assault was interrupted by their voices and bedroom lights. Each time the attacker returned. Yet nobody came to the victim's aid. No one even called the police.

Why? Some witnesses said matter-of-factly that they did not want to get involved. One said that he was tired. Still others said, "I don't know." As a nation, are we a callous bunch who would rather watch than help when others are in trouble? Perhaps nobody came to Kitty's aid because of the **bystander effect**; that is, they saw that other people were present or, because the murder took place in crowded New York City, they assumed that other people were also available to help.

WHEN DO WE HELP SOMEONE WHO IS IN TROUBLE? Many factors are involved in helping behavior:

1. Observers are more likely to help when they are in a good mood (Schnall et al., 2010). Perhaps good moods impart a sense of personal power—the feeling that we can handle the situation.

2. People who are empathic are more likely to help people in need (Decety & Batson, 2009). Women are more likely than men to be empathic and thus more likely to help people in need (Yamasue et al., 2008).

3. Bystanders may not help unless they believe that an emergency exists (Cocking et al., 2009).

altruism unselfish concern for the welfare of others

bystander effect the tendency to avoid helping other people in emergencies when other people are also present and apparently capable of helping

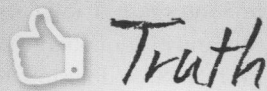

4. Observers must assume the responsibility to act (Nicksa, 2014). A lone person may have been more likely to try to help Kitty Genovese. *Diffusion of responsibility* may inhibit helping behavior in crowds.

5. Observers must know what to do (Baron et al., 2009). Observers who are not sure that they can take charge of the situation may stay on the sidelines for fear of making a social blunder or of getting hurt themselves.

6. Observers are more likely to help people they know (Nicksa, 2014). Evolutionary psychologists suggest that altruism is selfish from an evolutionary point of view when it helps close relatives or others who are similar to us to survive (Nicksa, 2014). It helps us perpetuate a genetic code similar to our own. This view suggests that we are more likely to be altruistic with our relatives rather than strangers, however.

7. Observers are more likely to help people who are similar to themselves. Being able to identify with the person in need promotes helping behavior (Nicksa, 2014).

A NOTE ON THE MOST PROSOCIAL BEHAVIOR Let us not end this chapter and this book on a negative note. Let us think, instead, about the altruism of the firefighters, police officers, and ordinary people who came to the aid of the victims of the suicide terrorism of September 11, 2001. Following the attacks, thousands evacuated lower Manhattan by ferry to New Jersey. Residents of New Jersey drove up and down the streets near the ferry, asking if they could give evacuees rides or help in any other way. And people heading away from the devastation in Manhattan were happy to share their taxicabs, even with strangers. If you know a little about New York City, you know that's rather special—but it's also something done by ordinary people in extraordinary times.

STUDY TOOLS 14

READY TO STUDY? IN THE BOOK, YOU CAN:

☐ Check your understanding of what you've read with the quizzes below.

☐ Rip out the chapter review card at the back of the book to have a summary of the chapter and the key terms handy.

ONLINE AT CENGAGEBRAIN.COM YOU CAN:

☐ See how modern technology such as virtual reality devices are speeding up treatment for fear in a short video.

☐ Prepare for tests with quizzes.

☐ Review the key terms with Flash Cards.

☐ Play games to master concepts.

FILL-INS

Answers can be found in the back of the book, starting on page 393.

1. Attitudes are acquired through conditioning, observational learning, and _____ appraisal.

2. According to cognitive-_____ theory, we are motivated to make our cognitions consistent with one another and with our behavior.

3. One factor in prejudice is social _____, or the tendency to divide the world into us and them.

4. According to the _____-_____ hypothesis, we tend to be attracted to people who are similar to ourselves.

5. According to the triangular model of love, love can include combinations of intimacy, _____, and commitment.

6. The tendency to perceive others in terms of first impressions is an example of the _____ effect.

7. The following factors contribute to obedience: socialization, lack of _____ comparison, perception of experimenters as legitimate authority figures, the foot-in-the-door technique, and inaccessibility of values.

8. Social _____ refers to the enhancement of performance that results from the presence of others.

9. Members of a group may experience _____, which is a state of reduced self-awareness and lowered concern for social evaluation.

10. Kitty Genovese's death has been attributed to the _____ effect.

MULTIPLE CHOICE

1. **The A–B problem focuses on**
   a. activities we do and behaviors we avoid.
   b. attitudes and beliefs.
   c. the relationship between achievement and behavior.
   d. consistency between our attitudes and behavior.

2. **Mary prefers living in the country away from the noise and crowds of the city, but her sister Denise prefers the excitement and pace of city life. They differ in _____.**
   a. avoidance
   b. attitude
   c. polarization
   d. deindividuation

3. **One major reason that groups tend to take greater risks than their members would take as individuals is**
   a. diffusion of responsibility.
   b. the reciprocity norm.
   c. group intelligence.
   d. all of these.

4. **The _____ route is to facts and research results as the _____ route is to status and prestige.**
   a. peripheral; central
   b. central; peripheral
   c. secondary; primary
   d. primary; secondary

5. **The "Save the World by Praying" association predicted the world would end on Nov. 1, 1999. When the world did not end on that day their group made a statement that supported the theory of cognitive dissonance. Which of the statements below would fit that description?**
   a. "We were wrong, prayer does not help."
   b. "God did not listen to us."
   c. "Our praying must have saved the world."
   d. "We are confused about all this."

6. **The first time you met your fiancée you fell down and spilled a glass of wine on her dress. You obviously didn't make a very good first impression. However, it was several months later before you saw her again. Your second meeting went much better and it was almost as if your first encounter never happened. This change in her perception of you is probably due to the**
   a. primary effect.
   b. recency effect.
   c. repression.
   d. discrimination.

7. **Yevhen is standing in line in school. While he isn't looking, another boy steps on his toe. Yevhen says to himself: "He must have stepped on my toe because it's so crowded in here and somebody else pushed this guy; it was probably an accident." Yevhen is making a _____ attribution.**
   a. dispositional
   b. situational
   c. fundamental
   d. motivational

8. **If there had been two teachers acting together rather than one in Milgram's experiment, and the teachers could discuss the situation before complying with the demands of the experimenter, this change in procedure would probably have**
   a. decreased the level of obedience.
   b. had no effect on obedience.
   c. increased the level of obedience.
   d. none of these

9. **The process by which the presence of others improves our performance is known as**
   a. reciprocation.
   b. social facilitation.
   c. social lubrication.
   d. reciprocity.

10. **The self-serving bias is the tendency to**
    a. repeat ourselves when we think we're right.
    b. take care of our own needs first, and worry about others later.
    c. credit our successes to internal, dispositional factors and our failures to situational influences.
    d. describe our successes in greater detail than our failures.

LEARNING
YOUR WAY

Go to **www.cengagebrain.com**
to access **PSYCH Online!**

Appendix | Statistics

Pixland/Jupiterimages

PhotoSpin

LEARNING OUTCOMES

After studying this chapter, you will be able to...

App-1 Explain how statistics are used in psychology

App-2 Calculate values using descriptive statistics

App-3 Describe and apply the normal curve

App-4 Calculate values using the correlation coefficient

App-5 Explain the logic behind inferential statistics

App-1 STATISTICS

Imagine that aliens from outer space arrive outside Madison Square Garden in New York City. Their goal this dark winter evening is to learn all they can about planet Earth. They are drawn inside the Garden by lights, shouts, and warmth. The spotlighting inside rivets their attention to a wood-floored arena where the New York Big Apples are hosting the California Quakes n a briskly contested basketball game.

Our visitors use their sophisticated instruments to take measurements of the players. Some statistics are sent back to their home planet: It appears that (1) 100% of Earthlings are male and (2) the height of Earthlings ranges from 6'1" to 7'2".

These measurements are called **statistics**. Statistics is the name given to the science concerned with obtaining and organizing numerical information or measurements. Our visitors have sent home statistics about the gender and size of humans that are at once accurate and misleading. Although they accurately measured: he basketball players, their small sample of Earth's population was distorted.

A **population** is a complete group of people, other animals, or measures from which a sample is drawn. For example, all people on Earth could be defined as the population of interest. So could all women, or all women in the United States. A **sample** is a group of measures drawn from a population. Fortunately for us Earthlings, about half of the world's population is female. And the

> To what degree do you think the people in your school represent the population of the United States? North America? The world?

range of heights observed by the aliens, of 6'1" to 7'2", is both restricted and too high—much too high. People vary in height by more than 1 foot and 1 inch. And our **average** height is not between 6'1" and 7'2"; rather, it is a number of inches below.

Psychologists, like our imagined visitors, are concerned with measuring human as well as animal characteristics and traits—not just physical characteristics as height, but also psychological traits such as intelligence, aggressiveness, and depression. By observing the *central tendencies* (averages) and variations in measurement from person to person, psychologists can say that one person is average or above average in intelligence, or that someone else is less anxious than, say, 60% of the population. But psychologists, unlike our aliens, attempt to select a sample that accurately represents the entire population. Professional basketball players do not represent the entire human species.

In this appendix, we survey some statistical methods used by psychologists to draw conclusions about the measurements they take. First we discuss *descriptive statistics* and learn what types of statements we can make about height and other human traits. Then we discuss

statistics numerical facts assembled in such a manner that they provide useful information about measures or scores (from the Latin *status*, meaning "standing" or "position")

population a complete group from which a sample is selected

sample part of a population

average the central tendency of a group of measures, expressed either as the mean, median, or mode of a distribution

Truth

| T | **F** | Professional basketball players could be said to be abnormal. |

Basketball players could be said to be abnormal in the sense that they are taller, stronger, and more agile than the rest of us.

Truth or Fiction?

WHAT DO YOU THINK? Folklore, common sense, or nonsense? Select T for "truth" or F for "fiction," and then check the accuracy of your answers as you read through the chapter.

T	F	Professional basketball players could be said to be abnormal.
T	F	Being a "10" is not always a good thing.
T	F	You should not assume that you can walk across a river with an average depth of 4 feet.
T	F	Adding people's incomes and then dividing them by the number of people can be an awful way of showing the average income.
T	F	Psychologists express your IQ score in terms of how deviant you are.
T	F	An IQ score of 130 is more impressive than an sat score of 500.

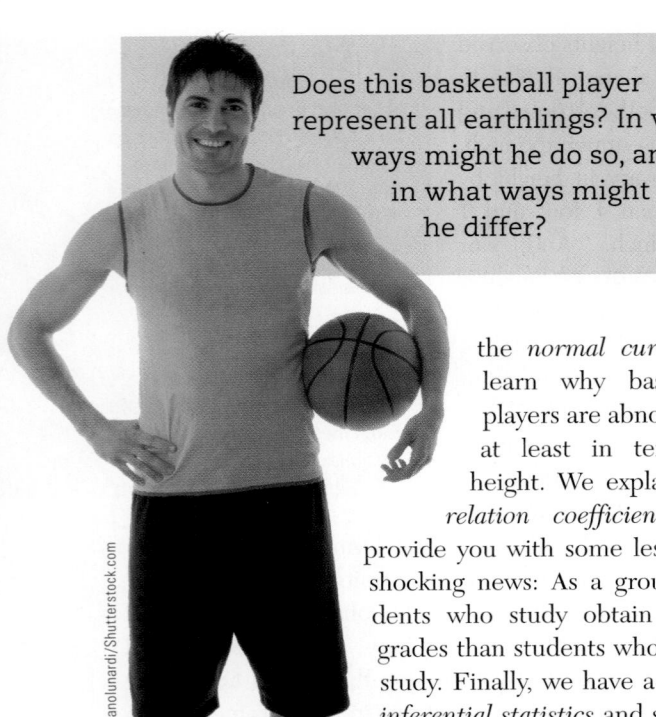

Does this basketball player represent all earthlings? In what ways might he do so, and in what ways might he differ?

the *normal curve* and learn why basketball players are abnormal—at least in terms of height. We explain *correlation coefficients* and provide you with some less-than-shocking news: As a group, students who study obtain higher grades than students who do not study. Finally, we have a look at *inferential statistics* and see why basketball players are in fact *statistically significantly* taller than the general population.

Being A "10" is not always a good truth thing because a scale can vary, say, from 0 to 100, in which case a score of 10 would place one nearer to the bottom of the scale, making a score of 50 the center point of the scale.

DESCRIPTIVE STATISTICS

App-2

Being told that someone is a "10" may sound great at first. However, it is not very descriptive unless you know something about how the scores on the scale are distributed and how frequently one finds a 10. Fortunately—for 10s, if not for the rest of us—one usually means that the person is a 10 on a scale of from 1 to 10, and that 10 is the highest score. If this is not sufficient, one will also be told that 10s are few and far between—unusual statistical events.

The idea of the scale from 1 to 10 may not be very scientific, but it does suggest something about descriptive statistics. **Descriptive statistics** is the branch of statistics that provides information about distributions of scores. We can use descriptive statistics to clarify our understanding of a distribution of scores such as heights, test grades, IQs, or even increases or decreases in measures of aggressive behavior following the drinking of alcohol. For example, descriptive statistics can help us

descriptive statistics the branch of statistics that is concerned with providing descriptive information about a distribution of scores

frequency distribution an ordered set of data that indicates the frequency (how often) with which scores appear

determine measures of central tendency (averages) and to determine how much fluctuation or variability there is in the scores. Being a 10 loses much of its charm if the average score is an 11. Being a 10 is more remarkable in a distribution whose scores range from 1 to 10 than it is in a distribution whose scores range from 9 to 11.

Let's now consider some of the concerns of descriptive statistics: the frequency distribution, measures of central tendency (types of averages), and measures of variability.

App-2a THE FREQUENCY DISTRIBUTION

A **frequency distribution** takes scores or items of raw data, puts them into order from the lowest to the highest, and indicates how often a score appears. Table A.1 shows the rosters for a recent basketball game between

Being a 10 may not be such a good thing if the average score is 11.

TABLE A.1 ROSTER OF QUAKES VERSUS BIG APPLES AT NEW YORK

A glance at the rosters for a recent basketball game in which the New York Big Apples "entertained" the California Quakes shows that the heights of the team members, combined, ranged from 6'1" to 7'2". Do the heights of the team members represent those of the general male population? What do you think?

California Quakes			New York Big Apples		
2	Callahan	6'7"	3	Roosevelt	6'1"
5	Daly	6'11"	12	Chaffee	6'5"
6	Chico	6'2"	13	Baldwin	6'9"
12	Capistrano	6'3"	25	Delmar	6'6"
21	Brentwood	6'5"	27	Merrick	6'8"
25	Van Nuys	6'3"	28	Hewlett	6'6"
31	Clemente	6'9"	33	Hollis	6'9"
32	Whittier	6'8"	42	Bedford	6'5"
41	Fernando	7'2"	43	Coram	6'2"
43	Watts	6'9"	45	Hampton	6'10"
53	Huntington	6'6"	53	Ardsley	6'10"

the California Quakes and the New York Big Apples. The players are listed according to the numbers on their uniforms.

It would also be possible to list players according to class intervals, such as a 1-inch class interval as shown in Table A.2, or a 3-inch class interval as shown in

TABLE A.2 REQUENCY DISTRIBUTION OF BASKETBALL PLAYERS (QUAKES AND BIG APPLES COMBINED), WITH A 1-INCH CLASS INTERVAL

Class Interval	Number of Players in Class
6'1"–6'1.9"	1
6'2"–6'2.9"	2
6'3"–6'3.9"	2
6'4"–6'4.9"	0
6'5"–6'5.9"	3
6'6"–6'6.9"	3
6'7"–6'7.9"	1
6'8"–6'8.9"	2
6'9"–6'9.9"	4
6'10"–6'10.9"	2
6'11"–6'11.9"	1
7'0"–7'0.9"	0
7'1"–7'1.9"	0
7'2"–7'2.9"	1

TABLE A.3 FREQUENCY DISTRIBUTION OF HEIGHTS OF BASKETBALL PLAYERS, USING A 3-INCH CLASS INTERVAL

Class Interval	Number of Players in Class
6'1"–6'3.9"	5
6'4"–6'6.9"	6
6'7"–6'9.9"	7
6'10"–7'0.9"	3
7'1"–7'3.9"	1

Table A.3. In determining the size of a class interval, the researcher tries to collapse the data into a small-enough number of classes to ensure that they will be meaningful at a glance. But the researcher also tries to keep a large-enough number of categories (classes) to ensure that important differences are not obscured.

Table A.3 obscures the fact that no players are 6'4" tall. If the researcher believes that this information is important, a class interval of 1 inch may be maintained.

Figure A.1 shows two methods of graphing the information in Table A.3: the **frequency histogram** and the **frequency polygon**. Students sometimes have difficulty interpreting graphs, but the purpose of graphs is to reveal key information about frequency distributions at a glance. Note that in both kinds of graph, the frequency histogram and the frequency polygon, the class intervals are usually drawn along the horizontal line. The horizontal line is also known as the x-axis. The numbers of cases (scores, persons, or events) in each class interval are shown along the vertical line, which is also known as the y-axis. In the histogram, the number of scores in each class interval is represented by a bar—a rectangular solid—so that the graph looks like a series of steps. In the polygon, the number of scores in each class interval is plotted as a point. The points are connected to form a many-sided geometric figure (polygon). Note that empty class intervals were added at each end of the frequency polygon so that the sides of the figure could be brought down to the x-axis to close the geometric figure.

App-2b MEASURES OF CENTRAL TENDENCY

Measures of central tendency are "averages" that show the center, or balancing points, of a frequency distribution. There are three commonly used types of measures of central tendency: the *mean*, the *median*, and the *mode*. Each attempts to describe something about the scores in a frequency distribution through the use of a typical or representative number.

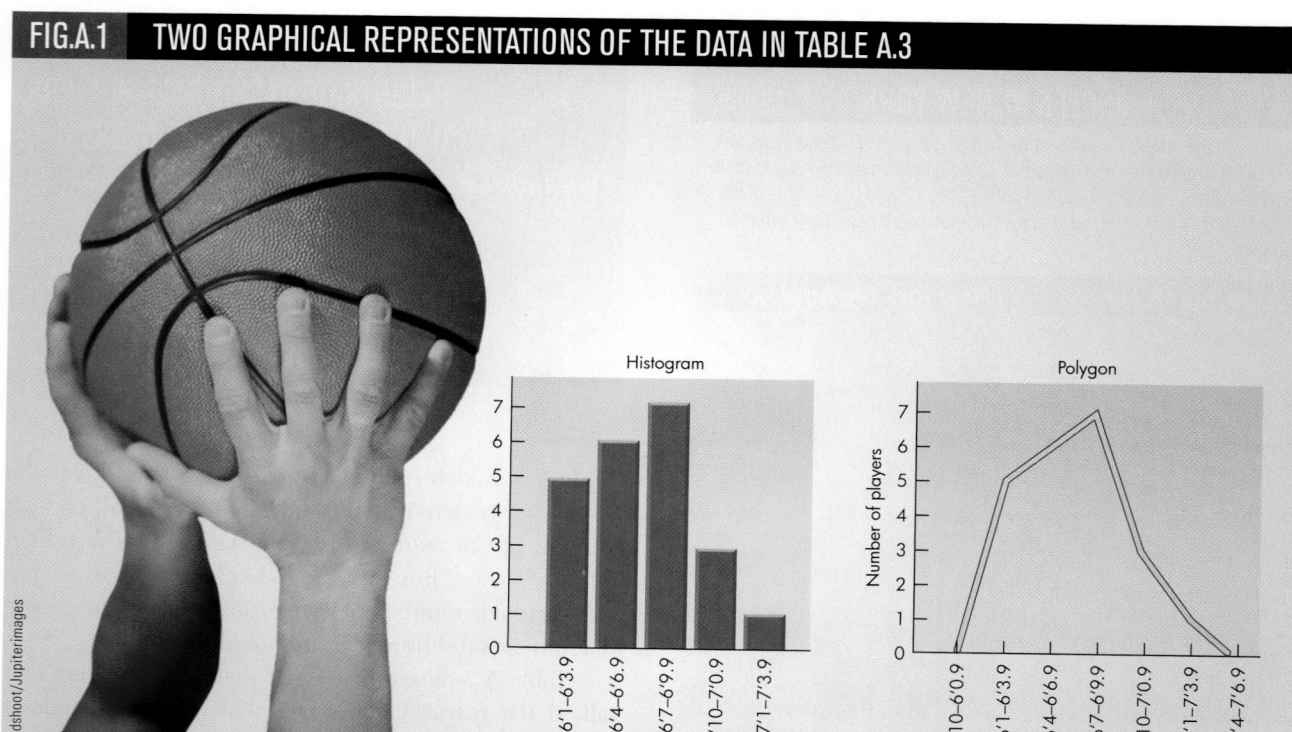

FIG.A.1 TWO GRAPHICAL REPRESENTATIONS OF THE DATA IN TABLE A.3

The graph on the left is called a frequency histogram, or bar graph. The graph on the right is called a frequency polygon.

The **mean** is what most people think of as "the average." We obtain the mean of a distribution by adding up the scores and then dividing the sum by the number of scores. In the case of the basketball players, it would be advisable to first convert the heights into a single unit, such as inches (6'1" becomes 73", and so on). If we add all the heights in inches and then divide by the number of players (22), we obtain a mean height of 78.73". If we convert that number back into units of feet and inches, we obtain 6'6.73".

The **median** is the score of the *middle case* in a distribution.

> *Never try to walk across a river just because it has an average depth of four feet.*
>
> —Martin Friedman

It is the score beneath which 50% of the cases fall. In a distribution with an even number of cases, such as the distribution of the heights of the 22 basketball players as shown in Table A.2, we obtain the median by finding the mean of the two middle cases. When we list the 22 cases in ascending order (moving from lowest to highest), the 11th case is 6'6" and the 12th case is 6'7". Therefore, the median of the distribution is (6'6" + 6'7") /2, or 6'6.5".

When we analyze the heights of the basketball players, we find that the mean and the median are similar. Either one serves as a useful indicator of the central tendency of the data. But suppose we are trying to find the average savings of 30 families living on a suburban block. Let's assume that 29 of the 30 families have savings between $8,000 and $12,000, adding up to $294,000. But the 30th family has savings of $1,400,000! The mean savings for a family on this block would thus be $56,467. The mean can be greatly distorted by one or two extreme scores. An IQ score of 145 would similarly distort the mean of the IQ scores of a class of 20 students, among whom the other 19 IQ scores ranged from 93 to 112. Then, too, if a few basketball players signed up for one of your classes, the mean of the students' heights would be distorted in an upward direction.

mean a type of average that is calculated by adding all the scores and then dividing by the number of scores

median the central score in a frequency distribution; the score beneath which 50% of the cases fall

When there are a few extreme scores in a distribution, the median is a better indicator of central tendency. The median savings on our hypothetical block would lie between $8,000 and $12,000. Thus it would be more representative of the central tendency of savings. Studies of the incomes of families in the United States usually report median rather than mean incomes just to avoid the distortion of findings that would occur if the incomes of a handful of billionaires were treated in the same way as more common incomes. On the other hand, one could argue that choosing the median as the average obscures or hides the extreme scores, which are just as "real" as the other scores. Perhaps it is best to use the median and a footnote—a rather big footnote.

The **mode** is simply the most frequently occurring score or measure in a distribution. The mode of the data in Table A.1 is 6'9" because this height occurs most often among the players on the two teams. The median class interval for the data shown in Table A.3 is 6'6.5" to 6'9.5". With this particular distribution, the mode is somewhat higher than the mean or the median.

In some cases the mode is a more appropriate description of the central tendency of a distribution than

the mean or the median. Figure A.2 shows a **bimodal** distribution—that is, a distribution with two modes. This is a hypothetical distribution of test scores obtained by a class. The mode at the left indicates the most common class interval (45 to 49) for students who did not study, and the mode to the right shows the most common class interval (65 to 69) for students who did study. (Don't be alarmed. I'm sure that the professor, who is extremely fair, will be delighted to curve the

mode the most frequently occurring number or score in a distribution

bimodal having two modes

FIG.A.2 A BIMODAL DISTRIBUTION

This hypothetical distribution represents students' scores on a test. The mode at the left represents the central tendency of the test scores of students who did not study. The mode at the right represents the mode of the test scores of students who did study.

grades so that the interval of 75 to 79 is an A+ and the interval of 65 to 69 is at least a B.) The mean and median test scores would probably lie within the 55 to 59 class interval, yet use of that interval as the measure of central tendency could obscure rather than reveal the important aspects of this distribution of test scores. It might suggest that the test was too hard, not that a number of students chose not to study. Similarly, one of the distribution's modes might be a bit larger than the other, so one could follow the exact rule for finding the mode and report just one of them. But this approach would also hide the meaning of this particular distribution of scores. All in all, it is clearly best to visualize this distribution of scores as bimodal.

App-2c MEASURES OF VARIABILITY

Our hypothetical class obtained test scores ranging from class intervals of 35 to 39 to class intervals of 75 to 79. That is, the scores *varied* from the lower class interval to the higher class interval. Now, if all the students had obtained scores from 55 to 59 or from to 65 to 69, the scores would not have varied as much; that is, they would have clustered closer to one another and would have had lower variability.

The measures of the variability of a distribution inform us about the spread of scores—that is, about the typical distances of scores from the average score. Two commonly used measures of variability are the *range* of scores and the *standard deviation* of scores.

The **range** of scores in a distribution is defined as the difference between the highest score and the lowest score. The range is obtained by subtracting the lowest score from the highest score. The range of heights in Table A.2 is obtained by subtracting 6'1" from 7'2", or 1'11". It is useful to know the range of temperatures when we move to an area with a different climate so that we may anticipate the weather and dress for it appropriately. A teacher must have some understanding of the range of abilities or skills in a class to teach effectively. An understanding of the range of human heights can be used to design doorways, beds, and headroom in automobiles. Even so, the typical doorway is 6'8" high; and, as we saw with the California Quakes and New York Big Apples, some people will have to duck to get through.

The range is an imperfect measure of variability because of the manner in which it is influenced by extreme scores. The range of savings of the 30 families on our suburban block is $1,400,000 minus $8,000, or $1,392,000. This is a large number, and it is certainly true. However, it tells us little about the *typical* variation of savings accounts, which lie within a more restricted range of $8,000 to $12,000.

The **standard deviation** is a statistic that does a better job of showing how the scores in a distribution are distributed (spread) about the mean. It is usually better than the range because it considers every score in the distribution, not just the extreme (highest and lowest) scores. Consider Figure A.3. Each distribution in the figure has the same number of scores, the same mean, and the same range of scores. However, the scores in the distribution on the right side cluster more closely about the mean. Therefore, the standard deviation of the distribution on the right is smaller. That is, the typical score deviates less from the mean score.

The standard deviation is usually abbreviated as S.D. It is calculated by the formula

$$\text{S.D.} = \sqrt{\frac{\text{Sum of } d^2}{N}}$$

where d equals the deviation of each score from the mean of the distribution and N equals the number of scores in the distribution.

Let's find the mean and standard deviation of the IQ scores listed in column 1 of Table A.4. To obtain the mean we add all the scores, attain 1,500, and then divide by the number of scores (15) to obtain a mean of 100. We obtain the deviation score (d) for each IQ score by subtracting the score from 100. The d for an IQ score of 85 equals 100 minus 85, or 15, and so on. Then we square each d and add the squares. The S.D. equals the square root of the sum of squares (1,426) divided by the number of scores (15), or 9.75.

As an additional exercise, we can show that the S.D. of the test scores on the left (in Figure A.3) is greater than that for the scores on the right. First, we assign the grades a number according to a 4.0 system. Let A = 4,

range a measure of variability defined as the high score in a distribution minus the low score

standard deviation a measure of the variability of a distribution, obtained by the formula

$$\text{S.D.} = \sqrt{\frac{\text{Sum of } d^2}{N}}$$

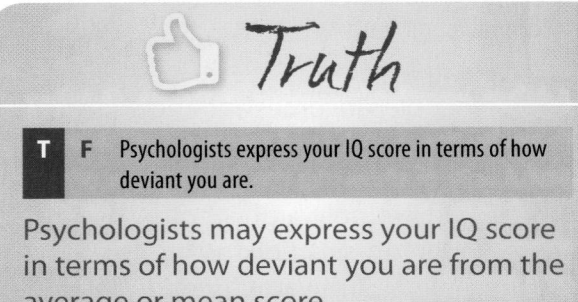

Truth

T F Psychologists express your IQ score in terms of how deviant you are.

Psychologists may express your IQ score in terms of how deviant you are from the average or mean score.

FIG.A.3 HYPOTHETICAL DISTRIBUTIONS OF STUDENT TEST SCORES

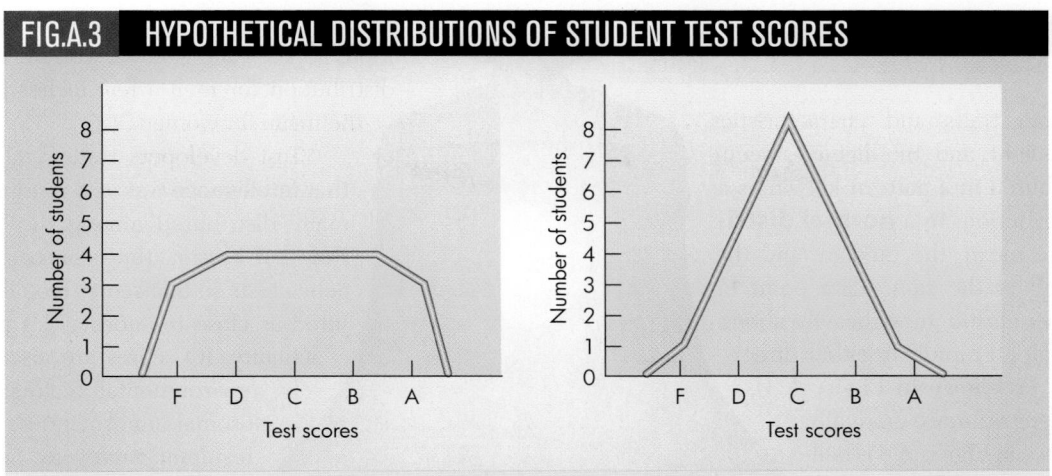

Each distribution has the same number of scores, the same mean, even the same range, but the standard deviation (a measure of variability) is greater for the distribution on the left because the scores tend to be farther from the mean.

B = 3, C = 2, D = 1, and F = 0. The S.D. for each distribution is computed in Table A.5. The larger S.D. for the distribution on the left indicates that the scores in that distribution are more variable, or tend to be farther from the mean.

TABLE A.4 HYPOTHETICAL SCORES OBTAINED FROM AN IQ TESTING

IQ Score	d (Deviation Score)	d^2 (Deviation Score Squared)
85	15	225
87	13	169
89	11	121
90	10	100
93	7	49
97	3	9
97	3	9
100	0	0
101	−1	1
104	−4	16
105	−5	25
110	−10	100
112	−12	144
113	−13	169
117	−17	289

Sum of IQ scores = 1,500   Sum of d^2 scores = 1,426

$$\text{Mean} = \frac{\text{Sum of scores}}{\text{Number of scores}} = \frac{1,500}{15} = 100$$

$$\text{Standard Deviation (S.D.)} = \sqrt{\frac{\text{Sum of } d^2}{N}} = \sqrt{\frac{1,426}{15}} = \sqrt{95.07} = 9.75$$

TABLE A.5 COMPUTATION OF STANDARD DEVIATIONS FOR TEST-SCORE DISTRIBUTIONS IN FIGURE A.3

Distribution at Left			Distribution to the Right		
Grade	d	d^2	Grade	d	d^2
A (4)	2	4	A (4)	2	4
A (4)	2	4	B (3)	1	1
A (4)	2	4	B (3)	1	1
B (3)	1	1	B (3)	1	1
B (3)	1	1	B (3)	1	1
B (3)	1	1	C (2)	0	0
B (3)	1	1	C (2)	0	0
C (2)	0	0	C (2)	0	0
C (2)	0	0	C (2)	0	0
C (2)	0	0	C (2)	0	0
C (2)	0	0	C (2)	0	0
D (1)	−1	1	C (2)	0	0
D (1)	−1	1	C (2)	0	0
D (1)	−1	1	D (1)	−1	1
D (1)	−1	1	D (1)	−1	1
F (0)	−2	4	D (1)	−1	1
F (0)	−2	4	D (1)	−1	1
F (0)	−2	4	F (0)	−2	4

Sum of grades = 36
Mean grade = 36/18 = 2
Sum of d^2 = 32
Sum of grades = 36
Mean grade = 36/18 = 2
Sum of d^2 = 32
S.D. = $\sqrt{32/18}$ = 1.33

Sum of grades = 36
Mean grade = 36/18 = 2
Sum of d^2 = 16
Sum of grades = 36
Mean grade = 36/18 = 2
Sum of d^2 = 16
S.D. = $\sqrt{16/18}$ = 0.94

THE NORMAL CURVE

Many human traits and characteristics, including height and intelligence, seem to be distributed in a pattern known as a normal distribution. In a **normal distribution**, the mean, the median, and the mode all fall at the same data point or score. Scores cluster most heavily about the mean, fall off rapidly in either direction at first (as shown in Figure A.4), and then taper off more gradually.

The curve in Figure A.4 is bell-shaped. This type of distribution is also called a **normal curve** or bell-shaped curve. This curve is hypothesized as the distribution of variables in which different scores are determined by chance variation. Height is thought to be largely determined by chance combinations of genetic material. A distribution of the heights of a random sample of the population approximates normal distributions for men and women, with the mean of the distribution for men a few inches higher than the mean for women.

Test developers traditionally assumed that intelligence was also randomly or normally distributed among the population. For that reason, they constructed intelligence tests so that scores would be distributed as close to "normal" as possible. In actuality, IQ scores are also influenced by environmental factors and chromosomal abnormalities, so that the resultant curves are not perfectly normal. The means of most IQ tests are defined as scores of 100 points. The Wechsler scales are constructed to have standard deviations of 15 points, as shown in Figure A.4. A standard deviation of 15 points causes 50% of the Wechsler scores to fall between 90 and 110, which is called the "broad average" range. About 68% of scores (two out of three) fall between 85 and 115 (within a standard deviation of the mean), and more than 95% fall between 70 and 130—that is, within two standard deviations of the mean. The more extreme high (and low) IQ scores deviate more from the mean score.

The Scholastic Assessment Tests (SATs) were constructed so that the mean scores would be 500 points and the S.D. would be 100 points. Thus a score of 600 would equal or excel that of some 84% to 85% of the test takers. Because of the complex interaction of variables that determine SAT scores, their distribution is not exactly normal either. Moreover, the actual mean scores and standard deviations tend to vary from year to year, and, in the case of the SAT IIs, from test to test. The normal curve is an idealized curve.

The IQ score of 130 is two standard deviations above the mean and exceeds that of more than 97% of the population. An SAT score of 500 is

normal distribution a symmetrical distribution that is assumed to reflect chance fluctuations; approximately 68% of cases lie within a standard deviation of the mean

normal curve graphic presentation of a normal distribution, which shows a characteristic bell shape

© iStockphoto.com/LordRunar/Marcus Lindström

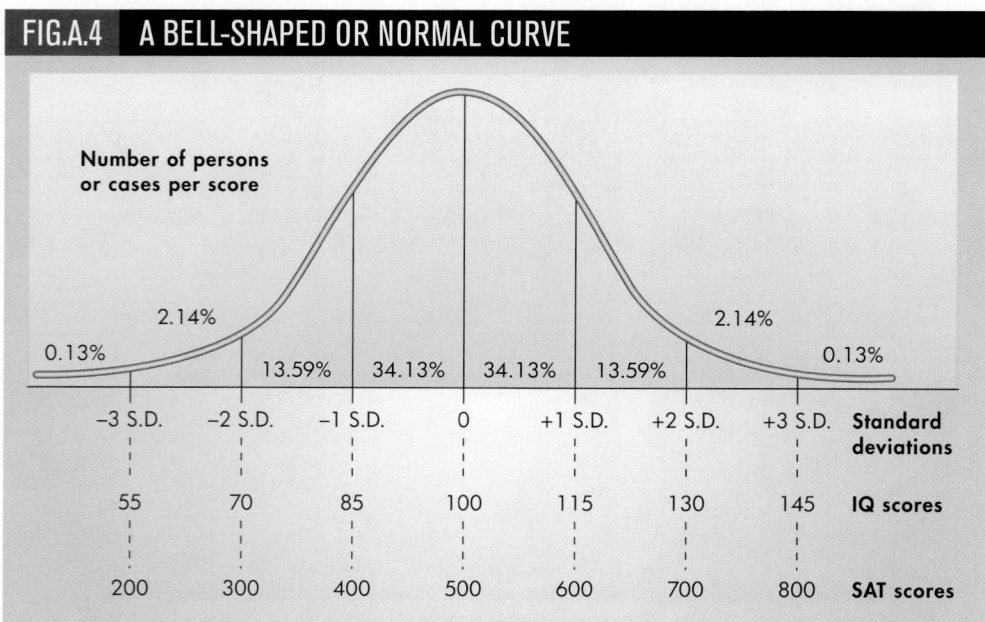

FIG.A.4   A BELL-SHAPED OR NORMAL CURVE

Number of persons or cases per score

0.13%   2.14%   13.59%   34.13%   34.13%   13.59%   2.14%   0.13%

−3 S.D.	−2 S.D.	−1 S.D.	0	+1 S.D.	+2 S.D.	+3 S.D.	Standard deviations
55	70	85	100	115	130	145	IQ scores
200	300	400	500	600	700	800	SAT scores

In a normal curve, approximately two out of three cases (68%) lie within a standard deviation (S.D.) from the mean. The mean, median, and mode all lie at the same score. IQ tests and the Scholastic Assessment Tests (SATs) are constructed so that their distributions approximate the normal curve.

the mean SAT score and thus equals or excels that of about 50% of the population.

App-4 THE CORRELATION COEFFICIENT

What is the relationship between intelligence and educational achievement? Between cigarette smoking and lung cancer among humans? Between the personality trait of introversion and numbers of dates among college students? We cannot run experiments to determine whether the relationships between these variables are causal, because we cannot manipulate the independent variable. That is, we cannot assign high or low intelligence at random. Nor can we (ethically) assign some people to smoke cigarettes and others not to smoke. People must be allowed to make their own decisions, so it is possible that the same factors that lead some people to smoke—or to continue to smoke after they have experimented with cigarettes—also lead to lung cancer. (Even if we were to assign a group of people to a nonsmoking condition, could we monitor them continuously to make sure that they weren't sneaking puffs?) Nor can we designate who will be introverted and who will be extraverted. True, we could encourage people to act as if they are introverted or extraverted, but behavior is not the same thing as a personality trait. We cannot run true experiments to answer any of these questions, but the *correlation coefficient* can be used to reveal whether there is a relationship between intelligence and achievement, a relationship between smoking and cancer, or a relationship between personality and dating. Correlational research shows that smoking and cancer are related but does not reveal cause and effect. However, experimental research with animals does strongly suggest that smoking will cause cancer in humans.

The **correlation coefficient** is a statistic that describes the relationship between two variables. A correlation coefficient can vary from +1.00 to −1.00. A correlation coefficient of +1.00 is called a perfect positive correlation, and it describes the relationship between temperatures as measured by the Fahrenheit and Centigrade scales. A correlation coefficient of −1.00 is a perfect negative correlation, and a correlation of 0 (zero) reveals no relationship between variables.

As suggested by Figures A.5 and A.6, most correlation coefficients in psychological research are less than perfect. The left graph in Figure A.5 reveals a positive relationship between time spent studying and grade point averages. Because there is a positive correlation between the variables but the relationship is not perfect, the correlation coefficient will lie between 0.00 and +1.00. Perhaps it is about +0.60 or +0.70. However, we cannot absolutely predict what a person's GPA will

> **correlation coefficient** a number between −1.00 and +1.00 that indicates the direction (negative or positive) and extent (from none to perfect) of the relationship between two variables

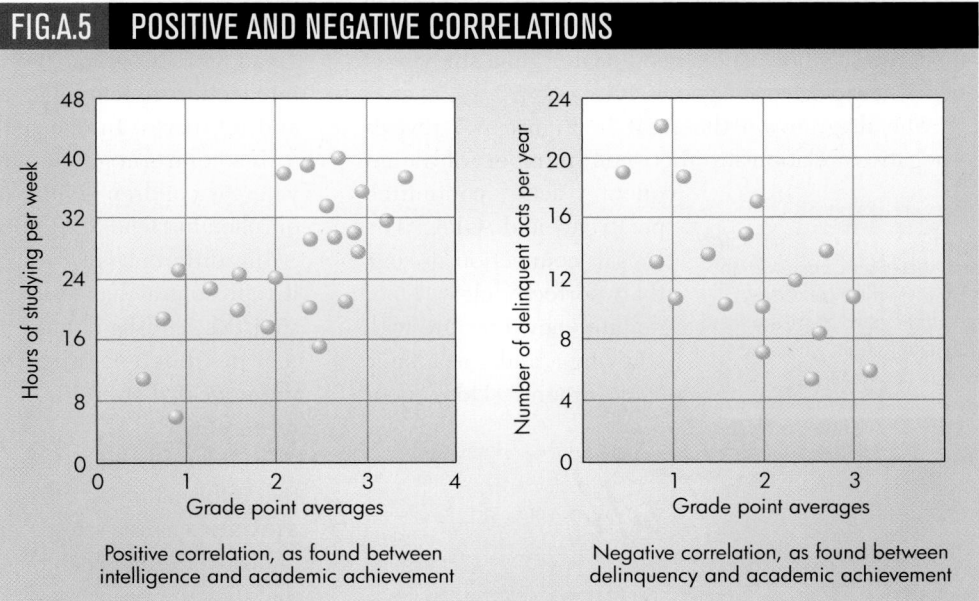

FIG.A.5 POSITIVE AND NEGATIVE CORRELATIONS

Positive correlation, as found between intelligence and academic achievement

Negative correlation, as found between delinquency and academic achievement

When there is a positive correlation between variables, as there is between intelligence and achievement, one increases as the other increases. By and large, the more time students spend studying, the better their grades are likely to be, as suggested in the diagram to the left. (Each dot represents the amount of time a student spends studying each week and his or her grade point average.) But there is a negative correlation between grades and juvenile delinquency. As the number of delinquent acts per year increases, one's grade point average tends to decline. Correlational research may suggest but does not demonstrate cause and effect.

Other variables

Cultural belief in the value of education?
Enjoyment of learning?
Parental pressure to do well?

| Variable X | → | Variable Y |

A

| Academic grades | → | Time spent studying |

B

Correlational relationships may suggest but do not demonstrate cause and effect. In part A, there is a correlation between variables X and Y. Does this mean that either variable X causes variable Y or that variable Y causes variable X? Not necessarily. Other factors could affect both variables X and Y. Consider the examples of academic grades (variable X) and time spent studying (variable Y) in part B. There is a positive correlation between the two. Does this mean that studying contributes to good grades? Perhaps. Does it mean that good grades encourage studying? Again, perhaps. But there could also be other variables—such as cultural belief in the value of education, enjoyment of learning, even parental pressure to do well—that contribute both to time spent studying and good grades.

be if we know the hours per week that he or she spends studying (nor can we predict exactly how much time the person spends studying on the basis of his or her GPA). Nevertheless, it would seem advisable to place oneself among those who spend a good deal of time studying if one wishes to achieve a good GPA.

The diagram on the right in Figure A.5 reveals a negative relationship between number of delinquent acts committed per year and GPA. The causal connection is less than perfectly clear. Does delinquency interfere with studying and academic achievement? Does poor achievement weaken a student's commitment to trying to get ahead through work? Do feelings of distance from "the system" contribute both to delinquent behavior and a low GPA? The answers are not to be found in Figure A.5, but the negative correlation between delinquent behavior and GPA does suggest that it is worthwhile to study the issues involved and—for a student—to distance himself or herself from delinquent behavior if he or she wishes to achieve in the academic world.

inferential statistics the branch of statistics that is concerned with the confidence with which conclusions drawn about samples can be extended to the populations from which the samples were drawn

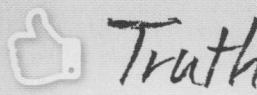

T **F** Psychologists express your IQ score in terms of how deviant you are.

An IQ score of 130 is more impressive than an sat score of 500. The IQ score is two standard deviations above the mean, and the sat score is the mean for that test.

App-5 INFERENTIAL STATISTICS

Head Start programs have apparently raised children's intellectual functioning, as reflected in their grades and IQ scores. In one such study, children enrolled in a Head Start program obtained a mean IQ score of 99, whereas children similar in background who were not enrolled in Head Start obtained a mean IQ score of 93. Is this difference of six points in IQ *significant*, or does it represent a chance fluctuation in scores? Inferential statistics help us determine whether we can conclude that the differences between such samples reflect real differences that are found in the populations that they represent.

Descriptive statistics enables us to provide descriptive information about samples of scores. **Inferential statistics** assist us in determining whether we can generalize differences among samples to the populations that they represent.

Figure A.7 shows the distribution of heights of 1,000 men and 1,000 women who were selected at random from the general U.S. population. The mean height for men is greater than the mean height for women. Can we conclude, or *infer*, that this difference in height is not just a chance fluctuation but represents an actual difference between the general populations of men and women? Or must we avoid such an inference

FIG.A.7 DISTRIBUTION OF HEIGHTS FOR RANDOM SAMPLES OF MEN AND WOMEN

Number of persons

1,000

500

0

Women   Men

4'10"   5'5"   6'   6'10"
    5'   5'10"   6'5"

Height

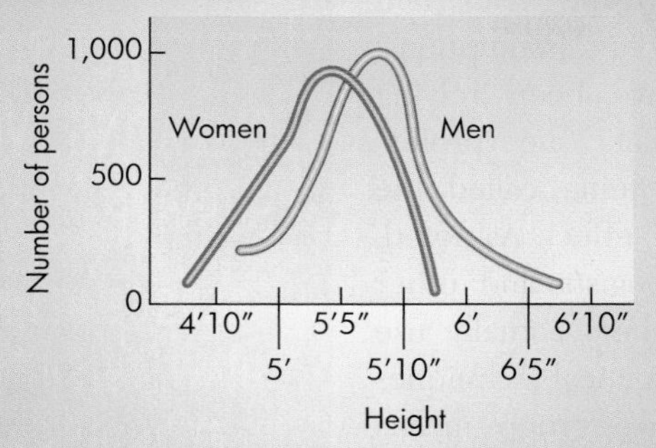

Note that the mean height of the men is greater than that of the women. Is the group mean difference in height statistically significant? Researchers use a tool called inferential statistics to determine the answer.

and summarize our results by stating only that the mean height of the sample of men in the study was greater than the mean height of the sample of women in the study?

If we could not draw inferences about populations from studies of samples, our research findings would be limited indeed. We could speak only about the specific individuals studied. There would be no point to learning about any study in which you did not participate because it would not apply to you! Fortunately, that is not the case. Inferential statistics permits us to extend findings with samples to the populations from which they were drawn.

App-5a STATISTICALLY SIGNIFICANT DIFFERENCES

We asked whether the differences in height between our samples of men and women were simply a chance fluctuation or whether they represented actual differences between the heights of men and women. Researchers tend not to talk about "real differences" or "actual differences" between groups, however. Instead, they speak of statistically significant differences. Similarly, researchers asked whether differences in IQ scores between children in Head Start programs and other children from similar backgrounds were chance fluctuations or statistically significant differences.

Statistically significant differences are differences that are unlikely to be due to chance fluctuation. Psychologists usually do not accept a difference as being statistically significant unless the probability (p) that it is due to chance fluctuation is less than 1 in 20 (i.e., $p < 0.05$). They are more comfortable labeling a difference as statistically significant when the probability (p) that it is due to chance fluctuation is less than 1 in 100 (i.e., $p < 0.01$).

Psychologists use formulas involving the means (e.g., mean IQ scores of 93 versus 99) and the standard deviations of sample groups to determine whether differences in means are statistically significant. As you can see in Figure A.8, the farther apart group means are, the more likely it is that they are statistically significant. In other words, if the men are on average 5 inches taller than the women, it is more likely that the difference is statistically significant than if the men are only one-quarter of an inch taller on average. *Principle 1: Everything else being equal, the greater the difference between means, the greater the probability that the difference is statistically significant.* This makes sense. After all, if you were told that your neighbor's car had gotten one-tenth of a mile more per gallon of gas than your car in the past year, you would probably attribute the difference to chance fluctuation. But if the difference were greater, say 14 miles per gallon, you would probably assume that the difference reflected an actual difference in driving habits or the efficiency of the automobile.

FIG.A.8 DECREASING AND INCREASING THE MEAN GROUP DIFFERENCE IN HEIGHTS

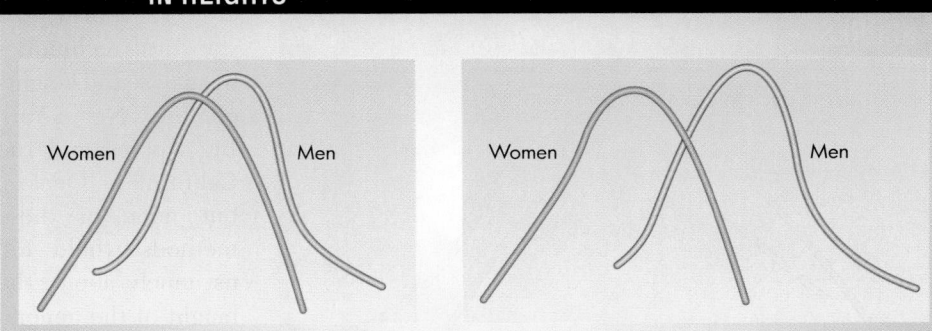

Women   Men   Women   Men

Everything else being equal, the greater the difference in group means, the greater the probability that the difference is statistically significant. The distribution on the right shows a greater difference in group means; therefore, there is a greater probability that the difference is statistically significant.

As you can see in Figure A.9, the smaller the standard deviations (a measure of variability) of the groups, the more likely it is that the difference between means is statistically significant. Consider the extreme example in which there is *no* variability within each group. That is, imagine that every woman in the randomly selected sample of 1,000 women is exactly 5'5" tall. Similarly, imagine that every man in the randomly selected sample of 1,000 men is exactly 5'10" tall. In such a case the heights of the men and women would not overlap at all, and it would appear that the differences were statistically significant. Consider the other extreme—one with unnaturally large variability. Imagine that the heights of the women vary from 2' to 14' and that the heights of the men vary from 2'1" to 14'3". In such a case we might be more likely to assume that the difference in group means of 5" was a chance fluctuation. *Principle 2: Everything else being equal, the smaller the variability of the distributions of scores, the greater the probability that the difference in group means is statistically significant.*

Therefore, we cannot conclude that men are taller than women unless we know the average heights of men and women and how much the heights within each group vary. We must know both the central tendencies (means) and variability of the two distributions of heights to infer that the mean heights are statistically significantly different.

We have been "eyeballing" the data and making assumptions. We have been relying on what one professor of mine called the "Wow!" effect. As noted, psychologists and other researchers actually use mathematical techniques that take group means and standard deviations into account to determine whether group differences are statistically significant. It is often the case that eyeballing real data does not yield clear results or even good guesses.

App-5b SAMPLES AND POPULATIONS

Inferential statistics are mathematical tools that psychologists apply to samples of scores to determine whether they can generalize or extend their findings to populations of scores. They must, therefore, be quite certain that the samples involved actually represent the populations from which they were drawn. Sampling techniques are crucial. Random sampling is the best method, and sampling is random only if every member of the target population has an equal chance of being selected.

It matters little how sophisticated our statistical methods are if the samples studied do not represent the target populations. We could use a variety of sophisticated statistical techniques to analyze the heights of the New York Big Apples and the California Quakes, but none of these methods would tell us much about the height of the general population. Or about the height of women. (Or about the height of people who can't pass the ball, shoot, or play defense.)

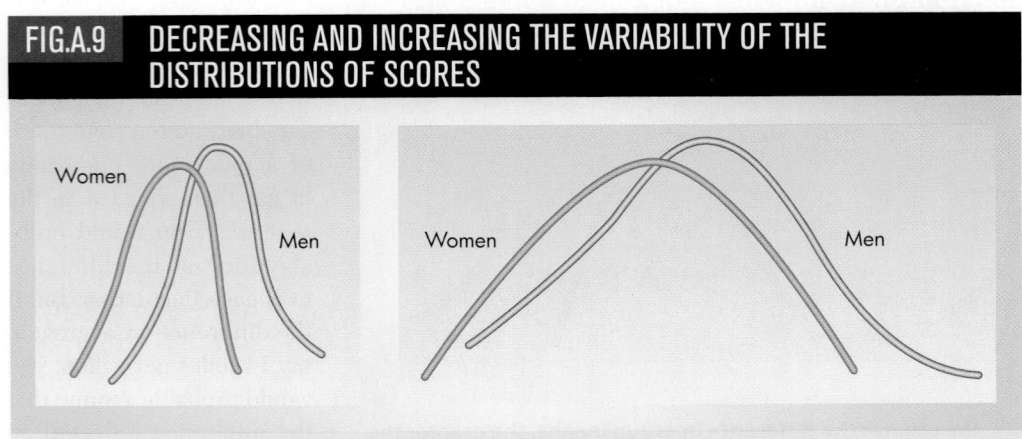

FIG.A.9 DECREASING AND INCREASING THE VARIABILITY OF THE DISTRIBUTIONS OF SCORES

Women   Men   Women   Men

Everything else being equal, the smaller the variability in group scores, the greater the probability that the difference in group means is statistically significant. The distribution on the right shows a greater difference in the variability of the groups; therefore, there is a *lower* probability that the difference in group means is statistically significant.

ONE APPROACH.
70 UNIQUE SOLUTIONS.

CENGAGE
Learning™

www.cengage.com/4ltrpress

ANSWERS TO STUDY TOOLS QUESTIONS

Chapter 1

FILL-INS

1. behavior
2. Clinical
3. Wilhelm Wundt
4. Gestalt
5. Evolutionary
6. Clark
7. population
8. survey
9. control
10. ethical

MULTIPLE CHOICE

1. A
2. B
3. C
4. A
5. D
6. D
7. A
8. A
9. C
10. C

Chapter 2

FILL-INS

1. neurotransmitters
2. axon
3. myelin
4. schizophrenia
5. autonomic
6. cerebellum
7. existence
8. instincts
9. Down
10. monozygotic (identical)

MULTIPLE CHOICE

1. C
2. B
3. A
4. B
5. A
6. D
7. D
8. A
9. A
10. D

Chapter 3

FILL-INS

1. Perception
2. absolute
3. rods; cones
4. optic
5. retina
6. olfactory
7. taste
8. position
9. semicircular
10. file-drawer

MULTIPLE CHOICE

1. C
2. B
3. A
4. D
5. C
6. C
7. A
8. D
9. A
10. B

Chapter 4

FILL-INS

1. awareness
2. paradoxical
3. five
4. activation
5. trance
6. mantra
7. control
8. abstinence
9. Cocaine
10. Hallucinogenic

MULTIPLE CHOICE

1. D
2. C
3. B
4. A
5. C
6. B
7. D
8. A
9. B
10. A

Chapter 5

FILL-INS

1. unconditioned
2. conditioned
3. extinguish
4. spontaneous
5. Albert
6. flooding
7. Negative
8. fixed-interval
9. Programmed
10. contingency

MULTIPLE CHOICE

1. B
2. D
3. C
4. C
5. A
6. C
7. D
8. D
9. C
10. A

Chapter 6

FILL-INS

1. episodic
2. Semantic
3. maintenance
4. elaborative
5. sensory; short-term; long-term
6. Eidetic
7. flashbulb
8. retroactive
9. proactive
10. synapses

MULTIPLE CHOICE

1. B
2. C
3. D
4. A
5. A
6. D
7. D
8. D
9. B
10. C

Chapter 7

FILL-INS

1. Concepts
2. algorithm
3. Heuristic
4. mental
5. linguistic
6. overregularization
7. g
8. multiple
9. practical
10. intelligence quotient

MULTIPLE CHOICE

1. D
2. D
3. B
4. B
5. C
6. D
7. C
8. D
9. B
10. C

Chapter 8

FILL-INS

1. Motives
2. incentive
3. homeostasis
4. self-actualization
5. Anorexia
6. excitement
7. organizing
8. Apperception
9. performance
10. action

MULTIPLE CHOICE

1. C
2. A
3. A
4. B
5. C
6. D
7. C
8. D
9. D
10. A

Chapter 9

FILL-INS
1. reflexes
2. concrete
3. zone
4. initial-preattachment
5. secondary
6. Formal
7. imaginary
8. diffusion
9. Fluid
10. do not

MULTIPLE CHOICE
1. B
2. A
3. C
4. D
5. B
6. C
7. D
8. B
9. C
10. B

Chapter 10

FILL-INS
1. id
2. superego
3. anal
4. collective
5. inferiority
6. antisocial
7. actualization
8. reference
9. collectivists
10. ambiguous

MULTIPLE CHOICE
1. B
2. A
3. C
4. C
5. B
6. D
7. A
8. D
9. C
10. B

Chapter 11

FILL-INS
1. hassles
2. conflict
3. Ellis
4. higher
5. commitment
6. alarm
7. fight; flight
8. befriend
9. immune
10. cholesterol

MULTIPLE CHOICE
1. B
2. D
3. C
4. B
5. A
6. C
7. D
8. C
9. A
10. B

Chapter 12

FILL-INS
1. perception
2. phobia
3. obsessive–compulsive
4. amnesia
5. identity
6. illness anxiety disorder
7. flight
8. internal
9. catatonic
10. Personality

MULTIPLE CHOICE
1. B
2. B
3. A
4. A
5. D
6. C
7. B
8. A
9. D
10. A

Chapter 13

FILL-INS
1. psychological
2. unconscious
3. Operant
4. free
5. Humanistic
6. Client-centered
7. Cognitive
8. desensitization
9. irrational
10. Minor

MULTIPLE CHOICE
1. C
2. B
3. B
4. B
5. A
6. B
7. B
8. D
9. A
10. C

Chapter 14

FILL-INS
1. cognitive
2. dissonance
3. categorization
4. attraction–similarity
5. passion
6. primacy
7. social
8. facilitation
9. deindividualization
10. bystander

MULTIPLE CHOICE
1. D
2. B
3. A
4. B
5. C
6. B
7. B
8. A
9. B
10. C

REFERENCES

A

Accardi, M., Cleere, C., Lynn, S. J., & Kirsch, I. (2014). Placebo versus "standard" hypnosis rationale: Attitudes, expectancies, hypnotic responses, and experiences. *American Journal of Clinical Hypnosis, 56*(2), 103–114.

Acevedo, B. P., Aron, A., Fisher, H. E., & Brown, L. L. (2012). Neural correlates of long-term intense romantic love. *Social Cognitive and Affective Neuroscience, 7*(2), 145–159.

Adams, A. L., Doucette, T. A., James, R., & Ryan, C. L. (2009). Persistent changes in learning and memory in rats following neonatal treatment with domoic acid. *Physiology and Behavior, 96*(4–5), 505–512.

Agrawal, A., Silberg, J. L., Lynskey, M. T., Maes, H. H., & Eaves, L. J. (2010). Mechanisms underlying the lifetime co-occurrence of tobacco and cannabis use in adolescent and young adult twins. *Drug and Alcohol Dependence, 108* (1–2), 49–55.

Ahonen, M. (2014). Mental disorders in ancient philosophy. *Studies in the History of Philosophy of Mind, 13*, 9–34.

Ahs, F., et al. (2009). Disentangling the web of fear: Amygdala reactivity and functional connectivity in spider and snake phobia. *Psychiatry Research, 172*(2), 103–108.

Ainsworth, M. D. S., Blehar, M. C., Waters, E., & Wall, S. (1978). *Patterns of attachment: A psychological study of the strange situation.* Hillsdale, NJ: Erlbaum.

Ainsworth, M. D. S., & Bowlby, J. (1991). An ethological approach to personality development. *American Psychologist, 46*, 333–341.

Aktar, E., et al. (2014). Parental social anxiety disorder prospectively predicts toddlers' fear/avoidance in a social referencing paradigm. *The Journal of Child Psychology and Psychiatry, 55*(1), 77–87.

Alarcón, R. D., et al. (2009). Issues for *DSM-V*: The role of culture in psychiatric diagnosis. *Journal of Nervous and Mental Disease, 197*(8), 559–660.

Albarracin, D., & Handley, I. M. (2011). The time for doing is not the time for change: Effects of general action and inaction goals on attitude retrieval and attitude change. *Journal of Personality and Social Psychology, 100*(6), 983–998.

Alberts, A., Elkind, D., & Ginsberg, S. (2007). The personal fable and risk-taking in early adolescence. *Journal of Youth and Adolescence, 36*(1), 71–76.

Alessi, S. M., & Petry, N. M. (2013). A randomized study of cellphone technology to reinforce alcohol abstinence in the natural environment. *Addiction, 108*(5), 900–909.

Alexander, G. M., Wilcox, T., & Woods, R. (2009). Sex differences in infants' visual interest in toys. *Archives of Sexual Behavior, 38*(3), 427–433.

Allen, J. P., & Antonishak, J. (2008). Adolescent peer influences: Beyond the dark side. In M. J. Prinstein & K. A. Dodge (Eds.), *Understanding peer influence in children and adolescents* (pp. 141–160). New York: Guilford Press.

Allene, C., et al. (2012). Dynamic changes in interneuron morphophysiological properties mark the maturation of hippocampal network activity. *The Journal of Neuroscience, 32*(19), 6688–6698.

Allport, G. W., & Odbert, H. S. (1936). Traitnames: A psycho-lexical study. *Psychological Monographs, 47*, 211.

Ambrosius, U., et al. (2008). Heritability of sleep electroencephalogram. *Biological Psychiatry, 64*(4), 344–348.

American Cancer Society. (2013). Secondhand smoke. http://www.cancer.org/cancer/cancercauses/tobaccocancer/secondhand-smoke (Accessed November 12, 2013).

American Lung Association. (2013). Smoking. Retrieved from http://www.lungusa.org/stop-smoking/about-smoking/health-effects/smoking .html (Accessed November 12, 2013).

American Psychiatric Association. (2013). *Diagnostic and statistical manual of mental disorders* (Fifth edition; DSM-5). Washington, DC: Author.

American Psychological Association. (2002). Ethical principles of psychologists and code of conduct. *American Psychologist, 57*(12), 1060–1073.

American Psychological Association. (2008). Award for distinguished scientific contributions: Michael S. Gazzaniga. *American Psychologist, 63*(8), 636–638.

American Psychological Association, Center for Workforce Studies. (2009). *Doctoral psychology workforce fast facts. Health service provider subfields.* Retrieved from http://research.apa .org/fastfacts-09.pdf

American Psychological Association. (2012). Stress in America 2009: Executive summary. Retrieved from www.apa.org/news/press/releases/stress/2011/final-2011.pdf

American Psychological Association. (2012). Guidelines for ethical conduct in the care and use of nonhuman animals in research. http://www.apa.org/science/leadership/care/guidelines.aspx

Amsel, E. (2011). Hypothetical thinking in adolescence: Its nature, development, and applications. In E. Amsel & J. G. Smetana (Eds.), *Adolescent vulnerabilities and opportunities* (pp. 86–116). New York: Cambridge University Press.

Anatomy of anxiety. (2002). *Time, 159*, 50.

Anderson, C. A., et al. (2010). Violent video game effects on aggression, empathy, and prosocial behavior in Eastern and Western countries: A meta-analytic review. *Psychological Bulletin, 136*(2), 151–173.

Anderson, O. (1995). The buzz on exercise. *Men's Health, 10*, 88–89.

Andreano, J. M., & Cahill, L. (2009). Sex influences on the neurobiology of learning and memory. *Learning and Memory, 16*, 248–266.

Ansburg, P.I. (2000). Individual differences in problem solving via insight. *Current Psychology, 19*, 143.

Apicella, C. L., Dreber, A., & Mollerstrom, J. (2014). Salivary testosterone change following monetary wins and losses predicts future financial risk-taking. *Psychoneuroendocrinology, 39*, 58–64.

Archer, J. (2009). The nature of human aggression. *International Journal of Law and Psychiatry, 32*(4), 202–208.

Arden, G. (2003, February 21). Test for color vision can save sight. *Optician,* p. 2.

Arendt, J. (2009). Managing jet lag: Some of the problems and possible new solutions. *Sleep Medicine Reviews, 13*(4), 249–256.

Arnett, J. J. (1999). Adolescent storm and stress, reconsidered. *American Psychologist, 54*(5), 317–326.

Arnett, J. J. (2000). Emerging adulthood. *American Psychologist, 55*(5), 469–480.

Arnett, J. J. (2012). New horizons in research on emerging and young adulthood. *National Symposium on Family Issues, 2*(5), 231–244.

Arthritis Foundation. (2000, April 6). Pain in America: Highlights from a Gallup survey. Retrieved from http://www.arthritis.org/answers/sop_factsheet.asp

Arya, R., & Jain, S. V. (2013). Sleepwalking in children and adolescents. In S. V. Kothare & A. Ivanenko (Eds.), *Parasomnias* (pp. 97–113). New York: Springer Science+Business Media.

Asch, S. E. (1952). *Social psychology.* Englewood Cliffs, NJ: Prentice Hall.

Ashtari, M., et al. (2009). Diffusion abnormalities in adolescents and young adults with a history of heavy cannabis use. *Journal of Psychiatric Research, 43*(3), 189–204.

Ashtari, M., & Cyckowski, L. (2012). Brain development during adolescence. In V. R. Preedy (Ed.), *Handbook of growth and growth monitoring in health and disease* (pp. 1213–1229). New York: Springer.

Atkins, M. S., et al. (2002). Suspensions and detention in an urban, low-income school: Punishment or reward? *Journal of Abnormal Child Psychology, 30*(4), 361–371.

Atkinson, R. C., & Shiffrin, R. M. (1968). Human memory: A proposed system and its control processes. In K. Spence (Ed.), *The psychology of learning and motivation* (Vol. 2). New York: Academic Press.

Auyeung, B., Baron-Cohen, S., Ashwin, E., Knickmeyer, R., Taylor, K., Hackett, G., & Hines, M. (2009). Fetal testosterone predicts sexually differentiated behavior in girls and in boys. *Psychological Science, 20*(2), 144–148.

B

Bae, S., Holloway, S. D., Li, J., & Bempechat, J. (2008). Mexican-American students' perceptions of teachers' expectations: Do perceptions differ depending on student achievement levels? *Urban Review, 40*(2), 210–225.

Bagchi, D., & Preuss, H. G. (2007). *Obesity: Epidemiology, pathophysiology, and prevention.* Boca Raton, FL: CRC Press.

Bagge, C. L., Lamis, D. A., Nadorff, M., & Osman, A. (2014). Relations between hopelessness, depressive symptoms, and suicidality: Mediation by reasons for living. *Journal of Clinical Psychology, 70*(1), 18–31.

Bahrick, H. P., Bahrick, P. O., & Wittlinger, R. P. (1975). Fifty years of memory for names and faces. *Journal of Experimental Psychology: General, 104,* 54–75.

Bahrick, H. P., Hall, L. K., & Da Costa, L. A. (2008). Fifty years of memory of college grades: Accuracy and distortions. *Emotion, 8*(1), 13–22.

Baker, L. A., DeFries, J. C., & Fulker, D. W. (1983). Longitudinal stability of cognitive ability in the Colorado adoption project. *Child Development, 54,* 290–297.

Bakst, S., Rabinowitz, J., & Bromet, E. (2009). Is premorbid functioning a risk factor for suicide attempts in first-admission psychosis? *Schizophrenia Research, 116*(2), 210–216.

Baltes, B. B., & Rudolph, C. W. (2013). The theory of selection, optimization, and compensation. In M. Wang (Ed.), *The Oxford handbook of retirement* (pp. 88–101). New York: Oxford University Press.

Baltes, P. B., & Staudinger, U. M. (2000). Wisdom: A metaheuristic (pragmatic) to orchestrate mind and virtue toward excellence. *American Psychologist, 55,* 122–136.

Banaji, M. R., & Heiphetz, L. (2008). Attitudes. In S. T. Fiske, D. T. Gilbert, & G. Lindzey (Eds.), *Handbook of social psychology* (5th ed., Vol. 1., pp. 353–393). Hoboken, NJ: Wiley.

Bandelow, B., et al. (2000). Salivary cortisol in panic attacks. *American Journal of Psychiatry, 157,* 454–456.

Bandelow, B., et al. (2012). Guidelines for the pharmacological treatment of anxiety disorders, obsessive–compulsive disorder and posttraumatic stress disorder in primary care. *International Journal of Psychiatry in Clinical Practice, 16*(2), 77–84.

Bandura, A. (1986). *Social foundations of thought and action: A Social-cognitive theory.* Englewood Cliffs, NJ: Prentice Hall.

Bandura, A. (1999). Social cognitive theory: An agentic perspective. *Asian Journal of Social Psychology, 2*(1), 21–41.

Bandura, A. (2008). An agentic perspective on positive psychology. In S. J. Lopez (Ed.), *Positive psychology: Discovering human strengths* (pp. 167–214). Santa Barbara, CA: ABC-CLIO.

Bandura, A. (2012). Social cognitive theory. In P. A. M. Van Lange, A. W. Kruglanski, & E. T. Higgins (Eds.), *The handbook of theories of social psychology, Vol. 1* (pp. 349–374). London: SAGE Publications.

Bandura, A., Blanchard, E. B., & Ritter, B. (1969). The relative efficacy of desensitization and modeling approaches for inducing behavioral, affective, and cognitive changes. *Journal of Personality and Social Psychology, 13,* 173–199.

Bandura, A., Ross, S. A., & Ross, D. (1963). Imitation of film-mediated aggressive models. *Journal of Abnormal and Social Psychology, 66,* 3–11.

Bandura, A., Taylor, C. B., Williams, S. L., Medford, I. N., & Barchas, J. D. (1985). Catecholamine secretion as a function of perceived coping self-efficacy. *Journal of Consulting and Clinical Psychology, 53,* 406–414.

Baraas, R. C., Foster, D. H., Amano, K., & Nascimento, S. M. C. (2010). Color constancy of red-green dichromats and anomalous trichromats. *Investigative Ophthalmology & Visual Science, 51*(4), 2286–2293.

Barber, J. G. (2001). Relative misery and youth suicide. *Australian and New Zealand Journal of Psychiatry, 35*(1), 49–57.

Barbor, C. (2001). The science of meditation. *Psychology Today, 34,* 54.

Bard, P. (1934). The neurohumoral basis of emotional reactions. In C. A. Murchison (Ed.), *Handbook of general experimental psychology.* Worcester, MA: Clark University Press.

Barden, J., & Tormala, Z. L. (2014). Elaboratio and attitude strength: The new meta-cognitive perspective. *Social & Personality Psychology Compass 8*(1), 17–29.

Barelli, C., Heistermann, M., Boesch, C., & Reichard, U. H. (2008). Mating patterns and sexual swellings in pair-living and multiple groups of wild white-handed gibbons, *Hylobates lar. Animal Behaviour, 75*(3), 991–1001.

Baron, R. A., Branscombe, N. R., & Byrne, D. R. (2009). *Social psychology* (12th ed.). Boston: Allyn & Bacon.

Barrett, E. S., Redmon, J. B., Wang, C., Sparks, A., & Swan, S. H. (2014). Exposure to prenatal life events stress is associated with masculinized play behavior in girls. *NeuroToxicology, 41,* 20–27.

Bartone, P. T., Roland, R. R., Picano, J. J., & Williams, T. J. (2008). Psychological hardiness predicts success in U.S. Army special forces candidates. *International Journal of Selection and Assessment, 16*(1), 78–81.

Bassok, M., & Novick, L. R. (2012). Problem solving. In K. J. Holyoak & R. G. Morrison (Eds.), *The Oxford handbook of thinking and reasoning* (pp. 413–432). New York: Oxford University Press.

Bates, E. (2001) Plasticity, localization and language development. In S. T. Parker, J. Langer, & C. Milbrath (Eds.), *Biology and knowledge revisited* (pp. 205–254). London: Routledge.

Baucom, D. H., & Boeding, S. (2013). The role of theory and research in the practice of cognitive-behavioral couple therapy: If you build it, they will come. *Behavior Therapy, 44*(4), 592–602.

Baumeister, R. F. (1996). *Evil: Inside human cruelty and violence.* New York: W. H. Freeman/Times Books/Henry Holt & Co.

Baumrind, D. (2013). Authoritative parenting revisited: History and current status. In R. E. Larzelere, A. S. Morris, & A. W. Harrist (Eds.), *Authoritative parenting: Synthesizing nurturance and discipline for optimal child development* (pp. 11–34). Washington, DC: American Psychological Association.

Bear, R. E., Fitzgerald, P., Rosenfeld, J. V., & Bittar, R. G. (2010). Neurosurgery for obsessive-compulsive disorder: Contemporary approaches. *Journal of Clinical Neuroscience, 17*(1), 1–5.

Beck, A. T., & Dozois, D. J. A. (2011). Cognitive therapy: Current status and future directions. *Annual Review of Medicine, 62,* 397–409.

Beck, A. T., Wright, F. D., Newman, C. F., & Liese, B. S. (2011). *Cognitive therapy of substance abuse.* New York: Guilford Press.

Beck, A. T., & Haigh, E. A. P. (2014). Advances in cognitive theory and therapy: The generic cognitive model. *Annual Review of Clinical Psychology,* DOI: 10.1146/annurev-clinpsy-032813-153734.

Beesdo, K., Pine, D. S., Lieb, R., & Wittchen, H.-U. (2010). Incidence and risk patterns of anxiety and depressive disorders and categorization of generalized anxiety disorder. *Archives of General Psychiatry, 67*(1), 47–57.

Behar, E., Dobrow DiMarco, I., Hekler, E. B., Mohlman, J., & Staples, A. M. (2009). Current theoretical models of generalized anxiety disorder (GAD): Conceptual review and treatment implications. *Journal of Anxiety Disorders, 23*(8), 1011–1023.

Belsky, J. (2006). Determinants and consequences of infant-parent attachment. In L. Baker & C. S. Tamis-LeMonda (Eds.), *Child psychology: A handbook of contemporary issues* (2nd ed.) (pp. 53–57). New York: Psychology Press.

Belsky, J., Weinraub, M., Owen, M., & Kelly, J. (2001, April). Quantity of child care and problem behavior. In J. Belsky (Chair), *Early childcare and children's development prior to school entry.* Symposium conducted at the 2001 biennial meetings of the Society for Research in Child Development, Minneapolis, MN.

Bem, D. J. (2011). Feeling the future: Experimental evidence for anomalous retroactive influences on cognition and affect. *Journal of Personality and Social Psychology, 100*(3), 407–425.

Benke, K., & Fallin, M. (2010). Methods: Genetic epidemiology. *Psychiatric Clinics of North America, 33*(1), 15–34.

Benson, H. (1975). *The relaxation response.* New York: Morrow.

Berkowitz, L. (2004). Two views of evil: Evil is not only banal. *PsycCRITIQUES.*

Bermudez, P., Lerch, J. P., Evans, A. C., & Zatorre, R. J. (2009). Neuroanatomical correlates of musicianship as revealed by cortical thickness and voxel-based morphometry. *Cerebral Cortex, 19*(7), 1583–1596.

Bernardin, H. J., Cooke, D. K., & Villanova, P. (2000). Conscientiousness and agreeableness as predictors of rating leniency. *Journal of Applied Psychology, 85*(2) 232–236.

Bernstein, D. M., & Loftus, E. F. (2009). How to tell if a particular memory is true or false. *Perspectives on Psychological Science, 4*(4), 370–374.

Berry, C. J., Shanks, D. R., Speekenbrink, M., & Henson, R. N. A. (2012). Models of recognition, recognition priming, and fluency: Exploring a new framework. *Psychological Review, 119*(1), 40–79.

Berscheid, E. (2009). Love in the fourth dimension. *Annual Review of Psychology, 61,* 1–25.

Berten, H., & Rossem, R. V. (2009). Doing worse but knowing better: An exploration of the relationship between HIV/AIDS knowledge and sexual behavior among adolescents in Flemish secondary schools. *Journal of Adolescence, 32*(5), 1303–1319.

Berthoud, H., & Levin, B. E. (2014). CNS regulation of energy balance. In G. A. Bray & C. Bouchard (Eds.), *Handbook of obesity—Epidemiology, etiology, & physiopathology* (pp. 161–172). Boca Raton, FL: CRC Press.

Best, C., & Fortenberry, J. D. (2013). Adolescent sexuality and sexual behavior. In W. T. O'Donohue, L. T. Benuto, & L. W. Tolle (Eds.), *Handbook of adolescent health psychology* (pp. 271–291). New York: Springer.

Bexton, W. H., Heron, W., & Scott, T. H. (1954). Effects of decreased variation in the sensory environment. *Canadian Journal of Psychology, 8,* 70–76.

Bidell, M. P., Turner, J. A., & Casas, J. M. (2002). First impressions count: Ethnic/racial and lesbian/gay/bisexual content of professional psychology application materials. *Professional Psychology: Research and Practice, 33*(1), 97–103.

Bierman, K. L., Domitrovich, C. E., Nix, R. L., Gest, S. D., & Welsh, J. A. (2008). Promoting academic and social-emotional school readiness: The Head Start REDI program. *Child Development, 79*(6), 1802–1817.

Binder, E. B., & Nemeroff, C. B. (2009). The CRF system, stress, depression, and anxiety—Insights from human genetic studies. *Molecular Psychiatry, 15*(6), 574–588.

Birt, D. F., & Phillips, G. J. (2014). Diet, genes, and microbes: Complexities of colon cancer prevention. *Toxicologic Pathology, 42*(1), 182–188.

Bishop, D. V. M. (2009). Genes, cognition, and communication. *Annals of the New York Academy of Sciences, 1156*, 1–18.

Blake, P., Fry, R., & Pesjack, M. (1984). *Self-assessment and behavior change manual.* New York: Random House.

Blass, T. (2009). From New Haven to Santa Clara: A historical perspective on the Milgram obedience experiments. *American Psychologist, 64*(1), 37–45.

Blechert, J., Wilhelm, F. H., Meuret, A. E., Wilhelm, E. M., & Roth, W. T. (2010). Respiratory, autonomic, and experiential responses to repeated inhalations of 20% CO_2 enriched air in panic disorder, social phobia, and healthy controls. *Biological Psychology, 84*(1), 104–111.

Blum, K., et al. (2009). Genes and happiness. *Gene Therapy and Molecular Biology, 13*, 91–129.

Bogen, J. E. (1969). The other side of the brain II: An appositional mind. *Bulletin of the Los Angeles Neurological Society, 34*, 135–162.

Bogen, J. E. (2000). Split-brain basics: Relevance for the concept of one's other mind. *Journal of the American Academy of Psychoanalysis, 28*(2), 341–369.

Bohner, G., & Dickel, N. (2011). Attitudes and attitude change. *Annual Review of Psychology, 62*, 391–417.

Bolinskey, K. P., & Gottesman, I. I. (2010). Premorbid personality indicators of schizophrenia-related psychosis in a hypothetically psychosis-prone college sample. *Scandinavian Journal of Psychology, 51*(1), 68–74.

Bond, B. J., Richards, M. N., & Calvert, S. L. (2013). Media and obesity. In D. Lemish (Ed.), *The Routledge international handbook of children, adolescents, and media* (pp. 232–239). New York: Routledge.

Bonds-Raacke, J.M., Fryer, L.S., Nicks, S.D., & Durr, R.T. (2001). Hindsight bias demonstrated in the prediction of a sporting event. *The Journal of Social Psychology, 141*, 349.

Bonini, L., Maranesi, M., Livi, A., Fogassi, L., & Rizzolatti, G. (2012). Influence of the sight of monkey's own acting hand on the motor discharge of ventral premotor mirror neurons. *International Journal of Psychophysiology, 85*(3), 319.

Bonn-Miller, M. O., Zvolensky, M. J., & Bernstein, A. (2007). Marijuana use motives: Concurrent relations to frequency of past 30-day use and anxiety sensitivity among young adult marijuana smokers. *Addictive Behaviors, 32*(1), 49–62.

Borelli, J., et al. (2010). Attachment and emotion in school-aged children. *Emotion, 10*(4), 475–485.

Bosmans, M. W. G., Benight, C. C., van der Knaap, L. M., Winkel, F. W., & van der Velden, P. G. (2013). The associations between coping self-efficacy and posttraumatic stress symptoms 10 years postdisaster: Differences between men and women. *Journal of Traumatic Stress, 26*(2), 184–191.

Bower, B. (1997). Forbidden flavors: Scientists consider how disgusting tastes can linger surreptitiously in memory. *Science News, 151*, 198–199.

Bower, B. (1991). Oedipus wrecked: Freud's theory of frustrated incest goes on the defensive. *Science News, 140*, 248–250.

Bowlby, J. (1988). *A secure base.* New York: Basic Books.

Boyatzis, R. E. (1974). The effect of alcohol consumption on the aggressive behavior of men. *Quarterly Journal for the Study of Alcohol, 35*, 959–972.

Boyd, J. (2014). Genetic predisposition to breast cancer: The next chapters. *Cancer*, DOI: 10.1002/cncr.28503

Brackett, M. A., Rivers, S. E., & Salovey, P. (2011). Emotional intelligence: Implication for personal, social, academic, and workplace success. *Social and Personality Psychology, 5*(1), 88–103.

Bradley, R. H., et al. (1989). Home environment and cognitive development in the first 3 years of life. *Developmental Psychology, 25*, 217–235.

Bradley, R. H. (2006). The home environment. In N. F. Watt, C. Ayoub, R. H. Bradley, J. E. Puma, & W. A. Lebeouf (Eds.), *The crisis in youth mental health: Critical issues and effective programs: Vol. 4. Early intervention programs and policies: Child psychology and mental health* (pp. 89–120). Westport, CT: Praeger/Greenwood.

Brand, J. (2000). Cited in McFarling, U. L. (2000, August 27). Sniffing out genes' role in our senses of taste and smell. *The Los Angeles Times online.*

Brand, J. S., & van der Schouw, Y. T. (2010). Testosterone, SHBG and cardiovascular health in postmenopausal women. *International Journal of Impotence Research, 22*, 91–104.

Braun, B. G. (1988). *Treatment of multiple personality disorder.* Washington, DC: American Psychiatric Press.

Bray, G. A., & Bouchard, C. (2014). *Handbook of obesity—Epidemiology, etiology, & physiopathology.* Boca Raton, FL: CRC Press.

Bravender, T., et al. (2010). Classification of eating disturbance in children and adolescents: Proposed changes for the *DSM-V. European Eating Disorders Review, 18*(2), 79–89.

Breckenridge, J. N., Zimbardo, P. G., & Sweeton, J. L. (2010). After years of media coverage, can one more video report trigger heuristic judgments? A national study of American terrorism risk perceptions. *Behavioral Sciences of Terrorism, 2*(3), 163–178.

Brewer, M.B. (1999). The psychology of prejudice: Ingroup love or outgroup hate? *Journal of Social Issues, 55*, 429.

Bricker, J. B., Liu, J., Ramey, M., & Peterson, A. V. (2012). Psychosocial factors in adolescent nicotine dependence symptoms: A sample of high school juniors who smoke daily. *Substance Use & Misuse, 47*(6), 640–648.

Brody, J. E. (2000, April 25). Memories of things that never were. *The New York Times,* p. F8.

Broesch, T. L., & Bryant, G. A. (2013). Prosody in infant-directed speech is similar across Western and traditional cultures. *Journal of Cognition and Development*, DOI: 10.1080/15248372.2013.833923

Broment, E. J. (2014). Emotional consequences of nuclear power plant disasters. *Health Physics, 106*(2), 206–210.

Brook, J. S., Zheng, L., Whiteman, M., & Brook, D. W. (2001). Aggression in toddlers: Associations with parenting and marital relations. *Journal of Genetic Psychology, 162*(2), 228–241.

Brown, A. S. (2007). Identifying risks using a new assessment tool: The missing piece of the jigsaw in medical device risk assessment. *Clinical Risk, 13*, 56–59.

Brown, A. S., & Derkits, E. J. (2010). Prenatal infection and schizophrenia: A review of epidemiologic and translational studies. *American Journal of Psychiatry, 167*, 261–280.

Brown, G. R. (2009). Evolutionary perspectives on sexual coercion in human beings and other primates: The future of the rape debate. *Journal of Evolutionary Psychology, 7*(4), 347–350.

Brown, A. S., Schrag, A., Krishnamoorthy, E., & Trimble, M. R. (2007). Are patients with somatization disorder highly suggestible? *Acta Psychiatrica Scandinavica, 117*(3), 232–235.

Brown, R., & McNeill, D. (1966). The tip-of-the-tongue phenomenon. *Journal of Verbal Learning and Verbal Behavior, 5*, 325–337.

Brownlee, S. (1997). The senses: They delight, heal, define the boundaries of our world. And they are helping unlock the brain's secrets. *U.S. News & World Report, 122*, 50–57.

Brownstein, A. L. (2003). Biased predecision processing. *Psychological Bulletin, 129*(4), 545–568.

Brun, C. C., Lepore, N., Luders, E., Chou, Y.-Y., Madsen, S. K., Toga, A. W., & Thompson, P. M. (2009). Sex differences in brain structure in auditory and cingulate regions. *NeuroReport: For Rapid Communication of Neuroscience Research, 20*(10), 930.

Bryant, R. (2006). Acute stress disorder. *Psychiatry, 5*(7), 238–239.

Buchanan, T. W., Driscoll, D., Mowrer, S. M., Sollers, J. J., Thayer, J. F., Kirschbaum, C., & Tranel, D. (2010). Medial prefrontal cortex damage affects physiological and psychological stress responses differently in men and women. *Psychoneuroendocrinology, 35*(1), 56–66.

Buckley, P. F., Buchanan, R. W., Tamminga, C. A., & Schulz, S. C. (2000). Schizophrenia research. *Schizophrenia Bulletin, 26*(2), 411–419.

Bulkeley, K. (2013, October 18). Data-mining our dreams. *The New York Times,* p. SR14.

Bull, N. J., Hunter, M., & Finlay, D. C. (2003). Cue gradient and cue density interact in the detection and recognition of objects defined by motion, contrast, or texture. *Perception, 32*(1), 29–39.

Bullough, V.L. (1998). Alfred Kinsey and the Kinsey Report: Historical overview and lasting contributions. *The Journal of Sex Research, 35*, 127–131.

Burger, J. M. (2009). Replicating Milgram: Would people still obey today? *American Psychologist, 64*(1), 1–11.

Bushman, B. J., Jamieson, P. E., Weitz, I., & Romer, D. (2013). Gun violence trends in movies. *Pediatrics*, DOI: 10.1542/peds.2013–1600)

Buss, D. M. (2009a). The great struggles of life: Darwin and the emergence of evolutionary psychology. *American Psychologist, 64*(2), 140–148.

Buss, D. M. (2009b). How can evolutionary psychology successfully explain personality and individual differences? *Perspectives on Psychological Science, 4*(4), 359–366.

Buss, D. M., & Schmitt, D. P. (2011). Evolutionary psychology and feminism. *Sex Roles, 64*(9–10), 768–787.

C

Cailhol, S., & Mormede, P. (2002). Conditioned taste aversion and alcohol drinking: Strain and gender differences. *Journal of Studies on Alcohol, 63*, 91–99.

Campbell, R. A., Machlus, K. R., & Wolberg, A. S. (2010). Smoking out the cause of thrombosis. *Arteriosclerosis, Thrombosis, and Vascular Biology, 30*(7), 75–79.

Campos, J. J., Hiatt, S., Ramsey, D., Henderson, C., & Svejda, M. (1978). The emergence of fear on the visual cliff. In M. Lewis & L. Rosenblum (Eds.), *The origins of affect.* New York: Plenum Press.

Cannon, W. B. (1927). The James-Lange theory of emotions: A critical examination and an alternative theory. *American Journal of Psychology, 39*, 106–124.

Cannon, W. B. (1932). *The wisdom of the body.* New York: Norton.

Cannon, W. B., & Washburn, A. (1912). An explanation of hunger. *American Journal of Physiology, 29*, 441–454.

Cantalupo, C., & Hopkins, W. D. (2001). Asymmetric Broca's area in great apes: A region of the ape brain is uncannily similar to one linked with speech in humans. *Nature, 414*(6863), 505.

Carey, B. (2009, November 27). Psychosurgery for mental ills offers both hope and risk. *The New York Times,* p. A1.

Carmichael, L. L., Hogan, H. P., & Walter, A. A. (1932). An experimental study of the effect of language on the reproduction of visually perceived form. *Journal of Experimental Psychology, 15*, 73–86.

Carpenter, S. (2001, March). Everyday fantasia: The world of synesthesia. *Monitor on Psychology, 32.* Retrieved May 22, 2003, http://www.apa.org/monitor.mar01/synesthesia.html

Carrard, A., Salzmann, A., Malafosse, A., & Karege, F. (2011). Increased DNA methylation status of the serotonin receptor 5HTR1A gene promoter in schizophrenia and bipolar disorder. *Journal of Affective Disorders, 132*(3), 450–453.

Carré, J. M., & Putnam, S. K. (2010). Watching a previous victory produces an increase in testosterone among elite hockey players. *Psychoneuroendocrinology, 35*(3), 475–479.

Carver, C. S., & Harmon-Jones, E. (2009). Anger is an approach-related affect: Evidence and implications. *Psychological Bulletin, 135*(2), 183–204.

Castelli, L., Zogmaister, C., & Tomelleri, S. (2009). The transmission of racial attitudes within the family. *Developmental Psychology, 45*(2), 586–591.

Castor, D., Pilowsky, D. J., Hadden, B., Fuller, C., Ompad, D. C., de Leon, C. L., ... Hoover, D. R. (2010). Sexual risk reduction among non-injection drug users: Report of a randomized controlled trial. *AIDS Care, 22*(1), 62–70.

Cattell, R. B. (1949). *The culture-free intelligence test.* Champaign, IL: Institute for Personality and Ability Testing.

Catts, V. S., & Catts, S. V. (2009). Psychotomimetic effects of PCP, LSD, and Ecstasy: Pharmacological models of schizophrenia? In P. S. Sachdev & M. S. Keshavan (Eds.), *Secondary schizophrenia* (pp. 141–168). Cambridge, England: Cambridge University Press.

Cavallaro, F. I., Cacace, I., Del Testa, M., Andre, P., Carli, G., De Pascalis, V., ... Santarcangelo, E. L. (2010). Hypnotizability-related EEG alpha and theta activities during visual and somesthetic imageries. *Neuroscience Letters, 470*(1), 13–18.

Cellard, C., Lefèbvre, A.-A., Maziade, M., Roy, M.-A., & Tremblay, S. (2010). An examination of the relative contribution of saturation and selective attention to memory deficits in patients with recent-onset schizophrenia and their unaffected parents. *Journal of Abnormal Psychology, 119*(1), 60–70.

Centers for Disease Control and Prevention. (2009). FastStats: Suicide and self-inflicted injury. Retrieved from http://www.cdc.gov/nchs/fastats/suicide.htm

Centers for Disease Control and Prevention. (2013a). Tobacco-related mortality. http://www.cdc.gov/tobacco/data_statistics/fact_sheets/health_effects/tobacco_related_mortality/ (Accessed November 12, 2013).

Centers for Disease Control and Prevention. (2013b). Suicide and self-inflicted injury. http://www.cdc.gov/nchs/fastats/suicide.htm (Accessed March 7, 2014).

Chafee, M. V., & Goldman-Rakic, P. S. (2000). Inactivation of parietal and pre-frontal cortex reveals interdependence of neural activity during memory-guided saccades. *Journal of Neurophysiology, 83*(3), 1550–1566.

Champagne, F. A., Curley, J. P., Swaney, W. T., Hasen, N. S., & Keverne, E. B. (2009). Epigenetic mechanisms mediating the long-term effects of maternal care on development. *Behavioral Neuroscience, 123*(3), 469–480.

Chance, W. T., Xiao, C., Dayal, R., & Sheriff, S. (2007). Alteration of NPY and Y1 receptor in dorsomedial and ventromedial areas of hypothalamus in anorectic tumor-bearing rats. *Peptides, 28*(2), 295–301.

Chang, E. C., Yu, E. A., & Lin, E. Y. (2013). An examination of ethnic variations in perfectionism and interpersonal influences as predictors of eating disturbances: A look at Asian and European American females. *Asian American Journal of Psychology,* DOI: 10.1037/a0034621

Chard, K. M., Schumm, J. A., Owens, G. P., & Cottingham, S. M. (2010). A comparison of OEF and OIF veterans and Vietnam veterans receiving cognitive processing therapy. *Journal of Traumatic Stress, 23*(1), 25–32.

Chen, J., & Rizzo, J. (2010). Racial and ethnic disparities in use of psychotherapy: Evidence from U.S. national survey data. *Psychiatric Services, 61*, 364–372.

Chen, J., & Li, X. (2014). Genetic and environmental etiologies of adolescent dysfunctional attitudes: A twin study. *Twin Research and Human Genetics: The Official Journal of the International Society for Twin Studies, 17*(1), 16–22.

Chen, Y., & Fouad, N. A. (2013). Asian American educational goals: Racil barriers and cultural factors. *Journal of Career Assessment, 21*(1), 73–90.

Cherniak, C. (2009). Brain wiring optimization and non-genomic nativism. In M. Piatelli-Palmarini, P. Salaburu, & J. Uriagereka (Eds.), *Of minds and language: A dialogue with Noam Chomsky in the Basque country* (pp. 108–122). New York: Oxford University Press.

Cheung, C-K., & Leung, K-K. (2008). Ways by which comparable income affects life satisfaction in Hong Kong. *Social Indicators Research, 87*(1), 169–187.

Chida, Y., & Steptoe, A. (2009). The association of anger and hostility with future coronary heart disease: A meta-analytic review of prospective evidence. *Journal of the American College of Cardiology, 53*(11), 936–946.

Ching, C. M., et al. (2014). The manifestation of traits in everyday behavior and affect: A five-culture study. *Journal of Research in Personality, 48*, 1–16.

Cho, S., et al. (2012). Hippocampal-prefrontal engagement and dynamic causal interactons in the maturation of children's fact retrieval. *Journal of Cognitive Neuroscience, 24*(9), 1849–1866.

Choi, B., Schnall, P., Ko, S., Dobson, M., & Baker, D. (2013). Job strain and coronary heart disease. *The Lancet, 381*(9865), 448.

Choi, D., et al. (2012). NADPH oxidase 1-mediated oxidative stress leads to dopamine neuron death in Parkinson's Disease. *Antioxidants & Redox Signaling, 16*(10), 1033–1045.

Clancy, S. A. (2008). How do people come to believe they were abducted by aliens? In E. Goode & D. A. Vail (Eds.), *Extreme deviance* (pp. 54–63). Thousand Oaks, CA: Pine Forge Press.

Clancy, S. A., McNally, R. J., Schacter, D. L., Lenzenweger, M. F., & Pitman, R. (2002). Memory distortion in people reporting abduction by aliens. *Journal of Abnormal Psychology, 111*(3), 455–461.

Clark, A., & Misyak, J. B. (2009). Language, innateness, and universals. In *Language universals* (pp. 253–261). *Oxford Scholarship* Online Monographs.

Clark, D. A., & Beck, A. T. (2011). Cognitive therapy for the anxiety disorders. New York: Guilford Press.

Clark, E. V., & Nikitina, T. V. (2009). One vs. more than one: Antecedents to plural marking in early language acquisition. *Linguistics, 47*(1), 103–140.

Clark, S. (2009). Sleep deprivation: Implications for obstetric practice in the United States. *American Journal of Obstetrics and Gynecology, 201*(2), 136. e1–136.e4.

Clark, S. E., & Loftus, E. F. (1996). Space alien memories and scientific scrutiny. *PsycCRITIQUES, 41*(3), 294.

Clark, T. T. (2010). Reviewing the connection between paradigms and theories to understand adolescent drug use. *Journal of Child and Adolescent Substance Abuse, 19*(1), 16–32.

Clasen, P. C., Disner, S. G., & Beevers, C. G. (2013). Cognition and depression: Mechanisms associated with the onset and maintenance of emotional disorder. In M. D. Robinson, E. R. Watkins, & E. Harmon-Jones. *Cognition and emotion* (pp. 443–461). New York: Guilford Press.

Cocking, C., Drury, J., & Reicher, S. (2009). The psychology of crowd behaviour in emergency evacuations. *Irish Journal of Psychology, 30*(1–2), 59–73.

Cohen, S., et al. (2012). Chronic stress, glucocorticoid receptor resistance, inflammation, and disease risk. *Proceedings of the National Academy of Sciences, 109*(16), 5995–5999.

Collaer, M. L., & Hill, E. M. (2006). Large sex difference in adolescents on a timed line judgment task: Attentional contributors and task relationship to mathematics. *Perception, 35*(4), 561–572.

Collins, R. L., et al. (2010). Off-premise alcohol sales policies, drinking, and sexual risk among people living with HIV. *American Journal of Public Health, 100*(10), 1890–1892.

Comas-Diaz, L. (2008). Latino psycho-spirituality. In K. J. Schneider (Ed.), *Existential-integrative psychotherapy: Guideposts to the core of practice* (pp. 100–109). New York: Routledge/Taylor & Francis Group.

Comas-Diaz, L. & Greene, B. (2013). *Psychological health of women of color: Intersections, challenges, and opportunities.* Santa Barbara: ABC CLIO.

Consortium of Social Science Associations. (2003). McQuery testifies to Homeland Security Science Subcommittee. *Washington Update, 22*(10), 1–7.

Contrada, R. J., & Baum, A. (Eds.), (2011). *The handbook of stress science: Biology, psychology, and health.* New York: Springer.

Cooper, C. A., Golden, L., & Socha, A. (2013). The Big Five personality factors and mass politics. *Journal of Applied Social Psychology, 43*(1), 68–82.

Cooper, M., Galbraith, M., & Drinkwater, J. (2001). Assumptions and beliefs in adolescents with anorexia nervosa and their mothers. *Eating Disorders: Journal of Treatment and Prevention, 9*(3), 217–223.

Corballis, M. C. (2009). The evolution and genetics of cerebral asymmetry. *Philosophical Transactions of the Royal Society, 364*(1519), 867–879.

Cornoldi, C. (2006). The contribution of cognitive psychology to the study of human intelligence. *European Journal of Cognitive Psychology, 18*(1), 1–17.

Coskun, O., Sener, K., Kilic, S., Erdem, H., Yaman, H., Besirbellioglu, A. B., & Eyigun, C. P. (2010). Stress-related Epstein-Barr virus reactivation. *Clinical and Experimental Medicine, 10*(1), 15–20.

Cotton, S. M., & Richdale, A. L. (2010). Sleep patterns and behaviour in typically developing children and children with autism, Down syndrome, Prader-Willi syndrome and intellectual disability. *Research in Autism Spectrum Disorders, 4*(3), 490–500.

Cox, W. M., & Alm, R. (2005, February 28). Scientists are made, not born. *The New York Times* online.

Craig, J.C., & Rollman, G.B. (1999, Annual). Somesthesis. *Annual Review of Psychology*, p. 305.

Craik, F. I. M., & Rose, N. S. (2012). Memory encoding and aging: A neurocognitive perspective. *Neuroscience & Biobehavioral Reviews, 36*(7), 1729–1739.

Crighton, D. A., & Towl, G. J. (Eds.), (2010). *Forensic psychology.* Hoboken, NJ: Wiley.

Crits-Christoph, P., Gibbons, M. B. C., & Mukberjee, D. (2013). Psychotherapy process-outcome research. In M. J. Lambert (Ed.), *Bergin and Garfield's handbook of psychotherapy and behavior change* (pp. 298–340). Hoboken, NJ: Wiley.

Crittenden, P. M., & Dallos, R. (2009). All in the family: Integrating attachment and family systems theories. *Clinical Child Psychology and Psychiatry, 14*(3), 389–409.

Crofoot, M. C., & Wrangham, R. W. (2010). Intergroup aggression in primates and humans: The case for a unified theory. In P. M. Kappeler & J. B. Silk (Eds.), *Mind the gap: Tracing the origins of human universals* (pp. 171–195). New York: Springer.

Crosnoe, R. (2011). Schools, peers, and the big picture of adolescent development. In E. Amsel & J. G. Smetana (Eds.), *Adolescent vulnerabilities and opportunities* (pp. 182–204). New York: Cambridge University Press.

Cuijpers, P., van Straten, A., Warmerdam, L., & Andersson, G. (2009). Psychotherapy versus the combination of psychotherapy and pharmacotherapy in the treatment of depression: A meta-analysis. *Depression and Anxiety, 26*(3), 279–288.

Cuijpers, P., et al. (2013). The efficacy of psychotherapy and pharmacotherapy in treating depressive and anxiety disorders: A meta-analysis of direct comparisons. *World Psychiatry, 12*(2), 137–148.

Cummings, J. A., Hayes, A. M., Newman, C. F., & Beck, A. T. (2011). Navigating therapeutic alliance ruptures in cognitive therapy for avoidant and obsessive-compulsive personality disorders and comorbid axis I disorders. *International Journal of Cognitive Therapy, 4*(Special section: Recent advances in BDD), 397–414.

Cummins, R. A., & Nistico, H. (2002). Maintaining life satisfaction: The role of positive cognitive bias. *Journal of Happiness Studies, 3*(1), 37–69.

Curry, K. (1993, October 22). Male menopause: Is it myth, or a reality of aging? *Knight Ridder/Tribune News Service.*

Curtis, A. (2001). Reward and punishment: In this regular feature examiners and teachers will explore baffling or taken for granted concepts and topics to give you clarity and insight into their meaning and their significance. *Psychology Review, 8,* 8–9.

D

Dabbs, J. M., Jr., Hargrove, M. F., & Heusel, C. (1996). Testosterone differences among college fraternities: Well-behaved vs. rambunctious. *Personality and Individual Differences, 20*(2), 157–161.

Dahl, A., Campos, J. J., et al. (2013). The epigenesis of wariness of heights. *Psychological Science, 24*(7), 1361–1367.

Danhauer, J. L. (2009). Survey of college students on iPod use and hearing health. *Journal of the American Academy of Audiology, 20*(1), 5–27.

Darley, J. M., & Latané, B. (1968). Bystander intervention in emergencies: Diffusion of responsibility. *Journal of Personality and Social Psychology, 8,* 377–383.

Darwin, C. A. (1872). *The expression of the emotions in man and animals.* London: J. Murray.

Daud, M. K. M., Mohd Noor, R., Abd Rahman, N., Suhaimi Sidek, D., & Mohamad, A. (2010). The effect of mild hearing loss on academic performance in primary school children. *International Journal of Pediatric Otorhinolaryngology, 74*(1), 67–70.

David, D., Lynn, S. J., & Ellis, A. (Eds.), (2010). *Rational and irrational beliefs: Research, theory, and clinical practice.* New York: Oxford University Press.

David, E. J. R., Okazaki, S., & Saw, A. (2009). Bicultural self-efficacy among college students: Initial scale development and mental health correlates. *Journal of Counseling Psychology, 56*(2), 211–226.

Davidoff, J., Fonteneau, E., & Goldstein, J. (2008). Cultural differences in perception: Observations from a remote culture. *Journal of Cognition and Culture, 8*(3–4), 189–209.

Davila-Ross, M., Allcock, B., Thomas, C., & Bard, K. A. (2011). Aping expressions? Chimpanzees produce distinct laugh types when responding to laughter of others. *Emotion, 11*(5), 1013-1020.

Dawood, K., Bailey, J. M., & Martin, N. G. (2009). Genetic and environmental influences on sexual orientation. In Y.-K. Kim (Ed.), *Handbook of behavior genetics* (pp. 269–279). New York: Springer.

Dede, A. J. O., Wixted, J. T., Hopkins, R. O., & Squire, L. R. (2013). Hippocampal damage impairs recognition memory broadly, affecting both parameters in two prominent models of memory. *Proceedings of the National Academy of Sciences of the United States of America, 110*(16), 6577–6582.

De Houwer, J., Thomas, S., & Baeyens, F. (2001). Associative learning of likes and dislikes: A review of 25 years of research on human evaluative conditioning. *Psychological Bulletin, 127*(6), 853–869.

De Michele, P. E., Gansneder, B., & Solomon, G. B. (1998). Success and failure attributions of wrestlers: Further evidence of the self-serving bias. *Journal of Sport Behavior, 21*(3), 242–255.

De Rooij, S. R., Painter, R. C., Swaab, D. F., & Roseboom, T. J. (2009). Sexual orientation and gender identity after prenatal exposure to the Dutch famine. *Archives of Sexual Behavior, 38*(3), 411–416.

DeCasper, A. J., & Prescott, P. A. (1984). Human newborns' perception of male voices. *Developmental Psychobiology, 17,* 481–491.

Decety, J., & Batson, C. D. (2009). Empathy and morality: Integrating social and neuroscience approaches. In J. Verplaetse et al. (Eds.), *The moral brain.* (pp. 109–127). New York: Springer.

Deecher, D., Andree, T. H., Sloan, D., & Schechter, L. E. (2008). From menarche to menopause: Exploring the underlying biology of depression in women experiencing hormonal changes. *Psychoneuro endocrinology, 33*(1), 3–17.

De Fruyt, F., & De Clercq, B. (2014). Antecedents of personality disorder in childhood and adolescence: Toward an integrative developmental model. *Annual Review of Developmental Psychology*, DOI: 10.1146/annurev-clinpsy-032813-153634.

De Houwer, J., Barnes-Holmes, D., & Moors, A. (2013). What is learning? On the nature and merits of a functional definition of learning. *Psychonomic Bulletin & Review, 20*(4), 631–642.

Del Giudice, M. J. (2010). What might this be? Rediscovering the Rorschach as a tool for personnel selection in organizations. *Journal of Personality Assessment, 92*(1), 78–89.

Delgado, J. M. R. (1969). *Physical control of the mind.* New York: Harper & Row.

DeLisi, M., Vaughn, M. G., Gentiel, D. A., Anderson, C. A., & Shook, J. J. (2013). Violent video games, delinquency, and youth violence: New evidence. *Youth Violence and Juvenile Justice, 11*(2), 132–142.

Demir, M., & Weitekamp, L. A. (2007). I am so happy 'cause today I found my friend: Friendship and personality as predictors of happiness. *Journal of Happiness Studies, 8*(2), 181–211.

Dennis, J., Markey, M., Johnston, K., Vander Wal, J., & Arriman, N. (2008). The role of stress and social support in predicting depression among a hypertensive African American sample. *Heart and Lung: Journal of Acute Critical Care, 37*(2), 105–112.

DeRigne, L., & Ferrante, S. (2012). The sandwich generation: A review of the literature. *Florida Public Health Review, 9,* 95–104.

DeRubeis, R. J., & Crits-Christoph, P. (1998). Empirically supported individual and group psychological treatments for adult mental disorders. *Journal of Consulting and Clinical Psychology, 66,* 37–52.

De Wild-Hartmann, J. A., et al. (2013). Day-to-day associations between subjective sleep and affect in regard to future depression in a female population-based sample. *British Journal of Psychology, 203*(5), DOI: 10.1192/bjp.bp.112.123794.

Dick, D. M., Prescott, C., & McGue, M. (2009). The genetics of substance use and substance use disorders. In Y-K. Kim (Ed.), *Handbook of behavior genetics* (pp. 433–453). New York: Springer.

Dickerson, B. C., & Eichenbaum, H. (2009). The episodic memory system: Neuro-circuitry and disorders. *Neuropsychopharmacology Reviews, 35,* 86–104.

Dickerson, F. D., Tenhula, W. N., & Green-Paden, L. (2005). The token economy for schizophrenia: Review of the literature and recommendations for future research. *Schizophrenia Research, 75*(2–3), 405–416.

Dienes, Z., & Hutton, S. (2013). Understanding hypnosis metacognitively: rTMS applied to left DLPFC increases hypnotic suggestibility. *Cortex, 49*(2), 386–392.

Difede, J. (2005). In Lake, M. (2005, May 2). Virtual reality heals 9/11 wounds. *CNN.* Retrieved from http://www.cnn.com/2005/TECH/04/29/spark.virtual/index.html

DiGiuseppe, R. A. (2009). Rational-emotive behavior therapy. In N. Kazantzis, M. A. Reinecke, F. M. Dattilio, & A. Freeman (Eds.), *Cognitive and behavioral theories in clinical practice* (pp. 115–147). New York: Guilford Press.

Dodge, K. A., & Godwin, J. (2013). Social-information processing patterns mediate the impact of preventive intervention on adolescent antisocial behavior. *Psychological Science, 24*(4), 456–465.

Doll, C., McLaughlin, T. F., & Barretto, A. (2013). The token economy: A recent review and evaluation. *International Journal of Basic and Applied Science, 2*(1), 131–149.

Dollard, J., Doob, L. W., Miller, N. E., Mowrer, O. H., & Sears, R. R. (1939). *Frustration and aggression.* New Haven, CT: Yale University Press.

Donovan, C.A., & Smolkin, L.B. (2002). Children's genre knowledge: An examination of K-5 student's performance on multiple tasks providing differing levels of scaffolding. *Reading Research Quarterly, 37,* 428–466.

Dotson, V. M., Kitner-Triolo, M. H., Evans, M. K., & Zonderman, A. B. (2009). Effects of race and socioeconomic status on the relative influence of education and literacy on cognitive functioning. *Journal of the International Neuropsychological Society, 15,* 580–589.

Dougherty, D. M., et al. (2013). Impulsivity, attention, memory, and decision-making among adolescent marijuana users. *Psychopharmacology, 226*(2), 307–319.

Drake, R. E., & Latimer, E. (2012). Lessons learned in developing community mental health center care in America. *World Psychiatry, 11*(1), 47–51.

Driessen, E., Cuijpers, P., de Maat, S. C., Abbass, A. A., de Jonghe, F., & Dekker, J. J. (2010). The efficacy of short-term psychodynamic psychotherapy for depression: A meta-analysis. *Clinical Psychology Review, 30*(1), 25–36.

Dube, S. R., Asman, K., Malarcher, A., & Caraballo, R. (2009). Cigarette smoking among adults and trends in smoking cessation—United States, 2008. *Morbidity and Mortality Weekly Report, 58*(44), 1227–1232.

Dubiela, F. P., et al. (2010). Inverse benzodiazepine agonist fi-CCM does not reverse learning deficit induced by sleep deprivation. *Neuroscience Letters, 469*(1), 169–173.

Duckworth, A. L., & Seligman, M. E. P. (2005). Self-discipline outdoes IQ in predicting academic performance of adolescents. *Psychological Science, 16*(12), 939–944.

Durlez, B. (2011). Adolescent ethnic prejudice: Understanding the effects of parental extrinsic versus intrinsic goal promotion. *The Journal of Social Psychology, 151*(4), 441–454.

Dweck, C. S. (2006). *Mindset: The new psychology of success.* New York: Random House.

Dweck, C. S. (2009). Self-theories and lessons for giftedness: A reflective conversation. In T. Balchin, B. Hymer, & D. J. Matthews (Eds.), *The Routledge international companion to gifted education* (pp. 308–316). New York: Routledge/Taylor & Francis.

Dworzynski, K., Happe, F., Bolton, P., & Ronald, A. (2009). Relationship between symptom domains in autism spectrum disorders: A population based twin study. *Journal of Autism and Developmental Disorders, 39*(8), 1197–1210.

E

Eaton, N. R., et al. (2012). An invariant dimensional liability model of gender differences in mental disorder prevalence: Evidence from a national sample. *Journal of Abnormal Psychology, 121*(1), 282–288.

Ebbinghaus, H. (1913). *Memory: A contribution to experimental psychology* (H. A. Roger & C. E. Bussenius, Trans.). New York: Columbia University Press. (Original work published 1885.)

Ebstein, R., Israel, S., Chew, S., Zhong, S., & Knafo, A. (2010). Genetics of human social behavior. *Neuron, 65*(6), 831–844.

Ecker, A. H., & Buckner, J. D. (2014). Cannabis use behaviors and social anxiety: The roles of perceived descriptive and injunctive social norms. *Journal of Studies on Alcohol and Drugs, 75*(1), http://www.jsad.com/jsad/article/Cannabis_Use_Behaviors_and_Social_Anxiety_The_Roles_of_Perceived_Descripti/4894.html

Egawa, T., Mishima, K., Egashira, N., Fukuzawa, M., Abe, K., Yae, T., … Fujiwara, M. (2002). Impairment of spatial memory in kaolin-induced hydrocephalic rats is associated with changes in the hippocampal cholinergic and noradrenergic contents. *Behavioural Brain Research, 129*(1–2), 31–39.

Ehde, D. M., Dillworth, T. M., & Turner, J. A. (2014). Cognitive-behavioral therapy for individuals with chronic pain: Efficacy, innovations, and directions for research. *American Psychologist, 69*(2), 153–166.

Eichenbaum, H., & Fortin, N. (2003). Episodic memory and the hippocampus: It's about time. *Current Directions in Psychological Science, 12*(2), 53–57.

Eisendrath, S. J., et al. (2014). A preliminary study: Efficacy of mindfulness-based cognitive therapy versus sertraline as first-line treatments for major depressive disorder. *Mindfulness,* DOI: 10.1007/s12671-014-0280-8

Ekman, P. (1980). *The face of man.* New York: Garland Press.

Ekman, P. (1993). Facial expression and emotion. *American Psychologist, 48,* 384–392.

Ekman, P. (2003). Cited in Foreman, J. (2003, August 5). A conversation with Paul Ekman: The 43 facial muscles that reveal even the most fleeting emotions. *The New York Times online.*

Ekman, P., Friesen, W. V., O'Sullivan, M., Chan, A., Diacoyanni-Tarlatzis, I., Heider, K., … Tzavaras, A. (1987). Universals and cultural differences in the judgments of facial expressions of emotion. *Journal of Personality and Social Psychology, 53,* 712–717.

Elkind, D. (1967). Egocentrism in adolescence. *Child Development, 38,* 1025–1034.

Elkind, D. (1985). Egocentrism redux. *Developmental Review, 5,* 218–226.

Elkins, D. N. (2009). Why humanistic psychology lost its power and influence in American psychology. *Journal of Humanistic Psychology, 49*(3), 267–291.

Ellickson, P. L., Tucker, J. S., Klein, D. J., & McGuigan, K. A. (2001). Prospective risk factors for alcohol misuse in late adolescence. *Journal of Studies on Alcohol, 62*(6), 773–782.

Elliot, A. J., et al. (2010). Red, rank, and romance in women viewing men. *Journal of Experimental Psychology: General, 139*(3), 399–417.

Elliot, A. J., Greitemeyer, T., & Pazda, A. D. (2013). Women's use of red clothing as a sexual signal in intersexual attraction. *Journal of Experimental Social Psychology, 48*(3), 599–602.

Elliot, A. J., & Mapes, R. R. (2005). Approach-avoidance motivation and self-concept evaluation. In A. Teaser, J. V. Wood, & D. A. Stapel (Eds.), *On building, defending, and regulating the self: A psychological perspective* (pp. 171–196). New York: Psychology Press.

Elliot, A. J., & Niesta, D. (2008). Romantic red: Red enhances men's attraction to women. *Journal of Personality and Social Psychology, 95*(5), 1150–1164.

Ellis, A. (2005). *How to stubbornly refuse to make yourself miserable about anything—yes, anything.* New York: Kensington.

Ellis, M. A., Weiss, B., & Lochman, J. E. (2009). Executive functions in children: Associations with aggressive behavior and appraisal processing. *Journal of Abnormal Child Psychology, 37*(7), 945–956.

Else-Quest, N. M., & Grabe, S. (2012). The political is personal: Measurement and application of nation-level indicators of gender equity in psychological research. *Psychology of Women Quarterly.* DOI: 10.1177/0361684312441592

Else-Quest, N. M., Hyde, J. S., & Linn, M. C. (2010). Cross-national patterns of gender differences in mathematics: A meta-analysis. *Psychological Bulletin, 136*(1), 103–127.

Engelhard, I. M., van den Hout, M. A., Janssen, W. C., & van der Beek, J. (2010). Eye movements reduce vividness and emotionality of "flash-forwards." *Behaviour Research and Therapy, 48*(5), 442–447.

English, T., & Carstensen, L. L. (2014). Selective narrowing of social networks across adulthood is associated with improved emotional experience in daily life. *International Journal of Behavioral Development,* DOI: 10.1177/0165025413515404

Erikson, E. H. (1963). *Childhood and society.* New York: Norton.

Eriksson, C. J. P. (2008). Role of alcohol and sex hormones on human aggressive behavior. In D. W. Pfaff, C. Kordon, P. Chanson, & Y. Christen (Eds.), *Hormones and social behavior* (pp. 177–185). Berlin: Springer-Verlag.

Eron, L. D. (1982). Parent-child interaction, television violence, and aggression of children. *American Psychologist, 37,* 197–211.

Eron, L. D. (1993). Cited in DeAngelis, T. (1993). It's baaack: TV violence, concern for kid viewers. *APA Monitor, 24*(8), 16.

Escorial, S., Rebollo, I., Garcia, L. F., Colom, R., Abad, F. J., & Juan-Espinosa, M. (2003). Abilities that explain the intelligence decline: Evidence from the WAIS-III. *Psicothema, 15*(1), 19–22.

Esser, J. K., & Lindoerfer, J. S. (2006). Groupthink and the space shuttle *Challenger* accident: Toward a quantitative case analysis. *Journal of Behavioral Decision Making, 2*(3), 167–177.

Etaugh, C. A., & Bridges, J. S. (2006). Midlife transitions. In J. Worell & C. D. Goodheart (Eds.), *Handbook of girls' and women's psychological health: Gender and well-being across the life-span* (pp. 359–367). Oxford series in clinical psychology. New York: Oxford University Press.

Eysenck, H. J., & Eysenck, M. W. (1985). *Personality and individual differences.* New York: Plenum Press.

F

Fairburn, C.G., & Harrison, P.J. (2003). Eating disorders. *The Lancet, 361*, 407.

Fantz, R. L. (1961). The origin of form perception. *Scientific American, 204*(5), 66–72.

Farb, N. A. S., Chapman, H. A., & Anderson, A. K. (2013). Emotions: Form follows function. *Current Opinion in Neurobiology, 23*(3), 393–398.

Farber, B. A., Brink, D. C., & Raskin, P. M. (1996). *The psychotherapy of Carl Rogers: Cases and commentary.* New York: Guilford Press.

Farmer, A., Elkin, A., & McGuffin, P. (2007). The genetics of bipolar affective disorder. *Current Opinion in Psychiatry, 20*(1), 8–12.

Farrell, S. (2012). Temporal clustering and sequencing in short-term memory and episodic memory. *Psychological Review, 119*(2), 223–271.

Farzan, F., et al. (2010). Evidence for gamma inhibition deficits in the dorsolateral prefrontal cortex of patients with schizophrenia. *Brain, 133*(5), 1505–1514.

Fasmer, O., Akiskal, H., Hugdahl, K., & Oedegaard, K. (2008). Non-right-handedness is associated with migraine and soft polarity in patients with mood disorders. *Journal of Affective Disorders, 108*(3), 217–224.

Fatemi, S. H., & Folsom, T. D. (2009). The neurodevelopmental hypothesis of schizophrenia, revisited. *Schizophrenia Bulletin, 35*(3), 528–548.

Fehr, B. (2008). Friendship formation. In S. Sprecher, A. Wenzel, & J. H. Harvey (Eds.), *Handbook of relationship initiation* (pp. 29–54). New York: CRC Press.

Feinstein, J. S., Adolphs, R., Damasio, A., & Tranel, D. (2010). The human amygdala and the induction and experience of fear. *Current Biology, 22*(1), 34–38.

Fenton, B. W. (2010). Measuring quality of life in chronic pelvic pain syndrome. *Expert Review of Obstetrics and Gynecology, 5*(1), 115–124.

Ferguson, C. J. (2013). Spanking, corporal punishment and negative long-term outcomes: A meta-analytic review of longitudinal studies. *Clinical Psychology Review, 33*(1), 196–208.

Ferguson, C. J., & Olson, C. K. (2013). Friends, fun, frustration, and fantasy: Child motivations for video game play. *Motivation and Emotion, 37*(1), 154–164.

Ferrario, M. M., et al. (2011). The contribution of major risk factors and job strain to occupational class differences in coronary heart disease. *Occupational and Environmental Medicine, 68,* 717–722.

Festinger, L., & Carlsmith, J. M. (1959). Cognitive consequences of forced compliance. *Journal of Abnormal and Social Psychology, 58,* 203–210.

Festinger, L., Riecken, H. W., Jr., & Schachter, S. (1956). *When prophecy fails.* Minneapolis: University of Minnesota Press.

Fields, R. D. (2005, February). Making memories stick. *Scientific American,* 75–81.

Finkelstein, E. A., Brown, D. S., Wrage, L. A., Allaire, B. T., & Hoerger, T. J. (2010). Individual and aggregate years-of-life-lost associated with overweight and obesity. *Obesity, 18*(2), 333–339.

Fisher, B. S., Daigle, L. E., & Cullen, F. T. (2008). Rape against women. *Journal of Contemporary Criminal Justice, 24*(2), 163–177.

Fisher, C. B. (2009). *Decoding the ethics code: A practical guide for psychologists* (2nd ed.). Thousand Oaks, CA: Sage.

Fisher, T. D., Moore, Z. T., & Pittenger, M. (2012). Sex on the brain? An examination of frequency of sexual cognitions as a function of gender, erotophilia, and social desirability. *Journal of Sex Research, 49*(1), 69–77.

Flavell, J. H., Miller, P. H., & Miller, S. A. (2002). *Cognitive development* (4th ed.). Upper Saddle River, NJ: Prentice Hall.

Flett, G. L., Besser, A., Hewitt, P. L., & Davis, R. A. (2007). Perfectionism, silencing the self, and depression. *Personality and Individual Differences, 43*(5), 1211–1222.

Fligor, B. J., & Cox, L. C. (2004). Output levels of commercially available portable compact disc players and the potential risk to hearing. *Ear and Hearing, 25,* 513–527.

Flor, H., Diers, M., & Andoh, J. (2013). The neural basis of phantom limb pain. *Trends in Cognitive Sciences, 17*(7), 307–308.

Flouri, E., & Buchanan, A. (2003). The role of father involvement and mother involvement in adolescents' psychological well-being. *British Journal of Social Work, 33*(3), 399–406.

Foell, J., & Flor, H. (2012). Phantom limb pain. In R. J. Moore (Ed.), *Handbook of pain and palliative care,* (pp. 417–430). New York: Springer.

Folkman, S. (Ed.), (2011). *The Oxford handbook of stress, health and coping.* New York: Oxford University Press.

Fontaine, R. G., et al. (2010). Does response evaluation and decision (RED) mediate the relation between hostile attributional style and antisocial behavior in adolescence? *Journal of Abnormal Child Psychology, 38*(5), 615–626.

Forrest, D. V. (2008). Alien abduction: A medical hypothesis. *Journal of the American Academy of Psychoanalysis and Dynamic Psychiatry, 36*(3), 431–442.

Foster, D. W., Yeung, N., & Neighbors, C. (2014). I think I can't: Drink refusal self-efficacy as a mediator of the relationship between self-reported drinking identity and alcohol use. *Addictive Behaviors, 39*(2), 461–468.

Franklin, K. B. (2014). Mental illness and crime. *The encyclopedia of criminology and criminal justice.* DOI: 10.1002/978118517383.wbeccj122

Frasure-Smith, N., & Lespérance, F. (2008). Depression and anxiety as predictors of 2-year cardiac events in patients with stable coronary artery disease. *Archives of General Psychiatry, 65*(1), 62–71.

Freeman, M. S., Spence, M. J., & Oliphant, C. M. (1993, June). *Newborns prefer their mothers' low-pass filtered voices over other female filtered voices.* Paper presented at the annual convention of the American Psychological Society, Chicago, IL.

Freud, S. (1964). A religious experience. In *Standard edition of the complete psychological works of Sigmund Freud* (Vol. 21). London: Hogarth Press. (Original work published 1927.)

Freud, S. (1998). The baby and the bathwater: Some thoughts on Freud as a postmodernist. *Families in Society: The Journal of Contemporary Human Services, 79,* 455–464.

Freund, M. (2009). On the notion of concept: II. *Artificial Intelligence, 173*(1), 167–179.

Friedlander, L. J., Connolly, J. A., Pepler, D. J., & Craig, W. M. (2013). Extensiveness and persistence of aggressive media exposure as longitudinal risk factors for teen dating violence. *Psychology of Violence, 3*(4), 310–322.

Frisby, B. N., Dillow, M. R., Gaughan, S., & Nordlund, J. (2010). Flirtatious communication: An experimental examination of social-sexual communication motivated by evolutionary forces. *Sex Roles, 64*(9–10), 682–694.

Fritsch, G., & Hitzig, E. (1960). On the electrical excitability of the cerebrum. In G. von Bonin (Ed.), *Some papers on the cerebral cortex.* Springfield, IL: Thomas. (Original work published 1870.)

Fuentes-Fernandez, R., Gomez-Sanz, J. J., & Pavon, J. (2014). Modelling culture through social activities. In V. Dignum & F. Dignum (Eds.), *Perspectives on culture and agent-based simulations: Studies in the philosophy of sociality, 3* (pp. 49–68). New York: Springer.

Fukushima, M., Sharp, S., & Kobayashi, T. (2009). Born to bond, collectivism, and conformity: A comparative study of Japanese and American college students. *Deviant Behavior, 30*(5), 434–466.

Fuller, T. (2011). Is scientific theory change similar to early cognitive development? Gopnik on science and childhood. *Philosophical Psychology.* DOI:10.1080/09515089.2011.625114

Fusar-Poli, P., & Meyer-Lindenberg, A. (2013). Striatal presynaptic dopamine in schizophrenia, part I: Meta-analysis of dopamine active transporter (DAT) density. *Schizophrenia Bulletin, 39*(1), 22–32.

Fusar-Poli, P., Nelson, B., Valmaggia, L., Yung, A. R., & McGuire, P. K. (2014). Comorbid depressive and anxiety disorders in 509 individuals with an at-risk mental state. *Schizophrenia Bulletin, 40*(1), 120–131.

G

Gao, Y., Raine, A., Venables, P. H., Dawson, M. E., & Mednick, S. A. (2010a). Association of poor childhood fear conditioning and adult crime. *American Journal of Psychiatry, 167,* 56–60.

Gao, Y., Raine, A., Venables, P. H., Dawson, M. E., & Mednick, S. A. (2010b). Reduced electrodermal fear conditioning from ages 3 to 8 years is associated with aggressive behavior at age 8 years. *Journal of Child Psychology and Psychiatry, 51* (5), 550–558.

Garb, H. N., Wood, J. M., Lilienfeld, S. O., & Nezworski, M. T. (2005). Roots of the Rorschach controversy. *Clinical Psychology Review, 25*(1), 97–118.

Garcia, J., & Koelling, R. A. (1966). Relation of cue to consequences in avoidance learning. *Psychonomic Science 4*, 123–124.

Garcia-Falgueras, A., & Swaab, D. F. (2010). Sex hormones and the brain: An essential alliance for sexual identity and sexual orientation. In S. Loche, M. Cappa, L. Ghizzoni, M. Maghnie, & M. O. Savage (Eds.), *Pediatric neuroendocrinology* (Vol. 17, pp. 22–35). Basel, Switzerland: Karger.

Gardner, H. (1983/1993). *Frames of mind.* New York: Basic Books.

Gardner, H. (2001, April 5). Multiple intelligence. *The New York Times*, p. A20.

Gardner, H. (2009). Birth and the spreading of a "meme." In J-Q. Chen, S. Moran, & H. Gardner (Eds.), *Multiple intelligences around the world* (pp. 3–16). Hoboken, NJ: Wiley.

Hayne, H. (2013). Verbal recall of preverbal memories: Implications for the clinic and the courtroom. In M. Garry & H. Hayne. (Eds.), *Do justice and let the sky fall: Elizabeth F. Loftus and her contributions to science, law, and academic freedom* (pp. 79–104). New York: Psychology Press.

Garza, Y., & Watts, R. E. (2010). Filial therapy and Hispanic values: Common ground for culturally sensitive helping. *Journal of Counseling and Development, 88*(1), 108–113.

Gatchel, R. J., Haggard, R., Thomas, C., & Howard, K. J. (2012). Biopsychosocial approaches to understanding chronic pain. *Handbook of pain and palliative care*, 1–16. DOI: 10.1007/978-1-4419-1651-8_1

Gatchel, R. J., & Kishino, N. D. (2010). Managing pain. In J. C. Thomas & M. Hersen (Eds.), *Handbook of clinical psychology competencies* (pp. 1181–1192). New York: Springer.

Gauvain, M., Perez, S. M., & Beebe, H. (2013). Authoritative parenting and parental support for children's cognitive development. In R. E. Larzelere, A. S. Morris, & A. W. Harrist (Eds.), *Authoritative parenting: Synthesizing nurturance and discipline for optimal child development* (pp. 211–233). Washington, DC: American Psychological Association.

Gay, P. (1999). Psychoanalyst: Sigmund Freud. *Time, 153*, 66.

Gegenfurtner, K. R., & Kiper, D. C. (2003). Color vision. *Annual Review of Neuroscience, 26*, 181–206.

Geher, G., Bauman, K. P., Hubbard, S. E. K., & Legare, J. R. (2002). Self and other obedience estimates: Biases and moderators. *The Journal of Social Psychology, 142*, 677–689.

George, M. R. W., Koss, K. J., McCoy, K. P., Cummings, E. M., & Davies, P. T. (2010). Examining the family context and relations with attitudes to school and scholastic competence. *Advances in School Mental Health Promotion, 3*(4), 51–62.

Gerdes, A. B. M., Uhl, G., & Alpers, G. W. (2009). Spiders are special: Fear and disgust evoked by pictures of arthropods. *Evolution and Human Behavior, 30*(1), 66–73.

Gershoff, E. T. (2002). Corporal punishment by parents and associated child behaviors and experiences: A meta-analytic and theoretical review. *Psychological Bulletin, 128*(4), 539–579.

Getzels, J. W., & Jackson, P. W. (1962). *Creativity and intelligence.* New York: Wiley.

Gigerenzer, G. (2010). Personal reflections on theory and psychology. *Theory & Psychology, 20*(6), 733–743.

Gigerenzer, G., Hoffrage, U., & Goldstein, D. G. (2008). Postscript: Fast and frugal heuristics. *Psychological Review, 115*(1), 238–239.

Gilbert, S. J., Bird, G., Brindley, R., Frith, C. D., & Burgess, P. W. (2008). Atypical recruitment of medial prefrontal cortex in autism spectrum disorders: An fMRI study of two executive function tasks. *Neuropsychologia, 46*(9), 2281–2291.

Gilovich, T., & Eibach, R. (2001). The fundamental attribution error where it really counts. *Psychological Inquiry, 12*(1), 23–26.

Giuliano, P. (2007). Living arrangements in Western Europe: Does cultural origin matter? *Journal of the European Economic Association, 5*(5), 927–952.

Glantz L. A., et al. (2010). Pro-apoptotic Par-4 and dopamine D2 receptor in temporal cortex in schizophrenia, bipolar disorder and major depression. *Schizophrenia Research, 118*(1–3), 292–299.

Glaser, R., Pearson, G. R., Bonneau, R. H., Esterling, B. A., Atkinson, C., & Kiecolt-Glaser, J. K. (1993). Stress and the memory T-cell response to the Epstein-Barr virus. *Health Psychology, 12*, 435–442.

Glasser, C. L., Robnett, B., & Feliciano, C. (2009). Internet daters' body type preferences: Race-ethnic and gender differences. *Sex Roles, 61* (1–2), 14–33.

Glenn, A. L., Johnson, A. K., & Raine, A. (2013). Antisocial personality disorder: A current review. *Current Psychiatry Reports, 15*, 427–434.

Glynn, R. J. (2010). The USPSTF recommendation statement on coronary heart disease risk assessment. *Annals of Internal Medicine, 152*, 403–404.

Goez, H., & Zelnik, N. (2008). Handedness in patients with developmental coordination disorder. *Journal of Child Neurology, 23*(2), 151–154.

Goghari, V. M., MacDonald, A. W., & Sponheim, S. R. (2014). Relationship between prefrontal gray matter volumes and working memory performance in schizophrenia: A family study. *Schizophrenia Research*, in press.

Goldman-Rakic, P. S. (1995). Cited in Goleman, D. (1995, May 2). Biologists find site of working memory. *The New York Times*, pp. C1, C9.

Goldstein, E. B. (2013). *Sensation and perception* (ninth edition). Belmont, CA: Cengage Learning.

Goldston, D. B., & Compton, J. S. (2010). Adolescent suicidal and nonsuicidal self-harm behaviors and risk. In E. J. Marsh & R. A. Barkley (Eds.), *Assessment of childhood disorders* (pp. 305–346). New York: Guilford Press.

Goleman, D. J. (1995). *Emotional intelligence.* New York: Bantam Books.

Golubovich, J., Chang, C., & Eatough, E. M. (2104). Safety climate, hardiness, and musculoskeletal complaints: A mediated moderation model. *Applied Ergonomics, 45*(3), 757–766.

Gone, J. P., & Trimble, J. E. (2012). American Indian and Alaska Native mental health: Diverse perspectives on enduring disparities. *Annual Review of Clinical Psychology, 8*, 131–160.

Gonneaud, J., et al. (2013). How do we process event-based and time-based intentions in the brain? An fMRI study of prospective memory in healthy individuals. *Human Brain Mapping*, DOI: 10.1002/hbm.22385

González, H. M., Vega, W. A., Williams, D. R., Tarraf, W., West, B. T., & Neighbors, H. W. (2010). Depression care in the United States: Too little for too few. *Archives of General Psychiatry, 67*, 37–46.

Gonzalez, R., & Swanson, J. M. (2012). Long-term effects of adolescent-onset and persistent use of cannabis. *Proceedings of the National Academy of Sciences in the United States of America, 109*(40), 15970–15971.

Goodenough, F. (1926). *Measurement of intelligence by drawings.* Yonkers, NY: World Book.

Goodman-Delahunty, J., & Sporer, S. L. (2010). Unconscious influences in sentencing decisions: A research review of psychological sources of disparity. *Australian Journal of Forensic Sciences, 42*(1), 19–36.

Gorelick, D. A., et al. (2013). Tolerance to effects of high-dose oral Δ9-tetrahydrocannabinol and plasma cannabinoid concentrations in male daily cannabis smokers. *Journal of Analytical Toxicology, 37*(1), 11–16.

Gotlib, I. H., & Joormann, J. (2010). Cognition and depression: Current status and future directions. *Annual Review of Clinical Psychology, 6*, 285–312.

Gottesman, I. I. (1991). *Schizophrenia genesis.* New York: Freeman.

Gould, S. J. (2002). *The structure of evolutionary theory.* Cambridge, MA: Belknap Press/Harvard University Press.

Greenberg, J. (1985) Family size tied to SAT, IQ scores. *Science News.* Science Service, Inc.

Greenberger, E., Chen, C., Tally, S. R., & Dong, Q. (2000). Family, peer, and individual correlates of depressive symptomology among U.S. and Chinese adolescents. *Journal of Consulting and Clinical Psychology, 68*, 209–219.

Greenhalgh, J., Dickson, R., & Dundar, Y. (2010). Biofeedback for hypertension: A systematic review. *Journal of Hypertension, 28*(4), 644–652.

Gregory, V. L., Jr. (2010). Cognitive-behavioral therapy for schizophrenia: Applications to social work practice. *Social Work in Mental Health, 8*(2), 140–159.

Greidanus, E., & Everall, R. D. (2010). Helper therapy in an online suicide prevention community. *British Journal of Guidance and Counselling, 38*(2), 191–204.

Greitemeyer, T., & Mugge, D. (2013). Rational bystanders. *British Journal of Social Psychology, 52*(4), 773–780.

Griebling, T. L. (2011). Sexual activities, sexual and life satisfaction, and successful aging in women. *The Journal of Urology, 185*(6), 2276–2277.

Grillon, M-L., Krebs, M-O., Gourevitch, R., Giersch, A., & Huron, C. (2010). Episodic memory and impairment of an early encoding process in schizophrenia. *Neuropsychology, 24*(1), 101–108.

Gross, A. L., Gallo, J. J., & Eaton, W. W. (2010). Depression and cancer risk: 24 years of follow-up of the Baltimore Epidemiologic Catchment Area. *Cancer Causes and Control, 21*(2), 191–199.

Gross, R. (2002). The prison simulation experiment. *Psychology Review, 8*, 15–17.

Grossman, I., & Na, J. (2014). Research in culture and psychology: Past lessons and future challenges. *WIREs Cognitive Science, 5*(1), 1–14.

Guan, S., et al. (2014). Chronic unpredictable mild stress impairs erythrocyte immune function and changes T-lymphocyte subsets in a rat model of stress-induced depression. *Environmental Toxicology and Pharmacology, 37*(1), 414–422.

Guidotti, T. L. (2012). Phineas Gage and his frontal lobe—The "American Crowbar Case." *Archives of Environmental & Occupational Health, 67*(4), 249–250.

Guo, X., et al. (2014). Hippocampal and orbital inferior frontal gray matter volume abnormalities and cognitive deficit in treatment-naive, first-episode patients with schizophrenia. *Schizophrenia Research, 152*(2), 339–343.

H

Haenen, J. (2001). Outlining the teaching-learning process: Piotr Gal'perin's contribution. *Learning and Instruction, 11*(2), 157–170.

Hafemeister, L., Gaussier, P., Maillard, M., Boucenna, S., & Giovannangeli, C. (2010). Perception: Insights from the sensori-motor approach. *European Workshop of Visual Information Processing.* Retrieved from http://hal .archives-ouvertes.fr/hal-00520433/

Haker, H., Kawohl, W., Herwig, U., & Rossler, W. (2013). Mirror neuron activity during contagious yawning—An fMRI study. *Brain Imaging and Behavior, 7*(1), 28–34.

Halim, M. L., Ruble, D., Tamis-LeMonda, C., & Shrout, P. E. (2013). Rigidity in gender-typed behaviors in early childhood: A longitudinal study of ethnic minority children. *Child Development, 84*(4), 1269–1284.

Hall, J. A., Park, N., Song, H., & Cody, M. J. (2010). Strategic misrepresentation in online dating: The effects of gender, self-monitoring, and personality traits. *Journal of Social and Personal Relationships, 27*(1), 117–135.

Hamilton, L. D., & Julian, A. M. (2014). The relationship between daily hassles and sexual function in men and women. *Journal of Sex & Marital Therapy,* DOI: 10.1080/0092623X.2013.864364

Hancock, J. (2007). Digital deception: When, where, and how people lie online. In K. McKenna, T. Postmes, U. Reips, & A. Joinson (Eds.), *Oxford handbook of Internet psychology* (pp. 287–301). Oxford, England: Oxford University Press.

Hansen, B. C. (2014). Animal models of obesity: Nonhuman primates. In G. A. Bray & C. Bouchard (Eds.), *Handbook of obesity—Epidemiology, etiology, & physiopathology* (pp. 149–160). Boca Raton, FL: CRC Press.

Harlow, H. F. (1959). Love in infant monkeys. *Scientific American, 200,* 68–86.

Harlow, J. M. (1868). Recovery from the passage of an iron bar through the head. *Publication of the Massachusetts Medical Society, 2,* 327.

Harris, J. L., Bargh, J. A., & Brownell, K. D. (2009). Priming effects of television food advertising on eating behavior. *Health Psychology, 28*(4), 404–413.

Harrison, K. (2013). Media, body image, and eating disorders. In D. Lemish (Ed.), *The Routledge international handbook of children, adolescents, and media* (pp. 224–231). New York: Routledge.

Hartley, C. A., & Casey, B. J. (2013). Risk for anxiety and implications for treatment: developmental, environmental, and genetic factors governing fear regulation. *Annals of the New York Academy of Sciences, 1304,* 1–13.

Hasin, D. S., Goodwin, R. D., Stinson, F. S., & Grant, B. F. (2005). Epidemiology of major depressive disorder. *Archives of General Psychiatry, 62,* 1097–1106.

Haupt, M., Sheldon, S. H., & Loghmanee, D. (2013). Just a scary dream? A brief review of sleep terrors, nightmares, and rapid eye movement sleep behavior disorder. *Pediatric Annals, 42*(10), 211–216.

Haustein, K-O., & Groneberg, D. (2009). Pharmacology and pharmakinetics of nicotine. In K-O. Haustein & D. Groneberg (Eds.), *Tobacco or health?* (pp. 61–86). New York: Springer.

Haworth, C. M. A., Dale, P. S., & Plomin, R. (2009a). Sex differences and science: The etiology of science excellence. *Journal of Child Psychology and Psychiatry, 50*(9), 1113–1120.

Haworth, C. M. A., et al. (2009b). A twin study of the genetics of high cognitive ability selected from 11,000 twin pairs in six studies from four countries. *Behavior Genetics, 39*(4), 359–370.

Health, United States (2010). http://www.cdc.gov/ nchs/data/hus/hus10.pdf (National Center for Health Statistics).

Helms, J. E. (2006). Fairness is not validity or cultural bias in racial-group assessment: A quantitative perspective. *American Psychologist, 61*(8), 845–859.

Henderson, A. S. (2009). Alzheimer's disease in its epidemiological context. *Acta Neurologica Scandinavica, 88*(S149), 1–3.

Henderson, T. L., Roberto, K. A., & Kamo, Y. (2010). Older adults' responses to Hurricane Katrina. *Journal of Applied Gerontology, 29*(1), 48–69.

Heng, M. A. (2000). Scrutinizing common sense: The role of practical intelligence in intellectual giftedness. *Gifted Child Quarterly, 44*(3), 171–182.

Henley, C. L., Nunez, A. A., & Clemens, L. G. (2010). Exogenous androgen during development alters adult partner preference and mating behavior in gonadally intact male rats. *Hormones and Behavior, 57*(4–5), 488–495.

Henry, D. B. (2008). Changing classroom social settings through attention to norms. In M. Shinn & H. Yoshikawa (Eds.), *Toward positive youth development* (pp. 40–57). New York: Oxford University Press.

Herbenick, D., et al. (2010a). Sexual behavior in the United States: Results from a national probability sample of males and females ages 14 to 94. *Journal of Sexual Medicine, 7*(Suppl. 5), 255–265.

Herbenick, D., et al. (2010b). Sexual behaviors, relationships, and perceived health among adult women in the United States: Results from a national probability sample. *Journal of Sexual Medicine, 7*(Suppl. 5), 277–290.

Herbenick, D., et al. (2010c). An event-level analysis of the sexual characteristics and composition among adults ages 18 to 59: Results from a national probability sample in the United States. *Journal of Sexual Medicine, 7*(Suppl. 5), 346–361.

Hergenhahn, B. R., & Henley, T. (2013). *An introduction to the history of psychology* (7th ed.). Belmont, CA: Cengage.

Herr, P. M., & Fazio, R. H. (2013). The attitude-to-behavior process. In A. A. Mitchell (Ed.), *Advertising exposure, memory and choice.* New York: Psychology Press.

Higgs, S., & Woodward, M. (2009). Television watching during lunch increases afternoon snack intake of young women. *Appetite, 52*(1), 39–43.

Hill, S. Y., et al. (2007). Cerebellar volume in offspring from multiplex alcohol dependence families. *Biological Psychiatry, 61*(1), 41–47.

Hilton, D. (2012). The emergence of cognitive social psychology: A historical analysis. In A. W. Kruglanski & W. Stroebe (Eds.), *Handbook of the history of social psychology* (pp. 45–79). New York: Psychology Press.

Hingson, R., Zha, W., & Weitzman, E. R. (2002). *A call to action: Changing the culture of drinking at U.S. colleges.* Washington, DC: National Institutes of Health: National Institute of Alcohol Abuse and Alcoholism.

Ho, M. Y., Cheung, F. M., & Cheung, S. F. (2010). The role of meaning in life and optimism in promoting well-being. *Personality and Individual Differences, 48*(5), 658–663.

Hobson, J. A. (2003). *Dreaming: An introduction to the science of sleep.* New York: Oxford University Press.

Hobson, J. A. (2009). REM sleep and dreaming. *Nature Reviews Neuroscience, 10,* 803–813.

Hobson, J. A. (2013). Ego Ergo Sum: Toward a psychodynamic neurology. *Contemporary Psychoanalysis, 49*(2), 142–164. http://www .wawhite.org/uploads/CPS.049.0142.pdf

Hoff, E. (2005). *Language development* (3rd ed.). Belmont, CA: Wadsworth.

Hoffman, H. G. (2004). Virtual reality therapy. *Scientific American, 291*(2), 58–65.

Hoge, C. W., et al. (2004). Combat duty in Iraq and Afghanistan, mental health problems, and barriers to care. *New England Journal of Medicine, 351*(1), 13–22.

Hoge, E. A., et al. (2013). Randomized controlled trial of mindfulness meditation for generalized anxiety disorder: Effects on anxiety and stress reactivity. *The Journal of Clinical Psychiatry, 74*(8), 786–792.

Hollenstein, T., & Lougheed, J. P. (2013). Beyond storm and stress: Typicality, transactions, timing, and temperament to account for adolescent change. *American Psychologist, 68*(6), 444–454.

Hollingshead, A. B., & Redlich, F. C. (1958). *Social class and mental illness.* New York: Wiley.

Honorton, C. (1985). Meta-analysis of psi Ganzfeld research. *Journal of Parapsychology, 49,* 51–91.

Honts, C. R., & Handler, M. (2011, January). *Interrogations, false confessions and the polygraph: Issues and concerns from psychological science.* Invited address at the Annual Meeting, American Association of Police Polygraphists, Boston, MA.

Hoover, R. N. (2000). Cancer—Nature, nurture, or both? *New England Journal of Medicine online, 343*(2).

Horcajo, J., Brinol, P., & Petty, R. E. (2014). Multiple roles for majority versus minority source status on persuasion when source status follows the message. *Social Influence, 9*(1), 37–51.

Horiguchi, H., Winawer, J., Dougherty, R. F., & Wandell, B. A. (2013). Human trichromacy revisited. *Proceedings of the National Academy of Sciences in the United States of America, 110*(3), E260–E269.

Horn, J. M. (1983). The Texas adoption project. *Child Development, 54,* 268–275.

Hornstein, E. P., Verweij, J., & Schnapf, J. L. (2004). Electrical coupling between red and green cones in primate retina. *Nature Neuroscience, 7*(7), 745–750.

House, S., Loud, K., & Shubkin, C. (2013). Female athlete triad for the primary care pediatrician. *Current Opinion in Pediatrics, 25*(6), 755–761.

Howard, G., Lau, M. Y., Maxwell, S. E., Venter, A., Lundy, R., & Sweeny, R. M. (2009). Do research literatures give correct answers? *Review of General Psychology, 13*(2), 116–121.

Howard, K. J., Ellis, H. B., & Khaleel, M. A. (2010). Psychological factors that may influence outcome after joint replacement surgery. *Current Orthopaedic Practice, 21*(2), 144–148.

Howard, M. E., et al. (2013). Deterioration in driving performance during sleep deprivation is similar and professional and non-professional drivers. *Traffic Injury Prevention,* DOI:10.1080/15389588.2013.800637

Hu, X., Yang, Y., Liu, L., Liu, X., & Tong, Y. (2010). Early psychological intervention following a natural disaster. *Social Behavior and Personality, 38*(1), 71–74.

Hubel, D. H., & Wiesel, T. N. (1979). Brain mechanisms of vision. *Scientific American, 241,* 150–162.

Huesmann, L. R., Dubow, E. F., & Yang, G. (2013). Why is it hard to believe that media violence causes aggression? In K. E. Dill (Ed.), *The Oxford handbook of media psychology* (pp. 159–171). New York: Oxford University Press.

Huesmann, L. R., Moise-Titus, J., Podolski, C., & Eron, L. D. (2003). Longitudinal relations between children's exposure to TV violence and their aggressive and violent behavior in young adulthood: 1977–1992. *Developmental Psychology, 39*(2), 201–221.

Hueston, C. M., & Deak, T. (2014). The inflamed axis: The interaction between stress, hormones, and the expression of inflammatory-related genes within key structures comprising the hypothalamic–pituitary–adrenal axis. *Physiology & Behavior, 124*(1), 77–91.

Hughes, T. F., Andel, R., Small, B. J., Borenstein, A. R., & Mortimer, J. A. (2008). The association between social resources and cognitive change in older adults. *Journals of Gerontology Series B: Psychological Sciences and Social Sciences, 63,* P241–P244.

Hunter, B.T. (2002). How food communicates with your taste buds: The chemistry of perception. *Consumers' Research Magazine, 85,* 26–28.

Hunter, D. J. (2005). Gene-environment interactions in human diseases. *Nature Reviews Genetics, 6,* 287–298.

Hurka, T. (2010). Morality and political violence. *Philosophical Review, 119*(1), 115–117.

Hustad, J. T. P., Barnett, N. P., Borsari, B., & Jackson, K. M. (2010). Web-based alcohol prevention for incoming college students: A randomized controlled trial. *Addictive Behaviors, 35*(3), 183–189.

Hutter, M., & Sweldens, S. (2013). Implicit misattribution of evaluative responses; Contingency-unaware evaluative conditioning requires simultaneous stimulus presentations. *Journal of Experimental Psychology: General, 142*(3), 638–643.

Hwang, C. H., et al. (2010). Role of bone morphogenetic proteins on cochlear hair cell formation. *Developmental Dynamics, 239*(2), 505–513.

Hyde, J. S., Lindberg, S. M., Linn, M. C., Ellis, A. B., & Williams, C. C. (2008). Gender similarities characterize math performance. *Science, 321,* 494–495.

Hyde, J. S., & Mertz, J. E. (2009). Gender, culture, and mathematics performance. *Proceedings of the National Academy of Sciences, 106*(22), 8801–8807.

Hyman, R. (2011). Cited in B. Carey. (2011, January 5). Journal's paper on ESP expected to prompt outrage. *The New York Times online.*

I

Iacono, W. G. (2008). Accuracy of polygraph techniques: Problems using confessions to determine ground truth. *Physiology and Behavior, 95*(1–2), 24–26.

IBTimes Staff Reporter (2011, January 26). Rise in pedestrian deaths renews call for an iPod bill. *International Business Times.* http://www.ibtimes.com/rise-pedestrian-deaths-renews-call-ipod-bill-259509

Ikeda, A., et al. (2013). Social support and cancer incidence and mortality: The JPHC study cohort II. *Cancer Causes & Control, 24*(5), 847–860.

Inaba, M., Maruyamab, T., Yoshimurab, Y., Hosoia, H., & Komatsu, Y. (2009). Facilitation of low-frequency stimulation-induced long-term potentiation by endogenous noradrenaline and serotonin in developing rat visual cortex. *Neuroscience Research, 64*(2), 191–198.

Inhelder, B., & Piaget, J. (1958). *The growth of logical thinking.* New York: Basic Books.

International Human Genome Sequencing Consortium. (2006). Finishing the euchromatic sequence of the human genome. *Nature, 431,* 931–945.

Isarida, T., & Isarida, T. K. (2006). Influences of environmental context on the recency effect in free recall. *Memory and Cognition, 34*(4), 787–794.

Isen, J., et al. (2010). Sex-specific association between psychopathic traits and electrodermal reactivity in children. *Journal of Abnormal Psychology, 119*(1), 216–225.

Ismail, S. A., & Mowafi, H. A. (2009). Melatonin provides anxiolysis, enhances analgesia, decreases intraocular pressure, and promotes better operating conditions during cataract surgery under topical anesthesia. *Anesthesia and Analgesia, 108,* 1146–1151.

Ito, H., et al. (2011). Prefrontal overactivation, autonomic arousal, and task performance under evaluative pressure. *Psychophysiology, 48*(11), 1563–1571.

Iverson, P., et al. C. (2003). A perceptual interference account of acquisition difficulties for non-native phonemes. *Cognition, 87*(1), B47–B57.

Iwasaki, A., & Medzhitov, R. (2010). Regulation of adaptive immunity by the innate immune system. *Science, 327*(5963), 291–295.

J

Jackson, E. C. (2009). Nocturnal enuresis: Giving the child a "lift." *Journal of Pediatrics, 154*(5), 636–637.

Jackson, H., & Nuttall, R. L. (2001). Risk for preadolescent suicidal behavior: An ecological model. *Child and Adolescent Social Work Journal, 18*(3), 189–203.

James, W. (1890). *The principles of psychology.* New York: Henry Holt.

Jamison, K. R. (2000). Suicide and bipolar disorder. *Journal of Clinical Psychiatry, 61*(Suppl. 9), 47–51.

Janis, I. L. (1982). *Groupthink* (2nd ed.). Boston: Houghton Mifflin.

Janowitz, H. D., & Grossman, M. I. (1949). Effects of variations in nutritive density on intake of food in dogs and cats. *American Journal of Physiology, 158,* 184–193.

Jennings, M., Heitner, K., & Heravi, N. (2009). Identification of factors associated with academic success and persistence to graduation in online learning environments. *Proceedings of World Conference on Educational Multimedia, Hypermedia and Telecommunications 2009* (pp. 4216–4219). Chesapeake, VA: AACE.

Jetten, J., & Hornsey, M. J. (2014). Deviance and dissent in groups. *Annual Review of Psychology, 65,* 461–485.

Johnson, D. P., & Whisman, M. A. (2013). Gender differences in rumination: A meta-analysis. *Personality and Individual Differences, 55*(4), 367–374.

Johnson, S. P. (2011). Development of visual perception. *WIREs Cognitive Science, 2,* 515–528. DOI:10.1002/wcs.128

Johnson, W., & Krueger, R. F. (2006). How money buys happiness: Genetic and environmental processes linking finances and life satisfaction. *Journal of Personality and Social Psychology, 90*(4), 680–691.

Johnston, L. D., O'Malley, P. M., Bachman, J. G., & Schulenberg, J. E. (2013a). *Monitoring the future national results on adolescent drug use: Overview of key findings, 2012.* Ann Arbor, MI: Institute for Social Research, The University of Michigan.

Johnston, L. D., O'Malley, P. M., Bachman, J. G., & Schulenberg, J. E. (2013b). *Monitoring the future national results on adolescent drug use, 1975–2012. Volume II: College students and adults ages 19–50.* Ann Arbor, MI: Institute for Social Research, The University of Michigan.

Jones, C., Hacker, D., Cormac, I., Meaden, A., & Irving, C. B. (2012). Cognitive behavior therapy versus other psychosocial treatments for schizophrenia. *The Cochrane Library.* Wiley.

Joska, J. A., Stein, D. J., & Grant, I. (2014). *HIV and psychiatry.* Hoboken, NJ: Wiley.

K

Kagan, J., & Saudino, K. J. (2001). Behavioral inhibition and related temperaments. In R. N. Emde & J. K. Hewitt (Eds.), *Infancy to early childhood: Genetic and environmental influences on developmental change* (pp. 111–122). New York: Oxford University Press.

Kamphuis, J., Meerlo, P., Koolhas, J. M., & Lancel, M. (2012). Poor sleep as a potential causal factor in aggression and violence. *Sleep Medicine, 13*(4), 327–334.

Kandel, E. R. (2009). The biology of memory: A forty-year perspective. *The Journal of Neuroscience, 29*(41), 12748–12756.

Kaplan, R. M., & Saccuzzo, D. P. (2008). *Psychological testing: Principles, applications, and issues.* Belmont, CA: Cengage.

Karatzias, T., et al. (2011). A controlled comparison of the effectiveness and efficiency of two psychological therapies for posttraumatic stress disorder: Eye movement desensitization and reprocessing vs. emotional freedom techniques. *Journal of Nervous & Mental Disease, 199*(6), 372–378.

Karolewicz, B., et al. (2009). Reduced level of glutamic acid decarboxylase-67 kDa in the prefrontal cortex in major depression. *International Journal of Neuropsychopharmacology. 13*(4), 411–420.

Karremans, J., Stroebe, W., & Claus, J. (2006). Beyond Vicary's fantasies: The impact of subliminal priming and brand choice. *Journal of Experimental Social Psychology, 42,* 792–798.

Katigbak, M. S., Church, A. T., Guanzon-Lapeña, M. A., Carlota, A. J., & del Pilar, G. H. (2002). Are indigenous personality dimensions culture specific? Philippine inventories and the five-factor model. *Journal of Personality and Social Psychology, 82*(1), 89–101.

Kawano, Y. (2010). Physio-pathological effects of alcohol on the cardiovascular system: Its role in hypertension and cardiovascular disease. *Hypertension Research, 33,* 181–191.

Kazdin, A. E. (2008). Evidence-based treatment and practice: New opportunities to bridge clinical research and practice, enhance the knowledge base, and improve patient care. *American Psychologist, 63*(3), 146–159.

Kazim, S. F., et al. (2008). Attitudes toward suicide bombing in Pakistan. *Crisis: Journal of Crisis Intervention and Suicide Prevention, 29*(2), 81–85.

Kegeles, L. S., et al. (2010). Increased synaptic dopamine function in associative regions of the striatum in schizophrenia. *Archives of General Psychiatry, 67*(3), 231–239.

Keller, S. S., Roberts, N., & Hopkins, W. (2009). A comparative magnetic resonance imaging study of the anatomy, variability, and asymmetry of Broca's area in the human and chimpanzee brain. *Journal of Neuroscience, 29*(46), 14607–14616.

Kelly, J. F. (2013). Alcoholics Anonymous science update. *Substance Abuse, 34*(1), 1–3.

Kendler, K. S., et al. (2000). Illicit psychoactive substance use, heavy use, abuse, and dependence in a U.S. population-based sample of male twins. *Archives of General Psychiatry, 57,* 261–269.

Kendler, K. S., Myers, J., Prescott, C. A., & Neale, M. C. (2001). The genetic epidemiology of irrational fears and phobias in men. *Archives of General Psychiatry, 58*(3), 257–265.

Kerlin, J. R., Shahin, A. J., & Miller, L. M. (2010). Attentional gain control of ongoing cortical speech representations in a "cocktail party." *Journal of Neuroscience, 30*(2), 620–628.

Kessler, R. C., et al. (2003). The epidemiology of major depressive disorder: Results from the National Comorbidity Survey Replication (NCS-R). *Journal of the American Medical Association, 289*(23), 3095–3105.

Kessler, R. C., et al. (2005a). Lifetime prevalence and age-of-onset distributions of DSM-IV disorders in the National Comorbidity Survey Replication. *Archives of General Psychiatry, 62*(6), 593–602.

Kessler, R. C., Berglund, P., Borges, G., Nock, M., & Wang, P. S. (2005b). Trends in suicide ideation, plans, gestures, and attempts in the United States, 1990–1992 to 2001–2003. *Journal of the American Medical Association, 293,* 2487–2495.

Kestemont, J., et al. (2014). Neural correlates of attributing causes to the self, another person, and the situation. *Social Cognitive and Affective Neuroscience,* DOI: 10.1093/scan/nsu030

Keyes, C. L. M., & Goodman, S. H. (Eds.), (2006). *Women and depression: A handbook for the social, behavioral, and biomedical sciences.* New York: Cambridge University Press.

Kibbe, M. M., & Leslie, A. M. (2013). What's the object of object working memory in infancy? Unraveling "what" and "how many." *Cognitive Psychology, 66*(4), 380–404.

Kikuchi, H., et al. (2010). Memory repression: Brain mechanisms underlying dissociative amnesia. *Journal of Cognitive Neuroscience, 22*(3), 602–613.

King, B. J. (2008). ME.ME.WASHOE: An appreciation. *Sign Language Studies, 8*(3), 315–323.

King, S. (2005). Virtual reality heals 9/11 wounds. Cited in M. Lake (2005). Retrieved from http://www.cnn.com/2005/TECH/04/29/spark.virtual/index.html

Kingsbury, S.J. (1997). What is solution-focused therapy? *Harvard Mental Health Letter, 13,* 8.

Kinsey, A. C., Pomeroy, W. B., & Martin, C. E. (1948). *Sexual behavior in the human male.* Philadelphia: Saunders.

Kinsey, A. C., Pomeroy, W. B., Martin, C. E., & Gebhard, P. H. (1953). *Sexual behavior in the human female.* Philadelphia: Saunders.

Kirke, D. M. (2009). Gender clustering in friendship networks. *Methodological Innovations Online, 4,* 23–36.

Kivimäki, M., et al. (2012). Job strain as a risk factor for coronary heart disease: A collaborative meta-analysis of individual participant data. *Lancet, 380,* 1491–1497.

Kiviniemi, M. T., & Rothman, A. J. (2010). Specifying the determinants of people's health beliefs and health behavior. In J. M. Suls, K. W. Davidson, & R. M. Kaplan (Eds.), *Handbook of health psychology and behavioral medicine.* (pp. 64–83). New York: Guilford Press.

Kleinmuntz, B., & Szucko, J. J. (1984). Lie detection in ancient and modern times. *American Psychologist, 39,* 766–776.

Klemfuss, J. Z., & Ceci, S. J. (2012). Legal and psychological perspectives on children's competence to testify in court. *Developmental Review, 32*(3), 268–286.

Klüver, H., & Bucy, P. C. (1939). Preliminary analysis of functions of the temporal lobe in monkeys. *Archives of Neurology and Psychiatry, 42,* 979–1000.

Knaapila, A., et al. (2012). Genetic analysis of chemosensory traits in human twins. *Chemical Senses, 37*(9), 869–881.

Knapp, L.G., Kelly-Reid, J. E., & Ginder, S. A. (2011). *Enrollment in Postsecondary Institutions, Fall 2009; Graduation Rates, 2003 & 2006 Cohorts; and Financial Statistics, Fiscal Year 2009 (NCES 2011-230).* U.S. Department of Education. Washington, DC: National Center for Education Statistics. Retrieved from http://nces.ed.gov/pubsearch

Knaus, L. K., & Knaus, J. W. (2012). Ethical issues in multiperson therapy. In S. J. Knapp et al. (Eds.), *APA handbook of ethics in psychology, Vol 2: Practice, teaching, and research. APA handbooks in psychology* (pp. 29–43). Washington, DC, US: American Psychological Association.

Knickmeyer, R., et al. (2005). Gender-typed play and amniotic testosterone. *Developmental Psychology, 41,* 517–528.

Knobloch-Westerwick, S., & Johnson, B. K. (2014). Selective exposure for better or worse: Its mediating role for online news' impact on political participation. *Journal of Computer-Mediated Communication, 19*(2), 184–196.

Koch, C. A., & Zitzmann, M. (2013). Testosterone deficiency of male hypogonadism. In C. A. Koch & G. P. Chrousos (Eds.), *Endocrine hypertension: Underlying mechanisms and therapy* (pp. 213–238). New York: Springer.

Koch, T., & Zerback, T. (2013). Helpful or harmful? How frequent repetition affects perceived statement credibility. *Journal of Communication, 63*(6), 993–1010.

Koenig, R., & VanRullen, R. (2013). SWIFT: A novel method to track the neural correlates of cognition. *NeuroImage, 81,* 273–282.

Koerber, A., et al. (2006). Covariates of toothbrushing frequency in low-income African Americans from grades 5 to 8. *Pediatric Dentistry, 28*(6), 524–530.

Kohlberg, L. (1969). *Stages in the development of moral thought and action.* New York: Holt, Rinehart and Winston.

Kohlberg, L. (1981). *The philosophy of moral development.* San Francisco: Harper & Row.

Kohn, N., & Smith, S. M. (2009). Partly versus completely out of your mind: Effects of incubation and distraction on resolving fixation. *Journal of Creative Behavior, 43*(2), 102–118.

Kong, L. L., Allen, J. B., & Glisky, E. L. (2008). Interidentity memory transfer in dissociative identity disorder. *Journal of Abnormal Psychology, 117*(3), 686–692.

Koss, M. P., Figueredo, A. J., & Prince, R. J. (2002). Cognitive mediation of rape's mental, physical and social health impact: Tests of four models in cross-sectional data. *Journal of Consulting and Clinical Psychology, 70*(4), 926–941.

Koster, E. H. W., Fox, E., & MacLeod, C. (2009). Introduction to the special section on cognitive bias modification in emotional disorders. *Journal of Abnormal Psychology, 118*(1), 1–4.

Kownacki, R. J., & Shadish, W. R. (1999). Does Alcoholics Anonymous work? The results from a meta-analysis of controlled experiments. *Substance Use and Misuse, 34,* 1897–1916.

Kráhenbühl, S., Blades, M., & Eiser, C. (2009). The effect of repeated questioning on children's accuracy and consistency in eyewitness testimony. *Legal and Criminological Psychology, 14*(2), 263–278.

Kriegel, U. (2014). *Current controversies in philosophy of mind.* New York: Routledge.

Krueger, F., et al. (2009). Integral calculus problem solving: An fMRI investigation. *Neuroreport, 19*(11), 1095–1099.

Kuhner, R., & Schemer, C. (2013). The emotional effects of news frames on information processing and opinion formation. *Communication Research,* DOI: 10.1177/0093650213514599.

Kukihara, H., Yamawaki, N., Uchiyama, K., Arai, S., & Horikawa, E. (2014). The trauma, depression, and resilience of earthquake/tsunami/nuclear disaster survivors of Hirono, Fukushima, Japan. *Psychiatry and Clinical Neurosciences,* DOI: 10.1111/pcn.12159.

Kuo, P-H., et al. (2010). Genome-wide linkage scans for major depression in individuals with alcohol dependence. *Journal of Psychiatric Research, 44*(9), 616–619.

Kurtz-Costes, B., Swinton, A. D., Skinner, O. D. (2014). Racial and ethnic gaps in the school performance of Latino, African American, and white students. In F. T. L. Leong et al. (Eds.), *APA handbook of multicultural psychology, Vol. 1: Theory and research* (pp. 231–146). Washington, DC: American Psychological Association.

L

Ladd, K. L., & Borshuk, C. (2013). Metaphysical chauvinism and perceptions of deviance in religion, atheism, and alien realms. *International Journal for the Psychology of Religion, 23*(4), 325–337.

Lahey, M., & Ernestus, M. (2013). Pronunciation variation in infant-directed speech: Phonetic reduction of two highly frequent words. *Language Learning and Development*, DOI: 10.1080/15475441.2013.860813

Lambert, M. J. (2013). The efficacy and effectiveness of psychotherapy. In M. J. Lambert (Ed.), *Bergin and Garfield's handbook of psychotherapy and behavior change* (pp. 169–218). Hoboken, NJ: Wiley.

Lambert, M. J. (Ed.), (2013). *Bergin and Garfield's handbook of psychotherapy and behavior change*. Hoboken, NJ: Wiley.

Lan, Y.-J., & Zuo, B. (2009). An introduction to social identity model of deindividuation effects. *Advances in Psychological Science, 17*(2), 467–472.

Landau, B. (2012). Editorial overview for this special issue on understanding cognitive development: Approaches from mind and brain. *Cognitive Neuropsychology, 29*(1–2), 1–6.

Lane, R. D. (2014). Is it possible to bridge the biopsychosocial and biomedical models? *Biopsychosocial Medicine, 8*, 3.

Lane, R. D., et al. (2009). Neural correlates of heart rate variability during emotion. *NeuroImage, 44*(1), 213–222.

Laney, C., & Loftus, E. F. (2009). Eyewitness memory. In R. N. Kocsis (Ed.), *Applied criminal psychology: A guide to forensic behavioral sciences* (pp. 121–145). Springfield, IL: Thomas.

Lang, A. R., Goeckner, D. J., Adesso, V. J., & Marlatt, G. A. (1975). Effects of alcohol on aggression in male social drinkers. *Journal of Abnormal Psychology, 84*, 508–518.

Lang, E. V., et al. (2000). Adjunctive non-pharmacological analgesia for invasive medical procedures: A randomised trial. *Lancet, 355*, 1486–1490.

Lange, R. A., & Hillis, L. D. (2010). Sudden death in cocaine abusers. *European Heart Journal, 31*(3), 271–273.

Langer, S. (1997). Break the chain-control stress with optimal nutrition. *Better Nutrition, 59*, 24–28.

Langin, D., & Lafontan, M. (2014). Adipose tissue metabolism, adipokines, and obesity. In G. A. Bray & C. Bouchard (Eds.), *Handbook of obesity—Epidemiology, etiology, & physiopathology* (pp. 225–236). Boca Raton, FL: CRC Press.

Larsen, J. T., Berntson, G. G., Poehlmann, K. M., Ito, T. A., & Cacioppo, J. T. (2008). The psychophysiology of emotion. In M. Lewis, J. M. Haviland-Jones, & L. F. Barrett (Eds.), *Handbook of emotions* (pp. 180–195). New York: Guilford Press.

Larzerele, R. E., Cox, R. B., & Mandara, J. (2013). Responding to misbehavior in young children: How authoritative parents enhance reasoning with firm control. In R. E. Larzelere, A. S. Morris, & A. W. Harrist (Eds.), *Authoritative parenting: Synthesizing nurturance and discipline for optimal child development* (pp. 89–111). Washington, DC: American Psychological Association.

Lashley, K. S. (1950). In search of the engram. In *Symposium of the Society for Experimental Biology* (Vol. 4). New York: Cambridge University Press.

Lawless, H. T., & Heymann, H. (2010). Measurement of sensory thresholds. In H. T. Lawless & H. Heymann (Eds.), *Sensory evaluation of food* (2nd ed., pp. 125–147). New York: Springer.

Lawson, T.J., & Reardon, M. (1997). A humorous demonstration of in vivo systematic desensitization: The case of eraser phobia. *Teaching of Psychology, 24*, 270–271.

Lazarus, R. S., DeLongis, A., Folkman, S., & Gruen, R. (1985). Stress and adaptational outcomes. *American Psychologist, 40*, 770–779.

Leaper, C. (2013). Gender development during childhood. In P. D. Zalazo (Ed.), *The Oxford handbook of developmental psychology, Vol. 2: Self and other* (pp. 326–377). New York: Oxford University Press.

LeBlanc, M., et al. (2009). Incidence and risk factors of insomnia in a population-based sample. *Sleep, 32*(8), 1027–1037.

Lee, J., & Zhou, M. (2014). The success frame and achievement paradox: The costs and consequences for Asian Americans. *Race and Social Problems*, DOI: 10.1007/s12552-014-9112-7

Lee, S. A. S., & Davis, B. L. (2010). Segmental distribution patterns of English infant- and adult-directed speech. *Journal of Child Language, 37*, 767–791.

Lee, S. J., Bellamy, J. L., & Guterman, N. B. (2009). Fathers, physical child abuse, and neglect. *Child Maltreatment, 14*(3), 227–231.

Lefcourt, H. M. (1997). Cited in Clay, R. A. (1997). Researchers harness the power of humor. *APA Monitor, 28*(9), 1, 18.

Lengen, C., Regard, M., Joller, H., Landis, T., & Lalive, P. (2008). Anomalous brain dominance and the immune system: Do left-handers have specific immunological patterns? *Brain and Cognition, 69*(1), 188–193.

Leonardo, E. D., & Hen, R. (2006). Genetics of affective and anxiety disorders. *Annual Review of Psychology, 57*, 117–137.

Leong, F., Park, Y. S., & Kalibatseva, Z. (2013). Disentangling immigrant status in mental health: Psychological and protective risk factors among Latino and Asian American immigrants. *American Journal of Orthopsychiatry, 83*(2), 361–371.

Leung, P., Curtis, R. L., Jr., & Mapp, S. C. (2010). Incidences of sexual contacts of children: Impacts of family characteristics and family structure from a national sample. *Children and Youth Services Review, 32*(5), 650–656.

Levin, E. D. (2013). Complex relationships of nicotinic receptor actions and cognitive functions. *Biochemical Pharmacology, 86*(8), 1145–1152.

Levinson, D. J. (1996). *The seasons of a woman's life*. New York: Knopf.

Levinson, D. J., Darrow, C. N., Klein, E. B., Levinson, M. H., & McKee, B. (1978). *The seasons of a man's life*. New York: Knopf.

Levy, R. A., & Ablon, J. S. (Eds.), (2009). *Handbook of evidence-based psychodynamic psychotherapy: Bridging the gap between science and practice*. New York: Humana Press.

Li, M., & Chapman, G. B. (2009). "100% of anything looks good": The appeal of one hundred percent. *Psychonomic Bulletin and Review, 16*, 156–162.

Li, X., Frye, M. A., & Shelton, R. C. (2012). Review of pharmacological treatment in mood disorders and future directions for drug development. *Neuropsychopharmacology Reviews, 37*, 77–101.

Liben, L. S., Bigler, R. S., & Hilliard, L. J. (2014). Gender development: From universality to individuality. In E. T. Gershoff, R. G. Mistry, & D. A. Crosby (Eds.), *Societal contexts of child development: Pathways of influence and implications for practice and policy* (pp. 3–18). New York: Oxford University Press.

Liebman, B., & Schardt, D. (2002). Tangled memories: Alzheimer's disease: The story so far. *Nutrition Action Healthletter, 29*, 1–8.

Lin, J-H. (2013). Do video games exert stronger effects on aggression than film? The role of media interactivity and identification on the association of violent content and aggressive outcomes. *Computers in Human Behavior, 29*(3), 535–543.

Lindgren, A. P., Mullins, P. M., Neighbors, C., & Blayney, J. A. (2010). Curiosity killed the cocktail? Curiosity, sensation seeking, and alcohol-related problems in college women. *Addictive Behaviors, 35*(5), 513–516.

Lippa, R. A. (2010). Sex differences in personality traits and gender-related occupational preferences across 53 nations: Testing evolutionary and social-environmental theories. *Archives of Sexual Behavior, 39*(3), 619–636.

Liu, A. (2009). Critical race theory, Asian Americans, and higher education: A review of research. *InterActions: UCLA Journal of Education and Information Studies, 5*(2). Retrieved from http://www.escholarship.org/uc/item/98h4n45j

Lochman, J. E., Powell, N. P., Boxmeyer, C. L., & Jiminez-Camargo, L. (2011). Cognitive-behavioral therapy for externalizing disorders in children and adolescents. *Child and Adolescent Psychiatric Clinics of North America, 20*(2), 305–318.

Loftus, E. F., & Davis, D. (2006). Recovered memories. *Annual Review of Clinical Psychology, 2*, 469–498.

Loftus, E. F., & Palmer, J. C. (1974). Reconstruction of automobile destruction. *Journal of Verbal Learning and Verbal Behavior, 13*, 585–589.

Lohman, D. F., & Lakin, J. M. (2009). Consistencies in sex differences on the Cognitive Abilities Test across countries, grades, test forms, and cohorts. *British Journal of Educational Psychology, 79*(2), 389–407.

Lohr, J. M., Lilienfeld, S. O., & Rosen, G. R. Anxiety and its treatment: Promoting science-based practice. *Journal of Anxiety Disorders, 26*(7), 719–727.

Longmore, M. A., Manning, W. D., & Giordano, P. C. (2013). Parent–child relationships in adolescence. In M. A. Fine & F. D. Fincham (Eds.), *Handbook of family theories* (pp. 28–50). New York: Routledge.

Lorenz, K. Z. (1981). *The foundations of ethology*. New York: Springer-Verlag.

Lowe, J. R., et al. (2013). Early working memory as a racially and ethnically neutral measure of outcome in extremely preterm children at 18–22 months. *Early Human Development, 89*(12), 1055–1061.

Lu, L. (2001). Understanding happiness: A look into the Chinese folk psychology. *Journal of Happiness Studies, 2*(4), 407–432.

Lubinski, D., & Benbow, C. P. (2006). Study of mathematically precocious youth after 35 years: Uncovering antecedents for the development of math-science expertise. *Perspectives on Psychological Science, 1*(4), 316–345.

Luchins, A. S. (1957). Primacy-recency in impression formation. In C. I. Hovland (Ed.), *The order of presentation in persuasion* (pp. 33–61). New Haven, CT: Yale University Press.

Ludescher, B. et al. (2009) Correlation of fat distribution in whole body MRI with generally used anthropometric data. *Investigative Radiology, 44*(11), 712–719.

Lukaszewski, A. W., & Roney, J. R. (2009). Estimated hormones predict women's mate preferences for dominant personality traits. *Personality and Individual Differences, 47*(3), 191–196.

Lykken, D. T. (2007). A more accurate estimate of heritability. *Twin Research and Human Genetics, 10*(1), 168–173.

Lykken, D. T., & Csikszentmihalyi, M. (2001). Happiness—Stuck with what you've got? *Psychologist, 14*(9), 470–472.

Lynn, B. M., McCord, J. L., & Halliwell, J. R. (2007). Effects of menstrual cycle and sex on progesterone hemodynamics. *American Journal of Physiology: Regulatory, Integrative, and Comparative Physiology, 292*, R1260–R1270.

Lyubomirsky, S., Dickerhoof, R., Boehm, J. K., & Sheldon, K. M. (2011). Becoming happier takes both a will and a proper way: An experimental longitudinal intervention to boost well-being. *Emotion, 11*(2), 391–402.

M

Macedo, R. H., & Machado, G. (2014). *Sexual selection: Perspectives and models from the neotropics.* London: Elsevier.

MacGeorge, E.L. (2003, February). Gender differences in attributions and emotions in helping contexts. *Sex Roles: A Journal of Research,* 175–182.

Machery, E. (2009). Three fundamental kinds of concept: Prototypes, exemplars, theories. In E. Machery (Ed.), *Doing without concepts* (pp. 76–121). Oxford Scholarship Online Monographs.

Machery, O., & Carlyon, R. P. (2010). Temporal pitch percepts elicited by dual-channel stimulation of a cochlear implant. *Journal of the Acoustical Society of America, 127*(1), 339–349.

MacNeill, I. (2003). Stressed: Warning signs that you could be hitting the danger zone. *BC Business, 31*, 60–63.

Maddi, S. R. (2008). The courage and strategies of hardiness as helpful in growing despite major, disruptive stresses. *American Psychologist, 63*(6), 563–564.

Maddi, S. R., Harvey, R. H., Khoshaba, D. M., Fazel, M., & Resurreccion, N. (2009). The personality construct of hardiness, IV. *Journal of Humanistic Psychology, 49*(3), 292–305.

Magno, C. (2010). Looking at Filipino pre-service teachers' values for education through epistemological beliefs about learning and Asian values. *Asia-Pacific Education Researcher, 19*(1), 61–78.

Mahar, I., Bambico, F. R., Mechawar, N., & Nobrega, J. N. (2014). Stress, serotonin, and hippocampal neurogenesis in relation to depression and antidepressant effects. *Neuroscience & Biobehavioral Reviews, 38*, 173–192.

Maiden, B., & Perry, B. (2010). Dealing with free riders in assessed group work: Results from a study at a UK university. *Assessment and Evaluation in Higher Education.* DOI:10.1080/02602930903429302

Maier, N. R. F., & Schneirla, T. C. (1935). *Principles of animal psychology.* New York: McGraw-Hill.

Mair, C., Martincova, M., & Shepperd, M. (2009). A literature review of expert problem solving using analogy. *EASE—Evaluation and Assessment in Software Engineering.* Retrieved from http://www.bcs.org/upload/pdf/ewic_ea09_s5paper1.pdf

Malgady, R. G. (2013). Culturally competent psychotherapy for Hispanic/Latino children and adolescents. In R. G. Malgady (Ed.), *Cultural competence in assessment and intervention with ethnic minorities* (pp. 51–60). Bentham Books.

Malgady, R. G., Rogler, L. H., & Costantino, G. (1990). Hero/heroine modeling for Puerto Rican adolescents. *Journal of Consulting and Clinical Psychology, 58*, 469–474.

Maltby, J., & Day, L. (2001). The relationship between exercise motives and psychological well-being. *The Journal of Psychology, 135*, 651–660.

Mallan, K. M., Lipp, O. V., & Cochrane, B. (2013). Slithering snakes, angry men and out-group members: What and whom are we evolved to fear? *Cognition & Emotion, 27*(7), 1168–1180

Mantovani, A., & Sica, A. (2010). Macrophages, innate immunity and cancer: Balance, tolerance, and diversity. *Current Opinion in Immunology, 22*(2), 231–237.

Marcus, D., Hughes, K., & Arnau, R. (2008). Health anxiety, rumination, and negative affect: A meditational analysis. *Journal of Psychosomatic Research, 64*(5), 495–501.

Marian, V., & Neisser, U. (2000). Language-dependent recall of autobiographical memories. *Journal of Experimental Psychology: General, 129*(3), 361–368.

Markham, B. (2006). Older women and security. In J. Worell & C. D. Goodheart (Eds.), *Handbook of girls' and women's psychological health: Gender and well-being across the lifespan* (pp. 388–396). Oxford series in clinical psychology. New York: Oxford University Press.

Markus, H. & Kitayama, S. (1991). Culture and the self. *Psychological Review, 98*(2), 224–253.

Marlatt, G. A. (2010). Update on harm-reduction policy and intervention research. *Annual Review of Clinical Psychology, 6*, 591–606.

Martignoli, S., Gomez, F., & Stoop, R. (2013). Pitch sensation involves stochastic resonance. *Scientific Reports, 3*(2676), DOI:10.1038/srep02676. http://www.nature.com/srep/2013/130917/srep02676/full/srep02676.html

Martin, C. L., & Ruble, D. (2004). Children's search for gender cues: Cognitive perspectives on gender development. *Current Directions in Psychological Science, 13*(2), 67–70.

Martin, R. A., & Lefcourt, H. M. (1983). Sense of humor as a moderator of the relation between stressors and moods. *Journal of Personality and Social Psychology, 45*, 1313–1324.

Martin, S. (2002). Easing migraine pain. *Monitor on Psychology, 33*(4), 71.

Martinez, E., et al. (2010). Correlates of smoking cessation self-efficacy in a community sample of smokers. *Addictive Behaviors, 35*(2), 175–178.

Martinez, G., Copen, C. E., & Abma, J. C. (2011). Teenagers in the United States: Sexual activity, contraceptive use, and childbearing, 2006–2010. *National Survey of Family Growth. National Center for Health Statistics. Vital Health Statistics, 23*(31).

Martin-Ordas, G., Atance, C. M., & Louw, A. (2012). The role of episodic and semantic memory in episodic foresight. *Learning and Motivation, 43*(4), 209–219.

Maslow, A. H. (1970). *Motivation and personality* (2nd ed.). New York: Harper & Row.

Mason, V., Andrews, H., & Upton, D. (2010). The psychological impact of exposure to floods. *Psychology, Health and Medicine, 15*(1), 61–73.

Masters, N. T., Casey, E., Wells, E. A., & Morrison, D. M. (2013). Sexual scripts among young heterosexually active men and women: Continuity and change. *The Journal of Sex Research, 50*(5), 409–420.

Masters, W. H., & Johnson, V. E. (1966). *Human sexual response.* Boston: Little, Brown.

Matsumoto, D., & Juang, L. (2013). *Culture and psychology,* 5th ed. San Francisco: Cengage.

Mattes, R. D., & Tan, S. Y. (2014). Obesity: The influence of the food environment on ingestive behaviors. In G. A. Bray & C. Bouchard (Eds.), *Handbook of obesity—Epidemiology, etiology, & physiopathology* (pp. 317–326). Boca Raton, FL: CRC Press.

Mattll, F., et al. (2013). Propspective memory across the lifespan: Investigating the contribution of retrospective and prospective processes. *Aging, Neuropsychology, and Cognition: A Journal of Normal and Dysfunctional Development,* DOI: 10.1080/13825585.2013.837860

Maurer, T. J., & Chapman, E. F. (2013). Ten years of career success in relation to individual and situation variables from the employee development literature. *Journal of Vocational Behavior, 83*(3), 450–465.

Maxwell, J. P., Visek, A. J., & Moores, E. (2009). Anger and perceived legitimacy of aggression in male Hong Kong Chinese athletes: Effects of type of sport and level of competition. *Psychology of Sport and Exercise, 10*(2), 289–296.

May, D. E., & Kratochvil, C. J. (2010). Attention-deficit hyperactivity disorder: Recent advances in paediatric pharmacotherapy. *Drugs, 70*(1), 15–40.

Mayer, J. D., Salovey, P., & Caruso, D. R. (2008). Emotional intelligence: New ability or eclectic traits? *American Psychologist, 63*(6), 503–517.

Mayers, A. G., Grabau, E. A. S., Campbell, C., & Baldwin, D. S. (2009). Subjective sleep, depression, and anxiety. *Human Psychopharmacology, 24*(6), 495–501.

Mazereeuw, G., et al. (2013). Platelet activating factors in depression and coronary artery disease: A potential biomarker related to inflammatory mechanisms and neurodegeneration. *Neuroscience & Biobehavioral Reviews, 37*(8), 1611–1621.

Mazur, A., & Booth, A. (2014). Testosterone is related to deviance in male army veterans, but relationships are not moderated by cortisol. *Biological Psychology, 96*, 72–76.

Mbwana, J., et al. (2008). Limitations to plasticity of language network reorganization in localization-related epilepsy. *Brain, 132*(2), 347–356.

McCardle, P., Colombo, J., & Freud, L. (2009). Measuring language in infancy. In J. Colombo, P. McCardle, & L. Freud (Eds.), *Infant pathways to language: Methods, models, and research disorders* (pp. 1–12). New York: Psychology Press.

McCarty, C. A., Rhew, I. C., Murowchick, E., McCauley, E., & Vander Stoep, A. (2012). Emotional health predictors of substance use initiation during middle school. *Psychology of Addictive Behaviors, 26*(2), 351–357.

McCauley, J. L., Ruggiero, K. L., Resnick, H. S., & Kilpatrick, D. G. (2010). Incapacitated, forcible, and drug/alcohol-facilitated rape in relation to binge drinking, marijuana use, and illicit drug use: A national survey. *Journal of Traumatic Stress, 23*(1), 132–140.

McClelland, D. C. (1958). Methods of measuring human motivation. In J. W. Atkinson (Ed.), *Motives in fantasy, action, and society.* Princeton, NJ: Van Nostrand.

McClelland, D. C. (1965). Achievement and entrepreneurship. *Journal of Personality and Social Psychology, 1,* 389–392.

McCormick, M.J. (2001). Self-efficacy and leadership effectiveness: Applying social cognitive theory to leadership. *Journal of Leadership Studies, 8,* 22–33.

McCrae, R. R., & Costa, P. T., Jr. (1997). Personality trait structure as a human universal. *American Psychologist, 52*(5), 509–516.

McCrae, R. R., & Costa, P. T., Jr. (2013). Introduction to the empirical and theoretical status of the five-factor model of personality traits. In. T. A. Widiger & P. T. Costa, Jr. (Eds.), *Personality disorders and the five-factor model of personality* (3rd ed.). (pp. 15–27). Washington DC: American Psychological Association.

McCrae, R. R., et al. (2000). Nature over nurture: Temperament, personality, and life span development. *Journal of Personality and Social Psychology, 78*(1), 173–186.

McDevitt-Murphy, M. E., et al. (2010). PTSD symptoms, hazardous drinking, and health functioning among U.S. OEF and OIF veterans presenting to primary care. *Journal of Traumatic Stress, 23*(1), 108–111.

McDougall, W. (1904). The sensations excited by a single momentary stimulation of the eye. *British Journal of Psychology, 1,* 78–113.

McDougall, W. (1908). *An introduction to social psychology.* London: Methuen.

McGovern, C.M. (1993). Asylum: The complex and controversial story of mental institutions in the U.S.A. *Journal of Social History, 26,* 668–669.

McGue, M., Bouchard, T. J., Jr., Iacono, W. G., & Lykken, D. T. (1993). Behavioral genetics of cognitive ability: A life-span perspective. In R. Plomin & G. E. McClearn (Eds.), *Nature, nurture & psychology* (pp. 59–76). Washington, DC: American Psychological Association.

McKenzie, C. R. M., Lee, S. M., & Chen, K. K. (2002). When negative evidence increases confidence: Changes in belief after hearing two sides of a dispute. *Journal of Behavioral Decision Making, 15*(1), 1–18.

McLachlan, N., & Wilson, S. (2010). The central role of recognition in auditory perception: A neurobiological model. *Psychological Review, 117*(1), 175–196.

McLaughlin, K. A., Conron, K. J., Koenen, K. C., & Gilman, S. E. (2010). Childhood adversity, adult stressful life events, and risk of past-year psychiatric disorder: A test of the stress sensitization hypothesis in a population-based sample of adults. *Psychological Medicine, 40,* 1647–1658.

McMurran, M., Blair, M., & Egan, V. (2002). An investigation of the correlations between aggression, impulsiveness, social problem-solving, and alcohol use. *Aggressive Behavior, 28,* 439–445.

McNally, R. J. (2012). Searching for repressed memory. *True and False Recovered Memories: Nebraska Symposium on Motivation, 58,* 121–147.

Medland, S. E., et al. (2008). Genetic influences on handedness: Data from 25,732 Australian and Dutch twin families. *Neuropsychologia, 47*(2), 330–337.

Mehta, P. H., & Gosling, S. D. (2008). Bridging human and animal research: A comparative approach to studies of personality and health. *Brain, Behavior, and Immunity, 22*(5), 651–661.

Meijer, J., & Elshout, J. J. (2001). The predictive and discriminant validity of the zone of proximal development. *British Journal of Educational Psychology, 71*(1), 93–113.

Meijer, W. M., Faber, A., van den Ban, E., & Tobi, H. (2009). Current issues around the pharmacotherapy of ADHD in children and adults. *Pharmacy World and Science, 31* (5), 509–516.

Meltzoff, A. N., & Brooks, R. (2009). Social cognition and language: The role of gaze following in early word learning. In J. Colombo, P. McCardle, & L. Freund (Eds.), *Infant pathways to language: Methods, models, and research disorders* (pp. 169–194). New York: Psychology Press.

Meltzoff, A. N., & Prinz, W. (2002). *The imitative mind: Development, evolution, and brain bases.* Cambridge, England: Cambridge University Press.

Meltzoff, A. N., Williamson, R. A., & Marshall, P. J. (2013). Developmental perspectives on action science: Lessons from infant imitation and cognitive neuroscience. In W. Prinz, M. Beisert, & A. Herwig (Eds.), *Action science: Foundations of an emerging discipline* (pp. 281–306). Cambridge, MA: MIT Press.

Melzack, R., & Katz, J. (2006). Pain in the 21st century: The neuromatrix and beyond. In G. Young, A. W. Kane, & K, Nicholson (Eds.), *Psychological knowledge in court* (pp. 129–148). New York: Springer.

Mendelsohn, F., & Warren, M. (2010). Anorexia, bulimia, and the female athlete triad: Evaluation and management. *Endocrinology and Metabolism Clinics of North America, 39*(1), 155–167.

Merari, A., Diamant, I., Bibi, A., Broshi, Y., & Zakin, G. (2010). Personality characteristics of "self martyrs"/"suicide bombers" and organizers of suicide attacks. *Terrorism and Political Violence, 22*(1), 87–101.

Mercado, E. (2008). Neural and cognitive plasticity: From maps to minds. *Psychological Bulletin, 134*(1), 109–137.

Mesoudi, A. (2009). How cultural evolutionary theory can inform social psychology and vice versa. *Psychological Review, 116*(4), 929–952.

Metcalfe, J. (1986). Premonitions of insight predict impending error. *Journal of Experimental Psychology: Learning, Memory, and Cognition, 12,* 623–634.

Metz, R. (2005, March 10). Think of a number… Come on, think! *The New York Times online.*

Metzger, K. L., et al. (2007). Effects of nicotine vary across two auditory evoked potentials in the mouse. *Biological Psychiatry, 61*(1), 23–30.

Meyer-Lindenberg, A., et al. (2001). Evidence for abnormal cortical functional connectivity during working memory in schizophrenia. *American Journal of Psychiatry, 158,* 1809–1817.

Meyersburg, C. A., Bogdan, R., Gallo, D. A., & McNally, R. J. (2009). False memory propensity in people reporting recovered memories of past lives. *Journal of Abnormal Psychology, 118*(2), 399–404.

Mignot, E. J. M. (2012). A practical guide to the therapy of narcolepsy and hypersomnia syndromes. *Neurotherapeutics, 9,* 739–752.

Mihura, J. L., Meyer, G. J., Dumitrascu, N., & Bombel, G. (2013). The validity of individual Rorschach variables: Systematic reviews and meta-analyses of the comprehensive system. *Psychological Bulletin, 139*(3), 548–605.

Milan, S., Zona, K., & Snow, S. (2013). Pathways to adolescent internalizing: Early attachment insecurity as a lasting source of vulnerability. *Journal of Clinical Child & Adolescent Psychology, 42*(3), 371–383.

Milgram, S. (1963). Behavioral study of obedience. *Journal of Abnormal and Social Psychology, 67,* 371–378.

Milgram, S. (1974). *Obedience to authority.* New York: Harper & Row.

Miller, A. L., et al. (2007). Dialectical behavior therapy for adolescents. In L. A. Dimeff & K. Koerner (Eds.), *Dialectical behavior therapy in clinical practice* (pp. 245–297). New York: Guilford Press.

Miller, D. I., & Halpern, D. F. (2014). The new science of cognitive sex differences. *Trends in Cognitive Sciences, 18*(1), 37–45.

Miller, G. A. (1956). The magical number seven, plus or minus two: Some limits on our capacity for processing information. *Psychological Review, 63,* 81–97.

Miller, L. M. (2013). Shaken, not stirred: Emergence of neural selectivity in a "cocktail party." *Neuron, 77*(5), 806–809.

Miller, M. A., Weafer, J., & Fillmore, M. T. (2009). Gender differences in alcohol impairment of simulated driving performance and driving-related skills. *Alcohol and Alcoholism, 44*(6), 586–593.

Miller, N. E. (1944). Experimental studies of conflict. In J. McVicker Hunt (Ed.), *Personality and the behavior disorders* (Vol. 1, pp. 431–465). Oxford, England: Ronald Press.

Miller, N. E. (1969). Learning of visceral and glandular responses. *Science, 163,* 434–445.

Miller, N. E. (1995). Clinical-experimental interactions in the development of neuroscience. *American Psychologist, 50,* 901–911.

Miller, P., McDonald, L., McKenzie, S., O'Brien, K., & Staiger, P. (2013). When the cats are away: The impact of sporting events on assault- and alcohol-related emergency department attendances. *Drug and Alcohol Review, 32*(1), 31–38.

Milne, R. D., Syngeniotis, A., Jackson, G., & Corballis, M. C. (2002). Mixed lateralization of phonological assembly in developmental dyslexia. *Neurocase, 8*(3), 205–209.

Milner, B. R. (1966). Amnesia following operation on temporal lobes. In C. W. M. Whitty & O. L. Zangwill (Eds.), *Amnesia* (pp. 109–133). London: Butterworths.

Mind and the immune system-part I. (2002). *Harvard Mental Health Letter, 18,* NA.

Mineka, S., & Oehlberg, K. (2008). The relevance of recent developments in classical conditioning to understanding the etiology and maintenance of anxiety disorders. *Acta Psychologica, 127*(3), 567–580.

Miniño A. M. (2010). *Mortality among teenagers aged 12–19 years: United States, 1999–2006* (NCHS Data Brief No. 37). Hyattsville, MD: National Center for Health Statistics.

MIT researchers ID gene involved in memory retrieval. (2002, June 21). *Genomics & Genetics Weekly,* p. 4.

Mitchell, K. S., & Bulik, C. M. (2013). Life course epidemiology of eating disorders. In K. C. Koenen et al. (Eds.), *A life course approach to mental disorders* (pp. 148–155). New York: Oxford.

Mohr, D. C., Ho, J., Duffecy, J., Baron, K. G., Lehman, K. A., Jin, L., & and Reifler, D. (2010). Perceived barriers to psychological treatments and their relationship to depression. *Journal of Clinical Psychology, 66*(4), 394–409.

Molfese, V. J., DiLalla, L. F., & Bunce, D. (1997). Prediction of the intelligence test scores of 3- to 8-year-old children by home environment, socioeconomic status, and biomedical risks. *Merrill-Palmer Quarterly, 43*(2), 219–234.

Montoya, R. M., & Horton, R. S. (2013). A meta-analytic investigation of the processes underlying the similarity-attraction effect. *Journal of Social and Personal Relationships, 30*(1), 64–94.

Moore, C. C., Romney, A. K., & Hsia, T. (2002). Cultural, gender, and individual differences in perceptual and semantic structures of basic colors in Chinese and English. *Journal of Cognition and Culture, 2*(1), 1–28.

Moruzzi, G., & Magoun, H. W. (1949). Brain stem reticular formation and activation of the EEG. *Electroencephalography and Clinical Neurophysiology, 1*, 455–473.

Moshman, D. (2011). *Adolescent rationality and development.* New York: Psychology Press.

Moyà-Solà, S., Köhler, M., Alba, D. M., Casanovas-Vilar, I., & Galindo, J. (2004). *Pierolapithecus catalaunicus*, a new middle Miocene great ape from Spain. *Science, 19*, 1339–1344.

Mund, M., & Mitte, K. (2012). The costs of repression: A meta-analysis on the relation between repressive coping and somatic diseases. *Health Psychology, 31*(5), 640–649.

Murata, A., & Fuson, K. (2006). Teaching as assisting individual constructive paths within an interdependent class learning zone: Japanese first graders learning to add using 10. *Journal for Research in Mathematics Education, 37*(5), 421–456.

Murphy, K., & Andalis, J. (2013). Unconscious priming: Masked primes facilitate change detection and change identification performance. *International Journal of Psychological Studies, 5*(1), 45–54.

Mystkowski, J. L., & Mineka, S. (2007). Behavior therapy for specific fears and phobias: Context specificity of fear extinction. In T. A. Treat, R. R. Bootzin, & T. B. Baker (Eds.), *Psychological clinical science: Papers in honor of Richard M. McFall* (pp. 197–222). London: Routledge.

N

Nadel, L., & Sinnott-Armstrong, W. P. (Eds.) (2012). *Memory and law.* New York: Oxford University Press.

Nader, K., Schafe, G. E., & Le Doux, J. E. (2000). Fear memories require protein synthesis in the amygdala for reconsolidation after retrieval. *Nature, 406*, 722–726.

Nagendra, R. P., Maruthai, N., & Kutty, B. M. (2012). Meditation and its regulatory role on sleep. *Frontiers in Neurology, 3*, 54, DOI: 10.3389/fneur.2012.00054.

Nampiaparampil, D. E. (2008). Prevalence of chronic pain after traumatic brain injury: A systematic review. *Journal of the American Medical Association, 300*(6), 711–719.

Naragon-Gainey, K. (2010). Meta-analysis of the relations of anxiety sensitivity to the depressive and anxiety disorders. *Psychological Bulletin, 136*(1), 128–150.

Nather, F. (2013). Exploring the impact of formal education on the moral reasoning of college students. *College Student Journal, 47*(3), 470–477.

National Center for Health Statistics. (2010). *Health, United States, 2009: With special feature on medical technology.* Hyattsville, MD: Author. Retrieved from http://www.cdc.gov/nchs/data/hus/hus09.pdf#032

National Center for Injury Prevention and Control. (2005, June 19). Suicide: Fact sheet. Retrieved from http://www.cdc.gov/ncipc/factsheets/suifacts.htm

National Eating Disorders Association. (2010). Retrieved from http://www.nationaleating-disorders.org/information-resources/general-information.php

National Institute on Alcohol Abuse and Alcoholism (NIAAA). (2005). Cage questionnaire. Retrieved from http://pubs.niaaa.nih.gov/publications/inscage.htm

National Sleep Foundation. (2001, November 19). Events of 9-11 took their toll on Americans' sleep, particularly for women, according to new National Sleep Foundation poll. Retrieved from http://www.sleepfoundation.org/whatsnew/crisis_poll.html

National Sleep Foundation. (2013). How much sleep do you really need? Retrieved from http://www.sleepfoundation.org/article/how-sleep-works/how-much-sleep-do-we-really-need

National Vital Statistics System. (2013). U.S. Census Bureau, 2010. http://www.cdc.gov/dhdsp/vital_signs.htm

Nee, D. E., et al. (2013). A meta-analysis of executive components of working memory. *Cerebral Cortex, 23*(2), 264–282.

Neelakantan, S. (2013). Psychology: Mind over myocardium. *Nature, 493*, S16–S17.

Neisser, U. (1997). Cited in Sleek, S. (1997). Can "emotional intelligence" be taught in today's schools? *APA Monitor, 28*(6), 25.

Neisser, U., Boodoo, G., Bouchard, Jr., T. J., Boykin, A. W., Brody, N., Ceci, S. J., … Urbina, S. (1996). Intelligence: Knowns and unknowns. *American Psychologist, 51*, 77–101.

Nestoriuc, Y., Rief, W., & Martin, A. (2008). Meta-analysis of biofeedback for tension-type headache: Efficacy, specificity, and treatment moderators. *Journal of Consulting and Clinical Psychology, 76*(3), 379–396.

Neve, K. A. (2009). *The dopamine receptors* (2nd ed.). New York: Springer.

Newman, S. D., Greco, J. A., & Lee, D. (2009). An fMRI study of the Tower of London: A look at problem structure differences. *Brain Research, 1286*, 123–132.

Nicholson, A. (2008). Socio-economic status over the life-course and depressive symptoms in men and women in Eastern Europe. *Journal of Affective Disorders, 105*(1–3), 125–136.

Nickell, J. (2001). Exorcism! Driving out the nonsense. *Skeptical Inquirer, 25*, 20.

Nicsa, S. C. (2014). Bystander's willingness to report theft, physical assault, and sexual assault: The impact of gender, anonymity, and relationship with the offender. *Journal of Interpersonal Violence, 29*(2), 217–236.

Nielsen, T. A., et al. (2003). The typical dreams of Canadian university students. *Dreaming, 13*, 211–235.

Nilsson, H., Juslin, P., & Olsson, H. (2008). Exemplars in the mist: The cognitive substrate of the representativeness heuristic. *Scandinavian Journal of Psychology, 49*(3), 201–212.

Nir, Y., & Tononi, G. (2010). Dreaming and the brain: From phenomenology to neurophysiology. *Trends in Cognitive Sciences, 14*(2), 88–100.

Nisbett, R. E. (2009). *Intelligence and how to get it: Why schools and cultures count.* New York: Norton.

Nock, M. K., & Kazdin, A. E. (2002). Examination of affective, cognitive, and behavioral factors and suicide-related outcomes in children and young adolescents. *Journal of Community Psychology, 31*(1), 48–58.

Nokes, T. J., & VanLehn, K. (2008). Bridging principles and examples through analogy and explanation. In *Proceedings of the eighth International Conference for the Learning Sciences* (Vol. 3, pp. 100–102). Utrecht, Netherlands: International Conference on Learning Sciences.

Nolan, J. M., Schultz, P. W., Cialdini, R. B., Goldstein, N. J., & Griskevicius, V. (2008). Normative social influence is underdetected. *Personality and Social Psychology Bulletin, 34*(7), 913–923.

Nolen-Hoeksema, S., Wisco, B. E., & Lyubomirsky, S. (2008). Rethinking rumination. *Perspectives on Psychological Science, 3*(5), 400–424.

Noltemeyer, A., Bush, K., Patton, J., & Bergen, D. (2012). The relationship among deficiency needs and growth needs: An empirical investigation of Maslow's theory. *Children and Youth Services Review, 34*(9), 1862–1867.

Nonaka, A. M. (2004). The forgotten endangered languages: Lessons on the importance of remembering from Thailand's Ban Khor Sign Language. *Language in Society, 33*(5), 737–767.

Norcross, J. C., & Wampold, B. E. (2011). Evidence-based therapy relationships: Research conclusions and clinical practices. *Psychotherapy, 48*(1), 98–102.

Norcross, J. C., & Karpiak, C. P. (2012). Clinical psychologists in the 2010s: 50 years of the APA Division of Clinical Psychology. *Clinical Psychology: Science and Practice, 19*, 1–12.

Norton, P. J. (2010). Adult measures. In D. W. Nange et al. (Eds.), *Practitioner's guide to empirically based measures of social skills* (pp. 383–418). ABCT Clinical Assessment Series. New York: Springer.

Novick, L. R., & Coté, N. (1992). The nature of expertise in anagram solution. In *Proceedings of the 14th annual conference of the Cognitive Science Society.* Hillsdale, NJ: Erlbaum.

O

O'Driscoll, M. P., & Brough, P. (2010). Work organization and health. In S. Leka & J. Houdmont (Eds.), *Occupational health psychology* (pp. 57–87). Hoboken, NJ: Wiley.

Ohayon, M. M., Guilleminault, C., & Priest, R. G. (1999). Night terrors, sleepwalking, and confusional arousals in the general population: Their frequency and relationship to other sleep and mental disorders. *Journal of Clinical Psychiatry, 60*(4), 268–276.

Ohman, A., & Mineka, S. (2001). Fears, phobias, and preparedness: Toward an evolved module of fear and fear learning. *Psychological Review, 108*(3), 483–522.

Ohman, A., & Mineka, S. (2003). The malicious serpent: Snakes as a prototypical stimulus for an evolved module of fear. *Current Directions in Psychological Science, 12*(1), 5–9.

Olatunji, B. O., & Wolitzky-Taylor, K. B. (2009). Anxiety sensitivity and the anxiety disorders: A meta-analytic review and synthesis. *Psychological Bulletin, 135*(6), 974–999.

Olds, J. (1969). The central nervous system and the reinforcement of behavior. *American Psychologist, 24*, 114–132.

Olds, J., & Milner, P. (1954). Positive reinforcement produced by electrical stimulation of the septal area and other regions of the rat brain. *Journal of Comparative and Physiological Psychology, 47,* 419–427.

Oliver, B. R., & Plomin, R. (2007). Twins' Early Development Study (TEDS): A multivariate, longitudinal genetic investigation of language, cognition and behavior problems from childhood through adolescence. *Twin Research and Human Genetics, 10*(1), 96–105.

Ormel, J., et al. (2013). Neuroticism and common mental disorders: Meaning and utility of a complex relationship. *Clinical Psychology Review, 33*(5), 686–697.

Orsi, J. M., Margellos-Anast, H., & Whitman, S. (2010). Black-White health disparities in the United States and Chicago: A 15-year progress analysis. *American Journal of Public Health, 100*(2), 349–356.

Osborn, K. A., Irwin, B. C., Skogsberg, N. J., & Feltz, D. L. (2012). The Kohler Effect: Motivation gains and losses in real sports groups. *Sport, Exercise, and Performance Psychology.* DOI: 10.1037/a0026887

Osborn, R., et al. (2013). Loss of control and binge eating in children and adolescents. In J. Alexander, A. B. Goldschmidt, & D. Le Grange (Eds.), *A clinician's guide to binge eating disorder* (pp. 170–181). New York: Routledge.

Owen, N., & Hamilton, M. (2014). Sedentary time and obesity. In G. A. Bray & C. Bouchard (Eds.), *Handbook of obesity—Epidemiology, etiology, & physiopathology* (pp. 367–376). Boca Raton, FL: CRC Press.

Oz, M., Lorke, D. E., Yang, K. H., & Petroianu, G. (2013). On the interaction of β-amyloid peptides and α7-nicotinic acetylcholine receptors in Alzheimer's disease. *Current Alzheimer Research, 10*(6), 618–630.

P

Packer, D. J. (2009). Avoiding groupthink. *Psychological Science, 20*(5), 546–548.

Panagioti, M., Gooding, P. A., Taylor, P. J., & Tarrier, N. (2014). Perceived social support buffers to impact of PTSD symptoms on suicidal behavior. *Comprehensive Psychiatry, 55*(1), 104–112.

Pani, P. P., Maremmanib, I., Trogua, E., Gessae, G. L., Ruizf, P., & Akiskalg, H. S. (2010). Delineating the psychic structure of substance abuse and addictions: Should anxiety, mood and impulse-control dysregulation be included? *Journal of Affective Disorders, 122*(3), 185–197.

Papadopoulos, F. C., Ekbom, A., Brandt, L., & Ekselius, L. (2009). Excess mortality, causes of death and prognostic factors in anorexia nervosa. *British Journal of Psychiatry, 194,* 10–17.

Park, J., & Spruston, N. (2012). Synergistic actions of metabolic acetylcholine and glutamate receptors on the excitability of hippocampal CA1 pyramidal neurons. *The Journal of Neuroscience, 32*(18), 6081–6091.

Park, J., & Kitayama, S. (2014). Interdependent selves show face-induced facilitation of error processing: Cultural neuroscience of self-threat. *Social Cognitive and Affective Neuroscience, 9*(2), 201–208.

Parr, L. A., Winslow, J. T., Hopkins, W. D., & de Waal, F. B. M. (2000). Recognizing facial cues: Individual discrimination by chimpanzees (*Pan troglodytes*) and rhesus monkeys (*Macaca mulatta*). *Journal of Comparative Psychology, 114*(1), 47–60.

Patterson, G. R., Dishion, T. J., & Yoerger, K. (2000). Adolescent growth in new forms of problem behavior: Macro- and micro-peer dynamics. *Prevention Science, 1*(1), 3–13.

Pavlov, I. (1927). *Conditioned reflexes.* London: Oxford University Press.

Pearson, M. R., Murphy, E. M., & Doane, A. N. (2013). Impulsivity-like traits and risky driving behaviors among college students. *Accident Analysis and Prevention, 53,* 142–148.

Penfield, W. (1969). Consciousness, memory, and man's conditioned reflexes. In K. H. Pribram (Ed.), *On the biology of learning.* New York: Harcourt Brace Jovanovich.

Perlstadt, H. (2013). Milgram's Obedience to Authority: Its origins, controversies, and replication. *Theoretical & Applied Ethics, 2*(2), 53–77.

Perrett, D. I., May, K. A., & Yoshikawa, S. (1994). Facial shape and judgments of female attractiveness, *Nature, 368,* 239–242.

Perusse, L., Rice, T. K., & Bouchard, C. (2014). Genetic component of obesity: Evidence from genetic epidemiology. In G. A. Bray & C. Bouchard (Eds.), *Handbook of obesity—Epidemiology, etiology, & physiopathology* (pp. 91–104). Boca Raton, FL: CRC Press.

Petersen, L., et al. (2014). Genetic and familial environment effects on suicide—An adoption study of siblings. *PLoS ONE 9*(1): 10.1371/annotation/41113674-7ca2-42a5-a364-f646ff-85c2e7. DOI: 10.1371/annotation/41113674-7ca2-42a5-a364-f646ff85c2e7

Peterson, C., & Seligman, M. E. P. (2004). *Character strengths and virtues: A handbook and classification.* Washington, DC: American Psychological Association.

Peterson, D. (2006). *Jane Goodall: The woman who redefined man.* Boston: Houghton Mifflin.

Peterson, L. R., & Peterson, M. J. (1959). Short-term retention of individual verbal items. *Journal of Experimental Psychology, 58,* 193–198.

Petrill, S. A., et al. (2010). Genetic and environmental influences on the growth of early reading skills. *Journal of Child Psychology and Psychiatry, 51* (6), 660–667.

Petty, R. E., Briñol, P., & Priester, J. R. (2009a). Mass media attitude change: Implications of the elaboration likelihood model of persuasion. In J. Bryant & M. B. Oliver (Eds.), *Media effects: Advances in theory and research* (pp. 125–164). Oxford, England: Taylor & Francis.

Petty, R. E., Fazio, R. H., & Briñol, P. (Eds.), (2009b). *Attitudes: Insights from the new implicit measures.* New York: Psychology Press.

Phalet, K., & Schoenpflug, U. (2001). Intergenerational transmission of collectivism and achievement values in two acculturation contexts: The case of Turkish families in Germany and Turkish and Moroccan families in the Netherlands. *Journal of Cross-Cultural Psychology, 32*(2), 186–201.

Phinney, J. S., & Baldelomar, O. A. (2011). Identity development in multiple cultural contexts. In L. A. Jensen (Ed.), *Bridging cultural and developmental approaches to psychology* (pp. 161–187). New York: Oxford University Press.

Phoenix, C. H. (2009). Organizing action of prenatally administered testosterone propionate on the tissues mediating mating behavior in the female guinea pig. *Hormones and Behavior, 55*(5), 566.

Piaget, J. (1963). *The origins of intelligence in children.* New York: Norton.

Piaget, J., & Smith, L. (Trans). (2000). Commentary on Vygotsky's criticisms of language and thought of the child and judgment and reasoning in the child. *New Ideas in Psychology, 18* (2–3), 241–259.

Pickens, C. L., & Holland, P. C. (2004). Conditioning and cognition. *Neuroscience & Biobehavioral Reviews, 28*(7), 651–661.

Piffer, R. C., Garcia, P. C., & Pereira, O. C. M. (2009). Adult partner preference and sexual behavior of male rats exposed prenatally to betamethasone. *Physiology and Behavior, 98*(1–2), 163–167.

Pihl, R. O., Peterson, J. B., & Finn, P. (1990). Inherited predisposition to alcoholism. *Journal of Abnormal Psychology, 99,* 291–301.

Pinker, S. (1994a, June 19). Building a better brain. *The New York Times Book Review,* pp. 13–14.

Pinker, S. (2007). *The stuff of thought: Language as a window into human nature.* New York: Penguin Books.

Pinker, S. (2011). *Words and rules.* New York: HarperCollins Publishers.

Piolino, P., Desgranges, B., & Eustache, F. (2009). Episodic autobiographical memories over the course of time: Cognitive, neuropsychological and neuroimaging findings. *Neuropsychologia, 47*(11), 2314–2329.

Pirbaglou, M., et al. (2013). Perfectionism, anxiety, and depressive distress: Evidence for the mediating role of negative automatic thoughts and anxiety sensitivity. *Journal of American College Health, 61*(8), 477–483.

Pizzagalli, D. A. (2014). Depression, stress, and anhedonia: Toward a synthesis and integrated model. *Annual Review of Clinical Psychology,* DOI: 10.1146/annurev-clinpsy-050212-185606.

Plomin, R. (2000). Behavioural genetics in the 21st century. *International Journal of Behavioral Development, 24*(1), 30–34.

Plomin, R., & Asbury, K. (2005). Nature and nurture: Genetic and environmental influences on behavior. *The Annals of the American Academy of Political and Social Science, 600*(1), 86–98.

Plomin, R., DeFries, J. C., McClearn, G. E., & McGuffin, P. (2008). *Behavioral genetics.* New York: Worth Publishers.

Plomin, R., & Haworth, C. M. A. (2009). Genetics of high cognitive abilities. *Behavior Genetics, 39*(4), 347–349.

Plomin, R., & Schalkwyk, L. C. (2007). Microarrays. *Developmental Science, 10*(1), 19–23.

Plomin, R., & Spinath, F. M. (2004). Intelligence: Genetics, genes, and genomics. *Journal of Personality and Social Psychology, 86*(1), 112–129.

Plomin, R., et al. (2013). Common DNA markers can account for more than half of the genetic influence on cognitive abilities. *Psychological Science, 24*(4), 562–568.

Polanczyk, G., Moffitt, T. E., Arseneault, L., Cannon, M., Ambler, A., Keefe, R. S. E., … Caspi, A. (2010). Etiological and clinical features of childhood psychotic symptoms. *Archives of General Psychiatry, 67*(4), 328–338.

Polina, E. R., Contini, V., Hutz, M. H., & Bau, C. H. D. (2009). Thesserotonin 2A receptor gene in alcohol dependence and tobacco smoking. *Drug and Alcohol Dependence, 101*(1–2), 128–131.

Popma, A., Vermeiren, R., Geluk, C. A. M. L., Rinne, T., van den Brink, W., Knol, D. L., … Doreleijers, T. A. H. (2007). Cortisol moderates the relationship between testosterone and aggression in delinquent male adolescents. *Biological Psychiatry, 61*(3), 405–411.

Porsolt, R. D., Moser, P. C., & Castagne, V. (2010). Behavioral indices in antipsychotic drug discovery. *Journal of Pharmacology and Experimental Therapeutics, 333*(3), 632–638.

Porter, R. (1997). Bethlem/Bedlam: Methods of madness? *History Today, 47,* 41–46.

Porter, S., & ten Brinke, L. (2008). Reading between the lies: Identifying concealed and falsified emotions in universal facial expressions. *Psychological Science, 19*(5), 508–514.

Postmes, T., & Spears, R. (1998). Deindividuation and antinormative behavior: A meta-analysis. *Psychological Bulletin, 123*(3), 238–259.

Power, T. G., Stewart, C. D., Hughes, S. O., & Arbona, C. (2005). Predicting patterns of adolescent alcohol use: A longitudinal study. *Journal of Studies on Alcohol, 66*(1), 74–81.

Pradhan, D. S., et al. (2010). Aggressive interactions rapidly increase androgen synthesis in the brain during the non-breeding season. *Hormones and Behavior, 57*(4–5), 381–389.

Preti, A., & Vellante, M. (2007). Creativity and psychopathology: Higher rates of psychosis proneness and nonright-handedness among creative artists compared to same age and gender peers. *Journal of Nervous and Mental Disease, 195*(10), 837–845.

Price, T. F., Hortensius, R., & Harmon-Jones, E. (2013). Neural and behavioral associations of manipulated determination of facial expressions. *Biological Psychology, 94*(1), 221–227.

Principe, C. P., & Langlois, J. H. (2011). Faces differing in attractiveness elicit corresponding affective responses. *Cognition & Emotion, 25*(1), 140–148.

Prochaska, J. O., & Norcross, J. C. (2014). *Systems of psychotherapy* (8th ed.). San Francisco: Cengage.

Proverbio, A. M., Riva, F., & Zani, A. (2010). When neurons do not mirror the agent's intentions: Sex differences in neural coding of goal-directed actions. *Neuropsychologia, 48*(5), 1454–1463.

Psychodynamic perspective. (1999). *Psychology Review, 6,* 32.

Pulley, B. (1998, June 16). Those seductive snake eyes: Tales of growing up gambling. *The New York Times,* pp. A1, A28.

Pusey, A., Murray, C., Wallauer, W., Wilson, M., Wroblewski, E., & Goodall, J. (2008). Severe aggression among female *Pan troglodytes schweinfurthii* at Gombe National Park, Tanzania. *International Journal of Primatology, 29*(4), 949–973.

Q

Qi, Z., & Gold, P. E. (2009). Intrahippocampal infusions of anisomycin produce amnesia: Contribution of increased release of norepinephrine, dopamine, and acetylcholine. *Learning and Memory, 16,* 308–314.

Qian, Z., Glick, J. E., & Batson, C. D. (2012). Crossing boundaries: Nativity, ethnicity, and mate selection. *Demography, 49,* 651–675.

R

Radcliffe, R. A., et al. (2009). A major QTL for acute ethanol sensitivity in the alcohol tolerant and non-tolerant rat lines. *Genes, Brain, and Behavior, 8*(6), 611–625.

Radel, R., Sarrazin, P., Jehu, M., & Pelletier, L. (2013). Priming motivation through unattended speech. *British Journal of Social Psychology, 52*(4), 763–772.

Raine, A. (2008). From genes to brain to antisocial behavior. *Current Directions in Psychological Science, 17*(5), 323–328.

Raine, A., Fung, A. L. C., Portnoy, J., Choy, O., & Spring, V. L. (2014). Low heart rate as a risk factor for child and adolescent proactive aggressive and impulsive psychopathic behavior. *Aggressive Behavior,* DOI: 10.1002/ab.21523.

Rainville, P., et al. (2002). Hypnosis modulates activity in brain structures involved in the regulation of consciousness. *Journal of Cognitive Neuroscience, 14*(6), 887–901.

Ramagopalan, S. V., Dyment, D. A., Handunnetthi, L., Rice, G. P., & Ebers, G. C. (2010). A genome-wide scan of male sexual orientation. *Journal of Human Genetics, 55,* 131–132.

Randolph, M. E., Torres, H., Gore-Felton, C., Lloyd, B., & McGarvey, E. L. (2009). Alcohol use and sexual risk behavior among college students. *American Journal of Drug and Alcohol Abuse, 35*(2), 80–84.

Raskind, M. A., et al. (2013). A trial of prazosin for combat trauma PTSD with nightmares in active-duty soldiers returned from Iraq and Afghanistan. *The American Journal of Psychiatry, 170*(9), 1003–1010.

Rathus, S. A., Nevid, J. S., & Fichner-Rathus, L. (2014). *Human sexuality in a world of diversity* (9th ed.). Upper Saddle River, NJ: Pearson Education.

Rawley, J. B., & Constantinidis, C. (2008). Neural correlates of learning and working memory in the primary posterior parietal cortex. *Neurobiology of Learning and Memory, 91* (2), 129–138.

Rayner, L., Kershaw, K., Hanna, D., & Chaplin, R. (2009). The patient perspective of the consent process and side effects of electroconvulsive therapy. *Journal of Mental Health, 18*(5), 379–388.

Reece, M., Herbenick, D., Schick, V., Sanders, S. A., Dodge, B., & Fortenberry, J. D. (2010). Sexual behaviors, relationships, and perceived health among adult men in the United States: Results from a national probability sample. *Journal of Sexual Medicine, 7*(Suppl. 5), 291–304.

Reed, S. K. (2013). *Cognition: Theories and applications* (9th ed.). Belmont, CA: Cengage Learning.

Reeder, G. D. (2001). On perceiving multiple causes and inferring multiple internal attributes. *Psychological Inquiry, 12*(1), 34–36.

Reeder, G. D. (2009). Mindreading: Judgments about intentionality and motives in dispositional inference. *Psychological Inquiry, 20*(1), 1–18.

Rees, T., Ingledew, D. K., & Hardy, L. (2005). Attribution in sports psychology: Seeking congruence between theory, research and practice. *Psychology of Sport and Exercise, 6*(2), 189–204.

Reeve, C.L. (2002). Race and intelligence: Separating science from myth. (Book Review). *Personnel Psychology, 55,* 778–781.

Reeve, J. (2002). Discussing prejudice with your child. *The Brown University Child and Adolescent Behavior Letter, 18,* S1.

Regan, P. C. (2013). Sexual desire in women. In D. Castaneda (Ed.), *The essential handbook of women's sexuality* (pp. 3–24). Santa Barbara, CA: ABC-CLIO.

Regier, T. (2005). The emergence of words: Attentional learning in form and meaning. *Cognitive Science: A Multidisciplinary Journal, 29*(6), 819–865.

Reichenbach, A., & Bringmann, A. (2013). Retina: Neuroanatomy and physiology. *Neuroscience in the 21st Century, 557–628.* DOI: 10.1007/978-1-4614-1997-6_22

Reinecke, M. A., DuBois, D. L., & Schultz, T. M. (2001). Social problem solving, mood, and suicidality among inpatient adolescents. *Cognitive Therapy and Research, 25*(6), 743–756.

Reis, H. T., Maniaci, M. R., Caprariello, P. A., Eastwick, P. W., & Finkel, E. J. (2011). Familiarity does indeed promote attraction in live interaction. *Journal of Personality and Social Psychology, 101*(3), 557–570.

Relation of child care to cognitive and language development. (2000). *Child Development, 71,* 960.

Rennels, J. L., & Langlois, J. H. (2014). A children's attractiveness, gender, and race biases: A comparison of their strength and generality. *Child Development,* DOI: 10.1111/cdev.12226

Renner, F., et al. (2013). Short-term group schema cognitive-behavioral therapy for young adults with personality disorders and personality disorder features: Associations with changes in symptomatic distress, schemas, schema modes and coping styles, *Behaviour Research and Therapy, 51*(8), 487–492.

Rescorla, R. A. (1967). Inhibition of delay in Pavlovian fear conditioning. *Journal of Comparative and Physiological Psychology, 64*(1), 114–120.

Rescorla, R. A. (1988). Pavlovian conditioning: It's not what you think it is. *American Psychologist, 43,* 151–160.

Rescorla, R. A. (1999). Partial reinforcement reduces the associative change produced by nonreinforcement. *Journal of Experimental Psychology: Animal Behavior Processes, 25*(4), 403–414.

Rhee, S. H., & Waldman, I. D. (2002). Genetic and environmental influences on antisocial behavior: A meta-analysis of twin and adoption studies. *Psychological Bulletin, 128*(3), 490–529.

Ricciardelli, L.A., & McCabe, M.P. (2001, February). Self-esteem and negative affect as moderators of sociocultural influences on body dissatisfaction, strategies to decrease weight, and strategies to increase muscles among adolescent boys and girls. *Sex Roles: A Journal of Research,* 189.

Richardson, L. K., Frueh, B. C., & Aciemo, R. (2010). Prevalence estimates of combat-related PTSD: A critical review. *Australia and New Zealand Journal of Psychiatry, 44*(1), 4–19.

Ringach, D. L., & Jentsch, J. D. (2009). We must face the threats. *Journal of Neuroscience, 29*(37), 11417–11418.

Riniolo, T.C., Koledin, M., Drakulic, G.M., & Payne, R.A. (2003). An archival study of eyewitness memory of the Titanic's final plunge. *The Journal of General Psychology, 130,* 89–95.

Risch, N., Herrell, R., Lehner, T., Liang, K.-Y., Eaves, L., Hoh, J., … Merikangas, J. R. (2009). Interaction between the serotonin transporter gene (*5-HTTLPR*), stressful life events, and risk of depression. *Journal of the American Medical Association, 301*(23), 2462–2471.

Robbins, J. (2000, July 4). Virtual reality finds a real place as a medical aid. *The New York Times online.*

Roberson, D., Davidoff, J., & Shapiro, L. (2002). Squaring the circle: The cultural relativity of good shape. *Journal of Cognition and Culture, 2*(1), 29–51.

Roberts, J., Lennings, C. J., & Heard, R. (2009). Nightmares, life stress, and anxiety. *Dreaming, 19*(1), 17–29.

Robertson, L. A., McAnally, H. M., & Hancox, R. J. (2013). Childhood and adolescent television viewing and antisocial behavior in early adulthood. *Pediatrics,* http://pediatrics .aappublications.org/content/early/2013/02/13/ peds.2012-1582.

Robins, R. W., Gosling, S. D., & Craik, K. H. (1999). An empirical analysis of trends in psychology. *American Psychologist, 54*(2), 117–128.

Robinson, E. (2011). *Disintegration: The splinter- ing of black America.* New York: Simon & Schuster.

Rodriguez, C. J., Burg, M. M., Meng, J., Pickering, T. G., Jin, Z., Sacco, R. L., ... Di Tullio, M. R. (2008). Effect of social support on nocturnal blood pressure dipping. *Psychosomatic Medi- cine, 70,* 7–12.

Roelofs, K., Hoogduin K. A., Keijsers G. P., Nàring G. W., Moene F. C., & Sandijck P. (2002). Hypnotic susceptibility in patients with conver- sion disorder. *Journal of Abnormal Psychology, 111*(2), 390–395.

Roepke, S., Schröder-Abé, M., Schütz, A., Jacob, G., Dams, A., Vater, A., ... Lammers, C.-H. (2011). Dialectic behavioural therapy has an impact on self-concept clarity and facets of self-esteem in women with borderline personality disorder. *Clinical Psychology and Psychotherapy, 18*(2), 148–158.

Rogers, C. R. (1951). *Client-centered therapy.* Boston: Houghton Mifflin.

Rogers, D. (2009). The other philosophy club: America's first academic women philosophers. *Hypatia, 24*(2), 164–185.

Roid, G. H., & Tippin, S. M. (2009). Assessment of intellectual strengths and weaknesses with the Stanford-Binet Intelligence Scales—5th edition. In J. A. Naglieri & S. Goldstein (Eds.), *Practitioner's guide to assessing intelligence and achievement* (pp. 127–152). Hoboken, NJ: Wiley.

Rojas, J. J., et al. (2013). Effects of daily environ- mental enrichment on behavior and dendritic spine density in hippocampus following neona- tal hypoxia-ischemia in the rat. *Experimental Neurology, 241,* 25–33.

Rolls, E. T. (2009). Functional neuroimaging of *umami* taste: What makes *umami* pleasant? *American Journal of Clinical Nutrition, 90*(3), 804S–813S.

Rose, N. S., & Craik, F. I. M. (2012). A process- ing approach to the working memory/long- term memory distinction: Evidence from the levels-of-processing span task. *Journal of Experimental Psychology: Learning, Memory, and Cognition, 38*(4), 1019–1029.

Rosekind, M. R., Gregory, K. B., Mallis, M. M., Brandt, S. L., Seal, B., & Lerner, D. (2010). The cost of poor sleep: Workplace productivity loss and associated costs. *Journal of Occupa- tional and Environmental Medicine, 52*(1), 91–98.

Rosenbaum, D. L., & White, K. S. (2013). The role of anxiety in binge eating behavior: A critical examination of theory and empirical literature. *Health Psychology Research, 1*(2), DOI: 10.4081/hpr.2013.e19.

Ross, C. A. (2006). Dissociative identity disorder. *Current Psychosis and Therapeutics Reports, 4*(3), 112–116.

Ross, S.E., Niebling, B.C., & Heckert, T.M. (1999). Sources of stress among college students. *Col- lege Student Journal, 33,* 312.

Roth, G. (2000). The evolution and ontogeny of consciousness. *Neural correlates of conscious- ness: Empirical and conceptual questions.* Cambridge, MA: MIT Press.

Roth, T. L., Lubin, F. D., Sodhi, M., & Kleinman, J. E. (2009). Epigenetic mechanisms in schizophrenia. *Biochimica et Biophysica Acta, 1790*(9), 869–877.

Rothbaum, F., Rosen, K., Ujiie, T., & Uchida, N. (2002). Family systems theory, attach- ment theory, and culture. *Family Process, 41,* 328–350.

Rotter, J. B. (1990). Internal versus external control of reinforcement. *American Psychologist, 45,* 489–493.

Rouder, J. N., & Morey, R. D. (2009). The nature of psychological thresholds. *Psychological Review, 116*(3), 655–660.

Rozanski, G. M., Li, Q., & Stanley, E. F. (2013). Transglial transmission at the dorsal root gangli- on sandwich synapse: Glial cell to postsynaptic neuron communication. *European Journal of Neuroscience, 37*(8), 1221–1228.

Rubia, K. (2009). The neurobiology of meditation and its clinical effectiveness in psychiatric dis- orders. *Biological Psychology, 82*(1), 1–11.

Ruiter, R. A. C., Abraham, C., & Kok, G. (2001). Scary warnings and rational precautions: A review of the psychology of fear appeals. *Psy- chology and Health, 16*(6), 613–630.

Ruiter, R. A. C., Kessels, L. T. E., Peters, G. Y., & Kok, G. (2014). Sixty years of fear appeal research: Current state of the evidence. *Inter- national Journal of Psychology, 49*(2), 63–70.

Rurak, D., et al. (2011). Third trimester fetal heart rate and Doppler middle cerebral artery blood flow velocity characteristics during prenatal selective serotonin reuptake inhibitor exposure. *Pediatric Research, 70,* 96–101.

Rushton, J. P., Skuy, M., & Fridjhon, P. (2003). Performance on Raven's Advanced Progressive Matrices by African, East Indian, and White engineering students in South Africa. *Intel- ligence, 31*(2), 123–137.

S

Safford, S., Alloy, L., Abramson, L., & Crossfield, A. (2007). Negative cognitive style as a predictor of negative life events in depression-prone individuals: A test of the stress-generation hypothesis. *Journal of Affective Disorders, 99*(1), 147–154.

Saffran, J. R. (2009). Acquiring grammatical pat- terns: Constraints on learning. In J. Colombo, P. McCardle, & L. Freud (Eds.), *Infant pathways to language: Methods, models, and research disorders* (pp. 31–47). New York: Psychology Press.

Salis, K. L., Salwen, J., & O'Leary, K. D. (2014). The predictive utility of psychological aggres- sion for intimate partner violence. *Partner Abuse, 5*(1), 83–97.

Salomon, K., & Jin, A. (2013). Diathesis-stress model. *Encyclopedia of behavioral medicine* (pp. 591–592). New York: Springer.

Salovey, P., Detweiler-Bedell, B. T., Detweiler- Bedell, J. B., & Mayer, J. D. (2008). Emotional intelligence. In M. Lewis, A. M. Haviland- Jones, & L. F. Barrett (Eds.), *Handbook of emotions* (3rd ed.) (pp. 533–545). New York: Guilford Press.

Salovey, P., Rothman, A. J., Detweiler, J. B., & Steward, W. T. (2000). Emotional states and physical health. *American Psychologist, 55,* 110–121.

Salthouse, T. A. (2001). Structural models of the relations between age and measures of cogni- tive functioning. *Intelligence, 29*(2), 93–115.

Samar, S. M., Walton, K. E., & McDermut, W. (2013). Personality traits predict irrational beliefs. *Journal of Rational-Emotive & Cognitive-Behavior Therapy, 31,* 231–242.

Sanchez, D. T., Shih, M., & Garcia, J. A. (2009). Juggling multiple racial identities: Malleable racial identification and psychological well- being. *Cultural Diversity and Ethnic Minority Psychology, 15*(3), 243–254.

Sanders, G. S. (1984). Effects of context cues on eyewitness identification responses. *Journal of Applied Social Psychology, 14,* 386–397.

Santarius, T., Shipley, J., Brewer, D., Stratton, M. R., & Cooper, C. S. (2010). Epigenetics and genetics: A census of amplified and overex- pressed human cancer genes. *Nature Reviews Cancer, 10*(1), 59–64.

Sarbin, T. R., & Coe, W. C. (1972). *Hypnosis.* New York: Holt, Rinehart and Winston.

Sava, S., & Yurgelun-Todd, D. A. (2008). Func- tional magnetic resonance in psychiatry. *Topics in Magnetic Resonance Imaging, 19*(2), 71–79.

Savin-Williams, R. C., & Cohen, K. M. (2007). Development of same-sex attracted youth. In I. H. Meyer & M. E. Northridge (Eds.), *The health of sexual minorities: Public health perspectives on lesbian, gay, bisexual, and transgender populations* (pp. 27–47). New York: Springer Science + Business Media.

Sawa, A., & Snyder, S. H. (2002). Schizophrenia: Diverse approaches to a complex disease. *Sci- ence, 296*(5568), 692–695.

Sayette, M. A., Reichle, E. D., & Schooler, J. W. (2009). Lost in the sauce: The effects of alcohol on mind wandering? *Psychological Science, 20*(6), 747–752.

Scarr, S., & Weinberg, R. A. (1983). The Minnesota adoption studies: Genetic differences and malleability. *Child Development, 54,* 260–267.

Schacter, D. L. (1992). Understanding implicit memory: A cognitive neuroscience approach. *American Psychologist, 47*(4), 559–569.

Schacter, D. L., Gallo, D. A., & Kensinger, E. A. (2007). The cognitive neuroscience of implicit and false memories: Perspectives on processing specificity. In H. L. Roediger & J. S. Nairne (Eds.), *The foundations of remembering: Essays in honor of Henry L. Roediger III* (pp. 355–379). New York: Psychology Press.

Schachter, S., & Singer, J. E. (1962). Cognitive, social, and physiological determinants of emotional state. *Psychological Review, 69,* 379–399.

Schmidt, N. B., Keough, M. E., Mitchell, M. A., Reynolds, E. K., MacPherson, L., Zvolensky, M. J., & Lejuez, C. W. (2010). Anxiety sensitiv- ity: Prospective prediction of anxiety among early adolescents. *Journal of Anxiety Disorders, 24*(5), 503–508.

Schmitt, D. P. (2003). Universal sex differences in the desire for sexual variety: Tests from 52 nations, 6 continents, and 13 islands. *Journal of Personality and Social Psychology, 85*(1), 85–104.

Schmitt, D. P., et al. (2012). A reexamination of sex differences in sexuality: New studies reveal old truths. *Current Directions in Psychological Science, 21*(2), 135–139.

Schnall, S., Roper, J., & Fessler, D. M. T. (2010). Elevation leads to altruistic behavior. *Psychological Science, 21* (3), 315–320.

Schott, B. H., et al. (2013). The relationship between level of processing and hippocampal-cortical functional connectivity during episodic memory formation in humans. *Human Brain Mapping, 34*(2), 407–424.

Schulte, M. T., Ramo, D., & Brown, S. A. (2009). Gender differences in factors influencing alcohol use and drinking progression among adolescents. *Clinical Psychology Review, 29*(6), 535–547.

Schutz, Y., & Dullou, A. G. (2014). Resting metabolic rate, thermic effect of food, and obesity. In G. A. Bray & C. Bouchard (Eds.), *Handbook of obesity—Epidemiology, etiology, & physiopathology* (pp. 267–280). Boca Raton, FL: CRC Press.

Schwartz, A. (2013). Dual roles: Employed caregivers of older adults. The Society for Social Work and Research: 2013 Annual Conference: San Diego.

Schwartz, B. L. (2008). Working memory load differentially affects tip-of-the-tongue states and feeling-of-knowing judgments. *Memory and Cognition, 36*(1), 9–19.

Schwartz, N. (2007) Evaluating surveys and questionnaires. In R. J. Sternberg, H. L. Roediger, & D. F. Halpern (Eds.), *Critical thinking in psychology* (pp. 54–74). New York: Cambridge University Press.

Scott, J. (1994, May 9). Multiple personality cases perplex legal system. *The New York Times*, pp. A1, B10, B11.

Second thoughts. (1989). *The Economist, 313*, 69.

Segerdahl, P., Fields, W., & Savage-Rumbaugh, S. (2006). *Kanzi's primal language: The cultural initiation of primates into language.* New York: Palgrave Macmillan.

Sekizuka, H., Kida, K., Akashi, Y. J., Yoneyama, K., Osada, N., Omiya, K., & Miyake, F. (2010). Relationship between sleep apnea syndrome and sleep blood pressure in patients without hypertension. *Journal of Cardiology, 55*(1), 92–98.

Seligman, M. (1975). *Helplessness: On depression, development, and death.* New York: Freeman.

Seligman, M. E. P. (1996, August). *Predicting and preventing depression.* Master lecture presented at the meeting of the American Psychological Association, Toronto, Canada.

Selye, H. (1976). *The stress of life* (Rev. ed.). New York: McGraw-Hill.

Shakelford, T. K., & Hansen, R. D. (2014). *The evolution of violence.* New York: Springer.

Shah, C., Trivedi, R. S., Diwan, J., Dixit, R., & Anand, A. K. (2009). Common stressors and coping with stress by medical students. *Journal of Clinical and Diagnostic Research, 3*, 1621–1626.

Shapero, B. G., et al. (2014). Stressful life events and depression symptoms: The effect of childhood emotional abuse on stress reactivity. *Journal of Clinical Psychology, 70*(3), 209–223.

Shapiro, F. (1989). Efficacy of the eye movement desensitization procedure in the treatment of traumatic memories. *Journal of Traumatic Stress, 2*, 199–223.

Shaw, P., Tafti, M., & Thorpy, M. J. (2013). *The genetic basis of sleep and sleep disorders.* New York: Cambridge University Press.

Shedler, J. (2010). The efficacy of psycho-dynamic psychotherapy. *American Psychologist, 65*(2), 98–109.

Shen, H., Mohammad, A., Ramroop, J., & Smith, S. S. (2013). A stress steroid triggers anxiety via increased expression of α4βδ GABA$_A$ receptors in methamphetamine dependence. *Neuroscience*, http://.dox.doi.org/10.1016/j.neuroscience.2013.08.033.

Sherratt, S., & Bryan, K. (2012). Discourse production after right brain damage: Gaining a comprehensive picture using a multi-level processing model. *Journal of Neurolinguistics, 25*(4), 213–239.

Sherwood, C. C., Rilling, J. K., Holloway, R. L., & Hof, P. R. (2008). Evolution of the brain: In humans—Specializations in a comparative perspective. In M. D. Binder, N. Hirokawa, U. Windhorst, & M. C. Hirsch (Eds.), *Encyclopedia of neuroscience* (pp. 1–5). New York: Springer-Verlag.

Shi, W., & Jia, F.-X. (2011). A review on the psychology of suicide terrorism. *Advances in Psychological Science.* Retrieved from http://en.cnki.com.cn/Article_en/CJFDTOTAL-XLXD201109017.htm

Shimizu, I., Kamochi, M., Yoshikawa, H., & Nakayama, Y. (2012). Gender difference in alcoholic liver disease. In I. Shimizu (Ed.), *Trends in alcoholic liver disease research.* Rijeka, Croatia: InTech.

Shirayamaa, Y., et al. (2010). Specific metabolites in the medial prefrontal cortex are associated with the neurocognitive deficits in schizophrenia: A preliminary study. *NeuroImage, 49*(3), 2783–2790.

Shneidman, E. S. (2001). *Comprehending suicide.* Washington, DC: American Psychological Association.

Short, S. J., et al. (2010). Maternal influenza infection during pregnancy impacts postnatal brain development in the rhesus monkey. *Biological Psychiatry, 67*(10), 965–973.

Shrager, Y., Kirwan, C., & Squire, L. R. (2008). Activity in both hippocampus and perirhinal cortex predicts the memory strength of subsequently remembered information. *Neuron, 59*(4), 547–553.

Shuper, P. A., Neuman, M., Kanteres, F., Baliunas, D., Joharchi, N., & Rehm, J. (2010). Causal considerations on alcohol and HIV/AIDS—A systematic review. *Alcohol and Alcoholism, 45*(2), 159–166.

Shyrack, J., Steger, M. F., Krueger, R. F., & Kallie, C. S. (2010). The structure of virtue: An empirical investigation of the dimensionality of the virtues in action inventory of strengths. *Personality and Individual Differences, 48*(6), 714–719.

Siegel, J. M. (2009). Sleep viewed as a state of adaptive inactivity. *Nature Reviews Neuroscience, 10*, 747–753.

Silver, E. (1994). Cited in DeAngelis, T. (1994). Experts see little impact from insanity plea ruling. *APA Monitor, 25*(6), 28.

Silver, S. M., Rogers, S., Knipe, J, & Colelli, G. (2005). EMDR therapy following the 9/11 terrorist attacks: A community-based intervention project in New York City. *International Journal of Stress Management, 12*(1), 29–42.

Simon, S. (2013, September 9). Electronic cigarette use doubles among teenagers. http://www.cancer.org/cancer/news/electronic-cigarette-use-doubles-among-teenagers (Accessed November 12, 2013).

Simon, T. R., et al. (2009). The ecological effects of universal and selective violence prevention programs for middle school students: A randomized trial. *Journal of Consulting and Clinical Psychology, 77*(3), 526–542.

Simons-Morton, B. G., Cheon, K., Guo, F., & Albert, P. (2013). Trajectories of kinematic risky driving among novice teenagers. *Accident Analysis and Prevention, 51*, 27–32.

Simonton, D. K. (2009). *Genius 101.* New York: Springer.

Singh, D., & Singh, D. (2011). Shape and significance of feminine beauty: An evolutionary perspective. *Sex Roles, 64*(9–10), 723–731.

Sio, U. N., & Ormerod, T. C. (2009). Does incubation enhance problem solving? *Psychological Bulletin, 135*(1), 94–120.

Sixsmith, R., & Furnham, A. (2010). A content analysis of British food advertisements aimed at children and adults. *Health Promotion International, 25*(1), 24–32.

Sizemore, R. C. (2012). How does stress affect the immune response? *Cell & Developmental Biology*, DOI: 10.4172/cdb.1000e101. Accessed February 9, 2014 from http://www.omicsgroup.org/journals/CDB/CDB-1-e101.pdf

Skinner, B. F. (1938). *The behavior of organisms: An experimental analysis.* New York: Appleton.

Skinner, B. F. (1948). *Walden Two.* New York: Macmillan.

Sleep and dreams. (2002). *Science Weekly, 19*, 1–12.

Slobin, D. I. (1983). *Crosslinguistic evidence for basic child grammar.* Paper presented at the biennial meeting of the Society for Research in Child Development, Detroit, MI.

Sloman, S. A., Harrison, M. C., & Malt, B. C. (2002). Recent exposure affects artifact naming. *Memory and Cognition, 30*(5), 687–695.

Small, E., et al. (2010). Tobacco smoke exposure induces nicotine dependence in rats. *Psychopharmacology, 208*(1), 143–158.

Smetana, J. G. (2011). Adolescents' social reasoning and relationships with parents: Conflicts and coordinations within and across domains. In E. Amsel & J. G. Smetana (Eds.), *Adolescent vulnerabilities and opportunities* (pp. 139–158). New York: Cambridge University Press.

Smillie, L. D., Cooper, A. J., Proitsi, P., Powell, J. F., Pickering, A. D. (2010). Variation in DRD2 dopamine gene predicts extraverted personality. *Neuroscience Letters, 468*(3), 234–237.

Smith, A. K., et al. (2012). The magnitude of genetic and environmental influences on parental and observational measures of behavioral inhibition and shyness in toddlerhood. *Behavior Genetics, 42*(5), 764–777.

Smith, A. R. Chein, J., & Steinberg, L. (2013). Impact of socio-emotional context, brain development, and pubertal maturation on adolescent risk-taking. *Hormones and Behavior, 64*(2), 323–332.

Smith, J. F. (2001). Biological evidence for evolution. *Journal of the Idaho Academy of Science, 37*, 102–104.

Smith, K. L. (2009). Humor. In M. Snyder & R. Lindquist (Eds.), *Complementary and alternative therapies in nursing* (pp. 107–122). New York: Springer.

Smith, M. L., & Glass, G. V. (1977). Meta-analysis of psychotherapy outcome studies. *American Psychologist, 32*, 752–760.

Smith, N. A., & Trainor, L. J. (2008). Infant-directed speech is modulated by infant feedback. *Infancy, 13*(4), 410–420.

Snyder, C. R., Lopez, S. J., & Pedrotti, J. T. (2010). *Positive psychology* (2nd ed.). Newbury Park, CA: SAGE Publications.

Snyder, D. J., & Bartoshuk, L. M. (2009). Epidemiological studies of taste function: Discussion and perspectives. *Annals of the New York Academy of Sciences, 1170,* 574–580.

Somerville, L. H. (2013). The teenage brain: Sensitivity to social evaluation. *Current Directions in Psychological Science, 22*(2), 121–127.

Soto, C. J. (2014). Is happiness good for your personality? Concurrent and prospective relations of the Big Five with subjective well-being. *Journal of Personality,* DOI: 10.1111/jopy.12081.

Souren, N. Y., et al. (2007). Anthropometry, carbohydrate and lipid metabolism in the East Flanders Prospective Twin Survey: Heritabilities. *Diabetologia, 50*(10), 2107–2116.

Soussignan, R. (2002). Duchenne smile, emotional experience, and autonomic reactivity: A test of the facial feedback hypotheses. *Emotion, 2*(1), 52–74.

Spencer, M. D., et al. (2008). Low birthweight and preterm birth in young people with special educational needs: A magnetic resonance imaging analysis. *BMC Medicine, 6*(1). DOI: 10.1186/1741-7015-6-1

Spencer, M. S., Chen, J., Gee, G. C., Fabian, C. G., & Takeuchi, D. T. (2010). Discrimination and mental health-related service use in a national study of Asian Americans. *American Journal of Public Health, 100*(12), 2410–2417.

Spencer, T. J., Montaldi, D., Gong, Q.-Y., Roberts, N., & Mayes, A. R. (2009). Object priming and recognition memory: Dissociable effects in left frontal cortex at encoding. *Neuropsychologia, 47*(13), 2942–2947.

Sperling, G. (1960). The information available in brief visual presentations. *Psychological Monographs, 74,* 1–29.

Sprecher, S., & Felmlee, D. (2008). Insider perspectives on attraction. In S. Sprecher, A. Wenzel, & J. H. Harvey (Eds.), *Handbook of relationship initiation* (pp. 297–314). New York: CRC Press.

Sprecher, S., Wenzel, A., & Harvey, J. H. (Eds.), (2008). *Handbook of relationship initiation.* New York: CRC Press.

Squire, L. R. (2004). Memory systems of the brain: A brief history and current perspective. *Neurobiology of Learning and Memory, 82*(3), 171–177.

Squire, L. R. (2009). The legacy of patient H. M. for neuroscience. *Neuron, 61* (1), 6.

Squire, L. R., & Kandel, E. R. (2008). *Memory: From mind to molecules.* Greenwood Village, CO: Roberts.

Stangor, C., & Crandall, C. S. (Eds.), (2013). *Stereotyping and prejudice.* New York: Psychology Press.

Stanley, B., & Siever, L. J. (2010). The interpersonal dimension of borderline personality disorder: Toward a neuro-peptide model. *American Journal of Psychiatry, 167,* 24–39.

Starratt, V. G., & Shackelford, T. K. (2010). The basic components of the human mind were solidified during the Pleistocene epoch. In F. J. Ayala & R. Arp (Eds.), *Contemporary debates in philosophy of biology* (pp. 243–252). Hoboken, NJ: Wiley.

Stasser, G. (1999). A primer of social decision scheme theory: Models of group influence, competitive model-testing, and prospective modeling. *Organizational Behavior and Human Decision Processes, 80*(1), 3–20.

Steenari, R., Vuontela, V., Paavonen, E. J., Carlson, S., Fjallberg, M., & Aronen, E. T. (2003). Working memory and sleep in 6 to 13-year old schoolchildren. *Journal of the American Academy of Child and Adolescent Psychiatry, 42,* 85–92.

Steiger, A. E., Allemand, M., Robins, R. W., & Fend, H. A. (2014). Low and decreasing self-esteem during adolescence predict adult depression two decades later. *Journal of Personality and Social Psychology, 106*(2), 325–338.

Stein, A. D., Pierik, F. H., Verrips, G. H. W., Susser, E. S., & Lumey, L H. (2009). Maternal exposure to the Dutch famine before conception and during pregnancy. *Epidemiology, 20*(6), 909–915.

Stener-Victorin, E. (2013). Hypothetical physiological and molecular basis for the effect of acupuncture in the treatment of polycystic ovary syndrome. *Molecular and Cellular Endocrinology, 373*(1–2), 83–90.

Stereotypes can affect memory when identifying criminal suspects. (2002, December 20). *Ascribe Higher Education News Service.*

Sternberg, R. J. (1988). Triangulating love. In R. J. Sternberg & M. J. Barnes (Eds.), *The psychology of love* (pp. 119–138). New Haven, CT: Yale University Press.

Sternberg, R. J. (2000). In search of the zipperump-a-zoo. *Psychologist, 13*(5), 250–255.

Sternberg, R. J. (2006). Creating a vision of creativity: The first 25 years. *Psychology of Aesthetics, Creativity, and the Arts, S*(1), 2–12.

Sternberg, R. J. (2007). Intelligence and culture. In S. Kitayama & D. Cohen (Eds.), *Handbook of cultural psychology* (pp. 547–568). New York: Guilford Press.

Sternberg, R. J. (2009). The assessment of creativity. *Creativity Research Journal, 24*(1), 3–12.

Sternberg, R. J. (2013). Searching for love. *The Psychologist, 26*(2), 98–101.

Sternberg, R. J., Gabora, L., & Bonney, C. R. (2012). Introduction to the special issue on college and university admissions. *Educational Psychologist, 47*(1), 1–4.

Sternberg, R. J., Grigorenko, E. L., & Kidd, K. K. (2005). Intelligence, race, and genetics. *American Psychologist, 60*(1), 46–59.

Stewart, A. J., & Ostrove, J. M. (1998). Women's personality in middle age: Gender, history, and midcourse corrections. *American Psychologist, 53*(11), 1185–1194.

Stocco, A., & Anderson, J. A. (2008). Endogenous control and task representation: An fMRI study in algebraic problem-solving. *Journal of Cognitive Neuroscience, 20*(7), 1300–1314.

Stocker, S. (1994). Stop a headache in 5 minutes. *Prevention, 46,* 65–72.

Stone, J., & Fernandez, N. C. (2008). How behavior shapes attitudes: Cognitive dissonance processes. In W. D. Crano & R. Prislin (Eds.), *Attitudes and attitude change* (pp. 313–336). Boca Raton, FL: CRC Press.

Story, P. A., Hart, J. W., Stasson, M. F., & Mahoney, J. M. (2009). Using a two-factor theory of achievement motivation to examine performance-based outcomes on self-regulatory processes. *Personality and Individual Differences, 46*(4), 391–395.

Stuart, K., & Conduit, R. (2009). Auditory inhibition of rapid eye movements and dream recall from REM sleep. *Sleep, 32*(3), 399–408.

Stice, E., Martti, C. N., & Rohde, P. (2013a). Prevalence, incidence, impairment, and course of the proposed DSM-5 eating disorder diagnoses in an 8-year prospective community study of young women. *Journal of Abnormal Psychology, 122*(2), 445–457.

Stice, E., Rohde, P., Shaw, H., & Marti, C. N. (2013b). Efficacy trial of a selective prevention program targeting both eating disorders and obesity among female college students: 1- and 2-year follow-up effects. *Journal of Consulting and Clinical Psychology, 81*(1), 183–189.

Stunkard, A. J., Harris, J. R., Pedersen, N. L., & McLearn, G. E. (1990). A separated twin study of the body mass index. *New England Journal of Medicine, 322,* 1483–1487.

Suinn, R. M. (2001). The terrible twos—anger and anxiety: Hazardous to your health. *American Psychologist, 56*(1), 27–36.

Suls, J. (2013). Anger and the heart: Perspectives on cardiac risk, mechanisms and interventions. *Progress in Cardiovascular Diseases, 55*(6), 538–547.

Sultanoff, S. M. (2013). Integrating humor into psychotherapy. *The Humanistic Psychologist, 41*(4), 388–399.

Sun-Edelstein, C., & Mauskop, A. (2012). Complementary and alternative approaches to the treatment of tension-type headache. *Current Pain and Headache Reports, 16*(6), 539–544.

Suslow, T., et al. (2010). Automatic brain response to facial emotion as a function of implicitly and explicitly measured extraversion. *Neuroscience, 167*(1), 111–123.

Susser, E., St. Clair, D., & He, L. (2009). Latent effects of prenatal malnutrition on adult health: The example of schizophrenia. *Annals of the New York Academy of Sciences, 1136,* 185–192.

Swami, V., Furnham, A., Haubner, T., Stieger, S., & Voracek, M. (2009). The truth is out there: The structure of beliefs about extraterrestrial life among Austrian and British respondents. *Journal of Social Psychology, 149*(1), 29–43.

Swan, G. E., et al. (2007). Joint effect of dopaminergic genes on likelihood of smoking following treatment with bupropion SR. *Health Psychology, 26*(3), 361–368.

Swartout, K. M., & White, J. W. (2010). The relationship between drug use and sexual aggression in men across time. *Journal of Interpersonal Violence, 25*(9), 1716–1735.

T

Tabassum, H., & Frey, J. U. (2013). The effect of acute swim stress and training in the water maze on hippocampal synaptic activity as well as plasticity in the dendate gyrus of freely moving rats: Revisiting swim-induced LTP reinforcement. *Hippocampus, 23*(12), 1291–1298.

Taber, K. S. (2013). Models of cognitive development. In K. S. Taber (Ed.), *Modelling learners and learning in science education* (pp. 257–276). New York: Springer.

Tahiri, M., et al. (2012). Alternative smoking cessation aids: A meta-analysis of randomized controlled trials. *The American Journal of Medicine, 125*(6), 576–584.

Tait, M., et al. (2010). Bilateral versus unilateral cochlear implantation in young children. *International Journal of Pediatric Otorhinolaryngology, 74*(2), 206–211.

Takemura, K. (1994). Influence of elaboration on the framing of decision. *The Journal of Psychology, 128,* 33–39.

Tamis-LeMonda, C. S., Cristofaro, T. N., Rodriguez, E. T., & Bornstein, M. H. (2006). Early language development: Social influences in the first years of life. In L. Balter & C. S. Tamis-LeMonda (Eds.), *Child psychology: A handbook of contemporary issues* (2nd ed., pp. 79–108). New York: Psychology Press.

Tanner, J. L., & Arnett, J. J. (2011). Presenting "emerging adulthood": What makes it developmentally distinctive? In J. J. Arnett, M. Kloep, L. B. Hendry, & J. L. Tanner. *Debating emerging adulthood: Stage or process?* (pp. 13–30). New York: Oxford University Press.

Taylor, A., Goehler, L., Galper, D., Innes, K., & Bourguignon, C. (2010). Top-down and bottom-up mechanisms in mind-body medicine. *EXPLORE: Journal of Science and Healing, 6*(1), 29–41.

Taylor, D., Paton, C., & Kapur, S. (2012). *Prescribing guidelines in psychiatry.* Hoboken, NJ: Wiley.

Taylor, S., et al. (2003). Comparative efficacy, speed, and adverse effects of three PTSD treatments: Exposure therapy, EMDR, and relaxation training. *Journal of Consulting and Clinical Psychology, 71,* 330–338.

Taylor, S. E. (2006). Tend and befriend: Biobehavioral bases of affiliation under stress. *Current Directions in Psychological Science, 15*(6), 273–277.

Taylor, S. E. (2012). Tend and befriend theory. In P. A. M. Van Lange, A. W. Kruglanski, & E. T. Higgins (Eds.), *Handbook of theories of social psychology, Vol. 1* (pp. 32–49). London: SAGE Publications.

Taylor, S. E., Klein, L. C., Lewis, B. P., Gruenewald, T. L., Gurung, R. A. R., & Updegraff J. A. (2000). Biobehavioral responses to stress in females: Tend-and-befriend, not fight-or-flight. *Psychological Review, 107*(3), 411–429.

Teachout, T. (2000, April 2). For more artists, a fine old age. *The New York Times online.*

Tenenbaum, H. R., Hill, D. B., Joseph, N., & Roche, E. (2010). "It's a boy because he's painting a picture": Age differences in children's conventional and unconventional gender schemas. *British Journal of Psychology, 101*(1), 137–154.

Terasawa, E., et al. (2012). Body weight impact on puberty: Effects of high-calorie diet on puberty onset in female rhesus monkeys. *Endocrinology, 153*(4), DOI: 10.1210/en.2011–1970

Terrace, H. S., & Metcalfe, J. A. (2005). *The missing link in cognition: Origins of self-reflective consciousness.* New York: Oxford University Press.

Tetlock, P. E., & McGraw, A. P. (2005). Theoretically framing relational framing. *Journal of Consumer Psychology, 15*(1), 35–37.

Thomas, K. R. (2008). An exploratory study of factors that relate to academic success among high-achieving African American males. *Dissertation Abstracts International, 69*(12) (UMI No. 3340955).

Thomas, S. L., Skitka, L. J., Christen, S., & Jurgena, M. (2002). Social facilitation and impression formation. *Basic and Applied Social Psychology, 24*(1), 67–70.

Thompson, B. R., & Thornton, H. J. (2002). The transition from extrinsic to intrinsic motivation in the college classroom: A first year experience. *Education, 122,* 785–782.

Thompson, L. E., Barnett, J. R., & Pearce, J. R. (2009). Scared straight? Fear-appeal anti-smoking campaigns, risk, self-efficacy and addiction. *Health, Risk, and Society, 11,* 181–196.

Thompson, M. G. et al. (2013). Subjective social status predicts wintertime febrile acute respiratory illness among women healthcare personnel. *Health Psychology,* DOI: 10.1037/a0032764

Thompson, P. M., et al. (2001). Mapping adolescent brain change reveals dynamic wave of accelerated gray matter loss in very early-onset schizophrenia. *Proceedings of the National Academy of Sciences USA. 98*(20), 11650–11665.

Thompson, S. C. (2009). The role of personal control in adaptive functioning. In I. C. R. Snyder & S. J. Lopez (Eds.), *Oxford handbook of positive psychology* (pp. 271–278). New York: Oxford University Press.

Thurstone, L. L. (1938). Primary mental abilities. *Psychometric Monographs, 1.*

Tigner, R. B., & Tigner, S. S. (2000). Triarchic theories of intelligence: Aristotle and Sternberg. *History of Psychology, 3*(2), 168–176.

Tinti, C., Schmidt, S., Testa, S., & Levine, L. J. (2013). Distinct processes shape flashbulb and event memories. *Memory & Cognition,* DOI: 10.3758/s13421-013-0383-9.

Tohidian, I. (2009). Examining linguistic relativity hypothesis as one of the main views on the relationship between language and thought. *Journal of Psycho-linguistic Research, 38*(1), 65–74.

Tolman, E. C., & Honzik, C. H. (1930). Introduction and removal of reward, and maze performance in rats. *University of California Publications in Psychology, 4,* 257–275.

Toma, C. L., Hancock, J. T., & Ellison, N. B. (2008). Separating fact from fiction: An examination of deceptive self-presentation in online dating profiles. *Personality and Social Psychology Bulletin, 34*(8), 1023–1036.

Tong, H. (2001). Loneliness, depression, anxiety, and the locus of control. *Chinese Journal of Clinical Psychology, 9*(3), 196–197.

Tonnesen, P. (2009). Smoking cessation: How compelling is the evidence? A review. *Health Policy, 91,* S15–S25.

Tost, H., Alam, T., & Meyer-Lindenberg, A. (2009). Dopamine and psychosis: Theory, pathomechanisms and intermediate phenotypes. *Neuroscience and Biobehavioral Reviews, 34*(5), 689–700.

Townsend, E., Hawton, K., Altman, D. G., Arensman, E., Gunnell, D., Hazell, P., … Van Heeringen, K. (2001). The efficacy of problem-solving treatments after deliberate self-harm: Meta-analysis of randomized controlled trials with respect to depression, hopelessness and improvement in problems. *Psychological Medicine, 31*(6), 979–988.

Treger, S., Sprecher, S., Hatfield, E., & Erber, R. (2013). Women's sexuality in close relationships. In D. Castaneda (Ed.), *The essential handbook of women's sexuality* (pp. 47–70). Santa Barbara, CA: ABC-CLIO.

Triandis, H. C. (2001). Individualism-collectivism and personality. *Journal of Personality, 69*(6), 907–924.

Triandis, H. C. (2005). Issues in individualism and collectivism research. In R. M. Sorrentino et al. (Eds.), *Cultural and social behavior: The Ontario Symposium, 10*(pp. 207–225). Mahwah, NJ: Erlbaum.

Triandis, H. C. (2006). Cultural aspects of globalization. *Journal of International Management, 12*(2), 208–217.

Triandis, H. C., & Suh, E. M. (2002). Cultural influences on personality. *Annual Review of Psychology, 53*(1), 133–160.

Trimble, J. E., King, J., LaFromboise, T. D., BigFoot, D. S., & Norman, D. (2014). American Indian and Alaska Native mental health perspectives. In R. Parekh (Ed.), *The Massachusetts General Hospital textbook on diversity and cultural sensitivity in mental health* (pp. 119–138). New York: Springer.

Truchot, D., Maure, G., & Patte, S. (2003). Do attributions change over time when the actor's behavior is hedonically relevant to the perceiver? *The Journal of Social Psychology, 143,* 202–208.

Tryphon, A., & Voneche, J. (2013). *Working with Piaget: Essays in honour of Barbel Inhelder.* New York: Psychology Press.

Tsai, P. (2012). The management of insomnia—biofeedback. *Intelligent Systems, Control and Automation: Science and Engineering, 64,* 165–182.

Tsang, Y. C. (1938). Hunger motivation in gastrectomized rats. *Journal of Comparative Psychology, 26,* 1–17.

Tsintsadze-Maass, E., & Maass, R. W. (2014). Groupthink and terrorist radicalization. *Terrorism and Political Violence,* DOI: 10.1080/09546553.2013.805094

Tumwesigye, N. M., Wanyenze, R. K., & Greenfield, T. K. (2012). Intoxication before last sexual intercourse and HIV risk behavior among men and women in Uganda: Evidence from a nationwide survey. *International Journal of Alcohol and Drug Research, 1*(1), 17.

Turner, M. M., Underhill, J. C., & Kald, L. L. (2013). Mood and reactions to political advertising. *Southern Communication Journal, 78*(1), 8–24.

Tversky, A., & Kahneman, D. (1982). Judgment under uncertainty. In D. Kahneman, P. Slovic, & A. Tversky (Eds.), *Judgment under uncertainty: Heuristics and biases* (pp. 3–22). New York: Cambridge University Press.

Tversky, A., & Kahneman, D. (2003). Emotional versus intuitive reasoning: The conjunction fallacy in probability judgment. In E. Shafir (Ed.), *Amos Tversky: Preference, belief, and similarity: Selected writings* (pp. 221–256). Cambridge, MA: MIT Press.

Tyagi, H., Brummond, L. M., & Fineberg, N. A. (2010). Treatment for obsessive compulsive disorder. *Current Psychiatry Reviews, 6*(1), 46–55.

U

U.S. Bureau of the Census. (2008). *Statistical abstract of the United States* (128th ed.). Washington, DC: U.S. Government Printing Office.

U.S. Bureau of the Census. (2011). Families and living arrangements. Retrieved from http://www.census.gov/population/www/socdemo/hh-fam.html

Uhlhaas, P. J., Roux, F., Rodriguez, E., Rotarska-Jagiela, A., & Singer, W. (2010). Neural synchrony and the development of cortical networks. *Trends in Cognitive Sciences, 14*(2), 72–80.

Uleman, J. S., Rim, S., Saribay, S. A., & Kressel, L. M. (2012). Controversies, questions, and proposals for spontaneous social inferences. *Social and Personality Psychology Compass, 6*(9), 657–673.

Umek, L. M., Podlesek, A., & Fekonja, U. (2005). Assessing the home literacy environment: Relationships to child language comprehension and expression. *European Journal of Psychological Assessment, 21*(4), 271–281.

Underhill, J. B. (2008). The politics of crisis management: Public leadership under pressure and lessons on leadership by terror: Finding Shaka Zulu in the attic. *Political Psychology, 29*(1), 139–143.

V

van den Hout, M. A., et al. (2011). EMDR: Eye movement superior to beeps in taxing working memory and reducing vividness of recollections. *Behaviour Research and Therapy, 49*(2), 92–98.

Van der Kolk, B. A., et al. (2007). A randomized clinical trial of eye movement desensitization and reprocessing (EMDR), fluoxetine, and pill placebo in the treatment of posttraumatic stress disorder. *Journal of Clinical Psychiatry, 68*, 1–10.

Van Horn J. D., et al. (2012), Mapping connectivity damage in the case of Phineas Gage. *PLoS ONE, 7*(5): e37454. DOI:10.1371/journal .pone.0037454

Van Swol, L. M. (2008). Performance and process in collective and individual memory: The role of social decision schemes and memory bias in collective memory. *Memory, 16*(3), 274–287.

Veenstra-Vanderweele, J., & Cook, E. H. (2003). Genetics of childhood disorders: XLVI. Autism, part 5: Genetics of autism. *Journal of the American Academy of Child and Adolescent Psychiatry, 42*(1), 116–118.

Velmans, M. (1999). When perception becomes conscious. *British Journal of Psychology, 90*, 543.

Vernon, D., et al. (2003). The effect of training distinct neurofeedback protocols on aspects of cognitive performance. *International Journal of Psychophysiology, 47*(1), 75–85.

Veselka, L., Schermer, J. A., Petrides, K. V., & Vernon, P. A. (2009). Evidence for a heritable general factor of personality in two studies. *Twin Research and Human Genetics, 12*(3), 254–260.

Viscusi, W. K., Phillips, O. R., & Kroll, S. (2011). Risky investment decisions: How are individuals influenced by their groups? *Journal of Risk and Uncertainty, 43*, 81–106.

Viulli, W. F. (2008). On Joseph Banks Rhine. *Monitor on Psychology, 39*(6), 4.

Vodosek, M. (2009). The relationship between relational models and individualism and collectivism: Evidence from culturally diverse work groups. *International Journal of Psychology, 44*(2), 120–128.

von Békésy, G. (1957, August). The ear. *Scientific American*, pp. 66–78.

Voorspoels, W., Vanpaemel, W., & Storms, G. (2008). Exemplars and prototypes in natural language concepts: A typicality-based evaluation. *Psychonomic Bulletin and Review, 15*(3), 630–637.

Voss, J. L. (2009). Long-term associative memory capacity in man. *Psychonomic Bulletin and Review, 16*, 1076–1081.

Vygotsky, L. (1978). *Mind in society: The development of higher psychological processes.* Cambridge, MA: Harvard University Press.

Vyse, S. (2014). *The psychology of superstition: Updated edition.* New York: Oxford University Press.

W

Wade, N. (1998, January 6). Was Freud wrong? Are dreams the brain's start-up test? *The New York Times online.*

Wadsworth, S. J., Corley, R. P., & DeFries, J. C. (2014). Cognitive abilities in childhood and adolescence. In D. Finkel & C. A. Reynolds (Eds.), *Behavior genetics of cognition across the lifespan* (pp. 3–40). New York: Springer.

Waite, L. J., Luo, Y., & Lewin, A. C. (2009). Marital happiness and marital stability: Consequences for psychological well-being. *Social Science Research, 38*(1), 201–212.

Waitt, C., Gerald, M. S., Little, A. C., & Krasielburd, E. (2006). Selective attention toward female secondary sexual characteristics. *American Journal of Primatology, 68*, 738–744.

Wallace, D. M., & Hinsz, V. B. (2009). Group members as actors and observers in attributions of responsibility for group performance. *Small Group Research, 40*(1), 52–71.

Walle, A. H. (2004). Native Americans and alcoholism therapy: The example of Handsome Lake as a tool of recovery. *Journal of Ethnicity in Substance Abuse, 3*(2), 55–79.

Wanchoo, S. J., Lee, M. J., Swann, A. C., & Dafny, N. (2010). Bilateral six-hydroxydopamine administration to PFC prevents the expression of behavioral sensitization to methylphenidate. *Brain Research, 1312*(2), 89–100.

Wang, A.-C., Hsieh, H.-H., Tsai, C.-Y., & Cheng, B.-S. (2011). Does value congruence lead to voice? Cooperative voice and cooperative silence under team and differentiated transformational leadership. *Management and Organization Review.* DOI: 10.1111/j.1740-8784.2011.00255.x

Wang, D. (2013). Cultural considerations for effective mental health treatment of Asian Americans. In R. G. Malgady (Ed.), *Cultural competence in assessment and intervention with ethnic minorities* (pp. 81–91). Bentham Books, Oak Park, Illinois.

Wang, L., et al. (2008). Prefrontal mechanisms for executive control over emotional distraction are altered in major depression. *Psychiatry Research: Neuroimaging, 163*(2), 143–155.

Wang, Q. (2008). Emotion knowledge and autobiographical memory across the preschool years: A cross-cultural longitudinal investigation. *Cognition, 108*(1), 117–135.

Wang, Y., et al. (2009). A doctrine of cognitive informics. *Fundamenta Informaticae, 90*(3), 203–228.

Wang, Y., & Chiew, V. (2010). On the cognitive process of human problem solving. *Cognitive Systems Research, 11* (1), 81–92.

Wann, D. L., Rogers, K., Dooley, K., & Foley, M. (2011a). Applying the team identification-social psychological health model to older sports fans. *The International Journal of Aging and Human Development, 72*(4), 303–315.

Wann, D. L., Waddill, P. J., Polk, J., & Weaver, S. (2011b). The team identification-social psychological health model: Sports fans gaining connections to others via sport team identification. *Group Dynamics: Theory, Research, and Practice, 15*(1), 75–89.

Wansink, B., & Shimizu, M. (2013). Eating behaviors and the number of buffet trips: An observational study of all-you-can-eat Chinese restaurants. *American Journal of Preventive Medicine, 44*(4), e49–e50.

Ward, C. P., McCoy, J. G., McKenna, J. T., Connolly, N. P., McCarley, R. W., & Strecker, R. E. (2009). Spatial learning and memory deficits following exposure to 24 h of sleep fragmentation or intermittent hypoxia in a rat model of obstructive sleep apnea. *Brain Research, 1294*, 128–137.

Warman, D. M., & Beck, A. T. (2003). Cognitive behavioral therapy for schizophrenia: An overview of treatment. *Cognitive & Behavioral Practice, 10*(3), 248–254.

Warman, D. M., & Cohen, R. (2000). Stability of aggressive behaviors and children's peer relationships. *Aggressive Behavior, 26*(4), 277–290.

Washburn, D. A., Gulledge, J. P., James, F., & Rumbaugh, D. M. (2007). A species difference in visuospatial working memory: Does language link "what" with "where"? *International Journal of Comparative Psychology, 20*, 55–64.

Waters, M. (2000). Psychologists spotlight growing concern of higher suicide rates among adolescents. *Monitor on Psychology, 31*(6), 41.

Watson, H. J., Raykos, B. C., Street, H., Fursland, A., & Nathan, P. R. (2011). Mediators between perfectionism and eating disorder psychopathology: Shape and weight overvaluation and conditional goal-setting. *International Journal of Eating Disorders, 44*(2), 142–149.

Watson, J. B. (1913). Psychology as the behaviorist views it. *Psychological Review, 20*, 158–177.

Watson, J. B. (1924). *Behaviorism.* New York: Norton.

Webster, J. D. (2003). An exploratory analysis of a self-assessed wisdom scale. *Journal of Adult Development, 10*(1), 13–22.

Weems, C. F., et al., (2010). Post traumatic stress, context, and the lingering effects of the Hurricane Katrina disaster among ethnic minority youth. *Journal of Abnormal Child Psychology, 38*(1), 49–56.

Weiner, B. (2006). *Social motivation, justice, and the moral emotions: An attributional approach.* Mahwah, NJ: Erlbaum.

Weiner, B. (2010). The development of an attribution-based theory of motivation: A history of ideas. *Educational Psychologist, 45*(1), 28–36.

Weiner, I. B. (2006). The Rorschach inkblot method. In R. P. Archer (Ed.), *Forensic uses of clinical instruments* (pp. 181–208). London: Routledge.

Weinmann, M., Bader, J., Endrass, J., & Hell, D. (2001). Sind Kompetenz- und Kontrollueberzeugungen depressionsabhaengig? Eine Verlaufsuntersuchung. *Zeitschrift fuer Klinische Psychologie und Psychotherapie, 30*(3), 153–158.

Weinstein, A., & Weinsten, Y. (2013). Exercise addiction-diagnosis, bio-psychological mechanisms and treatment issues. *Current Pharmaceutical Design*, PMID:24001300.

Weiss, A., et al. (2005). Cross-sectional age differences in personality among Medicare patients aged 65 to 100. *Psychology and Aging, 20*(1), 182–185.

Werner, L. A., & Bernstein, I. L. (2001). Development of the auditory, gustatory, olfactory, and somatosensory systems. In E. B. Goldstein (Ed.), *Blackwell handbook of perception, Handbook of experimental psychology series* (pp. 669–708). Boston: Blackwell.

Wessel, J., Moratorio, G., Rao, F., Mahata, M., Zhang, L., Greene, W., … O'Connor, D. T. (2007). C-reactive protein, an "intermediate phenotype" for inflammation: Human twin studies reveal heritability, association with blood pressure and the metabolic syndrome, and the influence of common polymorphism at catecholaminergic/β-adrenergic pathway loci. *Journal of Hypertension, 25*(2), 329–343.

Wetzler, S. E., & Sweeney, J. A. (1986). Childhood amnesia. In D. C. Rubin (Ed.), *Autobiographical memory* (pp. 191–201). New York: Cambridge University Press.

Whorf, B. (1956). *Language, thought, and reality.* New York: Wiley.

Wickens, C. M., Mann, R. E., & Wiesenthal, D. L. (2013). Addressing driver aggression: Contributions from psychological science. *Current Directions in Psychological Science, 22*(5), 386–391.

Widiger, T. A., & Simonsen, E. (2005). Alternative dimensional models of personality disorder: Finding a common ground. *Journal of Personality Disorders, 19*(2), 110–130.

Wienke, C., & Hill, G. J. (2009). Does the "marriage benefit" extend to partners in gay and lesbian relationships? *Journal of Family Issues, 30*(2), 259–289.

Wilen-Daugenti, T. (Accessed November 11, 2013). *Higher education trends and statistics.* Cisco. http://www.cisco.com/web/about/ac79/edu/trends/issue01.html

Wilhelm, K., Wedgwood, L., Parker, G., Geerligs, L., & Hadzi-Pavlovic, D. (2010). Predicting mental health and well-being in adulthood. *Journal of Nervous and Mental Disease, 198*(2), 85–90.

Willcutt, E., & McQueen, M. (2010). Genetic and environmental vulnerability to bipolar spectrum disorders. In D. J. Miklowitz & D. Cicchetti (Eds.), *Understanding bipolar disorder: A developmental psychopathology perspective* (pp. 225–258). New York: Guilford Press.

Wilner, P., Bergman, J., & Sanger, D. (2009). Behavioural pharmacology of impulse control. *Behavioural Pharmacology, 20*(5–6), 558–560.

Wilson, C. R. E., Baxter, M. G., Easton, A., & Gaffan, D. (2008). Addition of for-nix transection to frontal-temporal disconnection increases the impairment in object-in-place memory in macaque monkeys. *European Journal of Neuroscience, 27*(7), 1814–1822.

Wilson, I. B., Carter, A. E., & Berg, K. M. (2009). Improving the self-report of HIV antiretroviral medication adherence: Is the glass half full or half empty? *Current HIV/AIDS Reports, 6*(4), 177–186.

Wilson, R. S. (1983). The Louisville twin study: Developmental synchronies in behavior. *Child Development, 54*, 298–316.

Wisco, B. E., & Nolen-Hoeksema, S. (2009). The interaction of mood and rumination in depression: Effect on mood maintenance and mood-congruent autobiographical memory. *Journal of Rational-Emotive and Cognitive-Behavior Therapy, 27*(3), 144–159.

Wood, R. I., & Stanton, S. J. (2011). Testosterone and sport: Current perspectives. *Hormones and Behavior,* DOI:10.1016/j.yhbeh.2011.09.010

Wolitzky-Taylor, K., Bobova, L., Zinbarg, R. E., Mineka, S., & Craske, M. G. (2012). Longitudinal investigation of the impact of anxiety and mood disorders in adolescence on subsequent substance use disorder onset and vice versa. *Addictive Behaviors, 37*(8), 982–985.

Wooten, P. (1996). Humor: An antidote for stress. *Holistic Nursing Practice, 10*, 49–56.

World Health Organization. (2010a). Centers for Disease Control and Prevention. Birth to 24 months: Girls. Length-for-age and weight-for-age percentiles. From WHO Child Growth Standards (http://www.who.int/childgrowth/en). http://www.cdc.gov/growthcharts/data/who/grchrt_girls_24lw_9210.pdf

World Health Organization. (2010b). Centers for Disease Control and Prevention. Birth to 24 months: Boys. Length-for-age and weight-for-age percentiles. From WHO Child Growth Standards (http://www.who.int/childgrowth/en). http://www.cdc.gov/growthcharts/data/who/grchrt_boys_24lw_100611.pdf

Wright, D. B., & Loftus, E. F. (2008). Eyewitness memory. In G. Cohen & M. A. Conway (Eds.), *Memory in the real world* (3rd ed., pp. 91–105). New York: Psychology Press.

Wu, A. H., Yu, M. C., Tseng, C., Stanczyk, F. Z., & Pike, M. C. (2009). Dietary patterns and breast cancer risk in Asian American women. *American Journal of Clinical Nutrition, 89*, 1145–1154.

X

Xie, Y., & Goyette, K. (2003). Social mobility and the educational choices of Asian Americans. *Social Science Research, 32*(3), 467–498.

Xu, N., Burnham, D., Kitamura, C., & Vollmer-Conna, U. (2013). Vowel hyperarticulation in parrot-, dog-, and infant-directed speech. *Anthrozoos: A Multidisciplinary Journal of the Interactions of People and Animals, 26*(3), 373–380.

Y

Yamamoto, S., Tomoe, M., Toyama, K., Kawai, M., & Uneyama, H. (2009). Can dietary supplementation of monosodium glutamate improve the health of the elderly? *American Journal of Clinical Nutrition, 90*(3), 844S–849S.

Yamasue, H., et al. (2008). Sex-linked neuroanatomical basis of human altruistic cooperativeness. *Cerebral Cortex, 18*(10), 2331–2340.

Yazzie, A. (2010). Visual-spatial thinking and academic achievement: A concurrent and predictive validity study. *Dissertation Abstracts International: Section A, Humanities and Social Sciences, 70*(8-A), 2897.

Yeh, C., & Chang, T. (2004). Understanding the multidimensionality and heterogeneity of the Asian-American experience. *PsycCRITIQUES, 49*(5), 583–586.

Yehuda, R. (2002). Post-traumatic stress disorder. *New England Journal of Medicine, 346*(2), 108–114.

Yip, W., Wiessing, K. R., Budgett, S., & Poppitt, S. D. (2013). Using a smaller dining plate does not suppress food intake from a buffet lunch meal in overweight, unrestrained women. *Appetite, 69*, 102–107.

Yokota, F., & Thompson, K. M. (2000). Violence in G-rated animated films. *Journal of the American Medical Association, 283*, 2716–2720.

Yurgelun-Todd, D. A. (2007). Emotional and cognitive changes during adolescence. *Current Opinion in Neurobiology, 17*(2), 251–257.

Z

Zagrosek, A., et al. (2010). Effect of binge drinking on the heart as assessed by cardiac MRI. *Journal of the American Medical Association, 304*(12), 1328–1330.

Zanarini, M. C., Frankenburg, F. R., Reich, D. B., & Fitzmaurice, G. (2010). Time to attainment of recovery from borderline personality disorder and stability of recovery: A 10-year prospective follow-up study. *American Journal of Psychiatry, 167*, 663–667.

Zayas, L., Gulbas, L. E., Fedoravicius, N., & Cabassa, L. J. (2010). Patterns of distress, precipitating events, and reflections on suicide attempts by young Latinas. *Social Science and Medicine, 70*(11), 1773–1779.

Zhang, Y. (2013). The effects of preference for information on consumers' online health information search behavior. *Journal of Medical Internet Research, 15*(11), e234.

Zimbardo, P. G. (2004). A situationist perspective on the psychology of evil: Understanding how good people are transformed into perpetrators. In A. G. Miller (Ed.), *The social psychology of good and evil* (pp. 21–50). New York: Guilford Press.

Zimbardo, P. G., LaBerge, S., & Butler, L. D. (1993). Psychophysiological consequences of unexplained arousal. *Journal of Abnormal Psychology, 102*, 466–473.

Zimmer, C. (2002, December-2003, January). Searching for your inner chimp. *Natural History, 112.*

Zogg, J. B., Woods, S. P., Sauceda, J. A., Wiebe, J. S., & Simoni, J. M. (2012). The role of prospective memory in medication adherence: A review of an emerging literature. *Journal of Behavioral Medicine, 35*(1), 47–62.

Zosuls, K. M., Ruble, D. N., Tamis-Lemonda, C. S., Shrout, P. E., Bornstein, M. H., & Greulich, F. K. (2009). The acquisition of gender labels in infancy: Implications for gender-typed play. *Developmental Psychology, 45*(3), 688–701.

Zucco, G. M., Aiello, L., Turuani, L., & Koster, E. (2012). Odor-evoked autobiographical memories: Age and gender differences along the life span. *Chemical Senses, 37*(2), 179–189.

Zucker, A. N., Ostrove, J. M., & Stewart, A. J. (2002). College-educated women's personality development in adulthood: Perceptions and age differences. *Psychology and Aging, 17*(2), 236–244.

Zuffiano, A., et al. (2013). Academic achievement: The unique combination of self-efficacy beliefs in self-regulated learning beyond intelligence, personality traits, and self-esteem. *Learning and Individual Differences, 23*, 158–162.

NAME INDEX

A

Adler, A., 262
Ainsworth, M. S., 15, 240–241
Allport, G., 265
American Cancer Society, 113
American Lung Association, 112–113
American Psychiatric Association, 106, 114, 305
American Psychological Association, 15, 26, 40,
   49, 286
Aristotle, 7–8
Arnett, J., 247–248
Arthritis Foundation, 85
Atkinson, R., 150
Auyeung, B., 270

B

Bahrick, H., 160
Bandura, A., 138, 141, 268–269, 289, 337
Bard, P., 223
Barrett, E., 270
Basic Behavioral Science Task Force, 364
Baumrind, D., 242
Beck, A., 339–340, 343
Benoit, C., 52
Benoit, N., 52
Benson, H., 104
Bern, D., 88
Bernard, G., 390
Bhutto, B., 353
Binet, A., 191, 198
Binswanger, L., 272
Blake, P., 285
Bogen, J., 49
Boss, M., 272
Bowlby, J., 241
Brown, A. S., 322, 372
Brown, R. J., 313
Bryant, W. C., 253
Bucy, P., 46

C

Calkins, M. W., 15
Cannon, W. B., 223, 292, 294
Cartwright, J., 329–330
Cattell, R. B., 195
Centers for Disease Control and Prevention, 112,
   316–318

C

Cerletti, U., 347
Cho, S., 139
Chomsky, N., 187
Clark, K. B., 14
Clark, M. P., 14
Clark, S., 98
Clark, T. T., 107
Collette, T., 311
Comas-Diaz, L., 14
Consortium of Social Science Associations, 353
Costa, P. T. Jr., 265–266
Craik, F., 156
Crick, F., 55
Cuijpers, P., 348

D

Dabbs, J., 370
Danhauer, J., 81
Darwin, C., 9, 12, 52, 219
Delgado, J., 47
Democritus, 7–8
Difede, J., 336
Dix, D., 331
Domino, Fats, 346
Dweck, C., 217

E

Ebbinghaus, H., 159
Ekman, P., 219
Elizabeth II, 49
Ellis, A., 287, 307, 339–341, 343
Erikson, E., 13, 240, 247, 251–253, 262–263
Eysenck, H. J., 265, 343

F

Fantz, R., 232
Fechner, G. T., 8, 64
Festinger, L., 203
Fitz-Roy, R., 52
Flynn, J., 199
Foster, J., 304, 306
Frankl, V., 272
Franklin, B., 102
Freud, S., 12, 100, 112, 205, 258–261, 264,
   331–332, 370
Frost, R., 268

G

Galvani, L., 34
Gardner, H., 188
Gazzaniga, M., 49, 95
Genovese, K., 374
Glass, G., 343
Goleman, D., 189
Goodenough, F., 195
Gottfredson, L., 190
Gregson, T., 311

H

Hall, G. S., 246
Hannity, S., 356
Harlow, H. F., 241
Harris, E., 139
Heidegger, M., 272
Hering, E., 72–73
Hinckley, J., 305–306
Hinckley, W., 305
Hippocrates, 265, 305
Hitler, A., 368
Hofmann, H., 249–250, 329–330
Horney, K., 13, 262
Howard, M., 98
Hubel, D., 66
Hull, C., 205
Hyde, J., 196
Hyman, R., 87

I

International Human Genome Sequencing
   Consortium, 55

J

James, W., 9, 93, 150, 204, 222
Janis, I., 372–373
Johnson, S. P., 232
Johnson, W., 220
Jones, M. C., 126–127
Jung, C., 262, 265

K

Kabat-Zinn, J., 104
Kagan, J., 267
Kahneman, D., 179
Karremans, J., 65
Kennedy, J. F., 373
King, S., 336
Kinsey, A., 20
Klebold, D., 139
Klüver, H., 46
Kobasa, S., 290

Koffka, K., 10
Kohlberg, L., 233, 239–240, 246
Köhler, W., 10–11

L

Landon, A., 18
Lang, A., 24
Lange, K. G., 222
Lanza, A., 139
Lawrence of Arabia, 324
Le Bon, G., 373
Levinson, D., 251
Lewis, T., 219
Lief, H., 163
Limbaugh, R., 356
Lockhart, R., 156
Loftus, E., 15–16, 155, 163, 166
Lorenz, K., 242

M

Maddow, R., 356
Magoun, H., 44
Malgady, R., 345
Manning, P., 356
Maslow, A., 13, 206, 272
Matthews, C., 356
Mayer, J., 189
McClelland, D., 217
McCrae, R., 265–266
McDougall, W., 151, 204
Melzack, R., 86
Mesmer, F., 103
Milgram, S., 365–368
Miller, A. L., 316–317
Miller, G., 145, 153
Miller, L., 93
Miller, N. E., 105, 136, 287
Milner, P., 45, 105
Mineka, S., 126
Minnelli, L., 390
M'Naghten, D., 306
Molfese, V., 198
Moniz, A. E., 348
Monroe, M., 324
Morgan, C., 278
Moruzzi, G., 44
Murray, H., 278

N

National Center for Health Statistics, 249
National Center for Injury Prevention and Control, 318
National Eating Disorders Association, 210
National Sleep Foundation, 96, 98–99, 310
National Vital Statistics System, 297
Neisser, U., 190

A Name Index including References is available online.

SUBJECT INDEX

A

A–B problem, 354
Absolute threshold, 64
Absolutist thinking, 340
Abstinence syndrome, 106
Accessibility, 355
Accommodation, 233–234
Acculturation, 275
Accuracy of long-term memory, 155
Acetylcholine (ACh), 36, 112
Achievement motivation, 217–218
Acoustic code, 148
Acquired drives, 205
Acrophobia, 307
Action, 319
Action potential, 34
Activating effects, 213, 215
Activating event, 287
Activation-synthesis model, 100
Active touching, 85
Actor-observer effect, 364
Acupuncture, 86
Acute stress disorders, 311
Adaptation, 54
    dark, 70
    to light, 70
    negative, 66
    positive, 66
    sensory, 66–67
Adaptive thermogenesis, 210
Adderall, 110
Additive process, 71
Adjustment, 275, 330
Adjustment heuristic, 179
Adler, Alfred, 262
Adolescence, 243–247
    cognitive development during, 244–246
    defined, 243
    physical development during, 243–244
    social and emotional development during, 246–247
Adolescent egocentrism, 245–246
Adoption studies, 58
Adrenal glands, 51
Adrenaline, 51, 112, 295, 308
Adrenocorticotrophic hormone (ACTH), 51, 292
Adulthood, 248–253
    cognitive development during, 249–251
    early, 249, 251

emerging, 247–248
    late, 249, 252–253
    middle, 249, 251–252
    physical development during, 248–249
    social and emotional development during, 251–253
Adversive conditioning, 337
Advertisements, 355–356
Afferent neurons, 32–34
African Americans, 297, 345
Afterimages, 71–72
Age/aging
    chronological, 192
    of feeling in-between, 248
    of identity exploration, 247–248
    of instability, 248
    mental, 191
    of possibilities, 248
    of self-focus, 248
    successful, 253
Age quake, 249
Aggression, 26, 139–142, 369–371
    biology and, 369–370
    chemistry and, 369–370
    psychological aspects of, 370–371
Aggressive behavior, 17–18, 23
Aggressive memories, 140
Aggressive scripts, 140
Aggressive thoughts, 140
Aging parents, 252
Agoraphobia, 307–308
Agreeableness, 265
AIDS, 295
Alarm reaction, 292
Alcohol, 108–109, 298
Alcoholics Anonymous (AA), 343
Aldehyde dehydrogenase, 109
Algorithms, 175–176
All-or-none principle, 35
Alpha waves, 97
Altered states of consciousness, 96
Altering consciousness, 102–115
    biofeedback for, 105
    hypnosis for, 103–104
    meditation for, 104–105
    through drugs, 106–115
        depressants, 107–110
        hallucinogenics, 114–115
        stimulants, 110–113
        substance use, 106–107

Altruism, 374
Alzheimer's disease, 251
Ambivalent attachment, 240
America, stress in, 286287
American Polygraph Association, 225
American Psychiatric Association, 106
American Psychological Association (APA), 6, 15, 26
American Sign Language, 180
Amnesia, 163–164, 312
Amniotic sac, 230
Amphetamines, 110–111
Amplitudes, 97
Amygdala, 46
Anagrams, 175
Anal-expulsive traits, 261
Anal fixations, 261
Analogy, 176
Anal-retentive traits, 261
Anal stage, 260–261
Analytical intelligence, 188
Analytical psychology, 262
Anchoring heuristic, 179
Androgens, 230
Angel dust, 114
Anger, 218
Angular gyrus, 48
Animal magnetism, 103
Animal research ethics, 26
Animism, 235
Anorexia nervosa, 210–211
Anterograde amnesia, 164
Antianxiety drugs, 346
Antibodies, 293–294
Antidepressants, 346–347
Antidiuretic hormone, 51
Antigens, 293
Antipsychotic drugs, 346
Antisocial personality, 267
Antisocial personality disorders, 323
Anxiety, 297, 346
Anxiety disorders, 306–309
    biological views on, 308–309
    biopsychosocial views on, 309
    defined, 306–307
    generalized, 308
    origins of, 308–309
    panic disorder, 307–308
    psychological views on, 308
    social, 307
    specific phobic disorders, 307
Apes, 180–181
Aphagic, 209
Aphasia, 48
Appearance, 356
    physical, 359–360
Applied research, 5
Appraisal, 291

Approach–approach conflict, 287
Approach–avoidance conflict, 287
Approximation, 238
Aptitudes, 276
Archetypes, 262
Arguments, 17
Artificial ear, 84
Artificialism, 235
Asch's study on conformity, 368–369
Asian Americans, 297, 345
Assimilation, 233
Association, 137, 332
Association areas, 47
Assumptions, 17
Asylums, 330–331
Ativan, 346
Attachment, 240–242
Attachment-in-the-making phase, 241
Attention-deficit/hyperactivity disorder
    (ADHD), 110
Attitude-discrepant behavior, 357
Attitudes, 354–358
    congnitive dissonance for changing, 357–358
    defined, 354
    formation of, 355
    persuasion for changing, 355–357
    predicting behavior from, 354–355
    strength of, 354
Attraction, 359–362
    attraction-similarity hypothesis and, 360–361
    defined, 359
    gender differences and, 360
    physical appearance and, 359–360
Attraction-similarity hypothesis, 360–361
Attribution, 363
Attributional styles, 315
Attribution theory, 363–364
Audience, 245–246, 357
Auditory nerve, 82
Auditory stimulation, 80
Authoritarian parenting style, 242–243
Authoritarian parents, 242–243
Authoritative parenting style, 242–243
Authoritative parents, 242–243
Authority
    legitimate, 367–368
    obedience to, 365–368
Autobiographical memory, 146
Autonomic nervous system (ANS), 39, 218, 292
Autonomy, 240
Availability heuristic, 179
Average, 379
    grade point, 387–388
Aversion to taste, 122–123
Avoidance–avoidance conflict, 287
Avoidant attachment, 240
Avoidant personality disorders, 324

Collectivists, 274–275
Color. *See also* color vision
 blindness to, 73–74
 complementary, 71
 constancy of, 78
 cool, 71
 perceptual dimensions of, 71
 red, 361
 warm, 71
Color vision, 71–73. *See also* color
Columbine High School, 139
Command post of hearing, 82
Commitment, 290, 362
Common fate, 75
Commonsense theory, 222
Communication, 180–181, 356
Community mental health movement, 331
Complementary colors, 71
Compulsion, 309
Computerized axial tomography (CAT or CT scan), 42
Concepts, 173–174
Conclusions from evidence, 17
Concrete operational stage, 237
Conditional learning, 355
Conditional positive regard, 273
Conditional reflexes, 120–121
Conditioned reinforcers, 131
Conditioned response (CR), 121
Conditioned stimulus (CS), 121, 137–138
Conditions/conditioning
 adversive, 337
 classical, 120–127
 higher-order, 125–126
 operant, 128–137
 physiological, 296
 of worth, 273
Conductive deafness, 83
Cones, 69–70
Conflict, 287
 approach–approach, 287
 approach–avoidance, 287
 avoidance–avoidance, 287
 defined, 287
 multiple approach–avoidance, 287
Conformity, 368–369, 373
Congnitive dissonance, 357–358
Connection, 17
Consciousness, 258–259, 265
 altered states of, 96
 altering, 102–115
 as awareness, 93–94
 defined, 93–96
 during dreams, 96–102
 flavors of, 95
 non, 94–95
 as personal unity, 95
 pre, 94–95
 during sleep, 96–102

un, 94–95
 as waking state, 96
Consequences, 287
Conservation, 236
Consortium of Social Science Associations (COSSA), 365
Consumer psychologists, 7
Consummate love, 362
Consumption patterns, 296
Contact comfort, 242
Context-dependent memory, 159
Context of messages, 356–357
Contingency theory, 137–138
Continuity, 75
Continuous positive airway pressure (CPAP), 102
Continuous reinforcement, 133
Control, 290–291
Control groups, 23
Conventional level, 239
Convergence, 77–78
Convergent thinking, 191
Conversion disorder, 313
Cooing, 184
Cool colors, 71
Cornea, 68
Coronary heart disease (CHD), 296–298
 reducing risk for, 297
 risk factors for, 296–297
Coronary-prone behavior pattern, 289
Corpus callosum, 46
Correlation coefficient, 21, 387–388
Correlation methods, 21–22
Correlation's, 17–18
Cortex, 46–48
 defined, 46
 motor, 46–47
 somatosensory, 46
Corticosteroids, 51, 292
Corticotrophin-releasing hormone (CRH), 292
Cortisol, 292
Counseling psychologists, 5
Counterconditioning, 126–127
Couple therapy, 342
Crack, 111–112
Cravings, 106–107
Creative intelligence, 188–189
Creative self, 262
Creativity, 190–191
Cretinism, 51
Critical period, 242
Critical thinking, 16–17
Crying, 183–184
Crystallized intelligence, 250–251
Crystal super grass, 114
Cuento therapy, 345
Cultural bias, 195
Culture, 182–183
Curare, 36
Current cognition's, 339

D

Daily hassles, 285
Dark adaptation, 70
Deafness, 83–84
Debriefment, 26
Decentration, 237
Deception, 367
Decibels (dB), 81
Decision making, 178–180
    framing effect and, 179
    by groups, 372
    heuristics in, 178–179
    overconfidence and, 179–180
Deep-sleep disorders, 102
Defense mechanism, 260
Deindividuation, 373–374
Delayed reinforcers, 131
Delirium tremens (DTs), 107
Delta-9-tetrahydrocannabinol (THC), 114
Delta waves, 98
Delusional disorders, 319
Delusions, 319
Demonological model, 305
Dendrites, 32
Dependent variables, 23
Depersonalization–derealization disorder, 312
Depolarization, 34
Depressants, 107–110
    alcohol, 108–109
    barbiturates, 110
    defined, 106
    opiates, 109–110
Depression, 218, 297, 348
    in women, 316
Depressive disorders, 314–316
    biological views on, 315
    biopsychosocial perspective on, 315–316
    major, 314–316
    psychological views on, 314–315
Depth perception, 76–78
Descriptive statistics, 380–385
    central tendency, 381–384
    defined, 380
    frequency distribution, 380–381
    measures of variability, 384–385
Desensitization, 66
    eye-movement, 338
    systematic, 127
Despair, 252
Developmental psychologists, 5
Deviation IQ, 193
Diagnostic and Statistical Manual of Mental Disorders, 106, 267, 305
Diathesis–stress model, 305
Dichromats, 73
Difference stimulation, 65
Diffusion of responsibility, 372, 374

Direct inner awareness, 94. *See also* consciousness
Discrediting information, 373
Discrimination, 124–125, 358–359
Discriminative stimuli, 132–133
Disgust, 218
Disinhibition, 140
Displacement, 154, 181
Dispositional attribution, 363
Dissimilarities, 358–359
Dissociative amnesia, 163, 312
Dissociative disorders, 311–312
Dissociative identity disorder (DID), 303, 311–312
Divalproex sodium, 347
Divergent thinking, 191
Dizygotic (DZ) twins, 58, 198, 308
DNA (deoxyribonucleic acid), 55–56
Dopamine, 36, 112, 346
Double-blind studies, 24–25
Doubt, 240
Down syndrome, 56–57
Dreams, 99–100. *See also* sleep
    activation-synthesis model of, 100
    analysis of, 333
    as expression of unconscious desires, 100
    as "residue of the day," 100
Drive for superiority, 262
Drive-reductionism, 205
Drive-reduction theory, 205
Drives, 203–204
Drugs, 106–115
    antianxiety, 346
    antipsychotic, 346
    depressants, 107–110
    hallucinogenics, 114–115
    stimulants, 110–113
    substance use, 106–107
    therapy using, 346–347
Duct, 49
Ductless glands, 49–50

E

Ear, 81–82
    artificial, 84
    inner, 81–82
    middle, 81–82
    outer, 81–82
Eardrum, 81–82
Early adulthood, 249, 251
Eating disorders, 210–212, 346
Echoes, 152
Echoic memory, 152
Education, 199
Educational psychologists, 5
Efferent neurons, 32–34
Effort justification, 358
Ego, 259–260, 264
Ego analysts, 333

F

Facial-feedback hypothesis, 220–221
Factor analysis, 265
Factor theories, 187–188
Family history, 296
Family therapy, 342
Far-sighted, 70
Faulty perception, 304
Fear, 126
Fear appeal, 356
Fear-reduction methods, 336–337
Feature detectors in brain, 66
Feedback, 339
Feeling in-between, 248
Feeling-of-knowing experience, 158–159
Feelings, 330
    of invulnerability, 373
    subjective, 9
Female athlete triad, 211
Femininity, 14–15
Fetal stage, 230
Fields of psychology, 5–7
Fight-or-flight reaction, 292, 294
Figure-ground perception, 74–75
File-drawer problem, 88
Financial responsibility hassles, 285
Firing, 34–35
First-shift rule, 372
Fissures, 46
Five-factor model "Big Five," 265–266
Fixation time, 232
Fixed-interval scallops, 134
Fixed-interval schedule, 133–134
Fixed-ratio schedule, 135
Flashbacks, 114
Flashbulb memory, 156–157
Flavor, 84–85
Flooding, 127
Fluid intelligence, 250–251
Flynn effect, 199
Food and Drug Administration, 24
Foot-in-the-door technique, 368
Forced-choice format, 277
Forensic psychologists, 7
Forgetting, 159–164
    anterograde amnesia and, 164
    infantile amnesia and, 163–164
    interference theory on, 162–163
    memory tasks used in measuring, 160–161
    repression and, 163
    retrograde amnesia and, 164
Formal operational stage, 244–245
Formal operations, 237
Fovea, 69–70
Frames of reference, 272
Framing effect, 179
Free association, 332

Frequencies, 97
Frequency distribution, 380–381
Frequency histogram, 381
Frequency polygon, 381
Frequency theory, 83
Frontal lobe, 46
Functional fixedness, 178
Functionalism, 9
Functional magnetic resonance imaging (fMRI), 42–43, 244
Fundamental attribution error, 363–364

G

Galápagos Islands, 52
Gamma-aminobutyricacid (GABA), 37, 112
Gamma knife surgery, 348
Ganglion cells, 69
Ganzfeld procedure, 88
Gate theory, 86
Gay males, 216
Gender, 14–16
Gender differences, 360
    in intellectual functioning, 195–197
    in stress, 294
Gender-schema theory, 271
Gender-typing, 270–271
General adaptation syndrome (GAS), 291–293
    alarm reaction, 292
    defined, 291–292
    exhaustion stage, 293
    resistance stage, 292–293
General intelligence, 187
Generalizations
    classical conditioning and, 124–125
    psychological research, 19
Generalized anxiety disorders, 308
Generativity, 251–252
Genes, 55–57
Genetic code, 56, 180
Genetic differences, 180
Genetic influences, 197–198
Genetics, 54–55
Genetic whisperings, 369
Genital stage, 261
Genotype, 56
Genuineness, 334
Germinal stage, 229
Gestalt psychology, 10–12
Gestalt rules for perceptual organization, 75
Gestalt therapists, 12
Gestalt therapy, 335
Glands
    adrenal, 51
    defined, 49
    ductless, 49–50
    pineal, 51
    pituitary, 50–51
    thyroid, 51

processing information and, 156
storage in, 155–156
Long-term potentiation (LTP), 165
Loudness, 80–81
Love, 220, 359–362
Lysergic acid diethylamide (LSD), 114

M

Magnetic resonance imaging (MRI), 42–43, 180
functional, 42–43, 244
Magnification, 340
Maintenance rehearsal, 149
Major depressive disorders, 314
origins of, 314–316
Majority-wins scheme, 372
Major tranquilizers, 346
Malleus, 82
Manic, 313
Manic–depressive disorder, 313–314
Mantras, 104
Marijuana, 114
Masculinity, 14–15
Maslow's hierarchy of needs, 206–207
Masturbation, 214
Maturation of brain, 230
Mean, 381–382
Means–end analysis, 176
Measures/measurements
of central tendencies, 381–384
of variability, 384–385
Median, 381–383
Media violence, 139–142
Medical model, 305
Meditation, 104–105
Medulla, 43
Melatonin, 51
Memory
aggressive, 140
autobiographical, 146
biology of, 164–168
brain structures and, 167–168
challenges to, 146
childhood, 163
context-dependent, 159
defined, 149–150
echoic, 152
encoding and, 148
episodic, 145–146, 168
explicit, 145–146, 168
flashbulb, 156–157
forgetting, 159–164
iconic, 151–152
implicit, 146–147, 168
kinds of, 145–148
levels-of-processing model of, 156
long-term, 154–159
neural activity and, 164–167

nondeclarative, 146–147
procedural, 146
processes of, 148–150
prospective, 145, 147–148, 168
relationships among, 168
retrieval and, 149–150
retrospective, 147–148, 168
semantic, 146, 168
sensory, 150–152
short-term, 152–154
skill, 146
sleep and, 99
stages of, 150–159
state-dependent, 159
storage and, 149
Memory functioning, 250
Memory tasks, 160–161
Memory trace, 151
Menarche, 244
Menopause, 249
Menstruation, 244
Mental age (MA), 191
Mental hospitals, 331
Mental processes. *See* behavior and mental processes
Mental representation of problems, 175
Mental sets, 177
Mental structures, 137
Mescaline, 114
Messages, 356–357
Metabolism, 51
Metastasize, 298
Methedrine, 110
Method of savings, 160
Methods
correlation, 21–22
experimental, 22–25
observation, 19–21
sampling, 18–19
scientific, 17–18
Middle adulthood, 249, 251–252
Middle-aged children, 252
Middle ear, 81–82
Midlife crisis, 252
Midlife transition, 252
Milgram studies, 365–368
Mindfulness meditation (MM), 104–105
Mineral water, 347
Minnesota Multiphasic Personality Inventory (MMPI), 277
Mirror neurons, 138–139
Mistrust, 240
Mixing light, 71
Mob behavior, 373–374
Mode, 381, 383–384
Model, 138
Modeling, 269, 336–337
Monochromats, 73
Monocular cues, 76–77
Monozygotic (MZ) twins, 57–58, 198, 308

Nucleus, 32
Nurture, 56, 197–199, 305
   in language, 185–186

O

Obedience to authority, 365–368
   deception, 367
   Milgram studies, 365–368
   truth, 367
Oberlin College, 15
Obesity, 209–210
Obesogenic environment, 210
Objective responsibility, 236
Objective sensations, 9
Objective tests, 276–277
Object permanence, 234
Observable behavior, 10
Observation
   case studies as, 20
   methods of, 19–21
   naturalistic, 21
   surveys as, 20–21
Observational learning, 138–139, 269, 355
   defined, 138
   mirror neurons and, 138–139
   violence in media and, 140
Observer bias, 181
Obsession, 309
Obsessive-compulsive disorder (OCD), 309, 346, 348
Occipital lobe, 46
Oedipus complex, 261
Olfactory membrane, 84
Olfactory nerve, 84
Openness to experience, 265
Operant behavior, 129
Operant conditioning, 128–137
   applications of, 136–137
   biofeedback training, 339
   defined, 128–129
   discriminative stimuli and, 132–133
   extinction and, 131
   law of effect and, 128
   methods of, 129–130
   procedures for, 337–339
   reinforcement and, 128–135
   shaping and, 135–136
   social skills training, 339
   spontaneous recovery and, 131
   successive approximations, 339
   token economies, 338–339
Operants, 129
Opiates, 109–110
Opioids, 110
Opponent–process theory, 72–73, 83
Optic nerve, 69
Optimism, 220
Oral fixation, 260

Oral stage, 260
Organizational psychologists, 7
Organization in long-term memory, 157
Organizing effects, 215
Organ of Corti, 82
Orgasm, 214
Orgasmic phase, 214
Orienting reflex, 121
Outer ear, 81–82
Out-group, 373
Oval window, 82
Ovaries, 51–52
Overconfidence, 179–180
Overextension, 175
Overgeneralization, 17, 340
Overlapping, 77
Overregularization, 185
Oversimplification, 17
Overweight, 209–210
Oxcarbazepine, 347
Oxytocin, 51
Ozone, 114

P

Pain, 85–86
Paired associates, 160
Palmar reflex, 231
Panic disorder, 307–308, 346
Panic disorder with agoraphobia, 308
Paradoxical sleep, 98
Parallel processing, 177
Paralysis during sleep, 101
Paranoid personality disorders, 322
Parasympathetic division, 39
Parasympathetic nervous system, 218
Parental investment model, 360
Parenting style, 242–243
Parents
   aging, 252
   authoritarian, 242–243
   authoritative, 242
   permissive, 243
   relationships with, 247
   uninvolved, 243
Parietal lobe, 46
Partial reinforcement, 133
Partial-report procedure, 151
Passion, 362
Passive smoking, 113
Pathogens, 284
Peer relationships, 247
Penis envy, 262
Pentagon, 100, 365
Perception. *See* sensation and perception
   of color, 71
   defined, 63
   depth, 76–78

Positive correlation coefficient, 387
Positive instances, 174
Positive psychology, 219–220, 267
Positive punishments, 132
Positive regard, 272–273
Positive reinforcers, 130–131
Positive symptoms, 318
Positron emission tomography (PET scan), 42
Possibilities, 248
Postconventional level, 239, 246
Posttraumatic stress disorders, 163, 310
Practical intelligence, 188–189
Preconventional level, 239
Predictability, 291
Predicting behavior, 354–355
Predisposition's, 296
Prefrontal lobotomy, 347–348
Prefrontal region, 47
Pregenital fixations, 261
Prejudice, 358–359
Prelinguistic vocalizations, 183–184
Prenatal development, 229–231
Preoperational stage, 235–236
Preoperational thought, 235
Preparedness, 126
Presbyopia, 70
Pressure, 85
Pressured speech, 313
Pressures for conformity, 373
Primacy effect, 363
Primary drives, 205
Primary mental abilities, 188
Primary reinforcers, 131
Primary sex characteristics, 51–52
Priming, 147
Proactive inhibition, 162
Proactive interference, 163
Problems, 175
Problem solving, 174–178
    expertise and, 176–177
    factors affecting, 176–178
    functional fixedness and, 178
    incubation and, 177–178
    insight to, 177
    mental sets and, 177
    methods of, 175–176
Procedural memory, 146
Processing information, 156
Programmed learning, 136–137
Projective tests, 277–278
Project Pelican, 129
Project Pigeon, 129
Prolactin, 51
Propinquity, 361
Prospective memory, 145, 147–148, 168
Prostaglandins, 86
Prototypes, 174
Proximity, 75, 238

Prozac, 347
Psi communication, 87
Psi phenomena, 87–88
Psychic structures, 259
Psychoactive substances, 106. *See also* drugs
Psychoanalysis, 12, 259, 332–333
Psychoanalytic theory, 259
Psychodynamice theory, 258
Psychodynamic perspective, 13, 258–264
    evaluation of, 263–264
    non-Freudian theories, 262–263
    theory of psychosexual development, 258–261
Psychodynamic therapy, 331–333
    defined, 331
    modern approaches to, 333
    psychoanalysis, 332–333
    traditional approaches to, 332–333
Psychokinesis, 87
Psycholinguistic theory, 187
Psychological aspects of aggression, 370–371
Psychological disorders, 330
    acute stress disorders and, 311
    anxiety disorders and, 306–309
    classifying, 305
    contemporary models of, 305
    defined, 303–306
    delusional disorders and, 319
    demonological model of, 305
    dissociative disorders and, 311–312
    hoarding disorders and, 309–310
    medical model of, 305
    mood disorders and, 313–318
    obsessive-compulsive disorders and, 309
    personality disorders and, 322–324
    perspectives on, 304–305
    posttraumatic stress disorders and, 310
    prevalence of, 305–306
    schizophrenia and, 318–322
    somatic symptoms of, 312–313
    somatoform disorders and, 312–313
Psychological hardiness, 290
Psychological influences on hunger, 209
Psychological needs, 204
Psychological principles, 329
Psychological research generalizations, 19
Psychological views
    on anxiety disorders, 308
    on depressive disorders, 314–315
    on health problems, 296
    with personality disorders, 324
    on schizophrenia, 319–320
Psychologists. *See also* psychology
    animal research ethics of, 26
    behavior and mental processes
        studies on, 16–26
        view on, 12–16
    biological perspective of, 12
    clinical, 5

positive, 130–131
primary, 131
vs. punishments, 132
vs. rewards, 132
secondary, 131
types of, 130–131
Relationships
among memory, 168
with parents and peers, 247
Relative size, 77
Relaxation response, 104
Relearning, 160
Reliability, 276
REM rebound, 99
Representativeness heuristic, 179
Repression, 94–95, 155, 163, 259–260
Reprocessing, 338
Research
animal, 26
applied, 5
human, 25–26
psychological, 19
pure, 5
questions for, 17
Research evidence, 17
"Residue of the day," 100. *See also* dreams
Resistance, 332
Resistance stage, 292–293
Resistant attachment, 240
Resolution phase, 214
Response, 121–122
conditioned, 121
emotional, 126
to stress, 294
unconditioned, 121
Response set theory, 104
Responsibility
diffusion of, 372, 374
objective, 236
of psychologists, 5–7
Resting potential, 34
Reticular formation, 44
Retina, 69
Retinal disparity, 77–78
Retrieval, 149–150
Retroactive inhibition, 162
Retroactive interference, 162
Retrograde amnesia, 164
Retrospective memory, 147–148, 168
Reuptake, 36
Reversibility, 237
Rewards, 132
Right brain, 48–49
Rightness, 373
Risky shift, 372
Ritalin, 110
Rocket fuel, 114
Rods, 69–70

Role diffusion, 247
Role theory, 103–104
Romantic love, 362
Romantic partner selection, 360
Rooting, 231
Rorschach inkblot test, 277–278
Roy G. Biv, 68

S

Saccadic eye movements, 150–152
St. Mary's of Bethlehem, 330
Samples/sampling, 379
defined, 19
inferential statistics, 390
methods of, 18–19
random, 19
stratified, 19
"Sandwich generation," 252
Sandy Hook Elementary School, 139
Sanguine personality, 265
Satiety, 207–208
Saturation, 71
Savings, 160
Scaffolding, 238
Schedules
fixed-interval, 133–134
fixed-ratio, 135
interval, 133–135
ratio, 135
of reinforcement, 133–135
variable-interval, 134–135
variable-ratio, 135
Schemas, 137, 155, 233
Schizoid personality disorders, 323
Schizophrenia, 36–37, 303, 318–322
action and, 319
biological views on, 320–322
biopsychosocial views on, 322
defined, 318
emotions and, 319
explaining, 319–322
language and, 318–319
perception problems and, 319
psychological views on, 319–320
social interaction and, 319
sociocultural views on, 320
symptoms of, 318–319
negative, 318
positive, 318
thinking and, 318–319
Schizotypal personality disorders, 323
Scholastic Assessment Tests (SATs), 196, 386–387
School psychologists, 5
Scientific method, 17–18
Scientific study of behavior, 10
Sclera, 68–69
Secondary reinforcers, 131

of intelligence, 187–191
interference, 162–163
learning, 185, 187
moral development, 239
of motivation, 204–207
non-Freudian, 262–263
opponent–process, 72–73, 83
place, 83
psychoanalytic, 259
psychodynamice, 258
psycholinguistic, 187
of psychosexual development, 258–261
response set, 104
role, 103–104
self-, 272–273
of sexual orientation, 216
signal-detection, 65–66
social cognitive, 268–269
sociocultural, 238–239
trait, 265
triarchic, 188–189
trichromatic, 72, 83
Therapy
in asylums, 330–331
behavior, 335–339
biological, 345–348
client-centered, 273, 333–335
cognitive, 339–341
cognitive-behavioral, 341
community mental health movement for, 331
couple, 342
cuento, 345
drug, 346–347
electroconvulsive, 347
family, 342
Gestalt, 335
group, 341–343
history of, 330–331
humanistic, 333–335
in mental hospitals, 331
psychodynamic, 331–333
psychothearpy, 329–331, 343–345
rational-emotive, 341
rational emotive behavior, 340–341
virtual, 336
Theta waves, 97–98
Thinking/thoughts, 173–180, 330
absolutist, 340
aggressive, 140
cerebral cortex and, 47–48
concepts, 173–174
convergent, 191
decision making, 178–180
defined, 173
divergent, 191
judgment, 178–180
preoperational, 235
problem solving, 174–178
schizophrenia and, 318–319

Thyroid gland, 51
Thyroxin, 51
Time-based tasks, 148
Time out, 132
Time-pressure hassles, 285
Tip-of-the-tongue phenomenon, 158–159
Token economies, 338–339
Tolerance, 106
Top-down processing, 75–76
Touch/touching, 85
Trait perspective, 264–268
biology and, 266–268
evaluation of, 268
five-factor model "Big Five" on, 265–266
history of, 265
Traits
anal-expulsive, 261
anal-retentive, 261
defined, 264
virtuous, 267
Trait theory, 265
Trance, 102–103
Tranquilizers, 346
Transcendental meditation (TM), 104
Transference, 332–333
Traumatic events, 100
Triangular model of love, 362
Triarchic theories, 188–189
Trichromat, 73
Trichromatic theory, 72, 83
Trust, 240
Truth, 367
Truth-wins scheme, 372
Twins
dizygotic, 58, 198, 308
monozygotic, 57–58, 198, 308
studies on, 57–58
Two-thirds majority scheme, 372
Type A behavior patterns, 289, 296
Type B behavior pattern, 289

U

UCLA Higher Education Research Institute, 284
Umami, 84
Umbilical cord, 230
Unconditional positive regard, 273, 334
Unconditioned response (UCR), 121
Unconditioned stimulus (UCS), 121, 137–138
Unconscious desires, 100
Unconsciousness, 94–95, 259, 262
Uninvolved parenting style, 242
Uninvolved parents, 243

V

Validity, 276
Valium, 346
Value, 71, 368

X

Y

W

Z

CHAPTER OUTLINE

WHAT'S NEW

- Updated figures and captions

- Updated references

- Updated photos

- Updated information on the gender and ethnic backgrounds of new psychologists, illustrating the changes taking place in the profession

LEARNING OUTCOMES

1-1 Define psychology

1-2 Describe the various fields of psychology

1-3 Describe the origins of psychology and identify people who made significant contributions to the field

1-4 Identify the theoretical perspectives from which today's psychologists view behavior and mental processes

1-5 Explain how psychologists study behavior and mental processes, focusing on critical thinking, research methods, and ethical considerations

TEACHING SUGGESTIONS

MULTIMEDIA HIGHLIGHTS
Facial Analysis 5:16

Available through PSYCH Online. This video shows the scientific method in action as researchers explore whether computers could help us analyze facial expressions. Ask your students: What might be some real-world applications of facial analysis? Why might facial analysis be a more objective measure of emotions than our own perceptions? Why is the use of computers so important in research?

LECTURE TOPICS

1. **Student Expectations** Before going over the definition of psychology, break the students into groups and allow them to discuss the following questions:

   What is psychology?

   What would you like to learn in psychology?

   After giving them time to come up with their answers, have a member from each group report to the class what the group came up with. Write all their ideas on the board and discuss each concept. This helps students preview the course content and find out what they will learn versus what they wish they could learn.

2. **Preparing for a Future Class** End the first lecture by playing a tape of some unique music and invite students to sample a distinct aroma or taste as they file out. Provide numerous small samples of fresh basil leaves on top of summer tomatoes. Present this as simply something that is enjoyable and that you want the students to experience. Do not mention the purpose until the beginning of the unit on Memory, when you again play the music at the start of a class. If this works you will have several students spontaneously mention their association with the basil–tomato taste, and then you are off and running, having established associations as the basis for conditioning. (Note that this demonstration should work with any combination of novel and/or strong sensory stimuli.)

3. **Forensic Psychology** For this lecture topic, discuss with your students the topic of forensic psychology. This topic is typically not covered in an introductory text but is an area of interest to students. Forensic psychologists apply the modern approaches to psychology in the area of law. Psychologists in this field may focus on such things as the design of correctional facilities, interrogation methods, and examination of eyewitness testimony. To help your students understand this interesting, modern approach to psychology, access the American Board of Forensic Psychology website at: www.abfp.com.

(Continued)

CHAPTER PREP 1

KEY TERMS

TEACHING SUGGESTIONS *continued*

STUDENT PROJECTS

1. **American Psychological Association (APA)** One of the best resources on the web is the American Psychological Association's website, which can be found at www.apa.org. This extensive website has a plethora of information on psychology. Your textbook discusses many areas of study within the field of psychology. What career opportunities are there in psychology? The APA website can help answer this question. Use the site to explore five careers in psychology and explain each in your own words.

   Access the website at the above address. Once there, click on the Students link and then the Brochure link. Then you will be able to click on the Subfields link. You could go directly to the careers site by going to: http://www.apa.org/students/brochure/subfields.html.

2. **Samples of Populations** As you learn more about research methods used in psychology, you will find that much of the research is conducted using samples of people. This is commonly seen in election years when polling data is reported. Do samples used in research reflect human diversity (the whole population)? Why? For this project, bring in articles from newspapers or magazines, etc., that report research using samples. Be prepared to discuss the basic methods used in the research.

CLASSROOM DEMONSTRATIONS

1. **Current Perspectives in Psychology** This classroom activity works better after you have presented on the current perspectives in psychology. Between classes, create paper signs that you can hang on the walls in the classroom. On class day, hang the signs on the walls around the room. Have students stand in the center of the room and then ask them, "If you had to pick one perspective to study and explain behavior, which would it be?" Have students move to the appropriate sign on the wall. After all the students have made their decision, have each group explain why. This can lead to some interesting group discussions.

2. **"Star Trek"** *Preparation:* You will need copies of "Star Trek" and "Star Trek: the Next Generation" episodes that have captains as the main character. Students may have their own copies.

   One way to teach students the various aspects of research methods is to use an interesting methodology suggested by Herreinger (2000). His suggestions are found in the *Teaching of Psychology* journal and focus on the television series "Star Trek" and "Star Trek: the Next Generation." Herreinger has students watch episodes of each and analyze the personalities of Captain Kirk and Captain Picard. Students are instructed to use information that is reliable and objective, which typically involves operationally defining variables. This activity can help students apply the concepts of research methods.

CHAPTER PREP
Biology and Psychology

CHAPTER OUTLINE

WHAT'S NEW

- Updated figures and captions
- New interactive figures through 4LTR Online
- Updated photos

LEARNING OUTCOMES

2-1 Describe the nervous system, including neurons, neural impulses, and neurotransmitters

2-2 List the structures of the brain and their functions

2-3 Explain the role of the endocrine system and list the endocrine glands

2-4 Describe evolutionary psychology and the connections between heredity, behavior, and mental processes

TEACHING SUGGESTIONS

MULTIMEDIA HIGHLIGHTS

Action Potential 1:26

Available through PSYCH Online. This short clip describes the action potential. Ask your students: Can you define the action potential? Explain how an action potential travels along the axon of a neuron. Explain the relationship between the action potential and the resting potential.

Brain Organization, Structure and Function 5:52

Available through PSYCH Online. This video shows students how psychologists are learning to map the brain in a variety of organisms. They see how researchers use different procedures to identify which brain areas are connected and how they function, and how psychologists can trace a neural message in monkeys that travels from the finger to the brain.

LECTURE TOPICS

1. **The Neuron** After you have discussed how neurons work and how the synapse offers a wide range of variability in the nervous system, have students brainstorm ideas about how the neurons could be explained using real-life analogies. (For example: The students receive information from their instructor. Which part of the neuron would the instructor be?)

2. **Phineas Gage** No lecture on the brain can be complete without a discussion of Phineas Gage and the experience he had with a tamping iron. This historical experience is found in most introductory psychology textbooks as well as many neurology textbooks. In 1994, researchers were granted access to Gage's skull to determine exactly what happened when the tamping rod passed through his skull. To learn more about what they found, access an article found in most libraries titled "What Happened to Phineas?" written by Shreeve (1995). This brief article will aid you as you explain the fascination and the lessons learned from an experience that happened over century ago.

STUDENT PROJECTS

1. **Endorphins** Many students can easily relate to the concept of the "runner's high." The "runner's high," which is caused by the release of endorphins, helps the body compensate for pain. Research the following questions on the Internet. (You may wish to read the article, "The Buzz on Exercise," written by Anderson (1995). Then answer the following questions: (1) What types of exercise tend to facilitate the release of endorphins? (2) How long does a person typically have to exercise before experiencing the release of endorphins? (3) Have you ever experienced a runner's high? If so, be prepared to discuss your experience in class.

2. **Biological Evidence for Evolution** To aid in your understanding of what evolution is and the evidence that exists to support this theoretical approach, read "Biological Evidence For Evolution," by Smith (2001). Then answer the following questions: (1) What is the simple definition of evolution as presented in the article? (2) What is the crux of evolution? What does the term "heritable" mean? (3) What is natural selection? (4) What are the four things about evolution that the author says "need to be clear"?

(Continued)

CHAPTER PREP 2

KEY TERMS

TEACHING SUGGESTIONS *continued*

CLASSROOM DEMONSTRATIONS

1. **Timing the Neural Impulse** In order to demonstrate the time it takes for neural impulses to be processed, perform a variation of the "dollar drop." Take a dollar and ask a student to drop it from the thumb and index finger of one hand (holding onto the short side of the dollar) and catch it with the thumb and index finger of the other hand. The student should have no trouble with this part of the exercise. Then have the student try to catch it while a partner drops the bill. Ask the students to explain the difference in results.

2. **Behavioral Effects of the Split-Brain Operation** Ask for three volunteers from the class, one of whom has shoes with laces (volunteer 1). The other two volunteers should be right-handed (volunteers 2 and 3). (Make sure the rest of the class can see what will happen.) Have volunteer 1 stand on a table in the front of the classroom and untie one shoe. Have volunteer 2 retie that shoe while you explain that a "normal" functioning person has little problem tying a shoe. Explain that what will happen next is a demonstration of how it might be for someone who has experienced a split-brain operation (perhaps to help with a severe case of epilepsy). Have volunteer 1 untie the shoe. Have volunteers 2 and 3 sit on a chair in front of the table. Volunteer 2 and 3 should place their outside arms behind their backs (left hand for the left volunteer and right hand for the right volunteer). Volunteers 2 and 3 should place their inner arms on the table, one crossing over the other (to illustrate the crossing-over nature of the brain-body connection). The volunteer representing the left hand should not speak from this point on (to demonstrate the localization of brain functioning, specifically the speech areas). Now have volunteers 2 and 3 attempt to retie the shoe. *Adapted from: Morris, E.J. (1991). Classroom demonstration of behavioral effects of the split-brain operation. Teaching of Psychology, 18 (4), 226–228.*

   For the next two classroom demonstrations, you will need a computer, Internet access, and a projector.

3. **Hypothalamus and Pituitary** To help your students understand the endocrine system, show them the images at: http://arbl.cvmbs.colostate.edu/hbooks/pathphys/endocrine/hypopit/anatomy.html. The images of the hypothalamus and pituitary are from a real human cadaver, part of the Visible Human Project.

4. **Genetic Diseases** To discuss genetic diseases with your students go to: http://www.genome.gov/10001204

WHAT'S NEW

- Updated figures and captions
- New interactive figures through 4LTR Online
- Updated photos

LEARNING OUTCOMES

3-1 Define and differentiate between sensation and perception

3-2 Identify the parts of the eye; explain the properties of light and the theories of color vision

3-3 Describe the organization of visual perceptions

3-4 Identify the parts of the ear; explain how the sense of hearing works

3-5 Describe the chemical senses

3-6 Describe the skin senses and discuss theoretical explanations for pain

3-7 Describe the kinesthetic and vestibular senses

3-8 Explain why psychologists are skeptical about extrasensory perception

TEACHING SUGGESTIONS

MULTIMEDIA HIGHLIGHTS
Overview of the Functioning of the Eye and Retina 0:28

Available through PSYCH Online. This short clip provides a visual display of the eye's role in sight processes.

LECTURE TOPICS

1. **Synesthesia** Have your students imagine that they are eating something and instead of tasting the food, they see colors flashing in front of them; instead of hearing a song, they feel a soft brush on the back of their ankle. This interesting condition is known as synesthesia. To help your students understand this interesting condition, have them read "Everyday Fantasia: The World of Synesthesia," by Carpenter. This article, which was written for the *APA Monitor on Psychology*, discusses this interesting condition and provides examples of people with the condition and attempts to understand it.

2. **Somesthesis** To introduce your students to the area of the skin senses, ask them to read "Somesthesis," by Craig and Rollman (1999). This in-depth article explores the skin senses and focuses on touch, texture, touch in communication, thermal sensitivity, kinesthesis, and pain. This article will provide students with a complete understanding of the skin sense.

STUDENT PROJECTS

1. **Senses and the Brain** To better understand how our senses work, how they define our world, and how they interact with our brain, access an article found in most libraries titled "The Senses: They Delight, Heal, Define the Boundaries of our World. And They are Helping Unlock the Brain's Secrets" written by Brownlee (1997). This article explores each of the senses and suggests that most of our world is interpreted through a combination of senses working together. For this project, read the article and then write a one-page paper summarizing something interesting you learned about each of the five senses. You may also want to determine if you are a supertaster, which you can find at the end of the article.

2. **The Color Vision Test** For this project you will be exploring information regarding color vision and those who are colorblind. Effects have been made to improve the ability to assess color vision to detect possible vision problems. Access an article found in most libraries titled "Test for Colour Vision; -and save sight" written by Arden (2003). After reading this article, write a one-page response paper about color blindness and the attempts being made to assess this condition. You may also want to visit the following website at: http://colorvisiontesting.com. This website has information about color vision testing.

(Continued)

CHAPTER PREP 3

KEY TERMS

TEACHING SUGGESTIONS *continued*

CLASSROOM DEMONSTRATIONS

1. **Discussions of S & P** Divide the class into groups of four or five students. Ask them the following questions about sensation and perception:
   - What is the difference between sensation and perception?
   - Put out your arm and point your finger at an object across the room while you have one eye closed. Open that eye and close the other. Why isn't the finger still on the object?
   - Why is it easier to locate the source of a sound when it comes from the side than when it comes from behind?
   - Why doesn't food taste as good when you have a cold?

2. **Test for Color Blindness** *Preparation:* You will need a computer, Internet access, and a projector.

   In this demonstration, you will show your students a test to determine color blindness. You can find the test at: http://colorvisiontesting.com/ This website has a color-blindness test as well as some explanations of color blindness.

3. **The Food–Taste Bud Connection** *Preparation:* You will need three bottles of bottled water (different brands) with cups to illustrate taste preference, an artichoke and an apple to illustrate modifying proteins, an apple with salt to intensify the fruit's flavor, and soy sauce and chocolate syrup to illustrate muted tastes.

   In this demonstration, you will help students understand the complex sensation of flavor, which is an interaction of smell and taste. Taste and smell interact to help differentiate flavors. For example, bottled waters should have no taste, but do we have preferences for a certain brand? Have your students discuss this while volunteers sample different bottles of water and rank their preferences.

   Taste Modifiers: Foods can also taste different because of what you have recently eaten. For example, after you eat an artichoke, everything else you eat will taste sweet. Have a volunteer eat a piece of apple and rate its sweetness. Then have them eat some artichoke and then a piece of apple to see if the apple tastes sweeter. Putting salt on an apple should *also* intensify its taste.

   Taste Mute: Have a volunteer taste some soy sauce and then taste some chocolate syrup. The soy sauce should mute the sweet taste of the chocolate. *This information comes from* "How Food Communicates With Your Taste Buds: The Chemistry of Perception," *by Hunter (2002).* This demonstration takes some preparation time, but it can be very effective in illustrating taste and smell.

CHAPTER OUTLINE

WHAT'S NEW

- Expanded and updated coverage of dreams, hypnosis, meditation, and biofeedback

- Heavily revised coverage of substance use and substance use disorders, as viewed by the 2013 edition of the DSM–5

- New interactive figures through 4LTR Online

- New coverage on electronic cigarettes

- Updated references

LEARNING OUTCOMES

4-1 Define consciousness

4-2 Explain the nature of sleep and various sleep disorders

4-3 Explain the natures and uses of hypnosis, meditation, and biofeedback in altering consciousness

4-4 Define substance use disorders, identify categories of psychoactive drugs, and explain their allures and dangers

TEACHING SUGGESTIONS

MULTIMEDIA HIGHLIGHTS

Weight Loss Hypnosis 4:50

Available through PSYCH Online. Hypnosis helps one woman find the motivation to eat healthier and exercise. A look at the scientific side of hypnosis, how it can help, and its limitations.

LECTURE TOPICS

1. **When Perception Becomes Consciousness** To help your students better understand the construct of consciousness, access an article found in most libraries titled "When Perception Becomes Conscious" written by Velmans (1999). This article presents a model to represent the psychological transition between perceiving the world and how that analysis becomes consciousness. The author suggests that some of the difficulty in studying consciousness comes in defining the construct. Is something conscious when a person is conscious of the process, or is it consciousness when a third person can distinguish it? The article goes on to suggest ways to determine if something is conscious or not.

2. **Power Naps** Students often hear about cultures that take siestas or naps in the afternoon. In the fast-paced lifestyle of a college student, it would seem that the day isn't long enough to do that. But could taking a nap actually help? To help your students understand how this could benefit them, ask them to read "Siesta Time: Power Napping," written for *The Economist (2002)*. This article contains a summary of research conducted in which subjects took afternoon naps and describe the influence the naps had on their visual perception. The research suggests that an afternoon nap of 60 minutes can be beneficial, news that your students will love to hear.

3. **The Science of Meditation** Research is being conducted to determine the benefits of meditation. This ancient practice has been shrouded in mystery for many years. To help your students understand the scientific approach to meditation, have them read "The Science of Meditation," written by Barbor (2001). This article discusses how groups of people have integrated meditation into every aspect of their lives. The article also discusses research conducted at Harvard Medical School using MRI technology to investigate what happens to the brain during meditation. The article suggests that the autonomic nervous system seems to be affected.

(Continued)

CHAPTER PREP 4

KEY TERMS

TEACHING SUGGESTIONS *continued*

STUDENT PROJECTS

1. **Friend Survey** For this project, ask three female and three male friends if they have recently had any aggressive fantasies. Perhaps they were mad at someone and had a fantasy about getting even. With their permission and maintaining confidentiality, briefly summarize the fantasies and then evaluate the summaries to see if there is any difference in the type of aggressive fantasies that males and females have. Be prepared to share your findings in class.

2. **Teaching Children about Sleep** Sleep is a fact of life. It has been estimated that people spend about a third of their life sleeping. Because this experience is so common, people (including children) don't think a lot about it. Yet some of the common sleep disturbances happen during childhood. If you were to prepare a lesson plan to teach children about sleep, a great resource is an article titled "Sleep and Dreams," written for *Science Weekly (2002)*. This article provides information about sleep in a simplistic manner, though you may find some things that will be new to you. Your task for this assignment is to develop a lesson plan to educate children about sleep and dreams. You may want to include information such as different types of sleep, what nightmares are, dreams, circadian rhythms, sleepwalking, and the amount of sleep that is necessary for children.

3. **Awareness of Advertising** For this project, you will be exploring the world of advertising. Advertisers use various methods to sell their products. Are there techniques that may facilitate us in paying attention to their ads? The textbook suggests that sudden changes, novel stimuli, intense stimuli, and repetitive stimuli can all contribute to capturing our attention. For this project watch television and keep a log of the advertisements that you see. Indicate which advertisements you enjoyed and why you enjoyed them. Did the advertisers use some of the techniques suggested in the text? Be prepared to discuss your findings in class.

CLASSROOM DEMONSTRATIONS

1. **Biofeedback Computer Games** *Preparation:* You will need a computer, Internet access, and a projector. You may need to download the games from the site first, depending on your Internet provider.

   For this demonstration go to: www.bfbgames.com. This is the homepage for Biofeedback Computer Games, actual computer games that can be downloaded and played to help a person relax. For complete biofeedback, the website would like a person to purchase the "pulse detector," which can monitor the heart rate while a person plays the games. The pulse detector connects to the computer. For the demonstration, you can play the games without the detector.

2. **Prescribe a Good Night Sleep** *Preparation:* Be familiar with the suggested techniques from the article.

   In this demonstration, you will have a discussion with your students to elicit possible suggestions to help someone get a good night's sleep. Have the students suggest techniques that they use to help them sleep and list them on the board. You can suggest ideas that have been shown to be effective through research. These techniques can be found in an article titled "Getting a Good Night's Sleep with the Help of Psychology," on the American Psychological Association website at www.apa.org/research/action/sleep.aspx. The techniques these authors suggest are having good sleep hygiene, relaxation techniques, keeping a sleep diary, sleep restriction therapy, and psychotherapy. Then compare the student's suggestions to the suggestions from the article.

3. **Hypnotist** If you know a hypnotist or hypnotherapist, ask them to come to class and talk about what they do. Have them discuss clinical and stage hypnosis and then illustrate stage hypnosis. As the students are enjoying the stage hypnosis show, they are also learning various hypnotic concepts. When they finish the show, discuss clinical hypnosis and answer questions. It is a great way to teach the various aspects of hypnosis.

WHAT'S NEW

• Dozens of new references

• Updated discussion of the intersection of violence in the media with the Newtown shootings as an example

• A new figure helps students better understand the challenging concept of the four basic reinforcement schedules.

LEARNING OUTCOMES

5-1 Define learning

5-2 Describe principles and methods of classical conditioning

5-3 Describe principles and methods of operant conditioning

5-4 Discuss cognitive factors in learning

TEACHING SUGGESTIONS

MULTIMEDIA HIGHLIGHTS

Little Albert 0:38

Available through PSYCH Online. Watch this classic video clip of Little Albert and the conditioning he was exposed to as a baby. Ask your students to explain the learning theory of fear that underlies this experiment by John B. Watson and Rosalie Rayner. How would you go about reversing Little Albert's conditioning?

Fear Conditioning 6:04

Available through PSYCH Online. Many people suffer from phobias and anxiety disorders. Students learn how simple Pavlovian conditioning experiments with rats help to uncover the neurobiology of fear. Students see how surgical lesions in rats can help to determine which brain areas are critical for emotional content, and which are crucial for contextual learning.

LECTURE TOPICS

1. **Taste Aversion and Alcohol** Taste aversion research has focused on many areas of animal behavior. Comparative studies have been conducted with animals to investigate the possible influence that taste aversions could have with humans. One area of interest is alcohol consumption. Recent attempts to create taste aversion to alcohol in humans have been pursued as possible treatment options. Because of the various factors that contribute to alcohol consumption in humans, the research is ongoing. Reference the article "Conditioned Taste Aversion and Alcohol Drinking: Strain and Gender," by Cailhol and Mormede (2002). The authors investigate conditioned taste aversions in laboratory rats. One of the goals of the research was to determine the etiological basis of individual vulnerability to alcohol. This subject can be discussed with the class as ongoing research, trying to identify vulnerabilities as well as using classical conditioning procedures as possible treatment for alcohol abuse.

STUDENT PROJECTS

1. **Reinforcement or Reinforcer?** An integral part of operant conditioning is the concept of reinforcement. These "rewards" that increase the probability of responding can be powerful influences in a person's life. Students often get confused between positive and negative reinforcers. To aid in your understanding of these concepts, access an article in most libraries titled "Reward and Punishment: In the regular feature examiners and teachers will explore baffling or taken for granted concepts and topics to give you clarity and insight into their meaning and their significance" by Curtis (2001). After reading the article, define in your own words what a reinforcer and what a reinforcement is. Also, diagram the contingency table that explains positive and negative reinforcement, and punishment.

2. **Principles of Behavior Modification** This project will provide you with an opportunity to create a hypothetical plan to help a person overcome a problem behavior. Your first task will be to

(Continued)

CHAPTER PREP 5

KEY TERMS

TEACHING SUGGESTIONS *continued*

STUDENT PROJECTS *continued*

identify a problem behavior (in a person or animal) that needs to be changed. Then go to www.edpsychinteractive.org/topics/behavior/behmod.html. This website has proposed principles that can be used to help students in their task. Take the suggested principles and develop your plan to change the target behavior, then be prepared to discuss your plan in class.

3. **Forbidden Flavors** Researchers have surmised that how we taste may have evolved over time, and that placement of our taste buds may serve an evolutionary process, that being to warn us against poisons. Though we aren't often faced with having to detect poisons through our taste buds, we do develop taste aversions. To learn more about these aversions and the connection that flavors have with memory, access an article found in most libraries titled "Forbidden Flavors: Scientists Consider How Disgusting Tastes Can Linger Surreptitiously in Memory" by Bower (1997). After reading this article, write a one-page summary of what you learned. Connect the information presented in the article to the theory of evolution. Is it important that we remember?

CLASSROOM DEMONSTRATIONS

1. **Balloon** *Instructor Preparation:* You will need some balloons (full of air) and a pin to pop the balloons.

   Classical conditioning is difficult to demonstrate because the response that individuals have is reflexive or automatic. One demonstration that works is popping balloons. A popping balloon will typically elicit a startle response from students in the classroom. Take a few balloons and pop them with your pin. Point out the startle response in the students. Make sure you exaggerate the pin meeting the balloon. Now attempt to pop a balloon by sticking the pin in at the nipple of the balloon. The balloon will not pop. Typically students will still show the startle response. The response is in reaction to seeing the pin meet the balloon. If you do this a few times the students may develop an extinguished startle response. Toward the end of the lecture, try to pop the balloon again by going through the nipple, and see if there is a spontaneous recovery of the startle response.

2. **Invisible Fence** An interesting example of operant (and classical) conditioning principles is the invisible fence that many dog owners use. Draw a schematic of a house and yard. Ask for suggestions for how the owner might try to keep the dog in the yard. (They could tie the dog up, install a fence, or purchase a dog run.)

   The invisible fence solves this problem with a radio transmitter plugged into an electrical outlet in the home. This transmitter sends a signal to a wire embedded a few inches under the ground around the perimeter of the yard. The pet wears a radio receiver collar that emits "an audible warning tone" when the animal gets closer to the wire. If the animal ignores this signal, the collar delivers a "restraining correction" from the collar. This electrical shock is a punishment for the behavior of walking too close to the buried wire.

3. **Insight** This demonstration illustrates cognitive learning, latent learning, and insight. Challenge the students to specify the "rule" to a game wherein you state that you like X but don't like Y, X and Y being nouns. (Rule: The rule is that all Xs have double letters in their spelling whereas Ys do not.) Start with the following sentence:

   "I like cabbage, but I don't like spinach."

   If students want to suggest a solution, ask them to raise their hand and not blurt out the answer. The second sentence is:

   "I like school, but I don't like vacation."

   Presenting the words orally is tougher than presenting them in writing. You may want to create an overhead with the two sentences. It is not uncommon when conducting this demonstration to have a student blurt out the answer even though you have repeated the directions several times. Once they arrive at the solution, have the students think about how they got there. Some students will find it difficult to describe the process, i.e., it just came to them. This demonstration allows the students to experience the suddenness of insight while you explain that this type of learning could not have been conditioned.

WHAT'S NEW

- Dozens of new references to bring the study of memories of the past—and memories of what students plan to do in the future—up-to-date.

- New interactive figures through 4LTR Online

- Updated figures and captions

LEARNING OUTCOMES

6-1   Define memory and differentiate between types of memories

6-2   Explain the processes of memory

6-3   Explain the stages of memory

6-4   Identify contributors to forgetting

6-5   Describe the biological aspects of memory

TEACHING LESSONS

MULTIMEDIA HIGHLIGHTS

The Brain and Memory 5:19

Available through PSYCH Online. In this video, students learn how habit memory—a second robust, but unconscious memory system—plays a role in helping people with amnesia to learn a declarative task.

Reconstructive Memory 5:49

Available through PSYCH Online. Going beyond the book, this video discusses how an understanding of memory has implications for the police, the justice system, and eyewitness testimony. Ask your students: What kinds of factors influence a person's memory? How could these factors affect eyewitness testimony? What is a "leading" question? Why does it "lead"?

LECTURE TOPICS

1. **Working Memory and Sleep** College students are on the short side of sleep and relate to sleep deficits. To help them understand the connection between sleep and memory, ask the students to read "Working Memory and Sleep in 6- to 13-year-old School Children," by Steenari et al. (2003). This article presents a research study that demonstrates that lower sleep efficiency and not getting enough sleep can adversely affect memory performance. Although the study used children, many of your students will be able to relate to the findings.

2. **Eyewitness Testimony of the *Titanic*** For an interesting topic to discuss with your students, you can present a research study, which used subjects as eyewitnesses (their testimony) to the *Titanic* accident. This study is in "An Archival Study of Eyewitness Memory of the *Titanic's* Final Plunge," by Riniolo, Koledin, Drakulic, and Payne (2003). The authors suggest that the eyewitness testimony of this tragic event was mostly accurate, lending support to eyewitness testimony in traumatic events.

3. **Gene Involved in Memory** Researchers at MIT have attempted to locate the gene involved in memory retrieval. Their hypothesis is that older people have not lost their memories but are having difficulty in retrieving them. In their laboratories, researchers are working with mice, altering their hippocampus to see what happens. Researchers use electrodes to actually "see" memories as they are formed within the brains of the mice. To help your students understand this connection, have them read "MIT Researchers ID Gene Involved in Memory Retrieval," from *Genomics & Genetics Weekly* (2002). Discussing the comparative research conducted with mice can help your students see the relationship between brain structures and memory.

(Continued)

CHAPTER PREP 6

KEY TERMS

TEACHING LESSONS *continued*

STUDENT PROJECTS

1. **Learning and Memory** Although we use the words "learning" and "memory" in everyday speech, it can be instructive to start this unit by differentiating between the two. Both seem to involve the encoding, storage, and retrieval of information from our experiences. But how are they different? For this project, define the two terms in your own words, making sure to indicate the similarities and differences. Be prepared to discuss your answers in class.

2. **Memory and Misidentification** This student project will help you to better understand how memory can be affected by stereotypes. An article titled "Stereotypes Can Affect Memory When Identifying Criminal Suspects" that was written for *Ascribe Higher Education News Service*, describes a research study investigating this relationship. Read the article and then write a one-page summary of the research methods used and what the findings were.

CLASSROOM DEMONSTRATIONS

1. **Digits Forward** This class demonstration is very good at reinforcing the limitations of short-term memory. Ask your students to take out a sheet of paper. You will read a series of numbers to them. They are to write the numbers on the paper, but not until you have given them the "Go" signal. Prepare them for each set by saying "Ready."

DO NOT READ	READ	READ	READ
3 bits	Ready	9,6,3.	Go
4 bits	Ready	5,9,3,1.	Go
5 bits	Ready	8,2,7,4,5.	Go
6 bits	Ready	3,9,2,1,4,8.	Go
7 bits	Ready	4,1,8,7,9,3,6.	Go
8 bits	Ready	2,5,9,3,1,9,5,6.	Go
9 bits	Ready	9,6,3,2,5,1,7,4,8.	Go
10 bits	Ready	6,3,5,8,9,4,3,2,8,7.	Go
11 bits	Ready	3,1,8,5,1,6,4,2,7,5,1.	Go
12 bits	Ready	9,6,4,3,5,8,3,1,2,6,8,5.	Go

2. **Identifying Memory Types** *Preparation:* You will need to create a handout for each student or an overhead of the 10 memories listed below.

   After lecturing on the different types of memory, distribute the Episodic, Semantic, and Procedural Memory handout. Have students label the type of memory, and then write their own examples of each type of memory.

   Episodic, Semantic, and Procedural Memory Handout:

   1. Riding a bike
   2. Describing your trip to Texas last year
   3. Naming the 16th president of the United States
   4. Stating the details of your first kiss
   5. Executing a cartwheel
   6. Describing what you had for breakfast the day before yesterday
   7. Stating the definition of psychology
   8. Recalling the events of your 10th birthday
   9. Tying your shoelaces
   10. Knowing how to spell the word ENCYCLOPEDIA

WHAT'S NEW

- Updated figures and captions

- New interactive figures through 4LTR Online

- Updated photos

LEARNING OUTCOMES

7-1 Define thinking and explain how thinking is used in problem solving and decision making

7-2 Explain the nature of language

7-3 Describe language development—the "two-year explosion."

7-4 Discuss theories about the nature of intelligence

7-5 Discuss methods of measuring intelligence and the "testing controversy."

7-6 Discuss the roles of nature and nurture in the development of intelligence

TEACHING SUGGESTIONS

LECTURE TOPICS

1. **Child Care and Language Development** This lecture topic will provide you an opportunity to discuss various environmental factors that contribute to language and cognitive development. A study was conducted with children from 10 sites in the United States to determine the factors that contribute to language and cognitive development. The main independent variable explored in the study was day care and family environments. Access the article "The Relation of Child Care to Cognitive and Language Development," written for *Child Development* (2000). This article discusses quality of care, type of care, amount of care, and how these variables relate to development. One result from the article is that children in center care performed better than children in other types of care when compared at age 3.

2. **Race and Intelligence** Interesting topics to share with your students are race and intelligence. These areas more than any other in the field of psychology, are controversial. An article titled "Race and Intelligence: Separating Science from Myth," written by Reeve (2002), is a book review that focuses on this issue. Topics covered in the book (which would also make excellent topics for discussion in class) include race only as a socially defined category, racial categories used to justify and perpetuate social inequalities, the merits of intelligence testing, the misuse of statistical concepts, and alternative interpretations of the bell curve. Each of these areas can lead to lively discussions with your students.

STUDENT PROJECTS

1. **Individual Differences in Problem Solving** Insight is the solution to a problem that seems to be nonobvious and functional. For this project, you will be exploring the phenomenon of insight. Read "Individual Differences in Problem Solving via Insight," by Ansburg (2000). After reading this article, write a one-page response paper defining insight.

2. **Family Size and Intelligence** This project will give you an opportunity to explore the influence that family size can have on a person's intelligence. Before students read the assigned article, have them write down their hypothesis and answer the question, "What do you think is the influence of family size on intelligence?" The assigned article is "Family Size Tied to SAT, IQ Scores," by Greenberg (1985). After reading this article, write a one-page summary of what you learned and whether your initial hypothesis was supported by this article.

(Continued)

CHAPTER PREP 7

KEY TERMS

TEACHING SUGGESTIONS *continued*

CLASSROOM DEMONSTRATIONS

1. **Sporting Events and Hindsight Bias** *Preparation:* You will need to be familiar with this demonstration and use it at the time of a major sporting event (Super Bowl, NCAA basketball final, etc.). You will also need to create both a pre-event survey and a post-event survey similar to those discussed in the article.

   For an interesting example of the hindsight bias, read "Hindsight Bias Demonstrated in the Predictions of a Sporting Event," by Bonds-Raacke, Fryer, Nicks, and Durr (2001). This article discusses a research study that used college students and a popular sporting event to demonstrate the hindsight bias. To demonstrate how powerful the hindsight bias is, have students complete the pre-event survey. The survey will have students indicate how much they watch the actual sport being discussed in the survey, demographic information (gender and age), and the predicted outcome of the event. After the event is over and you meet again as a class, have the students complete the post-event survey, which asks the students who they predicted to win and whether they were surprised by the outcome. This collected data can help you demonstrate the hindsight bias.

2. **Framing Effect** *Preparation:* Be familiar with the framing example from the article. You may want to create an overhead of the framing example.

   To help your students understand the power of framing, have them read "Influence of Elaboration on the Framing of Decision," by Takemura (1994). This article describes a framing example that can be used in class to describe an unusual disease that is expected to kill 600 people. Two alternatives are presented for students to choose between. One option is positively framed, and one option is negatively framed. After presenting the scenario to your students, have them write down which option they would choose.

3. **Intelligence Meter** *Preparation:* You will need to be familiar with the scenario presented below and with the normal bell curve. In class, explain that a fictional intelligence meter has been developed that will measure an infant's intellectual potential. This meter is so modern that testing is no longer necessary; instead, the child is passed through what appears to be an airport metal detector, and a measurement is taken.

   In this fictional scenario, two children have been measured: "Child A" and "Child B." On the day of birth, both children are measured for intelligence, and both are shown to have a potential IQ score of exactly 100, which is at the 50th percentile in the normal bell curve and considered to be average. Child A and Child B are from different families and different environments. The parents of Child A want the best for all of their children but neither parent is well educated. They lack parenting skills, and both have to work extremely long hours in order to make ends meet.

   The parents of Child B are just the opposite. Child B is able to visit museums and zoos, and has a strong vocabulary because of the parents' involvement with books and reading. Each child, due to circumstances, experiences the world differently.

   Years later both children sit next to each other in a classroom and take an intelligence test. Ask your class if it seems reasonable that the enriched environment that has been provided for Child B would be worth 15 more points on an IQ test. Next ask them if it also seems reasonable that there could be a 15-point loss in Child A's score due to the less nurturing environment. After the response from your students, illustrate for them the normal bell curve; place Child B at the first standard deviation (84th percentile) and Child A at a standard deviation below the mean (16th percentile). Child A is headed for remedial education, and Child B is close to being gifted. Solicit students' reactions to this scenario.

CHAPTER OUTLINE

WHAT'S NEW

- Thoroughly updated coverage of the sections on being overweight and obese and the eating disorders of anorexia nervosa and bulimia nervosa.

- Updated figures and captions

- New interactive figures through 4LTR Online

LEARNING OUTCOMES

8-1 Define motivation including needs, drives, and incentives

8-2 Identify the theories of motivation

8-3 Describe the biological and psychological contributions to hunger

8-4 Explain the role of sex hormones and the sexual response cycle in human sexuality

8-5 Describe achievement motivation

8-6 Identify the theoretical explanations of emotions

TEACHING SUGGESTIONS

MULTIMEDIA HIGHLIGHTS
Weight Control 5:56

Available through PSYCH Online. In this clip, students learn how researchers are helping people respond to the obesity epidemic. They observe how researchers determine the relative importance of intensity and duration of exercise. They are also introduced to behavioral interventions that help people overcome "obstacles" to exercise, as well as interventions that help people learn to eat less and exercise more.

Culture and Emotion 4:55

Available through PSYCH Online. How does culture influence emotion, and how are emotional responses similar across cultures? Are there physiological differences, behavioral differences, or differences in emotional experience—depending upon the culture in which someone was raised? What implications might cultural differences have for clinical psychology? This video helps students explore these and other related questions.

LECTURE TOPICS

1. **Exercise and Well-Being** One topic that many of your students can relate to is motivation for exercise. To help your students understand the efforts made to study exercise motivation, ask them to read "The Relationship Between Exercise Motives and Psychological Well-Being," by Maltby and Day (2001). The article discusses extrinsic and intrinsic motives that people have when they exercise. The authors suggest that extrinsic motives for exercise may be what people begin exercise with, but for those who exercise for longer periods (six months or more) the motivation may change to intrinsic motivations. After discussing the article, ask your students to describe why they exercise.

2. **Eating Disorders** For an excellent review of eating disorders including: classification/diagnostic information, clinical features, and development and subsequent course of anorexia and bulimia nervosa, read "Eating Disorders," by Fairburn and Harrison (2003). This article also considers possible risk factors and management of the disorders.

3. **The Kinsey Report** Perhaps the most classic study conducted in the area of sex research was that of Alfred Kinsey. To help your students understand the research that Kinsey conducted and the lasting contributions from his research, have them read "Alfred Kinsey and the Kinsey Report: Historical Overview and Lasting Contributions," by Bullough (1998). This article summarizes sex research that took place prior to Kinsey, and then describes the research that Kinsey conducted with over 8,000 individuals that he interviewed. The summary presented in this article can help your students understand the impact that this research had.

(Continued)

CHAPTER PREP 8

KEY TERMS

TEACHING SUGGESTIONS *continued*

LECTURE TOPICS *continued*

4. **The College Transition** For the incoming freshman at college, the transition may prove difficult. Research has shown that nearly a third of college freshman do not enroll the following year. Why does this happen? In an article, "The Transition From Extrinsic to Intrinsic Motivation in the College Classroom: A First-Year Experience," by Thompson and Thorton (2002), this topic is discussed. The authors suggest that high school students are extrinsically motivated by grades, attendance, detentions, and suspensions. The college student, on the other hand, is not. The authors suggest that learning is intrinsically motivating, and the transition between the two experiences can be difficult. As an additional component to this lecture topic, you can have your students describe the difficulties they encountered when entering college.

STUDENT PROJECTS

1. **Prison Simulation** A classic study conducted in the field of psychology was initiated by Zimbardo at Stanford University and has come to be known as the Prison Simulation. This study had college students play the roles of prisoner and guard and was scheduled to last two weeks. After only six days, the experiment had to be abandoned due to unanticipated reactions. To find out more, read "The Prison Simulation Experiment," by Gross (2002), which summarizes the prison simulation study. After reading the article, write a one-page response paper focusing on your thoughts about this study and how it relates to aggressive behavior. What would you have done as a guard? As a prisoner?

2. **Emotional Intelligence** For this project, visit www.eqi.org/index.htm This website contains information about emotional intelligence and contains links to information about the construct. After you explore the website, write a one-page paper summarizing what you learned.

CLASSROOM DEMONSTRATIONS

1. **Motivation List** This classroom demonstration involves an assignment that the class will probably enjoy. Ask the students to rank-order a list of a dozen behaviors that reflect their preferences and, hence, their motivations. One way to do this is to create the list yourself ahead of time and distribute it to all the students. Typical items are studying, dancing, having sex, watching TV, shopping, buying fashionable clothes, exercising, meditating, being with friends, reading a book, and so on. You may want to let the class decide the contents of the list to ensure that you haven't left out something that is important to them.

   The fun comes when you assign them to rank-order the behaviors in two ways: first to represent their own preferences, and second to represent the preferences of a typical member of the other sex. Clarify the process, collect the data, and calculate the mean rank order to be distributed or shown on an overhead projector at the next class meeting. You can probably count on some surprises, as students eagerly debate the reasons for their accuracy or inaccuracy about the preferences of the other sex. (Typically, females state that "having sex" is the top male priority, while all those sensitive males deny such base instinctual drives.) This makes for a good review of perception, and a preview of social perception.

2. **TAT** *Preparation:* You will need to have a Thematic Apperception Test.

   It is always interesting to display some of the actual pictures from the Thematic Apperception Test (TAT). Show the pictures and allow the students to observe it for a minute. Then ask individuals what is happening in the picture. This also works well in demonstrating a projective test.

CHAPTER OUTLINE

KEY TERMS

WHAT'S NEW

- Thoroughly revised section on successful aging

- Updated references

- New interactive figures through 4LTR Online

- Updated figures and captions

LEARNING OUTCOMES

9-1 Describe the events of prenatal development and the role that sex hormones play

9-2 Explain the physical, cognitive, moral, social, and emotional development of children

9-3 Explain the physical, cognitive, moral, social, and emotional development of adolescents

9-4 Explain the features of emerging adulthood

9-5 Explain the physical, cognitive, moral, social, and emotional development of adults

TEACHING SUGGESTIONS

MULTIMEDIA HIGHLIGHTS

Newborns: Sensation and Perception 2:30
Available through PSYCH Online. Watch an infant and his early sensory experiences, and listen to the explanations of infant sight and hearing. Ask your students: What does research tell us about the sensory capabilities of newborns?

Adolescence: Moral Development 2:00
Available through PSYCH Online. Watch interviews with adolescents who are explaining their moral reasoning to understand moral development in this age group. Ask your students to describe the responses of the adolescents when presented with Kohlberg's Heinz dilemma. Are their responses typical for adolescents?

LECTURE TOPICS

1. **Scaffolding** The textbook refers to a cognitive technique known as scaffolding that helps children learn new material. Cognitive scaffolding refers to the temporary support given by a parent or teacher to a child who is learning a new task. To help students better understand scaffolding, have them read "Children's Genre Knowledge: An Examination of K–5 Students' Performance on Multiple Tasks Providing Differing Levels of Scaffolding," by Donovan and Smolkin (2002). This article discusses how scaffolding is used in children's writing. The authors suggest that it can help but can also hinder a child. Discuss scaffolding with students and ask them how they feel it both helps and hinders children.

2. **Attachment Theory** Attachment theory is discussed in the textbook, and Ainsworth's three stages of attachment are presented: 1) initial pre-attachment phase; 2) attachment, in-the-making phase; and 3) clear-cut attachment phase. Although this theory has gained acceptance in the United States, does it generalize to other societies? To help your students better understand this, have them read "Family Systems Theory, Attachment Theory, and Culture," by Rothbaum, Rosen, Ujiie, and Uchida (2002). This article discusses the similarities and differences in family systems theory and attachment theory. The authors also discuss how these theories apply in non-Western societies.

3. **Alzheimer's Disease** College students may appear to be indifferent to this Alzheimer's disease, but many may be able to relate to the experience because of grandparents who are in the age

(Continued)

CHAPTER PREP 9

TEACHING SUGGESTIONS *continued*

LECTURE TOPICS *continued*

category. To understand the disease, have the students read "Tangled Memories: Alzheimer's Diseases: The Story So Far," by Liebman and Schardt (2002). This article discusses the disease from various theoretical perspectives. These include plaques, the dead zones between the nerve cells that are filled with protein fragments called beta-amyloid and tangles, which are neurofibrillary tangles that come from deposits of tau.

STUDENT PROJECTS

1. **Visible Embryo** This project will allow you to explore the world of a developing fetus. Access the Visible Embryo website at www.visembryo.com/baby/. Explore the site and then write a one-page response paper discussing what you learned.

2. **U.S. Teenagers and Television** For this project, you will be exploring a website about U.S. adolescents' television watching and smoking. You can find this website at: http://www.nichd .nih.gov/new/releases/tv.cfm. This website is part of the National Institute of Child Health and Human Development site. After you read through the site, write a one-page response paper about what you learned. You may actually be surprised.

3. **Male Menopause?** Female menopause is an accepted phenomenon that females experience, formally thought of as the end of menses, the end of estrogen production, and the end of reproductive capability. Hormonal imbalances, mood disturbances, vaginal dryness, and hot flashes are often associated with menopause. In a 1992 book written by Sheehy, the concept of male menopause was promoted. Is it possible that males go through a similar experience? Read "Male Menopause: Is It Myth, or a Reality of Aging?" by Curry (1993).

CLASSROOM DEMONSTRATIONS

1. **Mini Experiment for Three- to Four-Year-Olds** *Preparation:* You will need to arrange with a parent of a three- to four-year-old child to come to your class. You will need a clear glass that is tall and thin, and a second glass that is wide and a pitcher of water. You will be conducting a version of the Piaget Conservation task. This experiment is described in the textbook.

   Once your "subject" has come to class, pour water from the pitcher into the tall, thin glass. Then, with the child watching, pour water into the wide glass. Then ask the child whether the low, wide glass has more, less, or the same amount of water that was in the tall, thin glass. If the child says they are the same, the child is correct. If the child errs, then ask your students "Why?" This can lead to a discussion of Piaget's theory of conservation.

2. **The Imaginary Audience** *Preparation:* You will need to have a student confederate who can drop something that will make a loud noise during the lecture.

   Because of the novelty of the noise, a number of students will turn toward the noise. After they do this, stop your lecture and discuss with the class what happened. First, ask the student who dropped the item to describe what it felt like to have everyone look at him or her. Then have the class members describe what they were thinking when they looked. For the most part, those who looked probably didn't think anything of what happened.

3. **What Is an Adult?** For this demonstration, have your students generate a list of characteristics that they think describe adults. Write their suggestions on the board. After the students have generated a list, ask them to decide if they "qualify." Many students in introductory courses are in the early adult stage. This will help them see how they are doing.

CHAPTER OUTLINE

WHAT'S NEW

- Dozens of new references and revised coverage of the relationships between personality traits and political preferences, prenatal influences on masculine- and feminine-typed behavior, and culture and personality

- Updated references

- New interactive figures through 4LTR Online

- Updated figures and captions

LEARNING OUTCOMES

10-1 Describe the psychoanalytical perspective and how it contributed to the study of personality

10-2 Explain the trait perspective and the "Big Five" trait model

10-3 Identify the contributions of learning theory to understanding personality

10-4 Describe the humanistic-existential perspective on personality

10-5 Describe the sociocultural perspective on personality

10-6 Describe the different kinds of tests psychologists use to measure personality

TEACHING SUGGESTIONS

MULTIMEDIA HIGHLIGHTS

Personality Traits 5:34

Available through PSYCH Online. How should we measure personality? Some researchers focus on broad traits, but others are looking at how we behave in different situations. In this clip students learn about the person-in-the-situation model of personality, how it differs from trait approaches, and how it might be used to help people learn to regulate their emotions. Ask your students to define the "person-in-the-situation" phenomenon. Can you think of a time you were in a social situation and behaved in such a way that you surprised yourself? Can you explain your behavior in terms of the requirements of the situation?

LECTURE TOPICS

1. **The Psychodynamic Perspective** For a succinct, organized approach to the psychodynamic perspective, read "The Psychodynamic Perspective," written for *Psychology Review (1999)*. This article describes the major components of the psychodynamic perspective in a manner that is easily understood and organized. The article begins with the levels of consciousness and then proceeds through the psychosexual stages of development and defense mechanisms. This is a nice review of this perspective.

2. **Karen Horney** In the history of psychology, women played major roles but often didn't get the recognition they deserved. Karen Horney was one of those women. To learn more about her life and contributions to the field of psychology, visit http://webspace.ship.edu/cgboer/horney.html. This website discusses her life and can provide you with information for your students.

3. **Leadership and Self-Efficacy** Often thought of as synonyms, self-efficacy and self-confidence are similar but not exactly the same. Both would seem to have an influence in the area of leadership ability. To help your students understand the relationship between these three concepts (self-efficacy, self-confidence, and leadership) access an article titled "Self-efficacy and Leadership Effectiveness: Applying Social Cognitive Theory to Leadership," by McCormick (2001). This article describes a model for leadership that includes self-efficacy and self-confidence as it relates to social cognitive theory. This article can help your students see an applied aspect to personality traits learned through social cognitive theory.

(Continued)

CHAPTER PREP 10

KEY TERMS

TEACHING SUGGESTIONS *continued*

LECTURE TOPICS *continued*

4. **Sociocultural Influences and Self-Esteem**   There is an interest in determining the factors that contribute to the self-esteem of those with eating disorders. People with eating disorders tend to have low self-esteem related to their poor body image. To help your students understand the complex interaction of self-esteem and sociocultural factors, read "Self-Esteem and Negative Affect as Moderators of Sociocultural Influences on Body Dissatisfaction, Strategies to Decrease Weight, and Strategies to Increase Muscles Among Adolescent Boys and Girls," by Ricciardelli and McCabe (2001). This article explores how media, family, and peers play an important role in transmitting sociocultural messages regarding the ideal body weight. The connection is then made to eating disorders.

STUDENT PROJECTS

1. **Oedipus Wrecked?**   One aspect of Freud's theory, which was controversial from the beginning, was that of the Oedipus complex. The idea that each child has incestuous desires toward their opposite-sex parent has left many cringing at the thought. To learn more about the difficulties that this theory has encountered, access an article found in most libraries titled "Oedipus Wrecked: Freud's Theory of Frustrated Incest Goes on the Defensive" by Bower (1991). This article discusses this controversial concept and explores the supposed evidence . . . or lack thereof.

2. **Defense Mechanisms**   Watch a favorite television show and record the various defense mechanisms that the characters use. Come to class prepared to summarize the episode, characters, and the defense mechanisms.

3. **Keirsey Sorter**   Complete the Keirsey Temperament Sorter, which you can access online at www.keirsey.com, and summarize the results. Do you think the results truly reflect yourself? Do you think the test is reliable and valid?

CLASSROOM DEMONSTRATIONS

1. **Sigmund Freud**   *Preparation:* Create note cards with the terms from the article. To help your students learn the terms from Freudian theory, play a version of the board game Taboo. An article titled "Psychoanalyst: Sigmund Freud," by Gay (1999), reviews a number of the terms found in Freudian theory. Take the terms and write them on the note cards. Have a student come up to the front of the room and randomly pick one of the cards. The student's task is to get the class to say what is written on the card without using the word(s) on the card. They also have to describe the word based on its psychological meaning. Continue playing the game, choosing other students from the class to pick a card.

2. **Traits of the Famous**   Before starting your presentation of the trait perspective of personality to the class, ask students to describe the personality of someone they know very well or a television or movie character. Students usually use an average of five traits to describe their person (you may need to screen out repetitive traits such as nice and kind, and things not considered personality traits such as intelligence or weight). Write down some of the descriptions on the board. Discuss the trait perspective and how one of the major theories describes personality along five dimensions (five-factor model).

WHAT'S NEW

- Updated coverage of the warning signs of stress, the effects of daily hassles, the value of social support when one is under stress, and of the relationships between ethnicity and chronic illnesses.

- Updated references

- New interactive figures through 4LTR Online

- Updated figures and captions

LEARNING OUTCOMES

11-1 Define stress and identify various sources of stress

11-2 Identify the psychological moderators of stress

11-3 Describe the impact of stress on the body

11-4 Explain the relationships between psychology and health

TEACHING SUGGESTIONS

MULTIMEDIA HIGHLIGHTS

Health and Stress 5:09

Available through PSYCH Online. In this clip your students will learn how researchers are determining the mechanisms by which stress affects the immune system, and how emotional states like happiness and loneliness may influence the ability to fight off infection. Ask your students to explain what happens to the immune system when a person becomes stressed. What is the role of cytokine? How can you differentiate between "good stress" and "bad stress"?

LECTURE TOPICS

1. **Road Rage** A phenomenon that is seen more and more is road rage. Road rage is a reaction to stress and frustration in which a person becomes aggressive in their driving, leading to unsafe situations for all. To begin the discussion you could share with them the article "Road Rage: Understandings and Experiences," by Lupton (2002). This article reports a qualitative study in which 77 people were interviewed about road rage. The results indicate that many people find driving to be a source of autonomy and self-expression. Driving can become frustrating when the roads become crowded and when the individuals experience frustrations at work. Drivers do characterize road rage as negative yet understandable, considering the stress people face.

2. **Nutrition and Health** For this topic you can help your students understand the connection between stress and nutrition. Have your students read "Break the Chain-Control Stress with Optimal Nutrition," by Langer (1997). This article discusses hardy personalities and less obvious signs of stress, and then suggests proper nutrition to alleviate and prevent stress. Suggestions include vitamin B-complex, vitamin C, vitamin E, and amino acids.

3. **The Mind and the Immune System, Part I and Part II** For this lecture topic you can help your students understand the connection between the mind and the immune system by accessing two articles written for the *Harvard Mental Health Letter (2002)*—"The Mind and the Immune System-Part I" and "The Immune System and the Mind-Part II." The first article introduces the immune system and suggests that the immune system can actually learn through association. The first article also discusses hormonal effects on stress, and how stress is related to physical illness. In part two the discussion expands to include HIV infection and cancer.

(Continued)

CHAPTER PREP 11

KEY TERMS

TEACHING SUGGESTIONS *continued*

STUDENT PROJECTS

1. **An Antidote for Stress** Find and read the article titled "Humor: An Antidote for Stress," by Wooten (1996). Although this article is written for nurses, who have a high-stress occupation, the suggestions are for all. Answer these questions in a one-page paper. (1) How does humor tie to the Middle Ages and what are the four humors mentioned in the article? (2) How does laughter stimulate the immune system? (3) What are the three hardiness factors discussed in the article? (4) How does humor influence locus of control? (5) How is humor processed in the brain?

2. **Stress Warning Signs** Experiencing stress is a natural reaction to situations in which our body needs to be in a state of readiness. But long-term exposure to stress can be negative. How much is too much? Find and read "Stressed: Warning Signs That You Could Be Hitting the Danger Zone," by MacNeill (2003) and write a one-page response paper focusing on the reactions our bodies have to stress.

CLASSROOM DEMONSTRATIONS

1. **Locus of Control** *Preparation:* You will need a computer, projector, and an internet connection.

   To illustrate how stress can come from within a person, have your students take the self-assessment found in Chapter 10 titled "Self-Assessment: Locus of Control Scale" at the book companion website. After they take the assessment, they can bring their scores to class and a class discussion can take place about locus of control and how a person's perceived control over situations can alleviate or lead to stress. While the discussion is taking place, you can revisit the questionnaire and discuss individual items found on the instrument.

2. **Stop a Headache in Five Minutes** *Preparation:* This demonstration will require you to prepare a guided imagery for relaxation.

   Many headaches that individuals suffer are tension headaches. People can find relief from these tension headaches by relaxing. If possible, the person should attempt to relax within the first five minutes of feeling the headache. To help your students learn how to relax, present your guided imagery. Examples of visualizations can be found in an article in *Prevention*, "Stop a Headache in 5 Minutes," by Stocker (1994). These visualizations include "imagine your pain is a dial and turn down the ache" and "imagine pain is a fiery color and see it turning a cool blue like calm water."

3. **Sources of Stress Among College Students** *Preparation:* You will need to create a handout of the list of stressful life events experienced by college students, as reported in the article, for each student. You may want to create an overhead to present the results for the class.

   There are many stress scales designed to assess stress in everyday life. In this demonstration you can show the results of a study designed specifically for college students. The list of stressful events can be found in "Sources of Stress Among College Students," by Ross, Niebling, and Heckert (1999). The student stress events are categorized under four areas: (1) Interpersonal, (2) Intrapersonal, (3) Academic, and (4) Environmental. For the demonstration you can have students check which events they have experienced and then tally the results, which can be presented in the next class period.

CHAPTER OUTLINE

WHAT'S NEW

Chapter 12 is completely revised to reflect the 2013 publication of the DSM-5 (Diagnostic and Statistical Manual of the Mental Disorders, 5th edition) of the American Psychiatric Association. Topic coverage in psychological disorders chapters typically follow the classification system of the DSM. The organization of the chapters in PSYCH followed the system of the DSM-IV-TR for many years, but that system has now changed.

This Prep Card will not only contain the usual features of Prep Cards—that is, Multimedia Topics, Lecture Topics, Student Projects, and Classroom Demonstrations. It will also summarize and discuss key changes in going from the DSM-IV-TR to the DSM-5 and suggest some topics for classroom discussion or debate as that text moves along. We will therefore discuss changes on a topic-by-topic basis.

In our discussion we will quote freely from the paper, "A Guide to DSM-5," by Jade Q. Wu, Hannah Boettcher, V. Mark Durand, David H. Barlow

LEARNING OUTCOMES

12-1 Define psychological disorders and describe their prevalence

12-2 Describe the symptoms and possible origins of anxiety disorders

12-3 Describe the symptoms and possible origins of obsessive–compulsive and related disorders

12-4 Describe the symptoms and possible origins of trauma- and stressor-related disorders

12-5 Describe the symptoms and possible origins of dissociative disorders

12-6 Describe the symptoms and possible origins of somatic symptom and related disorders

12-7 Describe the symptoms and possible origins of bipolar and depressive disorders

12-8 Describe the symptoms and possible origins of schizophrenia and other psychotic disorders

12-9 Describe the symptoms and possible origins of personality disorders

TEACHING SUGGESTIONS

MULTIMEDIA HIGHLIGHTS
Home Videos and Schizophrenia 5:44

Available through PSYCH Online. Can we learn to predict who will develop schizophrenia? In this video, students see how psychologists are using low-tech procedures like home videos, and high-tech procedures like hormonal measures and brain scans, to better understand who might develop this very serious mental health disorder.

Bipolar Disorder: Expression of Moods 1:38

Available through PSYCH Online. In this clip, Mary talks about her experience with bipolar disorder and expressions of mood.

Obsessive–Compulsive Disorder 1:22

Available through PSYCH Online. In this clip, Chuck explains his struggles with obsessive–compulsive disorder.

Antisocial Personality Disorder 0:57

Available through PSYCH Online. In this clip, George describes the symptoms of his antisocial personality disorder.

(Continued)

CHAPTER PREP 12

KEY TERMS

TEACHING SUGGESTIONS *continued*

LECTURE TOPICS

1. **Exorcism** From a historical perspective, disorders were once thought to be the work of demons possessing a person's body. One method of "therapy" was to perform exorcisms to drive the demon from the person's body. In an article titled "Exorcism! Driving Out the Nonsense," by Nickell (2001), this topic is discussed. The article discusses the possible reasons that people thought that disorders might be due to demon possession. The author continues into more modern days and focuses on people's opinions about the movie "The Exorcist." This article can help you present to your students the interesting history of psychological disorders and how some thoughts have endured through time.

2. **Medical Student Syndrome** Many students will be interested in the "medical student syndrome," also known as "intern's syndrome." First-year medical students read so much about symptoms of diseases that they convince themselves they are suffering from one or more of them. A little knowledge can be a dangerous thing, even for the highly intelligent. The chapter on abnormal behavior is usually introduced at a time in the semester when the workload has piled up for the students, and they may be feeling particularly vulnerable. Students will often approach you to discuss the symptoms of one of the disorders listed in the textbook. Warning students about medical student syndrome is not to deny that some students may be experiencing real problems, but it could provide an "inoculation" against seeing these troubles in their own behaviors.

3. **Experts Are Split** To help your students understand the controversy surrounding multiple personality disorder, read "Multiple Personalities: The Experts Are Split," by Sileo. This article describes one aspect of the controversy, the increased numbers of MPD patients seen. Are the larger numbers due to greater awareness or due to therapeutic misbehavior? The article presents information from both sides.

STUDENT PROJECTS

1. **Diagnosing** Research a famous person whom you believe has had a mental disorder. (Possible examples include Jeffrey Dahmer, Ted Kaczynski, Charles Manson, David Koresh, John Hinckley, Roseanne Barr, Sybil Lively, Karen Carpenter, Margot Kidder, Ted Bundy, Howard Hughes, Howie Mandel, Catherine Zeta Jones.) Write a one- to two-page paper on the evidence (or lack thereof) in support of a particular diagnosis of a mental disorder, using the DSM.

2. **Men and Depression** To learn more differences between men and women with depression, access a page from the National Institute of Mental Health website at http://menanddepression.nimh.nih.gov/. After exploring the site, write a one-page response paper summarizing what you have learned.

CLASS ROOM DEMONSTRATIONS

1. **Accuracy in the Media** *Preparation:* You will need to identify a specific media source that provides information about psychological disorders. An interesting source for your students is music lyrics, including songs by Pink Floyd, Jimi Hendrix, Metallica, etc. Share your source in class (you may want to create an overhead of the lyrics so that your students can see them while the song is playing) and then assign the students to find one of their own to bring to the next class for discussion.

2. **The 23-Year-Old Schizophrenic** *Preparation:* Be familiar with the article and provide either overheads or handouts of relevant sections of the article.

   To help your students understand the difficulties that a patient with schizophrenia encounters, share with them the story of Mr. X, a 23-year-old schizophrenic. His story can be found in most libraries in an article titled "A 23-Year-Old Man With Schizophrenia" written by Goff (2002). This article details the life of Mr. X. This article can help bring to life this devastating disorder.

3. **The Anatomy of Anxiety** *Preparation:* You will need overheads (presentation slides) of the brain (from your lectures in biopsychology).

   For this demonstration, you can show your students how anxiety impacts various structures in the brain. For this demonstration, access an article found in most libraries titled "The Anatomy of Anxiety" written for Time (2002). This article describes how the body responds to anxiety, targeting specific brain structures. This information can help your students understand the connection between biopsychology and anxiety.

TOPIC BY TOPIC

Anxiety Disorders

DSM-5 Changes to Anxiety Disorders:

In *DSM-5*, the *DSM-IV* category for anxiety disorders has been divided into three categories: anxiety disorders, trauma- and stressor-related disorders, and obsessive–compulsive and related disorders. All of these disorders involve a heightened level of anxiety. Trauma- and stressor-related disorders are grouped together because of their similarities in origin, while obsessive–compulsive and related disorders are grouped together because of their similar types of symptoms.

- Separation anxiety disorder, characterized by intense anxiety about being separated from important others, is newly classified as an anxiety disorder. It was grouped among childhood disorders in *DSM-IV*. For the first time, separation anxiety disorder may be diagnosed in adults. [Separation anxiety among children is discussed in this text in the chapter on lifespan development.]
- Agoraphobia, or a fear of being in situations from which escape would be difficult in the event of an unpleasant experience like a panic attack, is now a disorder in its own right. In the past, agoraphobia was linked to panic disorder or classified only in the context of other disorders.

FOR THE CLASS: Ask the class whether they "know people" (they usually talk about themselves, whether or not they admit it) who get highly anxious before tests, before dates, and so on. What are their symptoms like? What happens to their bodies? What thoughts go through their heads? Is their anxiety normal or abnormal? How do we define normal anxiety? Try to bring students around to the idea that anxiety is normal when it is appropriate for the occasion and not so excessive that it prevents people from functioning. For example, a phobia for injections can be abnormal when it prevents one from receiving important vaccinations or medical treatments.

Obsessive–Compulsive and Related Disorders

DSM-5 Changes to Obsessive–Compulsive and Related Disorders:

- In *DSM-IV*, these disorders were classified as anxiety disorders. The new *DSM-5* category of obsessive–compulsive and related disorders highlights the importance of obsessive thoughts and compulsive, repetitive behavior in these disorders.
- Body dysmorphic disorder, or an intense preoccupation with a perceived physical flaw, has been moved to this new category. In the past, it was classified among somatic symptom disorders.
- Hoarding disorder, characterized by amassing a large amount of items and having difficulty parting with items, was previously thought of as a type of OCD. It is now classified as a disorder in its own right.

FOR THE CLASS:

- It is common today for people to say they are obsessed with something. What do people mean when they say that? (Ask for examples.) Does their "obsession" reach the level of an obsessive–compulsive disorder?
- Reality shows on TV reveal the "horrors" of the households of hoarders. Although the show tends to sensationalize hoarding, there are interesting question-and-answer sessions with hoarders about what they have been thinking and feeling. Ask students if they know hoarders, what they hoard, and what they say about it.
- FOR THE CLASS: How do contemporary standards for slimness help create body dysmorphic disorder in many individuals? Do they know anyone who will stare at themselves in the mirror for many minutes at a time, focusing on imperfections such as a large nose, facial sores, or acne?

Trauma and Stressor-Related Disorders

DSM-5 Changes to Trauma- and Stressor-Related Disorders:

- In **DSM-IV**, these disorders were classified as anxiety disorders. The new category of trauma- and stressor-related disorders emphasizes that these disorders follow exposure to an acute or chronic stressor (e.g., assault, combat, abuse during childhood).
- Posttraumatic stress disorder was classified as an anxiety disorder in *DSM-IV*. It is now classified under the more specific category of trauma- and stressor-related disorders.
- In *DSM-5*, trauma exposure includes indirect exposure to a traumatic event through intense exposure to aversive elements of the event (as in performing rescue work).
- *DSM-5* no longer requires that the person react to the event with intense fear, helplessness, or horror.
- *DSM-5* acknowledges that exposure may consist of multiple events.
- *DSM-5* no longer includes the distinction between *acute* and *chronic* PTSD.

FOR THE CLASS: Does anyone know an individual experiencing PTSD after returning home from Iraq or Afghanistan, undergoing the aftermath of rape, or losing someone of great importance? What does the person report happening? Is he or she undergoing treatment? What kind?

Dissociative Disorders

DSM-5 Changes to Dissociative Disorders:

Compared to other categories of mental disorders, there have been relatively few alterations to the dissociative disorders from *DSM-IV* to *DSM-5*.

- The *DSM-IV* diagnosis of depersonalization disorder has been renamed to depersonalization/derealization disorder, accompanied by several changes to diagnostic criteria. This disorder is characterized by experiences of feeling disconnected from oneself or one's body (depersonalization), as well as experiences of unreality related to one's environment (derealization).
- Dissociative fugue, characterized by a dissociative experience where an individual wanders or travels away from home, is no longer classified as its own disorder. Instead, in *DSM-5* it is considered a type of dissociative amnesia.

FOR THE CLASS: Students are fascinated by the notion of multiple personalities. Early in the chapter we discuss "William," who was diagnosed with multiple personality disorder at the time of his crimes, but was found not guilty by reason of insanity. You can note that the authors of the DSM-5 question whether "multiple personalities," now called dissociative identity disorders," really exist.

CHAPTER PREP 12

Somatic Symptom and Related Disorders

DSM-5 Changes to Somatic Symptom and Related Disorders:

- In *DSM-5*, somatic symptom disorders were renamed from what were called "somatoform disorders" in *DSM-IV*.
- *DSM-5* reflects efforts to consolidate and rearrange *DSM-IV* diagnoses that were overlapping and poorly defined.

The following *DSM-IV* somatoform disorder diagnoses are not present in *DSM-5*: hypochondriasis, somatization disorder, pain disorder, and undifferentiated somatoform disorder. Some somatoform disorder diagnoses have been altered to become one or more new *DSM-5* diagnoses.

- Several new disorders were introduced in *DSM-5*, including illness anxiety disorder [formerly mainly "hypochondriasis," with some minor changes not necessary to discuss at the level of introductory psychology], somatic symptom disorder, and "psychological factors affecting other medical conditions." This last disorder occurs when there is both a diagnosed medical condition and a psychological or behavioral factor that is making that condition worse (e.g., the anxiety in panic disorder might worsen a person's asthma).
- Body dysmorphic disorder (BDD) was classified among somatic disorders in *DSM-IV*, but is now classified among obsessive–compulsive and related disorders, reflecting the important role played by obsessive thoughts and compulsions in BDD.

FOR THE CLASS: Ask students if they know anyone with "imaginary illnesses?" What do they mean by that? Do they know people who pop pills all the time? What pills? Why do they do that?

Mood Disorders

DSM-5 Changes to Mood Disorders:

Many of the changes to the mood disorders are minor and perhaps need not be discussed at the introductory psychology level. Of major interest here, perhaps, is that Premenstrual Syndrome ("PMS") is now classified as a mood disorder in the DSM-5: its technical name is "Premenstrual Dysphoric Disorder (PDD)." PMS/ PDD includes physical and mental symptoms: mood swings, tenderness in the breasts, bloating, joint or muscle pain, cravings for various foods, fatigue, too little sleep (insomnia) or too much sleep (hypersomnia), irritability and feelings of anger, anxiety and tension, feelings of depression, loss of interest in usual activities, and problems concentrating.

FOR THE CLASS:

- Explain the history of the symptoms of PMS/PDD being considered to be unimportant "women's problems" and reflecting some type of "hysteria." Ask the class if these symptoms are normal or abnormal. Point out that the statistical definition of abnormality is that relatively few people have the problem. How does this change their thinking of the symptoms being normal or abnormal? Will women in the class say it's time that the problem got sufficient recognition? It can also be noted that classification of PMS/PDD as a mental disorder might result in the coverage of treatments for PMS/PDD in health care plans.
- Do students know anyone who has contemplated suicide or attempted suicide? Anyone who has "succeeded" at it? What "drove" the individual to consider or attempt suicide? Did he or she warn others of his or her intentions? What can be done (or could have been done) to prevent the suicide?
- A number of states have passed "death with dignity" acts that allow terminally ill people who are in discomfort to take their own lives, assisted, perhaps, by a physician. Questions: Why is suicide illegal in most places? Do students agree or disagree with laws against suicide? Why?

Schizophrenia and Other Psychotic Disorders

DSM-5 Changes to Schizophrenia and Other Psychotic Disorders:

- *DSM-IV* subtypes of schizophrenia (i.e., paranoid, disorganized, catatonic, undifferentiated, and residual types) have been removed in *DSM-5*. This elimination was based on the subtypes' limited diagnostic stability, reliability and validity, as well as the subtypes' similarity in course and treatment response patterns.
- *DSM-5* now includes catatonia as a separate schizophrenia spectrum disorder. [The text refers to them as having "the condition called catatonia," not as having a specific subtype of schizophrenia.]
- *DSM-5* now includes a separate condition called *delusional disorder,* in which, as described in the text, the individual has one or more persistent, perhaps unshakeable, delusion but does not otherwise show odd behavior.

FOR THE CLASS: Do they know anyone with schizophrenia? Would they describe the symptoms and whether the individual is undergoing treatment? What kind of treatment? Looking at the research into the origins of schizophrenia, do they think schizophrenia is a psychological issue or a disease of the brain or nervous system?

Personality Disorders

DSM-5 Changes to Personality Disorders:

The DSM-5 diagnostic criteria for personality disorders remain unchanged from the DSM-IV.

FOR THE CLASS:

- Ask what is the difference between a personality disorder and having a "bad personality?"
- Students usually enjoy and learn from discussing the role of the antisocial personality disorder in aggression and crime. For example, could it be said that James Bond has the biological traits that contribute to antisocial personality disorder? What about professional football players or boxers? What are the differences between saying that a person is a criminal, even a violent criminal, and that he or she has an antisocial personality disorder?
- Use a Venn diagram showing two overlapping circles—one labeled "antisocial personality disorder," and the other labeled "criminal." Ask students how large the overlap should be and why.
- If a person with an antisocial personality disorder is biologically different from the rest of us, does that mean that we cannot really blame him or her for aggressive or criminal behavior? This question leads to a discussion of the intersections between antisocial drives and personal responsibility.

WHAT'S NEW

- Revised and updated coverage of topics such as the effects of psychotherapy, the effects of therapist factors such as empathy and showing positive regard, and the use of cognitive-behavior therapy with schizophrenia.

- Updated references

- New interactive figures through 4LTR Online

- Updated figures and captions

LEARNING OUTCOMES

13-1 Define psychotherapy and describe the history of treatment of psychological disorders

13-2 Describe traditional psychoanalysis and short-term psychodynamic therapies

13-3 Define humanistic therapy and contrast its two main approaches

13-4 Define behavior therapy and identify various behavioral approaches to therapy

13-5 Define cognitive therapy and describe Beck's approach and REBT

13-6 Identify various types of group therapy and discuss their advantages and disadvantages

13-7 Explain whether psychotherapy works and who benefits from it

13-8 Describe methods of biological therapy—their benefits and side effects

TEACHING SUGGESTIONS

MULTIMEDIA HIGHLIGHTS

Virtual Reality Therapy 4:59

Available through PSYCH Online. In this clip students learn how high-tech procedures—usually associated with the entertainment industry—are helping people overcome fear as virtual reality moves into the clinician's office. They also learn how virtual reality can speed up treatment, make treatment more convenient, and bridge the gap to real-life exposure.

LECTURE TOPICS

1. **Bethlem** Perhaps the most famous mental hospital is St. Mary of Bethlehem hospital in London. Possibly the oldest psychiatric facility in Europe, the hospital came to be known as Bethlem and subsequently Bedlam (a metaphor for madness). An excellent history of this hospital can be found in an article titled "Bethlem/Bedlam: Methods of Madness?" by Porter (1997). The article presents a history and descriptions of the facility and patients. Discussion of this early attempt to "house" individuals with psychiatric disorders is interesting to students.

2. **The Baby and the Bathwater** Some psychologists today suggest that Freudian concepts are outdated and should receive mention for historical perspective only. In essence, Freud did a fairly good job considering that he was one of the first to propose such a complete theory, but the theory has little relevance today. There are some who suggest that to throw it all away would be inappropriate. To see a postmodernist view of Freud's theory, read "The Baby and the Bathwater: Some Thoughts on Freud as a Postmodernist," written by Freud—that is, Sophie Freud (1998). Freud suggests that aspects of Sigmund's theory have relevance today: meaning making, the unconscious, defense mechanisms, and psychoanalytic treatment. Ask students to form their own opinions and be ready to discuss them in class.

(Continued)

CHAPTER PREP 13

KEY TERMS

TEACHING SUGGESTIONS *continued*

LECTURE TOPICS *continued*

3. **Solution-Focused Therapy** At the beginning of your lecture on therapy, ask students to describe what happens in therapy. You will probably get responses that suggest that a client goes to see a therapist to talk about their problems. The therapist then helps them work through their problems. This type of response implies that a majority of therapy may be spent talking about what is not working, i.e., the problems. In an interesting article titled "What is Solution-Focused Therapy?" by Kingsbury (1997) this topic is discussed. The author suggests that problem behaviors are present only intermittently. Solutions-based therapy attempts to help the client notice those times when symptoms are diminished or absent. It is actually that time that needs to be expanded. Kingsbury suggests that this type of approach works well with anxiety disorders, depression, dependence, and family conflicts. This short article can aid you as you present to your students that not all of therapy need focus on the negative.

STUDENT PROJECTS

1. **Asylums** Mental institutions, mental hospitals, asylums, etc., continue to be somewhat controversial aspects of therapy. With a checkered past, asylums have survived and continue to be used. What is the fate of the severely mentally ill? Should they be hospitalized, or not? For this project, read two articles. The first article is "Asylum: The Complex and Controversial Story of Mental Institutions in the U.S.A.," written by McGovern (1993). In this article, McGovern reviews a film that explores the history of asylums and the controversy surrounding them. The second article, "Second Thoughts," written for *The Economist* (1989), focuses on this issue in Britain. After reading these articles, write a response paper stating and supporting your view: Is there a need for mental institutions or not? Use evidence from these articles to support your view.

2. **What to Do?** Whether you or someone you know struggles with depression, there are resources available to help. To research the options that exist, explore the website at: http://depression .about.com. This site contains information for those who may be struggling with depression or for those who may have a friend or family member experiencing depression. For this assignment, explore the website and write a response containing information you learned while on the site.

CLASSROOM DEMONSTRATIONS

1. **Systematic Desensitization: The Eraser Phobia** *Preparation:* You will need a chalkboard eraser (white board eraser), a cage that the eraser can fit in, and a picture of an eraser. You will also need a student confederate, preferably one who sits away from the chalkboard.

   As you begin class, present to the students the three steps typically used in systematic desensitization: (1) relaxation techniques, (2) creating an anxiety hierarchy, and (3) progressive associations with each hierarchy item and relaxation. Explain to the class that you are going to demonstrate how systematic desensitization works. Take the photograph of the eraser and begin to approach the confederate student. Explain to the class that you have already worked with this student to overcome this hierarchical item. The student takes the photograph. Explain that you are going to work on the next item in the hierarchy. Remove the caged eraser from your case. Begin walking toward the student. The student should act somewhat nervous as you explain to the "client" to take deep breaths and to relax. As the demonstration continues, you can remove the eraser from the cage while the client continues to practice the relaxation techniques. Near the end of the demonstration the student should be able to actually hold the eraser. At this point, explain to the class that the student really has no eraser phobia and that actual systematic desensitization would take more than just one session. This humorous demonstration is adapted from an article written by Lawson and Reardon (1997) found in the *Teaching of Psychology* journal, a great teaching tool.

2. **Counselor Visit** Your campus's health or wellness center is an excellent resource for your students. Often these centers have a mental health component with therapists who work for the institution. Arrange for one of the counselors who conducts group therapy to come to your class and discuss the techniques they use in conducting group therapy.

WHAT'S NEW

- Updated information on suicide terrorism, genetics and attitude formation, sexual attraction and the color red, Amanda Knox, and groupthink.

- Updated references

- New interactive figures through 4LTR Online

- Updated figures and captions

LEARNING OUTCOMES

14-1 Define *attitude* and discuss factors that shape attitudes

14-2 Discuss prejudice and discrimination

14-3 Discuss factors that contribute to interpersonal attraction and love

14-4 Define *social perception* and describe factors that influence it

14-5 Explain why people obey authority figures and conform to social pressure

14-6 Discuss factors that contribute to aggression

14-7 Describe differences between the ways in which people behave as individuals and as members of a group

TEACHING SUGGESTIONS

MULTIMEDIA HIGHLIGHTS

Stereotype Threat 5:22

Available through PSYCH Online. Each of us belongs to groups that have stereotypes associated with them. Can belonging to a stereotyped group affect academic performance? In this clip, students learn about what's called stereotype threat—how it affects people and what might be done about it. Ask your students: What is the theory of stereotype threat, and what is its effect on people? Have you ever wondered whether people from your ethnic background or gender can do something as well as people from another ethnic background or gender? How did your uncertainty make you feel?

LECTURE TOPICS

1. **The Psychology of Prejudice** For this lecture, discuss with your students the underlying possibilities of prejudice. In an article titled "The Psychology of Prejudice: Ingroup Love or Outgroup Hate?" by Brewer (1999), two different possibilities are explored. The authors suggest that many prejudices are a result of attempts to maintain positive relationships within the group rather than any negative ideas of the outgroup. This information can lead to a classroom discussion about prejudice.

2. **Attribution Change** The fundamental attribution error suggests that individuals tend to overestimate the importance of personal variables and underestimate the importance of the situation when making judgments about other people's behavior. But do those attributions exist over time? To expand your student's knowledge of this area, read "Do Attributions Change Over Time When the Actor's Behavior Is Hedonically Relevant to the Perceiver?" by Truchot, Maure, and Patte (2003). This article explores whether the attributions made continue to exist over time with the added component that the behavior is negative to the observer. The results indicate that they do not.

3. **Gender Differences in Attributions** Use this lecture topic to help your students better understand the interaction of gender differences, attributions, and helping behavior. These three topics are discussed in an article titled "Gender Differences in Attributions and Emotions in Helping Contexts," by MacGeorge (2003). This article presents research findings suggesting that there are gender differences in attribution that are consistent with the application of moral orientation.

(Continued)

CHAPTER PREP 14

KEY TERMS

TEACHING SUGGESTIONS *continued*

LECTURE TOPICS *continued*

4. **Variations of Milgram** Milgram's classic study on obedience to authority spawned much research. These variations on his original work continue. To illustrate for your students the additional knowledge gained through similar research, read "Self and Other Obedience Estimates: Biases and Moderators," by Geher, Bauman, Hubbard, and Legare (2002). This article describes a project to determine how knowledge of Milgram's experiment would impact perceptions of self and another person in hypothetical replications of Milgram's original experiment. How far would they actually go? This information can help your students see the creative nature of research and how Milgram continues to influence the field.

STUDENT PROJECTS

1. **Family Observation** Make observations the next time you witness friends or family members having an argument. Ask afterward why the argument occurred—who had done something wrong and why. If an individual admits to having done something wrong himself or herself, does he or she make a dispositional or a situational attribution? If he or she blames the other person, does he or she make a dispositional or a situational attribution? Keep track of the responses and be prepared to share your results in class.

2. **Helping Behavior** The author presents information suggesting that women are more likely than men to help people in need. Yet in the South, it is traditional for men to help women. Gather some change and then "stage" a situation in which you drop the change on the ground while both men and women are present and note who helps and who doesn't. Bring your results to class for discussion.

3. **Discussing Prejudice with Your Child** Prejudice needs to be discussed, especially during periods of wartime or national crisis. For this project you will explore some suggestions on how to discuss prejudice with children. Read the article "Discussing Prejudice with Your Child." by Reeve (2002). This article presents five suggestions. For this project, list and briefly summarize each of the five suggestions and think of at least one additional factor to include in the discussion.

CLASSROOM DEMONSTRATIONS

1. **Persuasion** For this demonstration, assign your students to watch television (you probably won't get too much resistance to this assignment). Specifically, ask them to watch commercials. As they watch the commercials, have them note what type of persuasion method the commercial uses. Does the commercial utilize the foot-in-the-door technique, setting the context and mood, familiarity, pointing out weakness as well as strengths, or persuasive communicators? See if they can find an example of each and possibly even other attempts at persuasion. Have them write down the examples and be prepared to share what they found in class.

2. **Truth or Lie?** Before discussing with your class the idea that information can be transmitted through the eyes, have the students in the class pair up. Then have each student think of three things about themselves, two of which are truthful and one that is a lie. Then have them tell their partner the three things while the partner attempts to determine the lie. After they finish this activity, discuss with your students that when someone looks them squarely in the eye, they typically are being more honest and open. If they avoid eye contact, this may mean deception. Ask the students if they used these cues to help them determine the lie.

3. **Social Psychology Topics** For this demonstration, have your students take the following ten social psychology terms and try to provide current examples from the media that would support the psychological principles. Encourage them to use both their books and notes and to be prepared to support their examples. During the next class period have them share what they found.

   1. Gender polarization
   2. Fundamental attribution error
   3. Prejudice
   4. Obedience to authority
   5. Conformity
   6. Social Facilitation
   7. Group decision making
   8. Groupthink
   9. Mob behavior
   10. Bystander effect

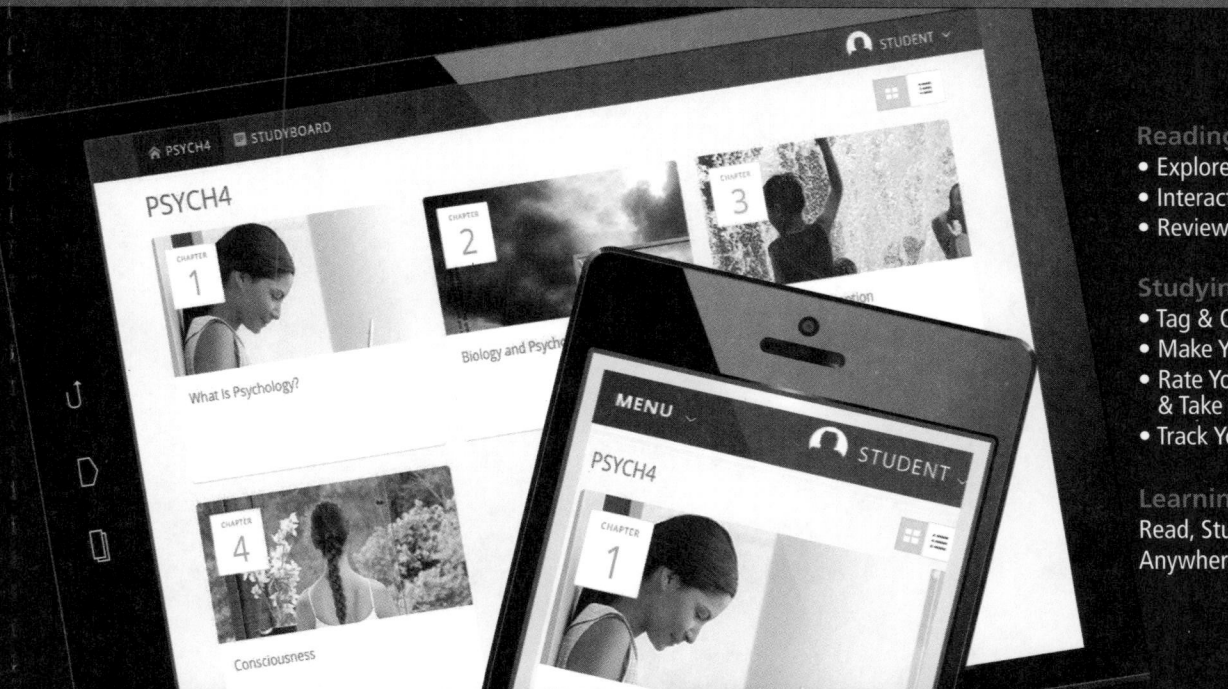